Biology of Termites

VOLUME 1

BIOLOGY OF TERMITES

Edited by

Kumar Krishna and Frances M. Weesner

DEPARTMENT OF ENTOMOLOGY
AMERICAN MUSEUM OF NATURAL HISTORY
NEW YORK, NEW YORK

AND

DEPARTMENT OF BIOLOGY
CITY COLLEGE
CITY UNIVERSITY OF NEW YORK, NEW YORK

NATIONAL PEST CONTROL
ASSOCIATION, INC.
ELIZABETH, NEW JERSEY

AND

DEPARTMENT OF ZOOLOGY
COLORADO STATE UNIVERSITY
FORT COLLINS, COLORADO

VOLUME 1

 1969

ACADEMIC PRESS *New York and London*

ACADEMIC PRESS, INC.
111 Fifth Avenue, New York, New York 10003

United Kingdom Edition published by
ACADEMIC PRESS, INC. (LONDON) LTD.
Berkeley Square House, London W.1

LIBRARY OF CONGRESS CATALOG CARD NUMBER: 68-26643

PRINTED IN THE UNITED STATES OF AMERICA

Contributors

Numbers in parentheses indicate the pages on which the authors' contributions begin.

BECKER, GÜNTHER, Technical University Berlin, Bundesanstalt für Materialprüfung, Berlin; (West) Germany (351)

COLLINS, MARGARET S., Department of Zoology, Howard University, Washington, D. C. (433)

GAY, F. G., Division of Entomology, CSIRO, Canberra, Australia (459)

KISTNER, DAVID H., Department of Biology, Chico State College, Chico, California (525)

KRISHNA, KUMAR, Department of Entomology, American Museum of Natural History, New York, New York, and Department of Biology, City College, City University of New York, New York (1)

MCMAHAN, ELIZABETH A., Department of Zoology, University of North Carolina, Chapel Hill, North Carolina (387)

MILLER, E. MORTON, Department of Biology, University of Miami, Coral Gables, Florida (283)

MOORE, B. P., Division of Entomology, CSIRO, Canberra, Australia (407)

NOIROT, CH., Laboratoire de Zoologie, Faculté des Sciences, Dijon, France (49, 89, 311)

NOIROT-TIMOTHÉE, C., Laboratoire de Zoologie, Faculté des Sciences, Dijon, France (49)

NUTTING, W. L., Department of Entomology, University of Arizona, Tucson, Arizone (233)

RICHARD, GASTON, Laboratoire d'Éthologie, Faculté des Sciences, Université de Rennes, Rennes, France (161)

v

SANDS, WILLIAM A., Termite Research Unit, c/o British Museum Natural History, London, England (495)

STUART, ALASTAIR M., Department of Zoology, North Carolina State University, Raleigh, North Carolina (193)

WEESNER, FRANCES M., National Pest Control Association, Inc., Elizabeth, New Jersey, and Department of Zoology, Colorado State University, Fort Collins, Colorado (19, 125)

Preface

Termites are a complex group of social insects that have a fascinating biology. Although termites have been associated mainly with damage, and while it is true that wherever they occur some species constitute a greater or lesser economic problem, less than 10% of the species have actually been recorded as pests. The attention accorded these few economically important species has obscured the important ecological role of termites in the breakdown of vegetative matter and their tremendous variety and complexity of structure, physiology, social behavior, caste differentiation and regulation, and other aspects of their biology.

No modern, comprehensive treatise on the biology of termites has hitherto been available, though some large works dealing with termites have been compiled in the past. The first work to deal extensively with termite biology was that of E. Hegh, "Les Termites," published in 1922. Although it approached its subject from a fundamental biological point of view and was comprehensive for its time, it is now outdated. A major work, which appeared in the United States in 1934, was "Termites and Termite Control," edited by C. A. Kofoid. This work, though it contains considerable basic biological information, is limited, as it deals with only a few North American species and approaches its subject from an economic point of view. Other widely known books are those of T. E. Snyder, "Our Enemy the Termite" (1948), H. Schmidt, "Die Termiten" (1955), and W. V. Harris, "Termites, Their Recognition and Control" (1961). These books give a good general account of termites and their social organization, again emphasizing control. Short accounts summarizing the more striking aspects of termite biology can be found in various textbooks. Most widely referred to are those of A. D. Imms' "General Textbook of Entomology" (1957, edited by O. W. Richards and R. G. Davies) and P. P. Grassé's "Traité de Zoologie" (1949). Among other general works on termites written for the informed layman are S. H.

Skaife's "Dwellers in Darkness" (1961), O. W. Richards' "The Social Insects" (1953), and C. D. Michener and M. H. Michener's "American Social Insects" (1951). All of these works are either limited from a fundamental biological point of view or are outdated, not only because of the development of new techniques and advances in traditional areas of investigation, but also because of the opening up of entirely new avenues of research.

In the last twenty years there has been a marked increase of interest in the study of termites, and a considerable new body of knowledge has accumulated. However, this information is widely scattered throughout various journals and other publications. The purpose of this two-volume treatise is to bring together the basic facts as currently understood and to reevaluate and review past research in the light of new discoveries, with the aim of presenting a comprehensive picture of the current status of our knowledge, incorporating a worldwide representation of termite species.

These chapters include both laboratory and field studies, and have been prepared by specialists who are actively engaged in research and are in a position to evaluate the accumulated knowledge and also to present here for the first time some of the results of their more recent research. Anatomical, physiological, biochemical, behavioral, and laboratory studies have been grouped in Volume I; Volume II is concerned primarily with taxonomy and the general biology of the termites of the different zoogeographical regions. The two volumes therefore incorporate material of interest not only to those with a primary interest in termite biology but also to the zoologist, botanist, ecologist, behaviorist, biochemist, endocrinologist, and economic entomologist.

The editors wish to express their deep appreciation to the authors, who have devoted a good part of their time to the preparation of their contributions. We must also express our gratitude for the active help and support provided by our spouses, Valerie Krishna and Robert R. Lechleitner.

January, 1969   KUMAR KRISHNA
                                             FRANCES M. WEESNER

Contents

Chapter 1   Introduction
KUMAR KRISHNA

Chapter 2   External Anatomy
FRANCES M. WEESNER

Chapter 3   The Digestive System
CH. NOIROT AND C. NOIROT-TIMOTHÉE

Chapter 9 Caste Differentiation in the Lower Termites

E. MORTON MILLER

Chapter 10 Formation of Castes in the Higher Termites

CH. NOIROT

Chapter 11 Rearing of Termites and Testing Methods Used in the Laboratory

GÜNTHER BECKER

Chapter 12 Feeding Relationships and Radioisotope Techniques

ELIZABETH A. MCMAHAN

Chapter 17 **The Biology of Termitophiles**

DAVID H. KISTNER

1

Introduction

KUMAR KRISHNA

Termites are found predominantly in the tropical regions of the world. Their role in the disintegration of wood and other cellulose material; their place in the food chains of many animals; their association with fungi, termitophiles, and parasites; their symbiotic relationships with protozoans and bacteria; their complex behavior and nest constructions; the adaptations, group integration, and polymorphism associated with their intricate social life — all these characteristics have made them unique objects of study by a wide variety of biologists.

I. WHAT ARE TERMITES? THEIR SOCIAL ORGANIZATION

Termites are social insects comprising the order Isoptera. The individuals are differentiated into various morphological forms, or castes, which exhibit division of labor, performing different biological functions, and which live in highly organized and integrated units, the societies or colonies. Termites differ from hymenopteran social insects (ants, bees, and wasps) in that they are hemimetabolous, their castes are usually bisexual, and they have no known subsocial groups.

Termites are structurally most closely related to the cockroaches (Blattidae): the primitive genus *Mastotermes* of Australia lays its eggs in an oothecal-like mass and has a folded anal lobe in the hind wing. They possess chewing and biting mouthparts, and the imagoes have two pairs of subequal wings which have the unique characteristic of breaking at the suture when shed, leaving only the base or "scale" on the thorax.

A termite colony consists of functional reproductives, workers, soldiers, and immature individuals. Immature individuals have been collectively termed "nymphs" by some investigators, particularly of the American school, or have been distinguished as "larvae" (lacking wing pads) and "nymphs" (possessing wing pads). The term larvae, as applied to immature termites, is not equivalent to the same term as it is used for holometabolous insects.

The functional reproductives are of two kinds, primary and supplementary. The primary reproductives, the king and queen, are highly sclerotized and pigmented and develop from winged (macropterous) adults. The supplementary reproductives are either slightly pigmented, with short wing pads (brachypterous), or very slightly pigmented, without wing pads (apterous). Both forms of supplementary reproductives may be termed neotenic, since they achieve sexual maturity without first reaching the imaginal form. There is usually only one pair of primary reproductives in a colony, but when they die they may be replaced by numerous supplementary reproductives.

Besides carrying out the fundamental function of reproduction, the reproductive caste also performs in distribution of the species by swarming or colonizing flights, choice of the site of a new colony, excavation of the first galleries, and the feeding and care of the first young in a new colony.

The sterile castes, the workers and soldiers, are wingless and, in the majority of the species, blind. The sterile castes sometimes exhibit polymorphism: in some species there are two types of worker—major (large) and minor (small)—and three types of soldier—major, intermediate, and minor. The worker caste is considered to be absent in the families Mastotermitidae and Kalotermitidae and in the subfamily Termopsinae of the family Hodotermitidae. In these groups the function of the workers is carried out by immature individuals, which may molt from time to time without appreciable change in size and which are termed pseudergates or pseudoworkers. The functions of the workers or pseudergates, which form the majority of the population in a colony, are tending the eggs and young, foraging for food, feeding and cleaning individuals of the other castes, and constructing and repairing the nest. The soldiers have long, powerful mandibles or other structural modifications to defend the community against predators.

The young individuals in the colony may develop into soldiers, workers, or winged alates. The male and female winged reproductives leave the parent colony in a mass exodus, the swarming or dispersal flight. After the dispersal flight, which is usually short, the alates lose their wings (dealation) and form pairs, usually on the ground. The paired reproductives dig a hole in the soil or in wood. Copulation follows establishment in the substrate, the first young develop into workers or pseudergates, and one or two soldiers may be produced. The male cohabits with the female, and copulation occurs at intervals throughout the life of the pair.

II. CLASSIFICATION

At the present time about 1900 living and fossil species of termites have been described. The classification of these into families and subfamilies which is generally followed in the present work is that proposed by Snyder (1949) and Emerson (1955). This classification is listed below:

> Family I   Mastotermitidae
> Family II   Kalotermitidae*
> Family III   Hodotermitidae
>   Subfamily 1   Termopsinae
>   Subfamily 2   Stolotermitinae
>   Subfamily 3   Porotermitinae
>   Subfamily 4   Cretatermitinae†
>   Subfamily 5   Hodotermitinae
> Family IV   Rhinotermitidae
>   Subfamily 1   Psammotermitinae
>   Subfamily 2   Heterotermitinae
>   Subfamily 3   Stylotermitinae
>   Subfamily 4   Coptotermitinae
>   Subfamily 5   Termitogetoninae
>   Subfamily 6   Rhinotermitinae
> Family V   Serritermitidae‡

*Snyder (1949) and Emerson (1955) included two subfamilies in the family Kalotermitidae, Kalotermitinae for living genera and Electrotermitinae for fossil genera. Krishna (1961) proposed that the distinctions between these two were not sharp enough to warrant their division into subfamilies.

†Emerson (1968) has recently described this new monotypic fossil subfamily.

‡Emerson (1965) elevated the subfamily Serritermitinae, previously included in the family Rhinotermitidae, to full family status.

Family VI   Termitidae
        Subfamily 1   Amitermitinae
        Subfamily 2   Termitinae*
        Subfamily 3   Macrotermitinae
        Subfamily 4   Nasutitermitinae

In this classification the families Mastotermitidae, Kalotermitidae, Hodotermitidae, Rhinotermitidae, and Serritermitidae are referred to collectively as the lower termites. The termites in these five families possess symbiotic protozoans in the hind intestine on which they depend for digestion of cellulose. The Termitidae, referred to as the higher termites, is the largest family, containing three-fourths of the known species. This family is the most advanced and diverse, exhibiting a wide variety of social specializations, and does not possess symbiotic protozoans.

Some current investigators, including a number of authors in the present work, follow the classification of Grassé (1949). Grassé divides the family Hodotermitidae of Snyder and Emerson into two families: (1) Termopsidae, to include the subfamilies Termopsinae, Stolotermitinae, and Porotermitinae, and (2) Hodotermitidae. The Termopsidae of Grassé includes all the species that are wood-dwelling, the Hodotermitidae those that are harvesters.

The generic and specific names used in this work follow the latest published synonymies and new combinations that are generally recognized. Specific names which are currently treated as synonyms when cited for the first time in each chapter are put in square brackets or parentheses.

III. RECENT HISTORY OF TERMITE RESEARCH

A detailed historical review of pertinent research is given in each chapter. Only the major areas and trends in termite research of the last 20–30 years are briefly touched upon here.

A. EVOLUTION

Termites have been used to illustrate various evolutionary principles. Among these the concept of the supraorganism has occupied a prominent

*Grassé and Noirot (1954) excluded from the subfamily Termitinae the genera *Apicotermes*, *Trichotermes*, *Jugositermes*, *Rostrotermes*, *Hoplognathotermes*, *Allognathotermes*, *Coxotermes*, and *Heimitermes* and erected a new subfamily, Apicotermitinae, for these genera. This division of the subfamily Termitinae is not, however, accepted by all investigators.

position. This concept, elaborated by Emerson (1939, 1952c), depicts the termite society, which is composed of many multicellular individuals, as a fundamental unit in evolution having analogies to an individual organism. For example, the supraorganism has division of labor, integration, and specialization between individual castes, with the sterile castes analogous to the somatic cells of an individual organism, the reproductive castes paralleling its gametes, and the functions of the workers and soldiers analogous to the functions of its nutritive and protective cells. The individuals in a termite society cannot exist by themselves, and their interdependence and integration resemble those of an organism (though of course the integration of a termite society is through trophallaxis, that is, mutual exchange of materials, and through sensory stimuli, not through protoplasmic continuity, as in an organism).

Emerson (1956) has further elaborated this concept, through field observations, to illustrate other similarities. He points out that, like organisms, termite nests are homeostatically regulated units. The nest wall serves as a barrier to predators in a manner similar to that of the shell of an animal. The internal environment is self-regulating, optimal for existence and survival, and to some degree independent of the external environment. Nest parts may be regenerated, like the lost parts of an organism. Similarities are also found in growth, development, symmetry, and adaptation. Lüscher (1953, 1961b) has further shown experimentally that the differentiation of termite castes has many similarities to cell differentiation in an organism and that analogous mechanisms (inhibitory and stimulatory factors) operate in both.

Though the concept of the supraorganism is not universally accepted, there is no doubt that it has been valuable as a conceptual framework and that information from such analogies may suggest experiments to be done and observations to be made in order to understand the underlying mechanisms operating in the social organization of the termite colony.

Termites have been used by Emerson (1961, 1962) in the illustration and analysis of other important evolutionary concepts and processes, such as homology, convergence, parallelism, divergence, and progressive, regressive, and adaptive evolution. Termites are particularly well suited for such studies: the taxonomy and phylogeny are unusually well worked out, because there are a great number of morphological characters available for study in the different castes of a species and also because the phylogeny is in many instances correlated with ecological, geographical, and paleontological data. Some of these characters are highly adaptive, such as the great variety of defensive modifications in the soldier, and, being highly adaptive, many of these clearly illustrate parallel and convergent trends. Also, because of the presence of numerous transitional

stages of the various characteristics, it is possible to analyze both pro-
gression and regression in detail.

B. Systematics

There has been a great deal of activity in termite taxonomy, phylogeny,
and evolutionary history. The main effort has been not merely to describe
new species but to understand basic phylogenetic relationships at the
level of higher categories (genera and above) and to speculate on evolutionary histories. These efforts have also contributed to making the
taxonomy and phylogeny better known for termites than for any group
of animals of comparable size.

The modern classification of Isoptera and the phylogenetic arrangement of genera in the various families that is most widely accepted today
and that has replaced the 1911—1913 classification of Holmgren and
others has been mainly the effort of Emerson and Snyder. As noted
above, this is the classification adopted by Snyder in his 1949 "Catalog
of the Termites of the World."

Phylogenetic trees for all the termite genera have been proposed by
Ahmad (1950), who based his evidence primarily on the imago-worker
mandible, which he considered a more conservative and less adaptive
character than the soldier mandible and the other characters of the
soldier caste. Ahmad thus avoided and corrected past errors that had
resulted from the use of adaptive characters of the soldier, which tend
to obscure the basic phylogenetic relationships due to convergent and
parallel evolution.

In connection with systematic revisions of different genera, phylogenetic relationships have been studied by many investigators, either
supporting the scheme proposed by Ahmad or suggesting changes in it.
These studies are too many to enumerate here, but among the more
important are Krishna (1961, 1963) on the family Kalotermitidae and
Foraminitermes; Sands (1957, 1965a) on the subfamily Nasutitermitinae;
Emerson (1950, 1952b, 1959, 1960a,b, 1965) on *Cornitermes* and other
genera of the subfamily Nasutitermitinae and genera of the families Termitidae and Mastotermitidae; and Roonwal and Chhotani (1965, 1966)
on *Eurytermes* and *Speculitermes.*

Significant contributions have been made to our knowledge of the
zoogeography of termites. Emerson has been a pioneer in this field also.
He has speculated (1952a, 1955) on the time and place of origin and
dispersal patterns of termite genera, correlating knowledge of phylogeny,

present geographical distribution, present ecological limitations, ancient climates, and ancient land bridges.

C. MORPHOLOGY

The external morphology of termites has received much attention, mainly due to its importance in systematics and classification. Comparative studies by taxonomists have focused in particular on the dentition of the imago-worker mandible, wing venation, and the mandible and labrum of the soldier. More direct contributions have been made by some morphologists, who have described in great detail the external morphology of a single species, rather than following a comparative approach, as was taken by Holmgren (1909). Recent studies of this type that have followed the studies of Imms (1919) on *Archotermopsis wroughtoni* Desneux and of Sumner (1933) on *Zootermopsis* are those of Gupta (1960) and Kushwaha (1960) on *Anacanthotermes macrocephalus* (Desneux) and *Odontotermes obesus* (Rambur), respectively.

Only very recently have investigators considered internal morphology in studies of phylogenetic relationships rather than relying solely on external morphology as observed in preserved specimens. Grassé and Noirot (1954) and Noirot and Kovoor (1958) have studied the digestive tube and associated structures—particularly the crop, the armature of the gizzard, and the enteric valves and Malpighian tubules—in *Apicotermes* and other genera of the subfamily Termitinae (see Chapter 3). The work of McKittrick (1964) on the proventriculus and the female genitalia substantiated for the first time on morphological grounds the long-postulated close relationship between *Mastotermes* and the wood-eating roach *Cryptocercus punctulatus* Scudder—a relation previously supported only by the fact of their similar protozoans. Other internal structures that have been studied are the musculature, by Vishnoi (1956); the nervous system, by Richard (1967), Hecker (1966), and Zuberi (1963) (see Chapter 6); the reproductive system, by Weesner (1955) (see Chapter 5); the genitalia, by Roonwal (1956) (see Chapter 2); and the sternal gland, by Stuart (1964) and Noirot and Noirot-Timothée (1965a) (see Chapter 4).

Some of these organ systems have attracted more attention than others. As soon as a particular structure is linked to an interesting function, it becomes the focus of attention. For example, as soon as trail laying was linked to the sternal gland, a great deal of research began to be concentrated on the details of this gland. This in turn has led to a detailed histological study of this and other structures with the aid of the electron microscope: Noirot and Noirot-Timothée (1965b) and others have so studied the sternal gland and Noirot-Timothée and Noirot (1965) the digestive tube.

D. Behavior and Nests

The areas in termite behavior that have received particular attention are dispersal, pairing, nest foundation and construction, feeding and foraging, defense, trail laying, communication, and regulation of castes (see Chapters 7 – 10, 12, 13). Early studies consisted mainly of observations made in the field, which were primarily descriptive and speculative. Only in recent years has the approach become experimental and analytical – an approach that, through modern techniques, had led not only to the confirmation of many of the earlier speculations based on field observations, but also to an understanding of the significance of behavior patterns and of their underlying physiological and biochemical mechanisms.

It is known that termites produce sound by convulsive movements, jerking and tapping their heads against the ground. This action had been especially noted in the soldier caste by early investigators. It was speculated (Emerson, 1929) that the sound produced by the soldiers was a means of communication of warning to other termites by means of the substratum vibrations produced.

Howse (1964a,b, 1965) has studied the problem of communication and sound production through oscillatory movements in termites by using cinephotography, kymographs, oscillographs, tape recorders, and electrophysiological techniques. His results indicated that, at least in *Zootermopsis*, the oscillatory movement results in the production of sound in both the soldiers and the nymphs and is accompanied by the laying of a trail of pheromone; that the termites respond to only the substratum vibrations and not to airborne sounds; that the subgenual organ is the one which picks up these vibrations; and that the significance and function of these substratum vibrations is to communicate alarm, as was speculated earlier.

The problem of the origin and mechanism of trail laying, of the nature of the trail, and of its significance has been studied in detail, mainly by Stuart (1961, 1963a,b). His studies have shown that the chemical scent trail is laid by the sternal gland, that its purpose is to communicate alarm, and that it is also important, at least in the higher termites, in foraging, or communicating the presence and direction of food. These studies by Stuart have also generated an interest in the biochemical analysis of trail-laying pheromones.

Feeding behavior in termites, e.g., the mutual exchange of nutrients between the members of a colony (trophallaxis), has been studied using radioactive isotope techniques by McMahan (1963, 1966), Alibert (1963), and Gösswald and Kloft (1960, 1963) (see Chapter 12). With these techniques the investigators have been able to confirm earlier observations and speculations and to quantify their results, which in the past had not been possible. Their studies have focused on solving such problems as the rate and pattern of food exchange between the members of a colony, which castes feed directly and which indirectly, and the manner in which the food is transferred from one individual to another. McMahan has been able to confirm with her studies the earlier speculation that soldiers are unable to feed themselves and are dependent on workers and nymphs for their food.

Every naturalist and collector who has traveled in the tropics has observed the striking nests built by termites, and termite literature abounds with descriptions of different nest forms constructed by various termite species. Details of the architecture of the nests of some species, as well as of the materials used in construction, have been recorded.

The evolution of termite behavior did not receive attention until Emerson (1938) pointed out that nests are visible and tangible expressions of behavior which can be studied like the morphological structure of an animal, and that the evolution of behavior can thus be traced in the same manner as morphological evolution. Similar evolutionary principles can be observed, such as convergence, divergence, adaptation, phylogeny, and ontogeny. Homologous parts of nest structures can be traced through a group of related species.

This approach has been followed through in the study of the African genus *Apicotermes* by Schmidt (1955), Bouillon (1964b), and others, where the nest structures of the various species have been studied in detail and arranged in a phylogenetic order which closely parallels the phylogeny based on the morphological characters of the animals. The study of the evolution of behavior is not unique to termites and is now being carried out on many other groups of insects (Emerson, 1958).

Because termites have a soft cuticle and are easily desiccated if exposed directly to the outside environment (see Chapter 14), they must live in the closed environment of the nests, where they are able to establish and regulate their microclimate—the humidity, temperature, carbon dioxide, and other factors suited to the needs of the individual species. This microclimate has been examined and studied in only a few species (mainly those of the higher termites that build large mounds) by Holdaway and Gay (1948), Lüscher (1955, 1961a), Emerson (1956), Ruelle (1964), and others. These studies have shown that this internal environment is relatively stable and that optimum conditions are usually maintained. The relative humidity is high (90—99%) in the nest interior. The temperature, generally higher inside the nest than outside, is not so closely regulated as the relative humidity and varies with that of the outside environment, though it is most stable in subterranean and thick-walled mound nests, such as those of *Macrotermes*. High concentrations of carbon dioxide are found in the nest interior; for example, 0.6—2.8% in *Macrotermes natalensis* (Haviland). In the final analysis, it is not known exactly how this microclimate is so carefully regulated, though behavioral activities, such as building and repairing the nest, are thought to play some part. The details of nest structure and the microclimate of the nest are given in Volume II.

E. CASTES

The area of caste differentiation, production, and regulation has received considerable attention (see Chapters 9, 10). Caste differentiation in termites cannot be due to genetic factors, as it is known that newly hatched nymphs are capable of developing into members of any one of the castes. Instead, so far as has been determined, extrinsic factors such as pheromones and hormones play a major role in this differentiation. The most adequate experimentally supported theory of caste differentiation is the inhibition theory, which was first proposed by Pickens (1932) and later elaborated and substantiated by the experiments of Castle (1934), Light (1942—1943, 1944), Lüscher (1952, 1960, 1961b), and others. This theory states that the members of the reproductive and soldier castes give off pheromones (earlier called ectohormones or socio-hormones), containing inhibiting substances, which are transmitted to nymphs through mutual feeding and grooming throughout the colony. In this way the reproductives and soldiers exert an inhibiting influence on the development of like forms. When, because of an increase in population due to colony growth or because of the loss or reduction of reproductives or soldiers, some undifferentiated nymphs fall beyond this inhibiting influence, they develop into additional members of these castes. Thus the production of the castes is regulated and the ratio kept in balance.

Studies of the total population and the fluctuations in the proportions of the different castes in natural colonies have been made in a few species by Gupta (1953), Sands (1965b), Bouillon (1964a), Bouillon and Lekie (1964), and other investigators.

F. ASSOCIATED ORGANISMS

All sorts of invertebrates (beetles, flies, and others) have become adapted to living in the nests of termites. They have become so adapted over the course of evolution to living in close association with termites that they cannot survive independently and have developed interesting structural and physiological modifications. These organisms are referred to as termitophiles (see Chapter 17).

These termitophiles attracted the attention of the early naturalists and collectors, to whom they were interesting curiosities that received only species descriptions. In the course of time, Seevers (1957) and Kistner (1958) realized that the host-termitophile relationship was species specific, with a taxonomic correlation between the termitophile and the host, and that the evolutionary history of the termitophiles closely paralleled the evolutionary history of the host termites. Thus, the phylogenetic study of either organism results in corroborative knowledge of the other. However, detailed biology of these organisms is still in the elementary stage.

Many termites are closely associated with different kinds of fungi, some symbiotic, some parasitic or pathogenic, and some saprophytic (see Chapter 16). The exact role of many of these fungi—whether they provide special nutrients in the diet of the termites, whether some of them decompose the cellulose and lignin in the wood on which the termites feed, or whether they play some other important role—is unknown. Research has progressed in trying to determine their role and has led to experimentation in the laboratory and correlation with data observed in nature.

The association between termites and fungi that has attracted the most attention of naturalists and biologists is the symbiotic relation between the subfamily Macrotermitinae and the fungal genus *Termitomyces*. It is well known that in the nests of all species of Macrotermitinae the termites construct sponge-shaped fungus gardens or combs, composed of excreta. In all species except *Sphaerotermes sphaerothorax* (Sjöstedt) the termites cultivate fungi on the combs, principally of the genus *Termitomyces*. There has been much speculation as to the function of the fungus comb and its associated fungi (as a possible source of food and vitamins, as producing heat and thus maintaining constant high temperature, as maintaining constant high humidity, and as serving as egg depositories and nurseries). Sands (1956) and others have shown experimentally that at least one of the most important functions is nutrition, since in laboratory cultures of *Odontotermes* small quantities of fresh combs with fungi, added to a diet of filter paper, increased the lifespan of individuals.

It has also been observed in nature that some termites are attracted to certain kinds of fungi (Esenther *et al.*, 1961; Esenther and Coppel, 1964), and the possibility presented itself that the fungal extracts could be used for control purposes. Attempts have been made to identify the attractant substances, and a number of workers are still engaged in this effort, though as yet it has not borne fruit.

The lower termites harbor in the hindgut a rich protozoan fauna. At least some of these flagellate protozoans have a definite symbiotic (mutualistic) relationship with their host termites (Volume II). The work of Cleveland (1923), Trager (1932), Hungate (1938), and others has demonstrated experimentally that the termites are dependent on the protozoans to provide the necessary enzymes for the digestion of cellulose. This spectacular discovery has overshadowed the fact that in the higher termites (Termitidae), which make up 75% of all termite species, these symbiotic protozoans are absent and only bacteria are present.

The physiology of cellulose digestion in the higher termites is not fully understood. It has been suggested that bacteria have taken over the functions performed by protozoans in the lower termites or that the enzymes are directly secreted by the gut epithelium. Misra and Ranganathan (1954) and Tracey and Youat (1958) have reported cellulase and cellobiase activity in the gut of some species of higher termites, but whether these enzymes are produced by the bacteria or directly by the gut epithelium is not known.

Because the symbiotic flagellate protozoans on which they are dependent are lost at each molt, and reinfection of the newly molted nymphs can only occur through association with other infected, nonmolting individuals, colony life is essential in the lower termites. Cleveland *et al.* (1934) suggested that this colony life in ancestral termites led to the origin of the social life of the termite society.

In addition to their importance to the study of digestion, the protozoans have been used as indicators of the phylogenetic relationships of their termite hosts (Kirby, 1937, 1949), since there has been reciprocal evolution of the protozoans and their hosts, with their close ecological association, for 100,000,000 years or more.

G. Culturing

Many attempts have been made to culture termites in the laboratory (see Chapter 11), since most centers of research and experimentation are far from the natural habitats of the majority of termite species. However, in most instances, termites have been difficult to rear, as the individuals in a colony have a delicate integration which is easily disturbed in handling and isolating them, resulting in a high mortality rate. In spite of this and other difficulties, many investigators have cultured termites in the laboratory with varying degrees of success, including Adamson (1941), Light and Weesner (1947), Lüscher (1949), Osmun

(1956), Gay *et al.* (1955), and Becker (1961, 1966). In general, it is possible to rear termites belonging to the family Kalotermitidae, the subfamily Termopsinae of the family Hodotermitidae, and the genus *Reticulitermes* of the family Rhinotermitidae with success, but many of the Rhinotermitidae and especially the Termitidae are very difficult to culture.

In conclusion, it can be said that some areas of termite research have received considerable more attention than others, a fact evidenced by the areas covered in the various chapters. We are far from a complete understanding of the physiological, ecological, and behavioral factors that govern the integration and stabilization of the termite society. However, with the development of new techniques and tools, beginnings have been made in the analysis of some of the mechanisms underlying these processes through controlled experimentation. It is hoped that the appearance of these volumes will alert biologists throughout the world to the many problems in the biology of termites awaiting further study.

REFERENCES

Adamson, A. M. (1941). Laboratory technique for the study of living termites. *Ecology* 22, 411-414.

Ahmad, M. (1950). The phylogeny of termite genera based on imago-worker mandibles. *Bull. Amer. Museum Nat. Hist.*, 95, 37-86.

Alibert, J. (1963). Echanges trophallactiques chez un termite supérieur. Contamination par le phosphore radio-actif de la population d'un nid de *Cubitermes fungifaber*. *Insectes Sociaux* 10, 1-12.

Becker, G. (1961). Beiträge zur Prüfung und Beurteilung der natürlichen Dauerhaftigkeit von Holz gegen Termiten. *Holz Roh-Werkstoff* 19, 278-290.

Becker, G. (1966). Einige Beobachtungen und Versuchsergebnisse an Zuchten von *Coptotermes*-Arten (Isopt.) im Laboratorium. *Z. Angew. Zool.* 53, 463-479.

Bouillon, A., (1964a). Etude de la composition des sociétés dans trois espèces d'*Apicotermes* Holmgren (Isoptera, Termitinae). *In* "Etudes sur les termites africains" (A. Bouillon, ed.), Chapter 18, pp. 180-194. Masson, Paris.

Bouillon, A. (1964b). Structure et accroissement des nids d'*Apicotermes*. *In* "Etudes sur les termites africains" (A. Bouillon, ed.), Chapter 26, pp. 295-326. Masson, Paris.

Bouillon, A., and Lekie, R. (1964). Populations, rythme d'activité diurne et cycle de croissance du nid de *Cubitermes sankurensis* Wasmann (Isoptera, Termitinae). *In* "Etudes sur les termites africains" (A. Bouillon, ed.), Chapter 19, pp. 197-213. Masson, Paris.

Castle, G. B. (1934). An experimental investigation of caste differentiation in *Zootermopsis angusticollis*. *In* "Termites and Termite Control" (C. A. Kofoid, ed.), 2nd ed., pp. 292-310. Univ. of California Press, Berkeley, California.

Cleveland, L. R. (1923). Symbiosis between termites and their intestinal protozoa. *Proc. Natl. Acad. Sci. U.S.* 9, 424-428.

Cleveland, L. R., Hall, S. R., Sander, E. P., and Collier, J. (1934). The wood-feeding roach *Cryptocercus*, its protozoa, and the symbiosis between protozoa and roach. *Mem. Am. Acad. Arts Sci.* [N.S.] 17, 185-342.

Emerson, A. E. (1929). Communication among termites. *Trans. 4th Intern. Entomol. Congr., 1928* Vol. 2, pp. 722-727, Ithaca, New York.

Emerson, A. E. (1938). Termite nests — a study of the phylogeny of behavior. *Ecol. Monographs* 8, 247-284.

Emerson, A. E. (1939). Social coordination and superorganism. *Am. Midland Naturalist* 21, 182-209.

Emerson, A. E. (1950). Five new genera of termites from South America and Madagascar (Isoptera, Rhinotermitidae, Termitidae). *Am. Museum Novitates* 1444, 1-15.

Emerson, A. E. (1952a). The biogeography of termites. *Bull. Am. Museum Nat. Hist.* 99, 217-225.

Emerson, A. E. (1952b). The Neotropical genera *Procornitermes* and *Cornitermes* (Isoptera, Termitidae). *Bull. Am. Museum Nat. Hist.* 99, 475-540.

Emerson, A. E. (1952c). The supraorganismic aspects of the society. *Colloq. Intern. Centre Natl. Rech. Sci. (Paris)* 34, 33-354.

Emerson, A. E. (1955). Geographical origins and dispersions of termite genera. *Fieldiana, Zool.* 37, 465-521.

Emerson, A. E. (1956). Regenerative behavior and social homeostasis of termites. *Ecology* 37, 248-258.

Emerson, A. E. (1958). The evolution of behavior among social insects. *In* "Behavior and Evolution" (A. Roe and G. G. Simpson, eds.), Chapter 15, pp. 311-335. Yale Univ. Press, New Haven, Connecticut.

Emerson, A. E. (1959). The African termite genera *Firmitermes, Hoplognathotermes, Acutidentitermes, Duplidentitermes* and *Heimitermes* (Termitidae, Termitinae). *Am. Museum Novitates* 1947, 1-42.

Emerson, A. E. (1960a). New genera on the *Subulitermes* branch of the Nasutitermitinae from the Ethiopian region (Isoptera, Termitidae). *Am. Museum Novitates* 1987, 1-21.

Emerson, A. E. (1960b). New genera of termites related to *Subulitermes* from the Oriental, Malagasy and Australian regions (Isoptera, Termitidae, Nasutitermitinae). *Am. Museum Novitates* 1986, 1-27.

Emerson, A. E. (1961). Vestigial characters of termites and processes of regressive evolution. *Evolution* 15, 115-131.

Emerson, A. E. (1962). Vestigial characters, regressive evolution, and recapitulation among termites. *Proc. New Delhi Symp. 1960*, pp. 17-30. UNESCO, Paris.

Emerson, A. E. (1965). A review of the Mastotermitidae (Isoptera), including a new fossil genus from Brazil. *Am. Museum Novitates* 2236, 1-46.

Emerson, A. E. (1968). Cretaceous insects from Labrador. 3. A new genus and species of termite (Isoptera, Hodotermitidae). *Psyche* [4] 74, 276-289.

Esenther, G. B., and Coppel, H. C. (1964). Current research on termite attractants. *Pest Control* 32 No. 2, 34, 36, 38, 42, 44, and 46.

Esenther, G. B., Allen, T. C., Casida, J. E., and Shenefelt, R. D. (1961). Termite attractant from fungus-infected wood. *Science* 134, 50.

Gay, F. J., Greaves, T., Holdaway, F. G., and Wetherly, A. H. (1955). Laboratory testing with termites. *Australia, Commonwealth Sci. Ind. Res. Organ., Bull.* 277, 1-60.

Gösswald, K., and Kloft, W. (1960). Untersuchungen mit radioaktiven Isotopen an Waldameisen. *Entomophaga* 5, 33-41.

Gösswald, K., and Kloft, W. (1963). Tracer experiments on food exchanges in ants and termites. *Proc. Symp. Intern. At. Energy Agency, Athens, 1963* pp. 15-42.

Grassé, P. P., (1949). Ordre des Isoptères ou Termites. *In* "Traité de Zoologie," (P. P. Grassé ed.) Vol. IX, pp. 408-544. Masson, Paris.

Grassé, P. P. and Noirot, C. (1954). *Apicotermes arquieri* (Isoptère) ses constructions, sa biologie. Considérations générales sur la sousfamille des Apicotermitinae nov. *Ann. Sci. Nat. Zool. Biol. Animale* [11] **16**, 345-388.

Gupta, S. D. (1953). Ecological studies of termites, Parts I and II. *Proc. Natl. Inst. Sci. India* **19**, 697-712.

Gupta, S. D. (1960). Morphology of the primitive termite *Anacanthotermes macrocephalus* (Desneux) (Isoptera: Hodotermitidae). *Records Indian Museum* **48**, 169-222.

Hecker, H. (1966). Das Zentralnerven system des Kopfes und seine postembryonale Entwicklung bei *Bellicositermes bellicosus* (Smeath.) (Isoptera). *Acta Trop.* **23**, 297-352.

Holdaway, F. G., and Gay, F. J. (1948). Temperature studies of the habitat of *Eutermes exitiosus* with special reference to the temperature within the mound. *Australian J. Sci. Res.* **B1**, 464-493.

Holmgren, N. (1909). Termitenstudien. I. Anatomische Untersuchungen. *Kgl. Svenska Vetenskapsakad. Handl.* [3] **44**, 1-215.

Howse, P. E. (1964a). The significance of sound produced by the termite *Zootermopsis angusticollis* (Hagen). *Animal Behaviour* **12**, 284-300.

Howse, P. E. (1964b). An investigation into mode of action of subgenual organ in the termite *Zootermopsis angusticollis* Emerson and in the cockroach *Periplaneta americana* L. *J. Insect Morphol.* **10**, 409-424.

Howse, P. E. (1965). On the significance of certain oscillatory movements of termites. *Insectes Sociaux* **12**, 335-346.

Hungate, R. E. (1938). Studies on the nutrition of *Zootermopsis*. II. The relative importance of the termite and the protozoa in wood digestion. *Ecology* **19**, 1-25.

Imms, A. D. (1919). On the structure and biology of *Archotermopsis*, together with descriptions of new species of intestinal protozoa, and general observations on the Isoptera. *Phil. Trans. Roy. Soc. London* **B209**, 75-180.

Kirby, H. (1937). Host-parasite relations in the distribution of protozoa in termites. *Univ. Calif. (Berkeley) Publ. Zool.* **41**, 189-212.

Kirby, H. (1949). Systematic differentiation and evolution of flagellates in termites. *Rev. Soc. Mex. Hist. Nat.* **10**, 57-79.

Kistner, D. (1958). The evolution of the Pygostenini (Coleoptera, Staphylinidae). *Ann. Musee Roy. Congo Belge: Ser. in 8°, Sci. Zool.* **68**, 1-198.

Krishna, K. (1961). A generic revision and phylogenetic study of the family Kalotermitidae (Isoptera). *Bull. Am. Museum Nat. Hist.* **122**, 303-408.

Krishna, K. (1963). The African genus *Foraminitermes* Holmgren (Isoptera, Termitidae, Termitinae). *Am. Museum Novitates* **2161**, 1-23.

Kushwaha, K. S. (1960). External morphology of the termite *Odontotermes obesus* (Rambur) (Isoptera: Termitidae) Part 1. Soldier, Part 2. Alate and worker. *Records Indian Museum* **55**, 209-250.

Light, S. F. (1942-1943). The determination of castes of social insects. *Quart. Rev. Biol.* **17**, 312-326; **18**, 46-63.

Light, S. F. (1944). Experimental studies on ectohormonal control of the development of supplementary reproductives in the termite genus *Zootermopsis* (formerly *Termopsis*). *Univ. Calif. (Berkeley) Publ. Zool.* **43**, 413-454.

Light, S. F., and Weesner, F. M. (1947). Methods for culturing termites. *Science* **106**, 131.

Lüscher, M. (1949). Continuous observation of termites in laboratory cultures. *Acta Trop.* **6**, 161-165.

Lüscher, M. (1952). New evidence for an ectohormonal control of caste determination in termites. *Trans. 9th Intern. Congr. Entmol., Amsterdam, 1951* Vol. 1, pp 289-294.

Lüscher, M. (1953). The termite and the cell. *Sci. Am.* **188** [5], 74-78.

Lüscher, M. (1955). Der Sauerstoffverbrauch bei Termiten und die Ventilation des Neste bei *Macrotermes natalensis* (Haviland), *Acta Trop.* **12**, 289-307.

Lüscher, M. (1960). Hormonal control of caste differentiation in termites. *Ann. N.Y. Acad. Sci.* **89**, 549-563.

Lüscher, M. (1961a). Air-conditioned termite nests. *Sci. Am.* **205** [1], 138-145.

Lüscher, M. (1961b). Social control of polymorphism in termites. *In* "Insect Polymorphism" (J. S. Kennedy, ed.), pp. 57-67. Roy. Entomol. Soc., London.

McKittrick, F. A. (1964). Evolutionary studies of cockroaches. *Cornell Univ., Agr. Expt. Sta. Mem.* **389**, 1-197.

McMahan, E. A. (1963). A study of termite feeding relationships, using radioisotopes. *Ann. Entomol. Soc. Am.* **56**, 74-82.

McMahan, E. A. (1966). Food transmission within the *Cryptotermes brevis* colony (Isoptera, Kalotermitidae). *Ann. Entomol. Soc. Am.* **59**, 1131-1137.

Misra, J. N., and Ranganathan, V. (1954). Digestion of cellulose by the mound building termite *Termes (Cyclotermes) obesus* (Rambur). *Proc. Indian Acad. Sci.* **39**, 100-113.

Noirot, C., and Kovoor, J. (1958). Anatomie comparée du tube digestif des termites. I. Sous-famille des "Termitinae." *Insectes Sociaux* **5**, 439-471.

Noirot, C., and Noirot-Timothée, C. (1965a). La glande sternale dans l'evolution des termites. *Insectes Sociaux* **12**, 265-272.

Noirot, C., and Noirot-Timothée, C. (1965b). Organisation de la glande sternal chez *Calotermes flavicollis* F. (Insecta, Isoptera). *Compt. Rend.* **260**, 6202-6204.

Noirot-Timothée, C., and Noirot, C. (1965). L'intestin moyen chez la reine des termites supérieurs. Etude au microscope éléctronique. *Ann. Sci. Nat. Zool. Biol. Animale* [12] **7**, 185-206.

Osmun, J. V. (1956). Rearing method of subterranean termites. *Proc. Indiana Acad. Sci.* **66**, 141-143.

Pickens, A. L. (1932). Observations on the genus *Reticulitermes* Holmgren. *Pan-Pacific Entomologist* **8**, 178-180.

Richard, G. (1967). Contribution a l'etude de la morphologie du systeme nerveux céphalique des termites. *Ann. Soc. Entomol. France* **3**, 609-617.

Roonwal, M. L. (1956). 8. Isoptera. *In* "Taxonomist's Glossary of Genitalia in Insects" (S. L. Tuxen, ed.), pp. 34-38. Munkgaard, Copenhagen.

Roonwal, M. L., and Chhotani, O. B. (1965). Revision of the termite genus *Eurytermes* (Termitidae, Amitermitinae). *Proc. Natl. Inst. Sci. India* **B31**, 81-113.

Roonwal, M. L., and Chhotani, O. B. (1966). Soldier and other castes in termite genus *Speculitermes* and the phylogeny of *Anoplotermes-Speculitermes* complex. *Biol. Zentr.* **85**, 183-210.

Ruelle, J. E. (1964). L'architecture du nid de *Macrotermes natalensis* et son sens fonctionel. *In* "Etudes sur les termites africains" (A. Bouillon, ed.), pp. 327-362. Masson, Paris.

Sands, W. A. (1956). Some factors affecting the survival of *Odontotermes badius*. *Insectes Sociaux* **3**, 531-536.

Sands, W. A. (1957). The soldier mandibles of the Nasutitermitinae (Isoptera, Termitidae). *Insectes Sociaux* **4**, 13-24.

Sands, W. A. (1965a). A revision of the termite subfamily Nasutitermitinae, (Isoptera, Termitidae) from the Ethiopian region. *Bull. Brit. Museum, Entomol.* Suppl. **4**, pp. 1-172.

Sands, W. A. (1965b). Mound population movements and fluctuations in *Trinervitermes ebenerianus* Sjöstedt (Isoptera, Termitidae, Nasutitermitinae). *Insectes Sociaux* **12**, 49-58.

Schmidt, R. S. (1955). The evolution of nest-building behavior in *Apicotermes* (Isoptera). *Evolution* 9, 157-181.

Seevers, C. (1957). A monograph on the termitophilous Staphylinidae (Coleoptera). *Fieldiana, Zool.* 40, 1-334.

Snyder, T. E. (1949). Catalog of the termites (Isoptera) of the world. *Smithsonian Misc. Collections* 112, 1-490.

Stuart, A. M. (1961). Mechanisms of trail-laying in two species of termites. *Nature* 189, 419.

Stuart, A. M. (1963a). The origin of the trail in the termites *Nasutitermes corniger* (Motschulsky) and *Zootermopsis nevadensis* (Hagen), Isoptera. *Physiol. Zool.* 36, 69-84.

Stuart, A. M. (1963b). Studies on the communication of alarm in the termite *Zootermopsis nevadensis* (Hagen), Isoptera. *Physiol. Zool.* 36, 85-96.

Stuart, A. M. (1964). The structure and function of sternal gland in *Zootermopsis nevadensis* (Hagen), Isoptera. *Proc. Zool. Soc. London* 143, 43-52.

Sumner, E. C. (1933). The species of termite genus *Zootermopsis* Emerson (=*Termopsis* Hagen). *Univ. Calif. (Berkeley) Publ. Entomol.* 6, 197-230.

Tracey, M. V., and Youat, G. (1958). Cellulase and chitinase in two species of Australian termites. *Enzymologia* 19, 70-72.

Trager, W. (1932). A cellulase from the symbiotic intestinal flagellates of termites and of the roach *Cryptocercus punctulatus*. *Biochem. J.* 26, 1762.

Vishnoi, H. S. (1956). The structure, musculature, and mechanism of the feeding apparatus of various castes of the termite *Odontotermes obesus* (Rambur). Part I, Clypeo-Labrum. *J. Zool. Soc. India* 8, 1-18.

Weesner, F. M. (1955). The reproductive system of young primary reproductives of *Tenuirostritermes tenuirostris* (Desneux). *Insectes Sociaux* 2, 323-345.

Zuberi, H. (1963). L'anatomie comparée du cerveau chez les termites en rapport avec le polymorphism. *Bull. Biol. France Belg.* 97, 147-207.

2

External Anatomy

FRANCES M. WEESNER

I. INTRODUCTION

The Isoptera have three distinct body regions: head, thorax, and abdomen (Fig. 1). A short cervix, or neck, is also present. The body, and particularly the head, is dorsoventrally flattened. The mouthparts are directed forward, or prognathous. A pair of large compound eyes is present in the imagoes, but poorly developed or absent in most other structural forms. A pair of ocelli may be present in addition to the compound eyes. There is a pair of moniliform antennae. The clypeus is divided into anterior and posterior sections and the mandibles are of the biting type. The maxillae have a hooded galea, stongly toothed lacinia, and five-jointed palps. The labium has a four-lobed ligula, and the labial palps are three-jointed.

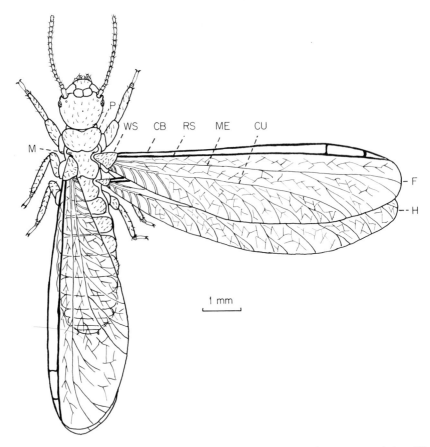

Fig. 1. The general structure of the termite imago. The right wings are extended, as if in flight; the left wings are shown in the resting position. (CB) Costal margin of the wing; (CU) cubitus vein; (F) fore wing; (H) hind wing; (M) mesonotum; (ME) media vein; (P) pronotum; (RS) radial sector vein; (WS) wing scale (from Weesner, 1965).

The thorax consists of three distinct segments, each bearing a pair of legs. The coxa of the second and third legs is divided into two distinct regions. The tarsus is four-jointed in most species. In the imago the last two thoracic segments bear a pair of wings more or less equal in size and venation and are usually deciduous along a basal suture. When at rest the wings are superimposed flat on the back of the abdomen and usually extend well beyond the tip of the abdomen.

The abdomen is ten-segmented and broadly joined to the thorax. In the females the seventh sternite is enlarged and the eighth and ninth reduced. In most individuals a pair of simple styli is present at the posteromedial edge of the ninth sternite. The tenth sternite is divided medially and bears cerci at its lateral margins. The cerci may have as many as eight joints, but are usually two-jointed.

The first major contribution to our knowledge of termite anatomy was the monograph of Holmgren (1909), in which he considered external and internal structure of the Isoptera on a comparative basis and presented a scheme of head segmentation. Fuller (1919, 1920, 1924) reported on various structures in African termites and made a critical examination of the postembryonic development of the antennae. Various studies have been made of the morphology of particular species (Imms, 1919; Crampton, 1920a,b, 1923; Tillyard, 1931; Sumner, 1933; Light, 1934; Kushwaha, 1955, 1959, 1960; Morgan, 1959; Gupta, 1960; and others). Various studies have also been made of certain external structures in the Isoptera, as they relate to similar structures in other insects, particularly the Blattoidea and Zoraptera (Walker, 1919, 1922; Browman, 1935; Delamere-Debouteeville, 1947; McKittrick, 1964). Specialized studies have been made of the comparative aspects of certain structures in the Isoptera, especially as they relate to termite taxonomy (Holmgren, 1911, 1912, 1913; Hare, 1937; Ahmad, 1950).

II. THE HEAD

A. THE IMAGOES

1. Dorsal and Lateral Structures

a. The Head Capsule. The head as viewed from above (Fig. 2A) is roundish or slightly elongated. On each side, at about the midpoint, or just anterior to the midpoint, lie the compound eyes. A pair of ocelli may be situated adjacent to the eyes. Anterior to the eyes, on each side, are the rather shallow *antennal depressions,* containing the *antennal fossae,* which bear the antennae. The upper margins of the head capsule curve around the medial sides of the antennal depressions. At about the level of the fore edge of the depressions, the head is transected by the *epistomal suture.* Anterior to this suture the head is continued medially as the clypeus, in front of which projects the labrum. The mandibles are visible to the sides of the labrum. The areas of the head lying adjacent to the bases of the mandibles and anterior to the antennal depressions are termed the *pleurostoma.*

The dorsal surface of the head capsule is usually considered to consist of two areas: the *frons,* anteriorly, and the *epicranium* (or parietal),

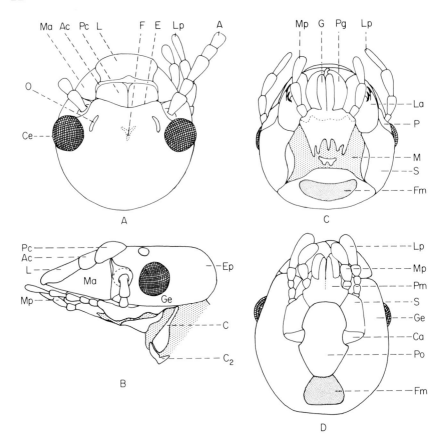

Fig. 2. A – C: The head of the alate of *Tenuirostritermes cinereus* (Buckley). A: Dorsal view; B: lateral view; C: ventral view. D: The head of *Incisitermes minor* (Hagen) in ventral view. (A) Antennae; (Ac) anteclypeus; (C) first cervical sclerite; (C₂) second cervical sclerite; (Ca) cardo; (Ce) compound eye; (E) epistomal suture; (Ep) epicranium; (F) fontanelle; (Fm) foramen magnum; (G) glossa; (Ge) gena; (L) labrum; (La) lacinia; (Lp) labial palp; (M) membrane; (Ma) mandible; (Mp) maxillary palp; (O) ocellus; (P) palpifer; (pc) postclypeus; (Pg) paraglossa; (Pm) prementum; (Po) postmentum; (S) stipes. (A – C, Alcohol preserved material from San Antonio, Texas; D, balsam mount.)

posteriorly. The limits of these two areas vary considerably with different authors. Snodgrass (1935) defines the frons as the area of the front of the head capsule which lies within a triangle formed by the two frontal sutures (when present) and the epistomal suture. This includes the area of the median ocellus (absent in the Isoptera) and excludes the lateral ocelli. Holmgren (1909) includes the lateral ocelli within the frons, encompassing the area from his "transverse suture" (Section II, A, 1, g) to the epistomal suture, and excluding the antennal depressions. However, he assigns the ocelli to the second preoral segment and the rest of the frons to the third segment.

In lateral view (Fig. 2B) the head capsule may be observed to curve downward and slightly forward in the posterior region and to extend beneath the eyes laterally to form the *genae* or cheeks. Anteriorly, the genae join the pleurostoma.

b. The Labrum. The labrum is the most anterior, dorsal, medial extension of the head. It arises from beneath the front of the clypeus, to which it is attached. It is rather tongue shaped and elongated, tending to be broader medially or distally than it is basally. The tip of the labrum is membranous and curves slightly over the tips of the mandibles. Within the imagoes, the labrum does not show any great variation in structure from group to group.

c. The Clypeus. The clypeus lies between the labrum and the head capsule. It is divided transversely into two sections: a distal, flexible region, the *anteclypeus,* to which the labrum is attached; and a caudal, well-sclerotized region, the *postclypeus,* adjacent to the head capsule. In the Rhinotermitidae and the Termitidae the postclypeus is divided by a longitudinal furrow. When not divided by a furrow, the postclypeus tends to be rather straight across the back and the front. When divided, it tends to be convex anteriorly and posteriorly, and the adjacent area of the head capsule, beyond the epistomal suture, is then concave. Usually the clypeus has a low, rounded profile (Fig. 2B). In the Rhinotermitinae, however, it projects dorsally to form a keel-like structure.

d. The Antennae. The antennae are moniliform. The basal segment, or *scape,* is relatively long. The second segment, or *pedicel,* is almost always shorter than the scape. The segments beyond the pedicel are referred to collectively as the *flagellum.* The third segment shows the greatest degree of variation from species to species, a characteristic which is probably related to the fact that this is the area of segment proliferation in the developing young (Fuller, 1920). It may be minute or greatly elongated, distinct, or poorly separated from the fourth segment. The number of antennal segments varies from 11 to 33. In the Mastotermitidae and Hodotermitidae,* as many as 33 antennal segments may occur, usually there are about 28. In the Kalotermitidae, Rhinotermitidae,

---

*The "Hodotermitidae," as used in this chapter, includes the subfamilies Termopsinae, Stolotermitinae, Porotermitinae, and Hodotermitinae.

and Termitidae, the number of segments does not often exceed 22 and the usual numbers are 14 – 18.

e. The Compound Eyes.   The compound eyes are fairly well developed in the termite imagoes. They are most frequently rounded in outline, but are often flattened somewhat at the anterior margin adjacent to the antennal depression. In some Hodotermitidae (*Zootermopsis*) they are elongated dorsoventrally. They tend to be proportionately larger and more protruding in the Termitidae than in the other families.

f. The Ocelli.   In addition to the compound eyes, a pair of simple eyes, or ocelli, is often present. These are situated above the compound eyes, usually at the midpoint or anterior to the midpoint of the compound eyes. They may lie adjacent to the eye, or be well removed from it. They vary considerably in size and shape in different species. Ocelli are absent in the Hodotermitidae and no median ocellus is present in the Isoptera. The structure termed the frontal ocellus by Wasmann (1902) is apparently comparable to the "mid-dorsal spot" associated with the fontanelle and defined by Roonwal and Sen-Sarma (1960).

g. The Epicranial Suture.   In some termites, especially in the Hodotermitidae and the Kalotermitidae, a Y-shaped line – the epicranial suture – may be observed on the top of the head. The stem of the Y runs caudally down the midline of the head. The arms of the Y extend from about the level of the back of the compound eyes toward the midpoint of the eyes, or toward the ocelli when they are present. The suture may be distinct, obscure, or absent. In many cases only the stem portion or a part of it is visible. In the Isoptera the arms of the epicranial suture do not appear to represent the true frontal suture of the insect head since they do not lie mesad of the antennal bases (Snodgrass, 1935). Holmgren (1909) refers to the lateral branches as the transverse sutures.

h. The Fontanelle.   In the imagoes of the Rhinotermitidae and the Termitidae, a small opening may be observed in the midline on the top of the head, just behind or between the compound eyes. This is the fontanelle, or opening of the frontal gland (Chapter 4). It may be a pore or a slit, conspicuous or obscure. It may be situated in a depression. In many Termitidae, a raised area, the fontanelle plate, is associated with the fontanelle. A shelflike infuscation may project over the fontanelle from behind. Sands (1957a) has documented the presence of a sexual dimorphism in the form of the fontanelle and associated areas of the imago head in certain Nasutitermitinae. When a dimorphism occurs, there is a tendency for the fontanelle to be Y-shaped in the female and U-shaped in the male; or V-shaped in the female and Y-shaped in the male.

In many species the fontanelle is associated with an unpigmented or lightly colored area which may be either small or very conspicuous. This zone of lighter pigmentation has been termed the mid-dorsal spot by Roonwal and Sen-Sarma (1960). It is obvious that most descriptions of the fontanelle refer not only to the actual opening of the frontal gland, but to the opening and associated depigmented areas. When the epicranial suture is visible in conjunction with a fontanelle, the latter lies at the fore edge of the stem of the suture, just posterior to the point where it joins the arms.

2. Ventral Structures

When the head is viewed in ventral aspect (Fig. 2C, D), the following structures may be noted. The posterolateral margins of the neck opening (*foramen magnum* or *occipital foramen*) are formed by the downward extension of the epicranium, termed the *postgenae*. The genae may be conspicuous (Fig. 2D) or obscure (Fig. 2C) in ventral view. Anterior to the foramen magnum, in the midline of the head, lies the labium. Anteriorly, and more or less obscured by the labium, lie the maxillae. In front of the maxillae, and generally concealed, are the mandibles. In lateral view (Fig. 2B), the most posterior appendage, the labium, appears ventral, and the maxillae, which are morphologically anterior, lie above it.

a. The Mandibles. The most anteroventral appendages of the head are the mandibles. Each mandible has two points of articulation with the head: at the lateral margin of the pleurostoma lies the socketlike, posterior (primary) mandibular articulation, and at the inner margin of the pleurostoma, adjacent to the base of the clypeus, lies the condyle of the anterior (secondary) mandibular articulation, which is usually pigmented. The primary articular point on the mandible, therefore, is a condyle; the secondary articular point is a socket (Fig. 3E).

The mandibles are of the biting type and have a relatively simple and conservative structure in the termite imago. They have played an increasingly important role in taxonomic groupings. Holmgren (1909, 1911, 1912) was the first to emphasize the importance of the imago-worker mandibles as a basis for taxonomic designations. Ahmad (1950) utilized the imago-worker mandibles as the basis for an extensive phylogenetic study of the termite genera.

The variations which occur in mandibular structure may be summarized as follows. Each mandible bears an apical tooth and a variable number of marginal teeth, as well as a molar plate at the base (Fig. 3E). In general, the right mandible shows less modification than the left. The Hodotermitidae demonstrate what are considered to be the most primi-

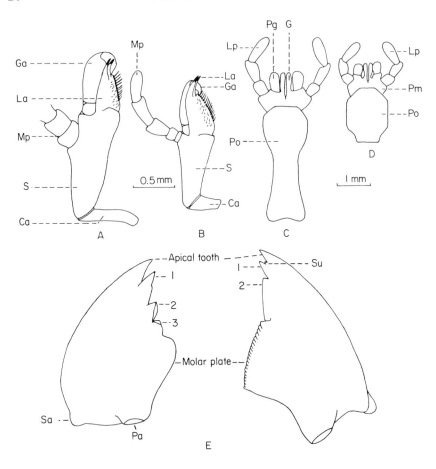

Fig. 3. A comparison of the maxillae (A, B) and labium (C, D) of the soldiers (A, C) and alates (B, D) of *Zootermopsis angusticollis* (Hagen). (Ca) Cardo; (G) glossa; (Ga) galea; (La) lacinia; (Lp) labial palp; (Mp) maxillary palp; (Pg) paraglossa; (Pm) prementum; (Po) postmentum; (S) stipes (from balsam mounts). Part E shows generalized imago-worker mandibles in dorsal view. (Pa) primary articulation point; (Sa) secondary articulation point; (Su) subsidiary tooth; (1–3) marginal teeth.

tive mandibular characters. In *Porotermes* (Fig. 4A) there are four marginal teeth on the left mandible. Most of the genera of Hodotermitidae have one apical and three marginal teeth on the left mandible and one apical and two marginal on the right mandible (Fig. 4B). A small subsidiary tooth is present at the base of the first marginal tooth of the right mandible. In the Mastotermitidae (Fig. 4C) oniy two marginal teeth occur on the left mandible, and there is no subsidiary tooth on the right. A similar situation occurs in the Kalotermitidae (Fig. 4D, E). In these cases the left marginal tooth referred to by Ahmad (1950) and others as the "first marginal" is considered to be the fused first tooth plus the second tooth by Krishna (1961). The "second marginal" tooth of Ahmad, therefore, is considered the third marginal tooth by Krishna.

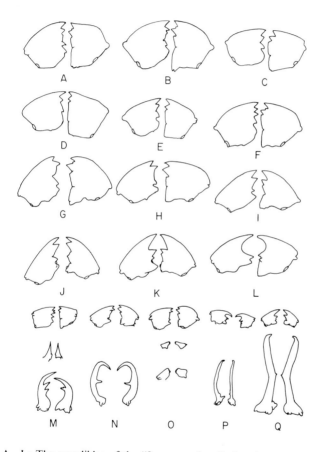

Fig. 4.   A–L: The mandibles of the "Imago-workers" of various groups of termites. A: *Porotermes*; B: *Zootermopsis*; C: *Mastotermes*; D: *Cryptotermes*; E: *Neotermes*; F: *Reticulitermes*; G: *Protermes*; H: *Nasutitermes*; I: *Subulitermes*; J: *Anoplotermes*; K: *Fastigitermes*; L: *Serritermes*. M–Q: A comparison of the alate, above, and soldier mandibles, below, of several genera of termites. M: *Rhinotermes*–imago, minor soldier (middle), and major soldier; N: *Armitermes*–imago and soldier; O: *Trinervitermes*–imago, minor nasute (middle), and major nasute; P: *Cavitermes*–imago and soldier; Q: *Orthognathotermes*–imago and soldier. [A–L, Redrawn from Ahmad (1950); M–Q, redrawn from Hare (1937).]

In the Rhinotermitidae (Fig. 4F) the left mandible has three marginal teeth, and a small subsidiary tooth is present at the base of the first marginal tooth of the right mandible, as in the Hodotermitidae.

In the large family Termitidae, there is a general trend for the right and left mandibles to become less asymmetrical. There are usually only two marginal teeth on the left mandible (three in *Protohamitermes*). As in the Kalotermitidae, the first (distal) marginal tooth of the left mandible is considered to represent the first plus the second tooth by Emerson (1959) and Krishna (1968). The basal marginal tooth, therefore, would be the "third marginal." In addition, there may be present beneath the molar plate of the left mandible a molar tooth, which may be visible from above (Krishna, 1968). In some cases the molar tooth is present, and the basal third marginal tooth is absent. Throughout the Termitidae there is usually a rather long space between the distal and basal marginal teeth.

In the Macrotermitinae (Fig. 4G) the second marginal tooth of the right mandible does not project from the mandibular face, and a small subsidiary tooth is present at the base of the first marginal tooth in most genera. The Nasutitermitinae are considered to include two distinct branches. In the *Triacitermes* branch* (Fig. 4H) the distal marginal teeth are generally larger than the apical teeth or, occasionally, almost the same size, and the right and left mandibles are quite asymmetrical. In the *Paracornitermes* branch† (Fig. 4I), the apical teeth are more pronounced than the distal marginal teeth, and the two mandibles tend toward a greater symmetry. In the Amitermitinae (Fig. 4J) the apical teeth and distal marginal teeth are similar in size, in some cases one, in other cases, the other, being somewhat larger. The second marginal tooth of the right mandible is fairly conspicuous and tends to project from the face of the mandible. In the Termitinae (Fig. 4K) there is a marked tendency for the apical teeth to predominate and for the right and left mandibles to approximate one another in structure. Finally, in *Serritermes* (Fig. 4L) the marginal teeth are represented by small basal projections, and the apical teeth are greatly enlarged. This monotypic genus has been variously assigned to the Rhinotermitidae (Holmgren, 1909; Grassé, 1949), the Termitidae, subfamily Serritermitinae (Snyder, 1949; Ahmad, 1950) and, most recently, to a separate family, the Serritermitidae (Emerson, 1965).

*The *Triacitermes* branch (Ahmad, 1950) approximates the *Procornitermes* branch of Sands (1957a) and the *Nasutitermes* branch of Noirot (Chapter 10).

†The *Paracornitermes* branch (Ahmad, 1950) approximates the *Paracornitermes-Subulitermes* branch of Emerson (1952) and *Subulitermes* branch of Noirot (Chapter 10).

The molar plates of the mandibles have received very little attention from either the anatomists or the taxonomists. Recently, they have been utilized as a basis for taxonomic groups of genera of Nasutitermitinae by Sands (1957b, 1965). The molar plate has grinding ridges and other characteristics which may be morphologically adaptive to the type of food eaten by the termites. In the humivores it may be smooth and concave (Sands, 1965; Deligne, 1966; Chapter 3).

b. The Maxillae. Posterior to the mandibles, and more or less displaced to the sides, lie the paired maxillae (Figs. 2C, D; 3A, B). The basal, elbowed portion is the *cardo.* The major plate is the *stipes*, which is elongated and supports the maxillary palps laterally and the lacinia and galea distally. The base of the palps may be set off from the stipes by a separate plate, the palpifer. The *maxillary palps* are five-jointed, and the first joint is often obscure. The *galea* is the most distal appendage of the maxillae and is an expanded, membranous, hoodlike structure with a short basal segment. The *lacinia* lies mesad and slightly proximal to the galea. It terminates in a double-toothed, heavily sclerotized portion, with a medial basal expansion bearing a row of large bristles and an area with numerous hairs. The general structure of the maxillae is consistent throughout the Isoptera.

c. The Labium. The labium is the most posterior head appendage. It consists of two major regions: the posterior (proximal) *postmentum* and the anterior (distal) *prementum.* The postmentum is often referred to as the gulamentum (Light, 1934; Grassé, 1949) or as the gula (Banks and Snyder, 1920). These terms, however, are not properly applied to the postmentum of the termites, since no gula plate is believed to be incorporated into this structure (Snodgrass, 1935, 1965). The postmentum is composed of two regions, usually undifferentiated in the Isoptera: the submentum proximally and the mentum distally. The postmentum varies considerably from group to group. In the lower termites it is a large, shieldlike plate (Fig. 2D) lying anterior and immediately adjacent to the foramen magnum. In some Termitidae it is somewhat reduced and surrounded by an extensive membranous area. In *Tenuirostritermes* (Fig. 2C) the anterior margin of the foramen magnum is bordered by a transverse plate which appears to be an extension of the postgenae. Anterior to this lies a small W-shaped plate, which may represent the submentum. The base of prementum is formed by an irregular sclerite, apparently the mentum. The prementum of the termites is quite consistent in structure, with a pair of three-jointed lateral appendages, the *labial palps,* and a four-lobed distal portion, the *ligula* (Fig. 3C, D). The outer lobes of the ligula are termed the *paraglossae* and the inner lobes are the *glossae*.

d. The Mouth. The labral-clypeal lobe anteriorly, the mandibles laterally, the maxillae posterolaterally, and the labium posteriorly enclose a chamber known as the *food meatus*. The floor of this chamber is formed by a tonguelike projection, the *hypopharynx*. At the upper limit of the food meatus, just in front of the opening of the esophagus, lies a small chamber termed the *cibarium*. It is in this chamber that food fragments are collected prior to ingestion into the gut. The epipharyngeal surface of the labral-clypeal lobe is referred to as the *palatum* and may bear a number of spines and peglike denticles arranged in a regular fashion (Vishnoi, 1956). Vishnoi, working with *Odontotermes obesus* (Rambur) concludes that the labral-clypeal lobe plays an important role in the manipulation of food within the food meatus and in the passage of food from the cibarium into the esophagus.

3. Segmentation of the Head

On the basis of innervation, muscle origins and insertions, and development, Holmgren (1909) designates the eye region of the termite head as the first segment (protocerebral lobe). He concludes that the area including the ocelli and antennae represents the second segment (deutocerebral lobe). The clypeus, labrum, and frons (exclusive of the area bearing the ocelli), as well as the region of the epicranium behind the first segment, are assigned to the oral or tritocerebral segment. Generally, however, the labrum and clypeus are considered to be preoral. Mukerji and Chowdhuri (1962) note that the labrum first appears as a median projection on the protocerebral lobe in *Odontotermes redemanni* (Wasmann). The oral segment is usually designated as the area containing the mouth and the epicranial region caudad of the eyes. The mandibles represent the appendages of the first postoral segment, the maxillae the appendages of the second, and the labium the appendages of the third.

B. The Immature Individuals and Workers

The head structure of the immature individuals of the colony and of the workers, when they are present, is similar to that of the imagoes. In most instances compound eyes and ocelli are lacking. When compound eyes are present, they are not as well developed as in the imago. The compound eyes are obvious in late nymphs well advanced toward alate development. The sequence and degree of eye development are discussed in Chapter 6. The nymphal antennae have fewer segments than the alates, and developing segments may be observed in the third segment in immature individuals. The labial, maxillary, and mandibular structures are comparable to those of the imagoes of the same species.

The epicranial suture, which may be obscure in the imago, is an important cephalic character in the immature individuals. This is the point of weakness in the cuticle which separates at the time of the molt, permitting escape from the old exoskeleton (Snodgrass, 1965). A "fontanelle," or "mid-dorsal spot," may be present in the workers of certain Termitidae, although no functional frontal gland is known to occur in these individuals (Chapter 4).

C. The Soldiers

The head structure of the soldiers is greatly modified from that of the alates and shows tremendous variation from group to group. In the Mastotermitidae and Hodotermitidae the soldiers have massive, heavily toothed mandibles and greatly enlarged heads (Fig. 5A). In the Kalotermitidae most of the soldiers have strongly elongated heads and stout, strongly toothed mandibles (Fig. 5B). In a few genera (*Calcaritermes, Cryptotermes*) the heads are phragmotic, being short and high in front (Fig. 5C, D). These apparently serve as plugs for openings in the colony workings. In the Rhinotermitidae many of the soldiers are of the mandibulate type, with elongated heads and well-developed mandibles, usually with a reduced marginal dentition. In some genera the frontal gland is functional as a defensive mechanism, and the fontanelle may be positioned at the anterior margin of the head and may be greatly enlarged as in *Coptotermes* (Fig. 5E). In some genera (*Rhinotermes, Dolichorhinotermes, Acorhinotermes*) the development of the frontal gland, and the anterior positioning of the fontanelle, are accompanied by a tremendous modification of the labrum. In these genera the labrum is elongated and grooved, and the tip may be bifurcated (Fig. 5G). These have been termed "*nasutoid*" soldiers (Grassé, 1949), but should not be confused with the true nasute soldiers of the Termitidae. Such nasutoid soldiers may be present in addition to soldiers of the mandibulate type (Fig. 5G, H). The nasutoid soldiers are smaller than the mandibulate soldiers and the two types are referred to as minor and major soldiers, respectively.

The Termitidae show a tremendous variation in the structural form of the soldiers. Many species have mandibulate soldiers, and these demonstrate a wide range of variation in the form (and the use) of the mandibles (Fig. 5F, I − M). They may be biting, pincerlike or snapping. In the case of the snapping mandibles, they may be strongly asymmetrical, as in *Pericapritermes* (Fig. 5L), *Capritermes, Neocapritermes,* and *Plani-*

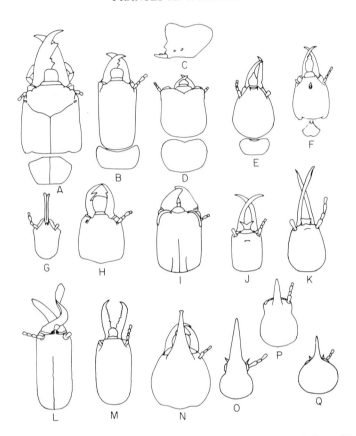

Fig. 5. Examples of soldier head form in various termites. Dorsal view of head and pronotum of A: *Archotermopsis wroughtoni* Desneux; B: *Rugitermes bicolor* (Emerson); D: *Cryptotermes verruculosus* (Emerson); E: *Coptotermes sjostedti* Holmgren; F: *Acanthotermes acanthothorax* (Sjöstedt), minor soldier. C: head of *Cryptotermes verruculosus* in lateral view. Dorsal view of the head capsule of G: *Rhinotermes hispidus* Emerson, minor soldier; H: major soldier; I: *Jugositermes tuberculatus* Emerson; J: *Procubitermes niapuensis* Emerson; K: *Promirotermes orthoceps* (Emerson); L: *Pericapritermes urgens* Silvestri; M: *Microcerotermes fuscotibialis* (Sjöstedt); N: *Armitermes grandidens* Emerson; O: *Angularitermes nasutissimus* (Emerson); P: *Coarctotermes suffuscus* (Emerson); Q: *Nasutitermes octopilis* Banks [A, Redrawn from Emerson (1933); B−D, G, H, N, O and Q, redrawn from Emerson (1925); E, F, I−M, and P, redrawn from Emerson (1928).]

capritermes; or they may be symmetrical, as in *Termes* (Chapter 10, Fig. 16). In the Nasutitermitinae many of the genera have true *nasute* soldiers with the head capsule prolonged in front to form a long nasus, at the tip of which opens the frontal gland. In *Armitermes* (Figs. 4N; 5N) the well-developed nasus is combined with well-developed mandibles. In most other nasute forms the mandibles are vestigial (Figs. 4O; 5O – Q). The deviation of the soldier mandibles from that of the alate mandibles of the same species is illustrated in Fig. 4M – Q.

The labrum of the soldiers is often greatly modified from that of the imago-worker. Its tip is often hyaline. It may be considerably elongated and grooved (as in the Rhinotermitinae), elongated with a trilobed tip (Fig. 5F), or rather frequently, distinctly bifurcated at the tip (Fig. 5J). In nasute soldiers it is reduced. Vishnoi (1956) notes that in *Odontotermes obesus* the labrum of the soldier lacks the hairs and bristles present on the palatum of the imagoes and workers and that the cibarium is smaller in the soldiers than in the other forms.

The maxillary structure in the soldiers remains rather stable and resembles that of the imagoes (Fig. 3A, B). The postmentum of the labium is greatly elongated in those soldiers with elongated heads; the prementum, however, retains its typical form (Fig. 3C, D). Compound eyes and ocelli may be present, but they are never as well developed as in the imago, and may be pigmented or colorless.

The number of antennal segments in the soldiers varies from 11 to 29 in different species. The structure of the antennae, especially with respect to the third antennal segment, varies considerably from that of the imagoes. In *Marginitermes hubbardi* (Banks), for example, the third antennal segment of the soldier is as long as the next six or seven segments together; in the alate of this species it is not noticeably enlarged. Two instances have been reported in the development of nasute soldiers in which the number of antennal segments is reduced during development, due to the fusion of two segments into one (Emerson, 1926; Weesner, 1953). The usual situation involves the addition of segments from one molt to the next (Fuller, 1920).

III. THE THORAX

A. THE IMAGOES

The thorax is a complex structure with three distinct segments: the *prothorax* (anteriorly), the *mesothorax*, and the *metathorax*, each bearing a pair of legs (Fig. 6). The mesothorax and metathorax also bear a pair of wings in the alate. The wing-bearing segments together are referred to as the *pterothorax*. The thorax is connected to the head by a short membranous area, the *cervix*, which is thought by some authors to represent a distinct segment, the microthorax, but is generally considered to include elements from the most posterior head segment and the anterior thoracic segment. There are two lateral cervical sclerites

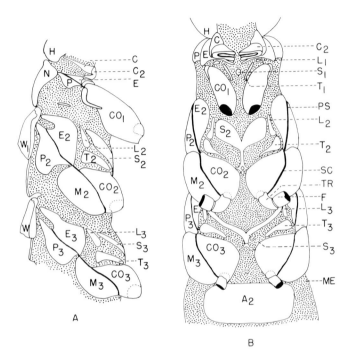

Fig. 6. The cervical and thoracic plates and the leg bases of the Isoptera. A: Lateral view; B: ventral view. (A_2) Second abdominal sternite; (C, C_2) first and second lateral cervical sclerite; (CO_1, CO_2, CO_3) coxa of first, second, and third pairs of legs; (E, E_2, E_3) episterum of pro-, meso-, and metathorax; (F) femur; (H) head capsule; (L_1, L_2, L_3) lateral sternal plates of the pro-, meso-, and metathorax; (M_2, M_3) meron of second and third pairs of legs; (ME) membrane; (N) pronotum; (P, P_2, P_3) epimeron of pro-, meso-, and metathorax (PS) pleural suture; (S_1, S_2, S_3) sternum of pro-, meso-, and metathorax; (SC) coxal suture (T_1, T_2, T_3) trochantine of pro-, meso-, and metathorax; (TR) trochanter of leg; (W_1, W) wing scale of fore and hind wing. (Sketched from an alcohol preserved specimen of *Tenuirostritermes cinereus*.)

which are set at right angles to one another (Figs. 2B; 6A, B). In some Hodotermitidae a small ventral cervical sclerite is present in the midline, but it is lacking in most termites.

1. Thoracic Sclerites

Laterally and ventrally, the thorax includes a number of sclerotized plates (Fig. 6A, B) which serve as attachment points for the muscles of the legs and the wings. These plates may be quite large and closely applied to one another, or considerably reduced and separated by an extensive membrane. In general, they are relatively large in the lower termites, but considerably reduced in the Termitidae. Although the plates vary in size from group to group, they are quite constant in their general form. The ventromedial plate of each segment is the *sternum*. It is very small in the prothorax and largest in the mesothorax. It is roughly triangular in shape and varies from a shieldlike structure to a Y-shaped form. At the posterior margins of the sternums of the meso- and metathorax lie the *mesosternellum* and *metasternellum*, respectively (Imms, 1948), also referred to as the furca (Light, 1934). These have the form of an inverted Y or inverted T. The sterna are bordered posterolaterally by the *trochantines* and laterally by the *lateral sternal plates*. Both of these are bordered laterally by the episterna, which lie adjacent to the *epimerons*. These latter pairs of plates are separated by the *pleural suture*. All of these structures are reduced and modified in the prothorax. The trochantines lie between the sterna and the bases, or coxae of the legs, with which they articulate. A small plate, the *subalaire* (post parapteron of Light, 1934), lies under the wing base. Another small plate, the *basisternum* (second parapteron of Light), may be observed between the upper arms of the epimeron and the episternum in the pterothorax.

Dorsally, the thorax is provided with three distinct plates, the *pronotum* (anteriorly), the *mesonotum*, and the *metanotum*. The pronotum is relatively simple and shieldlike. It may be almost flat, depressed at the sides, or elevated at the front. It may be as wide or slightly wider than the head, or much narrower. The mesonotum and metanotum have a yokelike plate, the *prephragma*, at the anterior margin. Both wing-bearing nota have anterior and posterior notal processes (Fig. 7A). The anterior portion of the mesonotum and metanotum, bearing the anterior notal processes, is referred to as the *scutum*. The posterior portion, bearing the posterior notal processes, is referred to as the *scutellum*. The anterior and posterior notal processes articulate with the axillary sclerites. These, in turn, articulate with the wing base. There are three axillaries. The first articulates with the anterior notal process and the third articulates with the posterior notal process. Both articulate with the second axillary, which in turn articulates with the base of the radius, media, and cubitus veins. An anterior projection of the first axillary extends toward the costal margin of the wing. A posterior projection of the third axillary articulates with the base of the anal veins or the anal field. In the hind wing of *Mastotermes* (Fig. 7B) the third axillary is clearly separated from the first and second axillaries. Posterior to the apex of the posterior notal process, a membranous outgrowth of the body wall extends to the hind edge of the wing; this is the axillary cord. At the anteromedial margin of each wing base lies a small lobe which is more or less sclerotized. This is the *tegula*, which bears a specialized set of sensory structures referred to as the tegular organ (Chapter 6).

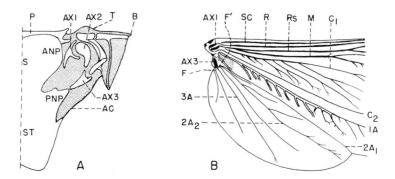

Fig. 7. A: The right half of the mesonotum and the right wing scale of *Tenuirostri-termes cinereus*. (ANP) Anterior notal process; (AC) axillary cord; (AX₁, AX₂, AX₃) first, second, and third axillary sclerites; (B) basal or humeral suture; (P) prephragma; (PNP) posterior notal process; (S) scutum; (ST) scutellum; (T) tegula. B: The hind wing of *Mastotermes darwiniensis* as illustrated by Tillyard (1931) to show wing veination and the anal lobe. (1A) First anal vein; (2A₁) first branch of second anal vein; (2A₂) second branch of second anal vein; (3A) third anal vein; (AX₁, AX₃) first and third axillary sclerites; (C₁) first or anterior cubitus vein; (C₂) second or posterior cubitus vein; (F − F′) line indicated by Tillyard as the usual point at which the hind wing is shed after flight (see text); (M) media vein; (R) radius; (Rs) radial sector vein; (SC) subcosta vein.

2. The Wings

The wings are dorsolateral outgrowths of the integument and are supported by a series of relatively simple veins whose arrangement and degree of development vary from family to family and from genus to genus. It should be noted that details of venation also vary somewhat from one individual to another within a species. There is considerable variation in the designations that have been given to the veins in the termite wing. The basis for these variations may be traced to different interpretations of the veins of the termite wing relative to that of the "theoretical" insect wing proposed by Comstock (1918). Comstock's scheme includes the following elements: a precosta vein (generally agreed to be absent in the Isoptera); a simple costa along the fore edge of the wing; a subcosta, which may bifurcate; a radius, which divides into two major sections, R_1 and the radial sector vein. The latter divides dicotomously into four branches $(R_2 - R_5)$. The next vein is the media, with several branches; and, finally, the anal veins. Snodgrass followed this general scheme in earlier works (1935), but later (1965) dropped the term "radial sector," utilizing only the term "radius" for the veins between the subcosta and media.

Emerson (1965) has revised the designations for the veins in the termite wings and presents synonymies for the terms utilized by various authors.

It should be noted that a true vein is one which is preceded in the developing wing by a tracheal tube. The fore edge of the wing is formed by a heavily sclerotized *costal margin* which does not represent a true vein. The precosta and costa veins are absent. A short *subcosta* may be present. It arises independently in the wing scale and joins the costal margin near the base (Fig. 8A). Three veins may follow, now designated first, second, and third *radius* (R_1, R_2, and R_3), any one of which may be absent or fused with another. The next vein is designated the *radial sector* (previously $R_4 + R_5$). This vein reaches or approaches the wing apex and may have a number of branches to the fore edge of the wing (Fig. 8A, E) or may be unbranched. As Emerson notes, the radial sector is not connected with any of the radius veins in the wing membrane.

The next vein, usually occupying the midarea of the wing membrane, and usually sending branches to the outer, posterior wing margin, is the *media*. Basally it is associated with the radial sector and in the hind wing usually arises from the radial sector in the wing membrane (Fig. 8B). The next vein is the anterior *cubitus*, which occupies the posterior basal area of the wing membrane and sends a number of branches to the posterior margin of the wing. In the Mastotermitidae a weak posterior cubitus is present. In most termites the *anal* veins are inconspicuous or lacking. In the hind wing of the *Mastotermes* there is a distinct anal lobe (Fig. 7B), and the anal veins are developed (Tillyard, 1931; Emerson, 1965). In the fore wing, even in the Mastotermitidae, the anal veins are not developed and are represented by an anal area or clavus, usually set off from the rest of the wing base by a clear area which Tillyard (1931) believes represents the base of the second (posterior) cubitus vein.

In those termites which are considered more primitive morphologically, most of these veins may be recognized (Figs. 7B; 8A – D). In the Rhinotermitidae and Termitidae, there is a marked reduction in the venation of the fore edge of the wing, which is supported by two parallel, heavily sclerotized areas (Fig. 8F, G). The sclerotization at the fore edge (costal margin) of the wing in usually designated in these families as the subcosta plus the radius. The vein which parallels it in the membrane is the radial sector.

The veins of the fore edge of the wing (through the radial sector) are usually well sclerotized and conspicuous, when present. The degree of development of the media vein is highly variable. In many Kalotermitidae it is closely associated with the radial sector, is heavy, and has few, if any, branches (Fig. 8A – D). In most other families it occupies a middle position in the wing membrane, is lightly sclerotized, and has a number of branches (Fig. 8E – G). In some species or in some individuals in some species, it may be very faint or even absent (as in *Prorhinotermes*).

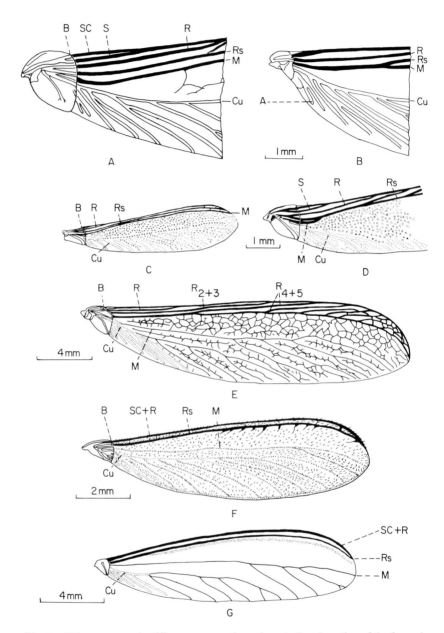

Fig. 8. Wing structure in different groups of termites. A: Basal portion of the fore wing of *Neotermes malatensis* (Oshima); B: basal portion of the hind wing of the same; C: fore wing of *Glyptotermes chapmani* (Light); D: basal portion of the fore wing of *Rugitermes athertoni* (Light); E: fore wing of *Zootermopsis angusticollis* (Hagen); F: fore wing of *Coptotermes pacificus* Light; G: fore wing of *Nasutitermes pictus* Light. (A) Anal vein; (B) basal or humeral suture; (Cu) cubitus vein; (M) media vein; (R, R_{2+3}) radius veins; (R_s, R_{4+5}) radial sector; (SC) costal margin; (S) subcosta (see text for discussion of designations). (All drawn from balsam mounts by projection.)

The cubitus is not heavily sclerotized, although rather conspicuous in the basal portion. If the media occupies an anterior position, or is absent, the cubitus tends to occupy a central position in the wing membrane. In either case it sends a number of branches to the posterior wing margin.

Generally, the termite wing is deciduous along a distinct basal suture (humeral suture). An examination of this area (Fig. 8A–G) shows a weakness in each of the veins where they transect it. In the case of the hind wing of *Mastotermes* Tillyard (1931) concludes that no basal suture is present. He indicates in his figure the point at which the wings are usually broken from the base and concludes that the hind wings are probably flexed upward against the bases of the fore wing after these have been shed, thus tending to break in a fairly uniform fashion. Emerson (1965) feels that a basal suture is present throughout the Isoptera, although it is very poorly defined or only "the beginning of an evolution of a suture" in the Mastotermitidae.

The portion of the wing lying between the thoracic nota and the humeral suture is referred to as the *wing scale* and persists after the wings have been shed. The base of the fore wing is larger than that of the hind wing. Their relative sizes, however, vary considerably from family to family. In the Termitidae, the fore wing scale is not much larger than that of the hind wing, and the two bases are clearly separated. In the other families the fore wing scale usually overlaps at least the base of the hind wing scale. Extensions of the wing veins may be quite distinct within the wing scale, especially in the forescale (Fig. 8A). As noted earlier, the subcosta arises independently. The radius branches are joined basally by the radial sector, then by the media, and finally by the cubitus, which often remains more or less distinct. In some cases, however, the media arises from a common trunk with the cubitus in the fore wing scale, although it arises from the radial sector in the wing membrane of the hind wing (e.g., *Kalotermes flavicollis* as figured by Krishna, 1961).

In general, the wing membrane of the Mastotermitidae, Kalotermitidae, and Hodotermitidae lack hairs, although some are present along the major anterior veins and on the wing scale. In the Rhinotermitidae some genera have numerous hairs on the wing membrane, as in *Coptotermes* (Fig. 8F), and in the Termitidae numerous minute hairs are usually present. Some of the Kalotermitidae have small nodules on the wing membrane (Figs. 8C, D). In the Mastotermitidae and Hodotermitidae the wing membrane is reticulated, with numerous, minute and rather weak cross veins (Fig. 8E). These veins, collectively, are referred to as the *archidictyon*. Some species of Kalotermitidae and Rhinotermitidae have weak reticulations in the wing membrane. In the Termitidae the wing membrane tends to be opaque, and the media and cubitus veins are generally conspicuously pigmented.

3. The Legs

In the Isoptera, the coxa of the second and third pair of legs is divided by a deep coxal suture into two sections, the *meron* and the *coxa* (Fig. 6A, B). The coxal suture is continuous with the line of the pleural suture. The first free leg joint is a short *trochanter*, which articulates distally with a rather long, fairly heavy *femur* (Fig. 9A). The femur articulates distally with the *tibia*, which is usually relatively long and thin. Finally, the leg terminates in the *tarsus* with a variable number of short proximal joints and an elongated distal portion ending in two claws (the pretarsus). In the Hodotermitidae and many Kalotermitidae an *arolium* is present between the claws (Fig. 9B).

In the Mastotermitidae the tarsi are five-jointed. In many Hodotermitidae they are imperfectly five-jointed with a partial joint between the first and second proximal joints (Fig. 9A). In the great majority of termites the tarsi are four-jointed. In *Stylotermes* (Rhinotermitidae, Stylotermitinae)

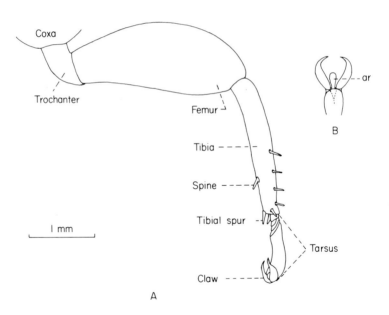

Fig. 9. A: The structure of the leg in *Zootermopsis angusticollis*. Note the spines on the shaft of the tibia (absent in many termites). (Sketched from a balsam mount of the right fore leg of a soldier.) B: The terminal portion of the tarsus of *Zootermopsis laticeps* (Banks) showing the arolium (ar) between the two claws. (Sketch from an alcohol preserved specimen.)

and in *Indotermes* and *Speculitermes* (Termitidae)* they are three-jointed (Roonwal and Sen-Sarma, 1960; Roonwal, 1962; Ahmad, 1963, 1965).

Conspicuous spines may be present on the shaft of the tibia in some Hodotermitidae and Kalotermitidae (Fig. 9A). In most termites a distinctive number of sclerotized *spurs* are present at the distal end of the tibia. The tibial spur formula for various species is expressed as 3:3:3, 3:2:2, 2:2:2, etc., indicating the number of spurs on the fore, mid, and hind tibia, respectively.

B. THE IMMATURE INDIVIDUALS AND WORKERS

The general structure of the thorax of the immature individuals and workers resembles that of the alates, except in the structure of the mesonotum and metanotum. These lack wings and do not have anterior and posterior notal processes (Chapter 10, Fig. 1). In these individuals the mesonotum and metanotum are usually more broad than long, and have simple, rounded margins. The metanotum frequently has the appearance of being the tergite of the first abdominal segment. In developing nymphs, the incipient wings appear as posterior projections of the lateral margins of the mesonotum and metanotum.

C. THE SOLDIERS

The thorax of the soldiers is variously modified from that of the alates. The pronotum may be large or small. It tends to be very broad in the Kalotermitidae (Fig. 5B, D), smaller than the width of the head in the Hodotermitidae (Fig. 5A), slightly smaller than the head in the Rhinotermitidae (Fig. 5E), and much smaller than the head in the Termitidae (Fig. 5F). The mesonotum and metanotum lack wings and notal processes typical of the imago. They are generally more wide than long and most frequently have simple rounded margins. In some groups, however, they are greatly modified and bear lateral spines or projections (Chapter 10, Fig. 6). In some genera soldiers with well-developed wing pads normally appear, as in *Pterotermes* (Kalotermitidae). In most genera they are the exception rather than the rule (Chapter 9, Fig. 3; Chapter 10, Fig. 16) and are termed intercastes. In mandibulate soldiers the legs tend to be stouter than those of the imagoes; in nasute soldiers the legs are usually thinner and more elongated. The tibial spurs may be variously modified

---

* Roonwal and Sen-Sarma (1960) place *Indotermes* in a separate family, Indotermitidae. Ahmad (1963, 1965), places *Indotermes* and *Speculitermes* in the subfamily Amitermitinae of the Termitidae.

and are often enlarged. The tibial spur formula of the soldier is the same as that of the alate of the same species.

IV. THE ABDOMEN

A. The Imagoes

The abdomen includes ten segments with a set of sclerotized plates: *tergites,* above, and *sternites,* below. These plates are interconnected by an extensive membrane. Depending upon the internal development and the condition of the individuals (presence or absence of large numbers of eggs or fatty deposits, lack or abundance of water, etc.), the membrane may be inconspicuous and the plates closely applied to one another, or the membrane may be greatly distended and the plates separated from one another. As in the case of the ventral sclerites of the thorax, the abdominal sternites of the Termitidae are generally reduced in size and the membranous areas more extensive when compared with those of the lower termites.

There are ten tergites which are more wide than long, except for the tenth, or *epiproct,* which is elongated and tapered caudally. The epiproct has been variously termed the supra-anal plate, the decapygidium or the pygidium (Roonwal, 1956). The tergites do not bear any appendages and are comparable in the male and female of a species.

The first abdominal sternite is greatly reduced or absent (Fig. 6B). The second through sixth sternites are more wide than long and are comparable in the female and the male. The seventh sternite (hypogynium, genital plate, or subgenital plate) of the female imago is elongated and often completely covers the eighth and ninth sternites, which are reduced and variously modified (Fig. 10C). In at least some Termitidae the divided eighth and ninth sternites of the female are visible to each side of the posterolateral margins of the hypogynium (Fig. 10D). Roonwal (1956) indicates that in the female of *Odontotermes obesus* the ninth sternite is entire and is visible posterior to the hypogynium; the margins of the eighth sternite are also visible.

In the male the seventh sternite is not enlarged and does not obscure the eighth and ninth sternites, which are not markedly reduced in size (Fig. 10A, B, E). In mature males there is usually a pair of unjointed *styli* on the posteromedial margin of the ninth sternite. These may be fairly large in those termites considered to be morphologically primitive (Fig. 10A), usually they are inconspicuous (Fig. 10B), and in some species they may be absent (Fig. 10E). Styli are usually lacking in the female imago, although they are present in immature females. In both the

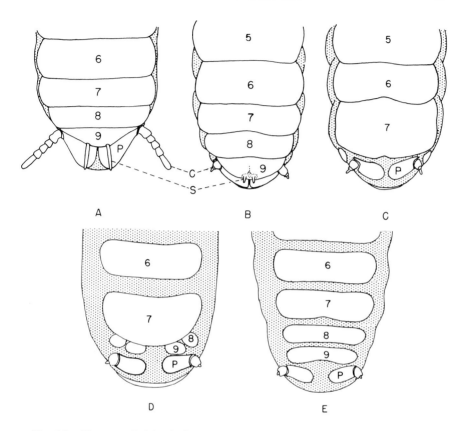

Fig. 10. The ventral abdominal structure in the male and female imagos. A: Male of *Zootermopsis laticeps*; B: male of *Coptotermes formosanus* Shiraki; C: female of *C. formosanus*; D: female of *Tenuirostritermes cinereus*; E: male of *T. cinereus*. (A: mature male from colony workings; B–E: alates taken at the time of flight.) (5–9) Fifth–ninth sternites; (C) cerci; (P) tenth sternite or paraprocts; (S) styli.

male and the female, the tenth sternite, or *paraproct,* is divided medially and bears cerci at the lateral margins (Fig. 10A – E). In the Mastotermitidae and some Hodotermitidae the cerci may have as many as five to eight joints, but in the other families they are usually two-jointed.

Although the details of the structure of the genital chamber of the female imagoes are discussed in Chapter 5, some general aspects of the anatomy of this region should be considered here. The female of the primitive *Mastotermes darwiniensis* has a genital chamber which resembles that of the roaches, with an ovipositer consisting of well-developed, unsclerotized ventral valves and distinct internal and dorsal valves

(Crampton, 1920b; Browman, 1935). These are greatly reduced or absent in all other termites. The eighth sternite of the female is consistently divided into two lateral plates (Browman, 1935) with the possible exception of *Archotermopsis* (Imms, 1919). Browman indicates that the ninth sternite of the female is reduced and variously modified, but entire in *Zootermopsis, Hodotermes, Stolotermes,* and *Porotermes.* It is divided and horseshoe-shaped in *Marginitermes,* and divided, simple, and reduced in most of the Rhinotermitidae and Termitidae which have been examined. There is no sclerotized copulatory organ in the male (Chapter 5).

B. OTHER INDIVIDUALS

The general form of the abdomen of the immature individuals, workers, and soldiers is comparable to that of the imago. In the Mastotermitidae, Hodotermitidae, and Kalotermitidae, the sex of well-developed individuals may be determined by the structure of the posterior abdominal sternites. As in the imagoes, the seventh sternite of the female tends to be elongated, although the eighth and ninth are not greatly reduced (Light, 1934; McMahan, 1959). In the Termitidae the sex of workers and soldiers cannot be determined by any external differences (Noirot, 1955).

V. CONCLUSION

The present account of the external morphology of the Isoptera has only touched upon the general form and more conspicuous differences and similarities between the various groups and the different castes. The morphological differences are most striking when one considers the general stability of the imago and the tremendous variability of the soldier. The soldier may be mandibulate (all families and subfamilies), nasutoid (Rhinotermitinae), or nasute (Nasutitermitinae); and monomorphic, dimorphic, or trimorphic (Chapter 10).

With few exceptions, the morphological variations have not been subjected to any critical comparative analysis. The soldier mandibles of the various families have been considered in detail by Hare (1937) and those of the imago-worker by Ahmad (1950). Comparative studies have been made of the mandibles within certain subfamilies, as in the Nasutitermitinae (Sands, 1965). Comparative aspects of wing venation have been considered by Emerson (1965). The genital chamber of the females of a number of genera have been the subject of a comparative study by Browman (1935). Of course, certain aspects of morphology are touched upon in all taxonomic works, and an increasing number of these are using a comparative approach and critical analysis of various morphological characters. Much remains to be done, however, in all areas of comparative morphology of the Isoptera, and a critical study of the ontogeny of even the most conspicuous structures has not even begun.

REFERENCES

Ahmad, M. (1950). The phylogeny of termite genera based on imago-worker mandibles. *Bull. Am. Museum Nat. Hist.* 95, 43-86.

Ahmad, M. (1963). On the phylogenetic position of *Indotermes*, with description of a new species (Isoptera, Termitidae). *Ann. Mag. Nat. Hist.* [13] 6, 395-399.

Ahmad, M. (1965). Termites (Isoptera) of Thailand. *Bull. Am. Museum Nat. Hist.* 131, 1-113.

Banks, N., and Snyder, T. E. (1920). A revision of the nearctic termites with notes on biology and geographic distribution. *U. S. Natl. Museum, Bull.* 108, 1-228.

Browman, L. G. (1935). The chitinous structures in the posterior abdominal segments of certain female termites. *J. Morphol.* 57, 113-129.

Comstock, J. H. (1918). "The Wings of Insects." Cornell Univ. Press (Comstock), Ithaca, New York.

Crampton, G. C. (1920a). The terminal abdominal structures of the primitive Australian termite *Mastotermes darwiniensis* Froggatt. *Trans. Roy. Entomol. Soc. London* 68, 137-145.

Crampton, G. C. (1920b). Some anatomical details of the remarkable winged Zorapterans, *Zorotypus hubbardi* Caudell, with notes on its relationships. *Proc. Entomol. Soc. Wash.* 22, 98.

Crampton, G. C. (1923). A comparison of terminal abdominal structures of the adult alate female of the primitive termite *Mastotermes darwiniensis* with those of the roach, *Periplaneta americana. Bull. Brooklyn Entomol. Soc.* 18, 85-93.

Delamere-Debouteeville, C. (1947). Sur la morpholgie des adultes, apteres et ailes de Zorapteres. *Ann. Sci. Nat. Zool. Biol. Animal* [11] 9, 145-154.

Deligne, J. (1966). Characteres adaptatifs au regime alimentaire dans la mandibles des termites (Insectes, Isopteres). *Compt. Rend.* D263, 1323-1325.

Emerson, A. E. (1925). The termites of Kartabo, Bartica District, British Guiana. *Zoologica* 6, 191-459.

Emerson, A. E. (1926). Development of a soldier of *Nasutitermes (Constrictotermes) cavifrons* (Holmgren) and its phylogenetic significance. *Zoologica* 7, 69-100.

Emerson, A. E. (1928). Termites of the Belgian Congo and the Cameron. *Bull. Am. Museum Nat. Hist.* 57, 401-574.

Emerson, A. E. (1933). A revision of the genera of fossil and recent Termopsinae (Isoptera). *Univ. Calif. (Berkeley) Publ. Entomol.* 6, 165-196.

Emerson, A. E. (1952). The Neotropical genera *Procornitermes* and *Cornitermes* (Isoptera, Termitidae). *Bull. Am. Museum Nat. Hist.* 99, 479-539.

Emerson, A. E. (1959). The African termite genera *Firmitermes, Hoplognathotermes, Acutidentitermes, Duplidentitermes, Heimitermes* (Termitidae, Termitinae). *Am. Museum Noviates* 1947, 1-42.

Emerson, A. E. (1965). A review of the Mastotermitidae (Isoptera), including a new fossil genus from Brazil. *Am. Museum Novitates* 2236, 1-46.

Fuller, C. (1919). The wing veination and respiratory system of certain South African termites. *Ann. Natal Museum* 4, 19-102.

Fuller, C. (1920). Studies on the post-embryonic development of the antennae of termites. *Ann. Natal Museum* 4, 235-295.

Fuller, C. (1924). The thorax and abdomen of winged termites. *Union South Africa, Dept. Agr. Entomol. Mem.* 2, 49-78.

Grassé, P.-P. (1949). Ordre des Isoptères ou Termites. *In* "Traité de Zoologie," (P.-P. Grassé, ed.), Vol. IX, pp. 408-544. Masson, Paris.

Gupta, S. D. (1960). Morphology of the primitive termite *Anacanthotermes macrocephalus* (Desneux) (Isoptera: Hodotermitidae). *Records Indian Museum* 48, 169-222.

Hare, L. (1937). Termite phylogeny as evidenced by soldier mandible development. *Ann. Entomol. Soc. Am.* 37, 459-486.

Holmgren, N. (1909). Termitenstudien. I. Anatomische Untersuchungen. *Kol. Svenska Vetenskapsakad. Handl.* [3] 44, 1-215.

Holmgren, N. (1911). Termitenstudien. II. Systematik der Termiten. Die Familien Mastotermitidae, Protermitidae and Mesotermitidae. *Kol. Svenska Vetenskapsakad.* [6] 46, 1-88.

Holmgren, N. (1912). Termitenstudien. III. Systematik der Termiten. Die Familie Metatermitidae. *Kol. Svenska Vetenskapsakad. Handl.* 48 [4], 1-166.

Holmgren, N. (1913). Termitenstudien. IV. Versuch einer systematischen Monographie der Termiten der orientalischen Region. *Kol. Svenska Vetenskapsakad. Handl.* 50 [2], 1-276.

Imms, A. D. (1919). On the structure and biology of *Archotermopsis,* together with descriptions of new species of intestinal Protozoa and general observations on the Isoptera. *Phil. Trans. Roy. Soc. London* B209, 75-180.

Imms, A. D. (1948). "A General Textbook of Entomology," 7th ed. Dutton, New York.

Krishna, K. (1961). A generic revision and phylogenetic study of the family Kalotermitidae (Ispotera). *Bull. Am. Museum Nat. Hist.* 122, 303-408.

Krishna, K. (1968). Phylogeny and generic reclassification of the *Capritermes* complex (Isoptera, Termitidae, Termitinae). *Bull. Am. Museum Nat. Hist.* 138, 261-324.

Kushwaha, K. S. (1955). External morphology of the soldier of *Odontotermes obesus* (Rambur). *Current Sci. (India)* 24, 203-204.

Kushwaha, K. S. (1959). A preliminary account of external morphology of the worker and alate of *Odontotermes obesus* (Rambur). *Current Sci. (India)* 28, 298-299.

Kushwaha, K. S. (1960). External morphology of the termite *Odontotermes obesus* (Rambur) (Isoptera: Termitidae). Part 1, Soldier. Part 2, Alate and worker. *Records Indian Museum, Delhi* 55, 209-250.

Light, S. F. (1934). The external anatomy of termites. *In* "Termites and Termite Control" (C. A. Kofoid, ed.), 2nd ed., pp. 50-57. Univ. of California Press, Berkeley, California.

McKittrick, F. A. (1964). Evolutionary studies on cockroaches. *Cornell Univ., Agr. Expt. Sta. Mem.* 389, 1-197.

McMahan, E. A. (1959). External sex characteristics of *Cryptotermes brevis* (Walker) and *Kalotermes immigrans* Snyder (Isoptera, Kalotermitidae). *Proc. Hawaiian Entomol. Soc.* 17, 270-272.

Morgan, F. D. (1959). The ecology and external morphology of *Stolotermes ruficeps* Brauer (Isoptera: Hodotermitidae). *Trans. Roy. Soc. New Zealand* 86, 155-196.

Mukerji, D., and Chowdhuri, R. (1962). Developmental stages of *Odontotermes redemanni* (Wasmann) *Proc. New Delhi Symp., 1960,* pp. 77-95. UNESCO, Paris.

Noirot, C. (1955). Recherches sur le polymorphisme des Termites supérieurs (Termitidae). *Ann. Sci. Nat. Zool. Biol. Animals* [11] 17, 399-595.

Roonwal, M. L. (1956). 8. Isoptera. *In* "Taxonomist's Glossary of Genitalia in Insects" (S. L. Tuxen, ed.), pp. 34-38. Munksgaard, Copenhagen.

Roonwal, M. L. (1962). Recent development in termite systematics (1949-60). *Proc. New Delhi Symp., 1960* pp. 31-50. UNESCO, Paris.

Roonwal, M. L., and Sen-Sarma, P. K. (1960). Contribution to the systematics of the oriental termites. *Indian Council Agr. Res., Entomol. Monograph* 1, 1-406.

Sands, W. A. (1957a). A revision of the east African Nasutitermitinae (Isoptera). *Bull. Brit. Museum, Entomol.* 5, 1-28.

Sands, W. A. (1957b). The soldier mandibles of the Nasutitermitinae (Isoptera), Termitinae). *Insectes Sociaux* 4, 13-24.

Sands, W. A. (1965). A revision of the termite subfamily Nasututermitinae (Isoptera, Termitidae) from the ethopian region. *Bull. Brit. Museum, Entomol.* Suppl. 4, 1-172.

Snodgrass, R. E. (1935). "Principles of Insect Morphology." McGraw-Hill, New York.

Snodgrass, R. E. (1965). "A Textbook of Arthropod Anatomy." Hafner, New York (facsimile of 1952 edition).

Snyder, T. E. (1949). Catalog of the termites (Isoptera) of the world. *Smithsonian Misc. Collections* 112, 1-490.

Sumner, E. C. (1933). The species of the termite genus *Zootermopsis* Emerson (=*Termopsis* Hagen). *Univ. Calif. (Berkeley) Publ. Entomol.* 6, 197-230.

Tillyard, R. J. (1931). The wing-venation of the order Isoptera. I. Introduction and the family Mastotermitidae. *Proc. Linnean Soc. N. S. Wales* 56, 371-390.

Vishnoi, H. S. (1956). The structure, musculature and mechanism of the feeding apparatus of various castes of the termite *Odontotermes obesus* (Rambur). Part I. Clypeo-labrum. *J. Zool. Soc. India* 8, 1-18.

Walker, E. M. (1919). The terminal abdominal structure of Orthopteroid insects: A phylogenetic study. *Ann. Entomol. Soc. Am.* 12, 267-316.

Walker, E. M. (1922). The terminal abdominal structure of Orthopteroid insects: A phylogenetic study. *Ann. Entomol. Soc. Am.* 15, 1-88.

Wasmann, E. (1902). Termiten, Termitophilen und Myrmekophilen gesammelt auf Ceylon von Dr. W. Horn 1899, mit anderm ostindischen Material bearbeitet. *Zool. Jahrb. (Syst.)* 17, 99-164.

Weesner, F. M. (1953). The biology of *Tenuirostritermes tenuirostris* (Desneux) with emphasis on caste development. *Univ. Calif. (Berkeley) Publ. Zool.* 57, 251-302.

Weesner, F. M. (1965). "The Termites of the United States, a Handbook." Natl. Pest Control Assoc., Elizabeth, New Jersey.

3

The Digestive System*

CH. NOIROT AND
C. NOIROT-TIMOTHÉE

I. INTRODUCTION

The digestive tube of the termites attains a considerable development and generally occupies a large part of the abdomen, as is the rule with

*Translated from the French by Mina Parsont and Frances M. Weesner.

those animals eating materials which are difficult to digest. In spite of its importance, anatomical studies are still few in number and are often inadequate. Thus, Holmgren, in his comprehensive monograph (1909), treated the digestive tube in a superficial manner, and most of the descriptions are unusable. Nevertheless, recent investigations have shown that this organ system has undergone considerable modification in the course of the evolution of the groups, and a comparative study could aid in clarifying the precise relationships of the forms existing at the present time (Grassé and Noirot, 1954).

The digestive physiology of the termites is dominated by two phenomena: the social life is accompanied by continuous exchanges of nutrients (trophallaxis) between individuals (Chapter 12) and the digestion of cellulose material necessitates the collaboration of symbiotic microorganisms (discussed in Volume II) localized in the proctodeum. In the lower termites these microorganisms are flagellate protozoans correlated with the proctodeal feeding (involving the paunch contents, which are swarming with the flagellates) that plays an essential role in the trophallactic exchanges. In the higher termites the flagellates are absent, but they are replaced by complex and variable associations of bacteria (Grassé and Noirot, 1959). Apparently these latter termites do not have an exchange of proctodeal food.

II. NUTRITIVE REGIME

As is the rule with the social insects, all of the individuals of the colony do not have the same nutrition. The crude nutrients are obtained by the workers or, in the lower termites without workers, by the older larvae and nymphs. The soldiers, the young brood, and the reproductives have an indirect nutrition, more or less different from the crude nutrients.

A. THE CRUDE NUTRIENTS

The xylophagous diet is certainly primitive in the termites and supposedly even existed in their Blattoid ancestors (Grassé and Noirot, 1959; McKittrick, 1964). This diet is retained, not only in the majority of the lower termites, but also by many higher termites (Termitidae). This is the case with the majority of the Macrotermitinae, numerous Nasutitermitinae (notably the large genus *Nasutitermes*), many of the Amitermitinae (*Amitermes, Microcerotermes, Globitermes, Cephalotermes*), and some of the Termitinae (certain *Termes*). There does not appear to be a specificity, or even a very marked preference for certain

types of vegetation. However, the condition of the wood is very important. Termites do not generally attack living wood, though there are
exceptions (many *Coptotermes*) which can cause considerable damage
on plantations (see Harris, 1961). Sound, dead wood is utilized by most
of the lower termites. Among the Termitidae the Macrotermitinae
particularly utilize this food, but certain *Amitermes*, *Microcerotermes*,
and *Nasutitermes* do so also. Many of the termites show a preference
for wood which is more or less altered by fungi, including those species
capable of attacking sound wood. The problem of the interactions between termites and fungi is complex (Chapter 16). Recent works show
that some fungi produce attractive substances, others produce substances
toxic to termites, and many facilitate the digestion of wood by the
termites. The interactions of termites and fungi attain a great specialization in the Macrotermitinae, or fungus-growing termites (Chapter 16).

The foraging termites (harvesters), which collect waste leaves, constitute a deviation from the xylophagous diet. Some have a mixed diet,
gnawing wood or cutting leaves depending upon the circumstances
(*Acanthotermes*, certain *Amitermes*, *Anacanthotermes*), but many are
strict foragers (*Hodotermes*, *Trinervitermes*, *Drepanotermes*) and may,
when they are abundant, destroy pastures in arid regions (Australia and
South Africa).

The eaters of humus have a regime which varies more from the primitive diet. The humivores are found only among the Termitidae and occur
in all the subfamilies with the exception of the Macrotermitinae. Most
of the Termitinae and all of the Apicotermitinae (sensu Grassé and
Noirot, 1954) have this mode of life. The humivores are numerous in the
Amitermitinae (*Eurytermes*, *Speculitermes*, *Anoplotermes*, *Euhamitermes*, *Firmitermes*, *Pseudhamitermes*, *Eburnitermes*, etc.). In the
Nasutitermitinae they are found in the *Subulitermes* line (*Mimeutermes*,
Eutermellus, *Afrosubulitermes*, *Postsubulitermes*, *Verrucositermes*). It
is unknown just how these termite utilize the humus, but they probably
use the more or less decomposed vegetable debris which it contains.

Let us note, finally, the very special case of the Australian genus
Ahamitermes (Calaby, 1956) which lives exclusively in the nest of
Coptotermes and whose nourishment is the wood carton which consti-
tutes the nest of these *Coptotermes*. *Termes inquilinus* (Emerson)
appears to have a similar relationship with *Constrictotermes cavifrons*
(Holmgren) in Guyana (Emerson, 1938).

On the whole, the nutritive regime of the termites has not varied very
much in the course of the evolution of the group and is always composed
of cellulose materials. One can say that this regime conditions the
biology of the termites as the exploitation of nectar and pollen conditions the biology of the bees.

B. Nutrients of the Dependent Castes

Proctodeal feeding appears to exist only in the lower termites provided with flagellates. The nutritive material consists of the contents of the paunch, swarming with protista, and is very distinct from the excrement (Grassé and Noirot, 1945).

The stomodeal nutrients may consist simply of regurgitated raw food, but, on the other hand, can be entirely liquid and, in all probability, composed of saliva.

The soldiers are incapable of nourishing themselves and generally receive solid stomodeal food; thus their diet is essentially the same as that of the workers. However, there are exceptions. In certain Termitidae the soldiers have an exclusively liquid food. This specialization is encountered in many of the Termitinae (*Procubitermes, Noditermes, Basidentitermes, Orthotermes, Fastigitermes, Proboscitermes, Promirotermes,* and *Pericapritermes*) (Noirot, 1955), and also in the Amitermitinae genus *Eburnitermes* (Noirot, 1966). It would be interesting to know the exact nutritive regimen of the soldiers whose digestive tube is more or less reduced as the result of the development of the frontal gland (*Coptotermes* and *Rhinotermes*) or the salivary gland (*Globitermes* and most of the Macrotermitinae).

In the lower termites the young larvae have a completely dependent nutrition (salivary and proctodeal food) and progressively come to procure their own nutrients (Grassé and Noirot, 1945). In the Termitidae the dependence of the larvae and nymphs is complete, with the possible exception of certain older nymphs. The larvae of the neuters are nourished by saliva, as are also the nymphs of the reproductives. Depending upon the species, the older nymphs receive saliva or a mixture of saliva and regurgitated food (Noirot, 1952).

In all of the termites the functional reproductives appear to be nourished by saliva (Jucci, 1924). The replacement reproductives also appear to receive salivary nutrients. However, the digestive tube of the ergatoid sexuals of *Termes hospes* (Sjöstedt) is always filled with wood (Noirot, 1955).

Thus, within a given species, the digestive processes and absorption can present considerable differences according to the types of individuals.

III. GENERAL STRUCTURE OF THE DIGESTIVE TUBE (WORKERS)

We will now consider the digestive tube of the workers (or of the larvae and older nymphs in the lower termites which lack workers) (Fig. 1).

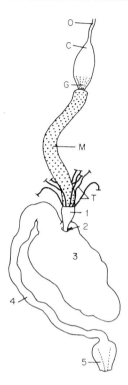

Fig. 1. Digestive tube of *Kalotermes flavicollis*. (C) Crop; (G) gizzard; (M) midgut; (O) esophagus; (T) Malpighian tubules; (1 – 5) the five segments of the hindgut; (1) segment preceding the enteric valve; (2) enteric valve; (3) paunch; (4) colon; (5) rectum.

A. THE MOUTH PARTS AND CIBARIUM

The mouth parts are of the common grinding type and have a very uniform structure throughout the entire order. The mandibles in particular have a very "conservative" dentition (Ahmad, 1950). However, the molar region can present adaptative variations: in the humivores it is smooth and hollowed out like a spoon, instead of having the mastication ridge that is present in the xylophagous forms (Sands, 1965; Deligne, 1966).

The mobility of the labrum and the clypeus appears to play an important role in mastication, ingestion, and the regurgitation of foods (Vishnoi, 1956). We have very little information regarding the hypopharynx and the cibarial region.

B. The Foregut

The *esophagus* is a simple, narrow tube which extends as far as the middle or posterior part of the thorax. The *crop* follows it and is not clearly separated, having practically the same structure: an unistratified epithelium, covered with a thin cuticle, enclosed by a well-developed muscular connective-tissue tunic in which may be distinguished internal longitudinal muscle fibers and an almost continuous layer of external circular fibers.

The *gizzard* is not generally separated from the crop, but its musculature is much more powerful. The epithelium forms a series of folds provided with a very well-differentiated cuticular armature. With most of the termites this armature has a remarkably constant arrangement (Fig. 2), which has often been described but not always correctly interpreted (Feytaud, 1912; Imms, 1919; Child, 1934; Mukerji and Raychaudhuri, 1943; Noirot and Kovoor, 1958; Schmidt, 1959; McKittrick, 1964; Kovoor, 1966, 1968). The wall of the gizzard has 48 longitudinal folds of 4 different types in regular alternation, giving a symmetry of the order of six. At the level of the folds the cuticle has characteristic thickenings. In the anterior part, the 6 folds of the first order and the 6 folds of the second order have practically the same structure and the same development, with a thick cuticle and partial sclerotization, but the folds of the first order are prolonged further into the posterior part, with a very thick but nonsclerotized cuticle (Fig. 2). This posterior region, sometimes called the pulvillus, is much less developed in the folds of the second order. The 12 folds of the third order, alternating with the first two, are less protruding and do not have the posterior pulvillus, but their cuticle is sclerotized. The 24 folds of the fourth order have a very thin longitudinal layer formed by unsclerotized cuticle. The various folds often have surface ornamentations, which can vary from one species to another. The form of the different folds is also slightly variable—as is the relative development of the pulvilli and the anterior region within the folds of the first and second order. The sclerotization can be more or less developed. A very detailed study could, perhaps, make evident the details characteristic of certain groups. We must, however, stress the remarkable uniformity of these structures in all of the termites. This stabilization of the gizzard of the termites contrasts with the considerable diversification which it has undergone in the ants (Eisner, 1957).

There exists, however, a frequent variation within the Termitidae: the almost complete absence of this armature of the gizzard (Section IV). This is surely an instance of a regressive evolution, which took place

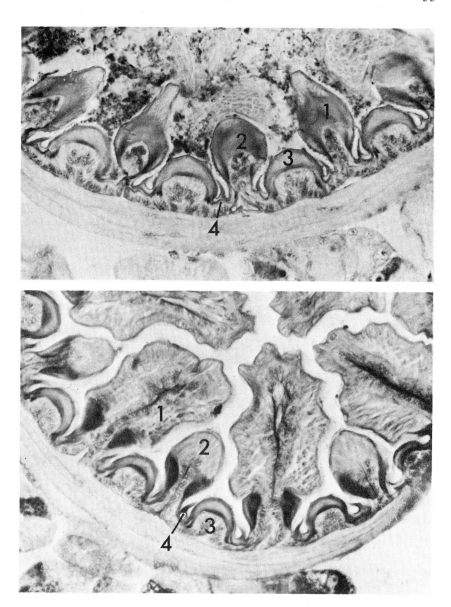

Fig. 2. Transverse sections of the gizzard of a worker of *Reticulitermes lucifugus.* Top: anterior region; bottom: posterior region. The four types of folds are numbered 1—4. Note, in the posterior region (bottom), the importance of the pulvilli of the folds of the first order (× 400).

independently in the various groups, and appears to have proceeded from the front to the back. The sclerotized anterior region of the folds is reduced first (Termitidae in the *Termes* series), after which these folds disappear, leaving only the pulvilli of the main folds (Termitidae of the *Thoracotermes-Cubitermes* series). The best proof that this is an instance of regression is that in certain genera the imagoes have a typical, though poorly developed, gizzard armature, while the workers have only a rudimentary armature (Section IV, C).

The gizzard, therefore, appears to have an extremely conservative structure since in spite of its complexity the only important evolution which it has undergone is regressive. It is not surprising, therefore, to find a plan of organization entirely analogous to that of the roaches (Judd, 1948) and particularly the Cryptocercidae (McKittrick, 1964).* However, in the roaches the gizzard has undergone a much more complex evolution.

The foregut terminates with an esophageal valve which is always well developed and which penetrates deeply into the midgut.

C. THE MIDGUT

The midgut is a tube of uniform diameter (with the exception of the anterior ceca present in some species), and its histological structure is remarkably constant (Fig. 3). The muscular connective envelope is only slightly developed; it includes a layer of almost continuous circular fibers and bundles of longitudinal fibers, some external and some internal to the circular fibers (Bonneville, 1936). The epithelium rests on a very distinct basement membrane and includes the regularly arranged *regenerative crypts* which produce the epithelial cells. This arrangement is frequent in the insects, especially the roaches and the orthopterans. In the termites the crypts are always numerous and are more or less close to one another. When they are very close together they protrude exteriorly and the basement membrane appears invaginated between adjacent crypts. The apical poles of the epithelial cells have a very regular brush border, and the cells are all of one type. They appear to pass through successive stages and then degenerate (Section V). Replacement of the functional cells by new cells results from the activity of the crypts and appears to be continuous. Moreover, at the time of the molt, the epithelium is rejected as a unit and a new epithelium is formed, arising from the crypts which remain in place. This regeneration of the midgut, studied by Weyer

*The homologies are even closer than indicated by McKittrick because she did not see, in the termites, the folds of the fourth order which are equivalent to the "intercalary folds" of the primitive roaches.

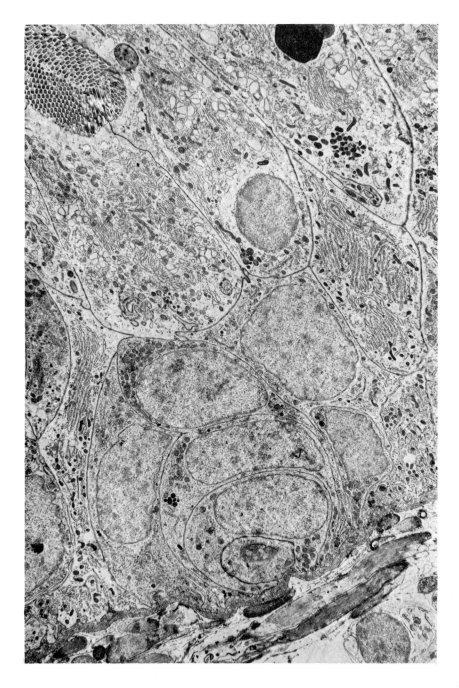

Fig. 3. Electron micrograph of the midgut of a worker of *Cephalotermes rectangularis*. In the center, at the bottom, is a regenerative crypt. At the top, to the left, the brush border (× 3300).

(1935) in *Microcerotermes amboinensis* Kemner, appears (on the basis of our unpublished observations) to be a phenomenon common to all termites. It occurs at every molt and in every caste.

A peritrophic membrane is generally present, but it has been studied only in *Kalotermes flavicollis* (Fabricius) and *Reticulitermes lucifugus* (Rossi) (Montalenti, 1930; Aubertot, 1934; Platania, 1938). It appears to arise from a ring of cells situated at the beginning of the mesenteron (at the junction of the esophageal valve) but might be reinforced by secretions coming from the whole of the mesenteron.

D. Limit between the Midgut and Hindgut; The Malpighian Tubules

In the lower termites the limit between the mesenteron and the proctodeum is normal. The proctodeal valve is a simple, slightly noticeable circular swelling at the beginning of the proctodeum. The Malpighian tubules empty at the exact limit between the two segments, just in front of this swelling.

In the Termitidae the arrangement is much more varied. There are always four Malpighian tubules. Sometimes (particularly in the Macrotermitinae) the structure is essentially the same as in the lower termites. In many cases, however, the mesenteron is considerably prolonged on one of the faces of the intestinal tube, resulting in a *mixed segment* (Grassé and Noirot, 1954), so-called because the intestinal lumen is limited on one side by the mesenteron and on the other by the proctodeum (Figs. 4 and 5c). At this level the Malpighian tubules form a cluster, closely adhering to the mesenteric part. The epithelium of the latter is thickened and possesses special characteristics. The Malpighian tubules are attached in different ways.

When such a mixed segment occurs, it always contains an abundance of bacteria, which have the appearance of a pure culture. These remain exterior to the peritrophic membrane and do not mix with the alimentary bolus (Grassé and Noirot, 1959; Kovoor, 1959, 1966, 1968). One may suppose that this constant association with bacteria is of a symbiotic character.

E. The Hindgut

The hindgut is always well developed, and it exhibits important variations according to different groups and their nutritive regime. Generally speaking, it is particularly long in the humivores. According to Holmgren (1909), five successive segments may be distinguished.

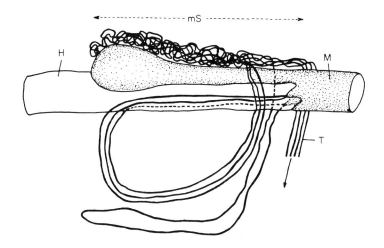

Fig. 4. The mixed segment and its relationships with the Malpighian tubules (worker of *Cephalotermes rectangularis*). (H) Hindgut; (M) midgut; (mS) mixed segment; (T) Malpighian tubules (after Noirot *et al.*, 1967).

The first has an extremely variable length and volume. It may be very short, long and tubular, or it may even have a more or less pronounced dilation. The second segment is formed by a differentiation which is characteristic of the termites, the *enteric valve* (Grassé and Noirot, 1954). This valve generally assumes the form of a muscular funnel invaginated into the following segment (Fig. 5B). The enteric valve often has folds, or longitudinal swellings, whose cuticle bears teeth or spines (having, at least primitively, a symmetry of the order of three) and whose structural details can furnish important characteristics for systematics (Fig. 5A).

The third segment, whose entrance is controlled by the enteric valve, always consists of a voluminous dilation, or *paunch*, in which the symbiotic microorganisms are very abundant (protozoan flagellates in the lower termites, bacteria in the Termitidae*). Sometimes the paunch possesses a lateral diverticulum of variable form. This segment narrows progressively in its posterior part and drains into the following segment without any clear limits.

The fourth segment is, in general, a narrow and contorted tube, often called the *colon*, of variable, but always considerable length. It sometimes possesses a dilation on one part of its course, but this dilation is

---

*Certain Termitidae harbor protozoans in the paunch or the colon (see Grassé and Noirot, 1959), but their role in digestion appears to be very limited.

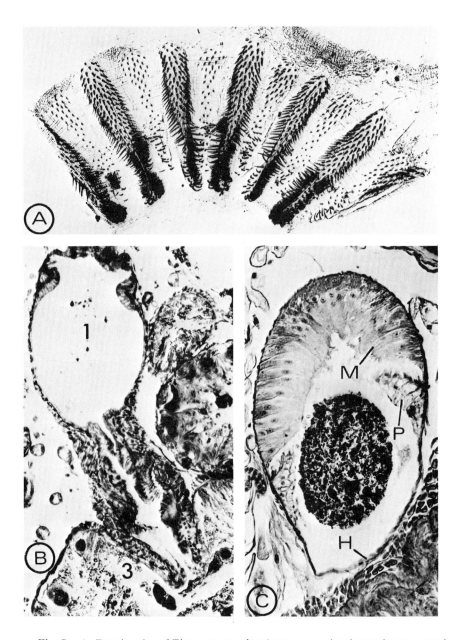

Fig. 5. A: Enteric valve of *Thoracotermes brevinotus*, opened and spread out to reveal the chitinized armature of the internal face (after Noirot and Kovoor, 1958) (× 75); B: enteric valve of a worker of *Mimeutermes giffardi* Silvestri, longitudinal section: (1) first proctodeal segment; (3) paunch (× 170); C: transverse section of the mixed segment of a worker of *Cephalotermes rectangularis:* (M) portion of mesenteron, separated from the hindgut (H) by the proctodeal valve (P) (× 220).

never as important as the paunch. In all of these cases the part preceding the rectum is narrow.

The fifth segment is the *rectum*, whose structure appears to be quite uniform, although it exhibits varying degrees of development. It is a sort of elongated ampul, very muscular, clearly larger than the preceding sections, and capable of strong dilation. As in many insects, the rectum of the termites has six more or less conspicuous longitudinal thickenings, forming the rectal papillae, or rectal glands. The papillae do not extend as far as the anus. The terminal part of the rectum is formed by a chamber with a thin pleated wall, which is capable of a considerable dilation. The importance of this terminal chamber varies greatly among the species.

The histological structure of the hindgut is rather uniform: its muscular connective tunic is composed of circular fibers and external longitudinal fibers. The importance of the musculature varies greatly with the different regions. With the exception of the rectum, the epithelium is unistratified, generally formed by flattened cells of the usual type; however, certain regions may possess a specialized epithelium, probably absorbant (Section V, E). Within the rectum one finds between the papillae a low epithelium of the usual type, but the papillae are comprised of two layers of cells: toward the interior tall cells with an apical part (under the cuticle) having very remarkable differentiations (Section V, F); externally a layer of very flat cells, rich in mitochondria (Fig. 6).

IV. COMPARATIVE ANATOMY

A. THE LOWER TERMITES

The arrangement of the digestive tube in the lower termites is not very variable (Fig. 1), probably due to the constant presence of symbiotic flagellates in the paunch, which indicates a rather uniform physiology.

The crop is essentially symmetrical. The gizzard always possesses a typical chitinized armature. The midgut, which is relatively long, always terminates in a normal manner, and the Malpighian tubules are inserted at the limit of the mesenteron-proctodeum. There are eight Malpighian tubules, except in *Mastotermes*. The first segment of the hindgut forms a cone, more or less elongated and regular, whose tip corresponds to the enteric valve. Internally the epithelium first forms a circular fold (proctodeal valve), which is often very distinct. It then has six thickenings or longitudinal swellings, frequently of two alternating types (symmetry of the order of three). These swellings are generally prolonged into the enteric valve. This valve invaginates more or less deeply into the paunch

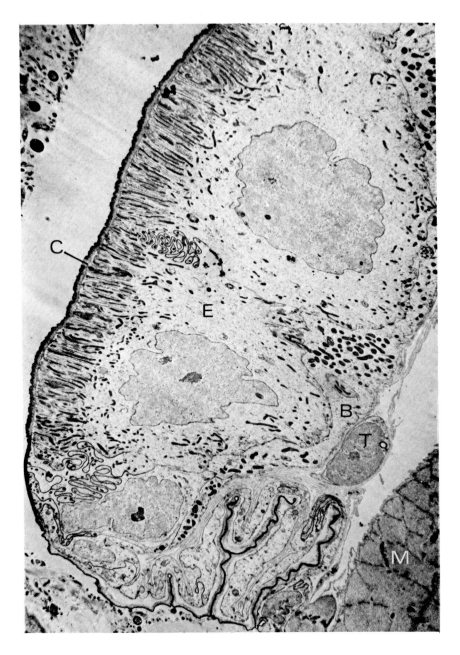

Fig. 6. Electron micrograph of a transverse section of the rectum of a worker of *Cephalotermes rectangularis*. The section intersects a rectal papillae and, at the bottom, the flattened epithelium situated between the papillae. The papillae consist of two layers of cells: beneath the cuticle (C), large cells (E), whose apical membrane possesses numerous invaginations, within which may be seen elongated mitochondria; and a layer of flattened basal cells (B) with globular mitochondria. (M) Muscle; (T) tracheal cell; (×3200).

but is never armed. The paunch, which is always very voluminous, is sometimes incompletely subdivided by a transverse constriction; the colon is always short.

1. Mastotermitidae

Our unpublished observations permit the complementing of the fragmentary work of Sutherland (1934). The crop is elongated and not separated from the gizzard, which has the typical chitinous armature (McKittrick, 1964). The midgut has, at the anterior extremity, two short ceca with a dorsal position. The Malpighian tubules are more numerous than in any other termites. We have observed from 12 to 15 in the few workers which were at our disposal; this question must be reexamined. The first proctodeal segment is typical: there are six longitudinal swellings which are clearly divided in two in a transverse plane; spines are situated on both sides of the division. The digestive tube of *Mastotermes* is thus entirely consistent with the general type, except for the number of Malpighian tubules, a characteristic which recalls the roaches.

2. Termopsidae (sensu Grassé, 1949)

We have a precise description for *Archotermopsis* (Imms, 1919) and particularly for *Zootermopsis* (Child, 1934) and some very fragmentary work by Sutherland (1934) on *Porotermes adamsoni* (Froggatt) [as *P. grandis*] and *Stolotermes victoriensis* Hill, which we have been able to complete by a study of *P. planiceps* (Sjöstedt) and *S. africanus* Emerson. The crop is very elongated and is not separated from the gizzard, which possesses a normal armature. The midgut has anterior ceca of variable number and importance: five in *Archotermopsis*, four in *Zootermopsis*, three in *Porotermes planiceps*. In *Stolotermes africanus* the beginning of the midgut is simply a lateral dilation (representing two dorsal ceca?). There are eight Malpighian tubules; the first segment of the hindgut is of the usual type; and the enteric valve is very clearly defined.

3. Hodotermitidae (sensu Grassé, 1949)

There is no good description of the digestive tube in the Hodotermitidae. We have been able to examine *Anacanthotermes ochraceus* (Burmeister), whose principal characteristic is an extremely elongated crop which pushes the gizzard to about the middle of the abdomen. The crop is clearly separated from the gizzard by a constriction. The gizzard bears a typical armature, but the folds of the first and second order are particularly strong, and the pulvilli are very conspicuous. The midgut is long and there are eight Malpighian tubules. The first proctodeal segment has the usual six swellings, bearing very small sclerotized tubercules at their anterior region. The enteric valve is well developed.

4. Kalotermitidae

Only fragmentary accounts are available for the Kalotermitidae. *Kalotermes flavicollis* (Fig. 1) has an elongated crop, symmetrical and muscular, which is not separated from the gizzard. The gizzard has the usual armature. There are eight Malpighian tubules; the first proctodeal segment is funnel-shaped and contains six folds with small projections, which are poorly separated in half in a transverse plane and which bear very fine spines. The enteric valve is clearly marked. The paunch is not subdivided.

Postelectrotermes amplus (Sjöstedt) has very similar characteristics; the crop is a little more developed.

Cryptotermes brevis (Walker) has an even more powerful crop. The first segment of the proctodeum is more elongated and does not have spines on the longitudinal swellings. The enteric valve is poorly developed. The paunch is divided into two parts by a very pronounced constriction, very close to the outlet of the enteric valve.

In these three genera the armature of the gizzard is always arranged on the same plan, but a detailed examination shows characteristic differences. A precise comparative study of the various Kalotermitidae would be useful to the systematists.

5. Rhinotermitidae

Our knowledge of this group is practically limited to *Reticulitermes lucifugus* (Feytaud, 1912; Platania, 1938; Baccetti, 1963), with the addition of a brief mention by Sutherland (1934) of *Coptotermes frenchi* Hill (as *C. flavus*), work which we have been able to complete with *C. sjöstedti* Holmgren. The digestive tubes of these two genera are extremely similar. The crop is oval, not very elongated, and not separated from the gizzard, which has a typical armature. There are eight Malpighian tubules. The first proctodeal segment has six longitudinal swellings in two parts; the posterior part of the three principal swellings bears a series of rather strong spines in front.

B. THE FAMILY TERMITIDAE

The digestive tube shows a great diversity of structure in the Termitidae. One character is common to the whole family: the Malpighian tubules number four. [Holmgren (1909) indicated only two in some species, but this statement appears doubtful to us.]

1. Macrotermitinae

Our personal observations, dealing with most of the genera, have permitted us to complement the work of Mukerji and Raychaudhuri (1943) on *Odontotermes obesus* (Rambur) and of Schmidt (1959) on *Bellicositermes natalensis* (Haviland).

The structure of the digestive tube is very uniform and very close to that of the lower termites, notably the Kalotermitidae and Rhinotermitidae. The gizzard always possesses a typical armature, which is well developed. The midgut is relatively long and terminates in the usual manner. The four Malpighian tubules are inserted in a symmetrical manner at the junction of the mesenteron-proctodeum. The hindgut begins with a very short, narrow segment and terminates in a muscular enteric valve, which commands the entrance to a voluminous paunch. From one genus to another the variations appear slight: ornamentation of the folds of the gizzard differs (for example, *Acanthotermes* possesses fine spines on the pulvilli of the folds of the first order); the enteric valve, which is generally conical, is tubular in *Sphaerotermes*; there are six longitudinal swellings, which are very weak in *Sphaerotermes* but very well developed in *Pseudacanthotermes* and which are sometimes armed by very small spines or tubercules (*Macrotermes*). In this uniformity, and the primitive characters of their digestive tube, the Macrotermitinae contrast with the other subfamilies.

2. Amitermitinae (Fig. 7)

The digestive tube of *Microcerotermes* has been studied in detail by Kovoor (1959, 1966, 1968). Noirot (1966) described that of *Pseudhamitermes* and *Eburnitermes* and compared these with the other Amitermitinae. *Cephalotermes* has been studied by Noirot and Noirot-Timothée (1967).

In this subfamily, considered to be primitive, the variations of the digestive tube are considerable. One type (Fig. 7A, D) is found in the genera *Eurytermes, Speculitermes, Indotermes,* and *Euhamitermes.* In these, the gizzard is without an armature; the mixed segment is as long as the true midgut but not much developed (mesenteric part not dilated), the Malpighian tubules being attached within the epithelium of the mesenteron toward the beginning of the mixed segment; the first proctodeal segment is very long but nondilated; the enteric valve is unarmed. *Firmitermes* is associated with this group, but the mixed segment is more differentiated.

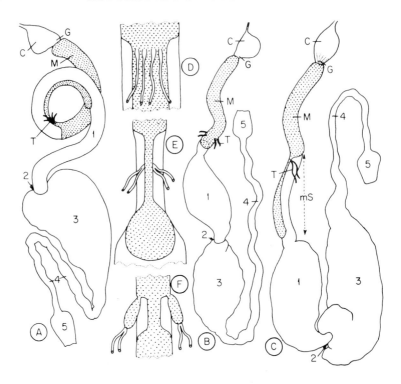

Fig. 7. Digestive tube of the Amitermitinae. A: *Euhamitermes lighti;* B: *"Anoplotermes"* sp. (see footnote on page 67); C: *Drepanotermes rubriceps* (Froggatt); D: attachment of the Malpighian tubules of *Euhamitermes lighti;* E: mixed segment and attachment of the Malpighian tubules of *Amitermes evuncifer* Silvestri; F: attachment of the Malpighian tubules of *Protohamitermes globiceps* Holmgren. (C) Crop; (G) gizzard; (M) midgut; (mS) mixed segment; (T) Malpighian tubules; (1) first proctodeal segment; (2) enteric valve; (3) paunch; (4) colon; (5) rectum. The areas of the mesenteron are stippled.

A second type occurs in the genera *Amitermes* (Fig. 7E), *Ahamitermes,* *Drepanotermes* (Fig. 7C), *Pseudhamitermes, Cephalotermes, Microcerotermes,* and *Eremotermes.* The gizzard has the typical armature; the mixed segment is always present, but attachment of the Malpighian tubules is at the mesenteron-proctodeum junction, generally in two pairs. The first proctodeal segment is generally dilated. The enteric valve has a chitinized armature, but it is not very pronounced. In the genera in which the mixed segment is most evolved (*Microcerotermes, Eremotermes*), the valve is unarmed. One may associate with this type of digestive tube the genera *Protohamitermes* (Fig. 7F), *Globitermes, Synhamitermes,* and *Prohamitermes,* where the Malpighian tubules are attached on two swellings formed by the evagination of the midgut. In the last three genera the mixed segment is particularly evolved.

In the genus *Anoplotermes** and some related forms there is no mixed segment (Fig. 7B), the Malpighian tubules are attached within the midgut, and the enteric valve lacks spines. The genus *Eburnitermes* does not have a mixed segment, but has an enteric valve which is strongly armed on the external face, arranged as in the Apicotermitinae (Fig. 11D).

One may thus detect in the Amitermitinae varied evolutionary tendencies, which foretell the arrangements observed in some other subfamilies.

3. Termitinae (Fig. 8)

According to the observations of Noirot and Kovoor (1958),† the principal characteristics of the digestive tube of the Termitinae are the following: there are four Malpighian tubules; the mixed segment is always present but of variable arrangement; the Malpighian tubules are inserted at the mesenteron-proctodeum limit at the anterior part of the mixed segment (Fig. 8); the first segment of the hindgut is long, dilated or not; and the enteric valve has a chitinous armature which is well developed on the internal face. One finds here the characters which have already been observed in the Amitermitinae of the *Amitermes* group.

Within this general outline, one may tentatively distinguish two different types. In the first [genera *Thoracotermes* (Fig. 8A), *Crenetermes*, *Apilitermes*, *Megagnathotermes*, *Cubitermes* (Fig. 8D, E), *Procubitermes*, *Noditermes*, *Ophiotermes*, *Euchilotermes*, *Basidentitermes* (Fig. 8F), *Orthotermes*, *Proboscitermes*, and *Fastigitermes*], the gizzard possesses a chitinized armature which is very regressed or even absent; the crop is often dilated, and the first segment of the hindgut is strongly dilated; the enteric valve is strongly armed with twelve longitudinal swellings on its internal face (Fig. 5A), has a symmetry of the third order (inclined to become bilateral); and the third proctodeal segment (paunch) possesses a lateral cecum of varying appearance.

In the second type [genera *Termes* (Fig. 8B), *Protocapritermes*, *Paracapritermes*, *Pericapritermes* (Fig. 8C), *Capritermes*, *Promirotermes*], the crop is not dilated. The armature of the gizzard is of the usual type, although not very well sclerotized; the first proctodeal segment is more or

* According to the observations of W. A. Sands (personal communication), *Anoplotermes pacificus* Fr. Müller, the type species of the genus, appears to have a digestive tube of the *Eurytermes-Euhamitermes* type, but this large genus appears to be heterogeneous, and the African species which we have studied should be placed in a different genus.

†An error occurred in this study since the facts described for *Tuberculitermes* actually concern another genus close to *Pilotermes*.

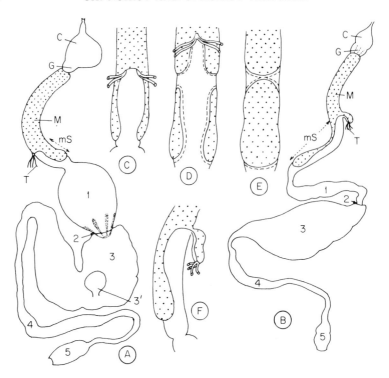

Fig. 8. Digestive tube of the Termitinae. A: *Thoracotermes brevinotus;* B: *Termes hospes;* C – F: mixed segment and attachment of the Malpighian tubules; C: *Pericapritermes urgens;* D and E: *Cubitermes severus* Silvestri (external face and internal face); F: *Basidentitermes mactus* (Sjöstedt). (3′) Lateral diverticulum of the paunch; other abbreviations as in Fig. 7 (after Noirot and Kovoor, 1958).

less dilated; the enteric valve is much less developed and has a reduced chitinized armature following six internal longitudinal folds; and the third segment does not bear a lateral cecum.*

4. Apicotermitinae (Fig. 9)

It is partly because of the character of the digestive tube that Grassé and Noirot (1954) proposed this new subfamily. The crop is rather voluminous and asymmetrical; the gizzard is very reduced, practically

*The genus *Foraminitermes* possesses a digestive tube which is completely different from that of other genera of the subfamily Termitinae. According to Krishna (1963) its systematic position is also unique as it does not have close relatives in the subfamily Termitinae. *Labritermes,* usually included in the Amitermitinae, has a digestive tube of the same type (Noirot, unpublished observations).

devoid of chitinous armor; there is no mixed segment; the four Malpighian tubules open into the midgut, each by a small ampulliform dilation; the first proctodeal segment is very short; and the enteric valve is
strongly armed on its *external* face (Fig. 11D), forming six chitinous lips
bearing spines which are often greatly differentiated. The third segment
(paunch) is not particularly developed, but the fourth is very long and
possesses one or two dilations, which are often voluminous. The enteric
valve has undergone a very complex evolution within this group. A symmetry of the third order seems to exist primitively, is retained in *Tricho-*
termes, and proceeds to a bilateral symmetry in *Jugositermes* and
Rostrotermes, but in the other genera the six valves are all dissimilar, so
that it is no longer possible to define any symmetry. One may, nevertheless, group the genera *Coxotermes* and *Heimitermes*, with their
spoonlike bristles, and the genera *Allognathotermes* and *Duplidenti-*
termes, with plumose bristles only borne by a single lip. Further research
is necessary in order to specify the condition in the genus *Apicotermes*.

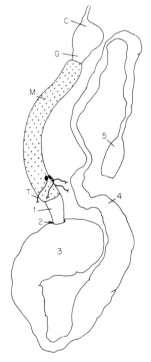

Fig. 9.   Digestive tube of the Apicotermitinae; *Allognathotermes hypogeus* Silvestri.
Abbreviations as in Fig. 7.

5. Nasutitermitinae (Fig. 10)

The investigations of Kovoor, which are as yet unpublished, reveal important details for this subfamily.

If one considers the forms having true nasute soldiers with atrophied mandibles, the distinction of the two phyletic lines, *Nasutitermes*, on one hand, and *Subulitermes*, on the other, appears very clearly in the digestive tube.

The genera of the *Nasutitermes* group (Fig. 10B) have a gizzard with normal armature. The mixed segment is long but little evolved; the prolongation of the mesenteron is simple and slightly dilated in its posterior part. The four Malpighian tubules are more or less dilated in their proximal region, but are always very narrow at the level of their insertion. This insertion is always at the level of the mesenteron-procto-deum limit. The first proctodeal segment is tubular or weakly dilated. The enteric valve is very weakly armed (genera studied: *Nasutitermes*, *Trinervitermes*, *Hospitalitermes*, *Leptomyxotermes*, *Fulleritermes*, and *Tumulitermes*). The genus *Occasitermes*, usually placed in the *Subulitermes* branch, must, on the basis of its digestive tube, be placed with the *Nasutitermes* group.

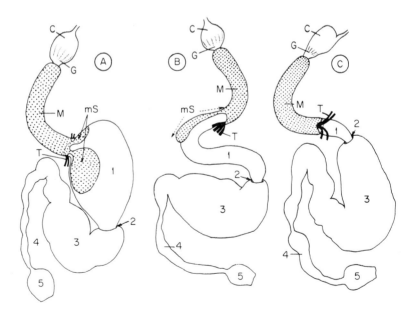

Fig. 10. Digestive tube of the Nasutitermitinae. A: *Syntermes dirus* (Burmeister); B: *Nasutitermes arborum* (Smeathman); C: *Postsubulitermes africanus* Emerson. Abbreviations as in Fig. 7 (after unpublished observations of Kovoor).

In the *Subulitermes* group (Fig. 10C) the armature of the gizzard is reduced. There is no mixed segment; the four Malpighian tubules are attached in two pairs at the mesenteron-proctodeal junction. The first proctodeal segment is very short; the enteric valve is well armed; the paunch is often subdivided into two sections; and the colon is very long. Among the genera examined two types of enteric valves may be distinguished. In *Eutermellus* and *Verrucositermes* the six longitudinal swellings protrude into the paunch in the form of sclerotized and thorny plates; in *Mimeutermes, Afrosubulitermes,* and *Postsubulitermes,* there are only 3 or 6 rows of spines on the internal face of the valve.

The facts are more complex with the forms having mandibulate soldiers. *Syntermes,* which is considered the most primitive type, has a gizzard with normal armature, but the mixed segment is very peculiar (Fig. 10A): the first proctodeal segment is considerably dilated, and the mesenteron sends two unequal prolongations over this dilation. The Malpighian tubules are inserted in two pairs at the mesenteron-proctodeal limit. The enteric valve is not very differentiated and lacks spines. *Labiotermes* and *Cornitermes* have a comparable appearance, but the prolongations of the mesenteron are less unequal. The enteric valve is armed with spines, especially in *Cornitermes. Procornitermes, Rhynchotermes* and *Armitermes* have only one prolongation of the mesenteron forming the mixed segment, and the first proctodeal segment is less dilated than in the preceding genera. The enteric valve is weakly armed in *Procornitermes* and *Rhynchotermes,* much more so in *Armitermes.* On the whole, all of these genera appear related, but the digestive tube does not permit us to state precisely their affinities with the two phyletic lines having true nasute soldiers.

C. VARIATIONS WITH POLYMORPHISM

The papers concerning this problem are few and often imprecise. Generally speaking, it does not appear that there are essential differences between different castes of a given species, but, at the very most, there are different degrees of development of one region or another of the digestive tube.

In the lower termites these differences are particularly slight [Feytaud, 1912: *Reticulitermes lucifugus;* Imms, 1919: *Archotermopsis wroughtoni* (Desneux)]. In certain Rhinotermitidae the soldier has an enormous frontal gland whose reservoir extends into the abdomen, and the digestive tube only occupies a reduced area. We have been able to ascertain that in *Coptotermes sjöstedti* the structure is similar to that of the worker, but the hindgut is very small, and the paunch, which is scarcely noticeable, only contains a few protozoans.

In the higher termites the digestive tube of the soldiers is built on the same plan as that of the workers, but certain regions may be less developed. Vishnoi (1956) observed a reduction of the cibarial cavity in the soldiers of *Odontotermes obesus*. The recent work of Deligne (1968) has contributed a precise documentation for the subfamily Termitinae. In the genera where the soldiers receive solid food, the differences between the workers and soldiers are not very important: the dilations of the hindgut are a little less voluminous, but the folding of the walls simply indicates that they are incompletely filled; the cuticular differentiations (gizzard, enteric valve) are a little reduced and less differentiated. Conversely, in soldiers receiving liquid food the digestive tube shows, by comparison with that of the workers from which they arise, a marked reduction. The length of the mesenteron is more or less reduced, but the degeneration is especially marked in the proctodeum, in which the dilations, which are especially marked in the worker, are hardly visible. An equally strong regression occurs in the spines of the gizzard and especially in the enteric valve. The spines of the enteric valve disappear completely in the soldiers of *Pericapritermes magnificus* Silvestri. In the imagoes (Noirot, unpublished observations) the hindgut is much less developed than in the workers, but nevertheless retains the same structure. The most interesting variation that we have observed concerns the gizzard. In certain Termitinae [*Cubitermes fungifaber* (Sjöstedt), *Thoracotermes brevinotus* Silvestri, and *Ophiotermes* sp.] the gizzard of the imago possesses a typical, although very slightly developed and nonsclerotized, armature, whereas the workers have a completely regressed armature. On the other hand, in *Euhamitermes lighti* (Snyder) the armature of the gizzard is absent in the imago and in the worker.

In the physogastric queens the midgut undergoes a considerable growth (Section V, D, 2); neither the stomodeum nor the proctodeum appear very much modified.

All these observations still remain very fragmentary; the study of the digestive tube as it relates to polymorphism has only begun.

D. PHYLOGENETIC CONSIDERATIONS

In the lower termites the intestinal structures are uniform. A very detailed study of the foregut (the crop and especially the armature of the gizzard) and the first proctodeal segment would, perhaps, aid us in a precise understanding of the phylogenetic relationships of certain genera. There are more than eight Malpighian tubules in *Mastotermes;* this approaches the number of tubules in the blattoids. The anterior ceca of the mesenteron, present in many Termopsidae, are likewise blattoid characters.

The evolution of the digestive tube has been much more varied in the Termitidae. The most striking features of this evolution concern, on one hand, the structure of the "mixed segment," and, on the other hand, the modifications of the first proctodeal segment and the enteric valve.

Is the mixed segment a primitive character in the Termitidae? Did their common ancestor already possess this specialization? The Macro-termitinae, whose digestive tube is very similar to that of the lower termites, have certainly never had a mixed segment. For the other sub-families the question cannot be answered with certainty. One may suppose that the mixed segment only appeared once in the course of evolution, and that, with the exception of the Macrotermitinae, its absence in a Termitidae is an instance of regressive evolution. On the other hand, one may advance the hypothesis of convergent evolution producing this specialization independently in various lines. At present the first hypothesis appears to us to be more consistent with the known facts.

The evolution of the anterior part of the proctodeum is less difficult to understand (Fig. 11). There is, first of all, a tendency for the most anterior region of the first proctodeal segment (the region situated in front of the six longitudinal swellings) to develop. This development is very limited in the Macrotermitinae, the Apicotermitinae, and the Nasuti-

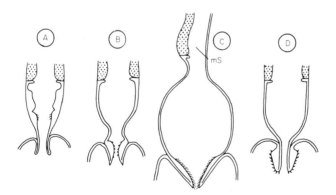

Fig. 11. Probable scheme of evolution of the first intestinal segment and the enteric valve. A: Lower termites; B: Macrotermitinae (*Pseudacanthotermes*); C: *Thoracotermes*; D: structure observed in the Apicotermitinae and *Eburnitermes* (Amitermitinae). (mS) Mixed segment. Stippled areas indicate the mesenteron.

termitinae of the *Subulitermes* branch, but is considerable with most of the other termites. The posterior region of the first proctodeal segment [which in the lower termites (Fig. 11A) bears six more or less spinose longitudinal thickenings] appears to have been incorporated within the enteric valve (Fig. 11B, C) and appears to form swellings, often strongly armed, of the valves of the Termitidae. In the Apicotermitinae and in *Eburnitermes* (Amitermitinae) this evolution goes farther: the enteric valve is much more profoundly invaginated into the paunch and has become extroverted; the thickenings of the wall and their chitinous armature are therefore passed onto its external face (Fig. 11D).

The intestinal anatomy confirms the distinctiveness of the Macrotermitinae, which is also indicated by their associations with fungi (Chapter 16) and the uniqueness of their polymorphism (Chapter 10). One may wonder if it would not be advisable to elevate this group to the rank of family, as has already been suggested by Grassé and Noirot (1951) and by Weidner (1956). At the very least, one must admit that the Macrotermitinae became separated at a very early stage from the common stock of the Termitidae. Among the other subfamilies the Amitermitinae appear the nearest to the stock (Emerson, 1955) and show very diverse intestinal types. One may conceive without difficulty the affiliation of the Termitinae and the Apicotermitinae, starting with the primitive Amitermitinae which had digestive tubes of the *Amitermes* and *Eburnitermes* type, respectively (Noirot, 1966). The origin of the Nasutitermitinae is much more difficult to define. The forms with the nasute soldiers of the *Nasutitermes* branch have a digestive tube very close to the Amitermitinae of the *Amitermes* group, but the forms with mandibulate soldiers, particularly *Syntermes* (considered the most primitive), present original characteristics, especially of the mixed segment. Are they derived from a group of Amitermitinae which is today completely extinct? Or else, have they undergone a special evolution, diverging very early from the stock of the Nasutitermitinae? At the present we are not able to make a choice between these two hypotheses.

V. PHYSIOLOGY

A. INTESTINAL TRANSIT

The problem of the passage of food through the digestive tube has been recently studied by Kovoor (1966, 1967b), in the workers of *Microcerotermes edentatus* Wasmann, by following, with X-rays, the alimentary bolus rendered opaque by barium sulfate. Under good culture conditions, the total duration of the passage is about 24 hours (with the temperature between 25° and 30°C). The passage is accelerated by increased temperatures and retarded by desiccation and isolation. The retention of the food in the foregut is from 1 to 2 hours. The emptying of the crop is continuous. Passage through the midgut is rapid ($1-1\frac{1}{2}$ hours), and it is a little slower in the mixed segment. The retention in the first proctodeal segment (dilated in this species) is from 4 to 5 hours, but 8 to 12 hours in the paunch. The final passage is rather rapid (2 to 3 hours).

The few observations which we have been able to make in *Kalotermes flavicollis* show us a comparable rapid passage of the food through the midgut (30 minutes − 1 hour). It is probable that in all of the termites (or at least in the castes having solid food) it is in the hindgut that the food remains for the longest time. It is here that the main part of digestion is accomplished.

One important fact must be emphasized: there is no reflux of the food from the hindgut to the midgut. The enteric valve prevents the return of the contents of the paunch toward the front. The radiographic observations of Kovoor have shown that such a reflux does not exist. Therefore, there is no mechanism present in the termites comparable to that described in *Cryptocercus* by Cleveland *et al.* (1934) and by Roessler (1961) in the larvae of *Oryctes,* where the content of the proctodeal dilation goes back to the midgut.

B. HYDROGEN ION CONCENTRATION

Table I presents a resume of the observations available regarding pH, utilizing ingestions by termites of papers impregnated with color indicators. The results are rather different from one species to another, but we may note that the foregut is quite acid in the lower termites and clearly alkaline in the only Termitidae studied. On the other hand, the paunch is always close to neutrality, whether the termite harbours flagellates (lower termites) or bacteria (*Microcerotermes*).

C. DIGESTIVE FLUIDS

We do not have any information on the role which the mandibular and salivary glands play in digestion (Chapter 4), but it is probable that this role is very limited. The secretion of enzymes takes place primarily in the midgut. The histological and histochemical studies (Kovoor, 1966, 1968) and the ultrastructures (Baccetti, 1963; Noirot and Noirot-Timothée, unpublished data, see Fig. 3) show that there is only one type of cell in the mesenteron, but that the absorptive functions and the secretory functions are performed successively by the same cells. But the investiga-

TABLE I

HYDROGEN ION CONCENTRATION IN THE VARIOUS SEGMENTS OF THE DIGESTIVE TUBE

Segment	Hydrogen ion concentration in:			
	Kalotermes flavicollis[a]	*Zootermopsis angusticollis*[b]	*Reticulitermes lucifugus*[c]	*Microcerotermes edentatus*[d]
Foregut	5.2 − 5.4	6.8 (esophagus) 5.2 (crop)	5.6	8.8 − 9.6
Midgut	6.8 − 7.5	5.2	6.8 − 7.2	8.8 − 9.6
Mixed segment	−	−	−	> 9.6
First proctodeal segment	5.0	3.0	−	> 9.6 then 7.6
Paunch	6.8 − 7.5	6.8	7.4	7.2 − 7.6
Colon				6.8 − 7.2
Rectum			5.0	6.0 − 6.8

[a] Noirot, unpublished observations.
[b] Randall and Doody, 1934.
[c] Grassé and Noirot, 1945.
[d] Kovoor, 1966, 1967c.

tions on the digestive fluids must take into account the symbiotic micro-organisms present in the proctodeum.

Montalenti (1932) observed an amylase and an invertase in the midgut, as well as a substance with a proteolytic action, but it is particularly the enzymes which are responsible for the degradation of cellulose (cellulase and cellobiase) with which most of the studies are concerned.

In the lower termites the investigations of Trager (1932) and of Hungate (1938) on *Zootermopsis* showed that the cellulolytic action is due to the symbiotic flagellates and that the termites do not have a cellulase proper. Yokoe (1964), working with *Reticulitermes*, concluded, on the contrary, that at least a part of the cellulase is secreted by the termites, but we do not feel that this conclusion is absolutely established.

In the higher termites Misra and Ranganathan (1954) found only a weak cellobiase activity in the midgut of *Odontotermes obesus*, and the cellulolytic activity of the hindgut could be due to the bacteria which it contains. Tracey and Youatt (1958) showed the existence of a cellulase and a chitinase in *Nasutitermes exitiosus* (Hill), but the assay involved total extracts and does not give us any information on the origin of these enzymes. The same is true for the chitinase observed by Waterhouse et al. (1961) in total extracts of the same species. Kovoor (1966) detected a cellulase (active on carboxymethylcellulose) and a cellobiase at the same time in the paunch and in the midgut (including the mixed segment) in *Microcerotermes*. In this latter case the enzymes could be produced either by the termites themselves or by the bacteria of the mixed segment.

Thus it appears that the microorganisms of the paunch produce the cellulases. The possibility of the production of a cellulase by the termites themselves calls for new investigations.

D. DIGESTION

1. Digestion of Wood

The few investigations which are available indicate that the termites assimilate a very important proportion of the wood which they ingest. We have found (unpublished observations) a coefficient of utilization of 55 – 60% in *Kalotermes flavicollis*, depending upon the species of wood consumed. Seifert and Becker (1965) found comparable values for *Kalotermes*, but their figures are higher for other species of termites (Table II).

Among the components of wood, cellulose is very strongly attacked (Hungate, 1938; Seifert and Becker, 1965, and Table II; Kovoor, 1966). The hemicelluloses, and notably the pentosans, also undergo a very important degradation (Kovoor, 1966). The problem of lignin appears complex. It was accepted, following the work of Hungate (1938), that the termites are incapable of digesting lignin. But the figures of Seifert and Becker (1965 and Table II) indicate an important degradation of this compound. However, these authors call attention to the fact that the conditions of culture may have provoked an unusual coprophagous behavior which may have falsified the results concerning *Reticulitermes* and *Nasutitermes*. Kovoor (1964a,b, 1966) shows that *Microcerotermes*

TABLE II

COEFFICIENTS OF THE UTILIZATION OF WOOD, CELLULOSE, AND LIGNIN IN FOUR SPECIES OF TERMITES[a]

Materials digested	Coefficients of utilization (%) in:			
	Kalotermes flavicollis	*Heterotermes indicola*	*Reticulitermes lucifugus santonensis*	*Nasutitermes ephratae*
Wood	54 – 64	62 – 69	86 – 93	75 – 85
Cellulose	74 – 91	78 – 89	96 – 99	91 – 97
Lignin	2 – 26	14 – 40	70 – 83	42 – 52

[a] After Seifert and Becker (1965).

edentatus degrades the lignin of sound wood to a slight extent (above all by demethoxylation), but that the digestion is more complete if the wood has been subjected beforehand to the attack of certain fungi. The digestion of lignin by the termites calls for new investigations.

On the whole, the documents, still too few in number, which we have available seem to show that there is no radical difference in the utilization of wood by the lower termites, provided with flagellates, and by the higher termites, which do not possess them.

In both cases the main part of the digestion takes place in the hindgut, especially in the paunch, under the action of the symbiotic microorganisms (flagellates in the lower termites, bacteria in the Termitidae). At the time of the rapid passage of food through the mesenteron, the fluids secreted by the termites cause the degradation of the easily available compounds (soluble sugars, amidon, proteins). Even if certain termites do possess a cellulase proper, it is the action of the symbionts which appears to predominate in the utilization of the cellulose. The cellulose is degraded by anaerobic fermentation by the flagellates (Hungate, 1938, 1939) or by the bacteria (Hungate, 1944; Pochon *et al.,* 1959; Kovoor, 1966), and these fermentations liberate volatile fatty acids in the paunch, particularly acetic acid (Hungate, 1939; Brown and Smith, 1954) and also, in *Microcerotermes,* propionic and butyric acids (Kovoor, 1966, 1967a). It is these fatty acids which are probably metabolized by the termites. The convergence with the phenomena observed in the mammalian ruminants has been emphasized by Hungate (1946).

We have very little information concerning the digestion and utilization of the hemicelluloses and lignin. It is possible the insects themselves contribute to the digestion of the pentosans, but as far as lignin is concerned, it is necessary certainly to call for intervention by the symbionts, for we do not know of any animal capable of digesting lignin.

2. *Other Nutritive Regimes*

a. *The Fungus-Growing Termites (Macrotermitinae).* The question of the nutrition of the Macrotermitinae is considered in Chapter 16. We will only mention that the utilization of vegetable material is indirect in this subfamily: the debris of wood or of leaves are first incorporated into fungus gardens and then consumed by the workers after having undergone the action of the fungus *Termitomyces.*

b. *The Humivores.* The humivorous regime exists in a very large number of Termitidae (Section II), but we do not have any information on the composition of the humus used by the workers, nor the manner by which its digestion is effected.

The digestive tube of the humivores is marked by a very considerable development of the hindgut, which distends the abdominal cavity and occupies it completely. As in the other Termitidae, this hindgut harbors a very rich population of bacteria, particularly at the outlet of the enteric valve and against the wall of the colon (Grassé and Noirot, 1959). It is permissible to think that it is the bacterial associations which are responsible for digestion.

c. *The Dependent Castes.* The individuals nourished by the workers may receive three types of nutrition (Grassé and Noirot, 1945; Chapter 10): solid stomodeal food (simple regurgitations of the contents of the crop), saliva, and, finally, proctodeal food.

The solid stomodeal food is not essentially different from the crude food of the workers, and its digestion would seem to occur in the same way. The other two types of food are, on the contrary, much more elaborate and probably easier to digest. The saliva of the workers appears as a clear liquid, optically transparent, but we do not know anything about its composition. The termites who receive only this type of food (larvae, functional reproductives, soldiers of certain species) have a bacterial flora which is reduced or absent. The saliva, readily assimilable, must be digested and absorbed at the level of the midgut. In the physogastric queens only the midgut undergoes a considerable enlargement, and the study of its ultrastructure indicates that the processes of absorption surpass the secretion of enzymes (Noirot-Timothée and Noirot, 1965).

Proctodeal food exists only in the lower termites having flagellates (Alibert, 1963, 1966; Grassé, 1949; Grassé and Noirot, 1945). It is formed by the contents of the paunch and contains protozoans; it is, therefore, entirely different from the excrements. Some of the protozoans are damaged in the foregut, especially by the mechanical action of the folds of the gizzard, and are then digested in the midgut, but some arrive intact in the paunch (Grassé and Noirot, 1945). This type of trophallactic exchange thus insures the inoculation of the individuals with protozoans and also constitutes a form of nutrition, particularly of proteins.

E. THE INTESTINAL ABSORPTION

The absorption at the level of the midgut appears limited to easily hydrolyzable compounds, which are broken down in this region. Indeed, we have seen (Section V, A) that the contents of the hindgut, particularly those in the paunch, cannot flow back into the middle intestine. The metabolites freed by the symbionts, especially the fatty acids, must, therefore, be absorbed at the level of the hindgut and across the cuticle.

Certainly, in the lower termites, trophallaxis may intervene, and the exchange of proctodeal food can permit absorption in the usual manner in insects (that is, in the midgut), but the trophallactic exchanges cannot account for all of the absorption. *Kalotermes* may be maintained in isolation from their congeners for a very long time, provided that following each molt the symbionts are restored to them (Grassé and Noirot, 1960). Finally, the exchange of proctodeal food does not seem to exist in the Termitidae.

In the lower termites the paunch is uniformly lined with an extremely thin epithelium. If there is, as we may suppose, a passage of the fatty acids at this level, this passage must be by simple diffusion. [However, Baccetti (1963) believes there is an active pinocytosis in *Reticulitermes lucifugus*.] In the higher termites there is often present in the posterior part of the paunch a more greatly thickened epithelium which could play a role in absorption (Kovoor, 1966, 1968; Noirot and Noirot-Timothée, 1967). These cells (Fig. 12) present characteristic ultrastructure usually encountered with epithelium where the transit of substances occurs; the folds of the apical membrane, under the cuticle, may be compared to a brush border. According to our unpublished observations, such an "absorbant" epithelium is found in the paunch of numerous Termitidae, belonging to all the subfamilies, but with a variable development according to the species.

F. EXCRETION AND HYDROMINERAL BALANCE

We do not have any precise information regarding excretion itself and the functioning of the Malpighian tubules of the termites. The cells usually possess refractive granulations, but the lumen of the tubules is optically clear (Jucci, 1924; Platania, 1939). Some histochemical data have been provided by Kovoor (1966, 1968). We do, however, have histophysiological works concerning the resorption of water and certain ions involved in the hydromineral balance.

1. *Role of the Rectum*

As in many insects, the excrements of termites may be more or less dehydrated before their expulsion. This dehydration is very marked in the Kalotermitidae (dry-wood termites) which eject hard pellets in the form of hexagonal prisms, which correspond to the form of the rectum. The Termopsidae (*Zootermopsis*) may also emit solid, but less desiccated, excrements. The other termites, particularly the Termitidae, emit liquid or rather pasty excrement, whose degree of dehydration is difficult to define.

Fig. 12. The ultrastructure of the absorbent epithelium of the paunch (worker of *Cephalotermes rectangularis*). (B) Brush border; (C) cuticle; (CL) connective lamellae; (D) septate desmosome; (m) microtubules; (M) mitochondria; (T) tracheoblast; (β) β-cytomembrane (after Noirot and Noirot-Timothée, 1967).

The resorptive power of the rectum probably varies considerably in the different species. It must play an important role in the ecological adaptation to an environment which is more or less rich in water (Chapter 14). The rectal papillae have their maximum development in the lower termites, especially in the Kalotermitidae, which are the termites of dry wood (M. S. Collins, personal communication). In the Termitidae the rectal papillae are less conspicuous and sometimes difficult to distinguish from the usual rectal epithelium. The comparative investigations which are underway (Collins) will perhaps allow us to determine if the development of the papillae is related to phylogeny or to the mode of life.

Investigations with the electron microscope (Noirot and Noirot-Timothée, 1966, and unpublished data) show that the basic structure of these papillae is constant (Section II, E, and Fig. 6). It does vary with respect to the height of the epithelial cells, which attain $50-60$ μ in *Kalotermes flavicollis*, but a maximum of only 15 μ in *Pericapritermes urgens* Silvestri. These cells have, beneath the cuticle, a folded membrane which is coated on its cytoplasmic face with particles of about 140 Å. This coating [which has been observed by Gupta and Berridge (1966) in the larvae of *Calliphora*] and the numerous mitochondria present between the apical folds could be involved in the active transport of certain ions, especially sodium. At the present time we cannot explain the functioning of these papillae, particularly in the absorption of water. We do not know the role of the flat basal cells (which at the present time have only been described in the termites).

Particular attention must be given to the mitochondria associated with the lateral membranes of the epithelial cells. We have described these associations in *Cephalotermes rectangularis* (Sjöstedt) (Termitidae) (Noirot-Timothée and Noirot, 1967), and they are much more developed in *Kalotermes flavicollis*, where their appearance is a little different (Fig. 13). We should perhaps compare them with the "mitochondrial pumps" described by Copeland (1964) in the mosquito larvae and with folds of the lateral membranes with associated mitochondria studied by Berridge and Gupta (1967) in the larvae of *Calliphora*. An experimental approach, on one hand, and a comparative approach, on the other, should reveal the significance of these structures and their role in the biology of the termites.

2. Functions of the Mixed Segment

In the Termitidae, where a mixed segment is present (Sections III, C; and IV, B), the proximal part of the Malpighian tubules forms a tight cluster at the surface of the mixed segment, usually on the mesenteric side (Fig. 4), and the whole is enclosed by a thin connective membrane. In this region the cells of the mesenteron possess very special ultrastructural characteristics (Noirot *et al.*, 1967). The brush border is very irregular, and no secretory activity is visible. There are deep invaginations of the plasma membrane at the basal pole with numerous associated mitochondria. This is very different from the β-cytomembranes present in the midgut proper since they are coated on their cytoplasmic face with particles which are entirely comparable to those of the apical membranes of the rectal papillae. In *Cephalotermes rectangularis* the Malpighian tubules are essentially closed near their junction with the digestive tube, and the urine cannot flow freely into it.

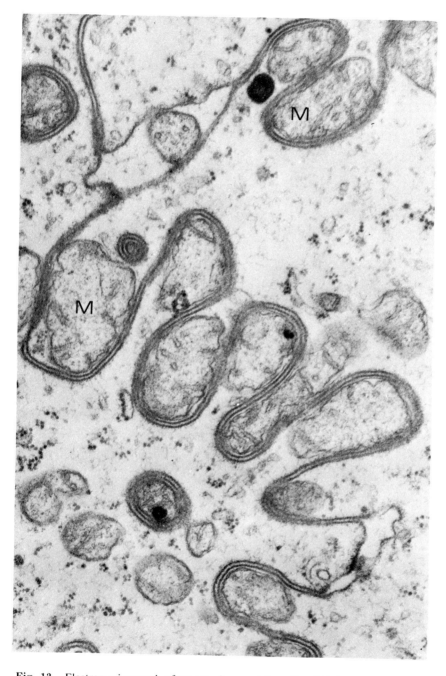

Fig. 13. Electron micrograph of an area in a rectal papilla of *Kalotermes flavicollis*. Association of the mitochondria with the lateral membranes of the tall cells: the mitochondria (M) are located in the coglike interdigitations of two adjacent cells and are closely associated with the plasma membrane (×23,000).

Apparently the products extracted from the blood by the Malpighian tubules pass through the wall of the mixed segment. The presence of coated membranes and of mitochondria indicates the possibility of a selective absorption and an active transport of materials. Histochemical studies have shown that sodium can be taken up in this way. Furthermore, an abundant population of bacteria, having the appearance of a pure culture, is consistently present in the cavity of the mixed segment. They are situated between the wall of the mesenteron and the peritrophic membrane. The presence of these bacteria may be related to the exchange of certain substances, for example, wastes of nitrogenous metabolism, which they could reutilize. New investigations are necessary in order to clarify the significance of this mixed segment, which is without an equivalent in other insects.

VI. CONCLUSIONS

Strangely enough, the social life of the termites does not appear to have greatly modified their digestive tube, contrary to the situation observed in ants (Eisner, 1957). Social life appears to have exerted its greatest influence on the salivary glands. Thus, these glands serve in the nutrition of the dependent castes and in building activities and are sometimes even transformed into organs of defense, while their digestive role appears to be reduced.

There are, on the other hand, symbiotic associations which affect the digestive morphology. The midgut is of little importance when compared with the considerable development of the hindgut, where the symbionts carry out the essential part of digestion and where the greatest part of absorption also occurs. In the Termitidae the existence of the mixed segment could be linked to a particular type of bacterial association.

The evolution of the symbiotic associations, notably the replacement of flagellates (lower termites) by bacteria (Termitidae), does not seem to have entailed essential modifications of the digestive physiology. But this evolution has been accompanied by considerable change in the interindividual behavior and the nature of the trophallactic exchanges. Thus, the disappearance of proctodeal food in the Termitidae appears to be correlated with the disappearance of the flagellates.

Many problems remain to be resolved: the chemical composition of the saliva and its nutritive role, the analysis of the bacterial associations of the Termitidae, the functioning of the mixed segment, excretion, etc. Despite the difficulties of experimental study, the digestive system of the termites constitutes a material of exceptional interest for the anatomist, the physiologist, and the biochemist.

REFERENCES

Ahmad, M. (1950). The phylogeny of termite genera based on imago-worker mandibles. *Bull. Am. Museum Nat. Hist.* 95, 39-86.

Alibert, J. (1963). Echanges trophallactiques chez un Termite supérieur. Contamination par le phosphore radio-actif de la population d'un nid de *Cubitermes fungifaber*. *Insectes Sociaux* 10, 1-12.

Alibert, J. (1966). La trophallaxie chez le Termite à cou jaune (*Calotermes flavicollis* Fabr.) étudiée à l'aide de radio-éléments. Doctoral Thesis, Univ. of Paris.

Aubertot, M. (1934). "Recherches sur la péritrophique des insectes," pp. 1-357. Thesis, Univ. of Nancy. George Thomas, Nancy.

Baccetti, B. (1963). Ricerche sull'ultrastruttura dell'intestino degli insetti. III. Il mesentero ed il colon nell'operaio de *Reticulitermes lucifugus* Rossi. *Symp. Genet. Biol. Ital.* 11, 230-255.

Berridge, M. J., and Gupta, B. J. (1967). Fine-structural changes in relation to ion and water transport in the rectal papillae of the blowfly, *Calliphora*. *J. Cell Sci.* 2, 89-112.

Bonneville, P. (1936). Recherches sur l'anatomie microscopique des Termites. *Arvernia Biol.* 15, 1-127.

Brown, B., and Smith, R. (1954). The relationship of the concentration of acetic acid in normal and defaunated termites. *Mendelian* 25, 19-20.

Calaby, J. H. (1956). The distribution and biology of the genus *Ahamitermes* (Isoptera). *Australian J. Zool.* 4, 111-124.

Child, H. J. (1934). The internal anatomy of termites and the histology of the digestive tract. *In* "Termites and Termite Control" (C. A. Kofoid, ed.), 2nd ed., pp. 58-88. Univ. of California Press, Berkeley, California.

Cleveland, L. R., Hall, S. R., Sander, E. P., and Collier, J. (1934). The wood-feeding roach *Cryptocercus*, its protozoa, and the symbiosis between protozoa and roach. *Mem. Am. Acad. Arts Sci.* 17, 185-342.

Copeland, E. (1964). A mitochondrial pump in the cells of the anal papillae of mosquito

Deligne, J. (1966). Caractères adaptatifs au régime alimentaire dans la mandibule des Termites (Insectes Isopteres). *Compt. Rend.* 263, 1323-1325.

Deligne, J. (1968). Doctoral Thesis, Univ. of Bruxelles.

Eisner, T. (1957). A comparative morphological study of the proventriculus of ants (Hymenoptera: Formicidae). *Bull. Museum Comp. Zool. Harvard* 116, 439-490.

Emerson, A. E. (1938). Termite nests. A study of the phylogeny of behavior. *Ecol. Monographs* 8, 247-284.

Emerson, A. E. (1955). Geographical origins and dispersions of termite genera. *Fieldiana, Zool.* 37, 465-522.

Feytaud, J. (1912). Contribution à l'étude du termite lucifuge. (Anatomie. Fondation de colonies nouvelles.) *Arch. Anat. Microscop. Morphol. Exptl.* 13, 481-607.

Grassé, P.-P. (1949). Ordre des Isoptères ou Termites. *In* "Traité de Zoologie" (P.-P. Grassé, ed.) Vol. IX, pp. 408-544. Masson, Paris.

Grassé, P.-P., and Noirot, C. (1945). La transmission des Flagellés symbiotiques et les aliments des Termites. *Bull. Biol. France Belg.* 79, 273-292.

Grassé, P.-P., and Noirot, C. (1951). Nouvelles recherches sur la biologie de divers Termites champignonnistes (Macrotermitinae). *Ann. Sci. Nat. Zool. Biol. Animale* [11] 13, 291-342.

Grassé, P.-P., and Noirot, C. (1954). *Apicotermes arquieri* (Isoptère): Ses constructions, sa biologie. Considérations générales sur la sous-famille des *Apicotermitinae* nov. *Ann. Sci. Nat. Zool. Biol. Animale* [11] 16, 345-388.

Grassé, P.-P., and Noirot, C. (1959). L'évolution de la symbiose chez les Isoptères. *Experientia* 15, 365-372.

Grassé, P.-P., and Noirot, C. (1960). L'isolement chez le Termite à cou jaune et ses conséquences. *Insectes Sociaux* 7, 323-331.

Gupta, B. J., and Berridge, M. J. (1966). A coat of repeating subunits on the cytoplasmic surface of the plasma membrane in the rectal papillae of the blowfly, *Calliphora erythrocephala* (Meig). studied in situ by electron microscopy. *J. Cell Biol.* 29, 376-382.

Harris, W. V. (1961). "Termites, their Recognition and Control." Longmans, Green, New York.

Holmgren, N. (1909). Termitenstudien. I. Anatomische Untersuchungen. *Kgl. Svenska Vetenskapsakad. Handl.* 44 [3], 1-215.

Hungate, R. E. (1938). Studies on the nutrition of *Zootermopsis*. II, The relative importance of the termite and the protozoa in wood digestion. *Ecology* 19, 1-25.

Hungate, R. E. (1939). Experiments on the nutrition of *Zootermopsis*. III, The anaerobic carbohydrate dissimilation by the intestinal protozoa. *Ecology* 20, 230-245.

Hungate, R. E. (1944). Studies on cellulose fermentation. I. The culture and physiology of an anaerobic cellulose-digesting bacterium. *J. Bacteriol.* 48, 499-513.

Hungate, R. E. (1946). The symbiotic utilization of cellulose. *J. Elisha Mitchell Sci. Soc.* 62, 9-24.

Imms, A. D. (1919). On the structure and biology of *Archotermopsis*, together with descriptions of new species of intestinal Protozoa and general observations on the Isoptera. *Phil. Trans. Roy. Soc. London* B209, 75-180.

Jucci, C. (1924). Sulla differenziazione delle caste nella societa dei termitidi. I, Neotenici (Reali veri e neotenici- l'escrezione nei reali neotenici-la fisiologia e la biologia). *Atti Accad. Nazl. Lincei, Rend., Classe Sci. Fis., Mat. Nat.* [5] 14, 269-500.

Judd, W. E. (1948). A comparative study of the proventriculus of the orthopteroid insects with reference to its use in taxonomy. *Can. J. Res.* D26, 93-161.

Kovoor, J. (1959). Anatomie du tractus intestinal dans le genre *Microcerotermes* (Silvestri) (Isoptera: Termitidae). *Bull. Soc. Zool. France* 84, 445-457.

Kovoor, J. (1964a). Modifications chimiques d'une sciure de bois de Peuplier sous l'action d'un Termitide: *Microcerotermes edentatus*. *Compt. Rend.* 258, 2887-2889.

Kovoor, J. (1964b). Modifications chimiques provoquées par un Termitide *Microcerotermes edentatus* Was. dans du bois de peuplier sain ou partiellement dégradé par des champignons. *Bull. Biol. France Belg.* 98, 491.

Kovoor, J. (1966). Contribution à l'étude de la digestion chez un Termite supérieur (*Microcerotermes edentatus* Was. Isoptera, Termitidae). Doctoral Thesis, Univ. of Paris.

Kovoor, J. (1967a). Présence d'acides gras volatils dans la panse d'un Termite supérieur (*Microcerotermes edentatus* Was., Amitermitinae). *Compt. Rend.* D264, 486-488.

Kovoor, J. (1967b). Etude radiographique du transit intestinal chez un Termite supérieur. *Experientia* 23, 820-821.

Kovoor, J. (1967c). Le pH intestinal d'un Termite supérieur (*Microcerotermes edentatus* Was., Amitermitinae). *Insectes Sociaux* 14, 157-160.

Kovoor, J. (1968). Le tractus intestinal d'un Termite supérieur (*Microcerotermes edentatus* Was., Amitermitinae). Histophysiologie et flore bactérienne symbiotique. *Bull. Biol. France Belg.* 102, 45-84.

Krishna, K. (1963). The African genus *Foraminitermes* Holmgren (Isoptera, Termitidae, Termitinae). *Am. Museum Novitates* 2161, 1-23.

McKittrick, F. A. (1964). Evolutionary studies of cockroaches. *Cornell Univ., Agr. Expt. Sta. Mem.* 389, 1-197.

Misra, J. N., and Ranganathan, V. (1954). Digestion of cellulose by the mound building termite *Termes (Cyclotermes) obsesus* (Rambur). *Proc. Indian Acad. Sci.* **39**, 100-113.

Montalenti, G. (1930). L'origine e la funzione della membrana peritrofica dell'intestino degli Insetti. *Boll. Inst. Zool. Univ. Roma* **9**, 36-69.

Montalenti, G. (1932). Gli enzimi digerenti e l'assorbimento delle sostanze solubile nell'intestino delle termiti. *Arch. Zool. Ital.* **16**, 859-864.

Mukerji, D., and Raychaudhuri, S. (1943). On the anatomy of the alimentary system of the termite *Termes redemanni* Wasmann. *Indian J. Entomol.* **5**, 59-88.

Noirot, C. (1952). Les soins et l'alimentation des jeunes chez les Termites. *Ann. Sci. Nat. Zool. Biol. Animale* [11] **14**, 405-414.

Noirot, C. (1955). Recherches sur le polymorphisme des Termites supérieurs (Termitidae). *Ann. Sci. Nat. Zool. Biol. Animale* **17**, 399-595.

Noirot, C. (1966). Description et affinités de deux nouveaux genres d'Amitermitinae (Isoptera, Termitidae). *Insectes Sociaux* **13**, 329-345.

Noirot, C., and Kovoor, J. (1958). Anatomie comparée du tube digestif des Termites. I. Sous-famille des "Termitinae." *Insectes Sociaux* **5**, 439-471.

Noirot, C., and Noirot-Timothée, C. (1966). Revêtement de la membrane cytoplasmique et absorption des ions dans les papilles rectales d'un Termite (Insecta, Isoptera). *Compt. Rend.* **D236**, 1099-1102.

Noirot, C., and Noirot-Timothée, C. (1967). L'épithélium absorbant de la panse d'un Termite supérieur. Ultrastructure et rapport possible avec la symbiose bactérienne. *Ann. Soc. Entomol. France* [N.S.] **3**, 577-592.

Noirot, C., Noirot-Timothée, C., and Kovoor, J. (1967). Revêtement particulaire de la membrane plasmatique en rapport avec l'excrétion dans une région specialisée de l'intestin moyen des Termites supérieurs. *Compt. Rend.* **D264**, 722-725.

Noirot-Timothée, C., and Noirot, C. (1965). L'intestin moyen chez la reine des Termites supérieurs. Etude au microscope électronique. *Ann. Sci. Nat. Zool. Biol. Animale* [12] **7**, 185-206.

Noirot-Timothée, C., and Noirot, C. (1967). Liaison de mitochondries avec des zones d'adhésion intercellulaires. *J. Microscopie* **6**, 87-90.

Platania, E. (1938). Richerche sulla struttura del tubo digerente di *Reticulitermes lucifugus* (Rossi), con particolare riguardo alla natura, origine e funzione della peritrofica. *Arch. Zool. Ital.* **25**, 297-326.

Platania, E. (1939). Prime osservazioni sulla struttura dei Malpighiani di *Reticulitermes lucifugus* (Rossi). *Atti Accad. Gioenia Sci. Nat. Catania* [6] **3**, 1-7.

Pochon, J., de Barjac, H., and Roche, A. (1959). Recherches sur la digestion de la cellulose chez le Termite *Sphaerotermes sphaerothorax*. *Ann. Inst. Pasteur* **96**, 352-355.

Randall, M., and Doody, T. C. (1934). Hydrogen-ion concentration in the termite intestine. *In* "Termites and Termite Control" (C. A. Kofoid, ed.), 2nd ed., pp. 99-104. Univ. of California Press, Berkeley, California.

Roessler, M. F. (1961). Ernährungsphysiologische Untersuchungen an Scarabaeiden-larven (*Oryctes nasicornis* L., *Melolontha melolontha* L.). *J. Insect Physiol.* **6**, 62-80.

Sands, W. A. (1965). A revision of the termite subfamily Nasutitermitinae (Isoptera, Termitidae) from the ethiopian region. *Bull. Brit. Museum, Entomol.* Suppl. 4, 1-172.

Schmidt, H. (1959). Beiträge zur Kenntnis der Ernährungsorgane und Ernährungsbiologie der Termiten. 2. Mitteilung. Kaumagen und Vorverdauung. *Z. Angew. Entomol.* **45**, 79-86.

Seifert, K., and Becker, G. (1965). Der chemische Abbau von Laub- und Nadelholzarten durch verschieden Termiten. *Holzforschung* **19**, 105-111.

Sutherland, J. L. (1934). Notes on the histology of the alimentary canal in some Australian termites. *Proc. Roy. Soc. Victoria* [N.S.] 47, 1-13.

Tracey, M. V., and Youatt, G. (1958). Cellulase and chitinase in two species of Australian termites. *Enzymologia* 19, 70-72.

Trager, W. (1932). A cellulase from the symbiotic intestinal flagellates of termites and of the roach *Cryptocercus punctulatus*. *Biochemical J.* 26, 1762.

Vishnoi, H. S. (1956). The structure, musculature and mechanism of the feeding apparatus of the various castes of the termite *Odontotermes obesus* (Rambur). Part I. Clypeolabrum, *J. Zool. Soc. India* 8, 1-18.

Waterhouse, D. F., Hackman, R. H., and McKeller, J. W. (1961). An investigation of chitinase activity in cockroach and termite extract. *J. Insect Physiol.* 6, 96-112.

Weidner, H. (1956). Beiträge zur Kenntnis der Termiten Angolas, hauptsächlich auf Grund der Sammlungen und Beobachtungen von A. de Barros Machado. *Publ. Cult. Comp. Diam. Angola* 29, 57-105.

Weyer, F. (1935). Epithelerneuerung im Mitteldarm der Termiten während der Häutung. *Z. Morphol. Oekol. Tiere* 30, 648-672.

Yokoe, Y. (1964). Cellulase activity in the termite *Leucotermes speratus*, with new evidence in support of a cellulase produced by the termite itself. *Sci. Papers Coll. Gen. Educ., Univ. Tokyo* 14, 115-120.

4

Glands and Secretions*

CH. NOIROT

I. INTRODUCTION

Recent works have shown the importance and the complexity of the exocrine secretions in the social insects (see the reviews by Wilson, 1965; Butler, 1967), but the termites have not been studied as much as the bees and ants. Our knowledge of the anatomy of the various glandular formations remains very fragmentary. The role and the nature of many of the secretions is still unknown. Conversely, various pheromones are known to play an important role in the formation of the castes (Lüscher, 1961; Chapter 9), but their origin remains unknown.

*Translated from the French by Mina Parsont and Frances M. Weesner.

We have better information on the endocrine glands, but the anatomical studies are based on a very small number of species, and the experimental works are concerned only with *Kalotermes flavicollis* (Fabricius)!

I have, nevertheless, tried to set up a general scheme of the termite glands, while complementing, whenever the opportunity arises, the scanty data of the literature with original observations.

II. EXOCRINE GLANDS

A. LABRAL "GLANDS"

Under the name "labral glands" Holmgren (1909) briefly described a pair of small organs coupled on the epidermis of the inferior face of the labrum. Deligne (1968) observed, on the labrum of workers of *Cubitermes heghi* Sjöstedt, five pairs of sensory organs, of which the most posterior appear to correspond to the "glands" of Holmgren. The "epipharyngeal ganglia," described in numerous insects, but whose significance remains debatable, appear to be of the same nature. These certainly contain sensory elements (probably chemoreceptors), but perhaps also glandular cells.

B. MANDIBULAR GLANDS

The mandibular glands were noted by Holmgren in 1909 and were observed in all of the species which he examined. Lambinet (1959) has studied these glands in *Kalotermes flavicollis*. Each gland is situated at the base of the mandible, between the inferior angle of the mandible and the maxillae. It consists (Fig. 1) of large, glandular, peripheral cells, each provided with a thin canaliculus secreted by small cells located at about the center of the gland. The different canaliculi end in a short common canal emerging in the cibarium. Each glandular cell contains a large vacuole, or intracellular reservoir, from which the evacuating canaliculus emerges. At the time of the molt these canaliculi are rejected, along with the exuviae of the common canal, and new canaliculi are secreted by some of the small cells, which penetrate the interior of the glandular cells and then degenerate.

In *Kalotermes* the mandibular glands show slight variations in the different castes. They are only slightly larger in the imagoes and neotenics than in the neuters.

The facts reported by Lambinet may be generally true for all of the termites. According to our observations, the histology of the mandibular glands is quite uniform, and the variation associated with different castes

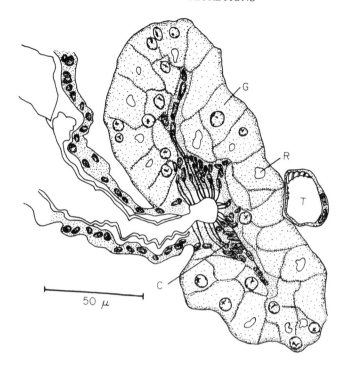

Fig. 1 Mandibular gland of *Kalotermes flavicollis* (old larvae), longitudinal section. (C) Canaliculi cells; (G) glandular cells; (R) intracellular reservoir; (T) trachea (after Lambinet, 1959).

is very slight. Mandibular glands are even present in the soldiers of *Nasutitermes*, despite the fact that their mandibles are atrophied.

We know nothing of the nature of the secretions or the function of the mandibular glands of termites.

C. LABIAL OR SALIVARY GLANDS

The salivary glands of the termites have the same general structure observed in the Orthoptera and Dictyoptera. Each gland consists of a series of lobes, or acini, connected by a salivary canal, which opens symmetrically at the base of the labium slightly before the margin of the buccal cavity. Furthermore, each gland possesses a salivary reservoir arising at the level of the base of the labium from the salivary canal corresponding to each gland. This general organization seems very uniform in all termites, but the glandular development and, even more, the development of the reservoirs vary from species to species and caste to caste.

The histological structure has been described by Child (1934) for *Zootermopsis*, by Pasteels (1965) for *Nasutitermes*, and by Kovoor (1966, 1968) for *Microcerotermes*. These works and our own unpublished observations on other species permit us to define the features which appear common to all the termites.

The glandular acini contain two types of secretory cells of rather large size. One type contains, in varying abundance, spherical inclusions whose size is more or less constant for a given species (the vacuole or glandular cells). The other type has a cytoplasm packed with inclusions of various sizes, which are sometimes dissolved by fixatives, giving these cells a foamy appearance (the foam cells). A third type of cell, of smaller size, occurs at the periphery of the gland. These small cells could be the precursors of either type of glandular cells. Finally, towards the center of the acini, there are small, elongated nuclei which probably belong to the secretory cells of the canaliculi (Fig. 5D).

The salivary canals are formed of an unistratified epithelium. The cells appear striated at their basal pole due to the presence of numerous mitrochondria and probably also due to β-cytomembranes. The lumen is provided with a thin cuticle, reinforced by a taenidia. The reservoirs have the same histological structure, but the epithelium is very flat. The canals ramify several times, in succession, to end in each glandular acinus (like a bunch of grapes). The canal of each acinus gives rise, in turn, to the internal canaliculi of the acinus, whose ramifications appear to penetrate into the different cells. The canaliculi appear to have a cuticular lining.

In spite of this uniformity of structure, there are important differences in the histochemical characteristics of the glandular cells from one species to another, and even among the individuals of a given species (Kovoor, 1966, 1968, and personal observations). The two types of glandular cells have very different reactions, and their products of secretion are certainly complex. In the workers of *Cephalotermes rectangularis* (Sjöstedt) (unpublished observations) the foam cells secrete lipids and perhaps also mucopolysaccharides; the secretion of the vacuole cells has the characteristic of glycoproteins. The role of the salivary canals may not be entirely passive. The cytological structure of the cells and the strong alkaline phosphatase activity which they demonstrate suggest a resorption of certain elements within the canals, as is observed in the salivary glands of the vertebrates.

We do not have any precise information regarding the composition of the saliva. It probably plays a minor role in digestion, although an amylase is present in *Kalotermes flavicollis* (unpublished observations). Nevertheless, its importance in the life of the society is considerable, because it serves, on one hand, as an important part of the nourishment for the dependent castes (Chapters 3 and 10) and is also involved, on the other hand, in building activities (Volume II).

We know very little of the function or the variations of the salivary glands in terms of polymorphism. According to our observations, the differences between castes in a given species are generally slight in structure and development of the glands, but could be more pronounced with regard to the nature of the secretions. Thus, in *K. flavicollis* the glandular acini of the larvae and nymphs are not colored by paraldehyde-fuchsin (after oxidation) and only slightly by PAS. On the other hand, these reactions are positive in the imagoes. The variations of the salivary glands of the workers merit a precise study. The work of Pasteels (1965) has shown that in *Nasutitermes lujae* (Wasmann) the workers of stages II and III have salivary glands which are less developed than those of workers of stage I. The latter workers, remaining voluntarily in the nest, could be specialized for the nutrition of the brood. Such a division of labor (although only relative) is probably frequent in the Termitidae.

A very special differentiation is noticed in certain soldiers of the Termitidae whose salivary glands become organs of defense. In *Globitermes sulphureus* (Haviland) (Amitermitinae) the salivary reservoirs occupy the entire front half of the abdomen. These are filled with a vivid yellow liquid which the soldiers throw out in abundance through the mouth when in combat; this liquid congeals in the air, becoming brownish, and irreparably entangles the soldier and his adversary. The emission of the fluid appears to result from the contraction of the abdomen. More-over, these contractions may be so violent that the abdominal wall bursts (Bathellier, 1927; Noirot, unpublished observations). A speciali-zation of this type seems frequent, even general, in the Macrotermitinae. The soldiers of *Protermes prorepens* (Sjöstedt) and *P. minutus* (Grassé), when they are disturbed, emit a drop of pure white saliva between their mandibles. When they bite, this liquid is spread out on their foe, other-wise it is reabsorbed (Grassé and Noirot, unpublished observations). The large soldiers of *Pseudacanthotermes spiniger* (Sjöstedt) have sali-vary reservoirs which occupy nine-tenths of the abdomen. At the time of combat, the saliva, transparent and viscous, enmeshes the combatants (Grassé, 1937). The large soldiers of *Bellicositermes natalensis* (Havi-land)* eject a brownish, corrosive saliva when they bite (Grassé, 1937). The salivary reservoirs of the soldiers of *Odontotermes redemanni* (Was-mann) are much more developed than those of the workers and contain a creamy liquid (Mukerji and Raychaudhuri, 1943). The soldiers of *Odon-*

---

*Bellicositermes natalensis (Haviland) is considered by other authors in this volume as *Macrotermes natalensis* (Haviland) (editors' note).

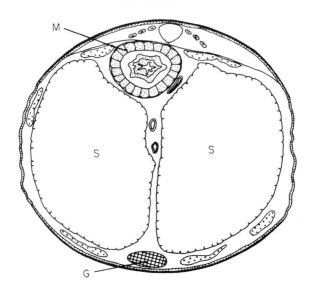

Fig. 2. Soldier of *Odontotermes magdalenae*, transverse section at the level of the second abdominal ganglion showing the enormous development of the salivary reservoirs. (G) Second abdominal ganglion; (M) midgut with esophageal valve; (S) salivary reservoirs.

totermes magdalenae (Grassé and Noirot) have a hyaline saliva which is probably utilized during combat. Their salivary reservoirs occupy the dorsal portion of the anterior segments of the abdomen (Fig. 2). The soldiers of *Ancistrotermes* have salivary reservoirs of considerable size (Noirot, unpublished observations).

We do not know the chemical composition of the "defensive" salivas. Their color, viscosity, and reaction in contact with air differ greatly from one species to another, probably indicating important differences in their composition.

D. FRONTAL GLAND

Despite its importance, this unpaired gland, without an equivalent in the other insects, remains poorly understood. We are indebted to Holmgren (1909) for our best knowledge of it. It was on the basis of the relative development of this gland that he established the large systematic divisions among the Isoptera.

He thus unites, in the family Protermitidae, the primitive forms in which the frontal gland is not differentiated. In these termites, corresponding to the current families Kalotermitidae, Termopsidae, and

Hodotermitidae, there is at most a slight, nonglandular expansion of the epidermis at the junction of the frontal suture and the transverse suture. In this region lie the attachments of a pair of muscles peculiar to the Isoptera. They are inserted on the tentorium and pass to both sides of the digestive tract just behind the brain. Holmgren comments on the uniqueness of these tentorial-fontanellar muscles, which appear to be present in all of the termites and in all the castes. We have found them in all of the species which we have examined.

In the Rhinotermitidae and the Termitidae (Mesotermitidae and Metatermitidae respectively of Holmgren) the frontal gland is generally differentiated in the soldier, but its development is quite variable. In the imagoes it may be well formed, or it can be represented only by an epidermal thickening subadjacent to a depigmented zone of the cuticle (fontanelle). This latter arrangement is generally found in the workers. In the Rhinotermitidae the frontal gland is well differentiated in imagoes, at least in the few types studied: *Heterotermes* and *Rhinotermes* (Holmgren, 1909); *Reticulitermes* (Feytaud, 1912, Noirot, unpublished observations). It is an invagination of the epidermis, forming a more or less ovoid sac behind the brain (Fig. 7B) and opening to the exterior by a very narrow pore [3μ in diameter in *Reticulitermes lucifugus* (Rossi)]. The cavity is lined by a continuous intima; the epithelium is formed by rather tall, narrow cells. The tentorial-fontanellar muscles are attached to the anterior part of the gland. According to our observations on *Reticulitermes*, this gland is differentiated at the imaginal molt. In the nymphs, as in the workers, there is only a thickening of the epidermis at the level of the fontanelle. The neotenic reproductives have an arrangement analogous to that of the nymphs. The soldiers of the Rhinotermitidae, on the other hand, possess a well-developed frontal gland (Fig. 7A), opening by a frontal pore which is very distinct. In *Coptotermes* (Bugnion and Popoff, 1910), in the large and small soldiers of *Schedorhinotermes* (Noirot, unpublished observations), and in the small soldiers of *Rhinotermes* (Holmgren, 1909) the gland occupies a large part of the dorsal abdominal cavity, forcing the digestive tube back into the posterior ventral region. The soldiers of *Coptotermes* emit from the frontal pore a white liquid which thickens in the air into a very viscous glue. In the course of combat (with ants, for example) the soldier is entangled with his adversary and probably is doomed to perish with him.

According to Holmgren (1909) the Termitidae are characterized by the existence in the imagoes of a frontal gland formed only by a plaque of glandular cells without a cavity proper, an arrangement which he described in *Nasutitermes chaquimayensis* (Holmgren) and which we have observed in *Cubitermes fungifaber* (Sjöstedt) and *Termes hospes*

(Sjöstedt). However, Bugnion (1913) describes a differentiated frontal gland with an excretory pore in the imago of *Odontotermes horni* (Wasmann). Furthermore, in the imago of *Bellicositermes natalensis* (Noirot, unpublished observations) the frontal gland resembles that of the Rhinotermitidae: it is a vesicle with a diameter approaching 0.5 mm, formed of a cylindrical epithelium and lined internally with a continuous intima. The cavity is filled with an amorphous coagulum and communicates with the exterior through a minute pore (about 6μ in diameter). Among the tall epithelial cells, cells occur which are a little larger and are provided with a vacuole from which a canaliculus emerges and enters the cavity of the gland. These cells with canaliculi are most numerous in the vicinity of the gland pore. It will be necessary to examine a much larger number of species in order to establish the phylogenetic significance of the frontal gland in the imagoes of the Termitidae. It would be especially desirable to know the development of this gland in the imagoes in which the fontanelle is very extended (*Apicotermes*, for example).

We have better information on the frontal gland in the neuter castes. In the workers there is a zone of more or less thickened epidermis at the level of the fontanelle. In the soldiers its development is extremely variable, but the existence of a frontal gland organ with an external pore appears to be general, and the absence of this organ is probably a case of regressive evolution. In the Macrotermitinae the existence of a frontal gland seems general, but it is weakly developed. We have seen that in this subfamily the secretions of the salivary glands are often utilized as a means of combat. Among the Amitermitinae the frontal gland is generally well developed, but cases of regression are numerous (*Microcerotermes, Eburnitermes*). The Termitinae possess types which are still more varied. Generally the development of the gland is moderate, but one finds genera in which the pore is situated at the tip of a veritable rostrum (*Prosbocitermes*). On the other hand, there is an almost complete regression in some genera with strongly asymmetrical mandibles. The Apicotermitinae (sensu Grassé and Noirot, 1954) appear to have a well-differentiated frontal gland. In these various subfamilies we know next to nothing of the role of the frontal gland in the soldiers, we are ignorant of the nature of the secretion, and we do not even know if it is utilized in the mode of combat of the soldiers.

The facts are much clearer in the subfamily Nasutitermitinae, where the enlargement of the frontal gland is accompanied, in the soldiers, by a more or less complete reduction of the mandibles, and the entire form of the head is more or less modified, terminating in soldiers of the "nasute" type (Fig. 3). In the genus *Nasutitermes*, for example (Holmgren, 1909; Bonneville, 1936), the gland is a pear-shaped vesicle, occupying

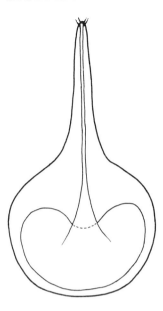

Fig. 3.   *Trinervitermes trinervius* (Rambur), head of a large soldier in dorsal view, showing the situation of the frontal gland.

all of the posterior part of the head, and opening at the extremity of the
rostrum. The wall of the gland is made up of unistratified epithelium, with
large glandular cells from place to place, each of which is provided with
a characteristic canaliculus. The epithelial cells are provided with a true
brush border at their apical poles, and they might also have a secretory
activity (secretions which would pass through the cuticle). The glandular
cells are especially abundant in the anterior region, notably around the
canal which runs to the rostrum. The tentorial-fontanellar muscles are
inserted on the anterior and ventral part of the dilation, but their function
remains unknown. The expulsion of the secretion is due to the action of
the mandibulary muscles, which remain very important in spite of the
extreme reduction of the mandibles. It is noteworthy that in the genera
with functional mandibles, such as *Armitermes*, the mandibular adductors
play a simultaneous role in closing the mandibles and contracting the
frontal gland (Holmgren, 1909). The nasute soldiers are capable of
projecting the contents of their glands for a distance of many centimeters,
and, though blind, are able to direct the jet with great precision toward
the adversary, probably located by its odor or by mechanical vibrations.
    The chemical nature of these secretions is generally unknown (see

Chapter 13). The work of Moore (1964) has demonstrated the presence of volatile terpenoids in the secretions of soldiers of *Nasutitermes*, probably serving as a solvent for the "resinous" material. These facts agree with the existence of two types of cells in the frontal glands of the termites. According to Ernst (1959) the glue of *Nasutitermes* has a purely mechanical action. It has often been postulated that a toxic action is produced by the products of the frontal gland, but this requires verification.

E. STERNAL GLANDS

The sternal glands were first pointed out by Grassi and Sandias (1893), then studied briefly by Holmgren (1909) and Montalenti (1928). Since the discovery of their role in trail laying (see Chapter 7), the studies have multiplied.

We have shown (Noirot and Noirot-Timothée, 1965b) that the position and number of the sternal glands vary from species to species (Fig. 4). Thus, *Mastotermes darwiniensis* Froggatt possess three sternal glands, on the middle of the third, fourth, and fifth sternites. In all the other species studied the sternal gland is single, but situated sometimes on the anterior part of the fourth sternite (subfamilies Stolotermitinae, Porotermitinae, and Hodotermitinae) and sometimes on the anterior part of

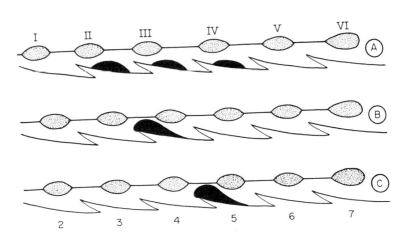

Fig. 4. Situation of the sternal glands of various termites. A: *Mastotermes;* B: Stolotermitinae, Porotermitinae, Hodotermitinae; C: Termopsinae, Kalotermitidae, Rhinotermitidae, Termitidae. (I–VI) Ganglia of the ventral nerve chain; (2–7) abdominal sternites (after Noirot and Noirot-Timothée, 1965b).

the fifth sternite (subfamily Termopsinae, families Kalotermitidae, Rhinotermitidae, and Termitidae).

The sternal gland always consists of an unpaired thickening of the middle of the epidermis, limited internally by a basement lamina well supplied with trachea and externally by a continuous cuticle without a pore. The secretion must therefore pass directly through the cuticle, which, at this level, possesses particular characteristics that require further investigation. Campaniform sensilla are always visible in the midst of the glandular mass; their presence has been confirmed, thanks to the electron microscope, in *Zootermopsis* (Stuart, personal communication) and *Kalotermes* (Noirot and Noirot-Timothee, unpublished observations). The histological structure is highly variable.

In *Mastotermes* (Noirot and Noirot-Timothée, 1965b) the cellular differentiation is not very marked, and there are no clearly distinguishable categories of cells. In *Porotermes planiceps* (Sjöstedt) the histological aspect is quite similar. However, in *Kalotermes flavicollis* (Bregeon, 1958; Noirot and Noirot-Timothée, 1965a,b) (Fig. 5A) one may readily distinguish large glandular cells filled with lipid vacuoles and the so-called intercalary cells, which are the only ones reaching the cuticle and which are furnished at their apex with a brush border make up of long microvilli. *Zootermopsis* (Stuart, 1964; Satir and Stuart, 1965) also possesses two similar types of cells and, in addition, small basal cells whose significance remains uncertain.

The sternal gland of *Reticulitermes* has been described by Mosconi-Bernardini and Vecchi (1964) in *R. lucifugus* and by Smythe and Coppel (1966) in *R. tibialis* Banks. The interpretations given by these two groups of authors are very different. Our personal observations on *R. lucifugus* confirm, in general, the interpretations of Smythe and Coppel. The gland includes an anterior part, in which the usual two categories of cells are encountered, and basal cells may also be present at the front. At the back of this region there is a group of very elongated cells which represent, at least in part, campaniform sensilla. The organization of the posterior region is less regular. One may distinguish small cells under the cuticle and large, vacuolarlike cells which are deeper. The sternal gland of *Reticulitermes* requires further research.

Anacanthotermes ochraceus (Burmeister) (Hodotermitidae) also possesses a sternal gland with two parts (Noirot, unpublished observations). The anterior region has the usual structure, but the posterior region, in particular, should be thoroughly examined.

In the Termitidae the sternal gland (Fig. 5B) is more individualized; its limits are clear, even though it is always continuous with the epidermis. The cells, which are often very regularly disposed, are of two types,

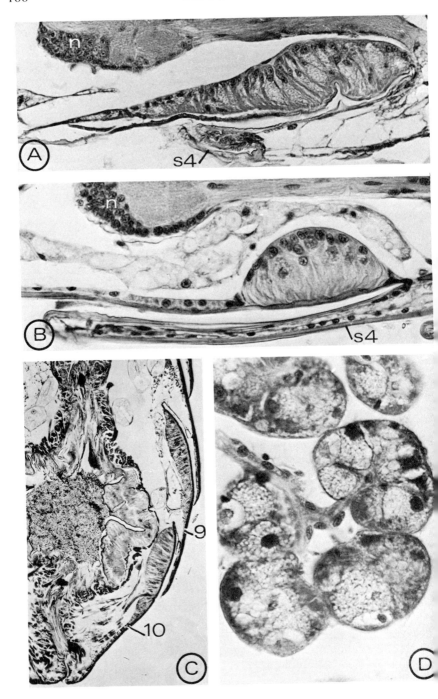

orresponding to the glandular and intercalary cells of other termites Pasteels, 1965; Noirot, unpublished observations). In certain cases the istological sections show grains of sharply stainable secretions between he cells and the cuticle (*Amitermes evuncifer* Silvestri, *Termes hospes, canthotermes*). Campaniform sensilla are present.

These glandular formations exist in all of the castes, and the variations vith polymorphism are generally slight, but there are exceptions. In Reticulitermes lucifugus the anterior part has its maximum development 1 the nymphs, neotenics (Mosconi-Bernardini and Vecchi, 1964), and nagoes (Noirot, unpublished observations). The posterior part, on the ontrary, is more developed in the workers and soldiers. The situation is imilar in *Anacanthotermes*. Moreover, there may be significant differnces in the development of the gland in different types of workers f a given species: in *Nasutitermes lujae* (Pasteels, 1965) the gland ttains its maximum development in the small workers of stage II nd the large workers of stage III (Fig. 6), which are responsible for 1e establishment of the foraging trail; in Nasutitermitinae, the sternal land of the imagoes is larger in the females than in the males (Sands, 965); and finally, the sternal gland regresses strongly in the old funconal reproductives, both imaginal and neotenic (Bregeon, 1958; Noirot nd Noirot-Timothée, 1965b).

The role of the sternal gland in trail laying has been established indeendently by Lüscher (Lüscher, 1962; Lüscher and Müller, 1960) with Zootermopsis and *Kalotermes* and Stuart (1961, 1963) with *Zootermopsis* and *Nasutitermes* (see Chapter 7). It is very probable that this also ccurs in other termites. The odoriferous secretion, probably stored in 1e intersternal fold, is deposited on the substrate when the insect applies s abdomen; the campaniform sensilla probably play a regulatory role 1 the deposition through a feedback mechanism (Stuart, 1964).

The chemical nature of the secretions is not yet known with certainty nd surely varies with the species, since the glands of *Zootermopsis* are 1effective for *Nasutitermes* and vice versa (Stuart, 1963). Stuart (1964) ipposes that the active substance is emitted in a solution with a lipid; 1is hypothesis agrees well with our observations on histochemistry and 1e electron microscopy on the gland of *Kalotermes* (Noirot and Noirot-

---

Fig. 5. A: Sternal gland of *Kalotermes flavicollis* (winged alate), sagittal section. (n) urth abdominal ganglion; (s4) fourth sternite; (×320). B: Sternal gland of *Trinervitermes* . (large soldier), sagittal section. Same abbreviations as in A (×500). C: Sagittal section the posterior extremity of a male imago of *Kalotermes flavicollis*, showing the tergal ands of the last two tergites (9 and 10); (×100). D: Group of acini of a salivary gland a large worker of *Trinervitermes* sp. (×525).

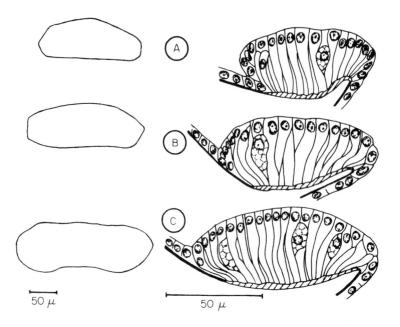

Fig. 6. Variations in the size of the sternal gland during the course of development i
the large workers of *Nasutitermes lujae*. Left: the contour of the gland in ventral vie₩
right: sagittal section. Large workers of – A: stage I; B: stage II; C: stage III (after Pasteel
1965).

Timothée, 1965a, and unpublished data) which indicate a metabolism ₡
the lipid type. The presence of a very active, nonspecific esterase in th
glandular cells and the cuticle itself could be linked to the extrusion ₡
the products of secretion. Very recently, Moore (1966) has isolated fro₩
extracts of entire *Nasutitermes exitiosus* (Hill) a terpenoid substanc
(Chapter 13) apparently responsible for the odor trail. It is reasonabl
to suppose that the sternal gland is responsible for the secretion. Th
production by the sternal gland of the attractive substances isolated b
Smythe *et al.* (1967) from *Reticulitermes* is more doubtful.

F. TERGAL GLANDS

The tergal glands appear to exist only in the imagoes of certain speci₡
but our knowledge of them is very poor. Apparently they were observ₡
by Montalenti (1928) in *Kalotermes*, but the only serious study is th
of Barth (1955) with *Syntermes dirus* (Burmeister). We shall compleme
these few data with some of our own unpublished observations.

In the female imago of *Syntermes* the epidermis of tergites nine and
ten is considerably thickened in its anterior region (usually overlapped
by the posterior margin of the preceding tergite). Two types of cells may
be distinguished: large glandular cells with vacuolated cytoplasm, possessing two nuclei, separated by narrow supporting cells in which the
cytoplasm has longitudinal striations. The glandular cells communicate
with the exterior through a system of ramifying canaliculi, probably
cuticular in nature and probably secreted by very small cells, of which
only the nuclei can be distinguished. The cuticle at this level has a
complex structure with striations perpendicular to the surface. These
tergal glands are absent in the male imago (Barth, 1955).

In *Kalotermes flavicollis* the tergal glands are present on the last two
abdominal tergites of the imagoes (Fig. 5C), with an approximately equal
development in both sexes but with slight differences in structure. In
the female imago we find a structure which is comparable to that of
Syntermes. The glandular cells are readily distinguished from the supporting cells by their size, their vacuolated cytoplasm, their central
nuclei, and the fact that they do not reach the cuticle. The supporting
cells with basal nuclei terminate beneath the cuticle in a very clear
brush border whose existence is confirmed by the electron microscope.
The canaliculi, which are difficult to see because of their very small
diameter (about 0.2μ), appear to have the same disposition. They have
strong esterase activity, as do the "vacuoles" of the glandular cells;
some very small nuclei are visible along their course. In the male imago
the glandular cells are very much narrower, not very different from the
intercalary cells, but otherwise their structure is the same as in the
females. In both cases the cuticle is very different from that of the rest
of the tergites, and the vertical striations are very distinct.

These structures are differentiated at the time of the imaginal molt.
In the functional reproductives the height of the epithelium diminishes
and the secretory activity appears reduced, but the tergal glands remain
clearly recognizable. The neotenic reproductives develop comparable
tergal glands, but in an irregular manner: at the time of the molt at which
the replacement reproductive is differentiated (see Chapter 10), the tergal
glands are formed on the last abdominal tergites, but on a variable
number of these (extreme cases observed: tergites 9 and 10 and tergites
10). The development of these glands is generally less than it is in
imagoes (the height of the epithelium remains in the neighborhood of
); a more or less important regression occurs when the neotenic
reproductive becomes functional.

The tergal glands do not seem to exist in all termites; we do know of
other cases, which are detailed below.

Kalotermitidae: the tergal glands are well developed in the last *thre*
abdominal tergites of *Neotermes castaneus* (Burmeister) and *N. joute*
(Banks) (M. S. Collins, personal communication).

Hodotermitidae: in the female imago of *Anacanthotermes ochrace*
there does not seem to be the exact equivalent of the tergal glands.
about the center of the last five tergites there are thickened regions
the epidermis where large cells become mixed with smaller cells, but su
thickenings are also visible in other regions, notably on the sternite
The cuticle at this level does not appear to be particularly differentiate
and we have not seen any excretory canals. A more detailed study
necessary in order to decide whether these represent a mass of oenocyt
or a glandular formation.

Rhinotermitidae: there are no tergal glands in the male and fem
imagoes of *Reticulitermes lucifugus*.

Termitidae: tergal glands are present only in the females (*Microterm*
sp., *Termes hospes, Cephalotermes rectangularis*); in these three cas
on the last *three* tergites. In *Bellicositermes natalensis* they are prese
on the last *five* tergites. Tergal glands are absent in *Cubitermes fun*
faber and *Procubitermes* sp.

We see, therefore, that the tergal glands appear to vary greatly a
cording to the species. New investigations are necessary in order
establish a correlation with the systematic position, the behavior at
time of flight, etc.

Indeed, the tergal glands appear to have an effect on the pairing of
reproductives after flight. Barth (1955) observed in *Syntermes dirus* t
the varnishing of the last abdominal segments of the female prevents
nuptial promenade: the male becomes indifferent to the presence of
female. In *Kalotermes flavicollis* where the tergal glands are presen
both sexes, it is frequent for the female to follow the male during
nuptial promenade (Grassé, 1942). In *Bellicositermes* and *Microterr*
this is never observed: the males lack tergal glands and do not att
the females (unpublished observations). We can, therefore, accept
idea of the production of a sexual pheromone by the tergal glands,
it is necessary, perhaps, to consider a similarity with the tergal gla
of certain roaches (Roth and Willis, 1954). In those species where
tergal glands are absent, the pairing, nevertheless, seems to be of the s
type (formation of tandems, nuptial promenade, see Chapter 8), but
have no knowledge of the mechanism involved.

We know nothing regarding the nature of the substances secrete
the tergal glands. The characteristics of the glandular cells, notably
presence of very active esterases within the cells and the canali
suggest a secretion of lipid or lipid-soluble substances. It is prob

that the secretion is complex. The intercalary cells, with their apical brush border, could also be engaged in a secretory role; the structure of the cuticle suggests the passage of certain substances through it.

G. OTHER EPIDERMAL GLANDS

There have often been described, notably in the reproductives, glandular cells in the epidermis which are either emptied to the exterior by a canaliculus proper (Ahrens, 1930) or without a canal (Jucci, 1924; Montalenti, 1928). All these studies need to be reexamined. Grassé (1949) has emphasized the resemblance of some of these elements to the *oenocytes*. A precise study of the epidermis in different regions of the body and for the different castes is indicated. In particular, we lack an explanation of the origin and the method of release of the liquid which is extruded in large quantities from the abdomen of the physogastric queens of the Termitidae. This is the liquid which the workers lick with avidness and which probably plays an important role in the attraction exerted by the queen on the workers (Grassé, 1945; Alibert, 1966). This problem was studied by Mukerji and Raychaudhuri (1942) in the queen of *Odontotermes redemanni*. They described, first, numerous secretory vesicles formed by thickened epidermal cells covered by a peculiar cuticula, the center of which bears a sensory hair; and, second, exudate glands opening in abdominal spiracles. The vesicles seem to be true secretory formations, but the "exudate glands" are probably strands of "royal fat body," which is not an exocrine tissue (Chapter 10, Section II, A, 3).

H. CONCLUSIONS

In the social organization of the termites, one may distinguish three main adaptations of external secretions: nutrition, defense, and chemical signals.

The role of the salivary glands in the nutrition of the brood, the reproductives, and the soldiers is generally acknowledged as being essential (see also Chapters 3 and 10) and has become increasingly important in the course of the evolution of the order. But nothing is known of the chemical composition of this social nutrient; we do not know if there are one or several varieties of saliva in a single species, and we only suspect a specialization of certain workers with regards to the salivary nutrition.

The defensive secretions are only known in the Rhinotermitidae and Termitidae where the frontal gland attains a more or less pronounced development in the soldiers and sometimes also in the imagoes (but in this caste its functions are not known). In certain Termitidae an analogous defensive role is filled by the salivary glands of the soldiers. But the study of the chemical nature of these secretions is hardly begun; in many cases, the role of the frontal gland is not known (as a matter of fact, in all of the Termitidae with the exception of the Nasutitermitinae). There may be other glandular formations with a repugnant role.

It is in the realm of chemical signals (pheromones) that there is the most to be done. If the sternal gland is actively studied and its role elucidated, the problem of the sexual pheromones (sex attractants) is scarcely begun. The studies by Verron (1963) showed that the inter-attraction of *Kalotermes* was based on olfaction, and that hexenol was one of the components of this mutual attraction, but we do not know the source of this product. There probably exists within the society a con-tinual exchange of information, much of which is chemical in nature, which guides the reciprocal behavior of the individuals, assuring the cohesion and the coordination of the social group (Stuart, 1967); however, we can only surmise the complexities of these exchanges. Certain of these pheromones have an effect on the formation of the castes (Lüscher, 1961), but we can only hypothesize on their origin and their constitution. The exploration of these unknown areas is a difficult, but very thrilling task.

III. ENDOCRINE GLANDS

A. ANATOMY AND HISTOLOGY

1. The Neurosecretory System

Little work has been devoted to the neurosecretory system. In the pars intercerebralis of the protocerebrum there occur the neurosecretory cells that are usually present in insects (Noirot, 1957; Bernardini-Mos-coni, 1958; Bernardini-Mosconi and Vecchi, 1961; Pasteels and Deligne, 1965). In certain lower termites neurosecretory cells are also stained in the subesophageal ganglia and other regions of the ventral nerve chain (Noirot, 1957; Bernardini-Mosconi and Vecchi, 1961); but in many cases, notably in the Termitidae with the exception of the queens, the tech-niques usually employed do not reveal any indication of neurosecretion (Pasteels and Deligne, 1965; Noirot, unpublished observations*).

---

*We have not taken into account the data of Zuberi and Peeters (1964) since the tech-nique employed (alcoholic fixation) seems inadequate to us.

2. The Retrocerebral Complex

a. Anatomy. The anatomical structure, studied notably by Holmgren (1909), Hanström (1940), and Cazal (1948), is of an entirely classic nature. The corpora cardiaca, situated just behind the brain in the anterior wall of the aorta, are in contact with the hypocerebral ganglia. The corpora allata are situated just in back, sometimes a little more laterally, but always dorsal to the esophagus. These two pairs of organs are associated with two pairs of cardiac nerves (*nervi corporis cardiaci*). The internal cardiac nerves are derived from the neurons of the pars intercerebralis, whose axons undergo an intracerebral decussation before their emergence in the customary manner. The origin of the external cardiac nerves remains to be clarified; their free course is very short because each one joins with the corresponding internal nerve a very short distance from the point of emergence. The corpora allata seem to be innervated by a more or less individualized prolongation of the cardiac nerve. In addition, there is a connection between the hypocerebral ganglion and the *corpora cardiaca*. Zuberi and Peeters (1964) described a nerve going from the corpora allata to the molt gland. This is perhaps the nerve seen by Hanström (1940) which emerged from the corpora allata in a ventral direction and whose destination he was unable to determine exactly. Obviously, the details of the nervous connections of this complex need to be studied precisely.

This arrangement is very constant in the different termites. The variations associated with polymorphism concern the relative development of the organs much more than their position. However, in the soldiers with elongated heads the allata-cardiac complex is a little more posterior, as noted by Imms (1919). In the large queens of the Termitidae the hypertrophied corpora allata extend back, even into the thorax.

b. The Corpora Cardiaca. Enclosed within the wall of the aorta, the two cardiac bodies are elongated from the front to the back, with a triangular cross section (Fig. 7C). Their posterior regions anastomose just behind the hypocerebral ganglion. The cardiac bodies contain cells distributed primarily in the external and ventral portion. In certain cases two types of cells may be distinguished: some with spherical nuclei, probably corresponding to the neurons; and others with small, elongated nuclei, which are probably the glia cells. The internal part (against the aorta) lacks nuclei and has a fibrous appearance. It is here that the products of neurosecretion are accumulated. In certain cases (section III, B, 1) the neurons of the cardiac bodies also show signs of secretory activity.

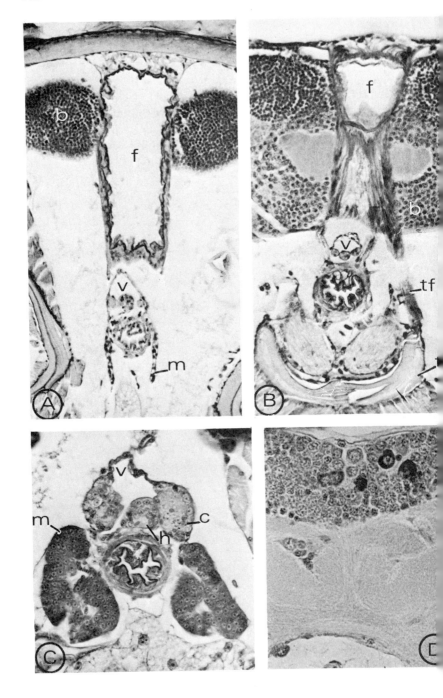

:. *The Corpora Allata.* The corpus allatum (Fig. 8) is a massive
;an which is generally spherical, but may be elongated longitudinally
rticularly in the soldier). The cells are more or less radially arranged.
en the glands are small, the nuclei are quite regularly arranged at
: periphery, and the internal parts of the cell are arranged like a whirl-
ol; when they are larger, the nuclei appear to be distributed throughout
: whole mass.

The Molt Glands

The molt glands were first described by Jucci (1924) as "tentorial
nds," by Pflugfelder (1947) under the name "ventral glands," and
:n by numerous authors (Section III, B, 3). They are often called
rothoracic glands," but this term is not very appropriate since they
: almost always entirely cephalic. Their position appears to be ex-
mely constant. Situated in the posteroventral part of the head, they
: formed by cords of cells attached to muscular fibers (Fig. 7C). These
scles are inserted, on one hand, on the digestive tube, lateral to the
el of the cardiac bodies and, on the other hand, on the rim of the
:ipital foramen. According to Herlant-Meewis and Pasteels (1961)
:se muscles correspond to the *dialatatores pharyngis posteriores*
erales of Holmgren (1909). The molt glands also rest upon the two
;e tracheal trunks which penetrate the head. The cords of cells form
:gular lobes, but the gland remains rather compact. In *Kalotermes*
icollis and in *Zootermopsis angusticollis* (Hagen) a lobe extends into
: anterior part of the prothorax (Bernardini-Mosconi, 1958; Lüscher,
50), but this arrangement seems to be exceptional. The histological
ect of the cells varies greatly with the physiological state of the animal.
he only innervation mentioned is a connection with the corpora
ta (Zuberi and Peeters, 1964), but this observation requires con-
nation.

---

ig. 7. A, B: Transverse sections of the head of *Reticulitermes lucifugus* at the level
he frontal gland. A: Soldier; B: winged imago. (b) Brain; (f) frontal gland; (m) molt
d; (t) tentorium; (tf) tentorial-fontanellar muscle; (v) dorsal vessel (×210). C: Trans-
se section of the head of a nymph with short wing pads of *R. lucifugus.* (c) Corpora
liaca; (h) hypocerebral ganglion; (m) molt glands; (v) dorsal vessel (×300). D: Queen
Microcerotermes parvus, transverse section through the posterior part of the brain,
wing the neurosecretory cells (stained with paraldehyde-fuchsin) in the pars inter-
ralis (×500).

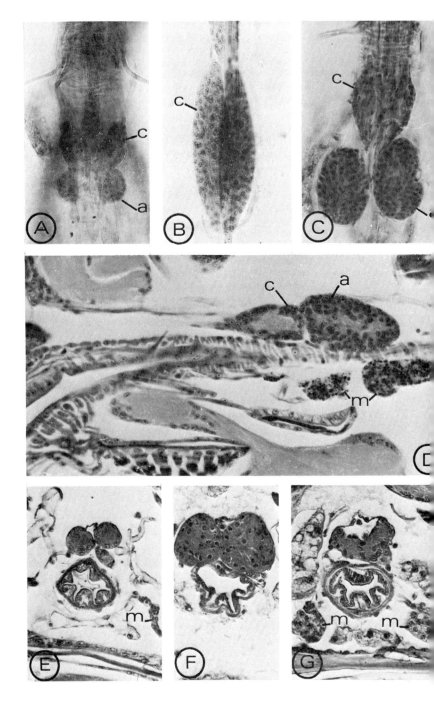

VARIATIONS WITH POLYMORPHISM (see also Chapters 9 and 10)

Neurosecretion and Corpora Cardiaca

The histological manifestations of the neurosecretions are often ob-
ure or absent. On this account, the variations are difficult to follow and
ould necessitate an experimental approach. It is justifiable to suppose
at, as in the other insects, the cerebral neurosecretory system controls
e activity of the endocrine glands. However, we cannot say anything
present about its role in the determination of the castes.
Nevertheless, a clear correlation exists between the histologically
ible neurosecretions and reproduction. In *Kalotermes flavicollis*
oirot, 1957) sexual maturity in both the imagoes and the neotenics is
companied by a general increase of neurosecretions and, above all,
the appearance of new neurosecretory cells, particularly in the dorso-
eral part of the protocerebrum, at the base of the optic ganglion.
e facts are even clearer in the physogastic queens of the Termitidae.
cording to the observations of Pasteels and Deligne (1965) the young
agoes of *Microcerotermes parvus* (Haviland) do not show any visible
1 of neurosecretion. However, in the old queens (just as in those of
bitermes heghi) certain neurons of the pars intercerbralis reveal, after
ning with paraldehyde-fuchsin, a very intense neurosecretion (Fig.
), which accumulates in the corpora cardiaca. These latter, which
enlarged, also possess a secretion proper which is acidophilic and
the form of spherical inclusions in the cells. The fuchsinophilic
rosecretion penetrates into the corpora allata by following the nerve
rs which join the latter to the corpora cardiaca. These facts appear
e general in the Termitidae. Pflugfelder (1938) noted the enlargement
he cardiac bodies in the physogastric queens of *Odontotermes re-
anni*. We have observed a situation parallel to that observed by Pas-
s and Deligne in the queens of *Nasutitermes* sp. and *Cubitermes*
gifaber. In these latter species, in addition to the cells of the pars
rcerebralis, there are some cells containing fuchsinophilic granula-
s within the laterodorsal part of the protocerebrum. These cells are

---

g. 8. A—C: Whole mounts of *Termes hospes* (×250). A: Corpora cardiaca and
ora allata of a worker; B: corpora allata of a soldier; C: corpora cardiaca and corpora
a of a male winged imago. D: Sagittal section of the head of a female sexual ergatoid
hospes just after the molt; the molt glands (m) are in an advanced stage of degeneration
5). E, F, G: Transverse sections of the head of *Noditermes curvatus* (×260). E: Normal
er; F and G: worker parasitized by a larva of *Noditermitomya*, showing the growth
e corpora allata in F and the molt glands in G. (a) Corpora allata; (c) corpora cardiaca;
nolt glands, except in B where (c) indicates the corpora allata.

perhaps homologous with the lateral cells of *Kalotermes*, but as Paste and Deligne (1965) have emphasized, there may be confusion with li fuscin accumulations. In the large queens of *Bellicositermes natalen* (Noirot, unpublished observations) the neurosecretory cells of the p intercerebralis appear rather low in secretions, but secretions are v abundant in the enlarged corpora cardiaca. Moreover, the corpora (diaca contain a great abundance of small drops of acidophilic secreti as pointed out in the previous case.

In *Kalotermes flavicollis* there are no very clear differences betw the neurosecretions of the males and the females. This is not true of Termitidae. In the imaginal kings which we have examined (*Nasutiter* sp., *Cubitermes fungifaber*, *Bellicositermes natalensis*), the cells of pars intercerebralis are very poor in fuchsinophilic granulations. corpora cardiaca, although more voluminous than those of the yo imagoes, are not as well developed as those of the queens. They con a moderate quantity of neurosecretions and also the small drop secretion proper. According to the histological picture the neurose tion of the kings in the Termitidae seems to be distinctly weaker t in the queens.

A precise physiological interpretation of these observations is diffi Do the substances produced by the brain and transmitted to the cor cardiaca act directly or do they stimulate the corpora allata? The ac on the corpora allata is suggested by the fact that the neurosecret penetrate effectively into these glands (Pasteels and Deligne, 1 Noirot, unpublished observations). There is also the question of significance of the secretion proper of the cardiac bodies. Experime tion will be necessary in order to answer these questions.

2. Corpora Allata

a. Kalotermes flavicollis. Numerous works have been devote this European dry-wood termite, dealing with the variation of the vo of the corpora allata during the course of postembryonic developr (Springhetti, 1957; Lüscher, 1957, 1960, 1965; Lebrun, 1967a) and their physiological role (Lüscher, 1958, 1960, 1965; Lebrun, 1 1967a,b).

In this primitive termite the corpora allata undergo rather rep growth up to the imaginal molt and are clearly developed in the funct imagoes. In addition, Lüscher (1965) observed a seasonal variation i pseudergates: the volume of these glands decreases in winter a minimal in March and again in July. Finally, he notes a decrease c volume of these glands at the time of the molt of these individuals. D the formation of the neotenic reproductives, the corpora allata onsiderably (volume multiplied 4 or 5 times) and very rapidly. The ormation of the soldiers is also accompanied by significant modifications f the corpora allata: at the time of the molt which produces the white- oldier, the volume of the corpora allata is tripled. In the adult soldiers he glands are a little smaller.

The enlargement of the corpora allata is therefore known to occur at he time of the maturation of the imagoes, at the time of the formation f the replacement sexuals, and at the time of the differentiation of the oldiers. The experimental studies have attempted to define precisely he role of the corpora allata in these phenomena (Chapter 9). We will nly note here that Lüscher comes to the conclusion, from his observa- ions, that several hormones are produced by the corpora allata (juvenile ormone, gonadotropic hormone, and a hormone responsible for the lifferentiation of the soldiers), but this interpretation is not accepted y everyone and is not supported by the recent experiments of Lebrun 1967a).

b. Termitidae. In the higher termites the enlargement of the corpora llata in the physogastic queens is considerable. By comparison with he imagoes with wings, the volume is multiplied 7 or 8 times (Kaiser, 956; Pasteels and Deligne, 1965); it becomes so great that these glands re often forced back into the thorax, and their form becomes irregular, ressing against the adjacent structures. This enlargement was inter- reted by Holmgren (1909) as a degenerative phenomena, but indicates, s a matter of fact, a hyperactivity. The cells, which are large, have lost heir radial disposition and have large nuclei (Fig. 9). They have probably ndergone one or more cycles of endomitosis (Pflugfelder, 1938; Kaiser, 1956). Their cytoplasm is filled with grains of secretions resem- ling lipofuscins (Pasteels and Deligne, 1965). Let us recall, finally, that he neurosecretions which emanate from the cardiac bodies penetrate o the interior of the corpora allata by following the nerve fibers con- ecting these two organs.

The modifications in the king are less pronounced. The increase in olume appears variable according to the species: in *Bellicositermes atalensis* it is a little larger than at the time of emergence (Noirot, unpub- ished observations): in *Anoplotermes pacificus* Fr. Müller the volume is imply doubled (Kaiser, 1956). On the other hand the size is only slightly ess than that of the queen in *Nasutitermes chaquimayensis* (Holmgren, 909) and *Cubitermes fungifaber* (unpublished observations). But even in his case the cells possess few modifications: the cytoplasm is much less acuolated than in the queens, and the enlargement of the nuclei is not s pronounced (Kaiser, 1956; Noirot, unpublished observations).

Similar facts have been observed in the replacement reproductives by

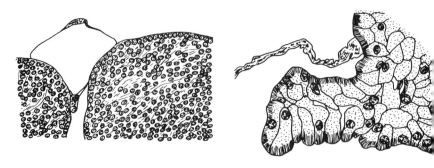

Fig. 9.   Histological structure of the corpora allata of a female winged imago (left) and
an old queen (right) of *Odontotermes redemanni* (after Pflugfelder, 1938).

Pflugfelder (1938). Kaiser (1956) found that female nymphoids of *Micro*
cerotermes amboinensis Kemner have corpora allata which are progres
sively larger as the neotenics are derived from more advanced nympha
stages. The ergatoid reproductives have a corpus allatum 7 times large
than that of the workers from which they are derived. This growth i
very pronounced by the time of the molt of transformation. In the male
(nymphs and ergatoids) the growth of the corpora allata is much less
In *Termes hospes* two molts are required for the transformation from
worker to ergatoid (Chapter 10). In the first the volume of the corpor
allata is doubled (a little more in the female, a little less in the male)
During the course of the intermediate stage (immature ergatoid) thei
growth is slight in the males, more pronounced in the females, and it i
after the second molt that the major growth occurs. Finally, the volum
is multiplied 8−10 times in the males and 15−20 times in the females
This growth is primarily the result of cellular multiplication, and ther
is little increase in cell size. The corpora allata of the ergatoid female
(Fig. 8, D) are slightly larger than those of the winged imagoes (Noirot
unpublished observations).

   During the course of postembryonic development of the imagoes, th
growth of the corpora allata is very slow at first. In the first stage larva
of *Anoplotermes pacificus* the glands appear identical in those of larva
which develop into neuters and those which develop into reproductive
(Fig. 10). It is during the last nymphal stage that a rapid growth occurs
and the volume is multiplied 8 times (Kaiser, 1956). We have been abl
to make comparable observations with *Termes hospes*.

   In the neuter castes Pflugfelder (1938) noted that the corpora allat
of the workers was small, and that their volume was a little larger in th
soldiers, being accompanied by a certain nuclear enlargement. Accordin

to the work of Kaiser (1956) the volume of the corpora allata of the workers of *Anoplotermes pacificus* is only 1/46 that of the winged imagoes. However, according to our observations (unpublished) the difference is less marked in *Nasutitermes arborum* (Smeathmann) (about one-tenth) and *Termes hospes* (one-fifteenth). Sexual dimorphism appears slight or absent, even when the male and female workers are of a very different size as in *Bellicositermes natalensis* (Noirot, unpublished observations). Similarly, when the workers go through several successive stages, the corpora allata do not grow in a regular manner, although there is a slight and temporary augmentation of the volume at the time of the molt (Kaiser, 1956; Noirot, unpublished observations).

The differentiation of the soldiers is accompanied by a more or less conspicuous enlargement of the corpora allata, depending upon the species. The increase in volume is visible before the molt giving rise to the white-soldier. In *Neocapritermes* sp. and an unidentified Nasutitermitinae, the corpora allata attain their maximum size at this time, and the volume then diminishes in the white-soldier and the soldier, although it is larger than in the workers (Kaiser, 1956). We have observed an analogous situation in *Bellicositermes natalensis* and *Mimeutermes giffardii* Silvestri, but the regression in the adult soldier is more accentuated in *Noditermes curvatus* (Silvestri). In *Termes hospes*, however, the growth continues during the white-soldier stage and even after the molt that gives rise to the soldier, so that the corpora allata of the adult soldier are larger than those of the winged imagoes (Fig. 8B, C).

3. The Molt Glands

As in all the Pterygote insects, the molt glands disappear in the imago and their degeneration begins *before* the imaginal molt (Herlant-Meewis and Pasteels, 1961). They also degenerate in the replacement reproductives of *Kalotermes* (Lüscher, 1960; Herlant-Meewis and Pasteels, 1961) and in both the nymphoid and ergatoid reproductives of the Termitidae (Kaiser, 1956; Noirot, unpublished observations), but are present in all the other individuals. During the course of the molt cycle, these organs undergo important variations in volume and in the histological characteristics of their cells. These variations, mentioned by different authors, remain to be studied in detail.

In the lower termites, which lack true workers, the molt glands undergo a rather regular growth in the course of development of the imagoes (Springhetti, 1957). In the Termitidae a very marked difference occurs in the molt glands of the neuter and reproductive lines. The first stage larvae are morphologically indifferent (Chapter 13), but at the end of this stage the future neuters and reproductives are distinct. According to Kaiser (1956) the molt glands of the future reproductives of *Anoplotermes pacificus* have a volume which is twice that of the future workers, although the number of cells remains about the same (Fig. 10). During the nymphal molts, the growth of the molt gland is considerable, whereas it remains slight in the neuter line. The workers (who never molt in this species) retain the molt gland, but it is small and appears inactive. Kaiser states that the growth of the molt gland in the nymph is much more rapid than that of the corpora allata (about 11-1 in the first stage larvae, and 42-1 in the last stage nymphs). Our unpublished observations on *Termes hospes*, although less thorough, permit us to extend Kaiser's observations to this species.

In the workers the molt glands are present but poorly developed. They usually have an inactive appearance, with small cells and inconspicuous cytoplasm (Fig. 8E). This changes at the time of the molt in those workers which are still capable of molting (Kaiser, 1956; Noirot, unpublished observations).

Similarly, the molt glands always persist in the soldiers (Pflugfelder, 1947; Kaiser, 1956; Lüscher, 1960; Herlant-Meewis and Pasteels, 1961) (Fig. 7A), and their development is comparable to that observed in the workers. The cells always appear inactive. The termite soldiers never molt, and this incapacity is thought to be due to the absence or insufficiency of the secretion of ecdysone by the molt glands. Lebrun (1963b, 1967b) has been able to provoke a molt in *Kalotermes* soldiers by implanting prothoracic glands of roaches. We do not yet know if the inactivity of the molt glands is definitive or only due to the absence of a cerebral stimulus.

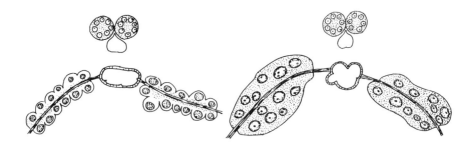

Fig. 10. First stage larvae of *Anoplotermes pacificus* approaching the first molt. Corpora allata and molt glands of a future worker (left) and a future imago (right) (after Kaiser, 1956).

We have little information regarding the development of the molt glands at the time the neotenic reproductives are formed apart from the commonly established fact that a swelling occurs at the time of the molt at which differentiation is effected. During the formation of ergatoid reproductives of *Termes hospes*, beginning with the workers and requiring two molts (Chapter 10), the molt glands are larger than those of the usual worker molt. However, the number of cells does not seem to be increased (Noirot, unpublished observations). The molt glands always degenerate in the different neotenics (Fig. 8D), but this degeneration may occur later than that which follows the imaginal molt (Kaiser, 1956; Springhetti, 1957; Noirot, unpublished observations).

C. CONCLUSIONS

Although the experimental research has only involved a single species — *Kalotermes flavicollis* — the data on anatomy and comparative histology permit the reasonable supposition that the hormonal conditioning of polymorphism is, in its broad outlines, the same in all termites. The endocrine system of the Isoptera does not seem to differ from other Pterygotes, as indicated by the activity of the roach endocrine glands implanted in *Kalotermes* (Lüscher, 1965; Lebrun, 1963a,b, 1967b).

The particularities of the postembryonic development of the termites, that is to say their polymorphism, reside, on the one hand, in the extra-individual mechanisms regulating the activities of the endocrine system (social factors and in particular pheromones, see Chapter 9) and, on the other hand, in the fact that the termites are capable of differentiation of different forms depending upon the hormonal equilibrium which occurs.

With the general concept of polymorphism developed by Wigglesworth (1961, 1966) the different types of morphogenesis are conditioned by the different genetic systems which coexist within the same individuals and whose repression or activation is regulated by a hormonal equilibrium. This interpretation could very well account for the facts observed in the termites (see Chapter 10, V, A). Without going into detail here (see Chapters 9 and 10) let us try to bring out the essential points concerning this orientation of the activity of the genes as a function of the endocrine secretions.

The differentiation of the *soldiers* is correlated with an activation of the corpora allata. Certain observations (Lüscher and Springhetti, 1960; Lüscher, 1960, 1965) have brought about the postulation of the existence of a hormone, distinct from the juvenile hormone (a hormone which stimulates metabolism in other insects). In spite of the importance of the arguments advanced, this hypothesis is not definitely demonstrated (see Lebrun, 1967a). According to Herlant-Meewis and Pasteels (1961) the persistence of the molt gland in the soldier could be due to the presence of a notable amount of juvenile hormone during the molt of differentiation.

The formation of the replacement reproductives is also accompanied by an activation of the corpora allata, but later than in the case of the soldiers. This activation would only intervene secondarily in the development of the genital apparatus. This phenomenon, still unexplained, might imply a cerebral action (Lüscher, 1960). Lüscher (1965) raises the question of a gonadotropic hormone distinct from both the juvenile hormone and the metabolic hormone; there might even be a secretion of distinct hormones for the male and the female. We do not propose to discuss the general problem of the unity or the plurality of the secretions of the allata bodies, but must emphasize the complexity of the problem associated with the development of the genital apparatus and with somatic differentiation. The work of Lebrun (1961, 1967b) has shown that in *Kalotermes* the differentiation of the neotenics is accompanied first of all by a growth of the genital tracts and the accessory glands (in the males as well as in the females); the development of the gonads themselves occurs only after the neotenic molt. On the other hand, so far as the somatic development is concerned, the neotenic molt in *Kalotermes* brings about a more or less marked differentiation of certain imaginal characters (compound eyes, tergal glands; Section II, F) but is almost always accompanied by a regression of the wing pads. Similar facts are observed with the neotenic nymphoids of *Reticulitermes lucifugus* (Buchli, 1958) and of *Microcerotermes amboinensis* (Weyer, 1930; Kaiser, 1956). In the cases of the ergatoid neotenics, the morphology of the worker may remain unchanged with the exception of the last abdominal sternites (*Termes hospes*; Noirot, 1955; *Microcerotermes amboinensis*, Noirot, 1955; Kaiser, 1956), but wing pads and compound eyes may also appear (*Cubitermes severus* Silvestri, Bodot, unpublished; see Chapter 10). In *Reticulitermes* the neotenics developing from workers may acquire wing pads if they arise from rather young stages (Buchli, 1958). These particular characteristics of the neotenic molt can indeed be explained by the hypothesis of a plurality of hormones of the corpora allata, and also by the unitarian hypothesis (balance between the rate of ecdysone and juvenile hormone, shifting in the secretion of the two hormones, reactivation of different tissues, intervention of neurosecretions . . .).

The few studies available on the differentiation between the neuters and the reproductives in the Termitidae suggest that the relative development of the corpora allata and the molt glands could provide an explanation for the formation of the workers, on one hand, and the imagoes, on the other hand (Kaiser, 1956; Section III, B, 3). What is important here is to take into account not only the differences in somatic development, but also the arrested development of the germinal tissue of the neuters. In the neuters of many Termitidae the germinal cells do not multiply after hatching (Noirot, 1955). Although many facts are known regarding the maturation of the gonads of insects (at least in the females), the growth and the differentiation of the genital apparatus remains one of the most obscure fields of the endocrinology of these animals. The termites offer numerous cases of separation between germinal and somatic development and should, in spite of the difficulties of experimentation, furnish material favorable for such research. Let us consider in this respect, the strange case of the workers of *Noditermes curvatus* parasitized by a dipteran larva (Noirot, 1953): these workers are morphologically normal, but do not perform any work, are nourished by their cogeners, and accumulate important reserves in the adipose tissue. Their genital apparatus is considerably developed but it does not become functional, and there is a very marked development of the corpora allata and molt glands (Fig. 8E−G).

In the last decade important progress has been made in the field of the endocrinology of the termites, concerning mainly the role of the corpora allata. One can hope that the question of the pluralities of the hormones of the corpora allata will soon be solved, but the role of the nervous system (neurosecretion, neural commands to other glands) and that of the molt glands remain to be studied. Above all, we must apply ourselves to a better understanding of the endocrine equilibrium realized during the course of the different stages of postembryonic development. By the very fact that their development is complex, the termites should contribute to a better understanding of the endocrinology of the insects.

REFERENCES

Ahrens, W. (1930). Über die Körpergliederung, die Haut und die Tracheenorgane der Termitenkönigin. *Jena. Z. Naturw.* **64**, 449-530.

Alibert, J. (1966). La trophalaxie chez le Termite à cou jaune (*Calotermes flavicollis* Fabr.) étudiée à l'aide de radio-éléments. Doctoral Thesis, Univ. of Paris, Paris.

Barth, R. (1955). Über die tergitalen Druesenfelder von *Syntermes dirus* (Isoptera). *Rev. Brasil. Biol.* **15**, 257-263.

Bathellier, J. (1927). Contribution à l'étude systématique et biologique des termites de l'Indo-Chine. *Faune Colonies Franc.* **1**, 125-365.

Bernardini-Mosconi, P. (1958). Le ghiandole endocrine e le cellule neurosecretici protocerebrali di ninfa di *Zootermopsis angusticollis*. *Symp. Genet. Biol. Ital.* **6**, 129-139.

Bernardini-Mosconi, P., and Vecchi, M. L. (1961). Neurosecrezione nel cervello e nei gangli di *Reticulitermes lucifugus* Rossi. *Symp. Genet. Biol. Ital.* 7, 322-330.

Bonneville, P. (1936). Recherches sur l'anatomie microscopique des Termites. *Arvernia Biol.* 15, 1-127.

Brégeon, A. (1958). Diplôme études supérieures, Univ. of Paris.

Buchli, H. (1958). L'origine des castes et les potentialités ontogéniques des Termites Européens du genre *Reticulitermes* Holmgren. *Ann. Sci. Nat. Zool. Biol. Animale* [11] 20, 263-429.

Bugnion, E. (1913). Le *Termes horni* Wasm. de Ceylan. *Rev. Suisse Zool.* 21, 299-330.

Bugnion, E. and Popoff, N. (1910). La termite à latex de Ceylan *Coptotermes travians* Haviland. Avec un appendice comprenant la description des *Coptotermes gestroi* Wasm. et *flavus* nov. sp. *Mem. Soc. Zool. France* 23, 107-123.

Butler, C. G. (1967). Insect pheromones. *Biol. Rev.* 42, 42-87.

Cazal, P. (1948). Les glandes endocrines retrocérébrales des insectes. Etude morphologique. *Bull. Biol. France Belg.* Suppl. 32, 1-228.

Child, H. J. (1934). The internal anatomy of termites and the histology of the digestive tract. *In* "Termites and Termite Control" (C. A. Kofoid, ed), 2nd ed., pp. 58-88. Univ. of California Press, Berkeley, California.

Deligne, J. (1968). Doctoral Thesis, Univ. of Bruxelles.

Ernst, E. (1959). Beobachtungen beim Spritzakt der *Nasutitermes* Soldaten. *Rev. Susisse Zool.* 66, 289.

Feytaud, J. (1912). Contribution à l'étude du Termite lucifuge. (Anatomie, Fondation de colonies nouvelles.) *Arch. Anat. Microscop. Morphol. Exptl.* 13, 481-607.

Grassé, P.-P. (1937). Recherches sur la systematique et la biologie des Termites de l'Afrique Occidentale Française. Premiere partie. Protermitidae, Mesotermitidae, Metatermitidae (Termitinae). *Ann. Soc. Entomol. France* 106, 1-100.

Grassé, P.-P. (1942). L'essaimage des Termites. Essai d'analyse causale d'un complexe instinctif. *Bull. Biol. France Belg.* 76, 347-382.

Grassé, P.-P. (1945). Recherches sur la biologie des Termites champignonnistes (Macrotermitinae). *Ann. Sci. Nat. Zool. Biol. Animale* [11] 7, 115-146.

Grassé, P.-P. (1949). Ordre des isoptères ou Termites. *In* "Traité de Zoologie," (P.-P. Grassé, ed.), Vol. IX, pp. 408-544. Masson, Paris.

Grassé, P.-P., and Noirot, C. (1954). *Apicotermes arquieri* n.sp.: ses constructions et sa biologie. Considérations générales sur les Apicotermitinae. *Ann. Sci. Nat. Zool. Biol. Animale* 16 [11], 345-388.

Grassi, B., and Sandias, A. (1893). Costituzione e sviluppo della societá dei termitidi. *Atti Accad. Gioenia Sci. Nat. Catania* [4] 6, 1-75; 71-76.

Hanström, B. (1940). Inkretorische Organe, Sinnesorgane und Nervensystem des Kopfes einiger niederer Insektenordnungen. *Kgl. Svenska Vetenskapsakad. Handl.* [3] 18, 1-265.

Herlant-Meewis, H., and Pasteels, J. M. (1961). Les glandes de mue de *Calotermes flavicollis* F. (Ins. Isopt.). *Compt. Rend.* 253, 3078-3080.

Holmgren, N. (1909). Termitenstudien. I. Anatomische Untersuchungen. *Kgl. Svenska Vetenskapsakad. Handl.* 44 [3], 1-215.

Imms, A. D. (1919). On the structure and biology of *Archotermopsis*, together with descriptions of new species of intestinal protozoa and general observations on the Isoptera. *Phil. Trans. Roy. Soc. London* 209, 75-180.

Jucci, C. (1924). Sulla differenziazione delle caste nella società dei termitidi. I, Neotenici Reali veri e neotenici-l'escrezione nei reali neotenici-la fisiologia e la biologia). *Atti Accad. Nazl. Lincei, Rend., Classe Sci. Fis., Mat. Nat.* [5] 14, 269-500.

Kaiser, P. (1956). Die Hormonalorgane der Termiten mit der Enstehung ihrer Kasten. *Mitt. Hamburgischen Zool. Museum Inst.* 54, 129-178.

Kovoor, J. (1966). Contribution à l'étude de la digestion chez un Termite supérieur (*Microcerotermes edentatus* Was. Isoptera, Termitidae). Doctoral Thesis, Univ. of Paris.

Kovoor, J. (1968). Le tractus intestinal d'un Termite superieur (*Microcerotermes edentatus* Was., Amitermitinae). Histophysiologie et flore bacterienne symbiotique. *Bull. Biol. France Belg.* 102, 45-84.

Lambinet, F. (1959). La glande mandibulaire du Termite à cou jaune (*Calotermes flavicollis*). *Insectes Sociaux* 6, 165-177.

Lebrun, D. (1961). Evolution de l'appareil génital dans les diverses castes de *Calotermes flavicollis*. *Bull. Soc. Zool. France* 86, 235-242.

Lebrun, D. (1963a). Implantation de glandes de la mue de *Periplaneta americana* dans les sexues néoténiques de *Calotermes flavicollis* Fabr. (Insecte, Isoptera). *Compt. Rend.* 257, 2181-2182.

Lebrun, D. (1963b). Implantation de glandes de la mue de *Periplaneta americana* dans des soldats de *Calotermes flavicollis* Fabr. *Compt. Rend.* 257, 3487-3488.

Lebrun, D. (1964). Le role de corps allates dans la formation des castes de *Calotermes flavicollis*. *Compt. Rend.* 259, 4152-4155.

Lebrun, D. (1967a). Hormone juvenile et formation des soldats chez le Termite à cou jaune *Calotermes flavicollis* Fabr. *Compt. Rend.* 265, 996-997.

Lebrun, D. (1967b). La détermination des castes du Termite à cou jaune *Calotermes flavicollis* Fabr. *Bull. Biol. France Belg.* 101, 139-217.

Lüscher, M. (1957). Ersatzgeschlechtstiere bei Termiten und die Corpora allata. *Verhandl. Deut. Ges. Angew. Entomol.* 14, 144-150.

Lüscher, M. (1958). Über die Enstehung der Soldaten bei Termiten. *Rev. Suisse Zool.* 65, 372.

Lüscher, M. (1960). Hormonal control of caste differentiation in termites. *Ann. N.Y. Acad. Sci.* 89, 549-563.

Lüscher, M. (1961). Social control of polymorphism in termites. *In* "Insect Polymorphism" (J. S. Kennedy, ed.), pp. 57-67. Roy. Entomol. Soc., London.

Lüscher, M. (1962). Sozialwirkstoffe bei Termiten. *Proc. 11th Intern. Congr. Entomol. Vienna, 1960,* Vol. 1, pp. 579-582, Christoph Reisser's Söhne, Vienna.

Lüscher, M. (1965). Functions of the corpora allata in the development of termites. *Proc. 16th Intern. Congr. Zool., Washington, D.C., 1963,* Vol. 4, pp. 244-250. Nat. Hist. Press, Garden City, New York.

Lüscher, M., and Müller, B. (1960). Ein spurbildendes Sekret bei Termiten. *Naturwissenschaften* 21, 503.

Lüscher, M., and Springhetti, A. (1960). Untersuchungen über die Bedeutung der Corpora allata für die Differenzierung der Kasten bei der Termite *Kalotermes flavicollis* F. *J. Insect Physiol.* 5, 190-212.

Montalenti, G. (1928). Sull'ipoderma e il tessuto adiposo nei neutri delle termiti. *Boll. Ist. Zool. Univ. di Roma* 5, 113.

Moore, B. P. (1964). Volatile terpenes from *Nasutitermes* soldiers (Isoptera, Termitidae). *J. Insect Physiol.* 10, 371-375.

Moore, B. P. (1966). Isolation of the scent trail pheromone of an Australian Termite. *Nature* 211, 746-747.

Mosconi-Bernardini, P., and Vecchi, M. L. (1964). Osservazioni istologiche et fluoromicroscopiche sulla ghiandola sternale di *Reticulitermes lucifugus* (Rhinotermitidae). *Symp. Genet. Biol. Ital.* 13, 169-177.

Mukerji, D., and Raychaudhri, S. (1942). The structure, function and origin of the exudate organs in the abdomen of the physogastric queen of the termite *Termes redemanni* Wasmann. *Indian J. Entomol.* 4, 173-199.

Mukerji, D., and Raychaudhuri, S. (1943). On the anatomy of the alimentary system of the termite *Termes redemanni* Wasmann. *Indian J. Entomol.* 5, 59-88.

Noirot, C. (1953). Un effet paradoxal du parasitisme chez les Termites. Developpement des gonades chez des ouvriers parasités. *Bull. Sect. Franc. Union Intern. Etudes Insectes Sociaux* 1, 11-28.

Noirot, C. (1955). Recherches sur le polymorphisme des Termites supérieurs (Termitidae). *Ann. Sci. Nat. Zool. Biol. Animale* [11] 17, 399-595.

Noirot, C. (1957). Neurosécrétion et sexualité chez le Termite à cou jaune *"Calotermes flavicollis* F." *Compt. Rend.* 245, 743-745.

Noirot, C., and Noirot-Timothée, C. (1965a). Organisation de la glande sternale chez *Calotermes flavicollis* F. (Insecta, Isoptera). *Compt. Rend.* 260, 6202-6204.

Noirot, C., and Noirot-Timothée, C. (1965b). La glande sternale dans l'évolution des Termites. *Insectes Sociaux* 12, 265-272.

Pasteels, J. M. (1965). Polyethisme chez les ouvriers de *Nasutitermes lujae* (Termitidae Isopteres). *Biol. Gabonica* 1, 191-205.

Pasteels, J. M., and Deligne, J. (1965). Etude du système endocrine au cours du vieillissement chez les "reines" de *Microcerotermes parvus* (Haviland) et *Cubitermes heghi* (Sjöstedt) (Isopteres Termitidae). *Biol. Gabonica* 1, 325-336.

Pflugfelder, O. (1938). Untersuchungen über die histologischen Veränderungen und das Kernwachstum der "Corpora allata" von Termiten. *Z. Wiss. Zool.* 150, 451-467.

Pflugfelder, O. (1947). Ueber die Ventraldrüsen und einige andere inkertorische Organe des Insektenkopfes. *Biol. Zentr.* 66, 211-235.

Roth, L. M., and Willis, E. R. (1954). The reproduction of cockroaches. *Smithsonian Inst. Misc. Collections* 122, 1-49.

Sands, W. A. (1965). A revision of the termite subfamily Nasutitermitinae (Isoptera, Termitidae) from the Ethiopian region. *Bull. Brit. Museum, Entomol.* Suppl. 4, 1-172.

Satir, P., and Stuart, A. M. (1965). A new apical microtubule associated organelle in the sternal gland of *Zootermopsis nevadensis* (Hagen), Isoptera. *J. Cell Biol.* 24, 277-283.

Smythe, R. V., and Coppel, H. C. (1966). A preliminary study of the sternal gland of *Reticulitermes flavipes* (Isoptera; Rhinotermitidae). *Ann. Entomol. Soc. Am.* 59, 1008-1010.

Smythe, R. V., Coppel, H. C., Lipton, S. H., and Strong, F. M. (1967). Chemical studies of attractants associated with *Reticulitermes flavipes* and *R. virginicus*. *J. Econ. Ertomol.* 60, 228-233.

Springhetti, A. (1957). Ghiandole tentoriali (ventrali, protoraciche) e corpora allata in *Kalotermes flavicollis* Fabr. *Symp. Genet. Biol. Ital.* 5, 333-349.

Stuart, A. M. (1961). Mechanism of trail laying in two species of termites. *Nature* 189, 419.

Stuart, A. M. (1963). Origin of the trail in the termites *Nasutitermes corniger* (Motschulsky) and *Zootermopsis nevadensis* (Hagen), Isoptera. *Physiol. Zool.* 36, 69-84.

Stuart, A. M. (1964). The structure and function of the sternal gland in *Zootermopsis nevadensis* (Isoptera). *Proc. Zool. Soc. London* 143, 43-52.

Stuart, A. M. (1967). Alarm, defense, and construction behavior relationships in termites (Isoptera). *Science* 156, 1123-1125.

Verron, H. (1963). Role des stimuli chimiques dans l'attraction sociale chez *Calotermes flavicollis* (Fabr.). *Insectes Sociaux* 10, 167-184 and 185-296.

Weyer, F. (1930). Über Ersatzgeschlechtstiere bei Termiten. *Z. Morphol. Oekol. Tiere* 19, 364-380.

Wigglesworth, V. B. (1961). Insect polymorphism. A tentative synthesis. *In* "Insect Polymorphism" (J. S. Kennedy, ed.), pp. 103-113. Roy. Entomol. Soc., London.

Wigglesworth, V. B. (1966). Hormonal regulation of differentiation in insects. *In* "Cell Differentiation and Morphogenesis" (W. Beerman, ed.), pp. 180-209. North-Holland Publ., Amsterdam.

Wilson, E. O. (1965). Chemical communication in the social insects. *Science* **149**, 1064-1071.

Zuberi, H., and Peeters, P. (1964). A study of the neurosecretory cells and the endocrine glands of Cubitermes exiguus. *In* "Etudes sur les Termites africains" (A. Bouillon, ed.), pp. 87-105. Masson, Paris.

5

The Reproductive System

FRANCES M. WEESNER

I. INTRODUCTION

The tremendous reproductive capacity of the queens of certain termite species which deposit thousands of eggs per day (Chapter 8) for periods of many years, has long aroused the interest of students of termites. Strangely enough, our knowledge of the structure of the reproductive system is limited to very few species, and we have almost no information regarding its physiology. Some of the studies have been rather superficial, and they are sometimes inconsistent from one author to another for the same species. Nevertheless, it has become evident that the reproductive system of both the male and female termite has undergone a considerable evolution within the various groups.

In the females, this evolution has involved an increase in the number of ovarioles and the development of a greater intricacy in the structure of the spermatheca in which the spermatazoa are stored. In the male the number of testicular elements has undergone a similar, but less marked increase in germinal elements from the primitive to the more highly evolved forms. The so-called "seminal vesicles" or accessory glands of the male show a great diversity from group to group. Finally, the spermatozoa have undergone a very marked alteration of form and size.

II. THE PRIMARY FEMALE

The reproductive system of the female termite includes the ovaries (Fig. 1A), made up of a number of panoistic ovarioles attached to the right and left oviducts. The ovaries lie to either side of the digestive system in the dorsolateral abdominal cavity. In young imagoes of the primitive species they may only occupy the posterolateral part of the abdomen. In egg-laying queens and even in imagoes of the Termitidae they may extend almost the full length of the abdomen. In physogastric queens they occupy the major part of the abdomen and greatly distend it. In the Rhinotermitidae, particularly the Termitidae, the sternites and tergites become widely separated by the intersegmental membrane, whose tremendous increase in surface area is not yet understood.

Anteriorly, each ovary terminates in a ligament, and these then approach or join each other to form the median ligament. This extends into the dorsal midthoracic region. The right and left oviducts pass almost vertically to either side of the digestive tube and join to form a short common oviduct at about the level of the anterior margin of the seventh sternite. The common oviduct opens via a median gonopore in the anterior *floor* of the genital chamber (Fig. 2). The opening of the spermatheca lies in the *roof* of the genital chamber at about the same level. An-

---

Fig. 1. *Tenuirostritermes tenuirostris.* A: Sketch of a whole mount of one ovary of a young imago after the initial egg-laying period. B: Terminal portion of one ovariole showing the various zones from the terminal filament through the anterior region of the middle growth zone. C and D: Cross sections of an ovary to show the arrangement of the ovarioles around the oviduct and the epithelial sheaths (young imago). The ovarioles are numbered in the order in which they arose from the oviduct, beginning with the most posterior. Note the small size of the basal ovarioles in D, which is typical of young individuals in which only the most posterior ovarioles are functional. (GR) Germarium; (MG) middle growth region; (OD) oviduct; (PR) prophase region; (TS) terminal strand (after Weesner, 1955).

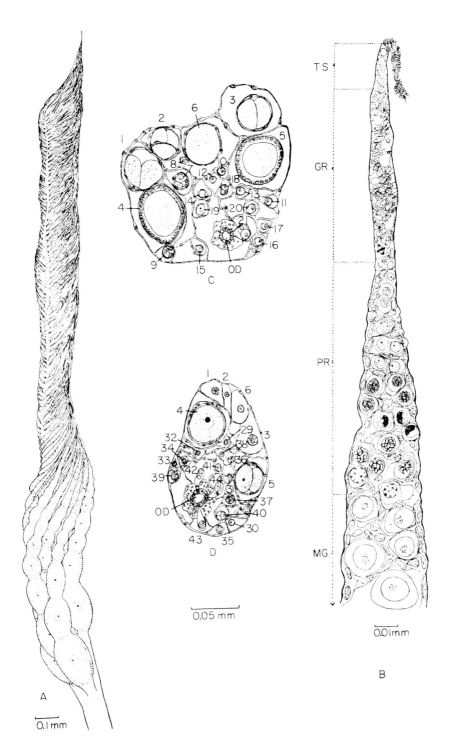

A

2

1

6

3

5

8

7

12

10

18

13

11

4

19

20

17

4

21

16

9

15

OD

C

1

2

6

4

29

3

32

38

34

33

36

41

39

42

44

5

OD

31

37

40

30

43

35

D

0.05 mm

TS

GR

PR

MG

B

0.01mm

0.1mm

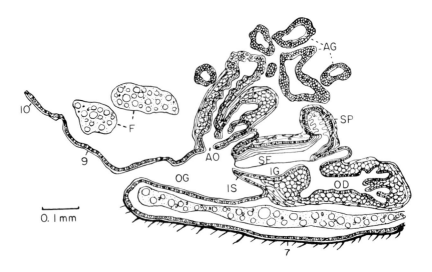

Fig. 2. Median section of the genital chamber of a female imago of *Tenuirostritermes tenuirostris*. (7, 9, 10) Sternites; (AG) lobes of the accessory gland; (AO) orifice of the accessory gland; (F) fat bodies; (IG) inner genital chamber; (IN) intersternal fold; (OD) oviduct; (OG) outer genital chamber; (SF) spermathecal furrow; (SP) base of spermatheca (after Weesner, 1955).

other structure associated with the female reproductive system is the bifurcated accessory gland. This opens through a median pore in the roof of the posterior portion of the genital chamber.

A. THE OVARIOLES

1. Structure

Each individual panoistic ovariole has a structure which appears to be fairly consistent from species to species and from group to group. The ovariole is enclosed in a noncellular layer, the *tunica propria* (Fig. 1B). Anteriorly, this layer extends beyond the tip of the ovariole, becoming incorporated into the mass of trachea and connective tissue forming the terminal ligament. The individual extension from each ovariole is known as the *terminal filament*. Posteriorly, the tunica propria appears to be continuous with the basement membrane of the epithlium of the oviduct (Weesner, 1955). In *Tenuirostritermes tenuirostris* (Desneux) a few flattened epithelial nuclei can be distinguished within the terminal filament. In addition, in immature ovarioles the apex of the ovarioles consists of a very regular row of $4-16$ cubodial cells about 4μ in diameter, with round nuclei which have been termed the terminal strand (Weesner, 1955). These are absent from some of the functional ovarioles in the young primaries. It may be that these cells represent the suspensorium of the developing ovarioles (Snodgrass, 1935). Exterior to the tunica propria, each ovariole is enclosed in a thin, irregular, epithelial sheath, which, in fixed material, only loosely surrounds the ovarioles (Fig. 1C,D).

In functional ovarioles a series of distinct regions may be recognized (Fig. 1B). The regions listed here are based on the study of *T. tenuirostris* (Weesner, 1955) and have been confirmed for *Reticulitermes hesperus* Banks (Weesner, 1956) and for the six species of Termitidae studied by Gabe and Noirot (1961) and listed in Section II, B. These agree, in general, with the accounts for various species by Grassi and Sandias (1893 – 1894), Brunelli (1904, 1905), Jucci (1924), Stella (1936, 1938), Ahrens (1935a,b), and others, and for the "typical" panoistic ovarioles discussed by Snodgrass (1935), Imms (1948), and Wigglesworth (1950).

In addition to the terminal filament, the panoistic ovariole is classically described as consisting of a terminal region, the *germarium*, followed by a growth region, the *vitellarium*, and connecting to the oviduct by a base or *pedicel*. In the termite ovariole there are three rather distinct regions of egg growth which may be designated from anterior to posterior as the prophase region, the middle growth region, and the terminal growth region.

a. The Germarium. Immediately posterior to the terminal strand cells or to the terminal filament when no strand cells are present lies a region with densely packed, small cells with elongated nuclei and little cytoplasm. These cells are irregular in shape. They may be arranged in a linear series with the nuclei oriented across the axis of the ovariole, or they may be arranged in an irregular fashion. Division figures are frequently observed in this region, particularly in the posterior portion. Ahrens (1935b) distinguishes between flat epithelial and round germinal cells in the germarium of *Odontotermes redemanni* (Wasmann). The cells of the germarium, without any distinct internal epithelial layer, are enclosed in the tunica propria.

b. The Prophase Region. The anterior portion of the prophase region is indicated by the clear distinction of flat epithelial cells with elongated nuclei and round germinal cells with round nuclei having a diffuse chromatin network and a small nucleolus. In *Tenuirostritermes* these cells are about 6 μ in diameter. In this species the size of the germinal cells increases to about 14 μ in the posterior portion of the prophase region. The epithelial cells may be observed dividing in this area, but no dividing germinal cells are encountered. These latter cells undergo a regular rearrangement of chromatin material corresponding to the typical pre-growth meiotic prophase. The nuceloli disappear and the chromatin becomes arranged in long, threadlike strands. These strands subsequently clump toward one pole of the nucleus. Chromatin threads then reappear throughout the nucleus, although they are now thicker and shorter than before. Finally, in the posterior oocytes of the prophase region the nuceoli reappear, and there are small clumps of chromatic material arranged throughout the nuclei (about 20 in *Tenuirostritermes*). Throughout this region the cytoplasm is strongly eosinophilic and the chromatin basophilic.

c. The Middle Growth Region. The oocytes now become surrounded by a rather irregular layer of thin follicular epithelium, and they are crowded together so that they are rather irregular and often polyhedral in shape. The cytoplasm becomes basophilic. The germinal vesicle is large and the nucleolus conspicuous. The peripheral clumps of chromatin become diffuse and oxyophilic. There is a considerable increase in the size of both the oocyte and germinal vesicle, and at the posterior portion of this region the nuclei are as large as the entire oocyte at the posterior prophase region.

d. The Terminal Growth Region. The final development of the eggs occurs in the posterior region of each ovariole. The terminal growth region may be distinguished by the regular arrangement of the follicular epithelium around each oocyte and by the positioning of the oocytes in a linear series in the ovariole. Anteriorly, the oocytes are as wide as they are long, but they gradually lengthen in the plane of the ovariole until they attain their maximum development (about $754 \times 232 \mu$ in *Tenuiro-stritermes*). The largest, central germinal vesicles observed in developing oocytes of *Tenuirostritermes* are 24 μ in diameter. Those of *Odonto-termes redemanni* are about 34 μ in diameter (Ahrens, 1935b). Stella (1938) concluded that the large central nucleus present just prior to yolk deposition represents the female pronucleus, but I do not feel that this conclusion has been established. The time at which meiotic division occurs warrants further investigation. In the posterior part of the ovariole, immediately adjacent to the oviduct, fully developed eggs enclosed in a chorion may be observed.

e. The Follicular Epithelium. The descriptions of follicular epithelium development are fairly consistent in the accounts for different species (Jucci, 1924; Stella, 1938; Ahrens, 1935b; Weesner, 1955, 1956; Gabe and Noirot, 1961). Ahrens (1935b) distinguished between epithelial and germinal cells in the germarium. His descriptions of the two types of cells correspond rather closely to those attributed here to the anterior portion of the prophase region. In the prophase region the cell boundaries of the epithelial cells are not clearly defined. In the middle growth region the cells are still irregular in arrangement and shape, but each nucleus appears incorporated in a clearly defined cell. In the terminal growth region the epithelial cells completely encircle each oocyte. In the prophase and middle growth regions and in the anterior part of the terminal growth region, these cells may frequently be observed in the process of mitosis.

In the terminal growth region the epithelial cells are at first irregular and flattened. They then become flattened cuboidal, then cuboidal, and finally columnar with a rounded inner margin (toward the oocyte). Jucci (1924) described these inner margins as pseudopodial and commented on the apparent secretory activity of the cells. At this time many of the follicular epithelial cells are binucleate, the nuclei apparently dividing amitotically and sometimes being only partly separated. The two nuclei are consistently arranged one above the other in the columnar cells (Ahrens, 1935b; Weesner, 1955). Ahrens notes that this amitosis occurs prior to the appearance of yolk in the oocyte. As the oocyte increases in size, the follicular epithelium is once again flattened and the nuclei are now arranged side by side in the cells. Binucleate cells are much larger than their uninucleate counterparts (Weesner, 1955).

Following the deposition of the egg a series of changes occurs in the residual follicular epithelium, terminating in the disintegration and probably the resorption of the cellular material. This process has been mentioned by a number of authors, but the most exhaustive account is that given by Ahrens (1935a) for *Odontotermes redemanni*. When the egg is discharged into the oviduct, the empty follicle shortens appreciably, probably due in part to the elasticity of the tunica propria, which may be thrown into a series of folds, but probably also due to the elasticity of the epithelium itself. The follicular epithelium assumes its earlier columnar form, and the nuclei are again arranged one above the other. Ahrens states that these cells appear perfectly normal. Eventually, however, they degenerate due to two processes: mechanical injury ("caryorrhixic degeneration") and nuclear atrophy ("pycnosis"). The mechanical injury results as the succeeding oocytes of the ovariole are released, forcing their way through the ovariole tube, past the old follicular cells. The latter are thus subjected to a sudden flattening and to a "grinding" action by the passage of the oocyte. When a series of empty follicles is present, those adjacent to the next oocyte are normal in appearance, those next in the series show considerable degeneration and damage, and in the subsequent follicle the cells have usually broken away from the tunica propria and lie free in the lumen (Ahrens, 1935a). These latter cells show advanced histolysis. Each group of degenerating follicular cells is referred to as a "corpus luteum" by Ahrens. This term has also been applied to the areas of yellow pigment granules discussed in Section II, A, 1, f.

It should be noted that there is disagreement regarding the origin of the follicular epithelium of the ovariole of the insects. It is generally believed to be derived from the mesodermal sheath of the primitive gonad and to arise either from the terminal cells closing the ovariole or from the ovarian pedicel. Its possible origin from the oogonia, as is true of the "nurse cells" of the meroistic ovarioles, must be kept in mind, although it seems unlikely. The ability of the termite ovariole to produce a large number of eggs without any specialized nurse cells is indeed puzzling. Any specialization would appear physiological rather than structural. Brunelli (1904) concluded that the follicular epithelium played a minor role, if any, in the growth of the oocyte, and that the development of the egg resulted from a special "perinuclear vitellarium zone" within the oocyte itself. Almost all other investigators, however, have concluded that the follicular epithelium is the immediate source of the nutrients which result in the rapid development of the oocyte and deposition of yolk in the terminal growth region.

f. The "Yellow Bodies."   In connection with the degenerating follicular epithelium, some consideration must be given to the yellow pigmented areas noted by many investigators in the ovarioles of termite queens, particularly mature, physogastric individuals (Grassi and Sandias, 1893-1894; Brunelli, 1904; Jucci, 1924; Stella, 1938; Ahrens, 1935a; and others). These areas were referred to by many authors as the "corpa lutea." (It should be noted that this usage is not the same as that applied by Ahrens to groups of degenerating follicular cells.) These yellow pigment bodies are apparently concretions of some material which is insoluble in alcohol, xylol, or ether. Brunnelli (1904) concluded that they represented concentrations of the by-products of the metabolism of the perinuclear yolk formation by the oocyte. Subsequent authors have felt that they represent wastes resulting from the breakdown of the follicular epithelium. Jucci (1924) noted their presence in both the ovarian calyx and in the oviduct proper. Ahrens (1935a) concluded that they represented waste products from the degeneration of the follicular cells which might be of a toxic nature. He found that most of these concretions, which are rather regular spheres, are contained in the epithelial cells at the base of the ovarioles. The size and the number of the concretions decrease with the distance from the area of disintegrating follicular epithelium. Ahrens terms these cells containing the spheres "pigment cells." He notes, however, that they do not differ from the normal epithelial cells of the oviduct except for the presence of these concretions.

termitidae, and for the desert Termitidae of the southwestern United States, at least in the high-altitude deserts of southern Arizona where the winters are relatively cold (Light and Weesner, 1947). Skaife (1961) found that egg laying is suspended during the winter months (in this region May through September) in colonies of *Amitermes hastatus* (Haviland) [as *Amitermes atlanticus* (Fuller)]. Apparently, in most of the tropical species egg laying continues throughout the year, although there may be seasonal fluctuations in the number of eggs laid (Chapters 8 and 10).

It has also been noted (Harvey, 1934; Castle, 1934; Stella, 1938; Skaife, 1961) that during periods of egg deposition the eggs may not be laid continuously. One group of eggs is deposited for a period of several weeks, followed by a "rest period" of several weeks, after which another group of eggs is deposited, etc.

Finally, it has been consistently noted that young queens of many termites deposit an initial group of eggs at varying periods after pairing, depending upon the species. This initial egg-laying period is followed by a period during which no eggs are deposited. In many cases the deposition of a second group of eggs corresponds to the time at which the first group of eggs hatches, and by the time the second group of eggs has developed, the first young have become functional in the colony (Castle, 1934; Harvey, 1934; Pickens, 1934; Buchli, 1950; Light and Weesner, 1955; Weesner, 1956; Grassé and Noirot, 1958; McMahan, 1962; Williams, 1959a,b; Sands, 1965).

A cyclic activity is also indicated by the structure of the ovarioles of the young queens. In these individuals only the most posterior ovarioles of each ovary are functional at the time of flight, and these are apparently the source of the initial group of eggs. In these ovarioles, the various growth stages are rather clearly distinguished from one another (prophase, middle, and terminal growth regions) so that there may actually be a rather marked increase in the diameter of the ovariole at the junction of each of these regions, rather than a perfectly continuous series of developmental stages. Furthermore, fully developed oocytes may adjoin oocytes in the prophase stage without any intervening middle growth region (Weesner, 1955). Ahrens (1935a) noted that in certain ovarioles in mature *Odontotermes redemanni* queens eggs adjacent to the oviduct were in the earliest stage of development typical of the terminal growth region, that is, almost as wide as long and without any yolk. He concluded that these ovarioles were attritic. However, it may be that this was merely an indication of a cyclic production of oocytes by the individual ovariole; in the cases he mentioned the earlier "wave" of oocytes may have fully matured and been discharged from the ovarioles, and the subsequent group of oocytes was just beginning its final development.

If the oocytes were produced continuously by all ovarioles which are functional, it would be expected that even with the limited number of functional ovarioles in young alates deposition of eggs would be more or less continuous. This cyclic activity of the gonads is another aspect of termite biology which should be investigated further.

B. THE OVIDUCTS

The oviducts are lined with a columnar epithelium resting upon a basement membrane and enclosed by a muscular tunic. The epithelium and basement membrane tend to be thrown into occasional inward projecting folds, which are not reflected in the muscular sheath (Ahrens, 1935b). The anterior region of the common oviduct is enclosed by a common muscular sheath, although the lumens of the right and left oviducts remain distinct throughout most of its length. The dorsal edges of the two ducts join, just anterior to the gonopore, to form a common, thin-walled chamber which lacks a muscular tunic. This opens via the gonopore through the floor of the genital chamber.

Although many illustrations suggest that the ovarioles are inserted into the oviduct in a lateral series (Imms, 1919; Thompson, 1922; Ahrens, 1935b), they are, in fact, inserted rather in a spiral fashion, as has been noted by these same authors and many others. Certainly, in the Rhinotermitidae and the Termitidae they arise from all sides of the oviduct (Fig. 1A). In *Kalotermes flavicollis*, Jucci (1924) notes that the ovarioles arise like "barbs from a feather."

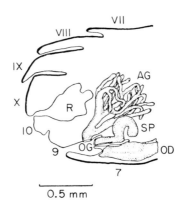

0.5 mm

Fig. 3. Reconstruction of the accessory gland and spermatheca of a female imago of *Tenuirostritermes tenuirostris* showing their relationship to other structures. (7–10) Sternites; (VII–X) tergites; (AG) accessory gland; (OD) oviduct; (OG) outer genital chamber; (R) rectum; (SP) spermatheca (after Weesner, 1955).

C. The Spermatheca

1. Structure

The presence of an organ for sperm storage is rather common in the insects and consistent in the Isoptera. Not much is known of the actual structure of this receptacle in the more primitive termites. In *Zootermopsis angusticollis* (Hagen), Thompson (1922) figures it variously as a doughnut-shaped, or a three- or four-lobed structure. She indicates that it opens directly into the oviducts "at their junction." However, it is evident that this structure has the usual position in this species, as noticed in other termites, and opens in the anterior roof of the genital chamber (Browman, 1935).

In the Rhinotermitidae and the Termitidae which have been examined, the spermatheca is an elongated, fingerlike tube extending dorsally and often having a recurved end (Fig. 3). In these families the spermatheca is lined with fingerlike projections of chitin resting on an esosinophilic layer which is underlaid by a zone of nuclei and then by tall columnar cells which appear to have a secretory function. In the Termitidae there are minute intracellular canals leading from the lumen of the spermatheca to the columnar epithelium (Ahrens, 1935b; Weesner, 1955). These do not appear to be present in *Reticulitermes hesperus* (Weesner, 1956). The vertical portion of the spermatheca joins a short duct (Fig. 4C) lined by a smooth, relatively thick laminated layer of chitin. This duct is enclosed in a muscular sheath. It runs posteriorly, paralleling the course of the paired oviducts, and opens in the roof of the genital chamber. In the more primitive forms such as *Incisitermes* (Browman, 1935) and *Neotermes* (Geyer, 1951), this opening appears to be a simple pore. In the Rhinotermitidae and the Termitidae, however, the opening may be extended posteriorly as a strongly chitinized arch in the roof of the genital chamber, the *spermathecal furrow* (Figs. 3, 4D). This structure (samenrinne) was noted by Holmgren (1909) in *Heterotermes tenuis* (Hagen). Although it was not specifically mentioned by many subsequent authors, it is suggested by figures of various species of Termitidae (Ahrens, 1935b; Browman, 1935; Geyer, 1951). It has been described in *Tenuirostritermes tenuirostris* and *Reticulitermes hesperus* (Weesner, 1955, 1956). In *R. hesperus* it is relatively short and has a sclerotized arch. The presence of such a furrow would appear to aid in the transfer of sperm from the outer genital chamber (Section II, E) to the spermatheca. On the other hand, the situation of the actual spermopore opposite the gonopore would seem to favor the fertilization of the eggs as they are extruded from the oviduct. *Reticulitermes hesperus* females fixed immediately after copulation had sperm in the spermathecal furrow (Weesner, 1956).

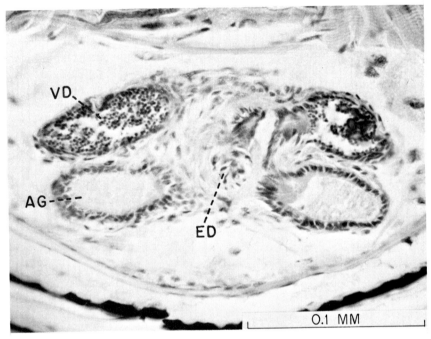

Fig. 4A

Fig. 4. *Reticulitermes hesperus.* A: Cross section of the abdomen of a male imago to show the bases of the vasa deferentia, filled with sperm, and the accessory glands. B: Cross section of a female imago immediately after copulation showing a mass of sperm in the outer genital chamber. Note the coagulum in which the sperm are suspended and the many inclusions. The spermatozoa are the small, deeply staining, regular spheres. C: Cross section of a female at the anterior end of the inner genital chamber showing the spermathecal duct (filled with sperm) and the common oviduct. D: Cross section at the posterior portion of the inner genital chamber showing the spermathecal furrow and the groove in the floor of the inner genital chamber. The intersternal fold separates the inner genital chamber from the anterior extension of the outer genital chamber. E: Section anterior to the genital chamber to show a portion of the spermatheca (containing sperm) and the paired oviducts which are enclosed in a common muscular sheath. (7, 9) Seventh and ninth sternites; (AD) duct of accessory gland; (AG) accessory gland; (ED) ejaculatory duct; (FB) fat body; (GR) groove in the floor of the inner genital chamber; (IG) inner genital chamber; (IF) intersternal fold; (OD) oviduct; (OG) outer genital chamber; (SD) spermathecal duct; (SF) sperma-thecal furrow; (S) sperm; (SP) spermatheca; (VD) vas deferens. (From Weesner, 1956; see pages 138-142.)

2. Sperm Storage

It is generally agreed that copulation is repeated throughout the life of the reproductives, although the frequency with which it occurs is not definitely known. There is some indication that copulation may be repeated more frequently in the more primitive species than in the more evolved forms. Thus Heath (1903) observed repeated copulations between pairs of *Zootermopsis* over a 12-month period. On the other hand, only an initial copulation was observed in a rather large series of pairs of *Reticulitermes hesperus* examined almost daily for over 7 months (Weesner, 1956). Parthenogenesis is known to occur rather readily in a few termite species, but it appears to be infrequent or absent in most (Chapter 8).

At the time of copulation, at least in *Reticulitermes*, the sperm are deposited in the outer genital chamber in a matrix which would appear to originate from the accessory gland (or seminal vesicle) of the males (Fig. 4B). Immediately after copulation sperm may be noted in the spermathecal furrow and the spermathecal duct, as well as the spermatheca proper, without the matrix in which they are suspended in the genital

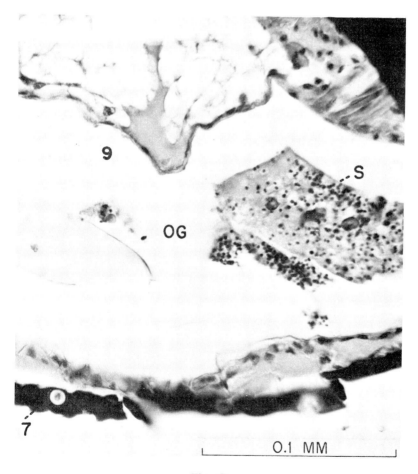

Fig. 4B

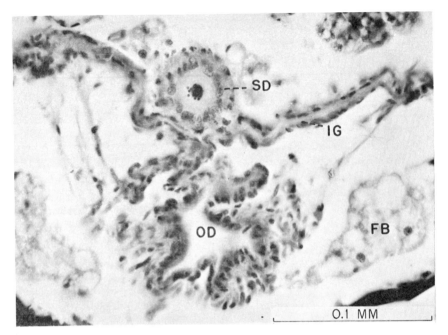

Fig. 4C

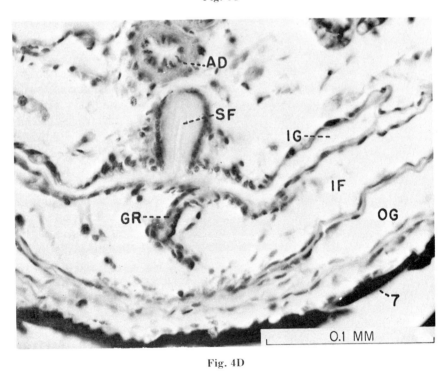

Fig. 4D

chamber. Sperm counts were made in *R. hesperus* immediately after copulation, and the maximum number observed was 9561, including those in all areas (Weesner, 1956). The maximum number counted in a single spermatheca was 5523. In the case of females which were isolated from males after the initial copulation as many as 1496 sperm were present 186 days after pairing and 156 days after the removal of the male. The counts in females with males were comparable at the same time, indicating that copulation had not yet been repeated. The pattern of egg development in these colonies indicated that the sperm from the initial copulation are functional for at least the first 6 months.

D. THE ACCESSORY GLANDS

The female accessory (colleterial) glands appear to be rather consistent throughout the Isoptera. The gland opens via a median pore in the roof of the outer genital chamber, lying between the dorsal valves when they are present (Figs. 2, 3, 5). There is a short, common, muscular canal which bifurcates into two arms, each of which divides into a number of narrow convoluted tubules. These apparently have a secretory function, and the lumen of the tubules may be more or less filled with a clear coagulum. The function of these glands in the Isoptera is not known. They serve a variety of functions in other insects.

E. THE GENITAL CHAMBER

The genital chamber of the female termite has been the subject of a series of studies (Knower, 1901; Holmgren, 1909; Imms, 1919; Crampton, 1920, 1923; Heberdey, 1931; Browman, 1935; Geyer, 1951; Weesner, 1955; Roonwal, 1955; McKittrick, 1964; and others). Many of these have been concerned with a single species or with a comparison of the genital chamber and associated structures of *Mastotermes darwiniensis* Froggatt with those of the roaches.

The genital chamber is clearly an invagination of the posterior, ventral intersegmental membranes of the abdomen. The eighth and ninth sternites are more or less reduced and are overlayed ventrally by the prolonged seventh sternite (Chapter 2). There are two rather distinct regions (Figs. 2, 3, 4). Posteriorly, there is a broad *outer genital chamber.* Anteriorly and dorsally there is a much narrower *inner genital chamber* into which open the spermatheca and the oviducts. The outer chamber has a more or less distinct ventral extension formed by the *intersternal fold,* which lies below the inner genital chamber (Figs. 2, 3, 4D). The opening of the accessory gland lies in the roof of the outer chamber,

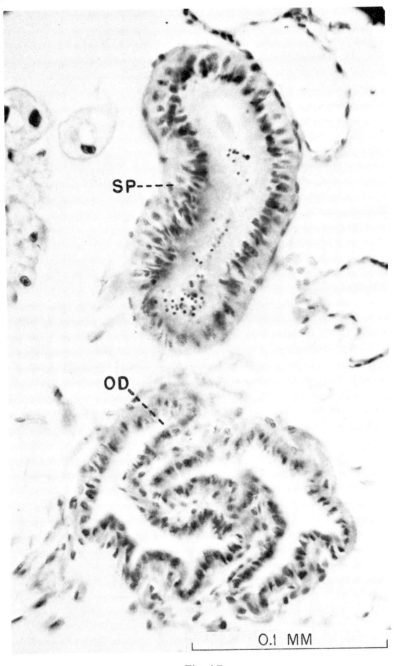

Fig. 4 E

immediately behind the opening of the inner chamber. In the Rhinotermitidae and the Termitidae the spermathecal furrow extends along
the dorsal midline of the inner genital chamber. There may be a fold in
the floor of this chamber, possibly allowing for its expansion when an
egg is extruded (Fig. 4D). The development of the intersternal fold and
the presence and importance of other structures varies from group to
group.

In *Mastotermes darwiniensis* the outer chamber is quite large and
resembles the vestibule of the roaches (Crampton, 1923; Browman,
1935). Both the floor and roof of the intersternal fold are well sclerotized.
A pair of well-developed ventral valves extend posteriorly from the sides
of the inner genital chamber (Fig. 5). These arise from well-developed
basivalvula. The opening of the accessory gland is flanked by a pair of
inner (internal) valves and subsequently by a pair of outer (dorsal)
valves. The gland opening is bordered anteriorly by a strongly chitinized
arch, the medisternite, and posteriorly by a smaller plate, the secondary
medisternite. The relatively complex, enlarged, outer genital chamber
in *Mastotermes* may be associated with the production of a cluster of
eggs arranged in a regular fashion similar to that in the ootheca of the
roaches (discussed in Volume II). This egg mass is not enclosed in a
capsule.

In *Zootermopsis angusticollis* the intersternal fold is also well sclerotized, but the ventral and basal valvula are greatly reduced from the
condition in *Mastotermes* (Browman, 1935) (Fig. 5). Dorsal valves are
absent. The mesosternite is present but reduced.

In most other species examined by Browman the intersternal fold is
membranous and not as well developed as in either *Mastotermes* or
Zootermopsis. When dorsal valves are present they are minute, and the
ventral valves have varying degrees of development but are never as
conspicuous as in *Mastotermes*. Usually, some remnants of the basivalve persist in the upper lateral margins of the inner genital chamber.

Holmgren (1909) did not recognize any intersternal fold in *Heterotermes tenuis*. He concluded that the gonopore, the spermatheca, and
the accessory gland all opened in the intersegmental membrane between
the seventh and eighth sternites. Imms (1919), from his studies of
Archotermopsis, concluded that the intersternal fold, the floor of the
inner genital chamber, and the gonopore were all situated on the eighth
abdominal segment and that the spermatheca and accessory glands were
associated with the ninth segment. The majority of the workers (Knower,
1901; Heberdey, 1931; Browman, 1935; Geyer, 1951; Weesner, 1955)
have concluded that the gonopore lies in the intersegmental membrane

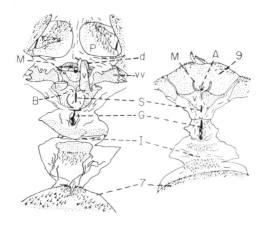

Fig. 5. Ventral view of a dissection of the genital chamber of a female of *Mastotermes darwiniensis* (left) and *Zootermopsis angusticollis* (right). The inner and outer genital chambers have been opened out so that the ventral structures (intersternal fold, gonopore) are now anterior to the structures of the roof of the chamber (openings of spermatheca and accessory gland) which they normally overlap. The ventral, dorsal, and inner valves have been removed from the left side of the sketch of *Mastotermes* to expose the horseshoe-shaped medisternite (M) and the small, sclerotized bar posterior to the opening of the accessory gland, the secondary medisternite (not lettered). (7, 9) Seventh and ninth sternites; (A) opening of accessory gland; (B) basivalve; (d) dorsal valve; (G) gonopore; (I) intersternal fold; (i) inner valve; (M) medisternite; (P) paraproct; (S) opening of spermatheca; (v) ventral valve; (vv) valvifer of eighth sternite (redrawn from Figs. 3 and 6, Browman, 1935).

between the seventh and eighth sternites; that the spermatheca is associated with the eighth sternite and the accessory glands with the ninth. This would seem to agree with Noirot's observations (1955) of various neuters of the Termitidae (Section IV).

III. THE PRIMARY MALE

The primary structures of the reproductive system of the male (Fig. 6A) are the paired testes lying to either side of the digestive system in the posterior region of the abdomen. From each testis there arises a vas deferens, which descends vertically and is inserted into a common, median ejaculatory duct. Accessory glands (or seminal vesicles) are present in the lower termites but appear to be absent in the Termitidae.

A. The Testes

The testes consist of a number of testicular lobes borne in a tight cluster at the ends of the paired vasa deferentia. There are usually between 7 and 10 lobes in each testis in the lower termites: 8—10 in *Archotermopsis* (Imms, 1919); 9 in *Kalotermes flavicollis* (Stella, 1938); 8 or 9 in *Reticulitermes lucifugus* (Jucci, 1924; Stella, 1938); and 7—9 in *Reticulitermes hesperus* (Weesner, 1956). In the Termitidae there is an increase in the number of testicular elements. Each testicular lobe is a compound structure with as many as 6 spermatic tubes, with those of each group opening into a small accessory chamber (the vas efferens) and subsequently into the vas deferens (Geyer, 1951; Weesner, 1955). As many as 50 spermatic tubes may be present in each testis, and there is a tendency for the ends of the tubes to be strongly recurved (Bugnion and Popoff, 1912; Bonneville, 1936; Geyer, 1951; Weesner, 1955).

The terminal portion of each testicular lobe consists of a mass of small, irregular, rather flattened and densely packed cells, among which dividing cells may be frequently noted (Fig. 7). The general appearance of this region is comparable to that of the germarium of the female. There is apparently no apical cell, as is encountered in the testis of some insects. Below the germarium the cells are rounded, or rather cuboidal, with round nuclei. They are arranged in groups or cysts, with all of the cells in a single cyst showing comparable stages of development. In the upper cysts the nuclei of the cells have a rather diffuse chromatin network. Other groups show typical meiotic prophase arrangements of the chromatin material, while some groups are undergoing meiotic division, with all of the cells in a cyst showing nearly identical stages (e.g., prophase or metaphase, etc.). In the basal portion of each spermatic tube lie cysts containing spermatids and spermatozoa. The cysts apparently break down and the spermatozoa are released into the vas deferens. In the case of both *Zootermopsis* (Stevens, 1905) and *Odontotermes redemanni* (Banerjee,

---

Fig. 6. *Reticulitermes hesperus.* A: Whole mount of the male reproductive system at the time of flight. The epithelial sheath has been removed from the testis on the right, showing the separate tubules. The membranous sheath which surrounds the ejaculatory duct has been extended. B and C: Accessory glands of males preserved about 70 days after copulation. Note the tremendous increase in size when compared with the alate at the time of flight as in A. D: Cross section of a male imago at the level of the testes and the vasa deferentia. E: Cross section of a male showing the condition of the accessory glands about 70 days after copulation. Note that they are filled with a clear coagulum. (AG) Accessory gland; (ED) ejaculatory duct; (S) sheath; (T) testis; (VD) vas deferens. (From Weesner, 1956; see pages 146-149.)

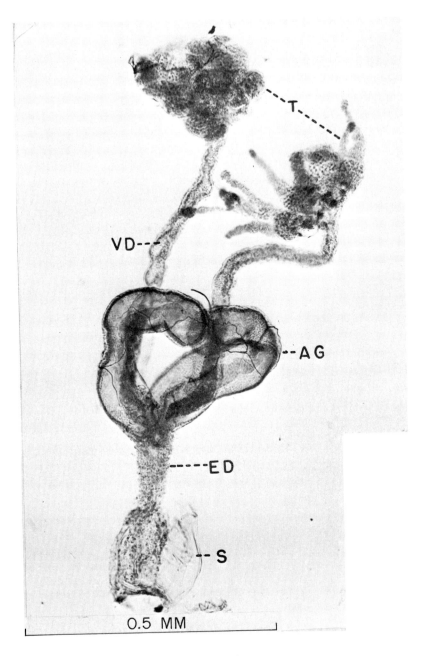

Fig. 6A

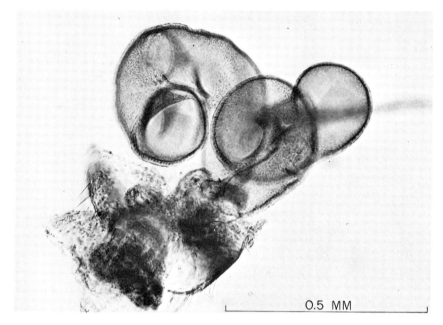

Fig. 6B

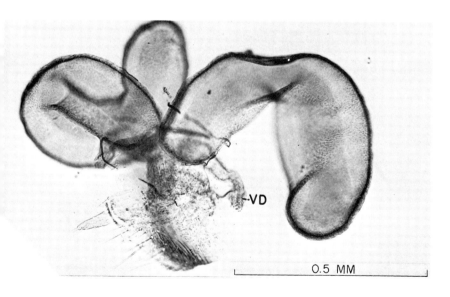

Fig. 6C

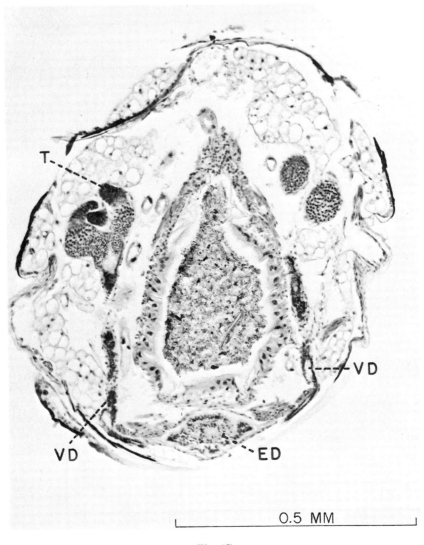

Fig. 6D

1961) sperm tetrads are formed since the division of the spermatocytes of the first order is not accompanied by a division of the cytoplasm of the cell.

Spermatogenesis has been described in varying detail for *Zootermopsis* (Stevens, 1905), *Kalotermes flavicollis* (Stella, 1938), *Reticulitermes fla-*

vipes (Benkert, 1930a,b, 1933), *Reticulitermes lucifugus* (Stella, 1936, 1938, 1939), *Reticulitermes hesperus* (Weesner, 1956), *Bellicositermes natalensis* (Grassé and Bonneville, 1936), *B. natalensis* and *Cubitermes fungifaber* (Grassé 1937), *Tenuirostritermes tenuirostris* (Weesner, 1955), and *Odontotermes redemanni* (Banerjee, 1961).

In addition to sperm which appear to be normal for the species, there are usually present abortive sperm, and entire cysts may undergo abnormal development (Jucci, 1924; Grassé and Bonneville, 1936; Grassé.

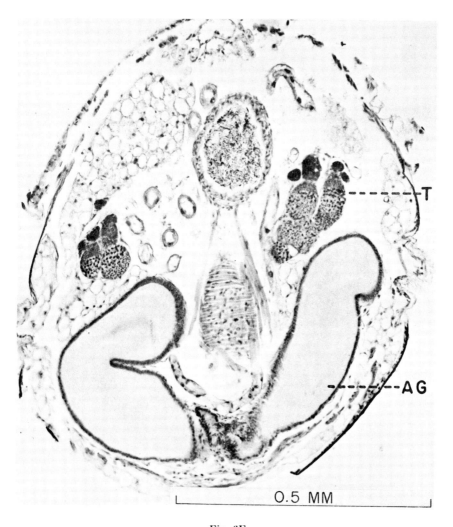

Fig. 6E

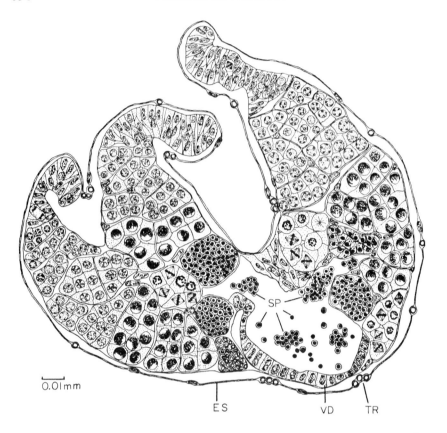

0.01mm

ES   VD   TR

Fig. 7.   Section of the testis of *Tenuirostritermes tenuirostris*. (See text for discussion.)
(ES) Epithelial sheath; (SP) spermatozoa; (TR) trachea; (VD) vas deferens (from Weesner,
1955).

1937; Stella, 1938; Weesner, 1955). Such aberrant sperm are more or
less numerous in the vas deferens, and Jucci (1924) concludes that these
constitute "sperm-nursing cells." In a number of species these cells
appear to be collected in the seminal vesicles (Section III, D).

B. THE SPERMATOZOA

The spermatozoa of most of the Isoptera are apparently nonflagellate.
There is a remarkable amount of confusion regarding this point. Grassi
and Sandias (1893–1894) indicated that the sperm in *Kalotermes flavicollis* have the form of a zinnia seed and are nonflagellate. Bugnion
and Popoff (1912) described the sperm in the Termitidae species they

examined as minute, round bodies lacking a flagellum. In a discussion of the achrestogonimes of *Glyptotermes parvulus* (Sjöstedt), Grassé and Bonneville (1935) remark that these earlier observations must have been in error since termites have typical flagellate spermatozoa. ("Les Termites ont des spermatozoides flagellés typiques . . . .") Later, however, Grassé (1949) states that the spermatozoa of the Isoptera are aberrant, lack a flagellum, and are immobile. It is evident that a considerable amount of variation occurs in the structure of the spermatozoa between the various termite families and that a critical comparative study of the spermatozoa is needed, particularly in the primitive groups.

Imms (1948) emphasizes that the sperm of *Archotermopsis wroughtoni* have the form usually encountered in insects, including a flagellum. The sperm also appear to be flagellated in *Zootermopsis* (Stevens, 1905; Weesner, unpublished). These two genera are both in the subfamily Termopsinae. *Kalotermes flavicollis* has sperm which are apparently nonflagellate and have the form of a zinnia seed (Grassi and Sandias, 1893 – 1894; Jucci, 1924; Stella, 1936, 1938) or of a flattened grain of barley (Grassé, 1949). Grassé indicates that such sperm in the Kalotermitidae vary from 12 to 20 μ in length. In the Rhinotermitidae and the Termitidae the sperm are minute round bodies, $1.5 - 4$ μ in diameter. They tend to be larger in the Rhinotermitidae and most minute in the Termitidae. They are nonflagellate and apparently immobile (see references regarding spermatogenesis).

It should be noted that the production of very small sperm by the male may be correlated with an increased egg-laying capacity on the part of the female. There may also be a correlation between the presence of a distinct spermathecal furrow in the female and the small, round, apparently immobile sperm produced by the male.

C. THE VASA DEFERENTIA

The paired vasa deferentia are simple tubes which apparently serve as areas of sperm storage as well as a means of conducting the spermatozoa from the testes to the ejaculatory duct. In the Termitidae the vasa deferentia may be considerably enlarged at the base. In *Archotermopsis wroughtoni*, Imms (1919) stated that the vasa deferentia join each other immediately before they are inserted into the anterior mid-dorsal portion of the ejaculatory duct. In all other species which have been studied, the vasa deferentia apparently enter the ejaculatory duct independently. Springhetti and Oddone (1963a) have described the arrangement of the vasa deferentia in a number of species. In *Mastotermes darwiniensis* (Mastotermitidae) the paired vasa deferentia curve through the projections of the accessory glands and open into the anterior region of the ejaculatory duct from the *ventral* side. In *Zootermopsis angusticollis* (Termopsinae) *Anacanthotermes ochraceus* (Burmeister) (Hodotermitinae) and *Kalotermes flavicollis* (Kalotermitidae) the ducts open from the *dorsal* side. This is also true in the Rhinotermitidae which have been examined: *Reticulitermes hesperus* (Weesner, 1956); *R. lucifugus, Psammotermes assuanensis* Sjöstedt, *Coptotermes sjöstedti* Holmgren, and *Schedorhinotermes javanicus* Kemner (Springhetti and Oddone, 1963b).

D. THE ACCESSORY GLANDS OR SEMINAL VESICLES

1. Structure

In the lower termites there are various structures associated with the male reproductive system which have been referred to by different authors as the accessory glands or seminal vesicles. Some confusion exists regarding the distinction between the ejaculatory duct and the accessory glands. Imms, Thompson, Weesner, and others have considered the structure into which the vasa deferentia open as the ejaculatory duct, which bears at its anterior region the paired accessory glands or seminal vesicles. Jucci and subsequent Italian workers have considered the structure into which the vasa deferentia open as the basal, common portion of the "seminal vesicles."

In *Mastotermes darwiniensis* Springhetti (1952) and Jucci and Springhetti (1952) indicated that the seminal vesicle is an ellipsoidal structure which bears sessile, cauliflowerlike glandular projections on its cephalic pole. Springhetti and Oddone (1963a) detailed the structure further and showed that in dorsal aspect the seminal vesicles are rather long, broad, paired structures with fingerlike projections at the cephalic pole. These projections arise in pairs from a very short, common trunk. In ventral aspect there is a pair of secondary trunks arising to the right and left almost immediately after the initial bifurcation (or base of the vesicle). These secondary trunks also bear fingerlike projections at their cephalic poles. The vasa deferentia pass from the dorsal to ventral surface between the primary and secondary trunks of the ventral side and are inserted immediately posterior to the initial bifurcation.

In *Archotermopsis wroughtoni* Imms (1919) describes the seminal vesicles as consisting of clusters of tubules arising from larger, paired basal tubes. The descriptions of the seminal vesicles in *Zootermopsis angusticollis* (Thompson, 1922; Child, 1934; Springhetti, 1953) indicate that they are similar to those of *Archotermopsis*, with small tubules arising from paired basal tubes. Springhetti and Oddone (1963a) found that the paired basal tubes give rise to a number of fingerlike tubules, each of which bifurcates about midpoint in its length. The basal tubes of the seminal vesicles are inserted on the *dorsal* surface of a rather distinct bulbous structure (ejaculatory duct?) into which the vasa deferentia also open. Jucci and Springhetti (1952) felt that *Masototermes, Archotermopsis,* and *Zootermopsis,* in that order, showed an evolutionary sequence.

In *Anacanthotermes ochraceus* (Hodotermitinae) the seminal vesicles consist of two basal trunks, each bearing numerous fingerlike tubules at the anterior pole. These tubules bifurcate several times in an irregular manner. Posteriorly, the two trunks unite to form a common chamber into which the vasa deferentia open (Springhetti and Oddone 1963a).

In *Kalotermes flavicollis* the seminal vesicles lack the fingerlike tubules at the cephalic pole and consist of two rather broad, sacklike structures (Jucci, 1924; Stella, 1938; Gelmetti, 1958). Springhetti and Oddone (1963a) indicate that the terminal portions of the vesicles have irregular, shallow, sacklike pockets. In this species the vasa deferentia enter the right and left seminal vesicles near the base.

In the Rhinotermitidae the seminal vesicles are simple, paired, elongated vesicles arising from the anterior margins of the ejaculatory duct ventral and immediately adjacent to the openings of the vasa deferentia (Figs. 4A, 6A). The accessory glands have been described in varying detail for *Reticulitermes lucifugus* (Grassi and Sandias, 1893 – 1894; Jucci, 1924); for *R. flavipes* (Kollar) (Thompson and Snyder, 1920); for *R. hesperus* (Weesner, 1956); and for *R. flavipes, R. lucifugus, R. hageni* Banks, *R. tibialis* Banks, and *R. hesperus* (Springhetti and Gelmetti, 1960). They have also been described in *Prorhinotermes simplex* (Hagen) (Thompson and Snyder, 1920) and for *Psammotermes assuanensis, Coptotermes sjöstedti,* and *Schedorhinotermes javanicus* (Springhetti and Oddone, 1963b). There is general agreement among these authors and in the different species regarding the general form and position of the accessory structures.

In the Termitidae there do not appear to be any structures which are comparable to the accessory glands of the lower termites. In the few Termitidae which have been studied, the basal portions of the vasa deferentia are more or less enlarged (Bonneville, 1936; Springhetti, 1952; Geyer, 1951; Weesner, 1955). These enlarged areas have been termed "seminal vesicles" by some of these authors. Apparently they serve as areas of sperm storage.

2. Function

There is general agreement that the various structures associated with the anterior portion of the ejaculatory duct in the male reproductive of the lower termites have a secretory function. Whether or not they serve as areas of sperm storage has not yet been resolved. Imms (1919) states that they do not contain sperm in *Archotermopsis*; Thompson (1922) states that they are not sperm storage sites in *Zootermopsis*; Springhetti (1952) indicated that the tubules in *Mastotermes* do not contain spermatozoa. Springhetti and Oddone (1963a) observed some sperm in the tips of the small tubules of *Mastotermes*, but they were not abundant. It has been pointed out (Weesner, 1955) that the close proximity of the openings of the accessory glands and the openings of the vasa deferentia might well account for the occasional presence of sperm in the accessory structures.

Jucci (1924) concluded that the seminal vesicles in *Kalotermes flavicollis* and *Reticulitermes lucifugus* represent areas of sperm storage. On one occasion he found a dense mass of spermatozoa, enclosed in a thin hyaline coat, within the seminal vesicle of *R. lucifugus*. He concluded that this was a spermatophore. Such a structure has not been described in related species, nor do I know of any other description of such a structure in the Isoptera. This may have been some artifact or unusual aggregation of sperm in the individual observed, and this problem should be reexamined.

The number of spermatozoa observed in the accessory glands of the species of *Reticulitermes* varies in different species. Weesner (1955) found that very few sperm were present in these structures in *R. hesperus*, either at the time of flight or after the individuals were well established in culture (Figs. 4A; 6B,C,D). The alates involved in this study were known to be sexually mature since other individuals, taken from the same colonies and flights, copulated, and sperm were transferred to the female and fertile eggs resulted.

In a comparative study of the seminal vesicles of various species of *Reticulitermes*, Springhetti and Gelmetti (1960) found that the numbers of sperms in the vesicles varied from species to species. Sperm were usually present in considerable numbers in alates of *Reticulitermes lucifugus* and *R. hageni*, but were few in *R. hesperus*, *R. tibialis*, and *R. flavipes*. In a later study of genera from other subfamilies of the Rhinotermitidae, Springhetti and Oddone (1963b) found that spermatozoa were commonly encountered in the vesicles in *Psammotermes assuanensis* and *Schedorhinotermes javanicus*, but not in *Coptotermes sjöstedti*.

In addition to the material which is apparently secreted by the accessory glands themselves, Jucci (1924) noted that the seminal vesicles contain various spherical inclusions, which he traced to the degenerative elements of the testes. These he termed sperm-nursing cells. He concluded that they might aid in maintaining the spermatozoa during the period when they are retained in the male. Subsequent studies of other species of termites have shown that such inclusions occur in varying abundance in the accessory structures in other groups of termites. It is generally agreed that they do not originate in the vesicles themselves.

The exact role of the accessory structures in the male reproductive necessitates much further study. It may be particularly profitable to study a sequence of individuals of a given species with known reproductive histories and ages. Thus in *R. hesperus* the accessory glands are well developed and filled with a clear coagulum (containing some spherical inclusions and a few sperm) at the time of flight. The primary concentration of spermatozoa in these individuals is in the vasa deferentia. At the time of copulation the contents of the accessory glands are apparently expelled along with the sperm from the vasa deferentia. The size of the glands is notably reduced. Following the initial copulation there is a very marked development of the glands so that by 70 days after flight they have more than doubled in size (Weesner, 1955; Fig. 6B,C). It would be interesting to know if this enlargement, following an initial copulation and establishment in the substrate, occurs in other species.

E. The Ejaculatory Duct

As has been noted earlier, the basal common tube into which the vasa deferentia open is considered by some to be the common portion of the accessory glands and by others as a distinct structure, the ejaculatory duct. The ejaculatory duct might be defined as a short, muscular tube into which open the vasa deferentia and (when they are present) the paired accessory structures. This duct may be rather bulbous anteriorly and narrow posteriorly. It opens via a medial pore at the posterior margin of the ninth sternite. The opening is usually described as a simple pore, and no sclerotized copulatory structures are present. However, Holmgren (1909) indicates that in *Rotunditermes rotundiceps* (Holmgren) the gonopore is situated on a papilla. A similar situation has been described by Geyer (1951) for *Hodotermes mossambicus* (Hagen). Roonwal (1956) indicates that these may represent a membranous penis. In *Tenuirostritermes tenuirostris* (Weesner, 1955) and *Reticulitermes hesperus* (Weesner, 1956) the gonopore is surrounded by an invagination of the intersegmental membrane, which forms a distinct sheath, suggesting that the proximal portion of the ejaculatory duct is actually a short, distendable penis (Fig. 6A). Such a structure may be more general than is now recognized.

IV. NEOTENICS AND NEUTERS

A. Neotenics

We have little data on the structure of the reproductive systems of replacement reproductives as compared with the primary reproductives. All indications are that the systems are comparable in individuals of the same species (Thompson and Snyder, 1920; Stella, 1938; Grassé and Bonneville, 1935; and others). It has been noted that the initial egg-laying rate of young neotenics may be greater than the initial egg-laying rate of young primary reproductives. However, as has been pointed out by McMahan (1962), these comparisons involve isolated pairs of primaries, on one hand, and groups of individuals, on the other. In this latter case it would be expected that reciprocal feeding might well effect the more rapid production of eggs by reproductives tended by their cohorts.

B. Neuters

Apparently the reproductive systems of nonfunctional individuals in the lower termites are relatively well developed as indicated by the studies of *Archotermopsis* (Imms, 1919); *Zootermopsis* (Heath, 1903, 1927; Thompson, 1922), and *Reticulitermes* and *Prorhinotermes* (Thompson and Snyder, 1920). The more recent studies of Springhetti and Oddone (1963a,b) also indicate that the reproductive systems of non-reproductive individuals in the lower termites are fairly well developed.

In the Termitidae, where there is a very early separation of the imago and neuter lines (Chapter 10), the gonads of the neuter individuals are very rudimentary (Noirot, 1955). Even in this family, however, at least some individuals in the neuter lines may become functional reproductives or ergatoids in some species. Generally, however, the replacement reproductives are nymphoids, developing from alate-line individuals. Noirot (1955, 1958) notes that in the female neuters of the Termitidae the incipient oviducts extend to the posterior margin of the seventh sternite. A minute rudimentary spermatheca is situated at the posterior portion of the eighth sternite, and a minute accessory gland just posterior to the ninth sternite. In the male neuters the incipient genital tract terminates at the posterior margin of the ninth sternite.

V. CONCLUSION

Although our information regarding the general structure of the reproductive systems of the Isoptera concerns only very few of the many existing species, it is evident that a marked evolution has occurred in the various groups. This evolution has affected the female and the male and involves both the germinal elements and the accessory structures. In the female there is a marked increase in the number of germinal elements, in the structure of the spermatheca, and in the structure of the genital chamber. In the male there is a notable variation in the number of germinal elements, in the structure of the spermatozoa, and in the form and presence or absence of accessory glands.

In addition to the need for purely descriptive comparative considerations of variations in and between different genera and species, there is an obvious need for precise studies of reproductives of a given species with different reproductive histories and of different ages. More detailed information is needed regarding the relative structures of imagoes and neotenics. Finally, the general physiology of the reproductives, the rate of egg production, the relationships between feeding and egg deposition, the storage of sperm in both the female and the male, etc., all call for further investigations.

REFERENCES

Ahrens, W. (1935a). Die entwicklung des "Corpus luteum" bei Insekten (nach Untersuchungen an *Termes redemanni*). *Z. Mikroskop.-Anat. Forsch.* 37, 467-500.

Ahrens, W. (1935b). Monographi des weiblichen Geschlechtsapparates der Termiten (nach Untersuchungen an *Termes redemanni*). *Jena. Z. Naturw.* 70, 223-302.

Banerjee, B. (1961). Chromosome morphology during the spermatogenesis of *Odontotermes redemanni* (Wasmann). *Caryologia* 14, 155-158.

Benkert, J. M. (1930a). Chromosomal study of *Reticulitermes flavipes*. *Proc. Penn. Acad. Sci.* 4, 1-3.

Benkert, J. M. (1930b). Chromosome number of the male of the first form reproductive of *Reticulitermes flavipes* Koll. *Proc. Penn. Acad. Sci.* 4, 97-99.

Benkert, J. M. (1933). Comparison of chromosomes of soldier and king of *Reticulitermes flavipes* Koll. *Proc. Penn. Acad. Sci.* 7, 121-122.

Bonneville, P. (1936). Recherches sur l'anatomie microscopique des termites. *Arvernia Biol.* 15, 1-127.

Browman, L. G. (1935). The chitinous structures in the posterior abdominal segments of certain female termites. *J. Morphol.* 57, 113-129.

Brunelli, G. (1904). Ricerche sull' ovario degli insetti sociali. *Atti Accad. Nazl. Lincei, Rend., Classe Sci. Fis., Mat. Nat.* [5] 12, 285 and 350-356.

Brunelli, G. (1905). Rulla struttura dell' ovario dei termitidi. *Atti Accad. Nazl. Lincei, Rend., Classe Sci. Fis., Mat. Nat.* [5] 15, 121-126.

Buchli, H. (1950). Recherches sur la fondation et le développement des nouvelles colonies chez le Termite lucifuge (*Reticulitermes lucifugus* Rossi). *Physiol. Comparata Oecol.* 2, 145-160.

Bugnion, E., and Popoff, N. (1912). Anatomie de la reine et du roi-termite (*Termes redemanii, obscuriceps* et *horni*). *Mem. Soc. Zool. France* 25, 210-231.

Castle, G. B. (1934). The damp-wood termites of Western United States, *Zootermopsis* (formerly, *Termopsis*). *In* "Termites and Termite Control" (C. A. Kofoid, ed.), 2nd ed., pp. 273-310. Univ. of California Press, Berkeley, California.

Child, H. J. (1934). The internal anatomy of termites and the histology of the digestive tract. In "Termites and Termite Control" (C. A. Kofoid, ed.), 2nd ed., pp. 58-88. Univ. of California Press, Berkeley, California.

Crampton, G. C. (1920). The terminal abdominal structures of the primitive Australian termite Mastotermes darwiniensis Froggatt. Trans. Roy. Entomol. Soc. London 68, Parts 1 and 2, 137-145.

Crampton, G. C. (1923). A comparison of the terminal abdominal structures of an adult alate female of the primitive termite Mastotermes darwiniensis with those of the roach Periplaneta americana. Bull. Brooklyn Entomol. Soc. 18, 85-93.

Gabe, M., and Noirot, C. (1961). Données histochimiques sur l'oogénèse chez les Termites. Bull. Biol. France Belg. 95, 411-425.

Gelmetti, B. L. (1958). Sul contenuto delle vescicole seminali di Calotermes flavicollis. Symp. Genet. Biol. Ital. 6, 48-54.

Geyer, J. W. C. (1951). The reproductive organs of certain termites with notes on hermaphrodites of Neotermes. Union S. Africa, Dept. Agr. Entomol. Mem. 2, 232-325.

Grassé, P.-P. (1937). La spermiogenése aberrante des Métatermitides. Compt. Rend. 204, 1677.

Grassé, P.-P. (1949). Ordre des Isoptères ou Termites. In "Traité de Zoologie," (P.-P. Grassé, ed.), Vol. IX, pp. 408-544. Masson, Paris.

Grassé, P.-P., and Bonneville, P. (1935). Les sexués inutilisés ou Achrestogonimes des Protermitides. Bull. Biol. France Belg. 69, 474-491.

Grassé, P.-P., and Bonneville, P. (1936). La spermatogénèse abortive ou atypique chez le Termite du Natal (Bellicositermes natalensis. Smeath). Compt. Rend. Soc. Biol. 122, 1009-1010.

Grassé, P.-P., and Noirot, C. (1958). La société de Calotermes flavicollis, de sa fondation au premier essaimage. Compt. Rend. 246, 1789-1795.

Grassi, B., and Sandias, A. (1893-1894). Costituzione e sviluppo della societa dei termitida. Atti. Accad. Gioenia Sci. Nat. Catania [4] 6 [13], 1-75; 7 [1], 1-76.

Harvey, P. A. (1934). Life history of Kalotermes minor. In "Termites and Termite Control" (C. A. Kofoid, ed.), 2nd ed., pp. 217-233. Univ. of California Press, Berkeley, California.

Heath, H. (1903). The habits of California termites. Biol. Bull. 4, 44 and 47-63.

Heath, H. (1927). Caste formation in the termite genus Termopsis. J. Morphol. Physiol. 43, 387-419.

Heberdey, R. F. (1931). Zur Entwicklungsgeschichte, vergleichenden Anatomie un Physiologie der weiblichen Geschlechtsausfuhrwege der Insekten. Z. Morphol. Oekel. Tiere 22, 416-586.

Holmgren, N. (1909). Termitenstudien. I. Anatomische untersuchungen. Kgl. Svegnska Vetenskapsakad. Handl. [3] 44, 1-215.

Imms, A. D. (1919). On the structure and biology of Archotermopsis, together with descriptions of new species of intestinal Protozoa and general observations on the Isoptera. Phil. Trans. Roy. Soc. London 209, 75-108.

Imms, A. D. (1948). "A General Textbook of Entomology," 7th ed., Dutton, New York.

Jucci, C. (1924). Sulla differeneziazione delle caste nella societa dei termitidi. I. Neotenici (Realie veri e neotenici—l'escrezione nei relai neotenici—la fisiologia e la biologia). Atti Accad. Nazl. Lincei, Mem., Classe Sci. Fis., Mat. Nat., Sez. III.ª [5] 14, 269-500.

Jucci, C., and Springhetti, A. (1952). Evolution of seminal vesicles in Isoptera. Trans. 9th Intern. Congr. Entomol. Amsterdam, 1951, Vol. 1, pp. 130-131.

Knower, H. McE. (1901). A comparative study of the development of the generative tract in termites. Bull. Johns Hopkins Hosp. 12, 135-138.

Light, S. F., and Weesner, F. M. (1947). Development of castes in higher termites. *Science* **106**, 244-245.

Light, S. F., and Weesner, F. M. (1955). The production and replacement of soldiers in incipient colonies of *Reticulitermes hesperus* Banks. *Insectes Sociaux* **2**, 347-354.

McKittrick, F. A. (1964). Evolutionary studies of cockroaches. *Cornell Univ., Expt. Agr. Sta. Mem.* **39**, 1-197.

McMahan, E. A. (1962). Laboratory studies of colony establishment and development in *Cryptotermes brevis* (Walker) (Isoptera: Kalotermitidae). *Proc. Hawaiian Entomol. Soc.* **18**, 145-153.

Noirot, C. (1955). Recherches sur le polymorphisme des Termites supérieurs (Termitidae). *Ann. Sci. Nat. Zool. Biol. Animale* [11] **17**, 399-595.

Noirot, C. (1958). Sur l'apparition de gonoductes hétérologues au cours du développement des Termites, des Blattes et des Orthopteres. *Proc. 10th Intern. Congr. Entomol., Montréal, 1956* Vol. 1, pp. 557-558.

Pickens, A. L. (1934). The biology and economic significance of the western subterranean termite *Reticulitermes hesperus. In* "Termites and Termite Control" (C. A. Kofoid, ed.), 2nd ed., pp. 157-183. Univ. of California Press, Berkeley, California.

Roonwal, M. L. (1955). External genitalia of termites (Isoptera). *J. Zool. Soc. India* **7**, 107-114.

Roonwal, M. L. (1956). 8. Isoptera. *In* "Taxonomist's Glossary of Genitalia in Insects" (S. L. Tuxen, ed.), pp. 34-38. Munksgaard, Copenhagen.

Sands, W. A. (1965). Alate development and colony foundation in five species of *Trinervitermes* (Isoptera, Nasutitermitinae) in Nigeria, West Africa. *Insectes Sociaux* **12**, 117-130.

Skaife, S. H. (1961). "Dwellers in Darkness." Doubleday, New York.

Snodgrass, R. (1935). "Principals of Insect Morphology." McGraw-Hill, New York.

Springhetti, A. (1952). Le vescicole seminali in *Mastotermes* e in *Macrotermes. Rend. 1st. Lombardo Sci. Lettere,* B**85**, 1-4.

Springhetti, A. (1953). Le vesciole seminali in *Zootermopsis* e in *Blattella. Rend. 1st. Lombardo Sci. Lettere* B**86**, 48-52.

Springhetti, A., and Gelmetti, L. (1960). Sull' apparato genitale maschile di *Reticulitermes. Insectes Sociaux* **7**, 377-382.

Springhetti, A., and Oddone, P. (1960). Sull' apparato genitale maschile di *Reticulitermes. Insectes Sociaux* **7**, 377-382.

Springhetti, A., and Oddone, P. (1963a). Funzionalita dell' apparto genitale maschile in caste diverse di alcune termite primitive. *Symp. Genet. Biol. Ital.* **11**, 311-334.

Springhetti, A., and Oddone, P. (1963b). Sugli organi genitali maschili del Rhinotermitidae (Isoptera). *Insectes Sociaux* **10**, 143-152.

Stella, E. (1936). Sulla maturazione delle gonadi nelle termiti italian. I. *Reticulitermes lucifugus.* II. *Calotermes flavicollis. Boll. Soc. Ital. Biol. Sper.* **11**, 731-734.

Stella, E. (1938). Richerche citologiche sui neutri e sui riproduittori delle termiti Italiane. (*Calotermes flavicollis* e *Reticulitermes lucifugus.) Atti Accad. Nazl. Lincei, Rend., Classe Sci. Fis., Mat. Nat.* **7**, 1-30.

Stella, E. (1939). Studi sulle termiti. I. Comportamento citologica delle gonadi in operai di *Reticulitermes lucifugus. Rev. Biol. Colon., Roma* **2**, 81-95.

Stevens, N. M. (1905). Studies in spermatogenesis with special reference to the accessory chromosomes. *Carneigie Inst. Washington, Publ. No. 36*, pp. 1-32.

Thompson, C. B. (1922). The castes of *Termopsis. J. Morphol.* **36**, 115-132.

Thompson, C. B., and Snyder, T. E. (1920). The "third form," the wingless reproductive type of termites: *Reticulitermes* and *Prorhinotermes. J. Morphol.* **34**, 591-633.

Weesner, F. M. (1955). The reproductive system of young primary reproductives of *Tenuirostritermes tenuirostris* (Desneux). *Insectes Sociaux* **2**, 321-345.

Weesner, F. M. (1956). The biology of colony foundation in *Reticulitermes hesperus* Banks, *Univ. Calif.* (Berkeley) *Publ. Zool.* **61**, 253-314.

Wigglesworth, V. B. (1950). "The Principles of Insect Physiology." Methuen, London.

Williams, R. M. C. (1959a). Flight and colony foundation in two *Cubitermes* species (Isoptera, Termitidae). *Insectes Sociaux* **6**, 203-218.

Williams, R. M. C. (1959b). Colony development in *Cubitermes ugandensis* Fuller (Isoptera, Termitidae). *Insectes Sociaux* **6**, 291-304.

6

Nervous System and Sense Organs*

GASTON RICHARD

I. CENTRAL NERVOUS SYSTEM

The general plan of the central nervous system of the termites is like that of other insects having a diffuse chain of ganglia. The cerebral ganglia and the subesophageal ganglion are contained in the cephalic capsule, and there are three thoracic ganglia and six abdominal ganglia. In addition, nerves belonging to the sympathetic system are attached to the central nerve chain.

A. CEREBRAL GANGLIA

1. Position and General Form (Figs. 1 and 2)

The cerebral ganglia are composed of the usual three parts recognized in other insects: protocerebrum, deutocerebrum, and tritocerebrum. The protocerebrum is associated with the eyes and the deutocerebrum with the antennae. The cerebral ganglia are located in the superior half of the cephalic capsule, of which they occupy a greater or lesser part, according to the caste or age of the individual. In young larvae of the reproductive

---

*The author expresses his deep gratitude to Mina Parsont and Frances M. Weesner for their fine translation from the French manuscript.

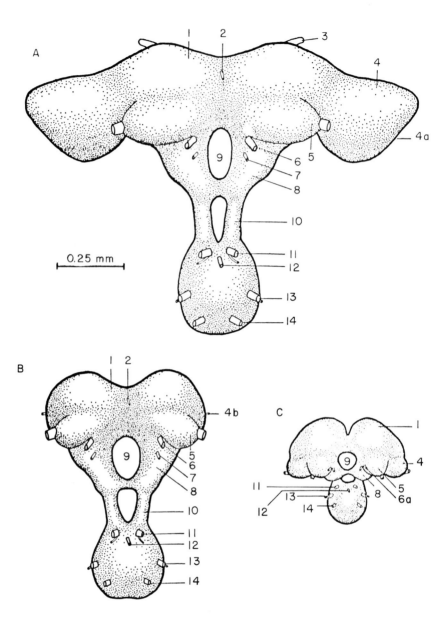

Fig. 1. Reconstruction of the supra and subesophageal ganglia. A: Front view winged sexual; B: small soldier; C: first larval instar. (1) Protocerebrum; (2) connective nerve; (3) ocellar nerve; (4) optic lobe; (4a) entrance surface of the optic filaments; (4b) rudimentary eye nerve; (5) deutocerebrum with antennal nerve; (6) frontolabral nerve; (6a) labral nerve (right) and frontal nerve (left) separated; (7) esophageal nerve; (8) tritocerebrum; (9) esophageal foramen; (10) esophageal connective; (11) mandibular nerve; (12) hypopharyngeal nerve; (13) maxillary nerve; (14) labial nerve [taken from Hecker (1966); translated by Dr. Kumar Krishna].

line the ganglia have a relatively large volume whereas in mature soldiers they have a relatively small volume. In the case of the nasutes, the cerebral ganglia are particularly compressed and deformed. The absolute volumes of the brains of *Bellicositermes bellicosus* (Smeathman) are similar in minor and major workers and minor soldiers, notwithstanding the different sizes of the heads (Hecker, 1966).

In general, the posterior part of the cerebral ganglia forms two convexities, slightly separated on the median line. The anterior part is slightly flattened and tilts in relation to the plane of the labium. This inclination varies with individuals of different castes. In *Kalotermes flavicollis* (Fabricius) (Vincent, 1964; Richard, 1967) the ganglia of the larvae, like those of the soldiers, are inclined at about 30° to the horizontal plane. The labium of the soldier, however, is parallel to the horizontal plane, whereas that of the larva is slanted in relation to the plane of the ganglia.

The posteroventral part of the cerebral ganglia is in contact with the digestive tube, especially in young individuals. In the older individuals there is a tendency for the ganglia to be more upright.

In the nasute soldiers the enormous development of the frontal gland may bring about a forward and ventral tipping of the brain and a lateral displacement of the symmetrical, ventrolateral portions (Zuberi, 1963).

Few precise evaluations of the volumes of the cerebral ganglia have been carried out on termites; only those of Hanström (1930) on *Zootermopsis nevadensis* (Hagen) and of Hecker (1966) on *Bellicositermes bellicosus* (planimetric evaluations) and those of Richard (unpublished) and Vincent (1964) on *Kalotermes flavicollis* (volumetric measurements based on reconstruction) will be considered here. Table I shows the general agreement of these evaluations which bring out the following points: the size of the cerebral ganglia increases during the course of development; the volume of the brain of mature soldiers is greater than that of individuals of the same age in the reproductive line; and, the pedunculate bodies show a consistent relative volume when compared with the volume of the total cerebral ganglia regardless of the species.

2. The Pedunculate Bodies (see Fig. 3)

In all the Isoptera the pedunculate bodies attain a considerable volume, which has often been related to their social habits. The structure of these bodies in the Isoptera, however, is far from that attained in the social Hymenoptera.

a. The Globuli Cells. The globuli cells are the characteristic neurons of the pedunculate bodies. They are situated in the dorsolateral region

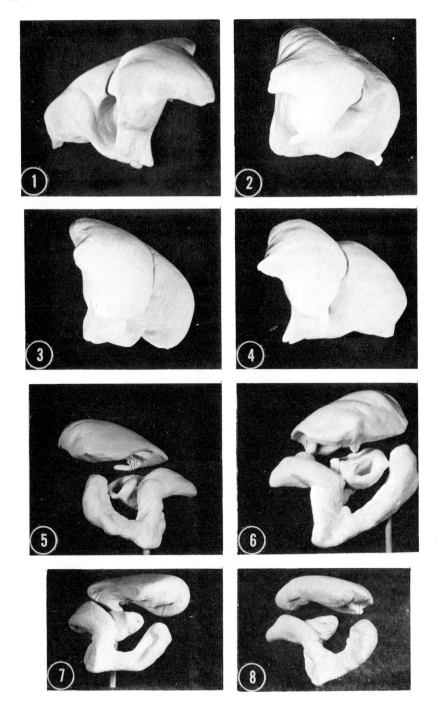

TABLE I

VOLUMETRIC EVALUATIONS OF THE CEREBRAL GANGLIA OF TWO SPECIES OF TERMITES

Species	Type of individual	Total volume of cerebral ganglia (mm³)	Percentage of total volume			
			Visual center	Antennal center	Pedunculate body	Central body
Zootermopsis	Nymph of soldier	0.109	12.2	11.7	31.4	0.6
nevadensis	Nymph of sexual	0.112	16.0	11.0	29.0	0.6
	Alate	0.129	14.1	12.8	28.0	0.6
Kalotermes	IX Stage soldier	0.0395			25.4	
flavicollis	VII Stage nymph	0.0276			23.1	
	V Stage soldier	0.0206			26.0	
	IV Stage larva	0.0219			26.1	

of the protocerebrum. They form two more or less contiguous symmetrical groups according to the species and the caste and are slightly raised from the surface of the cerebral ganglia. As in other insects, the cells are small, they have little cytoplasm, and their nuclei are strongly chromatic.

In *Kalotermes flavicollis* the globuli cells form a single mass in which no distinct groups can be recognized. However, Thompson (1916) describes three masses of cells successively enveloping a central point in *Reticulitermes flavipes* (Kollar). Zuberi (1963) also describes three poorly defined masses of globuli cells in *Trinervitermes oceonomus* (Tragärdh) (as *T. tchadensis*).

b. The Calyces. There are two pairs of calyces which are formed by the synaptic zone of the dendrites of the globuli cells and the processes of the axons and dendrites of other neurons. Each pair of calyces is tightly joined, side by side. In *Kalotermes flavicollis* they are inclined dorsoventrally and are flattened in the plane of this inclination. The walls of these calyces (synaptic glomeruli) are not very thick. The opening of each calyx is directed toward the superior face, whereas

---

Fig. 2.   Reconstruction of 1–4: the cerebral ganglia; 5–8: the peduculate bodies with the fibrous portion separated from the globuli cells. In each instance the reconstruction is shown in anterolateral aspect from the side indicated and the most complete reconstruction has been utilized. 1, 5: Seventh stage nymph, left aspect; 2, 6, ninth stage soldier, right aspect; 3, 7: fourth stage larva, right aspect; 4, 8: fifth stage soldier right aspect.

the bundle of axial fibers, forming the base of the peduncle, leave the calyces by an inferior orifice.

c. *The Pedunculus.* The pedunculus, or stalk, is formed primarily by the axons of the globuli cells. It penetrates deeply into the cerebral mass along the external, lateral edge of the protocerebrum. It then bends toward the saggital plane. Its distal extremity lies a little behind the posterior part of the deutocerebrum. At this level the bundle of fibers divides into two groups recrossing the protocerebral mass: the α lobe and the β lobe (terminology after Vowles).

d. *The α Lobe [Rameau (Racine) Anterieur, Cauliculus, Anterior Root, Obere rucklaufige Wurzel].* In the nymphs of *Kalotermes flavicollis* the α lobe has a broad base and arises from the pedunculus in an almost perpendicular plane. It extends toward the posterodorsal part of the protocerebrum while remaining anterior to the plane of the calyces. When it reaches the dorsal surface, this lobe bends abruptly toward the exterior, forming a very pronounced elbow. This portion is thickened anteroposteriorly and flattened along its large axis. It lies very close to the anterior wall of the calyces, although no actual connection can be detected. The distal extremity of the α lobe reaches the laterodorsal surface of the cerebral ganglia and terminates along the nerve cells of the anterior face of the dorsal part of the protocerebrum. At this level this distal extremity curves slightly ventrally. In addition to the fibers coming from the pedunculus, the α lobe receives bundles from the protocerebrum, as is the case with many insects. In *Trinervitermes oceonomus* (Zuberi, 1963) the α lobe is largely arcuate and bends at the level of the brain surface near the globuli. This secondary curve, preceding the distal curve, may be characteristic of the Termitidae.

e. *The β Lobe [Rameau (Racine) Interne, Balken, Posterior Root, Untere rucklaufige Wurzel].* The β lobe comes off of the pedunculus at the same level as the α lobe, but it remains in the plane of the stalk, that is, in the ventral part of the protocerebral lobe. It extends directly toward the sagittal plane, thus approaching the lobe from the opposite side. The two portions then proceed, parallel to each other, toward the posterior region of the cerebral ganglia. They pass ventral to the central body and the posterodorsal commissure. Slightly behind the protocerebral commissure, the sagittal edge of each lobe folds back slightly toward the dorsal region. This must not be mistaken for the tubercules of the central body, which are distinct and appear as two small protuberances on the ventral face of the corpus centrale and lodge in the groove formed by the fold of the β lobe's edge.

Beyond the posteriodorsal commissure, the β lobe bends abruptly upward while tilting toward the exterior and approaching the internal edge of the internal calyx. Its rounded, distal extremity is situated behind the posterior part of the calyces and terminates at the level of the globuli cells, although no fibrous connections are seen at this level. However, at the initial portion of its passage it is joined by numerous fibers, most of which arise from the protocerebrum. Some variation in detail was observed in different species studied by Zuberi (1963).

f. Variations in Different Castes. The morphological differences in the pedunculate bodies between individuals of different castes are not very marked. However, actual size does vary with the castes (Table I). In *Reticulitermes flavipes*, Thompson (1916) reported that the workers have the largest pedunculate bodies, the soldiers the smallest, and the pedunculate bodies of the nymphs are intermediate in size. However, these observations do not agree with those of Holmgren (1909), or those of von Rosen (1913) on *Kalotermes* and *Reticulitermes*. We have found that although few differences exist in *Kalotermes flavicollis* between the young larvae stage and the stage V soldiers, the stage IX soldiers have pedunculate bodies which have a greater volume than those of stage VII nymphs. In addition, Zuberi (1963) states that in *Trinervitermes oceonomus* similarities exist between workers and nymphs, but the small workers' pedunculate bodies are less inclined than those of the large workers, which, in turn, are less inclined than those of the nymphs. Furthermore, the α lobe of the small workers is curved further toward the back than it is in the larger workers. The β lobe forms a less obtuse angle with the pedunculus in the workers than in the nymphs.

In the soldiers Zuberi describes fissures in the pedunculus which are not thought to be histological artifacts since they are always present. A major difference lies in the precise position of the pedunculus in the protocerebrum of the soldier. The pedunculus of the soldier curves in a direction opposite to that of the nymphs and workers. This is more conspicuous in the large soldier than in the small soldier. Furthermore, the α lobe is oriented much more toward the back, and its compressed distal portion forms a crease; the β lobe gets much closer to the central body and bends in the shape of an S at its junction with the pedunculus. In other termites studied by Zuberi, the differences usually involve the curvature of the pedunculus or the lobes, and these are most frequently accentuated in the case of the workers. Hecker (1966) describes the ontogeny of the corpora pedunculata of *Bellicositermes bellicosus:* a small group of neuroblasts is present in the brain of the first instar larva; they divide and establish the globuli cells, which are quite similar in different castes.

3. The Corpus Centrale or Central Body

The central body is located in the middle region of the cerebral ganglia. It is relatively well-developed and resembles that of the ants or bees. It consists of two parts: a concave dorsal portion, composed of radial groups of fibers and synapses, and a flattened ventral portion. Two small protuberances are present on the ventral face, which have been interpreted by Thompson (1916) as being dependent on the β lobes of the pedunculate body. These are, in reality, an associated region, namely the "tubercules of the central body." Few differences have been noted in this structure in the different castes.

4. The Accessory Lobes (Copora Ventralis, Nebenlappen)

The accessory lobes are situated in the ventro-lateral region of the protocerebrum, very close to the pedunculate bodies and near the antennal glomeruli. In the nymphs of *Trinervitermes* they are linked by a slightly curved commissure. In the soldiers this commissure is strongly curved. The degree of separation of the accessory lobes from the protocerebral mass may vary with different species.

5. The Fiber Tracts (Fig. 3)

Few studies have been carried out on the bundles of fibers which pass through the protocerebrum. However, on the basis of the works of Holmgren (1909), Hanström (1940), Zuberi (1963), and Hecker (1966) it is possible to designate the following:

1. An optical globuli tract which connects the internal medulla of the optic lobes with the lateral part of the calyces of the pedunculate bodies. It is recognizable in the nymphs and imagoes; poorly developed or not recognizable in workers or soldiers.

2. An olfactory globuli tract that connects the deutocerebrum to the median part of the calyces.

3. A tract connecting the accessory lobes of the central body to the median part of the calyces.

4. A tract connecting the deutocerebrum to the central body.

5. A crossed tract, linking the tritocerebrum to the protocerebral zone, which is enclosed in the curve of the α lobes of the pedunculate bodies.

6. Diverse tracts connecting the protocerebral and deutocerebral areas with one another and with the subesophageal ganglion.

In addition, six commissures connect the right and left sides of the different regions of the cerebral ganglia:

1. A superior-anterior commissure which passes above the central body in the anterior region and links the lateral protocerebral lobes as

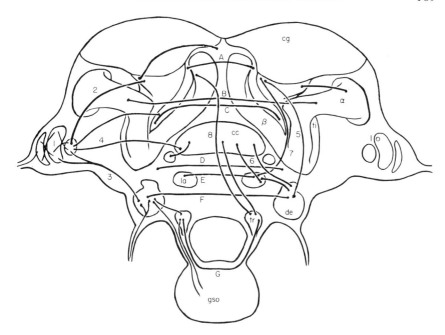

Fig. 3. Schematic representation of the main centers and fiber tracts of the cerebral ganglia of the termites (synthetized from the works of authors mentioned in the text). (cc) Corpus centrale; (cg) globuli cells; (de) deutocerebrum; (gso) subesophageal ganglion; (la) accessory lobe; (lo) optic lobe; (ti) stalk of the pedunculate body; (tr) tritocerebrum; (α) α lobe; (β) β lobe; (1) optic chiasmata; (2) optic globuli tract; (3) optic deutocerebral tract; (4) optic central tract; (5) olfactory globuli tract; (6) olfactory central tract; (7) accessory lobe-calyx tract; (8) prototritocerebral crossed tract; (A) superior-anterior commissure; (B) posterodorsal tract; (C) commissure of the α lobes; (D) ventral commissure; (E) commissure of the secondary lobes; (F) deutocerebral commissure; (G) tritocerebral commissure.

well as, perhaps, the optic lobes. It is often more arched in the soldiers than in the workers.

2. A posterior-dorsal commissure which passes behind the central body and forms a bridge (the protocerebral bridge) between the posterior ventral lobes.

3. A ventral commissure which goes behind and against the central body, joining the two ventral parts of the protocerebrum.

4. The commissure of the secondary lobes.

5. The deutocerebral commissure, connecting the two antennal lobes.

6. The tritocerebral commissure, connecting the right and left portions of the tritocerebrum.

6. The Optic Lobes

The optic lobes exhibit the greatest diversity of any portion of the cerebral ganglia during the course of development and in the different castes. They are always situated laterally, in contact with the protocerebral lobes, but are well developed only in the imagoes. At their maximum development, three masses can be recognized. These are the lamina ganglionaris and the external and internal medulla. Each consists of a cellular cover, enclosing fibrous bundles and synaptic glomeruli. The optic lobes are connected to each other by the two external-internal chiasmata, to the compound eyes by posterior retinal fibers which issue from the retinal cells and penetrate the lamina ganglionaris, and to the protocerebrum by a group of fibrous bundles making up the optic nerve.

In *Anacanthotermes ochraceus* (Burmeister) (Zuberi, 1963) the optic lobes of the workers are more developed than those of the nymphs. These termites have diurnal activities, but the morphological and behavioral facts are not necessarily connected.

In nymphs with long wing pads of *Reticulitermes flavipes*, the lamina ganglionaris is narrow and elongated in the dorsoventral direction, the external medulla is the most important of the three masses, and the internal medulla is closely associated with the protocerebral lobe. These structures are smaller in nymphs with short wing pads but have the same general form. These areas are less pronounced in the workers and even smaller in the soldiers, whose eyes are vestigal.

In *Kalotermes flavicollis* (Richard, 1950a) the development of the optic lobes parallels that of the eye. In the first larval stage the optic lobes are mixed with the protocerebral mass. It is only in the second and particularly in the third stages that the lobes themselves, and a fibrous mass giving rise to the optic nerve, are organized. In the fourth stage this mass is divided into a distal and proximal portion. The definitive organization into three optical masses is recognizable at the beginning of the fifth larval stage. In the old imagoes or the neotenic sexuals, the volume of the optic lobe diminishes due to a considerable regression of the fibrous tracts. The optic nerve follows the same regression.

The Ocellar Centers. In *Reticulitermes flavipes* the ocellar nerves penetrate the protocerebral lobes just above the anterior roots of the pedunculate bodies. They then follow a course posteriorly, and finally enter, via the dorsal surface of the protocerebral lobes, just in back of the dorsal protocerebral commissure. They disappear at this level, but Zuberi (1963) describes fibers reaching the antennal lobes in *Trinervitermes*.

These structures do not exist in the soldiers and workers.

7. The Deutocerebrum

The antennal lobes are ventral to the protocerebral lobes, and they are not very noticeable at the surface of the cerebral ganglia. Their structure is similar to that in other insects. Their size is not very different in the different castes. However, there is a slightly greater development in workers than in other individuals. The deutocerebral commissure is more concave in the soldiers than in the nymphs in *Trinervitermes*. There is general agreement among various authors regarding the relative homogeneity of the antennal region of the cerebral ganglia, as opposed to the great heterogeneity of the optic regions. It is possible to relate this situation to the behavior of the Isoptera. In these insects vision plays a very minor role in comparison to that of olfactory or tactile sensibility.

The nerves of the antennae are mixed nerves whose ventral motor element innervates the muscles of the antennal base. Zuberi (1963) traces these fibers to the subesophageal ganglion. Each sensory nerve is made up of the union of two branches in the scape. These are formed by the juxtaposition of the axons of the sensory cells corresponding to the group of external or internal sensilla described in the Section II, B.

8. The Tritocerebrum

In general, the tritocerebrum is not very conspicuous on the surface of the cerebral ganglia. The lobes are distinct from the olfactory lobes in many termites, but they are almost always associated with them in *Ancistrotermes latinotus* (Holmgren) and *Bellicositermes natalensis* (Haviland) (Zuberi, 1960, 1963). Hecker describes the connections in *Bellicositermes bellicosus* between the tritocerebron and protocerebral lobe, corpus centralis, mushroom bodies (indirect), deutocerebron, and subesophageal ganglion, and illustrates the frontal ganglion and its relations to the other parts of the brain. The two labial nerves emerge from the tritocerebral part.

B. VENTRAL NERVE CHAIN

1. The Subesophageal Ganglion

This ganglion has never been described very precisely. Zuberi (1963) however, has found a link between the subesophageal ganglion and the deutocerebral motor roots. Hecker (1966) adds some indications about the nerves of mouth parts and the ontogeny of this ganglion. The periesophageal ring closely encircles the esophagus. According to Feytaud (1912) the salivary canals pass to the exterior of the ring.

The nerves of the buccal area are derived from the subesophageal ganglion. There is a single hypopharyngeal nerve, which divides soon after its entry into the hypopharynx. Two systemic mandibular nerves branch out from the base of the mandibles. There are two pairs of maxillary nerves (a small nerve serving the base of the maxillae and a large nerve sending out branches in the various segments) and two pairs of labial nerves (a small one serving the base of the labium and a large one which sends out many branches to the extremity of the labial segments).

2. The Ventral Nerve Chain Proper

a. *Thoracic Portion.* The thoracic portion of the ventral nerve chain is composed of three ganglia typical of the insects' thorax. The internal structure of these ganglia has not been studied, but the nerves which are derived from them or enter them have been detailed by Pierre Duplessix (1964) and Richard (unpublished data) in *Kalotermes flavicollis*.

In addition to the sensory cuticular nerves or the motor nerves innervating the segmental muscles (these nerves are similar to those described elsewhere in the chapter), each thoracic ganglion sends out two pairs of nerves which proceed to the corresponding legs. In the imagoes the mesothoracic and metathoracic ganglia send out a pair of wing nerves.

The leg receives a small, composite anteroventral nerve which innervates different muscles of the coxa, trochanter, and femur, as well as the sensory organs of the anterior zones of the same joints. It terminates before the articulation of the femur and tibia. The main nerve, which arises from the lateroventral region of the ganglion, is also a composite nerve which innervates the majority of the muscles of the legs. It divides into numerous branches which serve all the sensory organs (see Section II, B) and terminates at the extremity of the tarsus.

This plan of innervation is recognizable in the first stage larvae of *Kalotermes*, but the number of ramifications of the nerves is relatively small. The number increases rapidly up to the fifth stage, at which time, and after which time, the definitive structure is recognizable (Denis, 1958a). The major lines of this innervation are the same in the different castes.

The wing nerves arise from the ganglia in the anterodorsal area (posterior and dorsal to the exit of the interganglionic connectives). An intercalary branch of the connective joins the wing nerve and innervates some longitudinal ventral muscles anteriorly. Each wing nerve supplies motor branches and is divided into a median branch, which innervates the major part of the tergite, and a dorsal branch, which twists around the transverse trachea and is divided into branches just before penetrating into the wing. The dorsal branch gives rise to the subcostal branch (innervating the tegular organs and the subcostal and costal bristles), the radial branch (divided in the wing into radial branch proper and the radial sector branch), the median branch (not very divided), and the cubitoanal branch (which branches out on the posterior side of the wing) (Fig. 4).

In stage II* larvae in *Kalotermes*, it is possible to distinguish the wing nerves, but the four branches are grouped by twos: the subcostal and radial, on the one hand, and the median-cubitoanal, on the other. The first two short nerves innervate the sensory bristles of the anterior region of the tergite. The other two, which are longer, extend toward the postero-lateral region where they innervate about twenty bristles. At stage III the distal extremity of the radial nerve shifts toward the posterior region, and the median and cubital nerves are still relatively conspicuous. At stage V the end of the radial nerve reaches the extreme lateroposterior regions of the wing sheath, which is beginning to become visible. The cubitoano-median nerve gives rise to the anal branch. In stage VII the tegular nerve and one costal branch appear and the cubital nerve becomes branched. In the case of regressive molting the nerves lose much of their rigidity, and the areas they serve become reorganized. In stage VIII the subcostal nerve is reduced; the radial nerve is regressed toward the anterior part of the tergite; the roots of the median and cubital nerves are less distinct; and the anal nerve serves a rather extensive field.

In *Reticulitermes*, Fudalewicz-Niemczyk and Richard (1965) found that the general plan is comparable to that of *Kalotermes*, although some differences appear in the organogenesis of the nervous system of the wing in the workers and the soldiers, on one hand (the subcostal nerve never reaches the posterior region of the tergite), and the nymphs, on the other hand (the subcostal nerve becomes elongated toward the extremity of the tergite although remaining shorter than the radial nerve). In *R. lucifugus* the separation between the castes is clearly marked in the third stage of development. In all the termites studied the costal and radial fields of the wing take shape starting with the anterolateral region of the tergites, whereas the posterolateral region of the same tergites supply the median and cubital fields. The anterior part of the tergite revolves around the posterior part. This is demonstrated by the fact that the middle branch of the thoracic nerve does not move in either the case of development or in the case of regression. The nerves seem to play an important role in these phenomena, serving particularly as leaders for the development of the trachea.

---

*In the case of *Kalotermes* and as used in this chapter, a stage II larvae is comparable to a second instar individual, a stage III to a third instar individual, etc. (editors).

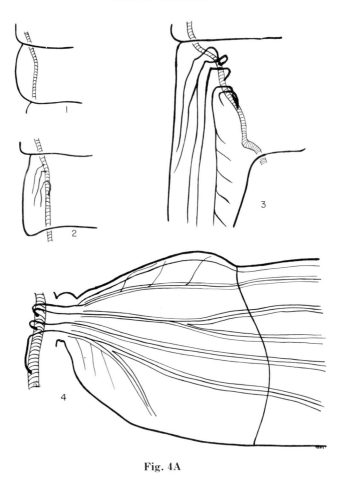

Fig. 4A

Fig. 4. Development of the wing region in *Kalotermes flavicollis*. Only the lateral sides of the tergites of the larvae are represented. The trachea are shown in A; the nerves in B. Drawings prepared from original preparations with methylene blue. 1: Larva of the first stage; 2: larva of the fifth stage; 3: young nymph of the seventh stage; 4: wing base of the imago.

b. Abdominal Portion. The abdominal portion of the ventral nerve chain includes six pairs of clearly separated ganglia located in the central portion of the sternites. The first five ganglia correspond to the first five abdominal segments. The last one results from the fusion of the ganglia belonging to segments seven through eleven.

Each ganglion of *Zootermopsis angusticollis* (Hagen) (Richard, unpublished data; Pierre Duplessix, 1964) emits two pairs of lateral nerves.

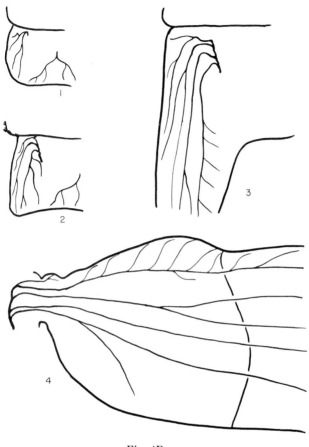

Fig. 4B

The anterior nerves come out posterodorsally from the ganglion in relation to the connectives. Soon after their origin they divide into two branches, A_1 and A_2. The A_1 nerve runs transversely through the sternite, forms a plexus with a branch of the median nerve, and reaches the lateral side of the tergite after crossing the pleural region without branching. It then innervates the sensilla of the lateral and posterior sides of the tergite. The A_1 branch is divided into two branches: one motor, for the longitudinal medial dorsal muscles; the other sensory, for the posterior medial sensilla of the tergite. The A_2 nerve is short and forms a broken line; it gives rise to numerous collateral nerves which innervate the medioventral longitudinal muscles of each segment (Fig. 5).

The posterior nerves, belonging to the second pair, B, emerge from the ganglia on the same horizontal plane as the A nerves and are divided

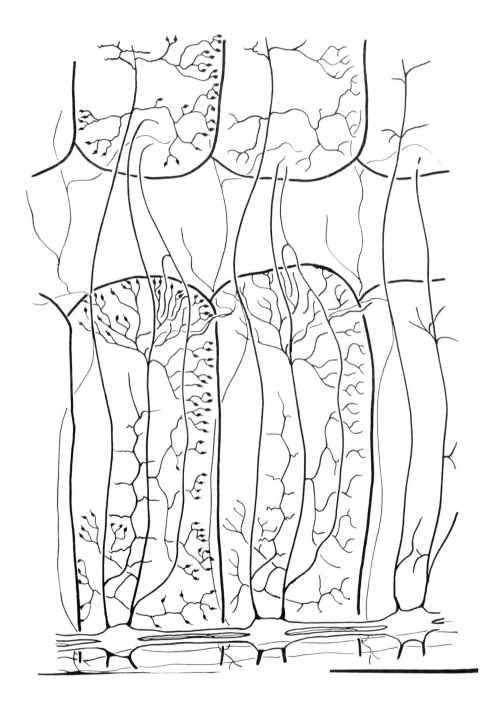

into two branches. B_1, the anterior branch, innervates the sternite sensilla by several branches perpendicular to its course, which reach the edge of the sternite. The last ramification of B_1 is a motor nerve and innervates the sterno-tergal muscle group. The B_2 branch is posterior and crosses the sternite and attaches to a branch of the median nerve. Following their common course, two branches may be noticed: one which innervates the sterno-pleural muscle; the other which proceeds to the stigmatic region.

The last ganglion, which is larger and more elongated than the others, gives rise to four pairs of nerves serving the posterior segments of the abdomen as well as the genital organs and the appendages (cerci and styli) in particular.

3. The Median Nerve

Between the roots of the two posterior connectives emerging from a ganglion, a small group of cells produce an uneven trunk, which is relatively conspicuous. This trunk runs along the connectives in the same plane for about three-fourths of the distance separating two successive ganglia. At this level the median nerve forms a bend of 90° and rises above the nerve chain. A thin, fibrous net joins this elbow to the zone of the following ganglion, enclosed between the two anterior connectives. After the vertical course, the sagittal nerve sends off branches, with each of the sections giving rise to the following:

1. A lateral ramification, M, which remains in the plane formed by the branches of the fork and which then obliquely crosses the segment in which it originates. It is this nerve which joins with a segment of the nerve A_1. A motor and a stigmatic nerve then arise from the common path; the motor nerve innervates the anterior sterno-tergal muscle, mentioned earlier.

2. An anterior longitudinal ramification, M_a.

3. A posterior longitudinal ramification, M_p.

These last two, combined with those of successive segments, form a ladderlike structure and a connection between the digestive tube and the nerve chain.

Macroscopically, this group of branches forms a plexiform network

---

Fig. 5. Distribution of the nerves in the middle of the abdominal region of *Kalotermes flavicollis*. For purposes of simplification, the sensory organs have not been shown. The heavy lines indicate the outlines of the sternites (below) and the tergites (above). The nerves arising from the ganglia of the ventral nerve chain are described in Section I, B, 2, b of the text. Drawn from original methylene blue preparations.

which is particularly complex in the anterior region of the body. These networks have not yet been completely analyzed.

II. SENSORY ORGANS

A. Photosensitive Organs

1. Compound Eyes (Figs. 6 and 7)

The compound eye of the imago is essentially hemispherical. It is positioned posterodorsally in relation to the base of the antennae and it never includes a very large number of ommatids.

Each ommatidium element includes a rather thin and very convex cornea. The corneagenous cells are usually still recognizable in the adult. The crystalline cells are of rather large size, with a large nucleus encircling the crystalline cone. The retina is elongated and has a small diameter. It includes seven retinal cells with very elongated nuclei. The rhabdome is rather slender. The whole group rests on a basement membrane and is enveloped by about ten pigmented cells (von Rosen, 1913; Jorschke, 1914; Bernard, 1937; Richard, 1950b, on various species of termites). Compared with the ommatids of other adult insects, this group possesses many embryonic characteristics.

The development of the eye is progressive. Von Rosen (1913) and Richard (1950b) have followed it in *Kalotermes flavicollis*. In stage I larvae the nuclei of the cells of the imaginal disc are visible. These cells number about ten and possess larger nuclei than those of adjacent hypodermal cells. They contact the cuticle and receive a short and relatively thin optic nerve. In stage II and especially in stage III there is a multiplication of the cells. The cells become organized into two layers, one internal, the other external. The cuticle thickens at the level of the developing eye, and the optic nerve becomes clearly defined. The stage IV larvae with 12 antennal segments (von Rosen, 1913) is characterized by a clearly defined separation of two cellular groups. The external group is composed of cells with small, elongated nuclei. The internal group is formed by cells with large, ovid nuclei. The cellular limits are not well defined, and many dividing cells are present. At the end of the fourth stage of development, the internal group is made up of seven large cells assembled near the basement membrane. No rhabdome is as yet noticeable between these cells, which will become the retinal cells. The external group is now composed of eight cells: four central ones with large nuclei which are the precursors of the crystalline cells and four peripheral cells with smaller nuclei which are the precursors of the pigment cells.

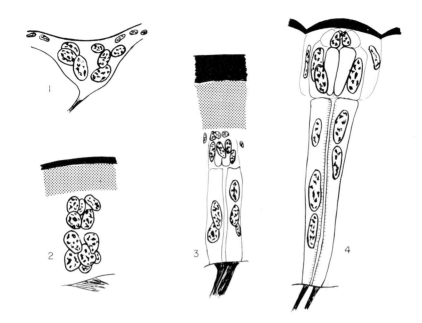

Fig. 6.   Development of the elements of the ommatidia of *Kalotermes flavicollis*. Drawn from original histological preparations. 1: Larva of the first stage; 2: larva of the fourth stage; 3: larva of the sixth stage; 4: the imago (see text).

In the fifth larval stage the rhabdome becomes visible although not attaining its definitive structure. The pigment cells are divided and form a crown with small and very chromatic nuclei. At the same time, the crystalline body appears between the crystalline cells. The fifth stage, therefore, can be considered as the developmental stage where the eye goes from a primitive, embryonic structure to a more evolved structure, since the perceptive and optical elements are present.

In the sixth and seventh stages of development, the characteristics of the adult eye become distinct, with growth in length and organization of the general definitive arrangement. The cuticle thickens at the level of the eye, making the general topography difficult to observe from the exterior. It is in the seventh stage that the distal pigment of the eye is deposited. While not very visible at first, it turns reddish brown and then dark brown. Shortly before the imaginal molt takes place, the eye becomes black and the cornea takes shape; the cuticle decreases in thickness and becomes convex.

Von Rosen (1913), working with neotenic reproductives of *Reticulitermes lucifugus* (Rossi), Jorschke (1914), with the queen of *Macro-*

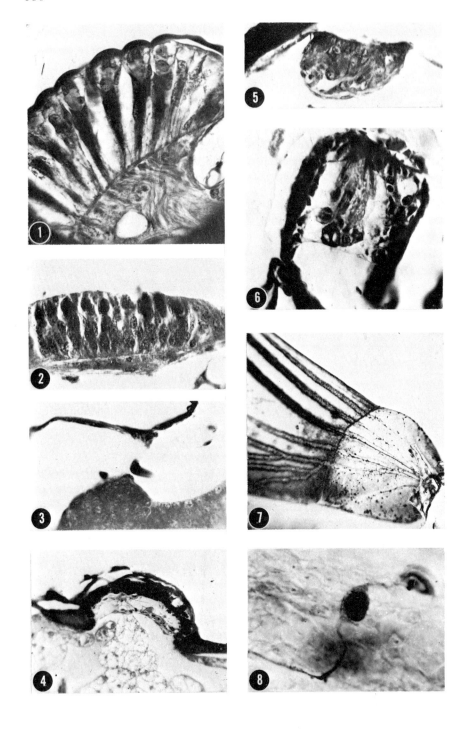

termes bellicosus, and Richard (1950b) with the imagoes and neotenics of *Kalotermes flavicollis,* have demonstrated the observable regression of the eye. The reduction of the ocular elements of the imagoes is very slow at first, but, in old individuals, it affects all the ommatidia and the sensitive elements (retina) regress before the optical elements (crystalline). Only pigmented granules which have escaped from the cells remain under the thickened cuticle. These granules may collect at different levels of the regressed eye.

In the neotenic reproductives the initial aspect of the eye varies according to the stage from which the animal developed. However, whatever its origin may be, the eye becomes pigmented, even though its coloration is not as intense as that of the adult eye. This raises the physiological problem of a relationship between the deposition of the pigment and sexual maturity. On the other hand, all of the cellular elements disappear, as in the primary reproductive form.

The pseudergates (developed from nymphs of the seventh stage) show another type of regression since the ommatidium regains the characteristics of that of the larvae of the fifth stage: a return to cells with globular nuclei, disappearance of the rhabdomes, and less distinct refractive organs.

2. The Ocelli

The ocelli have been described in *Reticulitermes* (von Rosen, 1913) and *Kalotermes* (Richard, 1950b). Two ocelli are present in the individuals of the reproductive line. They do not occur, or are regressed, in the other castes. The cuticle is not modified at the level of the ocelli. Immediately under the cuticle a very compact layer of cells with stainable nuclei may be observed; these constitute the corneagenous cells. Deeper, there is a layer of large cells which also have stainable nuclei. These are associated with the distal ends of the ocellan nerve. The development of the ocelli have been followed in *Kalotermes* (Richard, 1950b). The precursors become clearly visible during the fourth stage and the ocelli are completely formed at the seventh stage.

B. Other Sensory Organs

The entire body of the termite is provided with bristles and pores of different sizes, chordotonal organs, and diffuse nerve endings.

Fig. 7. Photographs of original microscopic preparations of *Kalotermes flavicollis.*
1: Eye of an imago; 2: eye of a fifth stage larva; 3: optic precursor of the first stage larva; 4: regressed eye of an old queen; 5: ocellus; 6: section of the antennal scape showing the chordotonal organ of the scape and the various rods of the organ of Johnston; 7: methylene blue preparation of the nerves of the wing scale; 8: innervation of a sensory pore of the tibia.

The sensory organs can be readily classified in accordance with the terminology of Snodgrass (1935) — Type I of Snodgrass: sensilla trichodea, sensilla basiconica, sensilla campaniforma, peg organs, and chordotonal organs; Type II of Snodgrass: diffuse sensory elements of the mouth parts and the articulations.

1. Organs with External Cuticular Processes

a. Trichodea Sensilla. The sensilla of the trichodea type are distributed over the entire body. They are especially concentrated on the antennae, the mouth parts, the cerci, and the legs. They form roughly concentric crowns on these appendages. Their length is from six to ten times the diameter of their cuticular base, and they are always innervated by a bipolar cell whose distal process penetrates into the base of the sensillum. Their function is probably tactile.

b. Basiconica Sensilla. The sensilla of the basiconica type are short thorns with thin walls, and their length is at the most four times their diameter at the base. They are innervated by a bipolar cell whose distal extremity reaches the base without penetrating very far into the sensillum. In general, they are concentrated in groups on some precise points of the cuticle: the articular regions of the appendages in particular, the base of the antennae, the coxal base of the legs, the base of the mobile mouthparts, or palps; the base of the wings, the tergal, and sternal intersegmental junctions, etc. These groups may contain as many as twenty sensilla, and their function is without doubt proprioceptive.

c. Campaniformia Sensilla. The sensilla of the campaniformia type belong to two categories, elliptical pores and circular pores whose diameter approximates 5 μ in primitive termites. These pores occupy fixed positions on the body. They can be observed on the wings, the antennae, and the mouth parts (maxillary and mandibular especially). On the external side of the tibia, there are a group of five or eight pores which are placed at the level of the subgenual organ, in accordance with a very precise pattern, forming a right angle. The function of this structure is not clear, but rather similar pores occur in different orthopterans where they are associated with the tibial tympanic organ.

Each of these sensilla is innervated by a bipolar cell whose distal process, often very twisted, reaches the center of the pore, which is usually occupied by a membrane bearing a slightly raised area at the point where the process ends.

d. Peg Organs. The peg organs are small cuticular protuberances which are innervated but not articulated. They are sometimes located at the center of a slight depression in the cuticle. Each peg organ is innervated by a single bipolar cell, and a grouping of the organs results in a similar grouping of the nerve cells. These organs occur on the labrum, the extremity of the buccal palps, and the antennae. Many organs of the Type I of Snodgrass are olfactory or chemical receptors. Some works (Abushama, 1964, 1965; Prestage *et al.*, 1963) give information about these functions.

2. The Chordotonal Organs

The chordotonal organs are very numerous on the termites' body, and they are found in the same position as in other insects. Isolated scolopic rods are recognized here and there on the body (thorax and abdomen). Complex scolopalia exist at the base of the wings, the antennae, and the legs. Each mouth part has scolopalia, with most of them situated at the bases of the maxillae and the mandibles.

a. The Tegular Organ. The tegular organ is made up of a rather small number of scolopic rods, and its position in the termite tegula approximates that in many other insects (Zacwilichowky, 1930). Its role must be very important in the dynamics of wing movement and also in the general dynamics of the body. (We must remember that this organ persists in the reproductives after shedding of the wings, which follows swarming, and that the early removal of the deciduous part of the wing raises the level of activity of the insects.)

b. The Chordotonal Organs of the Legs. The types of chordotonal organs of the termite legs are the types described in the legs of insects by Debaisieux (1938), namely: proximal and distal chordotonal organs, subgenual organs, distal tibial organs, and tarsal organs. The subgenual organ is the most remarkable one. It includes a variable number of scolopic rods, usually about ten, distributed into two groups: one medio-dorsal and the other laterodistal. The whole group of rods rests on the tibial trachea, which are divided into two parts in this area. The right-angled external sensilla campaniformia (Section II, B, 1, c) are situated at this level. The innervation of this organ is provided by a branch of the anterior tibial nerve. Its structure, like that of other chordotonal organs, is already present in the first stage larvae. The only change one can mention is a slight increase in the number of scolopic rods (Fig. 8).

The work of Howse (1962, 1963, 1965), particularly on *Zootermopsis*, demonstrates the possibility that this organ receives external mechanical

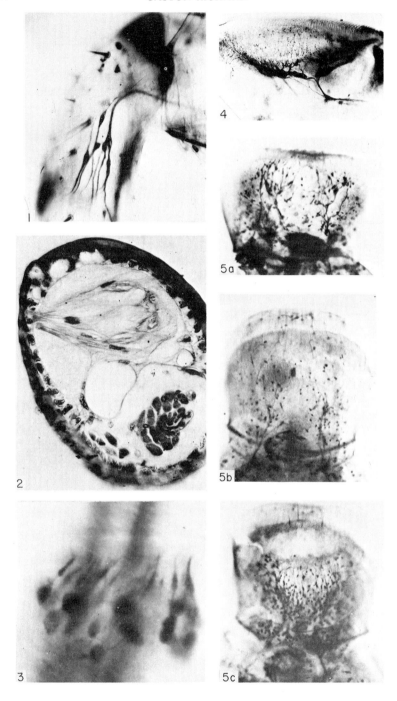

stimuli. Its structure and its physiology make it especially apt to react to the variations in the intensity of the stimuli.

c. *The Antennal Chordotonal Organs.* The base of the antenna possesses three groups of chordotonal organs.

1. The chordotonal organ of the scape, whose cells are situated toward the proximal third of the joint. The rods are attached on the scape at the articulation of the scape and the pedicel, near the distal insertion of the elevator muscle of the pedicel. It is innervated by a special branch of the anterior antennal nerve (Fig. 9).

2. The chordotonal organ of the pedicel, which consists of cells located at the base of the joint. The rods are attached at one point of the internal distal wall of the pedicel, after an oblique course in the latero-anterior plane.

3. The Organ of Johnston is relatively simple in the termites. It is composed of a crown of scolopic rods, attached to the articular membrane near the distal side of the pedicel. It is organized in two symmetrical halves, which are both attached to one of the anterior antennal nerve branches. In *Kalotermes* and *Reticulitermes* (Fudalewicz-Niemczyk, 1965) it is asymmetrical. The rods are more regularly spread out in *Zootermopsis angusticollis* (Noyes, 1930) than in *Kalotermes flavicollis* (Richard, 1950a). The role of this organ may consist of receiving vibrations and appraising the curvature of the antennal flagellum; but it also seems to play the role of a dynamogenic organ, increasing the tonus of the insect. Grassé (1949) has emphasized the apathy of a termite with the antennae severed at the level of the head capsule. Just as the wing mutilations never reach the tegular chordotonal organs, so the antennal mutilations, practiced on the reproductives of termites, never reach the pedicel.

The antennal chordotonal organs are already present in the larvae of the first stage, and the general plan does not vary during the course of development. Only the number of scolopic rods and some modalities of the innervation change (for example, the organ of Johnston in the first stage larvae of *Kalotermes* has 15 – 17 rods; in the second and third stages, 20 rods; in the fourth, 25; in the fifth through seventh, 30 – 45; in the imago, 40).

Fig. 8. Photographs of original preparations of *Kalotermes flavicollis*. 1: Methylene blue preparation of the nerve cells of the subgenual organ; 2: section of the tibia showing the subgenual organ resting on the two branches of the trachea; 3: methylene blue preparation of the organ of Johnston (pedicel of the antenna); 4: methylene blue preparation of the hypopharynx; 5a–c: three preparations of the labrum using methylene blue; 5a: resting stage; 5b: just prior to molting; 5c: at the time of the molt.

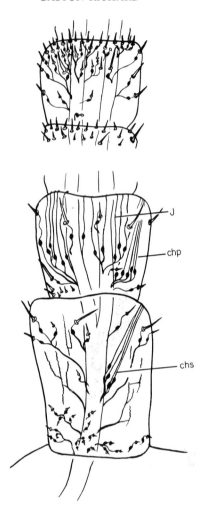

Fig. 9.   Distribution of the sensory organs and nerves in the antenna of *Kalotermes flavicollis*. Based upon original preparations with methylene blue. (chp) Chordotonal organ of the pedicel; (chs) chordotonal organ of the scape; (J) organ of Johnston.

3. Type II Organs of Snodgrass

These organs are most frequently sensory endings issuing from a multipolar cell, and they belong, without doubt, to two functional groups:

a. Endings which are probably proprioceptive and which are situated in the articular regions (the two sides of the articulations of the femur-tibia, tibia-tarsus, and glossae-paraglossae joints). These endings disappear in a diffuse manner in the hypodermis.

b. Endings which are probably chemoreceptive are situated on the mouth parts (labium, hypopharynx, mandibles); they end on the cuticular surface in a minute pore at the level of which no thickening of the cuticle is observable.

4. Development of the Peripheral Nervous System

In the larvae the plan of the peripheral innervation and the main groups of sensory organs are in place at the time of emergence from the egg. On the entire body and on the appendages, the sensilla increase in number and in size during the course of aging, but the sensilla of newly emerged young are almost always recognizable by their position, their larger size, and their heavy coloration. In the course of postembryonic development, the sensilla of the larvae of the first stage multiply, while maintaining their relative positions.

The differentiation of new sensilla marks off well-defined regions, of which certain ones are particularly well supplied. Correlated with this differentiation is the formation of numerous branches of the sensory nerves. The principal nerves increase in diameter, and important secondary branches appear.

The increase in the number of new sensory organs does not always take place at the same rate (Denis, 1958a, b; Table II). In *Kalotermes flavicollis* the rate is rather slow for the leg of the larvae of the first four stages, and the sensory organs are few in number and not well differentiated. Beginning with the fifth stage, the rhythm of multiplication increases, territories appear, and the plan of organization reaches the peak of precision. The imago resembles the nymphs quite closely, but the pseudergates derived from nymphs with long wing sheaths show regressions of sensory organs in contrast to those of the nymphs.

At the time of each molt, the distal process of the bipolar cells innervating the sensilla is cut across, but it serves as a support for the development of the new sensilla and the prolongation of the elements which innervate it. The stainability by the vital nerve dyes (methylene blue) of the nerve cells adjacent to the sensilla is variable in the course of the intermolt period (Denis, 1958b). When at rest, only one bipolar cell under each sensillum is stainable, but when the molting period approaches, groups of cells with different degrees of stainability and which send out distal and proximal processes are observed. In certain cases it is possible to observe division of these cells. After the molt the stainability becomes normal again. It would seem that the new nerve cells,

TABLE II

STAGES OF LINEAR GROWTH OF THE MESOTHORACIC LEGS OF *Kalotermes flavicollis*
AND THE NUMBER OF SENSILLA WHICH EACH SEGMENT BEARS

Stage	Coxa		Femur		Tibia	
	Length (μ)	Number of sensilla	Length (μ)	Number of sensilla	Length (μ)	Number of sensilla
I	200	14 – 17	260	19 – 21	260	26 – 28
V	600	170	670	115	670	135
Imago	840	240	750	185	750	165

innervating the new sensilla, can develop from hypodermic elements
which are modified as the time of molting approaches.

5. The Peripheral Sense Organs in the Different Castes

A precise comparison of the peripheral sense organs in the members
of the different castes is not very advanced. In *Reticulitermes lucifugus
santonensis* Feytaud, Fudalewicz-Niemczyk (1965) shows (Table III)
that when the antenna is considered few significant differences exist

TABLE III

STAGES OF LINEAR GROWTH AND THE NUMBER OF SENSILLA TRICHODEA OF
THE ANTENNA OF *Reticulitermes lucifugus*

Type	Stage	Segment of the antenna												
		Scape		Pedicel		3		9		11		13		16 – 18	
		L[a]	N[b]	L	N	L	N	L	N	L	N	L	N	L	N
Larva	I	10	3 – 4	85	5	70	5	70 – 75	10	–	–	–	–	–	–
Worker	III	25	7 – 8	28	6	35	5	60		5	60	5	–	–	–	–
Nymph	III	24	8	28	6	38	5	70		5	60	5	–	–	–	–
Worker	V	30	10	33	8	35	6	55		6	55	6	55	6	–	–
Nymphs	V	40	10	40	8	35	6	70		6	60	6	60	6	–	–
Worker	VII	35	10	45	8	55	6	60		6	55	6	55	6	55	10 – 12
Nymph	VII	35	10	45	8	60	6	60		6	55	6	55	6	55	1 – 12

[a] Length of segment in microns.
[b] Number of trichodea sensilla.

TABLE IV

PILOSITY OF THE MAXILLARY PALPS (NOT INCLUDING THE PROPRIOCEPTIVE SENSILLA BASICONICA OF THE BASE OF THE SEGMENTS) OF *Cubitermes heghi*[a]

Segment	No. considered	Value[b]	Worker bristles					Soldier bristles				
			Sum of lengths (μ)	Number	Sig.[c]	Mean length (μ)	Sig.	Sum of lengths (μ)	Number	Sig.	Mean length (μ)	Sig.
1	10	Mean	86.9	3.2	S	27.2	H	31.1	2.4	S	13.3	H
		95% level	±26	±0.6		±3.4		±6.2	±0.6		±1.2	
		Variance	1281	0.6222		22.82		75.21	0.7111		2.863	
2	10	Mean	314.7	4.9	N	64.6	H	198.7	4.5	N	42.6	H
		95% level	±18	±0.2		±6.0		±22	±0.5		±4.7	
		Variance	626.2	0.1000		70.36		968.5	0.5000		43.39	
3	10	Mean	850.6	20.0	N	42.5	H	580.6	19.50	N	29.83	H
		95% level	±74	±1.5		±1.6		±28	±0.8		±1.6	
		Variance	10711	4.667		4.729		1532	1.389		4.727	
4	10	Mean	2009.9	38.7	N	51.9	H	1268.2	37.10	N	34.24	H
		95% level	±119	±1.9		±1.8		±88	±1.7		±2.3	
		Variance	27667	7.344		6.249		15140	5.656		10.76	
5	3	Mean	7813.0	199	N	39.3	S	8923.6	182.7	N	49.0	S
		95% level	±1730	±38		±8.1		±513	±26		±4.3	
		Variance	485577	78.00		10.60		42597	110.4		2.931	

[a] Unpublished data provided by J. Deligne.
[b] Values indicated for each group are mean value of measurements; 95% confidence level of the mean (95% level); and σ^2 (variance).
[c] N indicates no significant difference; S indicates statistically significant difference; H indicates highly statistical significance.

between members of the same age and of different castes. However, the differences are more evident if one studies the tergal sides of the meso- and metathoracic segments. Beginning with the third stage, the members of the reproductive line are distinguishable from the class of workers by the presence of the tegular chordotonal organ and by the fact that the radial nerve always reaches and innervates the posterior extremity of the tergal margin. The most precise studies are those of Deligne* which demonstrate, using statistical methods, the differences between soldiers and workers in the higher termites. An important regression of the bristles of the mouth parts is noticed in soldiers of *Bellicositermes natalensis* (Haviland), compared with the workers. Measurements carried out on *Cubitermes heghi* Sjöstedt (Table IV) demonstrate that

TABLE V

THE NUMBER OF SENSILLA OF THE LEFT MANDIBLES OF TEN WORKERS AND TEN SOLDIERS OF *Cubitermes heghi*[a]

| Sensillia | Sig.[b] | Worker | | | Soldier | | |
		Mean	95% Confidence level of the mean	Variance	Mean	95% Confidence level of the mean	Variance
External apical canals	N	14.7	±0.6	0.6776	14.8	±0.9	1.956
Internal apical canals	H	20.5	±0.7	1.167	3.1	±0.5	0.5444
Ventral canal I	S	15.4	±1.1	2.489	13.4	±1.7	5.376
Ventral canal II	N	8.1	±0.7	0.9889	8.5	±0.7	0.9444
Marginal canal	H	38.0	±1.3	3.111	7.3	±0.9	1.567
Molar canal	H	234.5	±5.4	56.28	117.4	±9.8	189.4
Ventral pore I	S	7.8	±0.7	0.8444	8.9	±0.8	1.211
Ventral pore II	H	4.2	±0.7	1.067	7.0	±1.3	3.111
Dorsal pore III	N	2.5	±0.4	0.2788	2.6	±0.6	0.7111
Dorsal pore IV	N	6.0	±0.6	0.6667	5.4	±0.5	0.4889
Dorsal pore V	H	8.3	±0.8	1.344	14.8	±1.7	5.733
Molar bristles	N	25.2	±1.7	5.956	24.2	±2.7	13.96
External bristles	H	8.4	±1.3	3.378	25.1	±1.6	4.989
Basal bristles	H	100.±			0		

[a] Unpublished data provided by J. Deligne.

[b] N indicates that there is no significant difference between the worker and soldier; S indicates the difference between the worker and soldier is significant at the 95% level; H indicates the difference between the worker and soldier is highly significant (99% level).

*I wish to thank most sincerely Mr. J. Deligne who willingly agreed to send me some important unpublished results.

although the number of bristles of the basal joints of the maxillary palps varies little from the worker to the soldier the size of the bristles, at least 60μ in the worker, diminishes very significantly in the soldier. On the last joint (joint five) the average size of the bristles of the soldier is greater than that of the bristles of the worker. Deligne (1962, 1965) believes that this results in a lessening of the capacity for topographical discrimination of the soldier's environment. On the other hand, its sensitivity for "all or none" would be increased by the lengthening of some average and large bristles.

In a similar way the mandible (Table V) possesses considerable modifications of its sensory plan. The actual number and the density of the sensory canals is reduced in the soldier; the basal bristles disappear, but certain pores and bristles maintain or increase their number. It appears that the sensilla involved in nutrition undergo a regression, which is all the more conspicuous since they are more apical in position. The opposite is true for the sensilla concerned with transmitting information regarding the position and bending of the mandibles.

REFERENCES

Abushama, F. T. (1964). Electrophysiological investigation on the antennal olfactory receptors of the moist termite *Zootermopsis angusticollis* (Hagen). *Entomologist* 97, 48-150.

Abushama, F. T. (1965). The olfactory receptors on the antennae of the damp wood termite *Zootermopsis angusticollis*. *Entomologists' Monthly Mag.* 100, 145-147.

Bernard, F. (1937). Recherches sur la morphogenèse des yeux composés d'Arthropodes. Developpement, croissance, reduction. *Bull. Biol. France Belg.* Suppl. 23, 1-155.

Debaisieux, P. (1938). Organes scolopidiaux des pattes d'Insectes. *Cellule Rec. Cytol. Histol.* 47, 77-168.

Deligne, J. (1962). Observations sur la transformation de l'ouvier en soldat chez le Termite du Natal, *Bellicositermes natalensis* (Haviland). *Insectes Sociaux* 9, 7-21.

Deligne, J. (1965). Morphologie et fonctionnement des mandibules chez les soldats des Termites. *Biol. Gabonica* 1, 179-186.

Denis, C. (1958a). Contribution a l'étude de l'ontogenèse sensori-nerveuse du Termite *Calotermes flavicollis* Fab. *Insectes Sociaux* 5, 171-188.

Denis, C. (1958b). Cytologie des terminaisons nerveuses au cours de l'ontogenèse de *Calotermes flavicollis* Fab. (Insecte Isoptère). *Bull. Biol. France Belg.* 92, 240-247.

Feytaud, J. (1912). Contribution à l'étude du Termite lucifuge. (Anatomie. Foundátion de colonies nouvelles.) *Arch. Anat. Microscop. Morphol. Exptl.* 13, 481-607.

Fudalewicz-Neimczyk, W. (1965). Ontogenèse de l'innervation des organes sensoriels des antennes chez *Reticulitermes lucifugus santonensis* Feyt. *Insectes Sociaux* 12, 241-252.

Fudalewicz-Niemczyk, W., and Richard, G. (1965). Organogenèse des nerfs et trachées alaires du Termite *Reticulitermes lucifugus santonensis* Feyt. *Insectes Sociaux* 12, 309-320.

Grassé, P.-P. (1942). L'essaimage des Termites. Essai d'analyse causale d'un complexe instinctif. *Bull. Biol. France Belg.* 76, 347-382.

Grassé, P.-P. (1949). Ordre des Isoptères ou Termites. *In* "Traité de Zoologie," (P.-P. Grassé, ed.) Vol. IX, pp. 408-544. Masson, Paris.

Hanström, B. (1930). Über das Gehirn von *Termopsis nevadensis* und *Phyllium pulchrifolium* nebst Beiträgen zur Phyllogenie der corpora pedunculata der Arthropoden. *Z. Morphol. Oekol. Tiere* 19, 732-773.

Hanström, B. (1940). Inkretorische Organe, Sinnesorgane und Nervensystem des Kopfes einiger niederer Insektenordnungen. *Kgl. Svenska Vetenskapsakad. Handl.* [3] 18, 1-265.

Hecker, H. (1966). Das Zentralnervensystem des Kopfes und sein postembryonale Entwicklung bei *Bellicositermes bellicosus* (Smeath) (Isoptera). *Acta Trop.* 23, 297-352.

Holmgren, N. (1909). Termiten studien. I. Anatomische Untersuchungen. *Kgl. Svenska Vetenskapsakad. Handl.* 44 [3], 1-215.

Howse, P. E. (1962). The perception of vibration by the subgenual organ in *Zootermopsis angusticollis* and *Periplaneta americana*. *Experientia* 18, 457-459.

Howse, P. E. (1963). Zur Evolution der Erzeugung von Erschutterungen als Benachrichtigungsmittel bei Termiten. *Rev. Suisse Zool.* 70, 19-26.

Howse, P. E. (1965). The structure of the subgenual organ and certain other mechanoreceptors of the Termite *Zootermopsis angusticollis*. *Proc. R. Ent. Soc.* Lond. (A) 40, 137-146.

Jorschke, H. (1914). Die Facettenaugen der Orthopteren und Termiten. *Z. Wiss. Zool.* 3, 153-280.

Noyes, B. (1930). The peripheral sense organs in the termite *Termopsis angusticollis* (Hagen). *Univ. Calif. (Berkeley) Publ. Zool.* 33, 259-286.

Pierre Duplessix, F. (1964). Contribution à l'étude du système nerveux abdominal des Termites. *Dip. Et. Sup. Fac. Sci. Renne* pp. 1-50.

Prestage, J. J., Slifer, E. H., and Stephens, L. B. (1963). Thin-walled sensory pegs on the antenna of the termite worker *Reticulitermes flavipes*. *Ann. Entomol. Soc. Am.* 56, 874-878.

Richard, G. (1950a). L'innervation et les organes sensoriels de la patte du Termite à cou jaune (*Calotermes flavicollis* F.) *Ann. Sci. Nat. Zool. Biol. Animale* [11] 12, 65-83.

Richard, G. (1950b). La phototropisme du Termite à cou jaune (*Calotermes flavicollis* Fabr.) et les organes sensoriels. *Ann. Sci. Nat. Zool. Biol. Animale* [11] 12, 487-604.

Richard, G. (1967). Contribution a l'étude de la morphologie du système nerveux cephalique des Termites. *Ann. Soc. Entomol. France* 3, 609-617.

Snodgrass, R. (1935). "Principles of Insect Morphology." McGraw-Hill, New York.

Thompson, C. B. (1916). The brain and frontal gland of the castes of the "white ant" *Leucotermes flavipes* Kollar. *J. Comp. Neurol.* 26, 553-603.

Vincent, M. P. (1964). Contribution à l'étude des centres nerveux cérébroides des Insectes Isoptères. Cas particulier de l'ontogenèse de *Calotermes flavicollis*. *Dipl. Et. Sup. Fac. Sci. Rennes* pp. 1-70.

von Rosen, K. (1913). Studien am Sehorgan der Termiten nebst Beitragen sur Kenntnis des Gehirns derselben. *Zool. Jahrb., Abt. Anat. Ontog. Tiere* 35, 625-664.

Zacwilichowski, J. (1930). Unerwienie skrydel owadow. I. *Rozpravy Wydzialu Mat.-Przyr. Pay* 70, 1-154.

Zuberi, H. (1960). Sur quelques particularités de la structure du cerveau chez *Anacanthotermes ochraceus* Burmeister (Isoptère). *Compt. Rend.* 250, 3506-3508.

Zuberi, H. (1963). L'anatomie comparée du cerveau chez les Termites en rapport avec le polymorphisme. *Bull. Biol. France Belg.* 97, 147-207.

7

Social Behavior and Communication

ALASTAIR M. STUART

"If I should write you all the interesting things I see among the termites, it would read like a Munchaüsen story, ..."

J. Beaumont, June 2, 1889, Panama

I. INTRODUCTION

Many naturalists have observed termites over the centuries, and the more spectacular parts of their behavior, such as their building and fighting, have been mentioned many times. Some of the "ants" mentioned by Réaumur in 1742 were undoubtedly termites, while Smeathman gave an account of the building activities of *Termes bellicosus** in a paper presented to the Royal Society of London in 1781. The beginnings of critical observations and experiments are to be found, however, in the latter part of the nineteenth century. Beaumont (1889 – 1890) in particular noted many facets of the behavior of the termites of Panama and conducted simple experiments, while Grassi and Sandias (1896 – 1897) made similar observations on the European species. Some of the early experimental work was excellent for its time, and Andrews' (1911) classic work on trail laying and colony odor must be mentioned here. Such work was continued through the first half of this century, and Grassé (1952), Emerson (1939), and others have published extensively on the behavior of many species of termites.

Today, work on the social behavior of termites and other insects is progressing from the purely observational and descriptive stages. There are perhaps two main approaches being actively taken today. The more classic of the two is the strictly evolutionary one founded on the early work of the late William Morton Wheeler of Harvard. This approach is concerned with the importance of behavioral interactions on the evolution of sociality and with the present day adaptiveness of the different degrees of social cooperation. It attempts to answer such questions as: "Why are some insects social?" "What is the origin of sociality?" "How did the specialization of the various castes of social insects come about?". This field has been excellently delineated recently by Wilson (1966). In the past it has relied heavily on intelligent speculation based on observations, but with the advent of the computer and the contributions of mathematics it promises to yield important quantified information on the significance and evolutionary effectiveness of social behavior.

The other line of study attempts to answer questions of a more immediate nature by using the specialized approaches of physiology, biochemistry, and other modern techniques which are available. Here again the questions are framed within the evolutionary theory. A given piece of behavior is examined by critically analyzing it at the organismic and cellular levels by experimentation and then relating the results to that actually occurring in the field. By such analysis it is possible to understand more fully the adaptive significance of the behavior, as well as the underlying physiological mechanisms. This approach has been used

---

*Grassé and Noirot (1961) have the following comment to make on the species of termite actually observed by Smeathman: "It is almost certain that the *Termes bellicosus* of Smeathman is really what we call today *B. natalensis*. The shape and dimensions of the large soldiers and especially the architecture of the nest [plage VI (editors' note: error for VII) of Smeathman] attest to this . . ." (editors' translation).

recently in termite studies (e.g., Lüscher, 1960; Stuart, 1960, 1963a), and it is the approach which Sudd (1967) has advocated for ants. Though not recognized as a "school" in animal behavior, such as ethology or comparative psychology, this approach is really quite old and established. Such an analytical and zoological approach should be distinguished from present day ethology and comparative psychology, and perhaps the name suggested by Griffin (1958)—Experimental Natural History—could be used to designate it.

Both the evolutionary and experimental approaches to the study of the behavior of social insects are quite compatible, and the results obtained from them should be collated in order to gain as complete an understanding of the whole animal as possible.

Communication being the prime essential of social life (Wigglesworth, 1966), it will be treated as part of the total behavior of termites. As Huber (1810) says ". . . tous ces rapports supposent entre les individus de différens ordres une liaison qui ne sauroit exister sans l'intervention du langage."*

In the past decade reviews dealing at least in part with the social behavior of termites (Noirot, 1958-1959; Weesner, 1960; Harris and Sands, 1965) have appeared as well as other reviews on the behavior of social insects in general (Lindauer, 1965; Wilson, 1966). Most of the references to previous work on termite behavior are contained in these reviews and in the excellent bibliography of Snyder (1956, 1961). Rather than attempting to include all the countless previous observations on behavior, the present chapter will confine itself to outlining current trends in the investigation of social behavior and communication in the Isoptera and in endeavoring to resolve conflicting views on certain aspects of behavior. At the same time an attempt will be made, where relevant, to relate the behavior of termites to that of the better known ants and to evaluate some old ideas in light of recent work. Certain points of behavior treated elsewhere (Chapters 6, 8, and Volume II) will be considered in part at the risk of some repetition in order to ensure continuity.

II. SEXUAL BEHAVIOR

It is in sexual behavior that all animals can be considered "social" (Wheeler, 1928; Lindauer, 1961), and this aspect of termite social behavior may be considered first before treating behavior involving more individuals than two.

*". . . . . all these relations imply a coordination of activities that could not exist without the occurrence of language."

In most termites sexual behavior in the perfect insect can be subdivided into the temporal sequence of Preflight, Dispersal Flight, Dealation and Pairing, Nest Founding, and Copulatory Behavior. Descriptions of this behavior and its variations in different species may be found in many papers, particularly in the classic paper of Fuller (1915), in the reviews of Harris and Sands (1965) and Weesner (1960), as well as in Chapter 8 of the present work. In this chapter, therefore, attention will be paid mainly to the parts where some comments can be made from the point of view of communication.

A. PREFLIGHT BEHAVIOR

Anyone who has observed termites in culture can see that the imagoes and preimagoes congregate in certain parts of the nest. They may do this by means of a mutual attraction, or it may be that the behavior of the other members of the colony forces them together. Most of the evidence seems to suggest that it is the behavior of the other members of the colony that is important. Verron (1963) in his extensive study on chemical attraction between the various instars and castes of *Kalotermes flavicollis* (Fabricius) has shown that there is little or no attraction between alates that have not yet flown (Fig. 1), though after the flight males are attracted

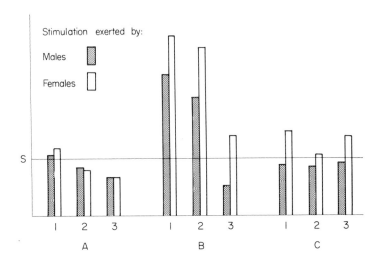

Fig. 1. Stimulation exerted by the imagoes of *Kalotermes flavicollis* at different stages on nymphs and other imagoes. The ordinate indicates the relative degree of "stimulation." The abscissa indicates stimulation exerted: (A) before the flight; (B) after the flight; (C) by the reproductives; (1) on nymphs without wing pads; (2) on wing padded nymphs; (3) on alates. Only the results above the line "S" are significant (after Verron, 1963).

to females. This would seem to rule out aggregation by mutual chemical attraction between the unflown imagoes and also between the preimagoes. Verron has also shown in his experiments that the larvae are somewhat attracted to the unflown imagoes, though nowhere to the extent they are to the imagoes that have flown (Fig. 1). This reaction of the larvae in Verron's experimental setup could be a reflection of the phenomenon of worker antagonism towards young imagoes that Buchli (1961) observed in *Reticulitermes lucifugus* (Rossi). Mild antagonism could explain, at least to some extent, the congregation of winged forms at the periphery of a nest. Harris and Sands (1965) did not observe such antagonism in their laboratory cultures of *Reticulitermes hesperus* Banks, but suggest that this may have been due to the small numbers in their colonies and to the absence of primary reproductives. The strong reaction of the larvae toward the newly flown imagoes in Verron's experiments could be indicative of the strong antagonism noted by Buchli (1961) when the workers of *Reticulitermes* actually killed imagoes that were attempting to return to their nests. Similar behavior has been noted by the present writer in laboratory cultures of *Reticulitermes flavipes* (Kollar), *Zootermopsis angusticollis* (Hagen), and *Z. nevadensis* (Hagen). Many mutilated imagoes of these species can be found when they are forced to return to the galleries they have just left. In Verron's experimental setup, where no actual contact occurred between the castes, it would be difficult to note this behavior.

B. DISPERSAL FLIGHT

Flight occurs in response to seasonal, immediate atmospheric, and other conditions. The flight is not a mating flight but a dispersal flight.

Usually the insects fly off clumsily, alight, and shed their wings by twisting their bodies and turning, and then pair. There are variations in this behavior, notably in *Pseudacanthotermes*, where the male clings to the abdomen of the female in flight, and in *Microtermes*, where a fold of the intersegmental membrane of the female abdomen is seized by the male and the tandem pair fly off (Harris and Sands, 1965). Other variations are described by Fuller (1915). This aspect of behavior is more fully treated in Chapter 8.

C. DEALATION

In many termites the sexes dealate separately, and the female may or may not take up a characteristic "calling" attitude (Fig. 2) where the abdomen bends at 90° to the horizontal. At this point it is likely that a pheromone is being given off which attracts the male. This behavior is

Fig. 2. A female of *Reticulitermes flavipes* immediately after dealation. Note the characteristic "calling" position which distends certain segments of the abdomen.

characteristic of many termites, including *Reticulitermes flavipes* and *R. lucifugus*. In *Zootermopsis*, however, the calling behavior is not observed, and after losing their wings the female and male tend to scurry into crevices. The insects move fast and may "jump" in a characteristic way. The jumping may be induced by prodding a newly dealated imago of *Zootermopsis*. This action must be useful in escaping some predators, as newly dealated termites are much more difficult to grasp and pick up than termites in the other stages, and their movement is quite erratic. The biological advantage of such erratic behavior has recently been emphasized by Humphries and Driver (1967). This behavior disappears later, after the excavation of the nest and the development of eggs or sperm. From recent observations (Stuart, unpublished) the "jumping" can be seen to be caused by the wing muscles contracting. The very fast vibration of these muscles can be reduced by cooling the insect, and when this is done it can be seen quite clearly by the vibration of the wing stubs that the wing muscles are responsible for the "jumping" component of this escape reaction. As these muscles are later resorbed, it can be seen why this aspect of behavior disappears in the functional reproductives. This is of interest in view of the recent popularity of the study of the ontogeny of behavior because we have here a case of behavior changing due to a very obvious and relatively simple factor. Only after dealation do the termites pair.

D. PAIRING

Tandem behavior is well known in termites and occurs in many species, including *Reticulitermes flavipes* and *R. lucifugus*. It has been excellently described in *Macrotermes natalensis* (Haviland) by Fuller (1915). In some species such as *Cryptotermes havilandi* (Sjöstedt) it is reported to be absent (Wilkinson, 1962), though it is present in *Cryptotermes cynocephalus* Light (Kalshoven, 1960). In others it is not at all spectacular, as is the case in *Zootermopsis*. In *Reticulitermes* it is often quite spectacular, and chains of up to six or seven dealates may be seen in tandem quite frequently (Grassé, 1949; personal observation). Grassé has indicated that a female never follows a male. Emerson (1933, 1949) made an experimental study of tandem following in *R. flavipes*. By ablating segments of a male antenna and then watching the response of the male to the female, he concluded that the behavior involves both an olfactory and tactile response. As has been mentioned, it is assumed that the female, when raising her abdomen, emits an odor. This, however, has not been proved experimentally.

Buchli (1960) has reinvestigated tandem behavior in *R. lucifugus* and substantiated the observation of Emerson that the female walks when touched by the male, but stops and takes up the calling attitude whenever contact is lost. Buchli, however, further analyzed the factors involved in this behavior. He claims that the female *Reticulitermes* produces a scent which the male recognizes and whose location is somewhere in vicinity of the genital area; he suggests that the accessory glands may be involved. Also, by separating the dealates by sex in petri dishes and placing them in the sunlight, he noted that only the males form chains with each other, while the females are dispersed and take up the characteristic calling position. Thus the males will follow any moving termite irrespective of sex or, as was shown in other experiments where a worker was followed, caste. Buchli's experiments on the formation of chains by males have been verified by the present writer in an independent study in *R. flavipes*. It was noted, in addition, that the males could be induced at will to produce chains of up to ten individuals by simply tapping the petri dish in which they were contained (Fig. 3). This same reaction could be obtained even after 12 days. Any other stimulus disturbing the termites produced the same response. In this connection the odor of the female may prove to be more of an excitatory pheromone, such as an alarm substance is, rather than an actual attractant. It would seem, therefore, that

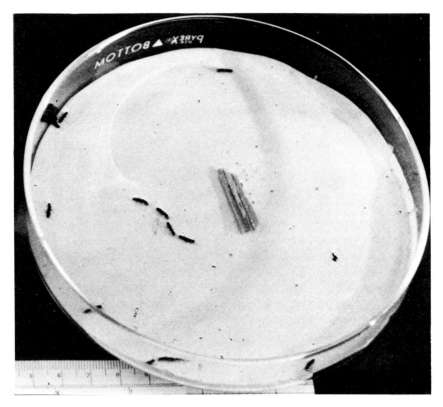

Fig. 3.   Tandem behavior. Males of *Reticulitermes flavipes* confined in a 150 mm diameter petri dish forming trains of individuals on being disturbed by tapping and the removal of the cover.

the stimulus for the actual tandem behavior is a high activity level caused by disturbance which stimulates the males to follow another termite in the manner described by the above workers. Tandem behavior, therefore, can be separated from the actual sexual attraction. Emerson's ablation experiments could not be substantiated: gross injury to the animals by cutting off the segments of the antennae seemed to cause abnormalities in the behavior.

It would appear, then, that a male is attracted to a female by the calling attitude, but thereafter the stimulus is mainly tactile. In the absence of females chains can still be formed. The females, on the other hand, do not form chains.

In preliminary studies on another genus (*Kalotermes*), Buchli (1960) found that males separated from females did not form tandems with each other, but when females were added, several tandems between males were seen to occur. In *Kalotermes* it would appear that the presence of females is needed to trigger tandem behavior. This species would seem to lie between *Zootermopsis* and *Reticulitermes* with regard to this behavior.

It should be noted that tandem behavior is a quite distinct category of behavior from that of trail laying.

E. NEST FOUNDING

The adaptive significance of tandem behavior is, of course, to ensure that the sexes pair, and the fact that only the males show the following response has probably evolved for the reason that two females founding a nest would be biologically uneconomical. Although parthenogenesis occurs in some termites, it appears to be the exception rather than the rule (Chapters 5 and 8). It is possible that the presence of a male may have a stimulatory effect on the production of eggs. In some termites the male and female share equally in the construction of the initial nest excavation (e.g., Fuller, 1915), though in others it is mainly the female, e.g., in *Zootermopsis*. It should be noted, however, that when males of *Zootermopsis* are allowed to dealate and are confined together in a petri dish with wood they live harmoniously and can excavate and indeed thrive. The present author has kept twelve males in such conditions for over 12 months. The male in this species is thus not incapable of excavation.

The behavior of nest selection has not been extensively studied in termites. Experiments have been conducted, however, by Light (1937), who studied the behavior of colonizing pairs of *Paraneotermes simplicicornis* (Banks). He showed that the colonizing pairs are unable to enter sound wood and that, unlike most known Kalotermitidae, they enter earth in preference to wood. Also, Sands (1965) gave alates of *Trinervitermes* a choice of various surfaces for nest founding. From his experiments he concluded that sites with a large number of crevices are preferred, showing that thigmotaxis is important. It is apparent, however, that the alates of different species must have different habits with regard to alighting on the ground or on trees to begin excavation. For example, *Nasutitermes* in Panama tends to build its "nigger head" nests in the branches of trees, indicating that this is the primary site of colony founding, while the imagoes of *Zootermopsis* merely scurry into crevices on the ground on dealating. As Harris (1961) points out, though, lack of the normal nesting site (posts and trees) may force such nasutes to become mound builders.

F. COPULATION

While the physiology of the mating behavior of the related cockroaches is well known (Roth and Barth, 1964) not a great deal is known of the similar behavior in termites. In a primary colony, of course, the normal number of individuals is two, and they have already paired. Copulation occurs only after a certain length of time—in *Zootermopsis* about 2 weeks—and is quite unspectacular when compared to the cockroaches. The reproductives remain close to each other all the time, and it is unlikely that an aphrodisiac pheromone such as that found in cockroaches is needed to indicate the presence of a receptive female. In *Zootermopsis* the male and female move very sluggishly past each other in opposite directions with their abdomens and antennae curving toward each other, their genital segments are distended and when they meet coupling occurs. This may last for several seconds. In supplementaries the behavior is quite similar and often the soldiers will take part in the act. Homosexuality has been observed many times in the supplementaries and soldiers of *Zootermopsis* (personal observation). In other termites copulation seems similar to that described for *Zootermopsis* (Chapter 8).

III. FEEDING BEHAVIOR AND FORAGING

A. GENERAL

The reader is referred to Chapter 12 for an extensive review of feeding behavior in a termite colony. Here a little will be said, however, about some mechanisms of feeding as shown in *Zootermopsis augusticollis* and *Z. nevadensis,* but attention will be paid more to the communication and foraging aspects of behavior than to the exchange of food.

Normally, a medium or large nymph of *Zootermopsis* pulls a small piece of wood from a relatively large piece and begins masticating until the wood is engulfed. Some of the smaller nymphs of approximately the third instar also feed on wood, but here it is common to see very fine particles being scavenged, with extensive use being made of the maxillae. This is often seen in colonies kept in glass containers. Soldiers seem to feed on proctodeal and perhaps stomodeal material.

Although all termites utilize cellulose, it should be noted that not all obtain this from wood (Chapter 3). Some obtain their cellulose by ingesting humus-containing soil, while others obtain nutriment from grass, e.g. *Hodotermes* (Skaife, 1955).

B. FORAGING

Many termites must forage to obtain their food, and the termite foraging columns seen in the tropics have long interested and amazed observers (Smeathman, 1781). As long ago as 1911 Andrews demonstrated that odor trails are connected with foraging in *Nasutitermes,* and more recently it has been shown that in this genus the origin of the odor and the trail lies in the sternal gland (Stuart 1960, 1961, 1963a). In *Nasutitermes* the construction of covered runways follows the formation of a trail; and this behavior has been noted in *N. corniger* (Motschulsky) by Stuart (1960) and in *N. lujae* (Wasmann) by Pasteels (1965). When a colony of *N. corniger* is confined with wood in a Wilson nest placed on a large piece of clean glass plate and then allowed access to the glass by the removal of a glass wool plug, the following behavior is noted. After a very short time a worker will encounter the virgin area; it will then give the characteristic "jerk," a variation of the reciprocating movement (Stuart, 1963b), and run off alerting other members of the colony by contact. The soldiers then leave the cover of the nest and cautiously venture into the open: in this case, over the large clean sheet of glass. A column is formed behind those first scouts and a tracing of the leader's path on a *"perspex"* sheet overlying the foraging area of the termites shows that the rest of the column follows these paths, indicating that a trail is being laid on the way out, though this trail is not visible on the glass. The termites at the head of the column frequently turn and run back along their own trails, much more quickly than they run on their progress outwards. The leaders are thus being constantly replaced by the individuals behind them. As more than one termite is in the lead, many trails are formed but soon one or two main trails supersede the others.* This "exploratory behavior" is remarkably similar to that described by Wilson (1962) for the ant *Solenopsis saevissima* (Fr. Smith). If a piece of decayed balsa is now placed on the glass plate so that the scouts find it, fast moving traffic will soon be observed along the trail between this food source and the nest once the workers traverse the trail. This probably results because the workers

---

*This was also noted by the present author in the field in Panama when, after a carton nest had been cut open and many termites had fallen to the ground, the termites quickly formed into trails and made their way up the trunk of the tree until they reached a runway or the nest. At first there were many trails, but soon one became the main stream and the others were relegated to tributaries. During this procession up the tree, workers were noticed, after the trail had been firmly established, to carry callow nymphs between their mandibles [as Emerson (1929a) also noted]. The nymphs were usually grasped by the thorax. When disturbed, the nymphs were dropped, and it was found that they were quite able to proceed on their own, if not so efficiently. These trails formed when the nest has been grossly disturbed are probably quite temporary, as when the nest was visited six days later no sign of new covered trails was seen though the nest had been repaired.

are larger than the soldiers and their sternal glands are also larger. It was noted that the termites tend to follow a worker trail in preference to a soldier trail when a choice was available. Pasteels (1965) has noted in *Nasutitermes lujae* that the larger workers of the 3rd stage have larger sternal glands than first stage workers have, and it is the former who seem to establish a foraging trail in that species. In *N. corniger* no track is at first visible on the clean surface, though the termites are following a trail, but once there is sufficient traffic, brown spots of fecal material appear marking the route taken by the termites. At this stage, where the route is quite distinct, soldiers are seen to line the edges with their heads pointing outwards. Such a trail may be temporary if the food source is not sufficiently attractive. If, however, the food source is a large piece of wood attractive to the termites and there is ample moisture, the workers will be seen depositing little pieces of chewed wood and anal cement at the edges of the trail. This happens at first proximally to the nest and food source, but soon two walls, on which the soldiers mount guard, are built along the edges of the trail from these pieces of chewed wood reinforced with anal cement. Eventually these walls bend inwards and ultimately join to form the classic covered runway or arcade. In a new arcade little gaps are left, and the antennae of the soldiers can usually be seen sticking through them. The arcade is subsequently reinforced with more chewed wood and anal cement, and an old arcade is quite opaque. In the field these arcades are about 10 mm wide and may run well over 150 feet.

It can thus be seen that in the foraging behavior of higher termites communication about presence and direction of food is carried out by the well-known contact movement and the laying of an odor trail. Some termites, of which *Zootermopsis* is one, do not forage but live in logs where nest and food are the same. As has been mentioned, *Zootermopsis* is quite capable of laying trails, but these are more noticeable in connection with alarm behavior (q.v.).

The actual mechanism of trail laying has been studied principally in *Zootermopsis* (Stuart, 1960, 1961, 1963a, 1964), where, as in *Nasutitermes,* a pheromone originating in the sternal gland is responsible for inducing trail following (Lüscher and Müller, 1960; Stuart, 1960, 1961). The termite first receives a certain stimulus which excites it and produces "alarm" behavior (Stuart, 1967). Among other events (described later under alarm behavior) the posture of the insect changes (Fig. 4), and its abdomen now touches and drags along the ground. The reservoir of the sternal gland is external and is formed by the overlapping of abdominal sternite 5 by abdominal sternite 4 (Fig. 5) so that when the termite's abdomen is pressed against the substrate the pheromonal secretion is passed out of this reservoir on to the ground.

A

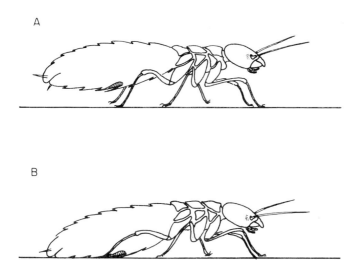

B

Fig. 4.   Schematic representation of the posture of a 12 mm nymph of *Zootermopsis,* A: during normal activity and B: while laying a trail. Note that in the latter position sternite 4, overlying the sternal gland (hatched area), is compressed (after Stuart and Satir, 1968).

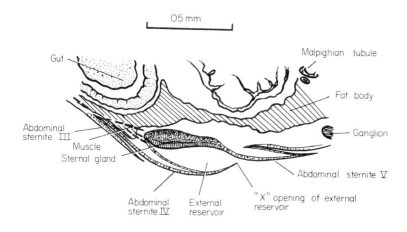

Fig. 5.   Diagrammatic longitudinal section through the abdomen of a nymph of *Zooter-mopsis nevadensis* (Hagen) showing the sternal gland. Notice that the 4th abdominal sternite is longer than the others and overlaps the 5th abdominal segment, forming a reservoir between the sternites, where pheromone could collect (from Stuart, 1964).

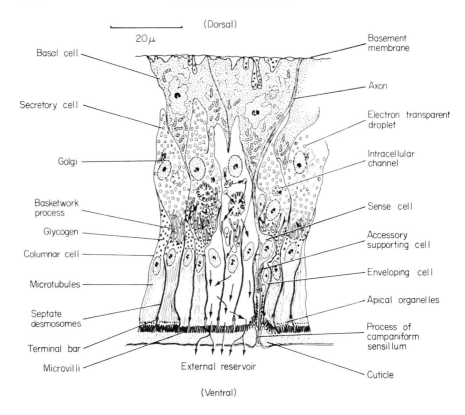

Fig. 6. Diagrammatic section, based on elecron micrographs, through the midportion of the sternal gland of a *Zootermopsis* nymph, showing the probable path of the trail pheromone from the secretory cells to the external reservoir, and one of the many campaniform sensilla (after Stuart and Satir, 1968).

The gland is unusual in having about 200 campaniform sensilla scattered through it (Fig. 6). These are generally considered to be propioceptors (Pringle, 1938) and in the present system must act as prcssure receptors (Stuart, 1964), coming into play when sternite 5 is compressed by sternite 4. The insect thus could receive information relating to the degree of compression of the sternites from these receptors. As the amount of pheromone pressed out of the external reservoir must be a function of this compression, some control could be exerted over the amount of pheromone laid down as a trail. The possible control system is diagrammed in Fig. 7. The sternal gland is thus a rather interesting organ since it has a propioceptive function combined with secretory functions (Stuart, 1964; Stuart and Satir, 1968). Perhaps, in view of its dual function of secretion and proprioception (Fig. 6), it might be more appropriate if it were called the sternal organ.

While other termites have not been studied in as much detail, it is most likely that the above mechanism, or a similar one, will be found to operate in other termites. Behavioral observations by the present author on trail laying in *Nasutitermes* and *Reticulitermes*, together with morphological studies of other workers in various other species, seem to indicate this. The sternal gland of *Reticulitermes lucifugus* seems to have campaniform sensilla (Bernardini-Mosconi and Vecchi, 1964) similar to those found in *Zootermopsis*, though Smythe and Coppel (1966a,b) are dubious about their presence in the very closely related *R. flavipes* and seem to disagree with Stuart (1964) in stating they find it difficult to conceive of a function necessitating so many sensilla in the sternal gland. In *Kalotermes* the sensilla are quite definitely present (Noirot and Noirot-Timothée, 1965), as they are in *Nasutitermes* (Pasteels, 1965). Smythe and Coppel (1966a) have inferred incorrectly that Stuart (1964) believes that *Zootermopsis* has no control over the laying of a trail. It should perhaps, therefore, be emphasized here that the view of the present writer is that in *Zootermopsis*, while the pheromone may be secreted continuously by the sternal gland, trail laying need not be continuous and, as has been mentioned, is probably under elaborate feedback control mediated in some measure by the campaniform sensilla (Fig. 7).

Smythe and Coppel (1966a) mention that the source of the trail in *Reticulitermes flavipes* is the same as in *Zootermopsis* and *Nasutitermes*, namely, the sternal gland. They have not, however, shown this in their published work. It seems, therefore, that their chemical work on the

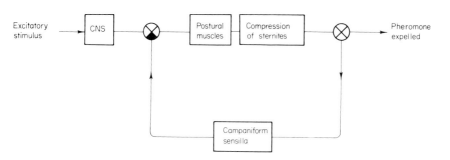

Fig. 7. Control diagram showing suggested proprioceptive feedback loop from campaniform sensilla during trail laying in *Zootermopsis*. The excitatory stimulus may be of several origins (see Stuart, 1967). Only the pathways leading to trail laying are indicated. Control systems notation is used: the shaded quadrant indicates subtraction.

identification of the pheromone from *Reticulitermes* may have proceeded without a proper biological foundation. This being so, it is difficult to evaluate the work of Esenther and Coppel (1964), Smythe and Coppel (1966b), and Smythe *et al.* (1967) on substances which they consider cause trail following in termites. Some comments, however, can be made on the validity of the type of bioassay for trail pheromones used in these later works. An assay for trail-following responses was devised by the above workers to test extracts from ground-up, whole *Reticulitermes* as well as from the fungus *Lenzites:* they consider that drawn-out extracts from *Lenzites* act in a manner similar to a trail. Basically, the assay for the extract consisted in drawing out the sample in a streak along a 60° arc of a 4 inch diameter circle with six termites placed within ½ inch of the streak. If two termites followed the trail in both directions or three in one direction, the extract was judged active. As has been pointed out (Stuart, 1963a), this type of assay cannot be considered definitive: a similar assay for trail following in the Panamanian *Nasutitermes corniger* was abandoned by the present author because, when a termite was given the choice between following any odor and nothing, it chose the former unless the substance being tested was actually repellent. The only trustworthy assay must use termites which are in as natural a condition as possible. In *Nasutitermes* the insects were first grouped together on one side of a large petri dish by placing a small portion of carton against the wall, the dish being set on a piece of paper on which several S-shaped lines had been drawn in red. The sample was then drawn out along one of the lines from the termites and was judged active only if the majority of the insects were drawn out along this trail. An assay basically similar to this has been used by B. P. Moore on his chemical work with Australian *Nasutitermes* (personal communication; see Chapter 13, Fig. 6).

In the case of *Zootermopsis* the assay was somewhat different, but here again it was considered positive when the termites were induced to cease other activities and were drawn out of an artificial nest on to a card on which an S-shaped artificial trail had been traced intersecting with a straight control trail. The termites thus left a nest where an optimal humidity of 100% prevailed to come onto a card outside the nest where the humidity was only about 50%.

Some unpublished experiments have been done recently by Stuart using the bioassay of Smythe *et al.* (1967) to test the effects of camphor drawn out in a trail. This substance was used as a standard attractant in the studies of Watanabe and Casida (1963). It was noted in several runs that the termites used, *Reticulitermes flavipes*, followed the artificial trail in the manner described by Smythe *et al.* (1967). When the standard assay of Stuart (1963a) was used no response was noted resembling the mass following of the trail observed in *Nasutitermes*. When a trail made from the squash of the integument containing the sternal gland was similarly presented to the same termites, then the classic response was noted. It would appear, therefore, that the sternal gland is the source of the trail in *Reticulitermes*. It can thus be seen that the type of assay used is important and should be adequately tested before chemical studies are carried out.

Other assays have been used by some of the above workers at various times. Esenther and Coppel (1964) and Smythe and Coppel (1966b), for example, gave termites a choice between pads placed on opposite sides of a plastic dish: one pad containing the test substance, the other being a control. The number occurring on either pad was counted at various time intervals. Such an assay may be all right for testing attractants, if carefully monitored, but it is of limited use in assaying trail substances, which are drawn out in nature. Caution must also be exercised in drawing the conclusion from the chemical investigations that the substances being assayed do have their origin in the sternal gland, as the isolation procedures used in these studies utilized whole termites (Moore, 1966; Smythe *et al.*, 1967). The various assays that have been used for trail-following responses are diagrammed in Fig. 8. As yet we have no information regarding the polarity of the trail in termites.

In the trail-following behavior in ants, similar precautions must be taken. While an ant may follow an extract of trail pheromone drawn out on a clean glass plate, similar behavior can be obtained by drawing a similar trail with, for example, a dilute solution of honey. Wilson (1959) was very aware of this, and, in his classic experiments on trail laying in *Solenopsis*, complete colonies were used to assay the pheromone. In Wilson's experiment, the ants were allowed to congregate around a piece of mealworm before a trail was drawn outwards from the aggregation so produced. When large numbers followed such a trail, the assay was considered positive.

In insects in general, Vité (1967) has cautioned against the drawing of conclusions from laboratory assays of chemical pheromones which have not adequately taken into consideration the normal behavior of the insect under investigation. In working with social insects it is even more important to have meaningful assays.

IV. NEST BUILDING AND CONSTRUCTION BEHAVIOR

A. EXCAVATION

Perhaps the simplest action in nest building is that of excavation. This is well known from primary colonies of several species of termites (e.g.,

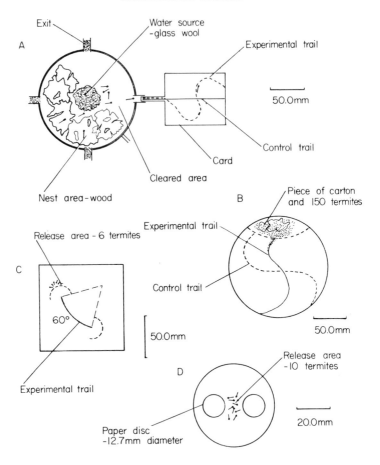

Fig. 8. Diagrams of the various types of assays used by different workers in testing material for trail-following responses of termites. For the reasons indicated in the text only assays similar to A and B are considered valid ones.

A. Assay for trail-following response in *Zootermopsis*. The experimental animals, numbering 35 or more, are an established subcolony in a Wilson nest. Substances and squashes to be tested are drawn out in an S-shaped trail on a card inserted into an exit of the nest: a straight control trail intersects with the experimental trail. Nymphs which follow the trail over a fixed time period are brushed off when they reach the end and are then counted. From Stuart (1963a).

B. Assay for trail-following response in *Nasutitermes*. Approximately 150 termites are placed with a small piece of their carton nest at one side of a 150 mm diameter petri dish. The number of termites actively drawn along an S-shaped trail made from the test material, during a period of 1 minute, is recorded. Control trails on paper under the dish are drawn, intersecting with the experimental one as shown. From Stuart (1963a). A somewhat similar assay, only using a rectangular, partitioned chamber, has been utilized by Moore (see Chapter 13), working with Australian *Nasutitermes*.

Fuller, 1915). During this behavior in *Zootermopsis angusticollis* and *Z. nevadensis* the slivers of wood are not eaten, but dropped and pushed behind the excavating termite by the action of the legs, principally the posterior ones. Such behavior is also found in nymphs which are enlarging their nest area (Stuart, unpublished). The nymph breaks off small slivers by gnawing with its mandibles, sometimes pulling away the sliver by twisting its head and body. The termite masticates the sliver slightly and then retreats no more than 4−5 mm and drops the sliver or sometimes, if the sliver has been more masticated, pushes the pulped wood into a crevice. When moving back this small distance, the nymph moves its legs in a characteristic way reminiscent of a dog burrowing or a chicken scratching for seed. This movement results in dropped slivers being pushed behind it; it can be designated the "Excavating Movement." This behavior is usually performed by several termites, quite often lined up in a row. The debris from the excavation is eaten by other termites or used to fill up crevices. Further work on this subject is in progress to ascertain how such behavior is coordinated and to find the cues responsible for its initiation and cessation.

B. CONSTRUCTION

The building behavior of termites has amazed many naturalists over the years. Smeathman (1781) observed the repairs to nests of *Macrotermes bellicosus* (Smeathman), while Beaumont (1889 − 1890) made exceedingly careful observations on the same behavior in a Panamanian nasute. Differences undoubtedly occur in various families and genera in the way and extent to which debris, fecal cement, malaxated wood, and other material are utilized and in the sequence of various actions involved in construction. Nonetheless, the behavior is remarkably similar in genera differing as much as *Zootermopsis* and *Nasutitermes* (Stuart, 1967).

C. Assay for trail-following response in *Reticulitermes*. A trail composed of the substance being tested is traced along a 60° arc (2.1 inches) of a 4-inch diameter circle drawn on the ground surface of a 4-inch square glass plate. Six workers are placed within $\frac{1}{2}$ inch of one end of the line. The response was regarded as positive if two termites ran along the trail in both directions or if three or more ran along the trail in at least one direction. Based on data in Smythe and Coppel (1966b); Smythe *et al.* (1967).
et al. (1967).
D. Assay for trail-following response in *Reticulitermes*. Ten termites are placed in the center of a plastic dish, 49 mm in diameter and are given the choice of two 12.7 mm paper pads: one being the experimental, the other the control. A response is considered positive if 5 or more termites (50%) are attracted to the experimental disk over periods of 1.0, 2.5, and 5.0 minutes. Based on data in Esenther and Coppel (1964); Smythe and Coppel (1966b); Smythe *et al.* (1967).

Basically and characteristically a nymph or worker gathers a piece of debris or dry fecal pellet in its mandibles and moves forward to the site where the object will be deposited. It then turns around and places a spot of fecal cement on the site, turns once more and, with a characteristic side to side motion of the head, places the debris or pellet on the wet cement. The process is then repeated. The most notable variation occurs in the order of the acts; in *Reticulitermes flavipes*, at least, the pellet may be positioned first and then the fecal cement deposited (personal observation). This genus is one which also makes use of malaxated material in its building. These various reactions in combination with others give rise to complicated nests in the higher termites, while in *Zootermopsis* the end constructions are walls or sheets sealing off galleries or areas. It has been noticed, however, that in older laboratory colonies of *Zootermopsis* tunnels are made through compacted fecal material, and an irregular structure reminiscent of the more organized carton nests and mounds is made.

Hypotheses to explain how the behavior of termites may lead to various constructions have been put forward principally by Grassé (1959) and more recently by Howse (1966) and Stuart (1967). The "stigmergy" hypothesis of Grassé is now well known and has been reviewed recently by Harris and Sands (1965). The principal idea in this hypothesis is that when building material at any one spot reaches a critical density this attracts other termites topochemically, foci of building activity occur, and constructions are made. Some objections to this hypothesis have been put forward by Harris and Sands (1965), among them the fact that the hypothesis would seem too simple to explain complicated structures like the launching platforms from which the imagoes of some termites take off on the swarming flight. One drawback to the hypothesis (that of their being no adequate stimulus to stop construction) has been pointed out by Stuart (1967).

Howse (1966), in his note on nest-building behavior, implies that the definitive stimulus causing building is a reaction to air movement. Stuart (1963b, 1967) has shown, however, that air movement is only one stimulus of a great number which can elicit building behavior. Howse does not comment on the hypothesis of Grassé, but suggests that the air ducts and chambers of the complicated nests found in the tropics may be constructed by the termites in response to air currents (Lüscher, 1955). Though termites are indeed exceedingly sensitive to air movement (e.g., Beaumont, 1889—1890), it is unlikely that major portions of a nest, such as *Macrotermes*, are built mainly by a response to such a single environmental stimulus. It is perhaps worth considering here whether the air currents in these nests are not the result, rather than the initiation, of building. The resolving of such speculations will await much further work. The possibility suggested by Stuart (1963b) that a sharp humidity gradient is one stimulus that could induce building was rejected by Howse on the basis of certain experiments. Howse (1966) found that when colonies of *Z. angusticollis* and *Z. nevadensis* were kept at a relative humidity of 92% they built at a rapid and fairly constant rate, while in colonies kept at relative humidities of 56% and 35% the building rate decreased and all building ceased after 24 hours. These experiments, however, seem to assume that a decrease in humidity is synonymous with a sharp humidity gradient. The results obtained might be expected since, in the species used, the low humidities are lower than normal for these animals and must affect them adversely. It can also be supposed that the reduced humidity would cause the insects to conserve water and that this in turn would lead to a reduction in the amount of fluid fecal cement necessary for building (Stuart, 1967). Snyder (1948) noted that in *Reticulitermes* such low humidities cause a reduction of shelter tube building.

The building of complicated nests, or even the less complicated constructions, will doubtless prove to be the result of no single stimulus, but rather of the interactions of many stimuli. Some of these stimuli may be normally present in the environment, or some may be self-created, as Grassé (1959) suggests in his stigmergy hypothesis. Nonetheless, it has been shown that the actual act of building is a response to a low level excitatory (or "alarm") stimulus (Stuart, 1967). This stimulus may be movement, air movement, odor, light, heat, etc. The common factor is that the stimulus upsets the normal state of the colony's environment. The response of a termite to such a stimulus is to first jerk backwards, turn, and deposit fecal cement and then to run back to the nest or central area of the colony, at the same time laying an odor trail. When another termite is met, alarm is transmitted by the well-known bumping movement (e.g., Goetsch, 1936; Stuart, 1963b). This is the same movement which Howse (1965) has called the "complex oscillatory movement." (Reference should be made to Table I for a comparison of the various names given to these different movements in termites.) The termite which receives the bumping then usually (depending on the intensity of the movement) follows the trail to the site where the first termite was alarmed; if the stimulus is still present, it will pick up a piece of debris or fecal pellet and, after depositing wet fecal cement, will place the debris or pellet in position in the usual way. As the structure forms, it gradually eliminates the causal stimulus and, when it is complete, the building activity in *Zootermopsis* is reduced and finally ceases. This structure, while it eliminates a primary stimulus, may itself give rise to a secondary stimulus (probably structural) which, in its turn, stimulates further building

TABLE I
THE TERMS APPLIED TO THE THREE WELL-KNOWN TERMITE MOVEMENTS[a]

Movement number	Authors: Various: e.g., Goetsch (1936)[b] Emerson (1929b) Morgan (1959)	Stuart (1960, 1963b)	Howse (1964a, 1965)
1	Head tapping, head banging	Head-tapping movement	Vertical oscillatory movement
2	Nudging, jittering, quivering, jerking	Horizontal reciprocating movement	Longitudinal oscillatory movement
3[c]	Alarm movement, running-dancing to all sides	Zigzag bumping move- ment ("alarm")	Complex oscillatory movement

[a]Including those utilized by Howse in his redescription of the movements with the aid of cinematography.
[b]The German of Goetsch has been translated.
[c]The third movement has been shown (Stuart, 1963b) to be implicated in the transmission from one termite to another of the excitation associated with alarm. An animal exhibiting it is in a high state of excitation ("alarm") and usually has been moving with a zigzag motion while laying a trail.

activity. Such a secondary stimulus would correspond to the second phase of coordination in the hypothesis of Grassé (1959) and, in this respect, would substantiate his idea of one of the mechanisms of building (stigmergy). The secondary stimuli created by the termites could also explain why termites can continue building in situations where humidity gradients, air movements, and other similar primary stimuli are no longer present, e.g., in sealed containers. It seems then that the initial phase in Grassé's hypothesis ("*La phase d'incoordination*"), as it applies to *Zootermopsis* and *Nasutitermes* at least, involves the transmission of directional (the trail) and excitatory information (the low level "alarm") from an "alarmed" termite, or termites, to the other members of the colony. Thus there actually is coordination even at this early stage. The second phase of stigmergy does occur in certain situations in *Zootermopsis*, but it is more apparent in those termites which build complicated nests.

It should be emphasized that the building reactions outlined above cannot explain by themselves how a complicated nest is constructed. The building of a nest must be a combination of many factors and the inter-actions of many sorts of stimuli, both primary and self-created. For example, as Harris (1961) has pointed out, various physical factors such as cold or lack of trees (a factor affecting in the first instance the paired primary reproductives) can affect the architecture of nests. The physiological state of the individual insects must also be important. Grassé and Noirot (1958) have shown that at certain times of the day building (in the form of closing exits) may occur, while at other times no building occurs and the termites forage in the open air. Whether this is due to subtle changes in the environment or to internal changes in the termite's physiology is not known. Again, in certain aspects of building the minor workers where present, as in *Nasutitermes lujae,* behave differently in this regard from the major workers (Pasteels, 1965); thus polyethism must certainly be important in nest building.

Emerson (1938, 1956) and Schmidt (1955), in their phylogenetic studies on termite nests, have regarded these nests as structures whose function is to homeostatically regulate several factors (e.g., humidity, entrance of intruders, invasion by fungi, temperature). The fact that "building" can now be shown to be a direct response to many such stimuli (Stuart, 1967) and that its immediate function is a homeostatic one of actively removing the stimulus which initiated the behavior supports the ideas of Emerson and Schmidt.

V. COLONY ODOR, ALARM, AND DEFENSE

It is becoming increasingly clear that dividing behavior into categories such as defense, feeding, and building has limitations in that, quite often, similar or even identical mechanisms are employed for these different activities. Recently Stuart (1967) pointed out certain relationships between defense behavior and building behavior. Perhaps it might be better merely to emphasize aspects concerned with homeostasis in the individual or in the colony, which is, after all, the "function" of behavior. For this reason colony odor, alarm, and defense will be considered together, and reference will be made, where appropriate, to aspects common to building and foraging behavior.

A. Colony Odor

Perhaps the most important stimuli in social behavior are chemical ones, and, indeed, as has been seen, termites are most sensitive to odors. It has been known for a long time that each colony of termites acquires an odor peculiar to it. A member of a colony, when introduced into a different colony, recognizes differences in odor from that of its own colony and will respond with a typical "alarm" reaction. A nymph may even attack a drop of distilled water which has been introduced into an experimental colony. It is possible, however, to amalgamate colonies despite the colony odor.

Andrews (1911) noticed this when he found that large numbers of termites from two different colonies showed no antagonistic behavior when mixed. Dropkin (1946) managed to mix colonies of various genera (e.g., *Kalotermes, Zootermopsis, Neotermes*) without the occurrence of fighting by partially freezing them and then placing them together. The individuals were immobilized by this treatment. When allowed to unfreeze and become mobile again no antagonism was noted. No physiological explanation for this has been given. It would be exciting if the cold somehow destroyed the "memory" for odor in the termites; however, when termites are brought out of the cold and examined under a dissecting microscope, their bodies can be seen to have minute droplets of condensation on them. It is possible that this could modify or mask the odor just as washing in water does. It is well known (e.g., Beaumont, 1889–1890; Andrews, 1911) that termites, when washed in water and replaced in their nest, are investigated vigorously, while if placed in an alien nest the attack reaction to them is somewhat reduced.

The source of the colony odor in termites has not been thoroughly investigated. Various people have considered that it may be genetic, metabolic (Verron, 1963), or that it may be derived from the environment by an odor being adsorbed onto the body (Emerson, 1929b, 1939). Free (1958) found that colony odor in bumblebees was due to a scent adsorbed on to the surface of the insect. It seems that at least part of the colony odor is environmental, as each half of a divided colony of *Zootermopsis* shows distinct hostility to the other after 3 months of separation (unpublished experiments by the present author and M. A. Schocken). There was a possibility that the changes in colony physiology with age might also be important in respect to change of odor. The work of Verron (1963), in particular, does show that colony composition must be a significant factor in the acquiring of a colony odor. As in other social insects the function of colony odor seems to be to enable the colony to recognize and deal with intruders quickly. More work is needed on this important aspect of termite biology.

B. DEFENSE

All termites share in the defense of the colony against enemies at one time or another. In the workers or worker-nymphs defense usually takes the form of building, but these animals may also snap or lunge at intruders. This is seen in some species of Panamanian nasutes where, if a nest is broken into, the workers will bite — their mandibles can penetrate the skin

of a man. In *Zootermopsis nevadensis* and *Z. angusticollis* the nymphs
are quite able to snap and bite alien insects introduced into the colony.
In most termites, however, certain individuals, members of the soldier
caste, have evolved in various ways to defend the colony specifically
against intruders rather than against physical factors such as humidity. In
the most primitive genera such as *Zootermopsis* the soldiers are relatively
few in number, and their modification is mainly in having sturdy mandibles longer than those of the workers or nymphs. In small colonies they
are normally present near the reproductives and quite often assume a
characteristic position of "rest." At other times (e.g., periods of flight
activity) they can be found in numbers at the periphery of the log they
inhabit. When confronted with an intruder the soldier points its head in
the direction of the intruder (presumably by a combination of kinesthetic
and chemical sense) and the mandibles open. The animal then closes its
mandibles quickly at the same time moving its body, but not its legs,
forward then backward in the horizontal plane. It is this action which can
disembowel another termite. This response can also occur as a low intensity reaction when the mandibles partly open but the lunge does not take
place and the mandibles then close slowly. The reaction and movement of
a nymph in snapping is quite similar to that just described for the soldier.
The soldiers of *Zootermopsis* are particularly effective against insects as
large or larger than themselves, but are rather ineffectual against very
small, hard-bodied insects such as small ants. Usually when an ant about
3 mm long is introduced into an experimental colony of *Zootermopsis* it
either escapes or else gets trapped in a *cul-de-sac* in the colony workings.
When the latter happens, the ant is walled off by nymphs depositing fecal
cement and pellets around it; rarely if ever does a soldier kill it, though
snapping occurs. The implications of this walling reaction will be considered below when alarm is discussed.

Soldiers of other families have evolved peculiar mandibles and various
methods of defense. In some cases the head has been modified in such a
way that it is very much sclerotized, and its shape just fits the tunnels
constructed by the termites in the wood (*Cryptotermes*). These phragmotic (Wheeler, 1927) soldiers thus act as living plugs. In other genera
the mandibles have been modified. Long slender curved mandibles are
present in species such as *Microcerototermes* and asymmetrical ones in
Capritermes. The soldiers of *Capritermes,* when they lock their mandibles together and release them with a loud click, spring backwards.
Emerson (1929b) has described this action, considering that this "snapping" type of mandible functions in communication rather than as an
escape mechanism. Recently, an analysis of the mandibles of soldiers of
Glyptotermes, Macrotermes, Termes, and *Pericapritermes* has been
undertaken by Deligne (1965). He considers that the slender mandibles

have evolved from the denticulated type of *Glyptotermes* through the slender symmetrical opposable types of *Termes* to the asymmetrical type of *Pericapritermes*. He considers that by virtue of its morphology and action the mandible has become more powerful in evolution. Kaiser (1954) described behavior in *Neocapritermes* similar to that reported by Deligne.

In some Rhinotermitidae and Termitidae the soldiers of certain genera are adapted for chemical defense. In *Coptotermes* this takes the form of a sticky white milky fluid, while in *Nasutitermes* a clear sticky substance is ejected from the modified "squirt gun" nasute head. The origin of these substances is the large frontal gland in the head of the soldiers. Ernst (1959) has shown the effectiveness of the nasute soldiers defense mechanism against ants. In certain Termitidae the salivary glands are specialized for defense and may be greatly enlarged. These chemical defense mechanisms are more fully dealt with in Chapters 4 and 13.

It is worth mentioning that most work on the defense behavior of termites has assumed that ants are the main enemy of termites, and little or no experimental work has been done on the effectiveness of defense mechanisms against vertebrates. While there is no doubt that ants are serious competitors and primary or secondary predators of termites (Wheeler, 1936; Bugnion, 1922), vertebrates are also extremely important (Hegh, 1922, p. 539). The nasute secretion, for example, has been described as "distasteful" to *Anolis* lizards in Hispaniola (A. S. Rand, personal communication). Again the writer has noted that many of the termites with long, slender mandibles, such as those described for *Armitermes*, tend to live underground or close to the ground. Their mandibles seem peculiarly effective against soft-skinned vertebrates, and when the skin is pierced the mandibles do not retract but stay crossed and embedded in the skin. When an attempt is made to dislodge the animal, the grip is so powerful that the thorax separates from the head, and the head and mandibles remain embedded in the skin. This situation has been noted principally in the Panamanian *Orthognathotermes,* but also in *Armitermes* where the mandibles are found in conjunction with a nasute head. A flexion of the mandibles similar to that described by Deligne in *Termes* and the quick snapping release could very easily pierce the skin of a human. It is therefore suggested here that these mandibles are more adapted to deal with vertebrates which may actively or passively open a nest, rather than to maim ants. More work is required on the ecology of termites to get a proper idea of the efficiency and extent of their predators.

As has been mentioned, the snapping reaction of the soldiers and certain workers and nymphs and the production of offensive secretions is not the only means of active defense that is available to termites. It has recently been emphasized (Stuart, 1967) that the deposition of fecal cement and the subsequent construction activity is quite an active defense mechanism. Here, however, the stimuli eliciting the response are of a lower order and, as has been mentioned, can include such physical factors as light, odor gradient, structure, or air movement. In the case of an insect intruder that has been immobilized by having its legs bitten off, for example, the nymphs or workers will commence to deposit fecal material and debris on and closely around it, thus burying it. The stimuli eliciting such a response in this situation must include odor. Sometimes burying behavior will be carried out, as in the case of the ant in a *cul-de-sac* previously mentioned, when the intruder has become immobile without actually having been killed. Burying behavior which appears similar to that described above has also been noticed in ants (Wheeler, 1910) but any significance in defense in these animals has not been pointed out.

C. COMMUNICATION OF ALARM

The defense behavior of termites just described dealt with the behavior of an individual toward a stimulus. It is a well-known fact, however, that in such instances the action taken is in conjunction with other members of the same colony. Smeathman (1781) noticed this in *Macrotermes bellicosus* when he stated:

"If you make a breach in a flight part of the building, and do it quickly with a strong hoe or pick-axe, in the space of a few seconds a soldier will run out, and walk about the breach, as if to see whether the enemy is gone, or to examine what is the cause of the attack. He will sometimes go in again, as if to give the alarm, but most frequently, in a short time, is followed by two or three others, who run as fast as they can, straggling after one another, and are soon followed by a large body who rush out as fast as the breach will permit them, and so they proceed, the number increasing, as long as any one continues battering their building."

In other words, information about the degree of excitation seems to be communicated to other members of the colony. There are several ways in which such "alarm" could be communicated, but sound (Grassi and Sandias, 1896−1897; Smeathman, 1781), odor, and contact (Grabensberger, 1933) have been the mechanisms most often implicated. The conclusions of these workers were, however, derived mainly from observations with little or no experimentation, and quite often the conclusions of different workers conflicted. Experimental studies were obviously called for to evaluate which of the suggested mechanisms were involved in alarm behavior and communication; one of the first such studies was that of Emerson's (1929b). He placed soldiers of *Reticulitermes flavipes* on a piece of wood which had replaced the diaphragm of a telephone transmitter and induced them, by disturbing them, to hammer their heads on the substratum. The sound produced was picked up by earphones after being amplified. It had been ascertained previously that the termites were unresponsive to various airborne sounds. Emerson concluded from his results, coupled with direct observation on other genera of termites (e.g. *Microtermes*), that sound produced by the soldiers is the means by which alarm is transmitted. Emerson noted that in the characteristic reciprocating movement (see Table I) well known in termites no sound is produced. He did not mention the third movement of termites where one actually makes contact with another when alarmed and performs a more zigzag bumping movement (Goetsch, 1936; Stuart, 1963b; Howse, 1965).

More recently Howse (1964a,b), using more sophisticated instruments than those available to Emerson, has reinvestigated the significance of sound in termite communication. By electrophysiological recording from the CNS he found that the subgenual organ has an "optimal frequency" for substratum vibrations of between 1000 Hz and 1150 Hz; while the sounds recorded from actively head-banging termites in wood have an approximate frequency of 1000 Hz. Howse, thus, considers that the subgenual organ in the leg is "tuned" to the sound pattern produced by the head banging of the termites. It is mainly on this basis that he claims the sound caused by head banging in *Zootermopsis* acts as a warning signal in this species also.

Howse, from other experiments, considers that the head banging (vertical oscillatory movement) produces more head banging by positive feedback, thus spreading the signal through the colony and tending to prolong the occurrence of the behavior. This physiological work, while elegant and showing the subgenual organ is extremely sensitive to substratum vibrations, is nonetheless indirect when the actual aspects of communication in a colony are considered. The conclusion that alarm transmission in *Zootermopsis* is by means of substratum vibrations was therefore based to a large extent on circumstantial evidence and cannot be considered unequivocal.

In the same studies Howse has shown quite definitely that *Zootermopsis*, like *Reticulitermes* (Emerson, 1929b), will not respond to airborne sound, and also that substratum vibrations optimally pulsating at about 2 pulses per second are needed to evoke a response. The pulsating of the sound is important as the subgenual organ will only respond to phenomena that precede or interfere with steady state.

Stuart (1963a,b) has reached a conclusion different from that of Howse

(1964a) with regard to the transmission of alarm in the primitive termite genus *Zootermopsis*. In experiments using whole colonies of *Zootermopsis* attempts were made to see whether alarm, as observed by increased activity and movements including "head banging," could be transmitted by naturally produced sound or chemicals. No alarm could be transmitted from one half of an experimentally separated colony to the other half, unless the termites were able to come in contact with each other. The termites in the experiment were kept in a 4-inch diameter Wilson nest, and in further experiments it was shown that when a nymph of *Zootermopsis* is excited by various stimuli it usually jerks back and runs off with a zigzag movement of the body, which becomes more violent when it bumps into another nymph. The second nymph in its turn becomes alarmed and a chain reaction is started. It seems that the intensity of the stimulus dissipates with secondary and tertiary bumpings of nymphs and with time. Thus, the numbers actually alarmed must depend on the degree of alarm the primary stimulus produces in a nymph and the numbers of nymphs exposed to the primary stimulus. It can be seen that with such a mechanism the activity of a whole colony need not be disrupted by the reaction of one nymph to a low-intensity alarm stimulus. A mechanism, however, which produces more head banging by positive feedback (Howse, 1964a), would tend to alarm almost every member of a colony in the situation just described, and the colony could only return to a normal state after being fatigued. In this case the normal activity of the colony would tend to be disrupted every time a quite small number of nymphs was alarmed; such a situation is unlikely.

Stuart (1963b) categorized alarm in a *Zootermopsis* colony into two types. The first, General Alarm, occurs when a large proportion of the colony is affected by the primary stimulus at the same time. The second, Specific Alarm, occurs when only one or a small number of termites is alarmed by the primary stimulus.

In General Alarm the level of excitation of every member of the colony increases as evidenced by increased activity; normal activities at first stop, and the termites seek crevices or bunch together (thigmotaxis). The soldiers and nymphs commence head banging, but the nymphs usually stop after approximately 10 minutes and begin building activities, a defense reaction (Stuart, 1967), which, when the alarm stimulus is lacking a focus, consists of filling in crevices and cracks (Stuart, 1963b). In General Alarm (Fig. 9,B) a specific focus for activities is usually lacking. It has been suggested by Stuart (1963b) that the head banging of soldiers probably keeps the insects in a higher state of activity and so speeds tasks such as building. As previously mentioned, Howse (1964a), feels

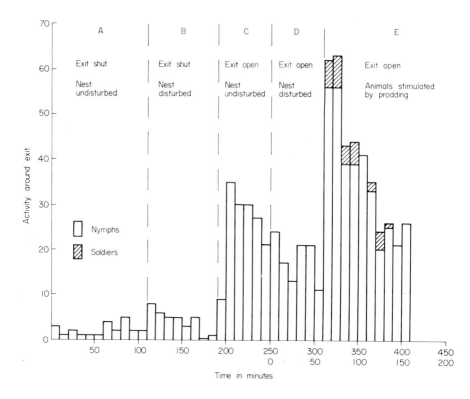

Fig. 9. Histogram showing the activity of individuals of *Zootermopsis nevadensis* around one exit of a Wilson nest, under various conditions of disturbance. Activity was measured by recording the numbers of termites entering a 3.0 cm area around the exit. Only termites remaining in the area for at least 15 seconds were recorded, and a nymph leaving the area was not recorded on a subsequent reentry unless it had been absent for at least 30 seconds. The colony was composed of 40 nymphs, 2 soldiers, and 2 secondary reproductives (♂ and ♀). Note that during General Alarm (B), when the insects are excited by banging the nest, that the activity around the exit does not increase appreciably even though all the termites are maximally excited. In Specific Alarm (C) and (E), though the external stimulus was less, the activity around the exit was greater, due to the presence of the directional vector in "alarm"—the odor trail. It should be noted that when the excitatory stimulus varies so does the activity: this can be seen in (E) where there is a greater response than in (C) where the additional stimulus of prodding with a clean needle was absent. In (E) the soldiers appear at the exit for the first time. Thus the number recruited to the site of excitation is related to the excitatory quotient of the stimulus.

In (D), where a directional vector is present but where the nest is also disturbed, numbers are less. This can be explained by the fact that each termite is alarmed individually, and the laying of trails in various parts of the nest would reduce the numbers following a trail to the exit. The experiment was interrupted after 250 minutes and re-started under the same conditions 20 hrs later: this is indicated by the dual scale (after Stuart, 1963b).

that head banging by producing vibrations acts as a warning signal. The interrelation of head banging with other activities of *Zootermopsis* will be considered below after some aspects of Specific Alarm (Fig. 9, C and E) have been treated.

The chain reaction described above, when only one or a few nymphs of a *Zootermopsis* colony are excited, is an example of Specific Alarm. In addition to the alarm transmission already mentioned, information indicating the direction of alarm is also transmitted (Fig. 10). This is done by the termite dragging its abdomen on the ground while running off, thus laying a trail. The alarmed nymphs eventually follow the trail back to the place where the first nymph was alarmed (Fig. 10). There they may carry out the defensive reactions (snapping, lunging, deposition of fecal cement) already described or run back along the trail, reinforcing it and further transmitting the alarm (Stuart, 1963b, 1967). Subsequently, Howse (1965), using the same termite (*Zootermopsis*) in experiments reminiscent of those just described (Stuart, 1963b), came to the same conclusions: that a trail is laid during alarm behavior; that the alarm is transmitted by bumping (Howse's complex oscillatory movement), and that termites so alarmed will normally follow the trail. The conclusions of Stuart (1963b) have thus been tested and confirmed in another laboratory. In this latest paper, Howse unfortunately did not comment on his previous ideas of the transmission of alarm being by sound nor on the pertinent aspects of the prior study of Stuart (1963b).*

Howse (1965) states that a nymph of *Zootermopsis*, when excited by the bumping movement (see Table I and Stuart, 1963b) and given the choice of following a trail or moving downward will choose the latter. Recent unpublished observations by Stuart on large laboratory cultures of both *Zootermopsis angusticollis* and *Z. nevadensis* have shown that when nymphs which are working on the surface of a log contained in a plastic box, the walls of which can be considered the "outside" of the

---

*It should perhaps be pointed out that Howse tended to use *Zootermopsis angusticollis* rather than *Z. nevadensis*. It is well known, however, that the two Californian species of *Zootermopsis* appear identical in all known aspects of their behavior; e.g., either species will follow artificial trails made from sternal gland extracts of the other (Stuart, 1963a). Apart from the alates of the two species being of different size and color, their morphology is identical; the nymphs are indistinguishable; the soldiers cannot be separated with any confidence; and there is still doubt as to whether *Z. angusticollis* and *Z. nevadensis* can be considered separate species. The present author has several hybrid primary colonies in the laboratory. It can be mentioned here that parallel, but less extensive, experiments to those reported in Stuart (1960, 1963a,b) were carried out at the same time on *Z. angusticollis*. The results in any experiment conducted were identical to those using *Z. nevadensis*. To avoid needless duplication and to standardize material *Z. nevadensis* was used in the majority of the experiments.

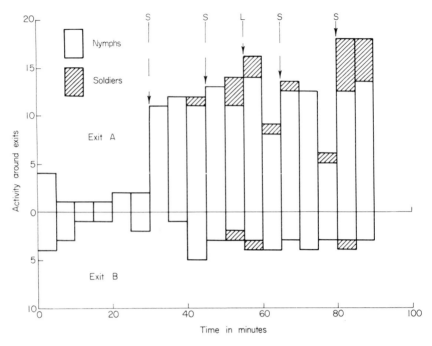

Fig. 10. Histogram showing the activity of individuals of *Zootermopsis nevadensis* around two open exits of a Wilson nest when an additional stimulus is presented at one of them. Activity was measured in a manner similar to that described in Fig. 9. Termites coming to exit A were excited by prodding (S) with a clean flamed needle, while those coming to exit B were not disturbed. Once prodding is initiated, the activity around A increases, showing that the excitation produced by the original stimulus is related to the numbers of termites recruited. It is interesting to note that if classic conditioning were operating results opposite to those actually obtained might be expected. L = 180° change in the direction of diffuse light falling on the animals. The numerical value of activity cannot be compared with Fig. 9, as the number of experimental animals tested was different (after Stuart, 1963b).

nest, are alarmed by a pulsating whistle or slight jarring, they often move upward along what is presumably a trail. A situation which has been photographed with a cine-camera is shown in Fig. 11. It would seem that under conditions approximating those found in nature termites will choose a trail. Howse in his experiments used batches of approximately 10 nymphs which were displaced from their nest or culture, and he used a severed cockroach leg as the excitatory stimulus. In the corresponding experiments of Stuart (1960, 1963b), which showed that recruitment to the "alarm" site occurs by excitation coupled with the laying of a trail, established colonies of termites were used and "alarm" was initiated by the mechanical stimulus of prodding a termite with a clean flamed needle. The smaller numbers and artificial conditions used by Howse could well explain the discrepancies in the conclusions.

D. RELATIONSHIPS BETWEEN ALARM, DEFENSE, AND CONSTRUCTION

Recently Stuart (1967) emphasized the relationships between the communication of alarm, defense, and construction. These relationships are summarized in Fig. 12. Here a single nymph excited by a stimulus follows a certain course of action. Certain stimuli are regarded as maximally evoking "alarm," as a nymph exposed to them will exhibit the complete repertoire of actions coupled with faster movement, while "low alarm stimuli" will produce less excitation and movement. In all cases a trail is laid, and, depending on the stimulus, a greater or smaller number of other nymphs are alerted and recruited. It can be seen that the results of certain of the actions modify the original stimulus by eliminating certain components of it. There are thus extracorporeal, homeostatic, feedback mechanisms operating. In an actual case when a nymph meets an intruder such as an ant or a termite from another colony it will snap at the intruder, perhaps injuring it, and then transmit the alarm to other nymphs and soldiers, which will follow the trail laid by the first nymph. If the intruder is still in the same spot, the nymphs will again snap, as will the soldier. Eventually the intruder is immobilized and the stimulus now becomes a nonmoving one. A nonmoving stimulus is a lower intensity one than a corresponding moving one, and the snapping responses decrease and are replaced more and more by the deposition of fecal cement and debris. The intruder thus becomes buried and the important odor component of the stimulus neutralized. Again the burying reaction is a negative feedback one with regard to the primary stimulus.

VI. REGULATORY BEHAVIOR

In social insects the proportion of the castes in a colony is kept in nice balance, even though the proportion itself may vary at different times. To a large extent this is done through physiologically acting pheromones and hormones responsible for polymorphism. However, the proportion of castes is also regulated in a more negative manner in that individuals are actively eliminated by the remainder of the colony. In termites this elimination is well known (e.g., Lüscher, 1952) and takes the form of selective cannibalism. At certain times both soldiers and reproductives, when in excess, may be thus eliminated.

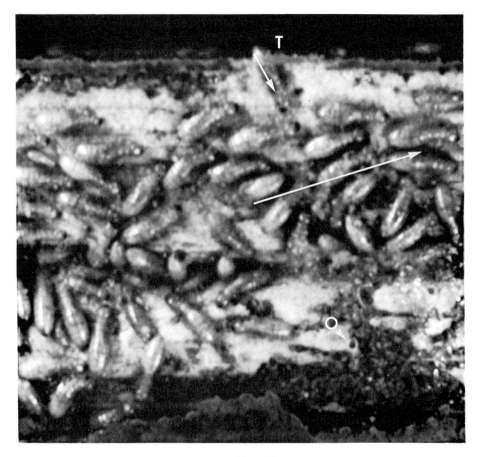

Fig. 11A

Fig. 11.   Photographs from a cine-film of a laboratory colony of *Zootermopsis nevaden-sis* in a clear plastic container. (A) The animals are undisturbed and show no common orientation. (B) The termites have just been alarmed by a series of sharp taps. Note that they are all moving upward toward a narrow gap in a lamella constructed of cemented fecal material. The position of the gap is indicated by "T" in both photographs, and the point marked by "0" in both photographs is the same.

Lüscher (1952, 1961) has investigated the social factors involved in the production and elimination of supplementary reproductives of *Kalotermes flavicollis*. He found that there appear to be sex-specific phero-mones, in addition to the inhibitory pheromones produced by reproduc-tives, which are perceived by the pseudergates with their antennae. The pheromones seem, however, not to be volatile, as actual antennal contact with the reproductives is needed before any newly produced supplementaries, formed when the original reproductives have been cut off from the rest of the colony by single wire gauze, are eliminated. No explanation for the manner in which these pheromones operate has been worked out. Less is known about soldier elimination. Similar phenomena found in the social hymenoptera have been reviewed by Wilson (1966). Wilson (1966) has observed the execution of queens of *Solenopsis*, but it is not known whether chemical substances, akin to those postulated by Lüscher in *Kalotermes*, are involved here. The reader is referred to Chapters 9 and 10 for further discussion.

Fig. 11B

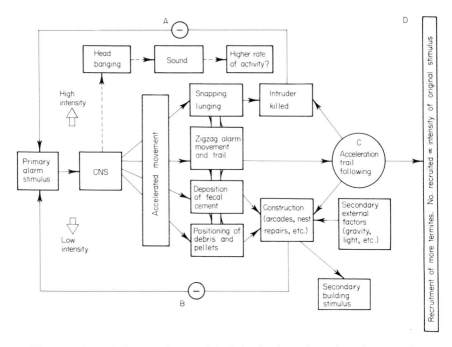

Fig. 12. Control diagram of some of the behavioral reactions of termites to excitatory stimuli causing varying degrees of "alarm." At high intensities a nymph may snap or lunge, while the response to low intensity stimuli is to jerk and deposit fecal cement or build. (A) and (B) are negative feedback pathways which modify the primary stimulus causing the excitation. The probable relationship of head banging, occurring when a colony is maximally alarmed (General Alarm), is indicated by broken lines. (C) represents another termite alarmed by the first, and (D) represents further recruitment of more animals. It can be seen that the relatively immediate reactions lead to social homeostasis quite quickly (after Stuart, 1967).

VII. CONCLUSION

Many aspects of the social behavior of termites need much more investigation. In particular, more information is needed concerning the division of labor in a colony. Pasteels (1965) has shown that in *N. lujae*, at least, there is a significant difference in behavior (caste polyethism) between the major and minor workers. Also, the evolutionary aspects need more consideration. It would be interesting to know, for example, why in the Isoptera the male has been retained in the colony to continually inseminate the female, while in the ants such a "king" is lacking.

There is no doubt that the superorganism analogy of the social insect colony put forward by Wheeler (1911) and elaborated in termites principally by Emerson (e.g., 1939) and Lüscher (1953), has provided a useful background for the investigation of social behavior. More work, however, should be carried out on the behavior of single termites as individual organisms, but always with the very important fact in mind that a single termite isolated from its colony is in quite an unnatural situation. In *Zootermopsis*, *Nasutitermes*, and *Reticulitermes*, at least, a termite under normal conditions is always in "contact" with its companions, even when separated from them by some distance, because a trail is laid down.

Not much is known about the development of behavior and modified behavior in termites. Colony odor, however, would seem to be a phenomenon involving modified behavior, and the factors responsible for appearance and disappearance of the characteristic "jumping" behavior of recent dealates of *Zootermopsis* are now known.

ACKNOWLEDGMENTS

The writing of this chapter and much of the original work first reported here was supported by grant No. GB-5051 from the U.S. National Science Foundation.

Thanks are due to Dr. R. T. Yamamoto for critically reading the manuscript.

REFERENCES

Andrews, E. A. (1911). Observations on termites in Jamaica. *J. Animal Behavior* 1, 193-228.

Beaumont, J. (1889-1890). Observations on the termites or white ants of the isthmus of Panama. *Trans. N. Y. Acad. Sci.* 8, 85-114; 9, 157-180.

Bernardini-Mosconi, P., and Vecchi, M. L. (1964). Osservasioni istologiche e fluoromicroscopiche sulla ghiandola sternale di *Reticulitermes lucifugus* (Rhinotermitidae). *Symp. Genet. Biol. Ital.* 13, 169-177.

Buchli, H. (1960). Les tropismes lors de la pariade des imagos de *Reticulitermes lucifugus* R. *Vie Milieu* 11, 308-315.

Buchli, H. (1961). Les relations entre la colonie naternelle et les jeunes imagos ailés de *Reticulitermes lucifugus*. *Vie Milieu* 12, 627-632.

Bugnion, E. (1922). La guerre des fourmis et des termites, la genése des instincts expliquée par cette guerre. *In* "Le monde social des fourmis" (A. Forel), Vol. III, Appendix, pp. 173-225, Genève.

Deligne, J. (1965). Morphologie et fontionnement des mandibules chez les soldats des Termites. *Biol. Gabonica* 1, 179-186.

Dropkin, V. H. (1946). The use of mixed colonies of termites in the study of host-symbiont relations. *J. Parasitol.* 32, 247-251.

Emerson, A. E. (1929a). Ecological relationships between termites and termitophiles in British Guiana. *Proc. 10th Intern. Congr. Zool.* Budapest (1927), Vol. 2, pp. 1008-1009.

Emerson, A. E. (1929b). Communication among termites. *Trans. 4th Intern. Congr. Entomol., Ithaca* (1928) Vol. 2, pp. 722-727.

Emerson, A. E. (1933). The mechanism of tandem behavior following the colonizing flight of termites. *Anat. Record* 57, 61 (Abstr.).

Emerson, A. E. (1938). Termite nests. A study of the phylogeny of behavior. *Ecol. Monographs* 8, 247-284.

Emerson, A. E. (1939). Social coordination and the superorganism. *Am. Midland Naturalist* **21**, 182-209.

Emerson, A. E. (1949). The organization of insect societies. *In* "Principles of Animal Ecology" pp. 419-435. Saunders, Philadelphia, Pennsylvania.

Emerson, A. E. (1956). Regenerative behavior and social homeostasis of termites. *Ecology* **37**, 248-258.

Ernst, E. (1959). Beobachtungen beim spritzakt der *Nasutitermes* soldaten. *Rev. Suisse Zool.* **66**, 289-295.

Esenther, G. R., and Coppel, H. C. (1964). Current research on termite attractants. *Pest Control* **32** [2], 34-46.

Free, J. B. (1958). The defence of bumblebee colonies. *Behaviour* **12**, 233-242.

Fuller, C. (1915). Observations on some South African termites. *Ann. Natal Museum* **3**, 329-505.

Goetsch, W. (1936). Beiträge zur biologie des termitenstaates. *Z. Morphol. Oekol. Tiere* **31**, 490-560.

Grabensberger, W. (1933). Untersuchungen über das zeitgedächtnis der ameisen und termiten. *Z. Vergleich. Physiol.* **29**, 1-54.

Grassé, P.-P. (1949). Ordre des Isoptères ou Termites. "Traité de Zoologie" (P.-P. Grassé, ed.), Vol. IX, pp. 408-544. Masson, Paris.

Grassé, P.-P. (1952). L'effet de groupe chez les insectes. *Bull. Sec. Franc. Union Intern. Etudes Insectes Sociaux* **1**, 32-43.

Grassé, P.-P. (1959). La reconstruction du nid et les coordinations inter-individuelles chez *Bellicositermes natalensis* et *Cubitermes* sp. La théorie de la stigmergie: Essai d'interpretation du comportment des Termites constructeurs. *Insectes Sociaux* **6**, 41-84.

Grassé, P.-P., and Noirot, C. (1958). Le comportement des Termites à l'egard de l'air libre. L'atmosphère des termitières et son renouvellement. *Ann. Sci. Nat. Zool. Biol. Animale* [11] **20**, 1-28.

Grassé, P.-P., and Noirot, C. (1961). Nouvelles recherches sur la systématique et l'éthologie des Termites champignonnistes du genre *Bellicositermes* Emerson. *Insectes Sociaux* **8**, 311-359.

Grassi, B., and Sandias, A. (1806-1897). The constitution and development of the society of termites: Observations on their habits; with appendices on the parasitic protozoa of Termitidae, and on the Embiidae. *Quart. J. Microscop. Sci.* **39**, 245-322; **40**, 1-82.

Griffin, D. R. (1958). "Listening in the Dark." Yale Univ. Press, New Haven, Connecticut.

Harris, W. V. (1961). "Termites, their Recognition and Control." Longmans, Green, New York.

Harris, W. V., and Sands, W. A. (1965). The social organization of termite colonies. *Symp. Zool. Soc. London* **14**, 113-131.

Hegh, E. (1922). "Les termites, partie générale." Brussels.

Howse, P. E. (1964a). The significance of the sound produced by the termite *Zootermopsis angusticollis* (Hagen). *Animal Behaviour* **12**, 284-300.

Howse, P. E. (1964b). An investigation into the mode of action of the subgenual organ in the termite, *Zootermopsis angusticollis* Emerson, and in the cockroach, *Periplaneta americana* L. *J. Insect Physiol.* **10**, 409-424.

Howse, P. E. (1965). On the significance of certain oscillatory movements of termites. *Insectes Sociaux* **12**, 335-346.

Howse, P. E. (1966). Air movement and termite behaviour. *Nature* **210**, 967-968.

Huber, P. (1810). "Recherches sur les moeurs des fourmis indigènes." Paschoud, Paris.

Humphries, D. A., and Driver, P. M. (1967). Erratic display as a device against predators. *Science* **156**, 1767-1768.

Kaiser, P. (1954). Ueber die funktion der mandibeln bei den soldaten von *Neocapritermes opacus* (Hagen). *Zool. Anz.* **152**, 228-234.

Kalshoven, L. G. E. (1960). Biological notes on the *Cryptotermes* species of Indonesia. *Acta Trop.* **17**, 263-272.

Light, S. F. (1937). Contributions to the biology and taxonomy of *Kalotermes (Paraneotermes) simplicicornis* Banks (Isoptera). *Univ. Calif. (Berkeley) Publ. Entomol.* **6**, 423-464.

Lindauer, M. (1961). "Communication among social bees." Harvard Univ. Press, Cambridge, Massachusetts.

Lindauer, M. (1965). Social behavior and mutual communication. *In* "The Physiology of Insecta" (M. Rockstein, ed.), Vol. 2, p. 124, Academic Press, New York.

Lüscher, M. (1952). Die produktion und elimination von ersatzgeschlectstieren bei der termite *Kalotermes flavicollis* Fabr. *Z. Vergleich. Physiol.* **34**, 123-141.

Lüscher, M. (1953). The termite and the cell. *Sci. Am.* **188** [5], 74-78.

Lüscher, M. (1955). Der sauerstoffverbrauch bei termiten und die ventilation des nestes bei *Macrotermes natalensis* (Haviland). *Acta Trop.* **12**, 289-307.

Lüscher, M. (1960). Hormonal control of caste determination in termites. *Ann. N. Y. Acad. Sci.* **89**, 549-563.

Lüscher, M. (1961). Social control of polymorphism in termites. *In* "Insect Polymorphism" (J. S. Kennedy, ed.), No. 1, pp. 57–67. Roy. Entomol. Soc., London.

Lüscher, M., and Müller, B. (1960). Ein spurbildendes sekret bei termiten. *Naturwissenschaften* **27**, 503.

Moore, B. P. (1966). Isolation of the scent-trail pheromone of an Australian termite. *Nature* **211**, 746-747.

Morgan, F. D. (1959) The ecology and external morphology of *Stolotermes ruficeps* Brauer (Isoptera, Hodotermitidae). *Trans. Roy. Soc. New Zealand* **86**, 155-195.

Noirot, C. (1958-1959). Remarques sur l'écologie des termites. *Ann. Soc. Roy. Zool. Belg.* **89**, 151-169.

Noirot, C., and Noirot-Timothée, C. (1965). La glande sternale dans l'évolution des termites. *Insectes Sociaux* **12**, 265-272.

Pasteels, J. M. (1965). Polyéthisme chez les ouvriers de *Nasutitermes lujae* (Termitidae, Isoptères). *Biol. Gabonica* **1**, 191-205.

Pringle, J. W. S. (1938). Proprioception in insects II. The action of the campaniform sensilla on the legs. *J. Exptl. Biol.* **15**, 114-131.

Réaumur, R. A. (1742). "Memoires pour servir à l'histoire des insectes." Paris.

Roth, L. M., and Barth, R. H. (1964). The control of sexual receptivity in female cockroaches. *J. Insect Physiol.* **10**, 965-975.

Sands, W. A. (1965). Alate development and colony foundation in five species of *Trinervitermes* (Isoptera, Nasutitermitinae) in Nigeria, West Africa. *Insectes Sociaux* **12**, 117-130.

Schmidt, R. S. (1955). The evolution of nest-building behaviour in *Apicotermes* (Isoptera). *Evolution* **9**, 157-181.

Skaife, S. H. (1955). "Dwellers in Darkness." Longmans, Green, New York.

Smeathman, H. (1781). Some account of the termites which are found in Africa and other hot climates. *Phil. Trans. Roy. Soc. London* **71**, 139-192.

Smythe, R. V., and Coppel, H. C. (1966a). A preliminary study of the sternal gland of *Reticulitermes flavipes* (Isoptera: Rhinotermitidae). *Ann. Entomol. Soc. Am.* **59**, 1008-1010.

Smythe, R. V., Coppel, H. C. (1966b). Some termites may secrete trail blazing attractants to lead others to food sources. *Pest Control* 34 [10], 73-78.

Smythe, R. V., and Coppel, H. C., Lipton, S. H., and Strong, F. M. (1967). Chemical studies of attractants associated with *Reticulitermes flavipes* and *Reticulitermes virginicus*. *J. Econ. Entomol.* 60, 228-233.

Snyder, T. E. (1948). "Our Enemy the Termite" Cornell Univ. Press (Comstock), Ithaca, New York.

Snyder, T. E. (1956). Annotated, subject-heading bibliography of termites 1350 BC to AD 1954. *Smithsonian Misc. Collections* 130, 1-305.

Snyder, T. E. (1961). Supplement to the annotated, subject-heading bibliography of termites 1955 to 1960. *Smithsonian Misc. Collections* 143, 1-137.

Stuart, A. M. (1960). Experimental studies on communication in termites. Ph.D. Thesis, Harvard University.

Stuart, A. M. (1961). Mechanisms of trail-laying in two species of termites. *Nature* 189, 419.

Stuart, A. M. (1963a). The origin of the trail in the termites *Nasutitermes corniger* (Motschulsky) and *Zootermopsis nevadensis* (Hagen), Isoptera. *Physiol. Zool.* 36, 69-84.

Stuart, A. M. (1963b). Studies on the communication of alarm in the termite *Zootermopsis nevadensis* (Hagen), Isoptera. *Physiol. Zool.* 36, 85-96.

Stuart, A. M. (1964). The structure and function of the sternal gland in *Zootermopsis nevadensis* (Hagen), Isoptera. *Proc. Zool. Soc. London* 143, 43-52.

Stuart, A. M. (1967). Alarm, defense and construction behavior relationships in termites (Isoptera). *Science* 156, 1123-1125.

Stuart, A. M., and Satir, P. (1968). Morphological and functional aspects of an insect epidermal gland. *J. Cell Biol.* 36, 527-549.

Sudd, J. H. (1966). "An Introduction to the Behaviour of Ants." Arnold, London.

Verron, H. (1963). Rôle des stimuli chimiques dans l'attraction sociale chez *Calotermes flavicollis* (Fabr.). Thèses présentées à la faculté des sciences de l'université de Paris, Ser. A, No. 4108, 167-335. Masson, Paris.

Vité, J. P. (1967). Sex attractants in frass from bark beetles. *Science* 156, 105.

Watanabe, T., and Casida, J. E. (1963). Response of *Reticulitermes flavipes* to fractions from fungus-infected wood and synthetic chemicals. *J. Econ. Entomol.* 56, 300-307.

Weesner, F. M. (1960). Evolution and biology of the termites. *Ann. Rev. Entomol.* 5, 153-170.

Wheeler, W. M. (1910). "Ants, their Structure, Development and Behaviour." Columbia Univ. Press, New York.

Wheeler, W. M. (1911). The ant colony as an organism. *J. Morphol.* 22, 307-325.

Wheeler, W. M. (1927). The physiognomy of insects. *Quart. Rev. Biol.* 11, 3-45.

Wheeler, W. M. (1928). "The Social Insects." Harcourt, Brace, New York.

Wheeler, W. M. (1936). Ecological relations to Ponerine and other ants to termites. *Proc. Am. Acad. Arts Sci.* 71, 159-243.

Wigglesworth, Sir V. B. (1966). "The Life of Insects." World, Cleveland, Ohio.

Wilkinson, W. (1962). Dispersal of alates and establishment of new colonies in *Cryptotermes havilandi* (Sjöstedt) (Isoptera, Kalotermitidae). *Bull. Entomol. Res.* 53, 265-286.

Wilson, E. O. (1959). Source and possible nature of the odor trail of fire ants. *Science* 129, 643-644.

Wilson, E. O. (1962). Chemical communication among workers of the fire ant *Solenopsis saevissima* (Fr. Smith). I. The organization of mass foraging. *Animal Behaviour* 10, 134-147.

Wilson, E. O. (1966). Behaviour of social insects. *In* "Insect Behaviour" (P. T. Haskell, ed.), Symp. No. 3, pp. 81-96. Roy. Entomol. Soc., London.

8

Flight and Colony Foundation*

W. L. NUTTING

I. INTRODUCTION

The majority of insects produce only winged adults, which may or may not take part in some form of migratory behavior. The termites, aphids, and ants, however, commonly produce both wingless adults

*This contribution and some of the unpublished work contained herein were supported by State Research Project 461 in the Agricultural Experiment Station, University of Arizona, Tucson.

and, periodically, winged adults whose sole function is participation in characteristic migration patterns. Indeed, the termite (or ant) colony has been likened to a sessile organism, wings having been retained by the sexual adults of one caste for a single seasonal migration or dispersal flight. A rather variable but complex sequence of behavior then normally intervenes between termination of the brief flight and copulation, which is delayed until a pair establish themselves within wood or beneath the soil. Foundation of successful colonies by such pairs in suitable vacancies or extensions of the habitat is accomplished by an extremely small proportion of those who participate in the flight. More limited dispersal may be achieved for certain species which sometimes found new colonies by "budding" (isolation of parts of a population) or by "sociotomy" (migration of complete units of a mature colony).

The subject of colonizing flights and associated activities has been rather comprehensively reviewed in the following: Hegh (1922), Light (1934), Grassé (1942, 1949), Snyder (1948), Herfs (1955), Harris (1958, 1961), Weesner (1960), and Harris and Sands (1965). From these and numerous other sources, examples have been selected to give a comparative view of typical behavior patterns and some of the factors concerned with their regulation. Also pertinent is the general work on animal dispersal in relation to social behavior by Wynne-Edwards (1962) and the review by Johnson (1966) in which he presents a scheme for the systematic study of the ecological, physiological, and behavioral aspects of insect dispersal by flight. Since so few comprehensive attempts have been made to interpret termite flight or to relate it to the dispersal of other insects, this approach might profitably be considered in the course of future observational and experimental work on the dispersal of termites.

II. PREFLIGHT ACTIVITIES OF THE COLONY

The swarming season provides the only occasion when the behavior of many species can be studied under natural conditions. Preliminary activities involving the production of mature alates and more immediate preparations for their exodus take place within the confines of the colony. Information on these phases has then obviously been accumulated from laboratory colonies and such drastic measures as opening up nests in the field. Through the efforts of several European workers (recently summarized by Buchli, 1961) these methods have probably provided more details on this phase of colonial life for *Reticulitermes lucifugus* (Rossi) than for any other termite.

A. PRODUCTION AND DEVELOPMENT OF ALATES

As with other castes, the production of alates is apparently under the immediate control of pheromones and nutrients which are exchanged in complex patterns of grooming and trophallaxis, so that a dynamic balance is continuously maintained among the various castes. The relative plasticity of immature forms, as well as the timing and other details of their development toward primary reproductives in each family, are considered in Chapters 9 and 10.

There is fragmentary evidence that a number of environmental factors influence alate production. Colony size or maturity is apparently fundamental in determining not only the number of alates, but whether they will be produced at all. For example, Lüscher (1961) found that alates were produced only in spring colonies of *Kalotermes flavicollis* (Fabricius) of 100 or more individuals. In laboratory colonies of the same termite maintained by Grassé and Noirot (1958), alates were not produced until after the second year, when most colonies had reached a comparable size. The effect of size may be modified by other factors (see below), for some alates were produced in colonies of only about 25 individuals. Snyder (1915) quoted Joutel, who kept a colony of two or three dozen workers of *Reticulitermes flavipes* (Kollar), in which a few alates were produced and swarmed each year. Among the higher termites, nymphs (with wing pads) appeared in colonies of *Apicotermes desneuxi* Emerson when total populations reached about 5000, including some 2000 workers. The largest societies of this species apparently produce two successive groups of alates and stage flights at the beginning of each phase of the rainy seasons (Bouillon, 1964). Two broods of alates may also occur in *Microcerotermes parvus* (Haviland) in Tanganyika (Kemp, 1955), and the same is often the case with *Reticulitermes lucifugus* under near-optimum laboratory conditions (Buchli, 1958). Buchli (1958) and Lüscher (1960) have expressed the conviction that nutrition, which is related to colony size, is also important in the differentiation of alates. Lüscher stated that good nutrition may favor development toward nymphs and alates of *Kalotermes flavicollis*, while less effective nutrition may lead to stationary or regressive molts. The possibility has also been raised that the appearance of nymphs in the alate line may be inhibited by the presence of mature alates in the parent colony (Weesner, 1953), and perhaps even by the primary reproductives (Grassé and Noirot, 1958; Snyder, 1915). Although there is no evidence that a colony founded by secondary reproductives cannot produce normal alates (Harris, 1958), Skaife (1954c) has stated that tertiary queens of *Ami-*

termes hastatus (Haviland) (as *A. atlanticus* Fuller) cannot lay eggs which will develop into alates.

While temperature obviously affects the rate of alate production (Buchli, 1958), growth potential is also influenced in unknown ways by environmental factors during winter in temperate zones and wet or dry seasons in the tropics (Brian, 1965a; Noirot, 1961). Alate development in mounds of *Trinervitermes geminatus* (Wasmann) (as *T. ebenerianus* Sjöstedt) is accelerated by moisture, and such a response may enable this species to take advantage of early rains (Sands, 1965b). It has also been noted that development of alates "may be quickened" in colonies of *Cryptotermes cynocephalus* Light confined in a small volume of wood (Kalshoven, 1960), and that the majority of individuals in declining colonies of *Zootermopsis* may mature as alates when colonies are isolated in old logs or drying limbs (Nutting, unpublished; Weesner, 1965). Among the lower termites a sharp contrast is provided by cases where alates are present in the nests and perhaps even produced more or less continuously throughout the year: *Neotermes tectonae* (Dammerman) (Kalshoven, 1930); *Cryptotermes havilandi* (Sjöstedt) (Wilkinson, 1962); *Zootermopsis angusticollis* (Hagen) (Castle, 1934). Although there may be periodic peaks, alate production in these species is certainly not so precisely synchronized with seasonal changes in the environment.

Buchli (1958) has reported an unequal sex ratio among alates of *Reticulitermes lucifugus* from a locality in France. He has discussed earlier (and occasionally disputed) reports on flights of this species in Italy composed either of one sex (Grassi and Sandias, 1893–1894) or of a preponderance of one sex (Herfs, 1951). He concluded that, in the above cases at least, *R. lucifugus* is probably not normally propagated by winged forms. This bears out earlier reports that the Italian form does not reproduce by dealated imagoes. His arguments involve the common lack of complete synchrony of flights from neighboring colonies, unequal production of the sexes, predation, and adverse climatic factors. A prevalence of females is produced among the alates of five species of *Trinervitermes* in Nigeria. Sands (1965b) attached selective value to this occurrence, since the females have a static calling behavior and may thus be more susceptible to predation than the wandering males.

The flights of termites are synchronized to varying degrees with specific seasonal weather patterns. The wide variation between the appearance of alates in the nest and the date of the first flight demonstrates a correlation between weather and flight, rather than between the systematic position and flight. For example, preflight delay for alates of *Reticulitermes lucifugus* was found to vary between 4 and 57 days by

Buchli (1961). An interval of several weeks has been noted for a variety of species: *Paraneotermes simplicicornis* (Banks) (Nutting, 1966a); *Pterotermes occidentis* (Walker) (Nutting, 1966b); *Zootermopsis laticeps* (Banks) (Nutting, 1965); *Trinervitermes* spp. (Sands, 1965b); and *Tenuirostritermes tenuirostris* (Desneux) (Weesner, 1953). Flight may be deferred for periods of a month and much longer as the following observations show: *Mastotermes darwiniensis* Froggatt (Hill, 1942); *Macrotermes natalensis* (Haviland) (Ruelle, 1964); and *Amitermes hastatus* [as *A. atlanticus*] (Skaife, 1954b). Perhaps the longest delay is one of 6 months reported for *Anacanthotermes ochraceus* (Burmeister) in the Sahara by Clément (1956a).

1. Numbers of Alates and Colony Size

Information on number of alates related to colony size is difficult to obtain, particularly where the largest populations occur, in subterranean forms. The following are examples of cases in which the percentages of alates in entire colonies were actually determined: *Pterotermes occidentis*, 30% (Nutting, 1966b); *Paraneotermes simplicicornis*, 14−16% (Nutting, 1966a); *Zootermopsis laticeps*, 39% (Nutting, unpublished); *Stolotermes victoriensis* Hill, 17.5% (Hill, 1942); *Nasutitermes exitiosus* (Hill), 2.4% (Holdaway et al., 1935); and *Odontotermes obesus* (Rambur), 28−43.3% (nymphs) (Roonwal, 1960). Ratcliffe et al. (1952) reported that a colony of *Coptotermes lacteus* (Froggatt), totaling approximately one million, might produce 60,000 alates in a year. After sampling mounds of *Trinervitermes geminatus* (as *T. ebenerianus*) in savannas of West Africa, with estimated populations between 19,000 and 52,000 individuals, Sands (1965a) calculated mean alate production at 950 per mound, with a probable number of one or two hundred thousand per acre. Counts of nymphs and alates are included in the extensive data collected by Bouillon (1964) on three species of *Apicotermes*, and by Bouillon and Lekie (1964) on *Cubitermes sankurensis* Wasmann.

2. Readiness of Alates for Flight

Except in those cases where only a single flight is staged each year, the final ecdysis and maturation of alates probably occur over a period proportional to the length of the flight season. In general, alates appear sufficiently well equipped for flight and colony foundation within a few days after molting into adults. Hardening and pigmentation of the cuticle seem to be complete in 2 days for *Reticulitermes lucifugus* (Buchli, 1961), in 7 days for *Marginitermes hubbardi* (Banks) (Nutting, unpublished), and in "several days" for *Zootermopsis nevadensis* (Hagen)

(Banks and Snyder, 1920). The neuromuscular flight mechanism is functional very early, but full flight capacity may not develop until 9 – 14 days after ecdysis in *M. hubbardi* (Nutting, unpublished) and 7 – 10 days in *Z. nevadensis* (Banks and Snyder, 1920). The gonads have matured to the point where copulation may be accomplished within a matter of hours or days and egg production begun within a few days or weeks after formation of the copularium (Section V, C).

It is occasionally ventured that alates do not feed while in the mother colony (Heath, 1927); indeed, Buchli (1958, 1961) concluded that alates and even last instar nymphs of *Reticulitermes lucifugus* may not feed or be fed. Yet, in laboratory colonies of *Zootermopsis nevadensis*, May (1941) found an increasing amount of wood and fluid in the digestive tracts of alates. However this may be, the fat body is generally well developed, and very obviously so in alates of the Termitidae. Even though it is evident that alates of the lower termites must fly with an inoculum of symbiotic protozoans, the details of its final acquisition are not agreed upon. In *Kalotermes flavicollis*, *Incisitermes minor* (Hagen), and *Z. nevadensis* and *Z. angusticollis* it is known that the protozoans are retained within the shed intima of the hindgut after the final ecdysis, so that refaunation is unnecessary (May, 1941; Grassé, 1949; Nutting, 1956). According to Grassé (1949) the symbiotes of *Reticulitermes lucifugus* are lost at the last ecdysis, and the young imagoes must regain their infection by proctodeal feeding. On the other hand, there is some evidence that the alates of certain Macrotermitinae do not fly similarly equipped with an inoculum for their fungus beds (Lüscher, 1951; Sands, 1960).

B. BEHAVIOR OF INDIVIDUAL CASTES

Grassé (1942) suggested that reciprocal stimulation between alates and the other castes is probably one of the most important factors inducing emergence in the day-flying Kalotermitidae and Rhinotermitidae. The following sections show that there are behavior patterns common to each group or caste within a colony, although the extent of their involvement in preparations for the exodus of alates is rather variable. Verron (1963) has investigated the complex and changing interattractions between the developing sexual forms and the other members in colonies of *Kalotermes flavicollis*. The analysis of preflight behavior in other families should benefit considerably from further application of this approach.

1. Larvae, Nymphs, and Workers

Preflight behavior is generally more complex among the higher termites, although the preparations made for the exodus of alates certainly depend on a variety of factors, including the location and architecture of the nest, number of alates involved, timing of the flight, and rate of predation. In the simplest cases immatures or workers drive tunnels to the surface of the wood (*Kalotermes flavicollis*), of the soil (*Reticulitermes lucifugus*, Grassé, 1942; *Coptotermes heimi* (Wasmann), Roonwal, 1959), or of the mound (*Macrotermes natalensis*, Ruelle, 1964), which end in unadorned emergence holes. Occasionally special waiting chambers are excavated to accommodate the alates prior to swarming: e.g., in *Odontotermes assmuthi* Holmgren (Sen-Sarma, 1962), *Microtermes havilandi* Holmgren (as *Termes incertus*) (Fuller, 1915). Abandoned tunnels of wood-boring beetles may sometimes serve as exits for the alates of *Porotermes adamsoni* (Froggatt) (Hill, 1942) and *Pterotermes occidentis* (Nutting, unpublished). In day- or twilight-flying subterranean species, where the holes are relatively exposed, immatures or workers and soldiers commonly guard the exterior vicinity of the exits during alate emergence. Such behavior is apparently unusual for night-flying or wood-inhabiting species, although Wilkinson (1962) cited a single observation where several larvae of *Cryptotermes havilandi* were found outside a flight exit.

Among certain subterranean species, workers build a diversity of special structures, which perhaps facilitate the takeoff of alates, but more likely reduce attack by small surface predators. These take the form of variously shaped walls, craters, and cones: *Odontotermes badius* (Haviland) (Harris, 1961), *Pseudacanthotermes spiniger* (Sjöstedt) (Grassé and Noirot, 1951a); funnels: *Allodontermes infundibuli* (Sjöstedt) (Hegh, 1922); and contorted or freestanding tubes or chimneys: *Reticulitermes flavipes* (Snyder, 1948), *Microtermes usambaricus* Sjöstedt (Grassé and Noirot, 1951a). To judge from the accompanying accounts, the workers and soldiers do not usually venture outside these structures during emergence of the alates. Although there are few enlightening observations on these particular activities, it appears that the workers may be stimulated by rainfall to dig emergence tunnels, either by the mechanical disturbance of raindrops on the mound (*Macrotermes natalensis*; Ruelle, 1964) or perhaps by the soaking of the soil (*Odontotermes badius*; Harris, 1958). Skaife (1954a) suggested that the exodus was controlled by the workers of *Amitermes hastatus*, since he saw them pulling imagoes back into the mound by their wings.

Immatures with well-developed wing pads sometimes become entrained in "pseudoflights" with the alates during emergence for flight. Such incipient adult behavior remains unexplained, although it has been observed and discussed for *Reticulitermes* and *Zootermopsis* (Snyder, 1948), *Pseudacanthotermes militaris* (Hagen) (Grassé and Noirot, 1951a), and also observed in *Gnathamitermes perplexus* (Banks) (Nutting, unpublished).

2. Soldiers

The soldiers are presumably adapted to deal with predators of particular sizes and types under commonly occurring sets of conditions. At the time of flight they are usually associated with other members of the colony, either within the exits or outside, to protect the emergence holes and issuing alates. Miscellaneous observations indicate that the soldiers occasionally play a major role in this connection, either by surrounding the hole, as in a species of *Cubitermes* (Harris, unpublished, in Williams, 1959a), or by perching on grass (larger soldiers) and crowding on the ground (smaller soldiers) with the workers as in *Pseudacanthotermes militaris* (Grassé and Noirot, 1951a). A single soldier of *Pterotermes occidentis* was seen within the open emergence tunnel, both day and night, during the latter half of the flight season (Nutting, unpublished). Harvey (1934) thought that the soldiers of *Incisitermes minor* might regulate the exit of the alates. Contrary behavior may also occur, like that described by Petch (1917), in which soldiers of *Hypotermes obscuripes* (Wasmann) attacked and drove off dealated imagoes trying to re-enter the nest. Very different tactics are illustrated by observations on several species of *Amitermes* in southern Arizona (Nutting, unpublished). Soldiers of *A. emersoni* Light, for example, wander widely in the vicinity of the holes during a period much longer than that taken for the actual flight. Such apparent "altruistic" behavior (Wiens, 1966) leads to rather effective diversion of the few small ants abroad at this time. Whether the soldiers survive these encounters or not, they are usually left outside when the holes are sealed (Hill, 1922).

3. Alates

As the time for flight approaches, the maturing nymphs and alates of many species become gregarious, with groups segregating in superficial or special chambers of the nest. This may take the form of short-term movement to warmer galleries, as in *Coptotermes* (Calaby and Gay, 1956), or may even include an additional response to increasing hostility of the rest of the colony, so far observed only in *Reticulitermes lucifugus* by Buchli (1961). References to a definite rule in the preparations for flight may even include an additional response to increasing hostility of the rest of the colony, so far observed only in *Reticulitermes lucifugus* by Buchli (1961). References to a definite rule in the preparations for flight are rare: Harvey (1934) believed that the alates of *Incisitermes minor* aid the nymphs in digging the exits; Nutting (unpublished) observed alates of *Amitermes emersoni* enlarging an exit while workers were attempting to close it. Because of an unseasonably delayed or short flight season, alates may be held in a colony for unduly long periods; or, indeed, in the absence of suitable flight conditions they may never fly at all. Imagoes of *Reticulitermes hesperus* Banks (Weesner, 1956) and of *R. lucifugus* (Buchli, 1961) so delayed may lose their wings while still within the colony, and some of these dealates may eventually emerge with alates to participate in the usual postflight behavior. Among several species of Kalotermitidae small numbers of alates sometimes remain after swarming. Even though they lose their wings and their gonads atrophy, they retain their protozoan fauna and continue to feed. Such individuals, called "achrestogonimes" by Grassé and Bonneville (1935), play no part in maintenance of the colony but are apparently tolerated by the other members.

Alates of *Pterotermes* confined in laboratory colonies died within a month after the end of the normal flight season (Nutting, unpublished). Light (1937) found evidence in natural colonies of *Paraneotermes* that unflown alates must sometimes die. Imagoes of *Reticulitermes lucifugus* were killed in Buchli's colonies if they were prevented from flying and the temperature remained above about 20°C (cf. Clément, 1956a). Alates of *Amitermes emersoni* reenter the nest if the wind is too strong for flight (Nutting, unpublished), and the observations of Williams (1959a), Harris and Sands (1965), and others suggest that the behavior of other species may be sufficiently flexible to enable unflown individuals to do likewise.

The complexities of preflight behavior may only be imagined among species of *Incolitermes* and *Ahamitermes* which are parasitic in the nests of either one of two species of *Coptotermes* in Australia. Calaby (1956) has found the imagoes of *Incolitermes pumilus* (Hill) in galleries with those of *Coptotermes acinaciformis* and believed that the workers of the host must release the parasitic alates along with their own.

III. FLIGHT

Dispersal of the winged males and females beyond the territory of the mother colony is accomplished in a number of ways, from the escape of a few individuals within a few seconds or minutes to the swarming exodus of many thousands lasting for an hour or more. Flight may occasionally be dispensed with where dealated forms leave the nest and participate directly in courtship (Section II, B, 3). It may be presumed that flights are staged during the season of the year and time of day when conditions are most favorable for consummation of postflight behavior. More than this perhaps, for in one or more species of *Trinervitermes*, Sands (1965b) has postulated that flight and early colony development may be scheduled so that the young workers are ready to begin foraging during the most favorable times of the rainy season.

A. THE FLIGHT SEASON AND REGIONAL WEATHER PATTERNS

Flight is essentially a seasonal phenomenon (Fig. 1). The seasonal cycles of various termite activities, from nest construction to reproduction, population fluctuations, and flight, have been reviewed and studied by Bodot (1962, 1966) and Noirot (1961; Chapter 10). Papers which contain general data and references relating the flights of specific faunas to regional weather patterns include: in the United States — Snyder (1954) and Weesner (1965); in Mexico — Light (1933); in Panama — Dietz and Snyder (1924); in Brazil — da Costa Lima (1960); in Africa — Fuller (1915), Kemp (1955), and Sands (1965b); in India — Beeson (1953) and Annandale (1923); in southeast Asia — Bathellier (1927); and in Australia — Ratcliffe *et al.* (1952).

In regions with definite, cold winters and evenly distributed rainfall, alate production and flight of the entire fauna are restricted to the warmer summer months (Grassé, 1949; Noirot, 1961). In some temperate deserts, however, there are species which fly during a rainy season in winter: for example, *Anacanthotermes ochraceus* in the Sahara of eastern Algeria (Clément, 1956a) and *Amitermes emersoni* in southern California and Arizona (Fig. 1) (Nutting, unpublished).

In the tropics, where seasons are not sharply divided by temperature, flights of many species are variously scheduled about a single rainy season (Noirot, 1961). Even in areas of high or more uniform rainfall, flights may still be related to a succession of wetter and drier periods (Williams, 1959a). Kemp's observations (1955) have suggested that a few species may stage flights during both rainy seasons in northeastern Tanganyika. On the other hand, certain *Microtermes* and *Microcerotermes* may fly during the dry season in forests or wooded savanna (Grassé, 1949).

Although there is little information on the point, it appears that the flight season may also be shifted by regional elevational differences. Over much of its wide range in the western United States, *Reticulitermes tibialis* Banks flies during late winter or spring and again in the fall (Weesner, 1965). Its flights are not associated with seasonal rains.

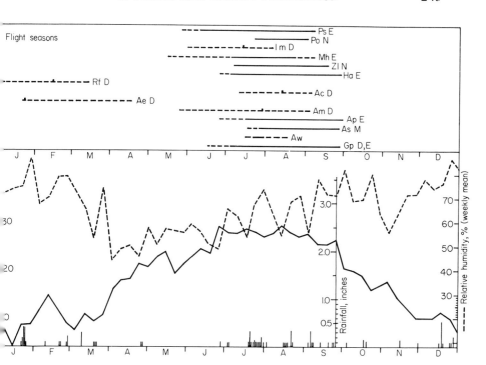

Fig. 1. Flight seasons of 14 species of termites in relation to rainfall, weekly mean temperature, and relative humidity at Tucson, Arizona. Dates showing 0.1 inch indicate amounts from a trace to 0.1 inch of rain. Solid lines and ticks represent the length of the flight seasons in 1962, dashed lines the seasonal limits determined over approximately 10 years. (Ac) *Amitermes coachellae* Light; (Ae) *Amitermes emersoni;* (Am) *Amitermes minimus;* (Ap) *Amitermes pallidus* Light; (As) *Amitermes silvestrianus;* (Aw) *Amitermes wheeleri;* (D) day flier; (E) evening flier; (Gp) *Gnathamitermes perplexus;* (Ha) *Heterotermes aureus;* (Im) *Incisitermes minor;* (M) morning flier; (Mh) *Marginitermes hubbardi;* (N) night flier; (Po) *Pterotermes occidentis;* (Ps) *Paraneotermes simplicicornis;* (Rt) *Reticulitermes tibialis;* (Zl) *Zootermopsis laticeps.*

Scattered records from Arizona indicate that it flies during summer above about 4000 feet and during winter below this elevation (Nutting, unpublished). Again, although data are scarce, there is an indication that flight seasons are shifted with change in latitude. *Heterotermes aureus* (Snyder) begins flying in early July in southern Arizona, but in early June about 800 miles south in west-central Mexico. These shifts are probably due to the earlier occurrence of the rainy season in the more southerly localities. Similar changes, but dependent on the advancement of seasonal temperatures, are known for species of *Reticulitermes* in the eastern United States (Snyder, 1948).

Probably the majority of species in all families have a moderate number of flights each year, generally restricted to one or a few successive months (Fig. 1). However, the flight season may vary from a period of only a few days each year to the entire year (or very nearly the entire year). Perhaps the most consistent example of narrow seasonal synchrony is the single swarming of *Odontotermes assmuthi* during the fourth week of June each year for 5 years at Dehra Dun (Sen-Sarma, 1962). One flight per year may be usual for many species, among them *Macrotermes natalensis* (Ruelle, 1964), *Odontotermes obesus* (Arora and Gilotra, 1959), and perhaps *Porotermes adamsoni* (Hill, 1942). In a small colony of *Reticulitermes flaviceps* (Oshima), Tang and Li (1959) reported that swarming occurred only once during the spring, while larger colonies produced flights on a number of successive, favorable days. Finally, species which fly throughout the year show, nevertheless, seasonal peaks in numbers flown (Castle, 1934; Wilkinson, 1962).

In summary, many authors have pointed out that the lower termites fly under a wide range of weather conditions and stage many flights of relatively small numbers over a prolonged season. The higher termites generally fly under more specific sets of conditions and produce fewer flights of much larger numbers, although the season often covers several months (Grassé, 1949; Harris, 1958). This may be a reasonable generalization; however, it is based on relatively few well-documented cases, and the exceptions are likely to increase as a wider variety of species is more carefully studied. Many of the factors which initiate the flight season are probably similar to, and closely integrated with, those regulating the daily flight periods. These factors are discussed, in connection with pertinent examples, in Section III, B, 1.

B. The Daily Flight Periods

Flight is subject also to a daily regimen within the season. Ruelle (1964) felt that the alates themselves may choose the combination of conditions suitable for their flight, while Skaife (1954a) suspected that the workers control the exit of the alates. However, the connections between many factors, both endogenous and exogenous, and the initiation of swarming remain largely speculative. The hormonal control of gonadal development and the resulting influence on migratory flights, particularly in locusts, have been reviewed by Johnson (1966). Activity rhythms have been detected in male alates of certain species of ants, and McCluskey (1965) suggested that they may be related to the timing of mating flights. Grabensberger (1933) was able to establish different feeding rhythms in laboratory colonies of ants and the termite, *Reticulitermes lucifugus.*

The subject of rhythms, particularly with relation to field periodicities of many insects, has been critically reviewed by Corbet (1966). Whether these factors are involved in the swarming of termites is not known; the above reviews should provide a stimulus for testing them.

The flight of the imagoes is further complicated by interactions among themselves and with the other castes, as the following behavioral situations show. For example, day-flying alates of two species of *Cubitermes* were negatively phototactic and gregarious when removed from the mound, but this behavior was reversed by the briefest use of their wings. They would not fly while in close contact with other members of the colony, even in the light (Williams, 1959a). The effect of many factors on the gregariousness and phototropic responses of alates is discussed by Grassé (1942), Noirot, Bouillon, and others (in Piraux and Hahirwa, 1964), and at some length by Williams (1959a); however, the intriguing problems recognized are far from resolution. One would expect responses of the alates to vary with their time of flight, day or night.

The hostility of the rest of the colony toward alates of *Reticulitermes lucifugus* may influence their exodus (Buchli, 1961). The attempts of *Amitermes emersoni* to open holes that workers were trying to close (Section II, B, 3) is another example of conflicting behavior. Hoell-dobler and Maschwitz (1965) raised an intriguing possibility with their report on the mediation of a pheromone in the swarming of the ant *Camponotus herculeanus*. Flight of the majority of both sexes is synchronized by a secretion from the male mandibular glands which stimulates takeoff by the females.

1. Relation between Time and Duration of Flight and Physical Factors

Climatic factors concerned with the initiation and synchronization of insect dispersal flights have been reviewed by Johnson (1966). Detailed studies on the flight of particular species of termites, with emphasis on accompanying meteorological conditions, have recently been made for *Anacanthotermes* (Clément, 1956a), *Paraneotermes* (Nutting, 1966a) (Fig. 2), *Macrotermes* (Ruelle, 1964), *Trinervitermes* (Sands, 1965b), *Cryptotermes* (Wilkinson, 1962), and *Cubitermes* (Williams, 1959a). Additional information is available in scattered sources, including the often overlooked biological sections of taxonomic works. Even though most of these accounts are purely descriptive of actual flight situations, they have nevertheless drawn attention to particular weather conditions.

In the following sections several climatic components are considered as factors which may singly, or in combination, influence the swarming (daily or seasonal) either through the setting of rhythms or the triggering of certain irregularly recurring reactions. Many correlations between

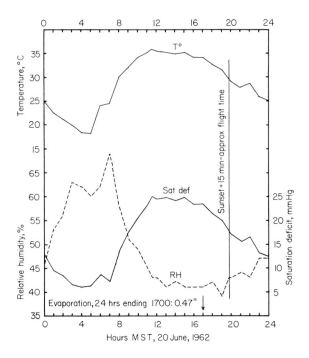

Fig. 2. Relationship between approximate flight time (sunset plus 15 minutes) of *Paraneotermes simplicicornis* and temperature, relative humidity, saturation deficit, and evaporation. June 20 was taken as a typical day during the 1962 flight season at Tucson, Arizona.

flight and various environmental factors are apparent, but it should be realized that a simple response to one may be modified or even reversed by changes in another. Wilkinson (1962) suggested the possibility of determining an optimum climatic formula for flight, although in the particular case of *Cryptotermes havilandi* he felt that changing conditions, rather than a fixed set of absolute values, provided the major climatic stimulus for flight. Such formulas, determined for the species of limited areas, might be useful for the prediction of flights on a regional basis.

a. Light — Time of Day. Light intensity is one of the principal factors affecting the time and duration of flights, which generally take place during very characteristic periods: day, night, or twilight, either morning or evening. Many specific examples are given by Weesner (1960) and in earlier general works.

Mastotermes is apparently an evening and early night flier (Gay, 1967, personal communication). The Kalotermitidae appear generally to be crepuscular fliers (Harris, 1958), although a few diurnal species are known even among the limited fauna of the southern United States: *Kalotermes approximatus* Snyder, *Incisitermes milleri* (Emerson), and *I. minor* (Snyder, 1954). *Pterotermes* flies throughout the night (Nutting, 1966b), and Kalshoven (1960) has reported *Cryptotermes cynocephalus* flying in the early morning soon after sunrise.

Many members of the Hodotermitidae* fly during the evening, but *Zootermopsis laticeps* flies throughout the night (Nutting, 1965). Afternoon flights have been described for *Anacanthotermes ochraceus* (Clément, 1956a) and *Archotermopsis wroughtoni* (Desneux) (Imms, 1919). A single alate of *A. wroughtoni* was taken by Ahmad (1955) at light. As Weesner (1965) has pointed out, the presence of alates at light after dark should be interpreted with caution, since stragglers from afternoon flights might occasionally be expected to appear at light. Diurnal or late afternoon and evening flights are common among the Rhinotermitidae; however, Kemp (1955) reported *Schedorhinotermes lamanianus* (Sjöstedt) flying at 0300 hours on a damp, foggy night in northeastern Tanganyika.

Although there are numerous examples in the Termitidae of diurnal, nocturnal, or evening flights, it is here that some of the most narrowly restricted flight periods are found. Among the most striking examples is that of *Amitermes silvestrianus* Light in the southwestern United States which occurs within a very short period of twilight before sunrise (Light, 1932; Nutting, unpublished). Since the diurnal and evening fliers have received so much attention, and the flights of so many more species are unknown, further generalizations on time of flight are unwarranted. Hazards of desiccation and predation are probably lessened for species which fly during twilight or at night, although those swarming at other times may also be avoiding the regular feeding hours of important predators.

Provided that other factors are suitable, twilight fliers apparently depend very closely on changing light intensity for the initiation of flight. This supposition is reinforced by observations on species that fly earlier in the evening on cloudy days (Kalshoven, 1930; Nutting, 1966a). With certain mosquitoes and other insects, Corbet (1966) has emphasized the importance of the gradual change in light intensity before the permissive range is reached. On the other hand, artificial dusk did not appreciably advance the flight time of *Cryptotermes havilandi* (Wilkinson, 1962). *Gnathamitermes perplexus* in the southwestern United States flies under a wide variety of conditions, not always associated with rainfall, from

---

*The Hodotermitidae, as considered in this chapter, includes the subfamilies Termopsinae, Stolotermitinae, Porotermitinae, and Hodotermitinae.

shortly after sunrise into evening twilight. In such cases responsiveness to light intensity may vary with changes in temperature, humidity, or some other factor (Johnson, 1966). It seems probable that, at least during the flight season, many species must obtain information on the photo-period and other external conditions, either by preliminary tunneling for exit holes or even through pores in the walls of superficial galleries in wood or soil. Particularly pertinent in this connection are the findings of Howse (1966) concerning the extreme sensitivity of *Zootermopsis* to air movement and of Loos (1964) relating air movement in mounds of *Macrotermes natalensis* directly to the wind outside. Apparently, no cor-relations have been made between time of flight and the lunar cycle, as has been done with mosquitoes (Bidlingmayer, 1964).

   b. Temperature.   Where light intensity is favorable, the closely inter-dependent factors of temperature and moisture are probably the most important in determining the daily flight periods. Many observers have recorded the temperature or range of temperatures during flights of particular species, but such values are, in the main, only of parochial interest (Nutting, 1966a; Fig. 1). Perhaps the widest range of temperature for the flight of any species is that from 12° to 30°C for *Anacanthotermes ochraceus* (Clément, 1956a). No one seems to have determined threshold temperatures above which flight is physiologically possible, although even these would undoubtedly vary with wide ranging species (Johnson, 1966).

   Evidence of minimum air temperatures operating to control exodus and flight has been provided by field observations; for example, Weesner (1956) noted flights of *Reticulitermes hesperus* to be earlier in sunny areas than those in shade. Interruptions of flight on cool days by passing clouds, e.g., *Reticulitermes hesperus* (Weesner, 1956) and *Amitermes emersoni* (Nutting, unpublished), were probably due to lowered tempera-ture rather than reduced light intensity. Tang and Li (1959) reported that swarming of *R. flaviceps* may be stopped by sudden drops in temper-ature accompanied by rising barometric pressure. In southern Arizona *Paraneotermes* begins flying when weekly mean temperatures remain consistently above about 23°C and may continue for somewhat longer than 3 months (Fig. 1). Swarming of *Pterotermes* was studied for an entire season and found to last for about 6 weeks during some of the highest weekly mean temperatures of the year (Fig. 1) (Nutting, 1966a,b). However, the length of the season for temperate species such as these is probably limited as much by the effect of temperature on alate production as it is by temperatures favorable for their flight.

   Clustered alates of *Paraneotermes* in laboratory colonies became in-creasingly excited, dissociated, and flew when the temperature was gradually raised from 34° to 38°C. They returned to quiet, gregarious behavior within a short time after the temperature was lowered to 36°C. It was suggested that rising soil or nest temperatures might be providing an important cue for the flight of this species, even though it flies at dusk, when the air temperature is falling steadily (Fig. 2) (Nutting, 1966a). In this connection it may be pertinent to note the temperature studies of Greaves (1964) on *Coptotermes frenchi* Hill nesting in living trees. The highest nursery temperatures were recorded in November when alates were present. It is conceivable that such a seasonal temperature trend may in some way set the stage for the flight season, which normally occurs in December.

   c. Rainfall and Moisture Conditions.   The annual distribution of rain and the accompanying seasonal increases in humidity probably affect the patterns of swarming more than the total amount of rainfall (Fig. 1). Many species fly in the rain, while others completely avoid it. Reports of flights during rain, at times in very heavy rain, most often involve members of the Termitidae. There are occasional records of lower termites flying during light rain: e.g., *Anacanthotermes macrocephalus* (Desneux) (Gupta, 1960) and *Coptotermes heimi* (Roonwal, 1959). It cannot be stated with certainty that this behavior is invariable with any species, except probably *Tenuirostritermes tenuirostris,* which has only been taken during nocturnal rains (Weesner, 1953; Nutting, unpublished). Most of the termites which fly during rain have also been reported flying at other times: e.g., *Stolotermes* (Gay, 1967, personal communication), five species of *Trinervitermes* (Sands, 1965b), *Pseudacanthotermes militaris* (Grassé and Noirot, 1951a), *Allognathotermes hypogeus* Silvestri (Noirot and Bodot, 1964) and *Gnathamitermes perplexus* (Nutting, unpublished). Some members of each family fly at variable but short intervals after rainfall, probably most commonly in the evening. Perhaps the most unusual and predictable are species such as *Amitermes silvestrianus* and *A. wheeleri* (Desneux) in southern Arizona, which fly before sunrise on summer mornings following at least 0.1 inch of rain the day before, and *A. emersoni,* which behaves similarly in the winter sunshine (Fig. 1).

   Whatever the pattern of rainfall, the kalotermitids generally avoid rainy periods, often by many hours or days. This includes the subterranean, dampwood species, *Paraneotermes simplicicornis* (Nutting, 1966a). Even though *Marginitermes hubbardi,* for example, flies during the summer rainy season in the southwestern United States—at the time of the highest weekly mean relative humidities (50−70%)—its flights are not consistently associated with rainfall. The same may be said for the hodotermitid, *Zootermopsis laticeps* (Fig. 1) (Nutting, unpublished).

However, the flights of *Cryptotermes havilandi* in West Africa were definitely suppressed by the higher relative humidity following rainfall, and only small flights or none at all occurred on days with heavy afternoon rains before 1800 hours. It was concluded that a sharp drop in relative humidity was the principal climatic stimulus for flight (Wilkinson, 1962). Rainfall apparently has little or no influence on the time of swarming for the species of *Reticulitermes* in the more humid central and eastern United States, although *R. hesperus,* in the southern part of its range in the far West, is more commonly associated with rainfall (Snyder, 1954; Weesner, 1965). In southwestern Australia, flights of *Coptotermes acinaciformis* (Froggatt) generally occur from a few hours to a day before rain (Calaby and Gay, 1956).

It is generally agreed that a high degree of soil moisture is distinctly advantageous to the dealated adults of subterranean species, since it greatly facilitates excavation of their initial cell and provides moisture during the early and critical months of the incipient colony. Wetting of the upper levels of the soil, perhaps by its effect on soil temperature, may be an important factor in signaling the start of the flight season or period. Clément (1956a) considered the increased humidity near the surface in desert soils to be critical for initiating flights of *Anacanthotermes ochraceus.* A nest of *Macrotermes natalensis* was induced to stage a flight, about 2 weeks before the normal time, by sprinkling it repeatedly with water (Ruelle, 1964). The effects of soil moisture on alate development and the mechanical effect of raindrops on worker behavior have already been mentioned (Sections II, A and II, B, 1).

Saturation deficit and evaporation rate were measured during two flight seasons in the study on *Paraneotermes simplicicornis* (Fig. 2). This desert species flies during a season of moderately high relative humidity, but, since the summer rains are in the form of sporadic thunderstorms, the saturation deficit and evaporation rate are at their highest levels of the year (Nutting, 1966a).

d. Wind and Atmospheric Pressure. Termites do not usually fly in windy weather, although limited dispersal of many species is undoubtedly favored by light air movement. Under apparently otherwise favorable conditions, alates of *Amitermes emersoni* have been observed at their exit holes during periods of gusty winds. While several individuals emerged briefly and managed to reenter the holes, a few were blown over the ground, apparently unable or unwilling to fly. On the other hand, certain species, such as *Gnathamitermes perplexus*, which may fly during thunderstorms, are occasionally scattered by very strong, turbulent winds (Nutting, unpublished). Any advantages of dispersal by such storm systems would seem to be negated by greatly reduced opportunities for postflight pairing of the more widely separated sexes.

Wellington (1946) has critically reviewed the work on effects of pressure changes on insects and concluded that extreme changes exert no direct influence. He found evidence that falling or slightly reduced pressures may increase the rates of development and of various activities, but that a decrease does not necessarily occur with the reverse conditions. Tang and Li (1959) have reported that *Reticulitermes flaviceps* swarms only on warm, sunny days in spring when the temperature rises to 20°C and the atmospheric pressure suddenly drops below 760 mm. Swarming may cease if the temperature suddenly drops and the pressure rises. Edwards (1961) has succeeded in determining that the flight of a blow-fly, *Calliphora vicina*, is stimulated by changes of natural amounts and rates in falling pressure. Such evidence implies that natural, prefrontal drops in pressure, when associated with appropriate conditions, can influence the activity of some insects. However, Edwards pointed out that caution must obviously be observed in this type of work so that the effects of pressure changes are clearly isolated from those of temperature, humidity, light, atmospheric electricity, etc., which also accompany storms. Wellington (1946) suggested that correlation between insect activities in the field and pressure cycles might be made in the tropics, where the complicating effects of storms are at a minimum.

e. Electric Properties of the Atmosphere. Edwards (1960a,b) has reviewed the largely speculative literature relating modifications of all types of insect behavior to certain electric properties of the atmosphere which are associated with storm conditions. He has also investigated the effects on insects of two important aspects of atmospheric electricity: potential gradient, or electric field and density of unipolar air-ions. He found no support for relating increase of insect activity before storms to the concomitant changes in electric fields (Edwards, 1960a); however, he did show that increased flight activity of *Calliphora vicina* follows an increased density of artificially produced, positive air-ions (1960b). None of this work pertained to termites, but Damaschke and Becker (1964) have recently determined that the oxygen consumption of certain species of termites varies inversely with the intensity of the electric field in the atmosphere. They also cited cases where *Kalotermes flavicollis* and *Reticulitermes lucifugus* have been observed emerging from wood in preparation for swarming before electric storms. Since some of these observations were made under known laboratory conditions, it is possible that they were responding to some factor such as atmospheric electricity. Alates of some macrotermitids and a few other groups are also known to orient themselves in definite positions with respect to both artificial and natural magnetic fields (Becker, 1963). These factors are easily overlooked and might also be masked by more obvious ones. However, since the swarming of many species is associated with storms, the effects of electric fields and related phenomena on termite behavior obviously must now be considered.

2. Concurrent Flights

It is generally assumed that flights of individual species are synchronized by similar meteorological conditions over rather wide areas, although records of concurrent flights beyond a few miles are uncommon. Concurrent flights of *Paraneotermes* were recorded just after sunset five times up to 13 miles apart (Nutting, 1966a). Perhaps one of the most notable records is that of the rare *Foraminitermes tubifrons* Holmgren in the Cameroun, which was collected at points over 200 miles apart at precisely the same time of the same day (Harris and Sands, 1965). Weesner (1965) listed flight data for several species over much of the eastern two-thirds of the United States; these included a number of flights, on the same days, of *Reticulitermes flavipes* which were several hundreds of miles apart, and a few over a thousand miles apart. Their relation to regional weather systems has not yet been determined.

On the other hand, it is certain that all colonies, even in limited areas, do not invariably stage synchronous flights. Weesner (1956) recognized that in the San Francisco Bay area the spring flights of *Reticulitermes hesperus* occurred from scattered colonies at different times. Even though *Amitermes emersoni* stages no more than about four flights each year, all colonies do not swarm on every favorable day (Nutting, unpublished). It is also obvious that flights would be synchronized over very scattered and irregular areas in those species depending upon thunderstorms, particularly in deserts. With the scarcity of regional data, speculation is unprofitable, although it seems reasonable to believe that flight schedules of individual species must be shifted in conformity with local meteorological conditions, which result from altitudinal and latitudinal differences over their entire range. Wynne-Edwards (1962) has made the interesting point that the remarkable synchrony of emergence, by both ants and termites, is probably the main reason for the generally short duration of their flight periods.

C. FLIGHT BEHAVIOR

It has frequently been observed that takeoff is delayed for several minutes after emergence of the alates at lower temperatures, but that exit and takeoff occur more closely together as it becomes warmer (Clément, 1956a). In the absence of flight towers and similar structures the alates of many species commonly climb up on pebbles, grass, herbs, etc., from which they leap into flight, for example: *Coptotermes michaelseni* Silvestri (Calaby and Gay, 1956), *Heterotermes aureus* (Nutting, unpublished), and species of *Reticulitermes* (Snyder, 1948). Fuller (1915) described a flight of *Microtermes havilandi* during which the alates emerged so thickly that they formed small columns above the holes, from which those in the lead took off. The dispersal of each individual is characteristically brief and, under the most favorable conditions, it leads quickly to pairing, which in rare instances may even take place in flight.

1. Dispersal

The effectiveness of dispersal obviously depends upon the meteorological conditions accompanying flight, the number of alates taking part, and the rate of predation; but it is also strongly influenced by the peculiarities and efficiency of postflight behavior which are considered in Section IV. The dry-wood termites obviously send out smaller numbers of alates per flight because of their generally smaller colonies; however, it has been pointed out (Tang and Li, 1959) that small colonies may produce fewer and briefer swarms each season, and this probably holds for all termites. There are few records where the number of alates flown from individual colonies is accurately known. Working with caged colonies during one season, Nutting (1966b) determined that one colony of *Pterotermes* staged 40 separate flights which consisted of from 1 to 199 alates; and that *Zootermopsis laticeps* staged 39 flights containing from 1 to 50 alates (Nutting, unpublished). Grassé (1942) stated that a large colony of *Kalotermes flavicollis* may produce from 30 to 60, and perhaps as many as 100, alates in a single flight. Field observations give some indication of the numbers of alates swarming, but the number of colonies participating is generally unknown. Wilkinson (1962) summarized data on the number of alates of *Cryptotermes havilandi* trapped over a period of about 1 year. A very large number of colonies was involved. Flights of the Rhinotermitidae and Termitidae, often containing hundreds to many thousands of alates, obviously present special problems, although it should be feasible to obtain this type of information by caging colonies and trapping the alates.

Most termites appear to be adapted for dispersal within a boundary layer of relatively calm air near the earth (Johnson, 1966), where they are perhaps able, not so much to control their course as, to at least avoid being carried away by the wind above it. The lower, wood-inhabiting termites are often considered to be strong fliers and thus probably able to fly farther (Weesner, 1965), but they also tend to fly under relatively quieter conditions. The distance flown by particular species is another area where there are relatively few precise data. The following observations, given in the units of each author, on the range and altitude, respectively, for several species may perhaps be typical: *Kalotermes flavicollis*, a few dozen meters (Grassé, 1942); *Cryptotermes havilandi*, 1–45 meters (Wilkinson, 1962); *Zootermopsis angusticollis*, 350 yards at 50 feet and probably much more (Castle, 1934); *Anacanthotermes ochraceus*, ca. 100 meters at 10–15 meters (Clément, 1956a); *Reticulitermes lucifugus*, 10–200 meters (Grassé, 1942); *Macrotermes*, a few kilometers at 4–5 meters (Grassé, 1949); *Odontotermes angustatus* (Rambur) [as *Termes vulgaris*] more than $\frac{1}{2}$ mile (Fuller, 1915); and *Amitermes minimus* Light, several hundred yards at 50 feet or more (Nutting, unpublished). Nothing is known about the physiology of flight and thus of the intrinsic maximum range of any species except in the form of judgments by experienced workers. As an example, Harvey (1934) observed flights of *Incisitermes minor* for distances of 125 yards and to altitudes of 75 feet, but he considered this species capable of flights from $\frac{1}{2}$ to 1 mile or more. Nineteen alates of *Reticulitermes virginicus* (Banks) were taken in traps by an airplane over Louisiana at altitudes ranging from 20 to 3000 feet (Glick, 1939). However, it must be very rare for colonies of this or any other species to be founded as a result of the pairing of wind-borne alates such as these.

Numerous accounts of swarming describe alates taking off in all directions (*I. minor;* Harvey, 1934), so that it is difficult to determine whether those species are guided by any particular environmental factor. Many species, particularly late afternoon or evening fliers, are attracted toward the setting sun (*Pseudacanthotermes militaris;* Grassé and Noirot, 1951a); some are borne along by light winds (*Amitermes emersoni;* Nutting, unpublished); others fly toward treetops, even against the wind (*Allognathotermes hypogeus*; Noirot and Bodot, 1964). Kalshoven (1960) observed that alates of *Cryptotermes cynocephalus* rose but little higher than the roofs of small houses. Diurnal species of *Amitermes* in Tucson, Arizona, commonly fly low along streets and alleys between houses, walls, and rows of trees and shrubs (Nutting, unpublished). Causes for terminating the flight and settling have apparently not been investigated, although some of the preceding examples suggest the pertinence of visual cues. The relations between flight and settling of other insects is reviewed and discussed by Johnson (1966).

2. Pairing during the Flight Period

Pairing, or the meeting and association of the sexes, generally takes place on the substrate after swarming (Section IV). A few instances have been described where the females apparently alight first, while the males seek them out in low, deliberate flight (Fuller, 1915). Fuller suggested that the males located the females by visual cues: the play of sunlight on the half-spread wings of *Macrotermes natalensis* poised on grass spears, and the fluttering wings of *Odontotermes badius* hanging from pendulous plants. This type of behavior, albeit in more subtle forms, may be much more common than has been suspected. In *Microtermes* (Harris and Sands, 1965) the male attaches himself to the underside of the female's abdomen, loses his wings, whereupon the female flies on. Williams (1959a) referred to earlier accounts of this behavior in which there is apparently some question as to the identity of the participants.

In the savannas of the Ivory Coast the alates of *Allognathotermes hypogeus* assemble in dense swarms on the leeward side of the tops of shrubs and trees which are spaced approximately one per hectare. Pairs are formed on the leaves and branches, the male attaching himself to the female as described for *Microtermes* above. Again it is the female which flies to the ground where both dealate quickly and begin the usual nuptial promenade (Noirot and Bodot, 1964). In this type of environment the trees provide rallying points for the alates from all nests within a certain radius and thus favor crossbreeding. Such an orientation toward high points or "hypsotaxis," has been observed for other termites — e.g., *Pseudacanthotermes militaris* (Grassé and Noirot, 1951a) and *Syntermes* (Snyder, 1948) — as well as for many other insects. Pairs of *P. militaris* have actually been taken in flight with dealated males clinging fast to the females (Grassé and Noirot, 1951a), and although pairing has not been observed it presumably takes place high in the air (Noirot and Bodot, 1964).

3. Predators

At swarming and during their subsequent overt behavior, the imagoes of many species are eaten by all sorts of animals, particularly other arthropods (scorpions, solpugids, spiders, centipedes, dragonflies, cockroaches, mantids, crickets, beetles, flies, and wasps) and vertebrates (fish, frogs, toads, lizards, snakes, birds, and mammals, including man) (Bathellier, 1927; Bryk, 1927; Emerson, 1938; Hegh, 1922; Mathur, 1962; Rothney, 1918; Snyder, 1948). Long lists of birds which feed in part upon winged termites are given by De Bont (1964) for Africa and by Snyder (1948) for the United States.

Although many predators harvest tremendous numbers of alates, nearly all appear to be opportunistic with regard to this food supply. Brian (1965b) pointed out that such predation as a control, by birds for example, is not reciprocal; however, De Bont (1964) believed the swarming termites form the basic energy supply for the young of many birds in tropical Africa. Of considerably more interest, he suggested that termites are vital to the survival of the insectivorous birds of Europe which winter in Africa during the swarming season. As yet there are no studies on the rate of predation and its possible significance in controlling the population of a single species of termite.

It has already been mentioned that many species probably avoid some predators by flying at particular times of day or night (Section III, B, 1, a), but almost nothing is known of this or any other possible adaptations for minimizing predation. Two examples are known where the alates feign death: *Trinervitermes occidentalis* (Sjöstedt) [as *T. auriterrae* (Sjöstedt)] (Sands, 1965b) and *Amitermes minimus* (Nutting, unpublished). Sands considered that this behavior might be an adaptation for avoiding vertebrate predators in flight rather than its having any survival value against terrestrial predators such as ants, which might be indifferent to the condition of their prey.

IV. POSTFLIGHT BEHAVIOR

With a few known exceptions, the activities immediately following flight provide for the formation of pairs and for their movement together to a suitable nesting site. Lüscher (1951) concluded that, in the Kalotermitidae at least, this sequence of behavioral acts was very flexible, but that among the higher families it was rigidly followed. It has been determined that some or all of the steps in the behavioral sequence, from swarming to construction of the initial cell, may be omitted and still result in successful colony foundation: Kalotermitidae, *Kalotermes flavicollis* (Grassé and Noirot, 1955; Lüscher, 1951); Rhinotermitidae, *Reticulitermes lucifugus* (Buchli, 1950b; Grassé and Noirot, 1955); Hodotermitidae, *Anacanthotermes ochraceus* (Clément, 1956b); Termitidae, *Macrotermes natalensis* (Grassé and Noirot, 1955); *Cubitermes* spp. (Williams, 1959a). Altogether, these examples scarcely provide sufficient grounds for generalizations; however, a certain degree of behavioral plasticity must be of great advantage in meeting the varied hazards of the postflight period (Williams, 1959a). Other notes show that this behavior may also be entrained before a normally scheduled flight. For example, Snyder (1915) observed that when a colony of *Reticulitermes* sp. is broken open during the proper season, the alates may be caused to make a short flight, dealate, and form tandems, presumably to continue toward the formation of new colonies.

Pairing between the sexes from different colonies is probably favored wherever the flights of several colonies are synchronized over a particular area as, for example, with *Allognathotermes hypogeus* (Noirot and Bodot, 1964). This view has been discussed and supported in recent reviews by Weesner (1960) and Harris and Sands (1965). Indeed, Wynne-Edwards (1962) has suggested that the need for cross-fertilization itself might be sufficient to account for the precise timing of the flights of both ants and termites. On the other hand, Grassé and Noirot (1951a) are inclined to believe that inbreeding is the general rule, even where synchronous flights are concerned, since the dispersal of imagoes from individual nests is often so limited (*Microtermes usambaricus*, for example). Snyder (1948) and Buchli (1958) have also favored this view with various species of *Reticulitermes*. There can be little doubt that flights from a single colony within a large area must lead to pairing between siblings. However, on the basis of present data it would be equally difficult to prove that either pattern provides a general rule for the pairing behavior of the entire order.

A. DEALATION

Although wings have been retained by the sexual adults of a single caste and are typically used for the dispersal flight, they are of little further use during the cryptobiotic life which follows. Perhaps the act of wing shedding is foreshadowed by the habit of the mature cockroaches (*Panesthia* sp.), which bite off their own tegmina and wings in preparation for their communal family life in subterranean burrows (Tillyard, 1926). The males of many cockroaches and other orthopteroid insects raise their wings in a characteristic courting response (Roth and Willis, 1954), but the use of wings during courtship may be a rare occurrence among the Isoptera. The females of *Macrotermes natalensis* rest head-downward, with half-opened wings, on grass spears, 15 – 20 inches above the ground, where the male generally alights on the female's back. The male initiates courtship by palpating the swollen tip of her abdomen, which successively stimulates the female and then the male to drop the wings. Females of *Odontotermes badius* (as *Termes latericius*) hang inverted on pendulous plants, violently fluttering their wings until a male alights nearby. The pair lose their wings as soon as contact is made. In both cases the females lead the way to the ground where the search for a suitable nesting site begins (Fuller, 1915).

Dealation is accomplished with relative ease and generally much more quickly by the Rhinotermitidae and Termitidae than by the Kalotermitidae or Hodotermitidae, apparently because of structural details at the base of the wings. Perhaps because of this peculiarity, some of the more primitive forms may retain their wings much longer after flight, occasionally until they are established within the nuptial cell (Snyder, 1948). Imagoes of *Marginitermes hubbardi* have been seen in the laboratory excavating the initial cell while retaining their wings. Fuller's observations (1915) show that males of some species may retain their wings longer than the females in order to seek out the resting females.

Some observers have ventured that imagoes may be stimulated to shed their wings because of their isolation from the other individuals after flight: *Anacanthotermes ochraceus* (Clément, 1956a), *Odontotermes assmuthi* (Sen-Sarma, 1962). Others have thought flight itself to be a prerequisite to dealation (Williams, 1959a), although it is certainly not necessary in all cases. However, many species, particularly subterranean forms, become dealated on landing or shortly thereafter. This suggests that dealation may be influenced by unknown factors associated with the substrate which are indicative of its general suitability for nesting sites (Nutting, 1966a). Working with two species of *Cubitermes* in the laboratory, Williams (1959a) noted that wing shedding, particularly of the males, was stimulated by pairing or attempts at pairing, although not absolutely dependent upon it. Alates of *Amitermes emersoni* quickly dropped their wings on an agar surface in a petri dish which had recently been occupied by dealated individuals. This and other incidental observations raise the possibility that a pheromone may be released, perhaps by the females, which provokes dealation (Nutting, 1966a).

It is apparently common for many of the Kalotermitidae and Hodotermitidae to move back and forth or in circles until the wings are caught against the edges of cracks and protrusions and broken off one by one: e.g., *Paraneotermes* (Nutting, 1966a); *Zootermopsis* (Castle, 1934). This behavior is not invariable, for Wilkinson (1962) reported that the wings of *Cryptotermes havilandi* were suddenly raised and snapped off after the manner of the termitids. Grassé (1949) described the occasional use of the hind tarsi and even the mandibles in tearing off the wings, while Harris (1961) mentioned that one of the partners may sometimes chew off the wings of the other. The details of the very rapid dealation among the termitids are well described for *Cubitermes* spp. by Williams (1959a). The bases of the wings are restrained against the thorax and the blades raised to a point where they suddenly break at the basal suture. Snyder (1948) has mentioned that some termitids may lose one or more wings in flight. Imagoes of *Amitermes emersoni* are sometimes dealated by a strong breeze while awaiting takeoff with their wings pointing windward (Nutting, unpublished).

B. COURTSHIP

Among the termites courtship is a protracted affair since it may be considered to include the train of events from pairing to excavation of the initial cell where copulation is eventually accomplished. Yet, it would be very similar to that of many other insects if the digging were omitted and the whole sequence compressed in time from days to hours or minutes.

1. Calling and Tandem Behavior

The following remarks are largely from the penetrating analysis of this phase of courtship in *Reticulitermes lucifugus* by Buchli (1960a). The imagoes dealate on landing and the female then searches out elevated positions where she assumes a rigid stance with her abdomen raised in a typical calling attitude. Males excitedly seek these females and, upon meeting, the male touches the female with vibrating antennae and generally strokes her with his mouthparts. The female soon lowers her abdomen and in turn palpates the attentive male, whereupon she turns away to be followed by her mate. The pair then proceed in tandem to find a suitable nesting site, with the male maintaining almost constant contact on the posterior of the female's abdomen with his antennae and mouthparts. The female stops and calls if the male loses contact for long or becomes lost. Buchli has concluded that the male must be initially attracted and his following response sustained by a chemotropic factor produced more or less continuously during this nuptial promenade by an active female. Many earlier workers, e.g., Emerson (1933), have proposed that an attractant must be involved in this behavior. Final proof, including the source of such a substance, has yet to be found, but Buchli (1960a) suggested that it might be produced by the accessory glands of the female reproductive system (Chapter 4). On the basis of his experiments with *R. lucifugus* and more limited observations on *Kalotermes flavicollis,* he believed that abnormal tandems (reversed or all-male) could be explained by the brief persistence of the female odor in or near the substrate recently traversed by an active female. Although the accompanying conditions were not described, the intergeneric tandems (between *Amitermes, Gnathamitermes,* and *Tenuirostritermes*) noted by Light and Weesner (1955a) might be similarly interpreted.

Courtship behavior apparently follows a rather similar pattern throughout the order, although some important exceptions and variations have been described. Either calling and tandem behavior, or at least the latter, have been recorded for many of the kalotermitids and hodotermitids which have been carefully studied: *Kalotermes flavicollis* (Grassé, 1942), *Incisitermes minor* (Harvey, 1934), *Paraneotermes* (Nutting, 1966a), and *Zootermopsis angusticollis* (Castle, 1934). Although Kalshoven (1960) often observed tandems of *Cryptotermes cynocephalus*, Wilkinson (1962) was unable to detect any obvious calling or tandem behavior in *C. havilandi*; in fact, the dealated individuals were actually repelled whenever they met, no matter what the combination of sexes. In this species the sexes separately seek out nesting sites. Similar conduct was described for *Neotermes tectonae* (Kalshoven, 1930), and either sex may continue to attract or at least await a mate, from subsequent flights if necessary, for several weeks and probably months. No calling or tandem activity was observed for *Anacanthotermes ochraceus*, although brief antennal play might precede the digging in of a dealated pair (Clément, 1956a).

Some observers have suggested that the male may also use visual cues in locating the female; for example, the female of *Odontotermes assmuthi* remains stationary while calling but moves her abdomen rather violently from side to side (Sen-Sarma, 1962). The females of *Macrotermes natalensis* and *Odontotermes badius* call from vantage points on grasses and other plants several inches above the ground (Fuller, 1915; Section III, C, 2). Although visual cues may not be involved, females of *Microtermes usambaricus* alight and climb grasses to call, while the males climb in search of them (Grassé and Noirot, 1951a).

For most species nesting sites are probably located within a short time after pairing so that this phase of postflight behavior does not ordinarily last more than a few minutes or hours at most. Inside buildings Buchli (1960a) found tandem pairs still searching up to 23 hours after flight. In western Mexico a pair of *Tenuirostritermes* sp., a nocturnal flier, was discovered still actively running over open ground in intermittent sunlight at least 11 hours after flight (Nutting, unpublished). Grassé (1949) reported that the promenade of *Kalotermes* sp. might continue for hours or even days. Finally, Williams (1959a) noted, in cleaning his laboratory colonies of *Cubitermes ugandensis* Fuller, that the female might leave the cell accompanied by the male in tandem, and, if the male became separated, she would assume the calling attitude. This behavior was repeated as many as three times, but with decreasing efficiency, over a period as long as seven to eight weeks after their establishment in the primary cell. Such plasticity in postflight behavior has obvious advantages for the survival and ultimate success of the founding pairs. Buchli (1960a) also recorded calling, tandem behavior, and copulation among pairs of neotenic reproductives of *Reticulitermes lucifugus*, one entire sequence lasting for about 3 minutes. These observations thus strongly imply that normal postflight behavior is simply an extended courtship in which the final act of copulation must be delayed at least until the pair are settled in their copularium.

C. SELECTION OF NESTING SITE

Very little is known of the factors involved in the selection by the imagoes of a suitable substrate in which to establish the new colony, although miscellaneous observations and experiments suggest several possibilities. With wood-dwellers it seems reasonable to expect that the alates of some species might orient visually toward the forms of dead trees, branches, stumps, posts, and the like. This would appear probable in the case of desert species such as *Pterotermes,* which frequently attack the widely spaced skeletons of dead cacti and the trunks and branches of dead or leafless trees (Nutting, 1966b). Kalshoven (1960) reported that *Cryptotermes cynocephalus* appeared attracted by unpainted wood of buildings and the light surfaces of whitewashed walls. Thigmotactic responses are involved where initial entry is made via cracks and holes, particularly those made by wood-boring beetles: *Neotermes tectonae* (rarely) (Kalshoven, 1959), *Cryptotermes cynocephalus* (Kalshoven, 1960), and *Pterotermes* (Nutting, 1966b). Wilkinson (1962) has determined that imagoes of *C. havilandi* cannot bore into solid wood and thus require cracks or holes of a limited size range which allow sufficient space within for turning and yet are small enough to permit them to be sealed economically (see Section IV, D).

It is becoming increasingly apparent that the condition of the wood is of considerable importance to the susceptibility of attack by many species. Imagoes of *Zootermopsis laticeps* enter living trees via snags and wounds where the colony progressively invades only fungus-infected wood in the branches or trunk. This situation has suggested the possibilities that the alates may be attracted either by the odors of freshly exposed wood, fermenting sap, or perhaps by substances resulting from fungus infection (Nutting, 1965). *Neotermes tectonae* attacks living teak trees in a similar way through the dead or rotting wood at the ends of broken branches and wounds (Kalshoven, 1959). An incipient colony of *Stolotermes* sp. has also been found in a rotting knothole of *Pinus radiata,* which is indicative of similar behavior (Gay, 1967, personal communication). Light (1937) concluded that imagoes of *Paraneotermes* could probably detect wood through at least 2 inches of soil.

Studies with laboratory colonies have shown that certain species, particularly in the Kalotermitidae and Rhinotermitidae, definitely prefer woods attacked by specific fungi. Since the nutritive value of wood also

varies greatly according to the species of fungus involved, the relationships here are obviously of considerable importance to the success of
incipient colonies. Becker (1965) has made important contributions in
this area of research and has briefly summarized the pertinent literature.
Further, Becker (1964) and Smythe *et al.* (1967) have demonstrated the
presence of attractants in extracts from woods attacked by several species
of fungi. The sum of these observations suggests that the activity of
fungi in wood might thus focus the attention of imagoes of certain species
on suitable nesting sites in dead wood. The presence of repellents (Rudman and Gay, 1961) and feeding deterrents (Becker, 1965) in wood might
also be expected to influence the imagoes in this regard. Feeding preference tests suggested that conditioning might play a role in the selection of
the nesting site by the swarming alates of *Cryptotermes brevis* (Walker)
(McMahan, 1966a).

Thigmotactic responses appear to figure rather generally in the selection of nesting sites by subterranean species, although the operation of
attractants from wood on or in the soil in certain cases, i.e., *Paraneotermes* (Light, 1937), should also be considered. Most pairs probably
take advantage of plant litter and other debris and rarely dig in from the
open surface of the soil. Dealated females of *Reticulitermes hesperus*
(Weesner, 1956), *Cubitermes* spp. (Williams, 1959a), and *Trinervitermes*
spp. (Sands, 1965b) usually seek out small cracks and holes and thus
favor surfaces which provide protected situations from which to begin
their excavations. Many species also dig in beside pebbles, stones, and
pieces of wood: e.g., *Microtermes havilandi* (Fuller, 1915) and *Amitermes
hastatus* (Skaife, 1954a). However, Weesner (1965) has pointed out that
most species of *Reticulitermes* do not invariably enter wood in contact
with the ground but are quite capable of becoming established in any
workable substrate providing the necessary conditions of moisture and
temperature. Finally, it might be inferred from their habits that the
alates or dealated pairs of parasitic species, such as those of *Ahamitermes* and *Incolitermes*, must in some way home directly on the nests
of their hosts (Calaby, 1956).

Many observers have considered the search for a nesting site to signal
a return to photonegative behavior. If changes in the photic response
are indeed involved here, it would be interesting to determine whether
they are modified or reversed by changes in humidity or temperature
(Perttunen, 1963). On the other hand, the possibility also might be considered that it represents a search for higher humidity following some
desiccation during the flight period. In *Microcerotermes edentatus* Wasmann the presence of moist soil releases digging behavior (Lüscher,
1951).

Emerson (1955) briefly discussed the little-understood role of competition in the dispersal of termites and suggested that competition for colony and nesting sites may be greater than the nutritive resources, which are often incompletely exploited, even in areas supporting rich faunas. In one of the few pertinent studies, Greaves (1962) noted that young nests of *Coptotermes brunneus* Gay do not persist in territories occupied by mature colonies. He concluded that spacing of the colonies might result from active competition for food between them. In many areas of Mexico, and undoubtedly in many other regions, nesting sites for dry-wood termites are strictly limited to buildings, fence posts, and the dead wood of large trees and cacti because of the extremely efficient collection of firewood by the inhabitants (Nutting, unpublished). Finally, Emerson (1938) has pointed out that the nests of *Constrictotermes cavifrons* (Holmgren) are usually found on the smooth, undamaged underside of slanting trunks in the forests of British Guiana. He also reported the migration of an entire colony of *Nasutitermes costalis* (Holmgren). He concluded that the final nesting site must often be selected by the workers after a particular colony has begun to develop.

D. FORMATION OF THE COPULARIUM

In cases where a pair have selected a crack or hole in wood, rather specialized behavior may be involved in sealing the entrance. This has been described in detail for *Cryptotermes havilandi* (Wilkinson, 1962) and is ordinarily shared by the pair although one may initiate the closure and be assisted in its completion by a late-arriving partner. The preliminary latticework may be completed in an hour and the final seal after about 12 hours. The seal is made of rather quickly drying droplets of proctodeal fluid. The pair are quiet for a few days, then become more active and feed so that the original cavity is gradually enlarged.

Even though pairs of many wood-dwelling species are able to excavate their own chambers, they often take advantage of the shelter of cracks or holes from which to begin: *Incisitermes minor* (Harvey, 1934), *Pterotermes* (Nutting, 1966b), and *Kalotermes flavicollis* (Grassé, 1942). Both sexes usually cooperate in the operation, although Castle (1934) observed the males of *Zootermopsis angusticollis* to assist only occasionally while apparently otherwise occupied in guarding against intrusions by other males. In these four species the copularium typically consists of a short tunnel ending in a low chamber which at first allows only room for the pair to turn about in. The entrance is generally sealed with liquid fecal material although bits of wood and pellets may also be incorporated in it.

Among the subterranean species, Buchli (1950b) has described the construction of the initial cell from observations on *Reticulitermes lucifugus* in the laboratory. Some pairs even began digging before dealation. They generally excavated a chamber approximately 10×10×4 mm in sand next to wood, although some established themselves within buried wood. Both sexes cooperated in the work and lined the walls with fecal material. Similar observations were made on two species of *Cubitermes* by Williams (1959a). He found that the female did most of the initial digging in the hole she had chosen and covered it with a fragile dome of loose soil within about 10 minutes. The pair then worked more slowly until the final ovoid cell was completed about 2 days later. Fuller (1915) described the digging behavior of pairs of *Macrotermes natalensis*, which vigorously scratched out the loose soil with their feet and carried pebbles out in their mandibles. They dug 4−5 inches to the bottom of his jars and formed large globular cells about 1.75 inches in diameter and 0.75 inch high. The method used by *Microtermes havilandi* in driving shafts into the soil is probably widely followed by subterranean species (Fuller, 1915). The pair cooperate throughout and manage to conceal themselves by doming over the initial pit in 10−15 minutes. Working alternately they then excavate their way downward while packing the earth into the vault above them. Several pairs required about 18 hours to reach a depth of 4 inches. In his laboratory studies on five species of *Trinervitermes,* Sands (1965b) found *T. togoensis* (Sjöstedt) [as *T. suspensus* (Silvestri)] to be less capable of burrowing than the others, and he concluded from their behavior that they were probably adapted for settling in the nests of other termites. A pair of *Anacanthotermes ochraceus* may begin digging, or either sex may start alone, to be joined later by a partner. Clément (1956a) found two pairs in chambers 60 cm below the surface 15 days after the flight.

It is frequently noted, some time between pairing and settling in the copularium, that the mouthparts, legs, and most often the antennae of the founding pairs become mutilated to varying degrees. Williams (1959b) reviewed the suggestions of various authors relating this condition to courting behavior, mutual grooming, and nutritional needs and concluded that such mutilations are probably a manifestation of cannibalism.

V. FOUNDATION AND DEVELOPMENT OF THE COLONY

As a general rule, the foundation of a new colony begins with the establishment of a dealated royal pair in their nuptial chamber. Courtship is concluded there with copulation, although this act is periodically repeated throughout the life of the pair. The development of the colony begins with the appearance of the first eggs and larvae within days, sometimes weeks, thereafter. Deviations from this routine are rare, but the alternative modes of colony foundation are of considerable behavioral interest and apparently important in the economy of a few species.

A. COLONIZATION BY OTHER THAN A SINGLE PAIR OF PRIMARY REPRODUCTIVES

Occasionally three or more dealated reproductives dig in together to become established in the same or adjacent cells: *Anacanthotermes ochraceus* (Clément, 1956a), several species of *Trinervitermes* (Sands, 1965b), and a species of *Tenuirostritermes* in western Mexico (Nutting, unpublished). The sequel to this behavior has been reported in several instances. In the laboratory Kalshoven (1959) found that two young colonies of *Neotermes tectonae* placed together would fuse, with the resulting elimination of one parent couple. However, from field evidence he speculated that colonies might continue to live side by side in intertwining galleries without mixing. Wilkinson (1962) noted that third members of founding groups of *Cryptotermes havilandi* might either die within a few months or survive for at least a year. Multiple groups commonly fought until one pair was left, although two pairs sometimes separated themselves by partitioning a single compartment. The aggregation of neighboring incipient colonies of *Reticulitermes hesperus* results in larger, more efficient colonies, ultimately headed by a single pair of primary reproductives (Pickens, 1934). Weyer (1930) found that two or more primary pairs of *Microcerotermes amboinensis* Kemner and *Nasutitermes undecimus* (Kemner)* may cooperate in founding new colonies.

Harris (1958) has reviewed the details of colony foundation by budding and active social fragmentation. The phenomenon of budding or fission involves the division (either passive and gradual, or accidental and sudden) of a sizable and diffusely organized colony. Neotenic, or supplementary, reproductives are eventually produced to head the resulting fragments after isolation from the mother colony and its primary reproductives is complete. Formation of new colonies in this way is possible in at least some species of each family where a relatively extensive nesting habit is coupled with the capability of producing supplementary reproductives. Fairly well-documented examples of the habit have been reported in the following termites: several species of *Reticulitermes* (Pickens, 1934; Snyder, 1948); *Coptotermes amanii* (Sjöstedt) and *Schedorhinotermes lamanianus; Nasutitermes infuscatus* (Sjöstedt);

*A. E. Emerson has transferred this species to *Nasutitermes* (editors' note).

some species of *Trinervitermes* and *Cubitermes* (Harris, 1958). Circumstantial evidence suggests that independent colonies are also budded off from the parent colony in *Mastotermes* (Hill, 1942), many species of the Kalotermitidae (Harris, 1958), *Pterotermes* (Nutting, 1966b), and species of *Zootermopsis* (Castle, 1934). Finally, it is presumed that new colonies of *Reticulitermes lucifugus* in Italy are produced only by this means, since the dealated reproductives apparently fail at some point after formation of the copularium (Grasse, 1949; see Section II,A).

The foundation of new colonies by social fragmentation was described by Grassé and Noirot (1951b) from a case of migration by a species of *Anoplotermes* and two other instances of exposed marching and group activity by *Trinervitermes bettonianus* (Sjöstedt) in West Africa. In this very remarkable behavior, rather large groups, which may contain all ages and castes, emerge from the parent colony and move in fairly orderly fashion to one or more new nesting sites. The original pair of primary reproductives may even migrate to head one of the fragments, while supplementaries are produced to head those which are orphaned. This type of behavior, which is reminiscent of swarming by bees, has been termed "sociotomy" by Grassé and Noirot. Activity which might be similarly interpreted has been mentioned in a few other instances: at least two species of *Anoplotermes* and *Trinervitermes gratiosus* (Sjöstedt) (Harris, 1958); and *Syntermes territus* Emerson (Emerson, 1945). The wider dispersal of colonies founded by winged reproductives is thus sacrificed for the much greater chances of survival afforded those formed by budding or sociotomy. However, Harris and Sands (1965) warned that such atypical behavior may also result from raids by burrowing doryline ants.

B. COPULATION

Several accounts of mating in various species have been reviewed by Snyder (1915) and Becker (1952). In the absence of wings and complex external genitalia, this behavior is apparently relatively simple and brief. According to Grassé (1942) copulation in *Kalotermes flavicollis* takes place 10−15 days after establishment in the initial cell. Becker (1952) described the behavior of a pair of this species from a moderate-sized colony which mated three times within 2 hours. They moved very slowly and showed no signs of excitation. The male backed toward the female until, after a few slight sideward motions, the tips of their abdomens came together; contact was maintained for about 30 seconds in one instance and for about 2 minutes in another. Castle (1934) reported that mating lasted for 1−4 minutes for *Zootermopsis angusticollis;* Heath (1903) recorded mating for as long as 10 minutes. Pairs of *Reticulitermes lucifugus* may mate the day after establishment in the copularium (Grassé, 1942) and *R. hesperus* as early as 13 hours after setting in laboratory cultures (Weesner, 1956). Although it is not mentioned by most observers, Grassé stated that copulation is preceded by a certain amount of mutual licking or grooming, particularly about the head. Courtship between neotenic reproductives of *R. lucifugus* was described by Buchli (1960a), who considered the calling attitude of the female in this case to be a direct invitation to pairing. Williams (1959b) determined that copulation in *Cubitermes ugandensis* probably occurs on or soon after the third day following entry into the soil. Heath (1903) observed a laboratory pair of *Z. angusticollis* to mate at least 12 times in 11 months. On the basis of similar observations with *R. hesperus,* Pickens (1934) concluded that copulation probably occurs at intervals throughout the life of a royal pair.

1. Parthenogenesis

Accounts of parthenogenesis among termites are rare and in many instances the supporting evidence is largely circumstantial. In laboratory groups of *Zootermopsis angusticollis,* Light (1944) obtained female offspring from both virgin, pigmented nymphs and primary reproductives. Virgin, parthenogenetically derived females also produced offspring, presumably females, which died in early instars. Grassé (1949), referring to earlier work with Noirot, reported that neotenic and primary females in colonies of *Kalotermes flavicollis* deprived of males would lay eggs which develop into females. With the finding of only female dealates and alates in several colonies, Chhotani (1962) suspected that reproduction by parthenogenesis might be the rule in *Bifiditermes beesoni* (Gardner). Dealated virgin females of *Reticulitermes hesperus* produced eggs and very few young (Weesner, 1956), although in similar experiments with *R. lucifugus* all eggs eventually degenerated without hatching (Buchli, 1950a). Williams (1959b) concluded that parthenogenesis does not readily occur in *Cubitermes ugandensis.* Finally, Vishnoi (in Chhotani, 1962) reported finding a small colony of *Microcerotermes beesoni* Snyder apparently headed only by female neotenic reproductives. Although diploid, or thelytokous, parthenogenesis is apparently involved in some of these examples, its role in the lives of various species of termites under natural conditions is unknown. Further examples should be watched for and the whole matter subjected to critical experimentation and supporting cytological study.

C. The Young Colony

A colony may be considered young or immature during its first few years until it is capable of producing all castes characteristic of the species and capable of staging flights of winged reproductives. Initially, its size depends on the rate and the length of the periods of egg production as well as on the longevity of its members; these factors are in turn dependent on environmental conditions. This phase of termite biology is known largely from laboratory observations on the early development of no more than about two dozen species. Much of the work has been done under a variety of laboratory conditions, so that optimum temperatures for the growth of various stages and castes are imperfectly known for even fewer species. As a result, with this valuable but limited information, meaningful comparisons from family to family cannot yet be made. Becker (1961) conducted careful studies on the embryonic development and the progress of the first workers and soldiers of *Nasutitermes ephratae* (Holmgren) at various temperatures; he has also compared (1962) data on the first oviposition with those available for three other species. Lüscher (1951) made some similar comparisons with seven species at 25°C.

In the Kalotermitidae growth of the young colony has been followed in good detail on these species: *Neotermes tectonae* (Kalshoven, 1930), *Kalotermes flavicollis* (Grassé and Noirot, 1958), *Incisitermes minor* (Harvey, 1934), *Cryptotermes brevis* (McMahan, 1962), and *C. havilandi* (Wilkinson, 1962). In all cases progress is extremely slow at first since a very small number of eggs is laid (2−5 for *I. minor* and 12 or less for *K. flavicollis*) beginning 2 or more weeks after establishment of the pair and continuing over a prolonged period (30−35 days for the latter and for perhaps as long as 4 months or more in *C. havilandi*). The incubation period is long, even at "laboratory temperatures" (43−60 days for *C. havilandi*, 75−81 days for *C. brevis*). In temperate climates oviposition ceases during the colder months, while even in the laboratory there may be a pause of 10−40 days (*K. flavicollis*) or as long as 5 months (*C. brevis*) before another batch of eggs is laid. In this and the higher families, the reproductives often eat some of their eggs, even when nutrition appears to be adequate. Figures on the population of colonies at the end of the first year or so are *N. tectonae*, 30−60; *K. flavicollis*, 20−30 (max. 55) with 0−2 soldiers; *I. minor*, 0−20 with 1 soldier; *C. brevis*, 3−4, no soldiers; *C. havilandi*, 4−5 (max. 10).

Among the Hodotermitidae, *Anacanthotermes ochraceus* began oviposition 5−44 days after establishment, depending on laboratory temperature, deposited 40−50 eggs, then stopped until the first group had hatched (Clément, 1956b). *Zootermopsis angusticollis* deposited 6 – 22 eggs beginning 14 – 18 days after pairing in the laboratory (Castle, 1934). With both of these species oviposition is suspended during the winter, although Clément found that in the laboratory at 32°C young colonies of *A. ochraceus* might reach nearly 1000 individuals at the end of a year. No soldiers appeared in the first brood although they eventually occurred in a fairly constant ratio of 1:100 nonsoldiers. Castle stated that wild colonies of *Z. angusticollis* 1 year old averaged 12 – 20 larvae and 1 soldier. A laboratory pair of *Hodotermes mossambicus* (Hagen) began laying 7 days after swarming and averaged one egg every 2 days for 2 months. The first workers tunneled to the surface for foraging after another 2 months (Coaton, 1958).

Many details of colony development in the Rhinotermitidae may be found in Buchli (1950b, *Reticulitermes lucifugus*) and Light and Weesner (1955b; *R. hesperus*). The former may begin oviposition 6 or 7 days after establishment in laboratory colonies at 25°C and lay an initial group of 10 – 20 eggs in a month. Laying ceases with the hatching of the first larvae about 28 days after the first egg is laid; it is resumed 4 – 6 months later, after the first larvae molt to the fourth instar. In nature only one group of eggs is laid before winter, but at higher laboratory temperatures (26°C); oviposition is more nearly continuous (Buchli, 1960b). *Reticulitermes hesperus* paired under laboratory conditions laid a small number of eggs 15 – 60 days later, then produced a second group, usually 70 – 100 days after pairing and coinciding with the hatching of the first eggs. In further studies Weesner (1956) determined that variability in oviposition behavior of individual queens depended on a number of factors, including her colony of origin, time of year, and even the year in which she flew. Only a small percentage of laboratory colonies produced a single soldier during the first year. Pickens (1934) reported a primary colony of this species to contain about 250 individuals at the end of 20 months.

Most of the evidence on the Termitidae indicates that oviposition begins very soon after establishment of the pair in the copularium and starts at a relatively high rate. The following species begin laying within 3 – 4 days to produce a rather large clutch within about a month or less: *Nasutitermes ephratae*, 25 – 30 eggs (Becker, 1961); *Tenuirostritermes tenuirostris*, ca. 60 (Light and Weesner, 1955a); *Ancistrotermes guineensis* (Silvestri) 55 – 60 (Sands, 1960). *Trinervitermes geminatus* begins oviposition within about 5 days and may produce between 30 and 60 eggs in the first 12 days (Sands, 1965b). Although the rate was not determined, Sen-Sarma (1962) reported that *Odontotermes assmuthi* laid an initial clutch of 100 – 130 eggs beginning 6 – 9 days after swarming.

In several species egg production was considerably reduced or suspended after deposition of the first clutch and resumed shortly after these
had hatched (*Odontotermes assmuthi*), or roughly coincident with the
appearance of the first workers and the assurance of ample food (*Nasutitermes ephratae, Trinervitermes geminatus*, probable; *Ancistrotermes
guineensis*, probable). Preparatory to foraging, the first workers of
Tenuirostritermes tunneled out of the initial chamber to the surface about
2 months after the establishment of pairs at laboratory temperatures.
The initial brood in the larger incipient colonies may number 60−70
individuals with the ratio of nasute soldiers to workers approaching 1:2
(Light and Weesner, 1955a). The first workers of *Macrotermes natalensis* dug tunnels to wood in the soil of culture tubes between the 88th
and 95th days after founding, and between the 95th and 100th days they
built the first nest "*habitacle*" within the original copularium. After
$4\frac{1}{2}$ months these colonies exceeded 50 individuals (Grassé and Noirot,
1955).

Initial development may be considerably slower in some species: for
example, *Cubitermes ugandensis* began oviposition on about the fifth
day after foundation and laid at the rate of 1 egg/1.5 days for 2−3 weeks,
paused for about 4 weeks, then resumed at an even lower rate (Williams,
1959b). In the vicinity of Cape Town pairs of *Amitermes hastatus* become established in late autumn but, in the laboratory, wait until the following spring before laying about one-half dozen eggs. By the end of the
second year a colony may contain between 100 and 200 inhabitants
(Skaife, 1954a).

In keeping with their habit of nesting in wood, or else convenient to
a suitable food supply in or on the soil, the young dealates of the Kalotermitidae, Hodotermitidae, and Rhinotermitidae are generally capable
of feeding themselves for a relatively long period. Primary reproductives
of *Kalotermes flavicollis* are known to eat wood and to retain their symbiotes for at least $3\frac{1}{2}$ years so that they are not necessarily dependent
on their progeny during this time. They are, however, eventually fed
stomodeal food by older larvae and pseudergates in the colony. The first
and second instar larvae are fed both stomodeal and proctodeal food by
the king and queen, but, by the third instar, the larvae feed themselves
and maintain faunas of their own (Grassé and Noirot, 1958). In addition
to feeding individually on wood, young pairs of *Cryptotermes havilandi*
practiced reciprocal, and occasionally even autoproctodeal, feeding.
Wilkinson (1962) considered proctodeal feeding of the larvae to be essential until the fourth instar in this species. Pairs of *Anacanthotermes
ochraceus* are capable of feeding themselves for at least the first year
but are normally fed by the larvae as soon as they are sufficiently numerous. The king and queen feed the larvae until the third instar, when they

gradually become independent (Clément, 1956b). First instar larvae of *Zootermopsis angusticollis* are fed stomodeal food by the adults (Castle, 1934). Buchli (1950b) has noted that the larvae in incipient colonies of *Reticulitermes lucifugus* are fed on stomodeal and proctodeal food, mainly by the male, until the third instar, when they become more active and able to feed themselves. Later, workers must be fed until they mature in the fourth instar. When the colony numbers 30—50 workers, the pair lose their ability to feed themselves and digest wood and so must be fed by their brood (Buchli, 1958). Weesner (1956) found some evidence that the initiation of oviposition in *R. hesperus* was partly dependent on the nutritional status of the young dealates.

It is often stated that among the Termitidae the royal pair take no food during the rearing of their first brood and are not fed until the latter are nearly full grown, e.g. *Macrotermes natalensis*. Grassé and Noirot (1955) have reported that food reserves in the form of sawdust are gathered by the first workers of this species about 3 months after establishment of the royal pair, and the first fungus bed is ready about a week later. Largely on the basis of circumstantial evidence it is generally assumed that the royal pair subsist on, and feed their brood with, nutritional reserves derived from the fat body, flight muscles, and whatever might have been in the gut at the time of flight (Grassé, 1949; Light and Weesner, 1955a). However, there is evidence that royal pairs of some species supplement these reserves by feeding on soil, cast skins, and even some of their brood: *Tenuirostritermes tenuirostris,* primarily a forager (Light and Wessner, 1955a); *Cubitermes ungandensis,* a soil feeder (Williams, 1959b). In the latter species the young are groomed and fed on stomodeal food, primarily by the male. Skaife (1954a) suggested that the workers of *Amitermes hastatus* stimulated oviposition and regulated the rate of egg production of their queens through her food supply. The various types of food and the feeding habits of termites were reviewed by Grasse (1949). The mortality of young colonies resulting from natural causes has received passing attention by Skaife (1954a), Kalshoven (1959), and Williams (1959b).

D. THE MATURE COLONY

Maturity is normally reached after a variable number of years when a colony is sufficiently prosperous to complete its life cycle with the production of all typical castes, including alates (see Section II, A). The age of any colony at maturity is definitely known in very few instances, but it may be presumed to vary from somewhat beyond the second year for *Kalotermes flavicollis* (Grassé and Noirot, 1958); the fourth year for *Incisitermes minor* (Harvey, 1942); after the fourth year for *Zootermopsis* (Heath, 1927); after the sixth year for *Neotermes tectonae* (Kalshoven, 1930); and, perhaps in many species, after 5 or 10 years as in *Amitermes hastatus* (Skaife, 1954b, 1961). The growth of the colony now depends not only on the egg production of its queen and the longevity of its members but in many species on the contributions of supplementary females and in all species on the periodic losses of alates through swarming. Growth rates of a few social insects were discussed by Brian (1965a) and, although data were meager, they did suggest that termites and ants might have low, bees intermediate, and wasps high specific growth rates.

The fecundity of primary queens generally parallels increasing behavioral specialization from the Kalotermitidae to the middle and higher families as well as to the Mastotermitidae. At the lower end of the scale Wilkinson (1962) postulated that the slightly physogastric queens of *Cryptotermes havilandi* might average eight eggs per day, but perhaps not consistently. Grassé (1949) estimated that probably no more than 200–300 eggs per year are produced by mature colonies of various kalotermitids. Studies on the damp-wood inhabiting *Zootermopsis laticeps* (Nutting, unpublished) and on the soil-inhabiting *Anacanthotermes ochraceus* (Clément, 1956b) suggest that similar or perhaps somewhat higher rates may apply to the hodotermitids. Observations by Snyder (1948) on colonies of American *Reticulitermes* indicate oviposition rates of tens of thousands per year, while the capacity of some species of *Coptotermes* must be even greater, judging from the sizes of their colonies. Among the Rhinotermitidae, however, such high oviposition rates may often result from the combined efforts of a primary queen and numbers of supplementary females.

The physogastric queens of the Termitidae are undoubtedly capable of greater sustained egg laying than any other insects. Following are examples of 24-hour oviposition rates based on actual observations for an entire day or less: *Microcerotermes arboreus* Emerson, 1680 eggs; *Nasutitermes surinamensis* (Holmgren), 3917; *Speculitermes silvestrii* (Emerson), 8568 (Emerson, 1938); *Odontotermes obesus,* 26,208 (Arora and Gilotra, 1959), 86,400, at a rate of 1/second (Roonwal, 1960); and *Macrotermes natalensis,* 36,000 (Grassé, 1949). Although it has been assumed that these phenomenal rates may be sustained year after year with little variation (Emerson, 1938), Bodot (1962) found eggs in *Cubitermes* mounds to be more abundant toward the end of the lesser rainy season. On the other hand, such fecundity is not an unfailing characteristic of the Termitidae, as the more modest performance of the queens of *Amitermes hastatus* shows: she lays several hundred eggs in a few days, then rests for a few days or weeks before laying again; thus she continues, but only through the summer months from mid-October to the end of March (Skaife, 1954a). On the basis of the number of eggs found in nests,

Bouillon (1964) calculated an intermediate oviposition rate of some 400—500 eggs per day for three species of *Apicotermes*.

The length of life of the individuals in natural colonies cannot readily be determined except for the primary reproductives and this only in rare cases where the age of the nest is known. Probably the most comprehensive data on the longevity of the members of a colony are those presented by Buchli (1958) from his detailed laboratory studies on *Reticulitermes lucifugus*. Workers in primary colonies rarely lived more than $1\frac{1}{2}$ years at 25°C; in larger, more homogeneous colonies, under similar conditions, they may live for 5 years and perhaps longer. In nature they may reasonably be expected to live for 9 or 10 years. In the laboratory he maintained soldiers for 5 years and primary and neotenic reproductives for 7 years. On the basis of these data and considerable field experience he concluded that neotenic reproductives might live for 10 or 15 years and probably much longer. Among the incidental facts accruing from a number of other studies are the following longevity records for individuals kept in the laboratory: pseudergates of *K. flavicollis*, nearly 2 years (Grassé, 1949); workers and soldiers of *Coptotermes lacteus, C. acinaciformis*, and *Nasutitermes exitiosus*, about 2 years (Gay *et al.*, 1955), workers of *Amitermes hastatus*, nearly 2 years (Skaife, 1961). Of considerable interest in this connection is a proposal by Williams (1959b) for estimating the length of the worker's life based on the "worker immaturity period" which can be determined in the laboratory. Using a large sample from a colony of *Cubitermes ugandensis* and considering certain sources of error, he calculated the mean worker life-span to be between 196 and 339 days with 98.01% confidence.

Among the morphologically primitive termites, *Mastotermes* is exceptional in producing not only small communities numbering several thousands of individuals in natural situations, but much larger aggregations containing probably several millions in settled localities. Colonies may contain several apterous reproductives, and it seems likely that they may head independent, new colonies, subsidiary to older ones (Hill, 1942). Consistent with their habit of nesting within a limited volume of wood, most of the Kalotermitidae and many of the Hodotermitidae produce relatively small colonies of from several hundred to a few thousand members. Mature societies of *Cryptotermes brevis*, averaging less than 300 and with a soldier to nonsoldier ratio of 1:45, are apparently among the smallest known (McMahan, 1966b) although Wilkinson (1962) estimated that colonies of *C. havilandi* might exceed 3000. The following figures are generally consistent with the earlier data on colony size among the kalotermitids given by Grassé (1949): *Paraneotermes simplicicornis*, 1394 (max.), 1:12 (soldier to nonsoldier ratio) (Nutting, 1966a); *Pterotermes occidentis*, 2911, 1:68 (Nutting, 1966b); and *Marginitermes hubbardi*, 2267, 1:40 (Nutting, unpublished). A single colony of *Incisitermes minor* from southern Arizona, headed by primary reproductives, contained 9200 individuals with a soldier to nonsoldier ratio of 1:54 (Nutting, unpublished). These figures are considerably larger than the maximum estimate of 2750 and the average ratio of 1:28 given for this species by Harvey (1934, 1942). Emerson (1939) and Odenbach kept a colony of *Neotermes castaneus* (Burmeister) for 24 years and it finally died by accident. If the king or queen, or both, should die they are usually replaced by substitute reproductives, but it is generally held that mere aging reproductives of the drywood termite are not replaced, so that the colonies die out after some 10 — 15 years as a result of a gradual decline in egg production (Grassé, 1949).

   Although there is even less information on the wood- and soil-inhabiting Hodotermitidae, colony size and structure appear to be comparable with the Kalotermitidae: *Zootermopsis angusticollis*, 4000 — 8000 (max.), 1:50+ (soldier to nonsoldier ratio) (Castle, 1934; Grassé, 1949); *Z. laticeps*, 2367, 1:38 (Nutting, unpublished). The size and vigor of colonies of *Z. angusticollis* and *nevadensis*, at least, may be increased by the presence of several supplementary reproductives (Castle, 1934). Coaton (1958) found that nests of *Hodotermes mossambicus* may be headed by a primary pair, several secondary reproductives, or even by one or more pairs of dealated forms derived from the parent colony.

   It is extremely difficult to obtain accurate information on the Rhinotermitidae since their nests are frequently confined to the soil, tree trunks, or mounds from which their galleries may radiate for many yards. Grassé (1949), Pickens (1934), and Snyder (1948) have reported the colonies of various species of *Reticulitermes* to exceed one or more hundreds of thousands. Studies by Greaves (1964) have shown that a colony of *Coptotermes acinaciformis* may contain over 1.25 million and one of *C. frenchi* approximately 0.75 million individuals. Roonwal (1959) stated that the soldiers composed about one-third of a population of *C. heimi* found in a dead tree. Supplementary reproductives are known to occur very commonly in colonies of many members of this family.

   It is almost equally difficult to obtain representative samples from colonies of the Termitidae which nest in the soil, in mounds, or in trees; however, careful sampling techniques have been applied in detailed studies of some of the less prolific species. Sands (1965a) estimated populations of the small mounds of *Trinervitermes geminatus* to run between 19,000 and 52,000. Bouillon (1964) has provided extensive data for three species of *Apicotermes*. Thirty-six colonies of *A. desneuxi* averaged 11,638 with a maximum of 78,200 in one colony and a soldier to worker ratio of 1:25. Data of a comparable magnitude were given for colonies of *Cubitermes sankurensis* by Bouillon and Lekie (1964).

Similarly Skaife (1961) found the largest number in any mound of *Amitermes hastatus* to be approximately 40,000, and he has concluded that its populations probably never exceed 50,000. He also estimated the average age of colonies in this species to be 30 years and the maximum about 50 years. The soldier to worker ratio of this species is about 1:20 or 30 (Skaife, 1954a).

Among several genera known to produce much larger colonies are the following individual estimates which certainly do not all represent maximum populations: *Nasutitermes surinamensis,* ca. 3 million (Emerson, 1938); *Macrotermes natalensis,* ca. 2 million (Lüscher, 1955); *Odontotermes obesus,* 90,961 with no more than 7.7% soldiers (Gupta, 1953); and *Microcerotermes arboreus,* a small nest of 5876 with a soldier to nonsoldier ratio of 1:51 (Emerson, 1938). Grassé (1949) considered that the largest populations of all—several millions—are probably produced by species in the genus *Macrotermes* in equatorial Africa. A working familiarity with this group also led him to estimate the age of certain nests and their founding reproductives at about 80 years. Hill's (1942) often-quoted record of an already mature mound colony of *Nasutitermes triodiae* (Froggatt) apparently continuing a normal existence 63 years later ought at least to be noted here.

Colonies of Rhinotermitidae and Termitidae have been estimated to live for many decades. However, reliable data are obviously extremely difficult to obtain since it is entirely possible for abandoned nests to become reoccupied by later tenants. Greaves (1962) has found this to be true for *Coptotermes acinaciformis,* and Skaife (1961) for *Amitermes hastatus.* Although colonies of many species of Nasutitermitinae and Macrotermitinae appear to be headed regularly by primary pairs, neotenic reproductives may assume considerable importance in at least some members of the other subfamilies, particularly in the Amitermitinae (Grassé, 1949; Harris and Sands, 1965). Finally, in all families the size of a colony and the proportions of young and of each caste may vary sensibly according to its age, the ecological situation and the season (Castle, 1934; Weesner, 1956; Bouillon, 1964; Bouillon and Lekie, 1964).

VI. CONCLUDING REMARKS

In concluding a comprehensive treatment of the behavioral physiology of insects, Markl and Lindauer (1965) defended the discipline against complaints of too much phenomenology and so little causal analysis by emphasizing its concern with nothing less than the ultimate in biological complexity. Much of the research reviewed in this chapter is essentially comparative behavior which involves basic relations between insects and weather systems. It is through investigations of this sort that Haufe (1963) envisioned some hope for the development of unifying concepts between biology and meteorology, particularly where the large volumes of data accumulated in ecological and related studies can now be handled by computers. He added that the "eventual extension of analogue computer methods to behaviour problems may well facilitate an understanding of more complicated systems, especially those basic to the dispersal and migration of insects." This hope will require the concentrated efforts and at least regional cooperation of several disciplines. The research must include the generation of ideas through a continuation of observation and data collection in the field, balanced against essential experimentation with laboratory colonies where data can be analyzed, the hypotheses tested, and the phenomena explained in terms of physiological processes.

REFERENCES

Ahmad, M. (1955). Termites of West Pakistan. *Biologia (Lahore)* 1, 202-264.
Annandale, N. (1923). The fauna of an island in the Chilka Lake. The habits of the termites of Barkuda. *Records Indian Museum* 25, 233-251.
Arora, G. L., and Gilotra, S. K. (1959). The biology of *Odontotermes obesus* (Rambur) (Isoptera). *Res. Bull. Panjab Univ.* [N. S.] 10, 247-255.
Banks, N., and Snyder, T. E. (1920). A revision of the nearctic termites with notes on biology and geographic distribution. *U. S. Natl. Museum, Bull.* 108, 1-228.
Bathellier, J. (1927). Contribution à l'étude systématique et biologique des termites de l'Indo-Chine. *Faune Colonies Franç.* 1, 125-365.
Becker, G. (1952). Beobachtung der Kopulation bei *Calotermes flavicollis* Fabr. (Isoptera). *Zool. Anz.* 148, 270-273.
Becker, G. (1961). Beobachtungen und Versüche über den Beginn der Kolonie-Entwicklung von *Nasutitermes ephratae* Holmgren (Isoptera). *Z. Angew. Entomol.* 49, 78-93.
Becker, G. (1962). Die Temperaturabhängigkeit der Entwicklungsvorgänge in jungen Kolonien einer *Nasutitermes*-Art. *Symp. Genet. Biol. Ital.* 11, 286-295.
Becker, G. (1963). Ruheeinstellung nach der Himmelsrichtung, eine Magnetfeld-Orientierung bei Termiten. *Naturwissenschaften* 50, 455.
Becker, G. (1964). Termite-anlockende Wirkung einiger bei Basidiomyceten-Angriff in Holz entstehender Verbindungen. *Holzforschung* 18, 168-172.
Becker, G. (1965). Versüche über den Einfluss von Braunfäulepilzen auf Wahl und Ausnutzung der Holznahrung durch Termiten. *Mater. Organismen* 1, 95-156.
Beeson, C. F. C. (1953). "The Ecology and Control of the Forest Insects of India and the Neighboring Countries," 2nd ed. Dehra Dun, India.
Bidlingmayer, W. L. (1964). The effect of moonlight on the flight activity of mosquitoes. *Ecology* 45, 87-94.
Bodot, P. (1962). Le cycle saisonnier chez les termites des savanes de Basse Côte-d'Ivoire. *Compt. Rend.* 255, 789-790.
Bodot, P. (1966). Etudes écologique et biologique des termites des savanes de Basse Côte-d'Ivoire. Thèse présentée à la Faculté des Sciences de l'Université d'Aix-Marseille.

Bouillon, A. (1964). Etude de la composition des sociétés dans trois espèces d'*Apicotermes* Holmgren (Isoptera, Termitinae). *In* "Etudes sur les Termites africains" (A. Bouillon, ed.), pp. 181-196. Masson, Paris.

Bouillon, A., and Lekie, R. (1964). Populations, rythme d'activité diurne et cycle de croissance du nid de *Cubitermes sankurensis* Wasmann (Isoptera, Termitinae). *In* "Etudes sur les Termites africains" (A. Bouillon, ed.), pp. 197-213. Masson, Paris.

Brian, M. V. (1965a). Caste differentiation in social insects. *Symp. Zool. Soc. London* **14**, 13-38.

Brian, M. V. (1965b). "Social Insect Populations." Academic Press, New York.

Bryk, F. (1927). Termitenfang am Fusse des Mount Elgon. *Entomol. Rundschau* **44**, 1-3.

Buchli, H. (1950a). La Parthénogenèse, les rapports entre sexués et leur influence sur la ponte chez *Reticulitermes lucifugus* Rossi (Rhinotermitidae). *Compt. Rend.* **230**, 1697-1699.

Buchli, H. (1950b). Recherche sur la fondation et le développement des nouvelles colonies chez le termite lucifuge (*Reticulitermes lucifugus* Rossi). *Physiol. Comparata Oecol.* **2**, 145-160.

Buchli, H. (1958). L'origine des castes et les potentialités ontogéniques des termites européens du genre *Reticulitermes*. *Ann. Sci. Nat. Zool. Biol. Animale* [11] **20**, 263-429.

Buchli, H. (1960a). Les tropismes lors de la pariade des imagos de *Reticulitermes lucifugus* R. *Vie Milieu* **11**, 308-315.

Buchli, H. (1960b). Le premier accouplement et la fécondité de la jeune reine imaginale chez *Reticulitermes lucifugus santonensis* Feyt. *Vie Milieu* **11**, 494-499.

Buchli, H. (1961). Les relations entre la colonie maternelle et les jeunes imagos ailés de *Reticulitermes lucifugus*. *Vie Milieu* **12**, 627-632.

Calaby, J. H. (1956). The distribution and biology of the genus *Ahamitermes* (Isoptera). *Australian J. Zool.* **4**, 111-124.

Calaby, J. H., and Gay, F. J. (1956). The distribution and biology of the genus *Coptotermes* (Isoptera) in Western Australia. *Australian J. Zool.* **4**, 19-39.

Castle, G. B. (1934). The damp-wood termites of western United States, genus *Zootermopsis* (formerly, *Termopsis*). *In* "Termites and Termite Control" (C. A. Kofoid, ed.), 2nd ed., pp. 273-310. Univ. of California Press, Berkeley, California.

Chhotani, O. B. (1962). Further observations on biology and parthenogenesis in the termite *Kalotermes beesoni* (Kalotermitidae). *Proc. New Delhi Symp., 1960* pp. 73-75. UNESCO, Paris.

Clément, G. (1956a). Observations sur l'essaimage d'*Anacanthotermes ochraceus* Burm. [Isopt.]. *Bull. Soc. Entomol. France* **61**, 98-103.

Clément, G. (1956b). Premières étapes du développement de la colonie chez *Anacanthotermes ochraceus* Burm. [Isopt.]. *Bull. Soc. Entomol. France* **61**, 148-153.

Coaton, W. G. H. (1958). The hodotermitid harvester termites of South Africa. *Sci. Bull. Dept. Agr., Pretoria* **375**, 1-112.

Corbet, P. S. (1966). The role of rhythms in insect behavior. *Symp. Roy. Entomol. Soc. London* **3**, 13-28.

da Costa Lima, A. M. (1960). Ordem Isoptera, Capitulo XVI. *In* "Insetos do Brasil," No. 2, pp. 3-27 and No. 3, pp. 3-25. Agron, Rio de Janeiro.

Damaschke, K., and Becker, G. (1964). Korrelation der Atmungsintensität von Termiten zu Änderrungen der Impulsfolgefrequenz der Atmospherics. *Z. Naturforsch.* **19b**, 157-160.

De Bont, A.-F. (1964). Termites et densité d'oiseaux. *In* "Etudes sur les Termites africains" (A. Bouillon, ed.), pp. 273-283. Masson, Paris.

Dietz, H. F., and Snyder, T. E. (1924). Biological notes on the termites of the Canal Zone and adjoining parts of the Republic of Panama. *J. Agr. Res.* **26**, 279-302.

Edwards, D. K. (1960a). Effects of artificially produced atmospheric electrical fields upon the activity of some adult Diptera. *Can. J. Zool.* **38**, 899-912.

Edwards, D. K. (1960b). Effects of experimentally altered unipolar air-ion density upon the amount of activity of the blowfly, *Calliphora vicina* R. D. *Can. J. Zool.* **38**, 1079-1091.

Edwards, D. K. (1961). Activity of two species of *Calliphora* (Diptera) during barometric pressure changes of natural magnitude. *Can. J. Zool.* **39**, 623-635.

Emerson, A. E. (1933). The mechanism of tandem behavior following the colonizing flight in termites. *Anat. Record* **57**, 61-62.

Emerson, A. E. (1938). Termite nests—a study of the phylogeny of behavior. *Ecol. Monographs* **8**, 247-284.

Emerson, A. E. (1939). Populations of social insects. *Ecol. Monographs* **9**, 287-300.

Emerson, A. E. (1945). The Neotropical genus *Syntermes* (Isoptera: Termitidae). *Bull. Am. Museum Nat. Hist.* **83**, 427-472.

Emerson, A. E. (1955). Geographical origins and dispersions of termite genera. *Fieldiana: Zool.* **37**, 465-521.

Fuller, C. (1915). Observations on some South African termites. *Ann. Natal Museum* **3**, 329-505.

Gay, F. J., Greaves, T., Holdaway, F. G., and Wetherly, A. H. (1955). Standard laboratory colonies of termites for evaluating the resistance of timber, timber preservatives, and other materials to termite attack. *Australia, Commonwealth Sci. Ind. Res. Organ., Bull.* **277**, 1-60.

Glick, P. A. (1939). The distribution of insects, spiders and mites in the air. *U. S. Dept. Agr., Tech. Bull.* **673**, 60.

Grabensberger, W. (1933). Untersuchungen über das Zeitgedächtnis der Ameisen und Termiten. *Z. Vergleich. Physiol.* **20**, 1-54.

Grassé, P.-P. (1942). L'essaimage des termites. Essai d'analyse causale d'un complexe instinctif. *Bull. Biol. France Belg.* **76**, 347-382.

Grassé, P.-P. (1949). Ordre des Isoptères ou Termites. *In* "Traité de Zoologie" (P.-P. Grassé, ed.), Vol. IX, pp. 408-544. Masson, Paris.

Grassé, P.-P., and Bonneville, P. (1935). Les sexués inutilisés ou achrestogonimes des Protermitides. *Bull. Biol. France Belg.* **69**, 474-491.

Grassé, P.-P., and Noirot, C. (1951a). Nouvelles recherches sur la biologie de divers termites champignonnistes (Macrotermitinae). *Ann. Sci. Nat. Zool. Biol. Animale* [11] **13**, 291-342.

Grassé, P.-P., and Noirot, C. (1951b). La sociotomie: Migration et fragmentation de la termitière chez les *Anoplotermes* et les *Trinervitermes. Behaviour* **3**, 146-166.

Grassé, P.-P., and Noirot, C. (1955). La fondation de nouvelles sociétés par *Bellicositermes natalensis* Hav. *Insectes Sociaux* **2**, 213-220.

Grassé, P.-P., and Noirot, C. (1958). La société de *Calotermes flavicollis* (Insecte, Isoptère), de sa fondation au premier essaimage. *Compt. Rend.* **246**, 1789-1795.

Grassi, B., and Sandias, A. (1893-1894). Costituzione e sviluppo della società dei termitidi. *Atti Accad. Gioenia Sci. Nat. Catania* [4] **6**, No. 13, 1-75; **7**, No. 1, 1-76; Translation: *Quart. J. Microscop. Sci.* **39**, 245-322; **40**, 1-75 (1896-1897).

Greaves, T. (1962). Studies of foraging galleries and the invasion of living trees by *Coptotermes acinaciformis* and *C. brunneus* (Isoptera). *Australian J. Zool.* **10**, 630-651.

Greaves, T. (1964). Temperature studies of termite colonies in living trees. *Australian J. Zool.* **12**, 250-262.

Gupta, S. D. (1953). Ecological studies of termites. Part I. Population of the mound-building termite *Odontotermes obesus* (Rambur) (Isoptera: Family Termitidae). *Proc. Natl. Inst. Sci. India* 19, 697-704.

Gupta, S. D. (1960). Morphology of the primitive termite *Anacanthotermes macrocephalus* (Desneux) (Isoptera: Hodotermitidae). Part 2. External morphology of the alate and worker castes. *Records Indian Museum* 58, 195-222.

Harris, W. V. (1958). Colony formation in the Isoptera. *Proc. 10th Intern. Congr. Entomol., Montreal, 1956* Vol. 2, pp. 435-439.

Harris, W. V. (1961). "Termites, Their Recognition and Control." Longmans, Green, New York.

Harris, W. V., and Sands, W. A. (1965). The social organization of termite colonies. *Symp. Zool. Soc. London* 14, 113-131.

Harvey, P. A. (1934). Life history of *Kalotermes minor. In* "Termites and Termite Control" (C. A. Kofoid, ed.), 2nd ed., pp. 217-233. Univ. of California Press, Berkeley, California.

Harvey, P. A. (1942). The common dry-wood termite. *Univ. Calif. Coll. Agr., Agr. Expt. Sta., Berkeley* Unnumbered, 4 pp.

Haufe, W. O. (1963). Entomological biometeorology. *Intern. J..Biometeorol.* 7, 129-136. 7, 129-136.

Heath, H. (1903). The habits of California termites. *Biol. Bull.* 4, 47-63.

Heath, H. (1927). Caste formation in the termite genus *Termopsis. J. Morphol. Physiol.* 43, 387-425.

Hegh, E. (1922). "Les Termites." Imprimerie Industrielle et Financière, Bruxelles, Belgium.

Herfs, A. (1951). Der Schwarmflug von *Reticulitermes lucifugus* Rossi. *Z. Angew. Entomol.* 33, 69-77.

Herfs, A. (1955). Schwärmen und Koloniegründung der Termiten. *In* "Die Termiten" (H. Schmidt, ed.), pp. 121-130. Akad. Verlagsges., Leipzig.

Hill, G. F. (1922). Descriptions and biology of some North Australian termites. *Proc. Linnean Soc. N. S. Wales* 47, 142-160.

Hill, G. F. (1942). "Termites (Isoptera) from the Australian Region." Council Sci. Ind. Res., Melbourne, Australia.

Hoelldobler, B., and Maschwitz, U. (1965). Der Hochzeitsschwarm der Rossameise *Camponotus herculeanus* L. (Hymenoptera, Formicidae). *Z. Vergleich. Physiol.* 50, 551-568.

Holdaway, F. G., Gay, F. J., and Greaves, T. (1935). The termite population of a mound colony of *Eutermes exitiosus* Hill. *J. Council Sci. Ind. Res.* 8, 42-46.

Howse, P. E. (1966). Air movement and termite behaviour. *Nature* 210, 967-968.

Imms, A. D. (1919). On the structure and biology of *Archotermopsis,* together with descriptions of new species of intestinal protozoa, and general observations on the Isoptera. *Phil. Trans. Roy. Soc. London* B209, 75-180.

Johnson, C. G. (1966). A functional system of adaptive dispersal by flight. *Ann. Rev. Entomol.* 11, 233-260.

Kalshoven, L. G. E. (1930). Bionomics of *Kalotermes tectonae* Damm. as a base for its control. *Mededeel. Inst. Plantenziekten* 76, 1-154.

Kalshoven, L. G. E. (1959). Observations on the nests of initial colonies of *Neotermes tectonae* Damm. in teak trees. *Insectes Sociaux* 6, 231-242.

Kalshoven, L. G. E. (1960). Biological notes on the *Cryptotermes* species of Indonesia. *Acta Trop.* 17, 263-272.

Kemp, P. B. (1955). The termites of north-eastern Tanganyika: Their distribution and biology. *Bull. Entomol. Res.* 46, 113-135.

Light, S. F. (1932). Contribution toward a revision of the American species of *Amitermes* Silvestri. *Univ. Calif. (Berkeley) Publ. Entomol.* 5, 355-414.

Light, S. F. (1933). Termites of western Mexico. *Univ. Calif. (Berkeley) Publ. Entomol.* 6, 79-164.

Light, S. F. (1934). The life cycle: Colony foundation and development. *In* "Termites and Termite Control" (C. A. Kofoid, ed.), 2nd ed., pp. 34-41. Univ. of California Press, Berkeley, California.

Light, S. F. (1937). Contributions to the biology and taxonomy of *Kalotermes (Paraneotermes) simplicicornis* Banks (Isoptera). *Univ. Calif. (Berkeley) Publ. Entomol.* 6, 423-464.

Light, S. F. (1944). Parthenogenesis in termites of the genus *Zootermopsis*. *Univ. Calif. (Berkeley) Publ. Zool.* 43, 405-412.

Light, S. F., and Weesner, F. M. (1955a). The incipient colony of *Tenuirostritermes tenuirostris* (Desneux). *Insectes Sociaux* 2, 135-146.

Light, S. F., and Weesner, F. M. (1955b). The production and replacement of soldiers in incipient colonies of *Reticulitermes hesperus* Banks. *Insectes Sociaux* 2, 347-354.

Loos, R. (1964). A sensitive anemometer and its use for the measurement of air currents in the nests of *Macrotermes natalensis* (Haviland). *In* "Etudes sur les termites africains" (A. Bouillon, ed.), pp. 363-372. Masson, Paris.

Lüscher, M. (1951). Beobachtungen über die Kolonie-gründung bei verschiedenen africanischen Termitenarten. *Acta Trop.* 8, 36-43.

Lüscher, M. (1955). Der Sauerstoffverbrauch bei Termiten und die Ventilation des Nestes bei *Macrotermes natalensis* (Haviland). *Acta Trop.* 12, 289-307.

Lüscher, M. (1960). Hormonal control of caste differentiation in termites. *Ann. N. Y. Acad. Sci.* 89, 549-563.

Lüscher, M. (1961). Social control of polymorphism in termites. *In* "Insect Polymorphism" (J. S. Kennedy, ed.), pp. 57-67. Roy. Entomol. Soc., London.

McCluskey, E. S. (1965). Circadian rhythms in male ants of five diverse species. *Science* 150, 1037-1039.

McMahan, E. A. (1962). Laboratory studies of colony establishment and development in *Cryptotermes brevis* (Walker) (Isoptera: Kalotermitidae). *Proc. Hawaiian Entomol. Soc.* 18, 145-153.

McMahan, E. A. (1966a). Studies of termite wood-feeding preferences. *Proc. Hawaiian Entomol. Soc.* 19, 239-250.

McMahan, E. A. (1966b). Food transmission within the *Cryptotermes brevis* colony (Isoptera: Kalotermitidae). *Ann. Entomol. Soc. Am.* 59, 1131-1137.

Markl, H., and Lindauer, M. (1965). Physiology of insect behavior. *In* "The Physiology of Insecta" (M. Rockstein, ed.), Vol. 2, pp. 3-122. Academic Press, New York.

Mathur, R. N. (1962). Enemies of termites (white ants). *Proc. New Delhi Symp., 1960* pp. 137-139. UNESCO, Paris.

May, E. (1941). The behaviour of the intestinal protozoa of termites at the time of the last ecdysis. *Trans. Am. Microscop. Soc.* 60, 281-292.

Noirot, C. (1961). Le cycle saisonnier chez les termites. *Proc. 11th Intern. Congr. Entomol., Vienna, 1960,* Vol. 1, pp. 583-585.

Noirot, C., and Bodot, P. (1964). L'essaimage d'*Allognathotermes hypogeus* Silv. (Isoptera, Termitidae). *Compt. Rend.* 258, 3357-3359.

Nutting, W. L. (1956). Reciprocal protozoan transfaunations between the roach, *Cryptocercus,* and the termite, *Zootermopsis. Biol. Bull.* 110, 83-90.

Nutting, W. L. (1965). Observations on the nesting site and biology of the Arizona dampwood termite *Zootermopsis laticeps* (Banks) (Hodotermitidae). *Psyche* 72, 113-125.

Nutting, W. L. (1966a). Colonizing flights and associated activities of termites. I. The desert damp-wood termite *Paraneotermes simplicicornis* (Kalotermitidae). *Psyche* **73**, 131-149.

Nutting, W. L. (1966b). Distribution and biology of the primitive dry-wood termite *Pterotermes occidentis* (Walker) (Kalotermitidae). *Psyche* **73**, 165-179.

Perttunen, V. (1963). Effect of desiccation on the light reactions of some terrestrial arthropods. *Ergeb. Biol.* **26**, 90-97.

Petch, T. (1917). Note on the emergence of winged termites. *Spolia Zeylan.* **10**, 395-397.

Pickens, A. L. (1934). The biology and economic significance of the western subterranean termite, *Reticulitermes hesperus*. *In* "Termites and Termite Control" (C. A. Kofoid, ed.), 2nd ed., pp. 157-183. Univ. of California Press, Berkeley, California.

Piraux, M., and Hahirwa, A. (1964). Pterines chez les termites. *In* "Etudes sur les termites africains" (A. Bouillon, ed.), pp. 125-138. Masson, Paris.

Ratcliffe, F. N., Gay, F. J., and Greaves, T. (1952). "Australian Termites. The Biology, Recognition, and Economic Importance of the Common Species." Commonwealth Sci. Ind. Res. Organ., Melbourne, Australia.

Roonwal, M. L. (1959). Biology and ecology of Oriental termites (Isoptera). No. 4. The dry-wood termite *Coptotermes heimi* (Wasm.) in India. *J. Bombay Nat. Hist. Soc.* **56**, 511-523.

Roonwal, M. L. (1960). Biology and ecology of Oriental termites. No. 5. Mound structure, nest and moisture-content of fungus combs in *Odontotermes obesus*, with a discussion on the association of fungi with termites. *Records Indian Museum* **58**, 131-150.

Roth, L. M., and Willis, E. R. (1954). The reproduction of cockroaches. *Smithsonian Misc. Collections* **122**, 1-49.

Rothney, G. A. J. (1918). A flight of winged termites at Barrackpore. *Proc. Entomol. Soc. London* March 29, lxiv-lxvi.

Rudman, P., and Gay, F. J. (1961). The causes of natural durability in timber. V. The role of extractives in the resistance of tallowwood (*Eucalyptus microcorys* F. Muell.) to attack by the subterranean termite *Nasutitermes exitiosus* (Hill). *Holzforschung* **15**, 50-53.

Ruelle, J. E. (1964). L'essaimage de *Macrotermes natalensis* Haviland dans la region de Léopoldville (Isoptera, Macrotermitinae). *In* "Etudes sur les termites africains" (A. Bouillon, ed.), pp. 231-245. Masson, Paris.

Sands, W. A. (1960). The initiation of fungus comb construction in laboratory colonies of *Ancistrotermes guineensis* (Silverstri). *Insectes Sociaux* **7**, 251-263.

Sands, W. A. (1965a). Mound population movements and fluctuations in *Trinervitermes ebenerianus* Sjöstedt (Isoptera, Termitidae, Nasutitermitinae). *Insectes Sociaux* **12**, 49-58.

Sands, W. A. (1965b). Alate development and colony foundation in five species of *Trinervitermes* (Isoptera, Nasutitermitinae) in Nigeria, West Africa. *Insectes Sociaux* **12**, 117-130.

Sen-Sarma, P. K. (1962). Some observations on swarming in nature and colony foundation under laboratory conditions in *Odontotermes assmuthi* (Holmgren) at Dera Dun (Isoptera: Termitidae). *Beitr. Entomol.* **12**, 292-297.

Skaife, S. H. (1954a). The black-mound termite of the Cape, *Amitermes atlanticus* Fuller. *Trans. Roy. Soc. S. Africa* **34**, 251-271.

Skaife, S. H. (1954b). Caste differentiation among termites. *Trans. Roy. Soc. S. Africa* **34**, 345-353.

Skaife, S. H. (1954c). "African Insect Life." Longmans, Green, New York.

Skaife, S. H. (1961). "Dwellers in Darkness." Doubleday, New York.

Smythe, R. V., Coppel, H. C., and Allen, T. C. (1967). The responses of *Reticulitermes* spp. and *Zootermopsis angusticollis* (Isoptera) to extracts from woods decayed by various fungi. *Ann. Entomol. Soc. Am.* **60**, 8-9.

Snyder, T. E. (1915). Insects injurious to forests and forest products. Biology of the termites of the eastern United States with preventive and remedial measures. *U. S. Dept. Agr., Bull. Bur. Entomol.* **94**, 13-85.

Snyder, T. E. (1948). "Our Enemy the Termite," Rev. ed. Cornell Univ. Press (Comstock), Ithaca, New York.

Snyder, T. E. (1954). "Order Isoptera, the Termites of the United States and Canada," Tech. Bull. Natl. Pest Control Assoc., New York.

Tang, C., and Li, S. (1959). Forecasting the swarming of the yellow-thorax termite *Reticulitermes flaviceps* Osh. in Hangchow. *Acta Entomol. Sinica* **9**, 477-482.

Tillyard, R. J. (1926). "The Insects of Australia and New Zealand." Angus and Robertson, Sydney.

Verron, H. (1963). Rôle des stimuli chimiques dans l'attraction social chez *Calotermes flavicollis* (Fabr.). *Insectes Sociaux* **10**, 167-355.

Weesner, F. M. (1953). Biology of *Tenuirostritermes tenuirostris* (Desneux) with emphasis on caste development. *Univ. Calif. (Berkeley) Publ. Zool.* **57**, 251-302.

Weesner, F. M. (1956). The biology of colony foundation in *Reticulitermes hesperus* Banks. *Univ. Calif. (Berkeley) Publ. Zool.* **61**, 253-314.

Weesner, F. M. (1960). Evolution and biology of termites. *Ann. Rev. Entomol.* **5**, 153-170.

Weesner, F. M. (1965). "The Termites of the United States, A Handbook." Natl. Pest Control Assoc., Elizabeth, New Jersey.

Wellington, W. G. (1946). The effects of variations in atmospheric pressure upon insects. *Can. J. Res.* D24, 51-70.

Weyer, F. (1930). Ueber Ersatzgeschlechtstiere bei Termiten. *Z. Morphol. Oekol. Tiere* **19**, 364-380.

Wiens, J. A. (1966). On group selection and Wynne-Edwards' hypothesis. *Am. Scientist* **54**, 273-287.

Wilkinson, W. (1962). Dispersal of alates and establishment of new colonies in *Cryptotermes havilandi* (Sjöstedt) (Isoptera, Kalotermitidae). *Bull. Entomol. Res.* **53**, 265-286.

Williams, R. M. C. (1959a). Flight and colony foundation in two *Cubitermes* species (Isoptera: Termitidae). *Insectes Sociaux* **6**, 203-218.

Williams, R. M. C. (1959b). Colony development in *Cubitermes ugandensis* Fuller (Isoptera: Termitidae). *Insectes Sociaux* **6**, 291-304.

Wynne-Edwards, V. C. (1962). "Animal Dispersion in Relation to Social Behaviour." Hafner, New York.

9

Caste Differentiation in the Lower Termites

E. MORTON MILLER

I. INTRODUCTION

The literature dealing specifically with the problem of caste differentiation seems to start with the paper by Grassi and Sandias in 1893 – 1894, although Lespès (1856) and Mueller (1873) sensed the problem and gave it general mention. These observers were followed by Holmgren, Heath, Imms, Jucci, Snyder, Thompson, Kalshoven, Silvestri, Weyer, and others, but it is remarkable that work on such a fascinating biological phenomenon as polymorphism has been so infrequent and scattered. The excellent beginning by Grassi and Sandias drew few disciples, which, in retrospect, is regrettable. It was not until 1934 that Castle, Light, and Light's students, properly attacking the problem with experimental approaches, developed a firm working hypothesis and stimulated further critical research.

During this history, interpretations were of two sorts: some observers felt that the different castes — reproductive, soldier, and worker — were

---

*The Hodotermitidae, as considered in this chapter, includes the subfamilies Termopsinae, Stolotermitinae, Porotermitinae, and Hodotermitinae.

hereditarily determined and that the proportions of castes in a normal colony were segregants from heterozygous parental forms (Imms, 1919). This was the "intrinsic" school of thought. Others, beginning with Grassi and Sandias, Escherich (1909), Holmgren (1912), Feytaud (1912), Goetsch (1946), and especially Pickens (1932), suggested that all individuals possessed equal potential and were alike at hatching, and that specific caste development for a given proportion of the colony depended on "extrinsic" factors such as selective nutrition, influential exudates, or environmental factors. Pickens, working with *Reticulitermes,* suggested the additional idea that a functional queen produced an inhibiting substance which regulated the development of nymphs in the colony; at the same time he felt that soldiers came from a different kind of egg.

Of course, the fact that observers in different parts of the world have dealt with various species having differing habits and of different evolutionary status has produced some of the seeming contradictions, but it seems worth noting that analysis of the problem has progressed best when careful and continuous observations of living termites have been made; inferences from preserved specimens alone or from the development of other social insects have been unsatisfactory.

Only three families are included in this review. As far as can be determined, little study has been made of caste development in *Mastotermitidae,* although Hill (1925) described the occurrence and structure of apterous, third-form reproductives in the one living species of this family, *Mastotermes darwiniensis* Froggatt.

II. DEFINITION OF TERMS

In the review that follows, the terminology of the European investigators has been used, and, where possible, other usages have been converted to this. It seems important that standardization be achieved, but in order to reduce chances of misinterpretation synonymous terms are given parenthetically. Statements by Buchli (1958), Lüscher (1952a,b), Grassé and Noirot (1947), and Weesner (1960) have been useful in suggesting definitions.

Larva (apterous nymph) — an immature individual without any external signs of wing buds or of soldier morphology. The number of larval stages may vary with species and environment.

Nymph (brachypterous nymph) — an individual succeeding the larval stages and showing external wing buds.

Worker — a term occurring in the literature, but of questionable usage in the lower termites. It is intended to mean a permanently sterile form, without visible differentiation towards alate or soldier, which serves the colony in nutrition and construction. Recent observations suggest that supposed "workers" really may be pseudergates.

Pseudergate—literally, "false worker." An individual that has regressed from nymphal stages by molts that reduce or eliminate wing buds; or a form derived from a larva by undergoing "stationary," nondifferentiating molts. Buchli (1958) stated, however, that in *Reticulitermes lucifugus* (Rossi), a worker is distinguishable from a pseudergate in that the worker's mesonotum is narrower than its pronotum. Pseudergates retain caste-differentiating abilities.

Soldier—a form with defensive adaptations, such as enlarged mandibles (*Zootermopsis* and others) or stopperlike heads (*Cryptotermes* and *Calcaritermes*). In either case the head is heavily pigmented and sclerotized. A presoldier ("white" soldier, pseudosoldier, or soldier nymph) is an intermediate developmental stage between larva, pseudergate, or nymph and the definitive, mature soldier form; apparently the presoldier is nonfunctional for defensive purposes in the colony.

First-form reproductive (imago or primary)—the colony-founding type derived from winged adult or alate.

Second-form reproductive (brachypterous neotenic, nymphoid)—a functional male or female derived from a nymph and retaining, to some degree, wing buds.

Third-form reproductive (apterous neotenic, ergatoid)—a functional male or female without evidence of wing buds, usually larval in external form but more or less pigmented.

Replacement reproductive (supplementary or substitute or neotenic)—a general term including all second- or third-form functional reproductives which replace or, in some species, supplement the first-form reproductives. In the Termitidae imagoes may become functional in the colony of their origin in certain species (Chapter 10); these have been termed adultoids.

III. THE HODOTERMITIDAE

Almost all of the studies of castes in this family center around two species of *Zootermopsis: Z. angusticollis* (Hagen) and *Z. nevadensis* (Hagen). Heath in 1903 described the habits of these species and set forth the idea that the young are hatched without visible differences among them. Thompson later (1919, 1922) held that there are two sizes of eggs and two types of newly hatched larvae, distinguishable in preserved materials by differing brain sizes; however, she was uncertain of the implications of the two egg sizes and did not firmly correlate these with the two types of larvae. One type of larva was described as small headed, with a large brain, and large sex organs—the reproductive line; the other type represented the sterile line of development—the soldier and worker forms. Four "stable adult" castes were postulated: first-, second-, and third-form fertile or reproductive types; and sterile or soldier type. No permanent worker caste was recognized. Although clinging to this interpretation, Thompson (1922) did note that, "there is great variability in all organs (of *Termopsis*), and even in the degree of infertility of some female soldiers." She was aware also of the soldier-reproductive intercastes reported by others and she saw in her own material a suggestion that, compared to some young soldiers which had ovarian structures giving "promise of fertility," the older soldiers apparently had undergone arrest or regression in reproductive development. Observations at that time were scarce in respect to newly hatched larvae of the second-form line, and uncertainty existed as to size and antennal count. In evaluating these studies on *Zootermopsis*, it is worth noting that some of Thompson's concepts originated in work (1917) with *Reticulitermes*, which is in a higher family (see Section V).

Heath (1927, 1928) enlarged the study of *Zootermopsis* with collections of over 17,000 individuals from several hundred colonies of varying ages and sizes. At that time the possibility of confusing *Z. nevadensis* and *Z. angusticollis* material was reduced. This increased perspective permitted Heath to conclude that there were not two distinct types of eggs, although there was a normal variation in size. Nor could he detect any constant difference among newly hatched larvae. Differentiation into the reproductive and the soldier castes did not appear until the close of the sixth instar. Furthermore, fertile soldiers were observed, and the first instar progeny of one of these appeared to be normal.

Heath was unwilling to recognize as distinct castes the second- and third-form reproductives of Thompson's classification; he believed instead that these were modifications or transitional forms of the soldier-nymph line of development, brought about by "extrinsic factors—probably feeding." From his observations of living colonies he concluded that the larvae produced for the first 3 or 4 years in a primary colony were all of soldier potential, and that first-form reproductive nymphs appeared only in the larger, more populous colonies (Heath and Wilbur, 1927). In some experimental colonies from which the primary reproductives had been removed, replacement forms appeared within 82—154 days.

Since satisfactory evidence for both the intrinsic and the extrinsic theories of caste determination was lacking up to this time, Castle (1934) undertook to obtain some answers for the problem by experimentally testing Pickens' hypothesis of inhibiting hormones. By isolating individuals for 45 days or more and finding that they became replacement reproductives, Castle negated the idea of Holmgren and others that special feeding, stimulated by exudates or unknown factors, controlled differentiation into reproductives. It was shown, too, that such randomly selected and isolated individuals became reproductives in much higher proportion than could be expected by chance occurrence of genetically determined forms. In other experiments alcohol and ether extracts of functional supplementary female reproductives were fed on filter paper to groups of undifferentiated larvae, and these were compared to control groups. Those termites which received the extracts differentiated toward the replacement female condition more slowly than individuals of the control group, as indicated by the delay in egg laying. The extract of female bodies did not retard the development of males. In the presence of a functional reproductive of a given sex, no neotenic of that sex developed from the undifferentiated individuals, whereas in the control group, which lacked the functional reproductives, reproductives did arise. Such reproductives could be either brachypterous or apterous; the former type developed from individuals of the fifth or sixth instar, while the latter type arose from the fourth, fifth, sixth, or seventh instars.

Castle concluded from these studies that "all members of a colony are potentially reproductive and any individual (with the exception of the pseudo-soldier nymph, the adult soldier, the first form reproductive, and late seventh instar nymphs approaching alation) may develop into a supplementary reproductive of its sex."

Similar experimental comparisons on the development of the soldier caste led to the conclusions that (1) the presence of older individuals of the fifth and sixth instars in an incipient colony inhibited or greatly delayed the development of a soldier; and (2) in most cases the introduction of a soldier into an incipient colony before a presoldier (white soldier) appeared greatly delayed or prevented the origin of a new soldier within the group. Removal of each soldier as it developed in beginning colonies caused 50% of the laboratory colonies to produce more soldiers than normal for the first year of colony development.

From such studies Castle proposed a theory of caste differentiation, and because this was a sort of milestone in analysis of the problem, his statement is partially quoted:

At the time of hatching all nymphs [larvae] bear three sets of potentialities to the same degree, namely, 1) the reproductive potentiality resulting in sexual maturity; 2) the alate potentiality . . .; and 3) the soldier potentiality . . . . At a certain stage two groups are differentiated from the original group of nymphs [larvae]. Each of these groups retains the reproductive potentiality, but in one group the alate potentiality asserts itself and dominates further development, whereas in the other group the soldier potentiality induces further development. The assumption of the alate characteristics is dependent upon a time element in addition to the alate potentiality, whereas the development of the soldier form is dependent upon factors in the constitution of the colony . . . . Since reproductive potentiality is present in all nymphs [larvae] and since its expression has been shown to be inhibited by a substance produced by a functional reproductive and eaten by the nymphs, the absence of functional reproductives would allow the potentiality to express itself, resulting in the development of supplementary reproductives which are neotenics. At times this reproductive potentiality and the soldier potentiality operate together, resulting in the production of fertile soldiers.

As a result of further experiments in a pattern similar to those by Castle, Light (1942–1943) felt that some points were inconclusive, so he carried out a variety of additional studies (1944a,b). Many thousands of termites and various methods of preparing extracts of reproductives were used. In all of the experiments some degree of inhibition of reproductivity was obtained when extracts of functional reproductives were fed to the termites. However, the inhibition was not as complete as that found in natural colonies headed by primary reproductives; there was also considerable variability in results in different series. Although Light was reluctant to accept either Castle's or his own work as definitely proving the existence of an "ectohormonal" substance acting as an inhibiting agent and regulating the differentiation of replacement reproductives, he did state that the trend of the evidence was to support the theory.

In further studies, reported by Light and Illg (1945), it was found that reproductivity of experimental colonies was not effectively measured in terms of the number of replacements produced in a given time after separation from the parent colony. The troublesome variations were further analyzed, and although some of them could be considered random and normal variations, there were clear differences between the transformation potentials of different instars.

After refinement of experimental and culture techniques, further observations reported in 1951 by Light and Weesner made important points:

1. Segregated, homogeneous groups of second instars of *Zootermopsis angusticollis* did not survive; third and higher instars did.

2. Supplementary reproductives could be produced from all instar levels, fourth through tenth, within 102 days after separation from the primary reproductives of the donor colony.

3. Eggs were produced by the tenth instar replacement reproductives within 40 days. But a time gradient from the oldest to the youngest instars existed in the development of neotenic reproductives, the oldest developing most rapidly, and relatively few reproductives were produced in groups of brachypterous nymphs, as compared to groups of apterous individuals.

4. Replacement reproductives were developed after removal of the primaries from a colony, even if the primaries were returned, if the separation lasted 21 days. A 14-day separation reduced the number of groups developing replacements to 50%; 7-day, to 8.5%.

5. Within an instar-segregated group some individuals seemed to differentiate into replacements more readily than others. [The significance of this observation became apparent later in Lüscher's studies (1952b) with *Kalotermes*.]

6. Finally, each sex seemed to be more effective in inhibiting members of that same sex.

In comparing these studies with earlier ones from the "Light school," it seems clear that the use of primary reproductives as inhibitor sources gave more consistent (and perhaps more powerful) inhibition than the use of various extracts of replacement reproductives.

IV. THE KALOTERMITIDAE

In this family, as in the preceding one, investigations of the caste phenomenon have centered largely around a single species, *Kalotermes flavicollis* (Fabricius), found in parts of Southern Europe.

Grassi and Sandias (1893–1894, 1896–1897) made many observations on living colonies of *K. flavicollis*, both in nature and in the laboratory, noting details in regard to structure and size of newly hatched forms, types of individuals in normal colonies, culturing requirements, internal and external structures, intestinal protozoans, feeding habits, and caste development. In spite of their discursive and somewhat anthropomorphic style of description, natural to those years, these early observers set forth stimulating conclusions, which may be summarized as follows: "The normal development of *Calotermes* up to the perfect [winged] stage may undergo deviation at different ages. This . . . may lead to the formation of substitute royal forms or of soldiers . . . ." Artificial colonies of 15–40 individuals were carried about in vials by these authors and watched frequently. "Orphaned" colonies produced replacement reproductives detectable within 4–7 days. Grassi and Sandias claimed that formation of such substitute reproductives never occurred in colonies having the original reproductives (the "royal pair"), but that if the king and queen were removed from a small colony for even 24–48 hours a few substitutes would be produced at times. Substitutes were not formed from small larvae that had only 12 antennal segments, but could be from the "small-headed" forms having 14–16 segments. Colonies varying in size from 12–200 produced approximately the same number of reproductives.

It was said by Grassi and Sandias that the soldier "begins by possessing the characters of the worker." But artificial groups of nymphs produced, after a time, both replacement reproductives and soldier nymphs, which eventually became mature soldiers. The wing buds were resorbed until barely a vestige remained. Furthermore, Grassi and Sandias noted that soldiers could originate from various larval instars, thus producing the small, medium, and large soldiers often found. These size types differed not only in respect to head and body size, but in head proportions; thus we have a case of heterogonic growth. It was assumed in this study that the "large-headed" larvae all gave rise to soldiers, but descriptions are not clear as to what constituted "large-headed" and "small-headed" larvae.

The function of the protozoans in the hindgut of termites puzzled these authors. They assumed that the protozoans were parasites, yet were dissatisfied with this concept and noted that protozoans soon became absent in reproductives and soldiers. It was stated that "absence of protozoa is insufficient by itself to stimulate the maturation of the genital organs." Grassi and Sandias believed that "transformation of 'ordinary' forms into substitute forms must be dependent on a change, either quantitative or qualitative, in the character of the ordinary diet." They thought that this involved especially "saliva" since the frequent trophallactic exchanges were seen.

Escherich (1909) accepted the work of Grassi and Sandias, adding observations of his own, and attempting an hypothesis that the protozoans of larvae had a "castrating" effect and that only those individuals sufficiently released from protozoans could develop into neotenic reproductives. Holmgren (1912) likewise remarked upon the work of Grassi and Sandias and placed it in the perspective of his own observations on higher termites. This author recognized early the possibility that workers are "inhibited" forms between larvae and soldiers and/or imagoes.

Contributions to the study of caste determination in *Kalotermitidae* came next with Thompson's analysis (1919) of preserved material. Thompson rejected the Grassi and Sandias interpretations and thought that newly hatched *Kalotermes* larvae were separable into two types — the reproductive line and the soldier line. The former were said to have larger brains, larger sex organs, and a "white, dense abdomen." Thompson claimed that larvae with 9 antennal segments were separable into reproductive and soldier lines.

Kalshoven's observations (1930) on the bionomics of *Neotermes tectonae* (Dammermann) indicated that there were only two permanent castes in this species — winged and soldier — and that there were no special soldier-producing larvae. Neotenic reproductives could develop from various older nymph stages in orphaned colonies, and young members of a colony could become either soldiers or neotenics, depending on the population of the colony. Similar observations on *Postelectrotermes militaris* (Desneux) were made by Pinto (1941).

In the course of studies for the California Termite Investigations Committee, Harvey (1934) observed that *Incisitermes minor* (Hagen) was able to produce reproductives from undifferentiated larvae, more commonly from those in the sixth instar. As many as four such replacements often appeared in the small, isolated groups forming the experimental colonies. Harvey found wide variations in the duration of later instars and noted that these were related to "interpolated" molts, which apparently did not modify size or form. (This is probably the same phenomenon referred to by later authors as "stationary molts.") Large natural colonies sometimes contained not only primary but neotenic reproductives — hence the often-used term, supplementary. The origin of soldiers was not described.

Grassé and Noirot (1946a) began publications on caste in *Kalotermes flavicollis,* confirming and adding to the Grassi and Sandias observations on this species. They found that all larvae in or past the fourth instar had the ability to transform rapidly into neotenic reproductives if a molt preceded and if the gonad-inhibiting influence of already functioning reproductives was absent. But isolated couples of larvae became replacement reproductives without the colony salivary stimulus supposed by Grassi and Sandias. A colony, orphaned in the laboratory, rapidly produced several incipient reproductives, but only one pair of these was retained by the colony, the others being sometimes eaten or neglected to death.

In studies on the origin of the soldier caste, Grassé and Noirot maintained that there were not, in *K. flavicollis,* two categories of larvae at early stages, but that both sexuals and soldiers derived from a single stock. This seemed established when experimental groups of only wing-budded nymphs produced soldiers. Such soldier nymphs, passing through two molts, had their wing buds reduced in varying degrees. Individuals having a soldier head but retaining wing buds to a conspicuous degree were considered intercastes. There may have been a seasonal factor involved, since the greatest production of soldiers in both natural and experimental colonies took place in June and July. Soldiers of various sizes were developed in Grassé and Noirot's colonies, the smallest being from a third instar larva with 12 antennal segments and the others corresponding to larger and older instars.

Heretofore, it had been assumed that no worker caste occurred in *Kalotermes* and in a sense that remained true, but Grassé and Noirot (1947) found that large apterous individuals existed and that these were derived either from wing-budded nymphs by regressive molting which reduced the wing buds or by a sort of stationary molting of larvae during which no wing buds became visible. Such individuals they termed *pseudergates.* Although functioning as workers, perhaps for long periods, there was evidence that their reproductive and possibly their soldier potentials were not lost but merely arrested.

In 1952 Lüscher began a series of significant publications on *K. flavicollis,* studying with logical procedures the facts and factors of caste differentiation. To summarize his findings he proposed a developmental schema as follows (see also Fig. 1):

Normal development leads through a varying number of larval stages (5 – 10) to fully grown larvae, thence to the pseudergates. Depending

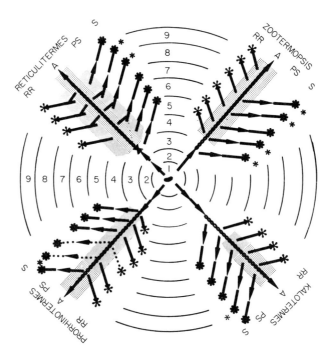

Fig. 1. Scheme generalizing the recorded differentiation paths possible in four genera. (A) Alate; (PS) presoldier; (RR) replacement reproductive; (S) mature soldier; (X) Buchli's workerlike form; (∗) recorded instance of brachypterous soldiers; (∗) definitive caste form reached; (1 – 9) stadia. Dotted line: postulated, not observed; chain line: period when either forward or regressive molts are possible; coarse screen; nymphal period; fine screen: pseudergate period (Based on data from Buchli, Castle, Grassé, Noirot, Light, Lüscher, Miller, and Weesner).

on the composition and size of the colony, such pseudergates can follow any one of several lines of further development. Some may undergo "stationary" molts and not change in form; others may molt into nymphs with wing buds and in two stages progress to the imago form. If no functioning reproductives are present, then some fifth-stage larvae (rarely) or pseudergates of later stage may become replacement reproductives. Likewise, if not inhibited by existing soldiers, some individuals may molt into presoldiers and eventually into the soldier caste. Finally, a nymph may undergo regressive moltings, reduce wing buds, and become a pseudergate or a soldier; but replacement reproductives, soldiers, and imagoes are final stages and cannot regress or change form.

To further elucidate and confirm certain parts of the problem Lüscher (1952a,b,c, 1956b) developed special techniques and devices. By marking and daily observation, it was found that differentiation from nymph to replacement reproductive involves a special molt, at which time the head width is usually reduced, wing buds are reduced, and the prothoracic gland atrophies. On the average, such a molt is preceded by a total loss of protozoans from the hind-gut. Replacement reproductives occur only when a colony is deprived of existing reproductives. Then undifferentiated nymphs, with reproductive "competence," may be determined as replacement reproductives within 24 hours. The differentiating competence decreases exponentially after a molt, so that only 54% of those nymphs that were 10 − 20 days past the molt changed, whereas 87% of those within the 0 − 10 day period after molt became reproductive. The curve of decreasing competence was of such form as to suggest that the loss was randomized, but perhaps regulated by some monomolecular physiological phenomenon (Lüscher, 1953a). Loss of competence was typically followed within 56 days by a molt.

Separating groups of planned composition from each other by wire gauze enabled Lüscher to deduce that two mechanisms existed for control of replacement reproductives in a colony. A group lacking reproductives would differentiate new ones, but would soon kill them if there were reproductives on the other side of the gauze fence, detecting by antennal contact the prior presence of reproductives. If two such groups were separated by a double fence, preventing antennal contact, the replacement reproductives in the orphaned group survived, as they would in an independent nest. Thus it was supposed that an inhibiting substance produced by reproductives and ordinarily passed by trophallaxis to all members of a colony was blocked by the single screen; but that another substance, sensed by antennae protruded through the screen meshes, was a stimulus for nymphs or larvae to kill the newer reproductives.

The postulated inhibitory substance was fully effective only when both sexes were present; often several males or females were produced before a competent member of the missing sex appeared. In such cases the supernumerary individuals of each sex were destroyed by the larvae and the nymphs of the colony, leaving only a functioning pair. Certain experiments showed that functional females had a measurable inhibitory effect on further development of females, but that a male alone had little or no effect on males. Further experiments (Lüscher, 1955), in which functioning female reproductives were fastened into a fence with the head on one side and abdomen on the other, showed that the inhibiting factor involved was given off from the abdominal end; the head end gave off no effective substance into the colony on that side. Furthermore, a larva or pseudergate fastened between an orphaned colony and one with a pair of reproductives could serve as a transmitter of inhibiting influence.

After reevaluating Light's experiments on *Zootermopsis*, Lüscher postulated that a pheromone originated in the head-thorax region, but was transmitted through the gut. Subsequently (1956b), experiments with head extracts in methanol were conducted, and it was suggested that such extracts would actually stimulate the development of replacement reproductives. Further, functioning reproductives had a complete inhibiting influence in a colony only if both sexes were present. A female alone partially inhibited the development of other females; two males were necessary to significantly inhibit the development of other males. Whether the "head factor" was brain hormone or some other substance was not clear from these experiments.

In view of previous observations (Grassé and Noirot, 1946a; Lüscher, 1952a) that differentiation of reproductives was definitely preceded by a molt, Lüscher next turned attention to possible effects of the prothoracic hormone, ecdysone (Lüscher and Karlson, 1958). Injection or feeding of α-ecdysone caused *K. flavicollis* nymphs or larvae to lose protozoans from the hind-gut and to molt, on the average, 10 days later. Such molting did not lead to differentiation or growth. Experiments (Lüscher, 1958) in which corpora allata from replacement reproductives were implanted into full-grown larvae or nymphs led unexpectedly to a number of presoldiers. If implantation of corpora allata was soon followed by injections of ecdysone, no presoldiers appeared, but if there were a few days intervening, presoldiers did develop.

Meanwhile, from Grassé and Noirot's laboratory (1958), details were added to the knowledge of primary colony development in *K. flavicollis*. Sixty-five percent of 250 such colonies were found to produce a small soldier, at the second or third instar, from the first-hatched larva. Soldiers formed after the first one were from older instars. Nymphs did not usually appear until colony population exceeded 100. Further studies (1960a) showed that in experimental colonies more female than male neotenics were formed in the first 10 days after starting. This may have been due either to easier reactivity of females or to more rapid transformation into recognizable reproductives. Female neotenics showed inhibiting specificity for female nymphs, and male for males; thus even in unisexual groups a stabilization occurred in the number of reproductives produced; but in the final regulation of numbers in male groups two or three male reproductives would persist, while in female groups only one functional female survived. Thus, there may be a quantitative difference either in reactivity or in the inhibiting powers of the different sexes.

In another series (1960b) it was found possible to keep isolated nymphs alive for prolonged periods (365 – 525 days), if each was refaunated after molting. This situation enabled Grassé and Noirot to follow accurately the molting history and individual differentiation. Although, as might be expected, the isolate had a slower physiological pace than groups, such single individuals could become neotenics, pseudergates, or imagoes; presoldiers were not formed, and regressive molting seemed most common. A few hatching eggs were obtained from female isolates that converted into neotenics, thus establishing the possibility of parthenogenesis. Although these authors felt at this time that Lüscher's hypothesis of a molt-stimulating hormone from the head was not supported in the evidence from the isolate series (no trophallactic companions), they did not mention the possibility that the refaunation necessary might communicate to the isolate some hormones as well as protozoans.

Significant and difficult sets of experiments were performed by Lüscher and Springhetti (1960). Corpora allata from various termite caste donors were transplanted into 365 K. flavicollis pseudergates; the receiving individuals were then kept in small supporting colonies. When corpora allata from primary and secondary reproductives, from preimago nymphs, and from soldiers were implanted, a large number of the recipients differentiated into presoldiers. Transplants from pseudergates and nymphs not preparing to molt had no such effect, but those from pseudergates seemed to increase the occurrence of replacement reproductives as compared to controls. The absence of reproductives in the support colonies seemed to accelerate presoldier differentiation in the implanted animals. Some soldier – reproductive intercastes were produced.

Ligation of the head in molt-ready reproductives gave results that seemed to mean that the corpora allata enlargement that occurs in premolt is concerned with subsequent gonadotropic hormone production and growth of oocytes and not with external features of differentiation. The authors concluded from these experiments that corpora allata probably produce two separate hormones: a juvenile hormone which regulates competence for supplementary reproductive differentiation and a gonadotropic hormone which influences oocyte growth in female reproductives or initiates presoldier differentiation. Later work (Lüscher, 1963) indicated that the soldier-inducing substance may be different from the gonadotropic and, therefore, be a third hormone.

Further interest in the effects of insect hormones on molting behavior of termites was shown by Lebrun (1963a,b). He implanted molting glands (ventral, prothoracic) from *Periplaneta americana* into soldiers and replacement reproductives of *K. flavicollis*. The termites attempted to molt under this influence, but were unable to complete the action because of the heavier sclerotization in these castes. This reaction was interpreted to mean that soldiers and replacement reproductives, though considered terminal forms and definite castes, had not lost molting potential at the tissue-response level. Later, Lebrun (1964) reported that corpora allata from newly formed replacement reproductives, when transplanted into pseudergates at the beginning of the pseudergates' intermolt, would cause these recipients to form presoldiers or soldier intercastes. Corpora allata from roaches in gestation, although not as powerful as homotransplants, also caused a high percentage of the receiving termites to become presoldiers or intercastes. Thus the work of Lüscher and Springhetti was confirmed. Experiments by Lebrun (1967a,b) on late nymphs showed that injection of roach molting-glands could cause the termite nymphs to regress to pseudergates. Corpora allata injections led to presoldier and soldier intercaste forms. Injections of corpora allata from neotenics and "near neotenics" encouraged soldier development, and it appeared that the titer of corpora allata secretion in relation to the time of molt was important to the direction and the degree of caste metamorphosis.

In order to understand more precisely the relative functions of male and female replacement reproductives on inhibitions of others, Lüscher (1964) repeated and refined previous experiments of his own and of Grassé and Noirot (1960a). He confirmed the observation that a single male supplementary reproductive has, in the absence of a female, no inhibiting effect on other males, but that a single female reproductive strongly inhibits the development of other females. Extracts of male heads appeared to *stimulate* the differentiation of female replacement reproductives. In this work Lüscher thought that male reproductives needed the presence of either a female or of one or two other males to produce the inhibiting substance. One might suggest that he was dealing with a quantitative situation and that the amount of pheromone given off by a male was simply half or less than that of a female.

Although Grassé and Noirot (1946a, 1960a) and Lüscher (1952b) believed that the elimination of supernumerary replacement reproductives was accomplished through cannibalism by larvae and pseudergates,

Becker had suggested (1948) that some of the excess reproductives molted regressively into pseudergates. To clarify the matter Ruppli and Lüscher (1964) restudied the problem. It was discovered that if two pairs of *K. flavicollis* reproductives with amputated and sealed antennae were put together in colonies there was no reduction of numbers down to the typical single pair, but if to such a group there was added one reproductive with normal antennae, then the amputated individuals were attacked by the dominant reproductives and eventually eaten by the larvae and nymphs of the colony. These authors witnessed the process directly.

In an excellent series of papers (1960, 1961a,b, 1962, 1963) Lüscher has summarized the studies on *K. flavicollis*. These will be referred to in Section VI.

V. THE RHINOTERMITIDAE

In addition to their study of *Kalotermes flavicollis*, Grassi and Sandias (1893 – 1894) made many observations on the habits and occurrence of castes in *Reticulitermes lucifugus* although — as they remarked — the small size, more rapid motion, and greater difficulty of raising laboratory colonies were hampering factors and, consequently, their observations were less adequate. In this early paper the authors assumed that the species had a worker caste. They noted that in nature there were few first form "royal pairs" and many more substitute or supplementary reproductives (in contrast to *Kalotermes*). The types of individuals found in a large nest population were numerous in Grassi and Sandias' classification, which was based partly upon the number of antennal segments. Small-headed and large-headed individuals within the larval instars (except the first) were detected. A soldier-nymph intercaste was recorded. These observers thought that no parthenogenesis occurred in *R. lucifugus*, that apparently unmated females in fact often had sperm in their genital tracts. They concluded that "the regular development of *Termes* [*Reticulitermes*] up to the perfect insect may undergo a deviation at various periods of life which leads to the formation of workers, of complementary or substitute royal forms, or of soldiers, the last passing through the stadium of the young worker."

The origin of castes in *Reticulitermes flavipes* (Kollar) was reported by Thompson in 1917. As a strong adherent of the intrinsic or genetic theory of determination, Thompson set out to gather supporting data for that view. In her preserved material she claimed to see two types of newly hatched larvae: reproductive types with "large brains" and worker-soldier types with "small brains." "Adults"—called the first, second, and third forms — were found in the reproductive line; workers and soldiers in the other. Externally visible separation into the five "adult types" occurred about the fourth instar. This view of certain wing-budded nymphs as final, adult castes was maintained in a later paper (Thompson and Snyder, 1920).

Jucci in 1924 believed that diet was important in caste determination and that neotenics were produced by a special "alimentary regime."

Reticulitermes hesperus Banks was studied by Pickens (1932). He inserted an important view into the extrinsic vs. intrinsic discussion by suggesting that the worker caste may really be inhibited reproductive larvae or nymphs. After some experiments he postulated an inhibiting secretion, produced by queens, which prevented the development of other reproductives in the colony. At the same time he believed that "in the case of a soldier, a difference in the egg is indicated." Thus he suggested intrinsic factors for separation of eggs into a reproductive-worker line and a soldier line, but an extrinsic factor for differentiation of worker and reproductive. This concept of egg differences was not as firmly held later (1943), and a greater flexibility in caste nomenclature was proposed.

In 1934 Hare reported, after a reexamination of Thompson's histological material and after studies of her own on *Reticulitermes arenincola* Goellner and *R. flavipes*, that she was unable to confirm the idea that newly hatched larvae were separable into reproductive and worker-soldier lines. In Hare's material these lines were not distinguishable until the third stadium, at which time wing buds could be seen in the reproductive line; brain-width measurements were barely distinctive.

Another species of the family, *Prorhinotermes simplex* (Hagen), was the subject of my own studies, reported in 1942. Banks and Snyder (1920) had noted peculiar wing-padded forms in this species, with each pair of buds fused in the median line to form shieldlike extensions of the meso- and metanotum. They assumed these to be nymphs of the "second form," as did Thompson and Snyder (1920). They also noted that "third form" or supplementary reproductives, often more than one pair, were to be found in natural colonies. Otherwise, little was known of the life history although F. Weyer (1930) had held that in *Prorhinotermes rugifer* Kemner the apterous neotenics came from worker larvae.

In my colonies of *P. simplex* the distribution of head-width and mesonotum-width measurements failed to disclose any externally useful criteria for separating larvae into reproductive and soldier-worker lines until the fifth instar, at which time a bimodality appeared in the distribution of mesothorax measurements. Such individuals had 15 antennal segments.

Five hundred and seventy three of the conspicuously wing-padded individuals (with 17 or 18 antennal segments) were grouped and raised in laboratory colonies. Of these, 41.8% became workerlike, 17% became soldiers, and 41% became supplementary reproductives, all with variously reduced wing pads. Hence, any theory holding that there were a distinct worker-soldier line and a reproductive line with wing buds was untenable. These groups gave a striking display of *Prorhinotermes'* ability to adjust caste balance to the society's needs.

If to similar homogeneous groups of wing-padded nymphs one added replacement reproductives, only 4% of the nymphs would become reproductives, as judged by their increasing pigmentation and loss of protozoans. When, at the start, soldiers in a ratio of 1:4 were put into groups of nymphs, only 2.8% of the nymphs transformed into additional soldiers. Groups started with replacement reproductives produced more soldiers than those without.

Such differences were statistically significant, and I concluded, therefore, that not only were all caste potentials retained in the wing-padded forms, but that functional reproductives and soldiers exerted in experimental colonies an influence on the further differentiation of nymphs. This influence seemed to be a caste-specific inhibition. It was also found that small soldiers and replacement reproductives could develop within 45 days from workerlike larvae having 12 or 13 antennal segments. Hence, the plasticity for differentiation, depending on the composition of the society, which was suggested by investigators for other species, was demonstrated for *P. simplex*. Now, in the light of Grassé and Noirot's term, "pseudergate," it seems likely that *P. simplex* "workers" are often pseudergates and that the concept of an immutable worker caste is doubtful.

The question of worker caste was further examined by Grassé *et al.* (1950) in *Reticulitermes lucifugus*. They concluded that the so-called workers were not terminal, unchangeable forms, but under certain social circumstances could become soldiers or replacement reproductives or remain larvae functioning as workers. *Coptotermes* and *Schedrhinotermes* were said to behave similarly, but the latter possibly may have some permanent workers.

The regulation of soldier numbers and development in primary colonies of *Reticulitermes hesperus* was examined by Light and Weesner (1955); their data showed that not all colonies produced a soldier the first year and that among producing colonies 50% would produce a second soldier when the first soldier was removed. In some colonies the soldier came from the first set of eggs; in others from the second. Furthermore, some pairs of reproductives seemed to have a greater tendency to produce soldiers than others.

In an excellent report on 2040 primary colonies of *R. hesperus*, Weesner (1956) made numerous observations relative to the caste differentiation problem. Young presoldiers (white) appeared in the fourth stadium and matured into soldiers in the fifth. The production of soldiers in the first 6 months was low—occurring in 18 out of 2040 colonies—and no soldiers were found in "colonies" with a single larva. It could not be shown, as some authors had previously supposed, that a soldier was automatically produced from the first larva. It was inferred that soldier determination occurred in the third stadium and was correlated with a previous association of a young third instar with another molting individual which, perhaps, produced some stimulating substance. There was no evidence for genetic determination of caste, but neither was this possibility entirely precluded. Whatever the factor, it seemed to operate in the third stadium and more effectively in small colonies than large.

Buchli (1956a,b, 1958) next reported in remarkable detail more than 7 years of work with *R. lucifugus* and its subspecies *santonensis* Feytaud. He first established size ranges by numerous measurements on each caste and described morphological variations and classes to be found in the population of a colony. Then developments in experimental colonies were followed and compared in some instances with events in natural colonies. Important observations were made on feeding relationships of various forms. Buchli reached the following conclusions:

1. The larvae of the first two stages are all alike and undifferentiated, and they do not feed themselves. In small primary colonies these all become the form called "workers" at stage three, but in large natural colonies they may become nymphs, showing small wing buds.

2. "Workers" differentiating in stage three and remaining as workers thereafter may molt regularly through stage nine, but molts, indefinite in number, which may then occur subsequent to the ninth, produce almost imperceptible changes in form.

3. "Workers" can become sexuals, especially at stages five and six, and when numerous enough in laboratory colonies can reconstitute all castes for the colony. Hence, in the strict sense, no fixed adult form to be called "worker" exists in this species. The transfer of larvae in stage one from a large colony to a small primary colony causes them to become "workers" rather than nymphs.

4. Pseudergates can come from nymphs of stages three to six by regressing in character, or from larvae, by stationary molts which fix their characters between those of nymph and worker. Beyond stage five, pseudergates can form reproductive neotenics or soldiers, thus redifferentiating.

5. Soldiers can develop from workers, pseudergates, or nymphs of stages five to seven (stage four in primary colonies), always passing through a presoldier or white-soldier stage. Both sexes may produce soldiers.

6. Neotenic reproductives can develop from "workers" of stage four or later, from pseudergates of stage five or later, or from nymphs of stage six or later.

7. Even though the functional imagoes are present in a primary colony, neotenics are not suppressed if the nutritional equilibrium of the group is favorable; if not favorable, then further sexuals, as well as soldiers, may be suppressed or delayed in appearance.

8. Caste differentiation is regulated by extrinsic factors, with the first two larval stages being strongly affected by nutritive conditions and nymphs and workers by "perturbations" of the social equilibrium of the group. "It is the physiology of the whole colony which determines the destiny of the individual" (1958). Buchli did not believe that he found evidence of an inhibiting hormone as a major directive factor, but confirmed Lüscher's idea that within each larval or nymphal stadium there is a "critical phase" or "reactivity" period when the individual is susceptible to extrinsic influences.

Working with the Japanese termite, *Reticulitermes speratus* (Kolbe), Shimizu (1963) found that soldiers could emerge in artificial colonies of apparent "workers," but that the emergence ratio of soldiers increased with the number of larvae and "workers." Supplementary reproductives could develop from larva-workers and especially from nymphs, but in these cases the size of the colony was important, the larger colony being more conducive to development of replacements.

Different sizes of brachypterous neotenics in *Coptotermes intermedius* Silvestri have been reported by Roy-Noel (1966); apparently these come from at least two different nymphal stages.

VI. DISCUSSION AND SUMMARY

In evaluating the past work on caste differentiation in the lower termites and synthesizing it into present concepts, the recent excellent summaries by Lüscher (1960,1961a,b,1962), by Weesner (1960), and by Weaver (1966) are to be acknowledged. The integration of findings upon different species, arrived at by various methods, is at once hazardous and useful, and extrapolations must be made with care. Species differences may provide both contradictions and insights.

No evidence has yet shown that the various castes are genetically different; rather, the contrary seems to be the case — in the studied species of *Zootermopsis, Kalotermes, Reticulitermes,* and *Prorhinotermes* the newly hatched larvae are equipotent, and their caste destinies are the expression of social and environmental factors.

The existence of a permanent worker caste, unable to convert to another caste, has not been demonstrated for the lower termites, although such a condition may be approached in *Reticulitermes.* The "small and large" foraging workers of *Hodotermes mossambicus* (Hagen) (as *H. transvaalensis*) referred to by Hegh (1922) were distinguished from "larval forms," but experimental evidence about these interesting types is lacking.

The occurrence of intercastes such as fertile and wing-budded soldiers (Adamson, 1940; Heath, 1927) (Fig. 2) and pseudo-imagoes (Lüscher, 1960) in itself supports Castle's hypothesis that larvae possess three developmental tendencies — alate, reproductive, and soldier — and that these may respond somewhat individually to external factors at critical thresholds (Lebrun, 1964).

A. Comparisons of Four Genera

The demonstrated possibilities for development are diagrammed in Fig. 1. Differences in these genera seem to be largely differences of degree, of timing, and of relative reactivity to differentiating influences.

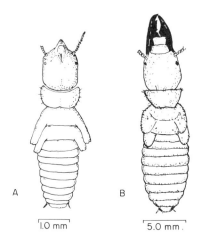

A   B

1.0 mm   5.0 mm.

Fig. 2. Examples of intercastes. A: Wing-budded presoldier of *Calcaritermes nearcticus* (Snyder), (Coll. Miller); B: wing-budded soldier of *Zootermopsis angusticollis* (redrawn from Fig. 15; Heath, 1927).

In *Zootermopsis* the overall pattern of caste development is similar to that of *K. flavicollis,* if one can assume that the versatile individuals of the sixth stage, as diagrammed by Castle (1934), are comparable to pseudergates. In *Zootermopsis,* soldiers in small colonies may begin differentiation one instar (third) earlier than in *K. flavicollis* although Becker's observations (1948) on the latter make even this difference uncertain. Possibly, fertile soldiers are more common in *Zootermopsis,* and numbers of replacement reproductives may occur in a single, natural colony (Castle) rather than one pair, as in *Kalotermes;* thus the behavior that leads to elimination of reproductives may be weaker in *Zootermopsis.*

In *Reticulitermes* visible differentiation in the form of small wing buds may appear earlier (third instar) than in *Kalotermes,* and early soldier development is also possible (Buchli, 1958) from that stage. A permanent, unchangeable adult worker caste does not exist, but, compared to more primitive genera, morphological signs of arrested development (the "worker") may appear earlier and be somewhat firmer, although under certain conditions "workers" retain reproductive and soldier potentials. Inhibition by functional reproductives and soldiers appears to be less diagrammatic, and nutritional factors may be relatively more important than in *Zootermopsis.* Experimental injections of hormones have not been performed with any *Rhinotermitidae;* hence, regulative mechanisms can only be inferred.

In *Prorhinotermes simplex* the apparently shorter "nymphal period" may be somewhat illusory because of the peculiar structure of the fused wing buds; this matter needs closer study. It seems reasonable to expect soldier development from sixth and seventh stadia although these have not been certainly observed.

These conclusions seem reasonably secure; it is in attempting to analyze the regulative factors that complexities arise.

B. MECHANISMS FOR CASTE REGULATION

Only with *Kalotermes flavicollis* have the thoroughgoing studies by Lüscher and associates progressed sufficiently to permit a theory (Lüscher, 1960, 1961a,b, 1962; Lüscher and Springhetti, 1960).

According to these investigators, regulative factors seem to operate at three levels: environmental, acting on the whole colony or society; social (pheromones), acting among the individuals; and individual (hormones), which act within the individual. Reasonably precise data are available only for the latter two levels.

Caste differentiation and molting are closely related. Influencing molting are the secretions from neurosecretory cells (described by Noirot, 1957) and corpora allata, which appear to stimulate the prothoracic glands to release ecdysone. Ecdysone brings about normal molts (Lüscher and Karlson, 1958). But, just before and after a molt, larvae and pseudergates are in a state of differentiation competence, which gradually declines until the next molt. "Competence" seems to be greatest during low corpora allata titer (Lüscher, 1963) and determination occurs then, to be followed in time by molting and differentiation. If male and female reproductives are present in the group, these give off sex-specific inhibiting pheromones, apparently through the anus, that are spread through the population by trophallaxis. Recently molted, competent individuals thus have their reproductive potential suppressed and continue as larvae or pseudergates. (Such suppression may be in the form of reduction of competence to zero.) The nature of the inhibiting substance is not known.

On the other hand, if competent individuals do not receive inhibiting substance, either directly or via pseudergates, then within 24 hours they become determined and in 6 or 7 days begin pigmentation and gonad development and become replacement reproductives. The effective factor for this reaction may be a massive release of the brain hormone which ordinarily is suppressed by the inhibiting pheromones (Lüscher, 1960). If more than one pair develop, the excess reproductives are recognized and eventually are eliminated by cannibalism (Fig. 3).

The production of soldiers presumably involves a similar mechanism but observations are less diagrammatic. Introduction of corpora allata (Lüscher and Springhetti, 1960; Lebrun, 1964) from replacement reproductives or preimagoes into competent pseudergates caused them to become presoldiers or soldier intercastes. However, corpora allata from pseudergates or younger nymphs did not. It was postulated (Lüscher, 1963) that the corpora allata produce two or three hormones, perhaps in different cycles: the juvenile hormone (neotenin); one which Lüscher called gonadotropic; and another (unnamed) that stimulated soldier development. However, since on other insects farnesol derivatives may have both juvenile and gonadotropic actions, it remains to be shown that corpora allata produce more than one hormone (Schneiderman and Gilbert, 1964). Corpora allata may have a rhythmic activity (Lüscher, 1960) which in turn affects other systems; within the intermolt period the allata may show two activity peaks, but different concentrations of hormone could be produced at these times. The tendency of primary colonies to produce a soldier early may be understandable in view of the "soldierizing effect" of corpora allata extracts from replacement reproductives and imagoes. In Miller's observations (1942) on *Prorhino-*

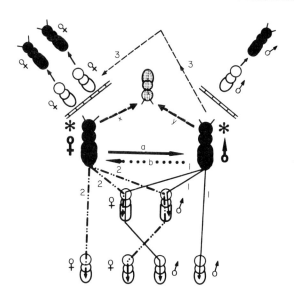

Fig. 3. Diagram to emphasize postulated actions of pheromones on replacement reproductive formation in *Kalotermes flavicollis* (Modified and redrawn after Lüscher, 1961b). The functional female and male (both black) at the center produce sex specific recognition substances, x and y, which may influence behavior of other individuals in the colony (shaded), leading to elimination of excess incipient functionals. Substance *a* from the female stimulates the production of male pheromone 1; similarly, but from less evidence, substance *b* from the male may stimulate the production of inhibitor 2. Substances 1 and 2 may pass directly to undifferentiated pseudergates or selectively through pseudergates or larvae, inhibiting transformation into reproductives. Competent individuals barred from receiving inhibiting pheromones (as above the double lines) may become replacement reproductives (small, black). Substance 3 from males only, may accelerate the differentiation of females into functionals.

termes there were strong indications that reproductives stimulated the differentiation of soldiers, but this was contrary to the findings of Lüscher and Springhetti (1960).

Lüscher postulated (1960) that, among pseudergates, those with greatest competence would become reproductives, and those with a lower degree of competence would differentiate into soldiers. At the same time it is useful to recall that Schneiderman and Gilbert (1964) have pointed out the chemical relatedness of insect hormones and the possibility of the same one producing different actions at different concentrations. But the regulation of soldier numbers at somewhat species-characteristic ratios is yet unexplained. The usual lack of fertility in soldiers may be due to the action of their persisting prothoracic glands, which have been shown in *Leucophaea* (Engelmann, 1959) to inhibit ovaries.

The development of larvae in a natural termite colony through the pseudergate period to become nymphs and eventually imagoes—the expected course of events—has not been well analyzed. Alates do not usually appear except in natural colonies of large size. This implies an optimum social and nutritive environment, which may condition not only reactive tissue substrates but also corpora allata activity. [In other insects there are complicated relationships among nervous stimuli, protein metabolism, and corpora allata activity (Davey, 1965); corpora allata and neurosecretory cells may influence some phases of protein synthesis and thus, indirectly, ovary development (Chen, 1966).] A large colony also introduces the possibility of effective distance of some of the population from inhibiting pheromone sources (the functioning king and queen), or a dilution of the inhibiting pheromones below some critical threshold (McMahan, 1966). Differing ages of the population and temperature fluctuation through the seasons provide rhythmical opportunities in the colony for some instars to escape the seeming rigidity of caste inhibition which is suggested by some of the previous statements about replacement reproductives and soldiers.

Preliminary observations on *Incisitermes snyderi* (Light) and *Neotermes jouteli* (Banks) by Miller (unpublished) suggest no basic contradictions of the general events described for *K. flavicollis*.

C. Future Problems

Future research needs seem obvious: no matter what the species, the background and identity of experimental individuals need to be precisely recognized; the regressive molting phenomenon and the fact of cyclic hormone titer introduce problems in obtaining homogeneous and controlled groups over a span of time for experimental use. Likewise, the nutritive conditions and the nature of the supporting group into which the experimental animal is placed need to be known (Grassé, 1952). Studies with endocrinological methods must be expanded to other species. Group-size effects need to be understood. Extension of studies to different genera is desirable.

Also, as Castle (1934), Emerson (1939), Noirot (1952), Buchli (1958), and Lüscher (1961b) have pointed out in varying phraseology, the termite colony must be viewed as a whole, as a supraorganism, involving many internal, interactive factors as well as environmental factors and with a physiological integrity that is easily disturbed. Furthermore, the careful use of analogies from studies of embryo and tissue physiology as already suggested by Lüscher (1953b, 1961b) may point the way to valuable methodology and interpretations. The establishment of small experimental laboratory groups of termites is a fragmenting of a natural colony comparable, in some respects, to so-called defect experiments with vertebrate embryos, or to tissue culture.

ACKNOWLEDGMENTS

Thanks are expressed for the assistance of Mrs. Dorothy B. Miller, Mr. Hector Hirigoyen, and Mr. George Scherer in preparing the material for this review. Drs. F. Gray Butcher and H. F. Strohecker kindly read and criticized the manuscript. Certain aid was received also from a portion of NSF Institutional Grant GU1218.

REFERENCES

Adamson, A. M. (1940). New termite intercastes. *Proc. Roy. Soc.* **B129**, 35-53.

Banks, N., and Snyder, T. E. (1920). A revision of the nearctic termites, with notes on biology and distribution. *U. S. Natl. Museum, Bull.* **108**, 1-228.

Becker, G. (1948). Uber Kastenbildung und Umwelteinfluss bei Termiten. *Biol. Zentr.* **67**, 407-444.

Buchli, H. (1956a). Die neotenie bei *Reticulitermes*. *Insectes Sociaux* **3**, 131-143.

Buchli, H. (1956b). Le cycle de developpement des castes chez *Reticulitermes*. *Insectes Sociaux* **3**, 395-401.

Buchli, H. (1958). L'origine des castes et les potentialités ontogéniques des termites européens du genre *Reticulitermes*. *Ann. Sci. Nat. Zool. Biol. Animale* [11] **20**, 263-429.

Castle, G. B. (1934). An experimental investigation of caste differentiation in *Zootermopsis angusticollis*. *In* "Termites and Termite Control" (C. A. Kofoid, ed.), 2nd ed., pp. 292-310. Univ. of California Press, Berkeley, California.

Chen, P. S. (1966). Amino acid and protein metabolism in insect development. *Advan. Insect Physiol.* **3**, 53-132.

Davey, K. G. (1965). "Reproduction in the Insects." Freeman, San Francisco, California.

Emerson, A. E. (1939). Social coordination and the superorganism. *Am. Midland Naturalist* **21**, 182-209.

Englemann, F. (1959). Uber die Wirkung implantierter Prothoraxdrusen in adulten Weibchen von *Leucophaea maderae*. *Z. Vergleich. Physiol.* **41**, 456-470.

Escherich, K. (1909). "Die Termiten" Klinkhardt, Leipzig.

Feytaud, J. (1912). Contribution à l'étude du Termite lucifuge (Anatomie. Fondation de colonies nouvelles). *Arch. Anat. Microscop. Morphol. Exptl.* **13**, 481-607.

Goetsch, W. (1946). Der Einflusz von Vitamin T auf körperform und entwicklung. *Naturwissenschaften* **33**, 149-154.

Grassé, P.-P. (1952). L'effet de groupe chez les insects. *Bull. Sect. Francaise Union Internatl. Etude Insectes Sociaux* **1**, 32-40.

Grassé, P.-P., and Noirot, C. (1946a). La production des sexués néoténiques chez le Termite à cou jaune: Inhibition germinale et inhibition somatique. *Compt. Rend.* **223**, 869-871.

Grassé, P.-P., and Noirot, C. (1946b). Le polymorphisme social du Termite à cou jaune (*C. flavicollis* Fabr.). La production des soldats. *Compt. Rend.* **223**, 929-931.

Grassé, P.-P., and Noirot, C. (1947). Le polymorphisme social du Termite à cou jaune. Les faux-ouvriers ou pseudergates et les mues régressives. *Compt. Rend.* **224**, 219-221.

Grassé, P.-P., and Noirot, C. (1958). La société de *Calotermes flavicollis* (Insecte, Isoptère), de sa fondation au premier essaimage. *Compt. Rend.* **246**, 1789-1795.

Grassé, P.-P., and Noirot, C. (1960a). Rôle respectif des mâles et des femelles dans la formation des sexués néoténiques chez *Calotermes flavicollis. Insectes Sociaux* **7**, 109-123.

Grassé, P.-P., and Noirot, C. (1960b). L'isolement chez le Termite à cou jaune et ses conséquences. *Insectes Sociaux* **7**, 323-331.

Grassé, P.-P., Noirot, C., Clement, G., and Buchli, H. (1950). Sur la signification de la caste des ouvriers chez les Termites. *Compt. Rend.* **230**, 892-895.

Grassi, B., and Sandias, A. (1893-1894). Costituzione e sviluppo della societa dei termitidi. *Atti Accad. Gioenia Sci. Nat. Catania* [4] **6**, No. 13, 1-75; **7**, No. 1, 1-76.

Grassi, B., and Sandias, A. (1896-1897). *Quart. J. Microscop. Sci.* **39**, 245-322; **40**, 1-82 (Translation of Grassi and Sandias, 1893-1894).

Hare, L. (1934). Caste determination and differentiation with special reference to the genus *Reticulitermes* (Isoptera). *J. Morphol.* **56**, 267-293.

Harvey, P. A. (1934). Life history of *Kalotermes minor. In* "Termites and Termite Control" (C. A. Kofoid, ed.), 2nd ed., pp. 217-233. Univ. of California Press, Berkeley, California.

Heath, H. (1903). The habits of California termites. *Biol. Bull.* **4**, 47-63.

Heath, H. (1927). Caste formation in the termite genus *Termopsis. J. Morphol. Physiol.* **43**, 387-425.

Heath, H. (1928). Fertile termite soldiers. *Biol. Bull.* **54**, 324-326.

Heath, H., and Wilbur, B. C. (1927). The development of the soldier caste in the termite genus *Termopsis. Biol. Bull.* **53**, 145-156.

Hegh, E. (1922). "Les Termites." Imprimerie Industrielle et Financière, Bruxelles, Belgium.

Hill, G. F. (1925). Notes on *Mastotermes darwiniensis* Froggatt (Isoptera). *Proc. Roy. Soc. Victoria* [N.S.] **37**, 119-124.

Holmgren, N. (1912). Termitenstudien. 4. Versuch einer systematischen Monographie der Termiten der orientalischen Region. *Kgl. Svenska Vetenskapsakad. Handl.* **48**, No. 4, 136-151.

Imms, A. D. (1919). On the structure and biology of *Archotermopsis*, together with descriptions of new species of intestinal Protozoa and general observations on the Isoptera. *Phil. Trans. Roy. Soc. London* **209**, 75-180.

Jucci, C. (1924). Sulla differenziazione delle caste nella società dei termitidi. I. Neotenici (Reali veri e neotenici- l'escrezionse nei reali neotenici-las fisiologia e la biologia). *Atti Accad. Naz. Lincei, Mem., Classe Sci. Fis., Nat., Sez. III.*[a] [5] **14**, 269-500.

Kalshoven, L. G. E. (1930). Bionomics of *Kalotermes tectonae* Damm. as a base for its control. *Mededeel. Inst. Plantzenziekten* **76**, 1-154.

Lebrun, D. (1963a). Implantation de glandes de la mue de *Periplaneta americana* dans les sexués néoténiques de. *Calotermes flavicollis* Fabr. (Insecte, Isoptera). *Compt. Rend.* **257**, 2181-2182.

Lebrun, D. (1963b). Implantation de glandes de la mue de *Periplaneta americana* dans des soldats de *Calotermes flavicollis* Fabr. *Compt. Rend.* **257**, 3487-3488.

Lebrun, D. (1964). Le rôle de corps allates dans la formation des castes de *Calotermes flavicollis. Compt. Rend.* **259**, 4152-4155.

Lebrun, D. (1967a). Nouvelles recherches sur le déterminisme endocrinien du polymorphisme de *Calotermes flavicollis. Ann. Soc. Entomol. France* [N.S.] **3**, No. 3, 867-871.

Lebrun, D. (1967b). La détermination des castes du Termite à cou jaune (*Calotermes flavicollis* Fabr.). *Bull. Biol. France Belg.* 101, No. 3, 141-217.

Lespès, C. (1856). Recherches sur l'organisation et les moeurs du Termite lucifuge. *Ann. Sci. Nat. Zool.* [4] 5, 227-282.

Light, S. F. (1942-1943). The determination of castes of social insects. *Quart. Rev. Biol.* 17, 312-326; 18, 46-63.

Light, S. F. (1944a). Parthenogenesis in termites. *Univ. Calif (Berkeley) Publ. Zool.* 43, 405-412.

Light, S. F. (1944b). Experimental studies on ectohormonal control of the development of supplementary reproductives in the termite genus *Zootermopsis* (formerly *Termopsis*). *Univ. Calif. (Berkeley) Publ. Zool.* 43, 413-454.

Light, S. F., and Illg, P. L. (1945). Rate and extent of development of neotenic reproductives in groups of nymphs of the termite genus *Zootermopsis*. *Univ. Calif. (Berkeley) Publ. Zool.* 53, 1-40.

Light, S. F., and Weesner, F. M. (1951). Further studies on the production of supplementary reproductives in *Zootermopsis* (Isoptera). *J. Exptl. Zool.* 117, 397-414.

Light, S. F., and Weesner, F. M. (1955). The production and replacement of soldiers in incipient colonies of *Reticulitermes hesperus* Banks. *Insectes Sociaux* 2, 347-354.

Lüscher, M. (1952a). New evidence for an ectohormonal control of caste determination in termites. *Trans. 9th Intern. Congr. Entomol., Amsterdam, 1951* Vol 1, pp. 289-294.

Lüscher, M. (1952b). Die Produktion und Elimination von Ersatzgeschlechtstieren bei der Termite *Kalotermes flavicollis* Fabr. *Z. Vergleich. Physiol.* 34, 123-141.

Lüscher, M. (1952c). Untersuchungen über das individuelle Wachstum bei der Termite *Kalotermes flavicollis* Fabr. (Ein Beitrag zum Kastenbildungsproblem). *Biol. Zentr.* 71, 529-543.

Lüscher, M. (1953a). Kann die Determination durch eine monomolekulare Reaktion ausgelöst werden? *Rev. Suisse Zool.* 60, 524-528.

Lüscher, M. (1953b). The termite and the cell. *Sci. Am.* 188 No. 5, 74-78.

Lüscher, M. (1955). Zur Frage der Ubertragung sozialer Wirkstoffe bei Termiten. *Naturwissenschaften* 42, 186.

Lüscher, M. (1956a). Die entstehung von Ersatzgeschlechtstieren bei der Termite *Kalotermes flavicollis* Fabr. *Insectes Sociaux* 3, 119-128.

Lüscher, M. (1956b). Hemmende und fördernde Faktoren bei der Entstehung der Ersatzgeschlechtstiere bei der Termite *Kalotermes flavicollis* Fabr. *Rev. Suisse Zool.* 63, 261-267.

Lüscher, M. (1958). Experimentelle Erzeugung von Soldaten bei der Termite *Kalotermes flavicollis*. *Naturwissenschaften* 45, 69-70.

Lüscher, M. (1960). Hormonal control of caste differentiation in termites. *Ann. N. Y. Acad. Sci.* 89, 549-563.

Lüscher, M. (1961a). Sozialwirkstoffe bei Termiten. *Proc. 11th Intern. Congr. Entomol. Vienna, 1960*, Vol. 1, pp. 579-582.

Lüscher, M. (1961b). Social control of polymorphism in termites. *In* "Insect Polymorphism" (J. S. Kennedy, ed.), pp. 57-67. Roy. Entomol. Soc., London.

Lüscher, M. (1962). Hormonal regulation of development in termites. *Symp. Genet. Biol. Ital., Univ. Pavia* 10, 1-11.

Lüscher, M. (1963). Functions of the corpora allata in the development of termites. *Proc. 16th Intern. Congr. Zool., Washington, D. C., 1963*, Vol. 4, pp. 244-250. Nat. Hist. Press, Garden City, New York.

Lüscher, M. (1964). Die spezifische Wirkung mannlicher und weiblicher Ersatzgeschlechtstiere auf die Entstehung von Ersatzgeschlechtstieren bei der Termite *Kalotermes flavicollis* (Fabr.). *Insectes Sociaux* 11, 79-90.

Lüscher, M., and Karlson, P. (1958). Experimentelle Auslösung von Häutungen bei der Termite *Kalotermes flavicollis* (Fabr.). *J. Insect Physiol.* 1, 341-345.

Lüscher, M., and Springhetti, A. (1960). Untersuchungen uber die Bedeutung der Corpora allata fur die Differenzierung der Kasten bei der Termite *Kalotermes flavicollis* F. *J. Insect Physiol.* 5, 190-212.

McMahan, E. A. (1966). Food transmission within the *Cryptotermes brevis* colony (Isoptera: Kalotermitidae). *Ann. Entomol. Soc. Am.* 59, 1131-1137.

Miller, E. M. (1942). The problem of castes and caste differentiation in *Prorhinotermes simplex* (Hagen). *Bull. Univ. Miami* 15, 3-27.

Mueller, F. (1873). Beiträge zur Kenntnis der Termiten. IV. Die larven von *Calotermes rugosus* Hagen. *Z. Naturw., Jena* 7, 333-358.

Noirot, C. (1952). Les soins et l'alimentation des jeunes chez les Termites. *Ann. Sci. Nat. Zool. Biol. Animale* [11] 14, 405-414.

Noirot, C. (1957). Neurosécrétion et sexualité chez le Termite à cou jaune *Calotermes flavicollis* F. *Compt. Rend.* 245, 743-745.

Pickens, A. L. (1932). Observations on the genus *Reticulitermes* Holmgren. *Pan-Pacific Entomologist* 8, 178-180.

Pickens, A. L. (1943). Suggested caste taxonomy for the common termite. *Science* 97, 116-118.

Pinto, M. P. D. (1941). Some observations on the biology of the Ceylonese Calotermitidae. *Indian J. Entomol.* 31, No. 1, 73-105.

Roy-Noel, J. (1966). Description de l'image et de quelques formes jeunes de néoténiques chez *Coptotermes intermedius* Silvestri (Isoptere). *Insectes Sociaux* 13, 217-224.

Ruppli, E., and Lüscher, M. (1964). Die Elimination uberzahliger Ersatzgeschlectstiere bei der termite, *Kalotermes flavicollis* (Fabr.). *Rev. Suisse Zool.* 71, 626-632.

Schneiderman, H. A., and Gilbert, L. I. (1964). Control of growth and development in insects. *Science* 143, 325-333.

Shimizu, K. (1963). Studies on the caste differentiation in termites. III. Emergence of soldiers and supplementary reproductives of the Japanese termite, *Leucotermes (Reticulitermes) speratus* (Kolbe). *Japan. J. Appl. Entomol. Zool.* 7, 207-212.

Thompson, C. B. (1917). Origin of the castes of the common termite *Leucotermes flavipes* Kol. *J. Morphol.* 30, 83-133.

Thompson, C. B. (1919). The development of the castes of nine genera and thirteen species of termites. *Biol. Bull.* 36, 379-398.

Thompson, C. B. (1922). The castes of *Termopsis*. *J. Morphol.* 36, 493-535.

Thompson, C. B., and Snyder, T. E. (1920). The "third-form," the wingless reproductive type of termites: *Reticulitermes* and *Prorhinotermes*. *J. Morphol.* 34, 591-633.

Weaver, N. (1966). The physiology of caste determination. *Ann. Rev. Entomol.* 11, 79-102.

Weesner, F. M. (1956). The biology of colony foundation in *Reticulitermes hesperus* Banks. *Univ. Calif. (Berkeley) Publ. Zool.* 61, 253-314.

Weesner, F. M. (1960). Evolution and biology of termites. *Ann. Rev. Entomol.* 5, 153-170.

Weyer, F. (1930). Uber Ersatzgeschlechtstiere bei Termiten. *Z. Morphol. Öckol. Tiere* 19, 364-380.

Weyer, F. (1931). Das problem der Kastendiffereuzierung bei den Termiten. *Biol. Zentr.* 51, 353-373.

10

Formation of Castes in the Higher Termites*

CH. NOIROT

I. INTRODUCTION

In the large family, Termitidae, the separation of the various castes is much more pronounced than in the lower termites. Workers, which are very distinct from larvae and nymphs, are always present. Polymorphism frequently occurs in both the workers and soldiers. By comparison with

*Translated from the French by Mina Parsont and Frances M. Weesner.

the lower termites, postembryonic development is much less variable and possesses certain characteristics common to the whole family.

II. GENERAL CHARACTERISTICS OF THE CASTES AND THEIR DIFFERENTIATION

A. THE IMAGOES

1. Sexual Dimorphism

The morphology of the imagoes is uniform. The genital plates are more reduced than in the Rhinotermitidae. In most cases the males and females are the same size, but slight differences sometimes occur. In general, the males are smaller, but occasionally the females are smaller (Table I).

TABLE I

SEXUAL DIMORPHISM OF THE IMAGOES AND WORKERS

Subfamily and species	Imagoes	Workers
Amitermitinae		
Amitermes evuncifer	♂ = ♀[f]	♂ = ♀[e]
Microcerotermes parvus	♂ = ♀[f]	♂ < ♀[e]
Termitinae		
Termes hospes	♂ = ♀[f]	♂ = ♀[e]
Cubitermes fungifaber	♂ = ♀[f]	♂ ≃ ♀[e]
Apicotermitinae		
Apicotermes arquieri	♂ < ♀[d]	♂ ≃ ♀[f]
Allognathotermes hypogeus	♂ < ♀[d]	♂ = ♀[f]
Duplidentitermes furcatidens	♂ < ♀[b]	♂ ≃ ♀[f]
Nasutitermitinae		
Syntermes magnoculus	♂ < ♀[a]	
Syntermes sp.		♂ > ♀[f]
Nasutitermes arborum	♂ = ♀[f]	♂ < ♀[e]
Trinervitermes bouvieri	♂ < ♀[a]	
Trinervitermes spp.		♂ < ♀[e]
Macrotermitinae		
Acanthotermes acanthothorax	♂ = ♀[f]	♂ > ♀[e]
Pseudacanthotermes militaris	♂ < ♀[c]	♂ > ♀[e]
Odontotermes magdalenae	♂ > ♀[f]	♂ > ♀[e]

[a]Emerson (1945).
[b]Emerson (1959).
[c]Grassé and Noirot (1951).
[d]Grassé and Noirot (1954).
[e]Noirot (1955).
[f]Noirot (unpublished observations).
[g]Sjöstedt (1926). *Microtermes*.

In at least two cases this dimorphism is related to special modes of pairing: in *Pseudacanthotermes militaris* (Hagen) (Grassé and Noirot, 1951) and *Allognathotermes hypogeus* Silvestri (Noirot and Bodot, 1964) pairing occurs before the return to the ground, and the female carries the male beneath her.

Sexual dimorphism can also affect certain anatomical characters. There is a considerable development of the tracheal network system of the abdomen of the female which allows for the enlargement of the ovaries in physogastric queens. Furthermore, the cuticle of the intersegmental membranes of the female abdomen has a number of folds which augment the surface. These are much less noticeable in the male (Bordereau, 1967). These folds can be considered an adaptation to the enlargement of the queen, but only allow for the initial growth of the imago (Section II, A, 3). This dimorphism is clearly defined in *Cubitermes fungifaber* (Sjöstedt) and *Cephalotermes rectangularis* (Sjöstedt) and much less so in *Bellicositermes natalensis* (Haviland).*

2. Development

The postembryonic development of the imagoes appears to be very uniform. Most authors agree that six stages precede the imaginal molt, and the alates are of the seventh stage (Bathellier, 1927; Noirot, 1952a; Weesner, 1953; Hecker, 1966; Bouillon and Mathot, 1964). Kaiser (1956) with *Anoplotermes pacificus* Fr. Müller, and Sands (1965b) with *Trinervitermes* spp. indicate one less stage. However, our own observations (unpublished) on other species of these two genera indicate that they do not differ from the usual pattern.

Morphologically, the newly emerged larvae all appear to be the same. After the first molt it is possible to recognize two categories of individuals (Fig. 1): (1) the *larvae* of the neuters, without any trace of wing development and with rudimentary gonads and (2) the *nymphs* of the reproductives, with very small wing pads and with gonads which have undergone a definite development. In the course of the subsequent molts the wing pads develop in a regular manner and the eyes become differentiated. The compound eyes usually acquire pigment toward the end of the penultimate stage.

There is little precise data on the duration of the different stages. Our observations and those of Bodot (1966) on the Ivory Coast indicate that the development of the imagoes requires about 5 or 6 months. Sands's data (1965b) on *Trinervitermes* of Nigeria indicate a similar duration. In *Anoplotermes pacificus* of Brazil each nymphal stage lasts 14 days, except for the penultimate stage whose development is arrested during the entire dry season (Kaiser, 1956).

Bellicositermes natalensis (Haviland) is considered by some other authors in this volume as *Macrotermes natalensis* (Haviland) (editor's note).

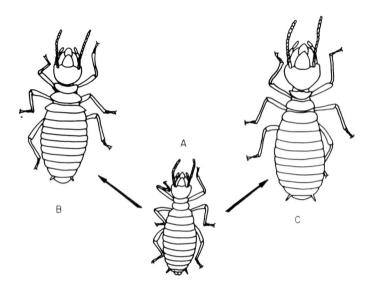

Fig. 1. *Cubitermes fungifaber.* Larva of the first stage (A) (undifferentiated) capable of giving rise at the first molt to a sexual nymph (B) or to a larva of the second stage (C).

The young nymphs never leave the nest and are entirely dependent on the workers for salivary nourishment. The older nymphs, especially those of the penultimate stage, are more active and are often encountered in the outer galleries along with the workers. In general, nymphs of the last two stages receive solid food, consisting primarily of regurgitations of the workers. It is probable that in certain genera (*Amitermes, Microcerotermes, Termes*) these nymphs also feed themselves. Sometimes salivary feeding is continued until just before the imaginal molt; this appears to be the case in many humivores (Noirot, 1952b).

After the imaginal molt the alates may remain in the nest for as much as 2 months. This delay appears to allow for a physiological maturation, regarding which we have little information. When the alates first appear they show little aptitude for flight or pairing. The development of the gonads appears to be very limited. During their retention in the nest, the alates are grouped in certain areas, and their primary nourishment appears to be the saliva of the workers (Alibert, 1963, 1966).

3. The Functional Reproductives

After flight and the foundation of new colonies (Chapter 8), the royal couple undergoes a series of transformations which are most pronounced in the female. There is a progressive degeneration of the flight muscles.

This process is very slow, requiring several years, and must play a minor role, if any, in nutrition, contrary to the situation in the ants. The mandibular muscles also undergo a marked but incomplete reduction. The compound eyes degenerate little by little (Chapter 6). All of these phenomena affect both the king and the queen. The abdomen of the king is only slightly modified, whereas that of the queen undergoes a considerable enlargement, or physogastry, which is correlated with the development of the gonads (Chapter 5). The cuticle of the intersegmental membranes is greatly distended, a process that is still unexplained and that even involves the epicuticle, whose unfolding (Section II, A, 1) can only account for a small part of this development. The tracheal system also undergoes important modifications (Bonneville, 1936). The sanguine mass is enlarged and can reach 17 ml in *Bellicositermes natalensis* (Grassé, 1949). The normal adipose tissue is replaced by "colonnettes" of cells probably derived from the tracheoblasts (Bonneville, 1936). The "royal adipose tissue," which remains limited in volume, has very different histochemical characteristics from the normal fat body of insects. There is an absence of lipids and a richness of ribonucleoproteins (Gabe and Noirot, 1960). The muscular system is also reorganized and provides for peristaltic contractions and movement of the abdomen. In certain species the queen is able to move by creeping, a little in the manner of a worm, but in most physogastric queens movement becomes impossible. Most of the growth of the digestive tube occurs in the midgut, whose epithelium undergoes notable modifications (Noirot-Timothée and Noirot, 1965). This growth is probably associated with the specialized nutrition of the queen, who is gorged incessantly by the salivary secretions of the workers.

B. THE WORKERS

1. Morphological Characteristics; Sexual Dimorphism

A true worker caste is present in all the Termitidae. This caste does not necessarily include only those individuals whose final morphological development has been reached. The workers are characterized by a complete absence of wings and a consequential reduction of the pterothorax. The compound eyes and ocelli are absent or greatly reduced, and the genital apparatus is infantile. Molt glands are always present, even when the workers appear incapable of molting. The head, which is rounded, is proportionately more voluminous, and the mandibular muscles are very powerful (the development of the head reaches its maximum in the Macrotermitinae). The digestive tube is well developed and occupies the major part of the abdominal cavity.

No external sexual characteristics are present. The structure of the last abdominal segments is identical in the male and the female, and the styli, when they are present, occur in both sexes. The identification of the sexes is dependent upon a study of the gonads. Nevertheless, a *sexual dimorphism* often occurs in the size of the workers (Noirot, 1955) (Fig. 2). Depending upon the species, the males or the females may be larger, and the direction of this dimorphism is not necessarily the same as that observed in imagoes of the same species (Table I).

Though polymorphism within the worker caste is usually associated with sexual dimorphism, in some species it also results from the fact that the workers are in different, successive stages. The molts are often accompanied by an increase in pigmentation and sometimes by a more or less conspicuous growth.

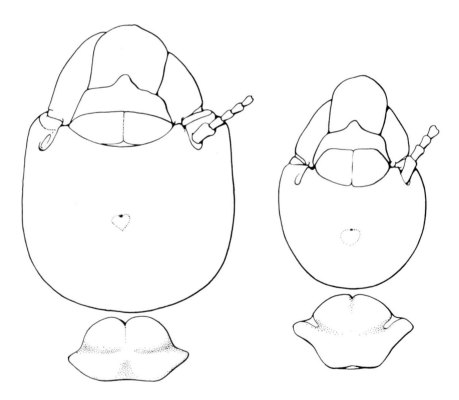

Fig. 2. *Bellicositermes natalensis.* Head and pronotum of the large male worker (left) and the small female worker (right) (after Noirot, 1955).

2. Development

In the Macrotermitinae the workers are preceded by three larval stages; in all of the other subfamilies there are only two. When the males and females differ in size, this difference is apparent in the second stage (Noirot, 1955) and sometimes even in the first (Sands, 1965b, with *Trinervitermes*).

The larvae of the Termitidae are unpigmented, their mouthparts are unsclerotized, and they are incapable of feeding themselves. They are nourished by the saliva of the workers. They are not very active and remain within the nest. The molt at which they are transformed into workers is accompanied by few important morphological modifications, but their physiology and behavior are completely transformed. This is in contrast with the lower termites, where passage of the larvae to workers is progressive (Chapter 9).

The workers of the Termitidae have not always achieved their final development. They may be capable of becoming soldiers (Fig. 3) (Section II, C, 2), and in many species they may undergo a series of molts while maintaining the worker state. In most of the latter cases the molt is not accompanied by any marked growth, except with respect to the antennae and the legs. The head may even be slightly reduced in diameter, as in *Microcerotermes fuscotibialis* (Sjöstedt). Generally there is an increase in pigmentation, especially of the head, but only precise measurements of the appendages permit one to distinguish the various stages with certainty (Noirot, 1955). More rarely the molts result in a progressive growth of the workers, as in *Trinervitermes*. When a number of successive stages exist, the number of individuals becomes less in the older groups; in other words, very few workers attain the ultimate stages (Noirot, 1955; Pasteels, 1965). This approaches the situation in the Rhinotermitidae (notably *Reticulitermes*), where the workers appear to run through an indefinite number of stages.

In other species the workers do not appear to be capable of molting, except in cases where they are transformed into soldiers. Evolution has occurred in the direction of a stabilization of the worker caste. There is a general stabilization in the subfamilies Macrotermitinae and Apicotermitinae, and examples may be found in all the other subfamilies.

3. Physiology and Behavior

The workers of the Termitidae play a role in the society which is exactly comparable to that of the workers in the societies of the Hymenoptera. The larvae, nymphs, soldiers, and reproductives are entirely dependent upon their activities. The workers construct the nest, collect

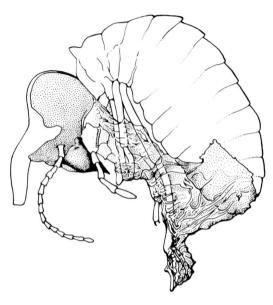

Fig. 3. Worker of *Nasutitermes arborum* in the process of molting into a white-soldier; the frontal projection has already emerged (after Noirot, 1955).

food from the exterior and distribute it (in a more or less elaborate form) to other individuals, and care for the eggs and the young. How are these different tasks divided between the different workers? The data that are available are very fragmentary, but suggest that a division of labor often exists which may be related to the age of the worker (as in certain bees) or to size (as in certain ants).

Thus, in many Macrotermitinae the large workers (females) usually collect food outside the nest, while the small workers appear to devote themselves mainly to work within the nest. The foraging columns are composed almost entirely of large workers in *Odontotermes magdalenae* (Grassé and Noirot) (Grassé and Noirot, 1950), *Macrotermes ivorensis* (Grassé and Noirot) and *M. mülleri* (Sjöstedt) (Grassé and Noirot, 1951). In *Odontotermes magdalenae* the small workers do not appear to participate in construction, but this is not true in *Bellicositermes natalensis*. Such a division of work between large and small workers is not a general occurrence, even in the Macrotermitinae, and the examples given above are the exception rather than the rule (it occurs within groups whose colonies are organized for foraging in the open). On the other hand, a specialization as a function of age could be very widespread. A good example of this is furnished by *Nasutitermes lujae* (Wasmann) (Pasteels, 1965) in which stage I workers (both large and small) do not participate in trail laying, but have greatly developed salivary glands (and perhaps a nutritive role). Similarly, in *Bellicositermes natalensis* (in which the workers are all of one stage) the workers participating in construction are frequently whitish in appearance due to the accumulation of urates in the fat body; this is a sign of age. All of these observations call for additional investigations.

C. THE SOLDIERS

1. Morphological Characteristics

In most cases the soldiers of the Termitidae have the same general characteristics as those of the other families: head elongated, prognathous, heavily sclerotized, and mandibles enlarged. However, the form and function of the mandibles have undergone a much more varied evolution than in the lower termites (Figs. 6, 15). In the Nasutitermitinae, on the other hand, there is a considerable regression of the mandibles and development of the frontal gland, giving rise to the nasute soldier. But a number of intermediate types exist (Fig. 4), permitting the conclusion that the nasute (Fig. 5) is homologous with the soldier of the usual type.

As in the case of the workers, there are no distinct external sexual characters, and the genital apparatus is rudimentary. Molt glands are always present, even though soldiers are apparently incapable of molting. In many species the soldiers are monomorphic (the majority of the Amitermitinae, Termitinae, Apicotermitinae), but in others there exist two, or more rarely three (Fig. 6), distinct types (many of the Macrotermitinae and some Nasutitermitinae). This polymorphism generally results from the fact that the different types of soldiers have undergone a different number of molts and is rarely caused by sexual dimorphism. When sexual dimorphism occurs, as in *Leptomyxotermes doriae* (Silvestri), it is not very pronounced (Noirot, 1955). In most species the soldiers are all of the same sex, either male or female, depending upon the species.

2. Development

In the lower termites the soldiers may arise in variable stages of development (Chapter 9). In the Termitidae, however, origin is generally fixed, and the stage at which they appear is very precise for each species. As is true in all termites, the differentiation of the soldiers occurs in two steps. The soldier is preceded by a stage which is larval in form (lacking pigment and unsclerotized) but with the morphological traits of the soldier. This is the "white-soldier" (soldier-nymph, Vorsoldat; Fig. 6). The duration of this stage is very short—generally about 2 weeks and 1

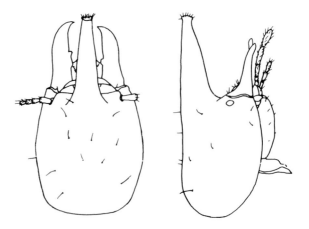

Fig. 4. Head of the soldier of *Armitermes parvidens* Emerson and Banks, dorsal view (left) and lateral view (right) (after Emerson and Banks, 1957).

week in *Nasutitermes ephratae* (Holmgren), at least in the young colonies (Becker, 1961, 1963).

Very frequently the white-soldier arises from a worker (Fig. 3) (Knower, 1894; Emerson, 1926; Bathellier, 1927; Light and Weesner, 1947; Noirot, 1955; Kaiser, 1956), but in other cases it develops from a larva (Bathellier, 1927; Weesner, 1953; Noirot, 1955; Becker 1961, 1963). These two origins may coexist in a single species. Some examples of different cases are given below. In the great majority of species there does not appear to be a special line giving rise to the soldiers. The workers that become soldiers are true workers in morphology and behavior, and, when the soldiers arise from larvae, these are identical with the larvae of the workers. However, this is not the case in some species, in which,

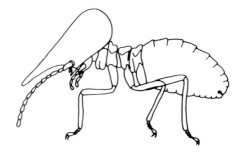

Fig. 5. Soldier of *Nasutitermes latifrons* (Sjöstedt) in lateral view.

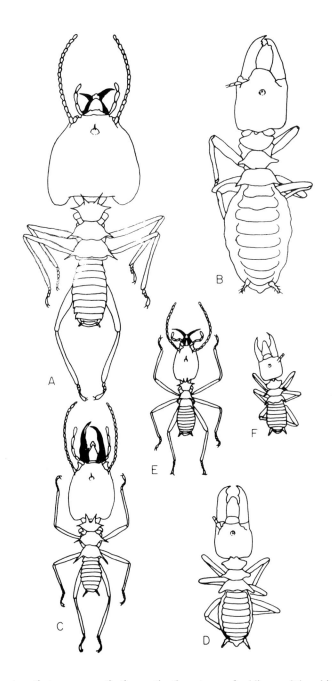

Fig. 6. *Acanthotermes acanthothorax*, the three types of soldiers and the white-soldiers from which they develop. A: Large soldier; B: large white-soldier; C: middle soldier; D: middle white-soldier; E: small soldier; F: small white-soldier (combined after Grassé, 1937, and Noirot, 1955).

after the first larval molt, there is a distinct group of stage II larvae which give rise to the white-soldier at the subsequent molt [*Acanthotermes acanthothorax* (Sjöstedt); Noirot, 1955] or after an additional larval stage [*Tenuirostritermes tenuirostris* (Desneux), Weesner, 1953; *Trinervitermes* spp., Noirot, 1955, and Sands, 1965b].

A specialization of the sexes in the formation of the soldiers is rather general (Noirot, 1955). Only a few species of Termitidae are known to have equal proportions of male and female soldiers (*Amitermes evuncifer* Silvestri, *A. santschi* Silvestri, *Leptomyxotermes doriae*). On the other hand, the soldiers are all males in most Nasutitermitinae studied and females in most of the Termitinae and Macrotermitinae.

3. Physiology and Behavior

The white-soldiers have the appearance and behavior of larvae: in the mandibulate form the mandibles are developed, but unsclerotized and motionless. These white-soldiers appear to be nourished by saliva. However, because of the briefness of this stage and the renovation which the digestive system undergoes at each molt (Chapter 3), the period during which they are fed is very short. It may be that the white-soldier is not fed at all in some instances.

The adaptation of the soldiers to the defense of the colony is accompanied by a complete trophallactic dependence upon the workers (Grassé, 1939). The soldiers are incapable of nourishing themselves. In general, they are provided with regurgitated material (consisting of a paste of wood or humus), but in certain species the soldiers receive only liquid food (saliva?), as in *Eburnitermes* (Amitermitinae; Noirot, 1966) and numerous genera of Termitinae (Noirot, 1955). The soldiers are also incapable of participating in construction, care of the eggs, etc. The few observations mentioning a soldier in the process of transporting a larva, wood debris, or pellets of earth between its mandibles are probably accidental occurrences.

In general, the behavior of the soldiers is closely adapted to combat and is related to the particular anatomy of each genus. It is necessary to distinguish between the general behavior when the soldier is faced with a situation which endangers the colony and the manner of combat when it is confronted by an enemy.

When a nest is opened, the reaction varies greatly from one species to another. The soldiers may rush in crowds to the opening and pour out to the exterior in an obvious state of excitement. This occurs in most species of *Nasutitermes* and *Trinervitermes*, in *Amitermes evuncifer*, *Globitermes sulphureus* (Haviland), and in *Bellicositermes natalensis*. Most of of the time the soldiers do not venture outside of the opening, but proceed to the edge of the breach with mandibles open and the antennae raised toward the front. Also, they may place themselves in the opening of the gallery with their heads blocking the opening (the *phragmosis* behavior of Wheeler). Finally, at times, these same circumstances may cause the entire population, including the soldiers, to retreat into the depths of the workings as in *Bellicositermes bellicosus* (Smeathman) and *Macrotermes ivorensis,* and the soldiers may often be observed closing the nest galleries as in the preceding case.

The defensive behavior of the soldiers is most apparent when the colonies venture openly into the air (to engage in foraging, or during organized migration or sociotomy). In groups which forage, such as *Hospitalitermes, Trinervitermes, Macrotermes,* and *Odontotermes magdalenae,* the foraging columns are flanked on each side by a row of soldiers, regularly aligned, and with their heads turned toward the exterior.

There is a great diversity in the manner of combat of the soldiers. In the mandibulate forms the manner in which the mandibles are employed varies greatly from genus to genus (Deligne, 1965). Thus, in the genus *Termes,* the mandibles, which can only be separated slightly, are pressed against one another when the soldier becomes excited, and they then intersect suddenly, causing deep wounds with their points. A similar arrangement, which is even more specialized, exists in the Termitinae with asymmetrical mandibles (Kaiser, 1954; Deligne, 1965). This is developed to such a point in *Pericapritermes,* that the soldiers only deliver a blow if their adversary is to their right side and thus within the range of the long left mandible.

In certain species a greatly developed salivary gland (Chapter 4) is associated with the defensive behavior of the soldiers. Thus, in *Globitermes sulphureus* (Bathellier, 1927; personal observations) a soldier which has seized an adversary within its mandibles (which are curved strongly outward) releases a flow or wave of bright yellow saliva. This coagulates and becomes brownish in the air and entangles the termite and his enemy. Frequently the muscular contractions of the soldier are so violent that the salivary reservoirs burst. The soldiers of *Protermes* separate their mandibles widely and allow a drop of white salivary fluid to gush from the opening.

The frontal glands of the soldiers exhibit quite a variable development in the different species (Chapter 4). We do not know anything of their role in the mandibulate soldiers, except in the Nasutitermitinae. According to Emerson (1961) only the mandibles are used in the primitive forms, as in *Corniternes,* which has a very short, only slightly projecting, frontal tube. In *Rhynchotermes* and *Armitermes,* in which the soldiers have well-developed mandibles, it is primarily the secretion of the frontal gland which is employed against ants. In the nasute soldiers the violent contraction of the mandibular muscles (Chapter 4) projects the content of the frontal gland for several centimeters. The tapering frontal tube gives a precise orientation to the jet, and the agility of the soldiers, along with the mobility of their heads, permits them to aim at the adversary with great precision. Since the soldiers are blind, we do not know how the target is located.

D. THE REPLACEMENT REPRODUCTIVES

Our knowledge of the replacement reproductives in the Termitidae is still very fragmentary and is based mostly on chance collections (Noirot, 1956). For a large number of species nothing is known of the possibilities of the formation of such sexuals. Nevertheless, three types of replacement reproductives may be distinguished on the basis of their origin: the *adultoids*, derived from imagoes; the *nymphoids*, derived from nymphs of various ages; and the *ergatoids*, derived from workers.

1. Adultoid Reproductives

It is only in the Termitidae that we have indisputable cases in which imagoes can acquire sexual maturity within the colony of their origin. The formation of imaginal sexual replacements has been obtained experimentally by Harms (1927) in *Macrotermes gilvus* (Hagen); by Coaton (1949) in various Macrotermitinae of South Africa; by Noirot (1956) in *Nasutitermes arborum* (Smeathman) and *Anoplotermes* sp.; and by Kaiser (1956) in *Anoplotermes pacificus*. Furthermore, the finding of numerous imaginal reproductives in natural colonies leads to the conclusion that such an origin does occur. Often, however, only a single pair is formed or persists, notably in the Macrotermitinae (Harms, 1927; Coaton, 1949). Under these circumstances it is difficult or even impossible to distinguish them from the founding pair. These reproductives may be formed by an *anticipated* imaginal molt. Thus, Kaiser (1956) found natural colonies of *Anoplotermes pacificus* with imaginal reproductives having incomplete pigmentation. However, they can also be derived from alates present in the nest at the time the normal reproductives disappear (our observations on *Anoplotermes* sp.).

2. Nymphoid Reproductives

In numerous species replacement reproductives have been observed which have pigmented eyes and more or less developed wing pads (brachypterous neotenics) and which are probably derived from nymphs.

In the few cases where good comparative data are available, these reproductives differ from the normal nymphs and must have undergone at least one special molt, as is the rule in the lower termites (Weyer, 1930; Noirot, 1956; Kaiser, 1956). According to the experimental studies of Weyer, whose material has been reexamined by Kaiser, the last three nymphal stages may give rise to neotenics in *Microcerotermes amboinensis* Kemner.

These nymphoid sexuals usually appear in large numbers, and the females are often more numerous than the males. In *Armitermes neotenicus* Holmgren only a single male is found for numerous females (Holmgren, 1906), but this is exceptional.

3. Ergatoid Reproductives

Very few positive examples of ergatoid sexuals are known. The literature contains quite a few cases of replacement reproductives which resemble the workers (Noirot, 1956). In these reproductives the most distinct characteristic is the absence of wing pads, but very often these ergatoid sexuals possess compound eyes, and the nota of the thorax are more developed than those of the workers. It is possible that such sexuals are derived from nymphs, for we know that the molt which transforms a nymph into a neotenic is often accompanied by a reduction, or even a disappearance, of the wing pads. The recent observations of Bodot (unpublished) show how difficult it is to determine *a posteriori* the origin of the replacement reproductive. Thus, in *Cubitermes severus* Silvestri the removal of the royal pair results in the differentiation of a part of the workers (up to 10%) which undergo two subsequent molts during which the wing pads appear! Ultimately the cuticle becomes dark brown and the gonads develop greatly although egg production has never been observed. These observations are similar to those of Buchli (1958) on *Reticulitermes*. Nonetheless, the morphology of the replacement reproductives is of the worker type in *Microcerotermes strunckii* (Sörenson) (Silvestri, 1901). *Microcerotermes amboinensis* (Noirot, 1955; Kaiser, 1956), and *Termes hospes* (Sjöstedt) (Noirot, 1955). In the latter case we have been able to show that the transformation requires two molts. According to Kaiser (1956) only one molt is necessary in *Microcerotermes amboinensis*.

Since the workers are considered to be individuals whose differentiation has stopped, and since they retain certain larval traits, the reproductives which are derived from them may be designated as neotenics. Although the molt glands are always present in the workers, they have disappeared in the true ergatoids (Kaiser, 1956; Noirot, unpublished observations).

III. COMPARATIVE STUDIES OF POLYMORPHISM IN THE TERMITIDAE

Since the development of the imagoes is very uniform, we will only consider the neuters and replacement reproductives.

A. AMITERMITINAE

This subfamily, which is probably the most primitive, has undergone a complex evolution (to be discussed in Volume II). Unfortunately, the formation of the castes is not yet known for the most primitive forms (*Eurytermes, Euhamitermes, . . .*). The genus *Amitermes*, which has undergone notable evolution, has the most primitive type of polymorphism among the higher termites (Fig. 7). There is an absence of sexual dimorphism in the neuters, with identical development of males and females. After two larval stages, the workers run through several successive stages without notable growth or modification. The soldiers arise from workers, especially from those of the first stage, and include males and females. On the other hand, *Microcerotermes* (Fig. 8) has a very

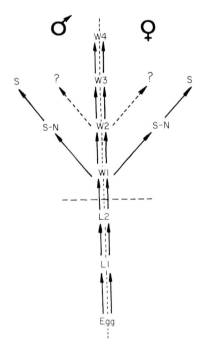

Fig. 7. *Amitermes evuncifer* (Amitermitinae): development of the neuters. There is no sexual dimorphism, and the development is identical for the males and the females. (L) Larvae; (S) soldier; (S-N) white-soldier; (W) worker (after Noirot, 1955).

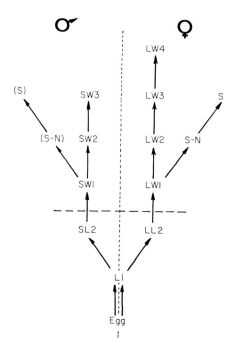

Fig. 8. *Microcerotermes* (Amitermitinae): development of the neuters. After the first molt it is possible to distinguish small, male, stage II larvae (SL2) and large, female, stage II larvae (LL2), giving rise, respectively, to small workers (SW) and large workers (LW). The white-soldiers (S-N) and the soldiers (S) develop almost always from large stage I workers and are almost always females (after Noirot, 1955).

marked sexual dimorphism, in which the males are smaller than the females. This is apparent in the second stage larvae. The workers go through three or four stages, and the soldiers arise from first stage workers and are almost always females. A sexual dimorphism of the same type is encountered in the workers of *Cephalotermes* and *Globitermes* (unpublished observations). On the other hand, we have not observed any dimorphism in the workers of *Anoplotermes,** and they belong to a single stage. The genus *Anoplotermes* lacks soldiers, and there seems to be a certain tendency for the disappearance of this caste in the Amitermitinae. Only very recently have soldiers been discovered in *Speculitermes,* and they remain unknown in *Protohamitermes* (a rare form, it is true). The proportion of soldiers is always very low in *Cephalotermes* (Grassé, 1939) and *Firmitermes* (Emerson, personal communication).

*According to Sands (personal communication), the genus *Anoplotermes* must be subdivided; the African species which we have studied apparently are in a genus other than *Anoplotermes.*

The formation of replacement reproductives has been studied experimentally by Weyer (1930) in *Microcerotermes amboinensis* (see also
Noirot, 1955; Kaiser, 1956). This species readily produces nymphoid
reproductives from the last three nymphal stages and also ergatoids from
the workers. Nymphoids have been found in quite a few species of
various genera, notably *Amitermes*. Adultoids have also been encountered [*Microcerotermes parvus* (Haviland) and *Anoplotermes* spp.]. In
spite of the numerous deficiencies in our knowledge, it appears that the
production of replacement reproductives is readily accomplished in this
subfamily.

B. TERMITINAE

The larvae and workers of the Termitinae do not possess any sexual
dimorphism (or else it is very slight, as in *Thoracotermes*). There is a
tendency toward a reduction of the number of stages of workers. In
Termes hospes the workers can pass through three successive stages, but
there is only one stage in the genera *Cubitermes, Noditermes* (Fig. 9),

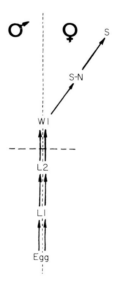

Fig. 9. *Noditermes curvatus* (Silvestri) (Termitinae): development of the neuters. There
is no sexual dimorphism and only one stage of workers (W1). The white-soldiers (S-N) and
soldiers (S) arise from female workers (after Noirot, 1955).

Pericapritermes, Orthotermes, Euchilotermes, Ophiotermes, and *Neo-capritermes.* In all of the cases studied the soldiers arise from workers. The soldiers are almost always females, although they are males in *Orthotermes depressifrons* Silvestri. In some genera two or three types of morphologically distinct soldiers are present *(Basidentitermes, Diho-plotermes),* but we do not know the nature of this polymorphism. Often these soldiers receive only salivary food (Chapter 3).

Most of the replacement reproductives which have been observed are adultoids. This is true of the large African genus *Cubitermes* in which reproductives are readily found. However, in *C. severus* (Section II, D, 3) very special ergatoids are found although it is not certain that they are functional. In *Termes hospes* the replacement reproductives may be adultoids or ergatoids (Noirot, 1956).

C. APICOTERMITINAE

On the basis of the fragmentary observations which we have been able to make, the polymorphism appears similar to that of the Termitinae. The workers are of a single stage, and their sexual dimorphism is not very marked. The soldiers are monomorphic and develop from female workers. We do not have any observations of replacement reproductives in this subfamily.

D. NASUTITERMITINAE

Beginning with the primitive forms, such as *Syntermes,* there are two different phyletic lines of evolution within the Nasutitermitinae which are rather distinct (the *Nasutitermes* and the *Subulitermes* lines). In *Syntermes* (according to our unpublished observations on *S. wheeleri* Emerson) the workers show a very marked sexual dimorphism. The males are the largest and pass through at least two stages. The majority of the soldiers are males and are probably derived from the large workers. In the *Nasutitermes* line the dimorphism of the workers appears to be general and is in the opposite direction so that the females are the largest. The workers generally go through several stages, and the soldiers are males (Fig. 10). However, in *Leptomyxotermes doriae* the soldiers are males and females. The soldiers usually arise from workers or from larvae of a special type as in *Tenuirostritermes tenuirostris* (Weesner, 1953) and the small soldiers of *Trinervitermes* (Noirot, 1955; Sands, 1965b).

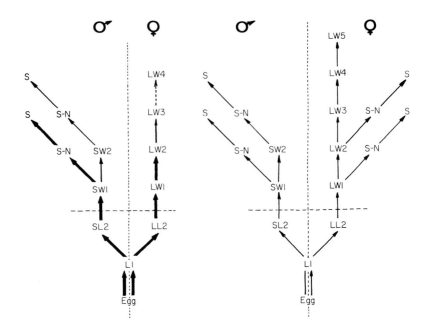

Fig. 10. *Nasutitermes arborum* (Nasutitermitinae): development of the neuters. To the left, development under natural conditions. Sexual dimorphism is very marked after the first molt. The small, male workers of stage I (SW1) mainly give rise to white-soldiers (S-N) and then soldiers (S), but sometimes they produce small workers of stage II (SW2). The large, female workers (LW) do not give rise to soldiers; they can pass through four successive stages, but very few attain stage III (LW3) and fewer stage IV (LW4). To the right is the scheme representing the total potentials of development; with the rearing of only large female workers, there may appear white-soldiers and soldiers from some of the large stage I and stage II workers (LW1, LW2); a fifth stage of worker (LW5) may also be obtained (after Noirot, 1955).

Soldier polymorphism is the exception in the *Subulitermes* line, but is frequent in the *Nasutitermes* line, and is the rule in the large genus *Trinervitermes*. The large soldiers develop from small workers, and the small soldiers from male larvae of a special type (Fig. 11). In this genus, where the soldiers are very numerous, the male workers do not do any work and are rapidly transformed into soldiers; thus all the functional workers are females and all the soldiers are males.

In the *Subulitermes* line, only the highly evolved genera *Mimeutermes* and *Eutermellus* have been studied (Noirot, 1955). Sexual dimorphism of the workers is very slight, and there is only one stage of workers. The soldiers, which are mostly males, arise from the workers (Fig. 12).

Little is known regarding the replacement reproductives in this sub-family. Nymphoid neotenics have been most frequently encountered, particularly in the genus *Armitermes*. Ergatoids have been described in certain *Nasutitermes* and *Lacessititermes*, but it is not certain that these are derived from workers. Under experimental conditions we have obtained adultoid reproductives in *Nasutitermes arborum*.

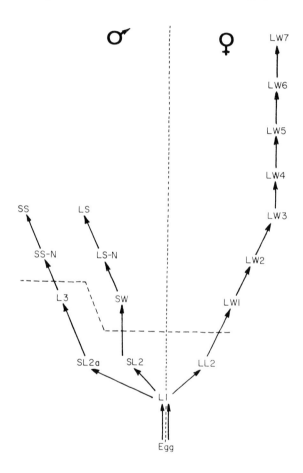

Fig. 11. *Trinervitermes* (Nasutitermitinae): development of the neuters. The sexual dimorphism is very marked; but the small male workers (SW) are not functional and evolve very rapidly into large white-soldiers (LS-N) and then to large soldiers (LS). The small soldiers (SS) develop from special male larvae (SL2a), differentiated at the first molt and passing through a third larval stage (L3). The large workers (LW) represent several successive stages (after Noirot, 1955).

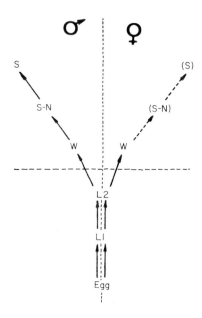

Fig. 12. *Eutermellus convergens* Silvestri: development of the neuters. Sexual dimorphism is not very marked. The white-soldiers (S-N) and soldiers (S) are almost always formed from a portion of the male workers. L: Larvae; W: workers (after Noirot, 1955).

E. MACROTERMITINAE

An important characteristic separates the fungus-growing termites from the other Termitidae: there are three stages of larvae (instead of two) in the development of the workers. Moreover, the very marked sexual dimorphism of the workers is the reverse of that in most species in that the large workers are males. The only analogous case is that of *Syntermes*. Also, there is only a single stage of workers. The soldiers are females except in *Sphaerotermes* where they are males. Two categories of soldiers frequently occur (Fig. 13): large ones, derived from small workers, and small ones, derived from stage III larvae (*Macrotermes, Bellicositermes, Ancistrotermes, Pseudacanthotermes*). The small workers which give rise to the soldiers can be normal and functional (*Ancistrotermes*) or they may be less sclerotized (*Bellicositermes, Macrotermes*). Frequently only one type of soldier is present, arising from stage III larvae (*Sphaerotermes, Protermes, Microtermes,* and certain *Odontotermes*). Finally, *Acanthotermes acanthothorax* has three types of soldiers (Fig. 14). The large and medium soldiers correspond to the preceding cases; the small soldiers, which are the most numerous, are derived from a special type of stage II larvae. As in the small soldiers of *Trinervitermes,* the determination occurs at the first molt.

Only adultoid replacement reproductives have been reported from the Macrotermitinae (Harms, 1927; Coaton, 1949).

IV. VARIATIONS OF POLYMORPHISM WITH TIME

The differentiation of castes undergoes important variations in the course of the life of a given colony. There is, on one hand, an evolution associated with the aging of the society, and on the other hand, a seasonal cycle which is usually very marked.

A. AGE OF THE COLONY

In spite of the small number of precise observations, it may be said that in the Termitidae the society undergoes a gradual aging, starting with

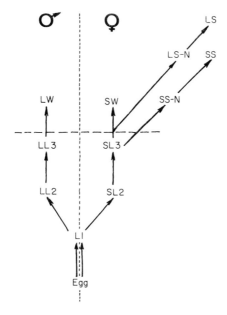

Fig. 13. *Bellicositermes natalensis* (Macrotermitinae): development of the neuters. Three larval stages are present; sexual dimorphism is very marked. The small white-soldiers and soldiers (SS-N and SS) arise from small female larvae of stage III (SL3); the large white-soldiers and soldiers (LS-N and LS) from small female workers (SW) which are incompletely pigmented. LL: Large larvae; LW: large workers (after Noirot, 1955).

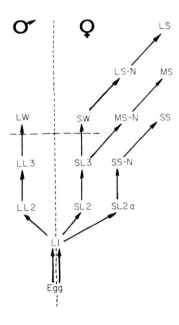

Fig. 14. *Acanthotermes acanthothorax* (Macrotermitinae): development of the neuters. The development is the same as in *Bellicositermes* (Fig. 13) except for the presence of three categories of soldiers, always females. The large soldiers (LS) and the middle soldiers (MS) are homologous to the large and small soldiers of *Bellicositermes*. The small white-soldiers and small soldiers (SS-N and SS) arise from stage II larvae of a special type (SL2a) (after Noirot, 1955).

its foundation and leading eventually to its death.* It is possible to recognize a *juvenile* period during which only the neuters (soldiers and workers) are differentiated; an *adult* period, when the society regularly produces winged imagoes; and finally, a *senile* period when this production diminishes and then stops, indicating the decline of the society. Thus, in *Cubitermes severus* the juvenile period lasts until the total population is about 10,000 individuals. Furthermore, there is, in this species, a progressive reduction in the proportion of larvae to workers (Table II), while the proportion of the soldiers remains more or less stable (about 0.8% of the total population) (Bodot, 1966). It would be very desirable to have comparable data for other species of Termitidae.

*We have very poor information regarding the longevity of the colonies, but it appears to be quite variable from one species to another. Hill (1942) indicates a nest of *Nasutitermes triodiae* (Froggatt) older than 70 years. Certainly the large nests of the Macrotermitinae persist for several decades. However, according to our observations, colonies of *Cubitermes fungifaber* must not persist for more than 5 years after the egress of the nest from the soil.

TABLE II

AVERAGE COMPOSITION OF COLONIES OF *CUBITERMES SEVERUS*[a]

	Young colonies, pop. <10,000	Adult colonies, pop. 10,000 – 40,000	Senile colonies, pop. >40,000
Number of colonies	25	45	12
Average population	5,600	30,000	50,000
Percentage of workers	47	58	85
Percentage of larvae	52	42	14
Percentage of soldiers	0.85	0.75	1.15

[a] After Bodot (1966).

We have better information on what happens in the very first stage of colony development (Chapter 8). Generally speaking, the workers and soldiers are smaller than normal (Harms, 1927; Noirot, 1955; Light and Weesner, 1955a). Nevertheless, the number of larval stages of the workers is the same as in the adult colonies (Light and Weesner, 1947, 1955a; Noirot, 1955; Williams, 1959b; Sands, 1965b). Usually this is also true for the soldiers [*Amitermes evuncifer* and small soldiers of *Bellicositermes natalensis* (Noirot, 1955) small soldiers of *Trinervitermes* (Sands, 1965b)]. Sometimes, however, as in *Pericapritermes urgens* Silvestri (Noirot, 1955), the first soldiers develop from stage II larvae and not from workers (Fig. 15). This is also probably true in *Nasutitermes,* but it cannot be confirmed since the observations on the development of the adult colonies (Knower, 1894; Bathellier, 1927; Noirot, 1955) are for different species than those studied by Becker (1961, 1963). Becker observed that in young colonies of *N. ephratae* the white-soldiers arise before the workers, developing from some stage II larvae. On the other hand, certain types of soldiers can be missing in the young colony, such as the large soldiers of *B. natalensis* (Noirot, 1955) and *Trinervitermes* spp. (Sands, 1965b). Finally, the workers may remain longer in the first stage as in *Gnathamitermes perplexus* (Banks) (Light and Weesner, 1947).

B. SEASONAL CYCLE

In the adult colonies the production of individuals with wings is not continuous, but usually responds to a very marked seasonal rhythm. The most visible manifestation of this cycle is the flight, which is generally produced at a definite time of the year for a given species and a given locality (Chapter 8). This seasonal cycle concerns not only the flight of the alates, but also their differentiation. This was noted as early as

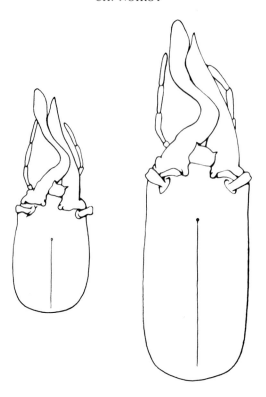

Fig. 15. *Pericapritermes urgens:* to the right, head of a normal soldier, developed from a worker; to the left, head of the first soldier to appear in the incipient colony, which arise from a larva of stage II (after Noirot, 1955).

1927 for the species of Indochina (Bathellier, 1927). Whereas the neuters (soldiers and workers) are produced during the entire year, the appearance of the young nymphs, the future imagoes, is much more limited in time. For example, in the tropical humid zone of the Ivory Coast the majority of the species (in the forest as well as in the savanna) fly at the end of the dry season or the beginning of the major rainy season (March to June). During most of the year the undifferentiated larvae of the stage I produce only soldiers and workers. During a period of about a month, toward October (the minor rainy season), the young nymphs appear, but the formation of the neuters is not interrupted during this period (Noirot, 1961; unpublished observations; Bodot, 1964, 1966). Such a cycle has been observed in representatives of all of the subfamilies, particularly in the genera *Amitermes, Microcerotermes, Cubitermes, Allognathotermes,*

Nasutitermes, Trinervitermes, Bellicositermes, and *Ancistrotermes.* In the much drier conditions in northern Nigeria, Sands (1965a,b) observed an entirely comparable cycle; this is also true for *Bellicositermes natalensis* near Kinshasa (Ruelle, 1962). In southeastern Asia the production of the young nymphs is spread out over a longer period, but their development always occurs during the dry season (Bathellier, 1927). The nymphs of *Anoplotermes pacificus* consistently appear during the dry season in Brazil (Kaiser, 1956).

All of these observations are in agreement with one another, but the facts are not always so simple. On the Ivory Coast an *Anoplotermes* of the forest produces reproductives in various seasons. *Cephalotermes rectangularis* has two cycles per year; flights occur in June and November, with nymphs appearing in December—January and in June. A single colony can produce two groups of reproductives in the same year, or only one (Noirot, unpublished observations). In East Africa, there may also be two cycles per year in *Microcerotermes parvus* (Kemp, 1955), *Cubitermes ugandensis* Fuller, and *Cubitermes testaceus* Williams (Williams, 1959a). *Cubitermes fungifaber* has a typical cycle in most of the forest region of the Ivory Coast, but, in a very limited area of the eastern part of this country, the cycle is shifted by 4 months (Noirot, 1961).

In all of the previous cases there is no interruption in either the development or the laying of eggs during the course of the year. This is not the case with *Tenuirostritermes tenuirostris* observed by Weesner (1953) in the mountains of southern Arizona. Egg laying is interrupted in the winter and not resumed until early April. Young nymphs appear at the end of August and probably spend the winter in the penultimate stage, with flight occurring in July and August. In spite of the complication introduced by the arrested development during the winter, these observations are comparable to those for tropical species, and the formation of reproductives is much more limited in time than the formation of neuters.

A detailed analysis of populations of *Cubitermes severus* in the savanna of the Ivory Coast (Bodot, 1966) brings out important seasonal fluctuations in the proportions of different castes. The proportion of larvae, in relation to the variations of the rate of egg laying by the queen, increases in the rainy season and diminishes in the dry season. The number of soldiers reaches a maximum at the time of flight (May and June) and the production of white-soldiers is at its maximum in April. Such studies should be conducted on other species in other environments. Our observations, although fragmentary, on *Cephalotermes rectangularis* in the forest of the Ivory Coast suggest that the production of new soldiers is maximal between the imaginal molt and flight, as in the preceding case.

According to Sands (1965a) *Trinervitermes geminatus* (Wasmann) (as *T. ebenerianus*) of northern Nigeria also shows a decrease in the proportion of larvae in the dry season, but the proportion of soldiers reaches its minimum at the time of flight. However, this analysis is based on nest fragments, and perhaps the movements of the population could distort the results. The observations of Bouillon and Mathot (1964) on *Cubitermes exiguus* Mathot provide figures which are quite variable from one colony to another and which hide the possible seasonal fluctuations. Such variations could be related to the replacement of the royal couple, which is very frequent in this species.

V. DETERMINATION OF POLYMORPHISM

A. Genetic Constitution

The facts available lead us to conclude that all of the individuals of a given species of termites have the same genetic constitution, with the exception of the factors which determine sex. In the lower termites (Chapter 9) this assertion is amply demonstrated. We will consider the main arguments which allow us to extend it to the Termitidae.

The fact that the soldiers (mandibulate and nasute) are most often formed from a portion of the workers clearly indicates that there is no genetic difference between these two categories of individuals. The question of a genetic difference between the neuters and reproductives may be raised when we consider that the separation of the two lines takes place before the first larval molt. However, the examination of certain intercastes indicates that such a difference does not really exist. Nymphal-soldier intercastes have been described in various Termitidae (Adamson, 1940; Gay, 1952; Noirot, 1955; Bouillon and Mathot, 1964). These individuals have a head which is almost identical to that of the normal soldier, but the thorax resembles that of the sexual nymphs. An analysis of such individuals (Fig. 16) shows that they must be derived from the nymphs (Noirot, 1955). The manner in which they differ from normal soldiers (flat pronotum, wing pads) probably results from the fact that these "soldiers" arise from forms different from the usual type (particularly in the thorax). Inversely, the observations of Bodot on the wing-padded neotenics developing from workers (Section II, D, 3) show that the workers retain the potential to develop a morphology of the imaginal type.

Fig. 16.   *Termes baculi* (Sjöstedt): nymph-soldier intercaste. The head is almost identical with that of the normal soldier, but the pronotum is flat and the wing pads on the meso- and metanotum indicate an origin beginning with a nymph (after Noirot, 1955).

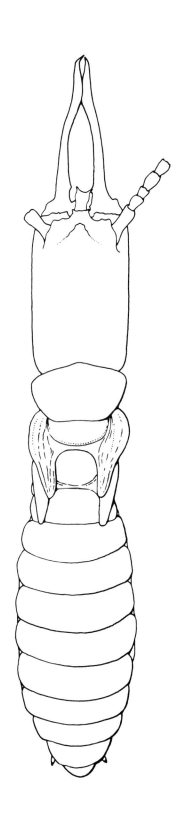

The polymorphism of the termites occurs, therefore, during the course of development of each individual. Wigglesworth (1954) suggested the hypothesis that the different forms (larvae, nymphs, imagoes) that an insect assumes during the course of its development depend upon the successive action of different genes; he has since extended this interpretation to the various cases of polymorphism (1961, 1966). It seems to us that this concept is particularly applicable to termites, and we believe (as inferred by Light in 1942) that *each individual possesses several genetic systems* conditioning the morphology and function peculiar to the different castes. Depending upon the influences which are exerted during postembryonic development (perhaps even embryonic), one of these systems is activated while the others are inhibited. We may postulate the existence of three systems determining the imago, worker, and soldier types, respectively, with each including two subsystems for the larval and terminal stages. We have seen, furthermore, that two very different types can succeed one another in the same individual (since the soldiers usually develop from workers), which clearly shows that polymorphism is a phenomenon of development. This interpretation permits us to understand the paradoxical aspects of sexual dimorphism: in certain species the differences in size between males and females are actually reversed in the imagoes and in the workers (Table I); this is easily understood if different genes are responsible for the formation of the two castes.

Nevertheless, it is probable that genetic differences occur between individuals for the determination of sex. We have seen (Section II, B, C; Section III) that the formation of soldiers usually involves one of the sexes. Our explanation is that the genetic differences between males and females create differences in sensitivity to the influences which determine the activity of the genetic "soldier" system. If these differences of sensitivity become very great, they may result in a situation (as in *Trinervitermes*) in which the determination appears to be genetic, since the soldiers are all males and the functional workers are females.

The differentiation of the castes may be represented as follows: external factors modify the physiological state of the individual, particularly the equilibrium of the endocrines. These modifications, in turn, act directly or indirectly on genes and determine the activation or repression of the different genetic systems, and, ultimately, the morphology resulting in the different castes.

In the concept of the social supraorganism, developed primarily by Emerson (1939, 1952), the formation of the castes may be compared to the cellular differentiation of a Metazoan.

One may thus distinguish, in the course of development, critical periods when the orientation toward one or the other types of morphology is decided. The primary problem will be to know the exact moment of this determination. It is necessary to examine what external factors can be responsible, and, finally, what physiological mechanisms are involved.

B. TIME OF DETERMINATION

1. Separation of the Imago and Neuter Lines

In all of the Termitidae, the distinction between the larvae and the nymphs becomes morphologically visible after the first molt. This implies, therefore, that the orientation is acquired at the time when the processes preparatory to the molt are initiated. Moreover, Kaiser (1956) has shown the histological differences which precede this molt (wing pads, eyes and molt glands). In other words, this orientation is acquired *at the latest* during the first larval stage. But is this early enough? Does it occur before or after the egg hatches? We are not yet able to answer these questions with certainty. On the basis of the size of the gonads, Bathellier (1927) thought he could recognize the future neuters and sexuals in *Nasutitermes matangensis* (Haviland) at the time of hatching or even before (while the larvae were still encased in the egg shell). However, his conclusions are based on too few observations and are especially obscured by the fact that he did not know how to tell the males from the females. The facts drawn from a study of the seasonal cycle are more easily interpreted to support the hypothesis of the determination preceding hatching. Thus, in the favorable season neuters and sexuals are produced simultaneously, and the young larvae and nymphs are mixed together in the same hatching chambers, a situation which does not favor a differential action of external factors such as the care given by the workers.

We are therefore faced with three possibilities regarding the time of determination of sexuals and neuters, which is rarely reversible: during the first larval stage, during the embryonic period, or during the oogenesis of the queen.

2. The Workers and Soldiers

a. Soldiers Originating from Workers. As a rule, the determination of the soldiers is late, since the workers that are transformed into soldiers do not differ from the others, either in morphology or in behavior. Moreover, it is possible, in experimental groups, to obtain soldiers from types of workers which very rarely or never produce them in nature (large female workers of *Nasutitermes*, small male workers in *Microcerotermes*). This determination must occur at the time when the processes leading to the molt are initiated in the worker.

There are exceptions, however. In *Bellicositermes* and *Macrotermes* the small workers that become soldiers are incompletely pigmented and do not seem to do any work. These workers, however, are morphologically identical with the other small workers. It is probable that determination occurs at the time of the molt of the stage III larvae into the workers or immediately afterwards.

  b. Soldiers Originating from Larvae. In the Macrotermitinae the small stage III larvae which give rise to small soldiers are morphologically identical with those which give rise to the small workers. Determination seems to occur in the stage III larvae and an earlier determination seems unlikely.

On the other hand, the small soldiers of *Acanthotermes* and *Trinervitermes* and the soldiers of *Tenuirostritermes* constitute a special line of neuters which are distinct after the first larval molt. Determination, therefore, must occur during the first stage at the latest.

3. The Replacement Reproductives

It is obvious that the determination of the replacement reproductives occurs late in development. In the case of the nymphoid and ergatoid reproductives, one or two special molts are required for the transformation into neotenics. This pattern is hardly compatible with an early determination of these types.

C. EXTRAINDIVIDUAL FACTORS

1. Neuters and Sexuals

Because of our uncertainty as to the time when determination occurs, we can only advance a hypothesis on the cyclic production of sexuals. Do the seasonal climatic conditions act upon the oogenesis of the queen, on the eggs, or on the very young larvae? We cannot say, but we may suppose that these influences are exerted through intermediaries, the workers, since the climatic variations are strongly moderated or even cancelled in many nests which are either subterranean or have a complex structure (to be discussed in Volume II). The workers are the only individuals which are in contact with the exterior environment and which experience variations which may modify their physiology or behavior. The seasonal modifications of the activities of construction and foraging have been made evident by Bodot (1966).

Weesner (1953) states that in *Tenuirostritermes* the young nymphs appear just after flight occurs and supposes that their differentiation could be due to the breaking up of inhibition emanating from the imagoes and exerting itself on the undifferentiated larvae of the first stage. The studies of tropical species do not favor this hypothesis. In a great number of species several months go by between flight and the formation of the new group of sexuals. In *Cephalotermes rectangularis* (where there may be two groups of sexuals each year) the young nymphs may appear while the alates of the preceding generation are still present in the nest.

2. Workers and Soldiers

In spite of seasonal fluctuations, the production of workers and soldiers is continuous, at least under tropical conditions (Section IV, B). We may note, however, that the proportion of soldiers varies greatly from one species to another, but this is less variable in a given species, suggesting a regulatory mechanism. Such a regulation is well evidenced in the rearing of workers all of the same type (Noirot, 1955). For example, the large female workers of *Nasutitermes* only produce soldiers when the small male workers, which normally produce soldiers, are absent.

This regulation could be due to the phenomenon of inhibition, the presence of soldiers in the society preventing (for example by the production of a pheromone) the differentiation of new soldiers. This theory is supported in the lower termites by the experiences of Castle (1934) and Light and Weesner (1955b) and provides a very satisfactory logical explanation with the interpretation of multiple genetics which we have developed (Section V, A). We must not forget, however, that there is no direct proof for this in the Termitidae. Bodot (1966), while observing the seasonal cycle of *Cubitermes severus,* noticed a *positive* correlation between the proportions of the white-soldiers and the soldiers, whereas the inhibition theory would indicate a negative correlation. This observation may be interpreted in different ways. For example, there may be a seasonal variation of the power of inhibition of the soldiers, or of the sensitivity of the workers. In any case, it points out the complexity of the phenomenon.

On the whole, it is clear that the stage and composition of the society influence the determination of the soldiers. The inhibition theory may be accepted as a working hypothesis, but calls for experimental research.

On the other hand, the frequent specialization of one of the sexes in the production of soldiers (Sections II, C and III) necessitates taking into account the genetic differences between males and females of the same species. In all probability, these differences affect the sensitivity to the factors which release or inhibit the development of the soldiers. This difference of sensitivity, pushed to the extreme, can result in a determination which appears to be purely genetic in the differentiation of the neuters into workers and soldiers as observed in *Trinervitermes* (Section V, A). It is not impossible that we may discover analogous cases in other genera, and we have expressed the hypothesis (Noirot, 1955) that it could be the case in *Tenuirostritermes*.

3. Replacement Reproductives

Although the problem of the regulation of replacement reproductives has been studied extensively in the lower termites, we have very little information regarding the Termitidae. Nevertheless, there is no doubt that the appearance of replacement reproductives is linked to the disappearance of the normal sexuals. One is able to suppose, therefore, that this differentiation results from the removal of an inhibition normally exerted by the functional reproductives. It is impossible at present to decide whether the theory of pheromone inhibitors (Chapter 9) can be extended to the higher termites. It must be emphasized that the loss of the functional reproductives leads to variable results, depending upon the different species. This may be interpreted as meaning that the stages which are sensitive to the removal of inhibition (and, therefore, capable of becoming reproductives) vary from one species to another. Thus, it may affect the imagoes, the nymphs, or the workers (Sections II, D, and III). It may even be that in certain species *none* of the individuals are capable of reacting. Thus, the removal of the royal couple from many nests of *Cubitermes fungifaber* on the Ivory Coast has never been followed by the appearance of replacement reproductives (Noirot, unpublished observations).

D. PHYSIOLOGICAL MECHANISMS

In the Kalotermitidae and the Termopsinae the role of the endocrine factors in the differentiation of castes is now well established (Chapter 9) although many of the details of this phenomenon remain to be explained. In the Termitidae we do not have any experimental work. However, anatomical and histological studies suggest that the facts are analogous, in spite of the complications introduced by the existence of a worker caste and the early separation of the neuters and sexuals.

The molt glands (Chapter 4) apparently play an essential role in the differentiation of the reproductives. Kaiser (1956) has shown in *Anoplotermes pacificus* that these glands are much more developed in the nymphs than in the larvae, and that this difference is already very apparent at the end of the first larval stage (which is still morphologically indifferent). We have been able to ascertain similar facts in *Termes hospes* (unpublished observations). The molt glands also have an effect on the formation of the neotenic sexuals since they become very enlarged at the time of the sexual molt (Kaiser, 1956; Noirot, unpublished observations), but degenerate in the functional neotenics as they do in the imagoes. The workers of *Noditermes*, parasitized by the larvae of *Noditermitomya* (Phoride), show a growth of the gonads which is correlated with an activation of the molt glands although these animals do not molt (Noirot, 1953). It seems, therefore, that the molt glands are involved in the differentiation of the imaginal characters, including the gonads. More precisely, the hyperactivity of the molt glands coincides with the growth of the gonads and the genital tract. The *maturation* of the gonads generally occurs after the degeneration of the molt glands in both the imagoes and the neotenics and seems to be associated with an activity of the corpora allata, which attains a considerable volume in the queens (Pflugfelder, 1938; Pasteels and Deligne, 1965). However, this enlargement of the corpora allata occurs late. Thus, in *Anoplotermes pacificus* (Kaiser, 1956) and *Termes hospes* (Noirot, unpublished observations), the larvae of the workers have corpora allata which are a little larger than those of the young nymphs.

In the Kalotermitidae and the Termopsinae the corpora allata also intervene in the differentiation of the soldiers, as has been demonstrated experimentally (Chapter 9). In the Termitidae we can only base our conclusions on anatomical observations, which indicate a notable growth of the corpora allata at the time of the molt transforming workers into soldiers (Kaiser, 1956; Noirot, unpublished). The intervention of the juvenile hormone in the formation of the soldiers may permit us to understand certain worker-soldier intercastes which originate from parasitism by Microsporidians in *Macrotermes gilvus* (Silvestri, 1945) and *Procubitermes* (Grassé and Noirot, unpublished). As a matter of fact, the work of Fisher and Sanborn (1964) has demonstrated the production of substances with an activity comparable to that of the juvenile hormone by a *Nosema* parasite in *Tribolium*. It is possible that the production of intercastes is linked to an excess of juvenile hormone (or an analogous substance) produced by the parasite.

We have very little information regarding the role of the neurosecretory cells, particularly those of the brain, which are so important in the development of insects. According to our observations (unpublished), the neurosecretory cells of the Termitidae are small and only slightly or nonstainable by the usual methods. Their study will probably necessitate special techniques. It is only in the physogastric queens that neurosecretory cells of the protocerebrum appear to be well differentiated and filled with products of secretion (Pasteels and Deligne, 1965; Noirot, unpublished observations). As in the Kalotermitidae (Noirot, 1957), the neurosecretions seems to intervene (directly or indirectly) in the activities of the gonads, but their eventual role in other aspects of the differentiation of the castes remains to be studied.

The few facts which are known clearly demonstrate that the endocrine glands have an effect on the different types of morphology ending in polymorphism, and suggest, also, that the mechanisms in the Termitidae are analogous with those of the lower termites. However, much remains to be done in this area.

VI. CONCLUSIONS

The Termitidae demonstrate postembryonic development which is much more stereotyped than that in the other families. This determination takes place at stages which are predetermined and are seldom reversible. It seems that the genetic systems of the different castes are much more individualized, and the passage from one to the other necessitates more precise conditions which are rarely reversible. One may conceive of a more rigid organization of the genome into distinct systems which cannot be activated simultaneously.

Within the Termitidae themselves, one may recognize several evolutionary trends which emphasize these features: a stabilization of the workers by reduction and then suppression of the molts that they may undergo; appearance of sexual dimorphism in the workers; a specialization of one of the sexes in the production of soldiers. The significance of these tendencies is much more difficult to establish since they manifest themselves in an independent manner in the different groups (the largest workers are sometimes males and sometimes females, and it is either the male or the female sex that produces the soldiers, etc.). Sometimes they even terminate in opposite results. Thus, the stabilization of the workers reduces the variability of this caste (tendency toward strict monomorphism), but sexual dimorphism increases the variability.

We cannot fail to be impressed by the fact that the neuter castes are particularly involved in this evolution. This is not only true for their development, as we have seen, but also for their morphology (in which the uniformity of the imagoes contrasts with the extraordinary diversity of the soldiers) and for their behavior. This latter evolution affects the workers, in particular, and their complex behavior, such as that involved in the construction of a nest with a clearly defined architecture. This clearly indicates that these societies are highly integrated. It is the social group which becomes the evolutionary unit. In order to comprehend its evolution, much remains to be learned regarding the roles of the different types of individuals in the society and the multiple interactions which are exerted within it.

REFERENCES

Adamson, A. M. (1940). New termite intercastes. *Proc. Roy. Soc.* B129, 35-53.
Alibert, J. (1963). Echanges trophallactiques chez un Termite supérieur. Contamination par le phosphore radio-actif de la population d'un nid de *Cubitermes fungifaber*. *Insectes Sociaux* 10, 1-12.
Alibert, J. (1966). La trophallaxie chez le Termite à cou jaune (*Calotermes flavicollis* Fabr.) étudiée à l'aide de radio-éléments. Doctoral Thesis, Univ. of Paris.
Bathellier, J. (1927). Contribution a l'étude systématique et biologique des Termites de l'Indo-Chine. *Faune Colonies Fran.* 1, 125-365.
Becker, G. (1961). Beobachtungen und Versuche über den Beginn der Kolonie-Entwicklung von *Nasutitermes ephratae* Holmgren (Isoptera). *Z. Angew. Entomol.* 49, 78-93.
Becker, G. (1963). Die Temperaturabhängigkeit der Entwicklungsvorgänge in jungen Kolonien einer *Nasutitermes*-art. *Symp. Genet. Biol. Ital.* 11, 286-295.
Bodot, P. (1964). Etudes écologiques et biologiques des Termites dans les savanes de Basse Côte d'Ivoire. *In* "Etudes sur les Termites Africains" (A. Bouillon, ed.), pp. 251-262. Masson, Paris.
Bodot, P. (1966). Etudes écologiques et biologiques des Termites des savanes de Basse Côte-d'Ivoire. Thèse présentée è la Faculté des Sciences de l'Université d'Aix-Marseille.
Bonneville, P. (1936). Recherches sur l'anatomie microscopique des Termites. *Arvernia Biol.* 15, 1-127.
Bordereau, C. (1967). Cuticule intersegmentaire des imagos de Termites supérieurs (Isoptera, Termitidae); Dimorphisme sexuel, ultrastructure, relation avec la physogastrie de la reine. *Compt. Rend.* 265, 197-200.
Bouillon, A., and Mathot, G. (1964). Observations sur l'écologie et le nid de *Cubitermes exiguus*. Description des nymphes-soldats et d'un pseudimago. *In* "Etudes sur les Termites Africains" (A. Bouillon, ed.), pp. 215-230. Masson, Paris.
Buchli, H. (1958). L'origine des castes et les potentialités ontogéniques des Termites européens du genre *Reticulitermes* Holmgren. *Ann. Sci. Nat. Zool. Biol. Animale* [11] 20, 263-429.
Castle, G. B. (1934). The experimental determination of caste differentiation in termites. *Science* 80, 314.
Coaton, W. G. H. (1949). Queen removal in termite control. *Farming S. Africa,* 14, 335-338.
Deligne, J. (1965). Morphologie et fonctionnement des mandibules chez les soldats des Termites. *Biol. Gabonica* 1, 179-186.
Emerson, A. E. (1926). Development of a soldier of *Nasutitermes (Constrictotermes) cavifrons* (Holmgren) and its phylogenetic significance. *Zoologica* 7, 69-100.
Emerson, A. E. (1939). Social coordination and the superorganism. *Am. Midland Naturalist* 21, 182-209.

Emerson, A. E. (1945). The Neotropical genus *Syntermes* (Isoptera: Termitidae). *Bull. Am. Museum Nat. Hist.* 83, 427-472.

Emerson, A. E. (1952). The supraorganismic aspects of the society. *In* "Structure et Physiologie des Sociétés Animales" (C. N. R. S., ed.), pp. 333-354. Imprimerie Nationale, Paris.

Emerson, A. E. (1959). The African termite genera *Firmitermes, Hoplognathotermes, Acutidentitermes, Duplidentitermes,* and *Heimitermes* (Termitidae, Termitinae). *Am. Museum Novitates* 1947, 1-42.

Emerson, A. E. (1961). Vestigial characters of termites and processes of regressive evolution. *Evolution* 15, 115-131.

Emerson, A. E., and Banks, F. A. (1957). Five new species and one redescription of the neotropical genus *Armitermes* Wasmann (Isoptera, Termitidae, Nasutitermitinae). *Am. Museum Novitates* 1841, 1-17.

Fisher, F. M. J., and Sanborn, R. C. (1964). *Nosema* as a source of juvenile hormone in parasitized insects. *Biol. Bull.* 125, 235-252.

Gabe, M., and Noirot, C. (1960). Particularités histochimiques du tissu adipeux royal des Termites. *Bull. Soc. Zool. France* 85, 376-382.

Gay, F. J. (1952). A rare termite intercaste. *Australian J. Sci.* 14, 127-128.

Grassé, P.-P. (1937). Recherches sur la systématique et la biologie des Termites de l'Afrique Occidentale Française. 1ᵉ partie. *Ann. Soc. Entomol. France* 106, 1-100.

Grassé, P.-P. (1939). Comportement et particularités physiologiques des soldats de Termites. *Bull. Soc. Zool. France* 64, 251-262.

Grassé, P.-P. (1949). Ordre des Isoptères ou Termites. *In* "Traité de Zoologie" (P.-P. Grassé, ed.), Vol. IX, pp. 408-544. Masson, Paris.

Grassé, P.-P., and Noirot, C. (1950). Documents sur la biologie de l'*Odontotermes magdalenae* n. sp. *Ann. Sci. Nat. Zool. Biol. Animale* [11] 12, 117-143.

Grassé, P.-P., and Noirot, C. (1951). Nouvelles recherches sur la biologie de divers Termites champignonnistes (Macrotermitinae). *Ann. Sci. Nat. Zool. Biol. Animale* [11] 13, 291-342.

Grassé, P.-P., and Noirot, C. (1954). *Apicotermes arquieri* (Isoptère): Ses constructions, sa biologie. Considérations générales sur la sous-famille des Apicotermitinae nov. *Ann. Sci. Nat. Zool. Biol. Animale* [11] 16, 345-388.

Harms, J. W. (1927). Koloniegründung bei *Macrotermes gilvus* Hag. *Zool. Anz.* 74, 221-236.

Hecker, H. (1966). Das Zentralnervensystem des Kopfes und seine postembryonale Entwicklung bei *Bellicositermes bellicosus* (Smeath.) (Isoptera). *Acta. Trop.* 23, 297-352.

Hill, G. F. (1942). "Termites (Isoptera) from the Australian Region." Council Sci. Ind. Res., Melbourne, Australia.

Holmgren, N. (1906). Studien über sudamerikanische Termiten. *Zool. Jahrb., Abt. Syst.* 23, 521-676.

Kaiser, P. (1954). Über die Funktion des Mandibeln bei den Soldaten von *Neocapritermes opacus* (Hagen). *Zool. Anz.* 152, 228-236.

Kaiser, P. (1956). Die Hormonalorgane der Termiten mit der Entstehung ihrer Kasten. *Mitt. Hamburgischen Zool. Museum Inst.* 54, 129-178.

Kemp, P. B. (1955). The termites of north-eastern Tanganyika; their distribution and biology. *Bull. Entomol. Res.* 46, 113-135.

Knower, H. (1894). Origin of the "Nasutus" (soldier) of *Eutermes. Johns Hopkins Univ. Circ.* 13, 58-59.

Light, S. F. (1942). The determination of castes of social insects. *Quart. Rev. Biol.* 17, 312-326; 18, 46-63.

Light, S. F., and Weesner, F. M. (1947). Development of the castes in higher termites. *Science* **106**, 244-245.

Light, S. F., and Weesner, F. M. (1955a). The incipient colony of *Tenuirostritermes tenuirostris* (Desneux). *Insectes Sociaux* **2**, 135-146.

Light, S. F., and Weesner, F. M. (1955b). The production and replacement of soldiers in incipient colonies of *Reticulitermes hesperus* Banks. *Insectes Sociaux* **2**, 347-354.

Noirot, C. (1952a). Le polymorphisme social chez les Termites et son déterminisme. *In* "Structure et physiologie des sociétés animales" (C. N. R. S., ed.), pp. 103-116. Imprimerie Nationale, Paris.

Noirot, C. (1952b). Les soins et l'alimentation des jeunes chez les Termites. *Ann. Sci. Nat. Zool. Biol. Animale* [11] **14**, 405-414.

Noirot, C. (1953). Un effet paradoxal du parasitisme chez les termites. Developpement des gonades chez des ouvriers parasités. *Bull. Section Française Union Intern. Etude Insectes Sociaux* **1**, 11-28.

Noirot, C. (1955). Recherches sur le polymorphisme des Termites supérieurs (Termitidae). *Ann. Sci. Nat. Zool. Biol. Animale* [11] **17**, 399-595.

Noirot, C. (1956). Les sexués de remplacement chez les Termites supérieurs (Termitidae). *Insectes Sociaux* **3**, 145-158.

Noirot, C. (1957). Neurosécrétion et sexualité chez le Termite à cou jaune "*Calotermes flavicollis* F." *Compt. Rend.* **245**, 743-745.

Noirot, C. (1961). Le cycle saisonnier chez les Termites. *Proc. 11th Intern. Congr. Entomol., Vienna, 1960* Vol. 1, pp. 583-585.

Noirot, C. (1966). Description et affinités de deux nouveaux genres d'Amitermitinae (Isoptera, Termitidae). *Insectes Sociaux* **13**, 329-345.

Noirot, C., and Bodot, P. (1964). L'essaimage d'*Allognathotermes hygogeus* Silv. (Isoptera, Termitidae). *Compt. Rend.* **258**, 3357-3359.

Noirot-Timothée, C., and Noirot, C. (1965). L'intestin moyen chez la reine des Termites supérieurs. Etude au microscope électronique. *Ann. Sci. Nat. Zool. Biol. Animale* [12] **7**, 185-206.

Pasteels, J. M. (1965). Polyéthisme chez les ouvriers de *Nasutitermes lujae* (Termitidae, Isoptères). *Biol. Gabonica* **1**, 191-205.

Pasteels, J. M., and Deligne, J. (1965). Etude du système endocrine au cours du vieillissement chez les "reines" de *Microcerotermes parvus* (Haviland) et *Cubitermes heghi* (Sjöstedt) (Isoptères, Termitidae). *Biol. Gabonica* **1**, 325-336.

Pflugfelder, O. (1938). Untersuchungen über die histologischen Veränderungen und das Kernwachstum der "Corpora allata" von Termiten. *Z. Wiss. Zool.* **150**, 451-467.

Ruelle, J. E. (1962). Doctoral Thesis, University of Lovanium, Leopoldville.

Sands, W. A. (1965a). Mound population movements and fluctuations in *Trinervitermes ebenerianus* Sjöstedt (Isoptera, Termitidae, Nasutitermitinae). *Insectes Sociaux* **12**, 49-58.

Sands, W. A. (1965b). Alate development and colony foundation in five species of *Trinervitermes* (Isoptera, Nasutitermitinae) in Nigeria, West Africa. *Insectes Sociaux* **12**, 117-130.

Sands, W. A. (1965c). A revision of the Termite subfamily Nasutitermitinae (Isoptera, Termitidae) from the Ethiopian region. *Bull. British Mus., Entomol. Suppl.* **4**, 1-172.

Silvestri, F. (1901). Operai ginecoidi di Termes con osservazioni intorno l'origine della varie caste nei termitidi. *Atti Accad. Nazl. Lincei., Rend., Classe Sci. Fis., Mat. Nat.* [A] **10**, 479-484.

Silvestri, F. (1945). Descrizione di intercaste di *Syntermes grandis* (Rambur) causate da un protozoo microsporidio. *Acta Pontif. Acad. Sci.* **9**, 77-89.

Sjöstedt, Y. (1926). Revision der Termiten Afrikas. *Kgl. Svenska Vetenskapsakad. Handl.* [3] **3**, No. 1, 1-419.

Weesner, F. M. (1953). Biology of *Tenuirostritermes tenuirostris* (Desneux) with emphasis on caste development. *Univ. Calif. (Berkeley) Publ. Zool.* **57**, 251-302.

Weyer, F. (1930). Über Ersatzgeschlechtstiere bei Termiten. *Z. Morphol. Oekol. Tiere* **19**, 364-380.

Wigglesworth, V. B. (1954). "The Physiology of Insect Metamorphosis." Cambridge Univ. Press, London and New York.

Wigglesworth, V. B. (1961). Insect polymorphism—a tentative synthesis. *In* "Insect Polymorphism" (J. S. Kennedy, ed.), pp. 103-113. Roy. Entomol. Soc., London.

Wigglesworth, V. B. (1966). Hormonal regulation of differentiation in insects. *In* "Cell Differentiation and Morphogenesis" (W. Beerman *et al.*, eds.). pp. 180-209. North Holland Publ., Amsterdam.

Williams, R. M. C. (1959a). Flight and colony foundation in two *Cubitermes* species (Isoptera: Termitidae). *Insectes Sociaux* **6**, 203-218.

Williams, R. M. C. (1959b). Colony development in *Cubitermes ugandensis* Fuller (Isoptera: Termitidae). *Insectes Sociaux* **6**, 291-304.

11

Rearing of Termites and Testing Methods Used in the Laboratory

GÜNTHER BECKER

I. GENERAL PRECONDITIONS FOR REARING, BREEDING, AND TESTING

A. BIOLOGY AND REPRODUCTION

The social behavior of termites is the most important biological factor to be considered in their breeding and testing.

A termite culture can be started with a dealated pair or with groups of preimaginal insects. For tests, workers are normally used, but pseudoworkers and larvae in suitable groups may be used; very seldom can tests be carried through with only a pair of imagoes.

As regards workers, pseudoworkers, nymphs, and larvae, single individuals can be kept alive for months in the case of Kalotermitidae species (Grassé and Noirot, 1960). Generally, however, groups of termites should be kept together. Kalotermitidae and Termopsidae are able to survive and to develop new colonies even in groups of only a few individuals, whereas Termitidae species can, in general, only be kept successfully in larger groups.

The development of neotenic reproductives takes place very easily with probably all Kalotermitidae (various authors) and Termopsidae species (Castle, 1934; Light and Illg, 1945; Light and Weesner, 1951; Lüscher, 1956) from nymphs, larvae (pseudoworkers), and even pre-soldiers. Within the Rhinotermitidae neotenic reproductives are usually formed by *Heterotermes* (Becker, 1953, 1962b) and *Reticulitermes* species (Grassé, 1949; Buchli, 1956, 1958; Shimizu, 1963), but not by most of the *Coptotermes* species investigated (Gay *et al.*, 1955; Hrdý, 1966; Becker, 1966f).

In the case of *Kalotermes flavicollis* (Fabricius) all neotenic individuals, save one pair, are killed by the group (Ruppli and Lüscher, 1964). This seems to apply also to other Kalotermitidae. Termopsidae and Rhinotermitidae colonies can contain several neotenic reproductives at the same time. With most Termitidae species the development of neotenics seems to be rare (Noirot, 1956; Harris, 1958); it occurs regularly in the genus *Microcerotermes*, however. In many other genera, only individuals of the last nymphal instar seem to be capable of transforming into functional reproductives.

The knowledge of the special behavior of reproduction by neotenic females and males is, of course, essential for breeding termite species and must be considered for setting up suitable groups for permanent cultures. The maintenance of active groups for tests and other purposes is, however, also possible with species of *Coptotermes, Nasutitermes*, and other genera (Gay *et al.*, 1955; Becker, 1961, 1966f) which—at least under laboratory conditions—do not produce neotenics. The time of survival of such groups depends on the normal lifetime of the individuals of the respective groups; it may last several months, sometimes even more than 2 years.

It should be noted that the "testing methods" dealt with in Section III are primarily oriented toward testing material with reference to termite attacks. However, the general conditions for maintaining termites in culture are obviously comparable for laboratory studies of other aspects of termite biology.

B. NUTRITION

Suitable wood species are essential for successful breeding and testing. Toxic timber must be avoided. Termites of the genus *Nasutitermes* reject coniferous wood species (Gay *et al.*, 1955; Becker, 1961, 1966c,f). Timber with low density is normally preferred to wood with high density. The spring wood is eaten first and the summer wood is frequently left only slightly destroyed. Pinewood can show a repellent effect, which disappears after leaching with water (Becker, 1966c). Hardwoods liked by termites are birch, poplar, beech, apple, pear, and some tropical hardwoods.

Attack of wood by fungi is of high significance and value for the termites. They are attracted by special Basidiomycetes of the brown-rot type (Esenther *et al.*, 1961; Becker, 1965c, 1966b; Lund, 1959). Slight deterioration by fungal action increases the nutritional value for the insects (Light and Weesner, 1947; Becker, 1948, 1965c). Also, Ascomycetes and Fungi Imperfecti, to which the soft-rot fungi belong, can be beneficial (Becker, 1948), whereas other species or even other strains of the same species may have no effect or else be toxic (Lund and Engelhardt, 1962; Becker and Kerner-Gang, 1964; Smythe and Coppel, 1966). It is known that white-rot fungi may be toxic too (Kovoor, 1964; Becker, 1965c).

For the breeding of termites it is advisable to use wood blocks with about $3-10\%$ weight loss due to attack by brown-rot Basidiomycetes, such as *Coniophora puteana*, *Lenzites* species, *Polyporus* species, or *Merulius lacrimans* (Becker, 1965c). Mycelium of beneficial, nontoxic fungi can be used as additional food (Becker, 1942b).

Filter paper is a suitable source of cellulose for termites. For nutritional studies special carbohydrates, proteins, and vitamins may be added. Avoidance of toxic mold development is always — even with special diets — a precondition for the maintenance and breeding of termites.

For small colonies the use of agar and wood has been suggested and applied successfully (Light, 1942-1943; Light and Weesner, 1947). Agar $(3-4.5\%)$ is mixed with chips or sawdust of wood. It is advisable to use wood which is slightly decayed by favorable brown- or soft-rot fungi (Light and Weesner, 1947; Becker, 1966f). Such a mixture provides nearly optimum food and humidity conditions.

Humus-containing soil may serve as a food basis for many termite species. *Cubitermes* species develop in the laboratory only when proper soil is freshly added at short intervals (Sands, personal communication by Harris).

It is very suitable for incipient and other colonies to be kept, for continuous observation, between glass plates (Adamson, 1941; Lüscher, 1949; Becker, 1966f) or in glass tubes (Grassé and Noirot, 1958, and others).

C. Aeration, Humidity, and Temperature

Every kind of aeration leads to desiccation unless the moisture content of the surrounding room is saturated or the termites have immediate access to a water supply. In the case of small groups of termites it is therefore recommendable to provide only the smallest possible exchange of air needed by the termites. Thus the source of moisture and the number of individuals kept in a container are decisive factors for the choice of an aeration system.

Termites, as compared with other insects, can tolerate air with a relatively high CO_2 content (Williams and Kofoid, 1934; Grassé, 1949; Lüscher, 1961). In order to avoid air movement, some termite species close holes or gauze windows of the containers with their fecal material or galleries.

Most termites require saturated relative humidity. The tolerance to desiccation is larger with many Kalotermitidae than with Termopsidae, Rhinotermitidae, and Termitidae. "Harvester" and some other termites leave their nests even in dry periods. Nest and gallery building takes place not only after rainfall at a high relative humidity but also under drier conditions. The ability to survive in unsaturated air depends, however, on the possibility of obtaining drinking water. The water needed by the termites is to some extent provided as a metabolic end product of their breakdown of cellulose and other carbohydrates. Thus, several genera do not require additional sources of water if the surrounding relative humidity is constantly kept high enough.

Termites produce their own microclimate in their nests and galleries. Larger groups can survive under drier conditions than groups of few individuals, which evaporate less water and suffer earlier from desiccation. Relative humidity is important in the development of incipient colonies of Kalotermitidae: larger groups may survive with $90-92\%$ relative air humidity, while incipient colonies die under such conditions, but develop at 95% relative air humidity (Becker, unpublished).

In laboratory cultures of soil-dwelling termites the necessary humidity conditions can be provided by the water content of the soil. The amount of water to be added depends on the water-holding capacity of the soil, which is very low in the case of pure sand, but high for peat and humus (Fig. 1). The optimum water content of sand is about $2-4\%$, of humus-containing soils $15-25\%$ (Becker, 1965a). In case of high-water-holding capacity, optimal conditions can occur in a rather broad range (Fig. 1). This is a convenient fact for the maintenance during tests (Becker, 1965a).

Temperatures can exercise a different influence on the various stages and activities of termites. Species can differ considerably in their reaction to temperature (Becker, 1966a, 1967) (Fig. 2).

Only species occurring in temperate climates, e.g., in Europe or in North America, are able to tolerate 20°C or lower temperatures for long periods (Weidner, 1954; Lund, 1962). Species from tropical countries survive only for a few weeks if kept constantly at 20°–22°C. *Zootermopsis angusticollis* (Hagen), however, cannot even tolerate 28°C for many weeks (Becker, 1967). The upper limit normally ranges be-

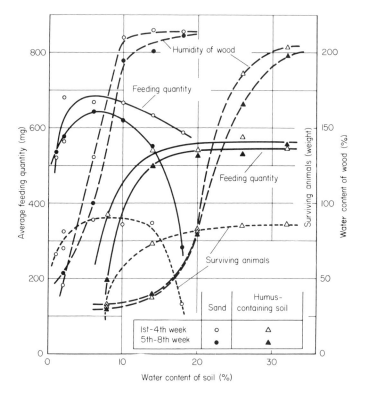

Fig. 1. Wood consumption by *Heterotermes indicola* at different soil and wood humidities (Becker, 1965a).

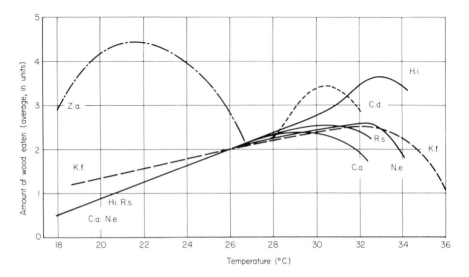

Fig. 2. Wood consumption by seven termite species at different temperatures (Becker, 1967). (C.a.) *Coptotermes amanii;* (C.d.) *Cryptotermes dudleyi;* (H.i.) *Heterotermes indicola;* (K.f.) *Kalotermes flavicollis;* (N.e.) *Nasutitermes ephratae;* (R.s.) *Reticulitermes lucifugus santonensis;* (Z.a.) *Zootermopsis angusticollis.*

tween approximately 32° and 34°C. For wood consumption and probably for other activities of larvae and workers, the optimum temperature may be higher than for the development of an incipient colony or for egg production. It is, therefore, advisable to use a somewhat lower temperature for breeding termites than for short-term testing of their destructive ability. The culturing of termite groups of the same colony at different temperatures may lead to the development of races with different temperature sensitivities (Becker, 1967). With the exception of few species, such as *Zootermopsis angusticollis,* a temperature between 26° and 28°C is, in general, most favorable for breeding and testing termites; for tropical species 30°C may also be suitable.

D. Toxic Factors, Diseases, Parasites, and Enemies

Timber species with toxic compounds are to be avoided in cultures. A large number of mold fungi, white-rot fungi, and bacteria can produce toxic substances. They are, nevertheless, eaten by termites (Lund and Engelhardt, 1962; Becker and Kerner-Gang, 1964; Kovoor, 1964; Smythe and Coppel, 1966). In some cases, such as with the frequently occurring *Aspergillus flavus* and *Trichoderma viride,* the toxic compounds are chemically known. The toxic fungi can develop on timber added to the culture. Hardwood species are, in general, more susceptible to attack by Ascomycetes and Fungi Imperfecti, but the toxic *Trichoderma viride* grows rapidly on pinewood. Water leaching and preattack by *Coniophora cerebella* diminish, to some extent, the mold development (Becker, 1965b).

Certain lower fungi and bacteria can cause diseases of termites. The fungal mycelium may enter living termites and cause their death. Some species, such as *Antennopsis* spec., parasitize termites (Buchli, 1952, 1960). Not much is known about the influence of bacteria (Smythe and Coppel, 1965; Lund, 1966).

Sterilization of soil and timber by heat reduces an infestation but does not prevent it. Small groups of termites are much more endangered than large, vigorous colonies. Groups brought freshly into the laboratory seem to be less tolerant to toxic microorganisms than cultures which — to some extent — may be selected as to natural tolerance to toxins and fungi. As long as the termites are undisturbed in their galleries in timber and soil, they are able to keep down fungal growth in their surroundings, but a change of the environmental conditions, especially a transfer to other containers and addition of timber, endangers them. Large and vigorous colonies soon cover freshly added timber with soil or enter it before toxic fungi can develop. Collembola in a culture are a useful control of fungi. The addition of antifungal substances to the culture media has been proposed. However, the success of such a procedure seems to be limited.

Some mites are parasitic to termites. They fix themselves on the head capsule or other parts of the body of the termites. Their development in a weak termite colony leads to its extinction. Application of special acaricides seems to involve hazards for the termites. Early removal of infested animals, if possible, is a way of controlling and reducing the mites. *Tyrolichus casei* Ouds. (Gallo, 1955) and *Pyemotes scolyti* Huds. (Weiser and Hrdý, 1962) have been reported to parasitize laboratory cultures. Chilopods are natural enemies of termites. They are not so harmful to large, vigorous colonies as they are to smaller groups, which can finally be killed by them. In order to prevent their development, soil taken to the laboratory from the field must be sterilized by heat.

E. CONTAINERS, PREVENTION OF ESCAPE, AND OBSERVATION

Containers for culturing termites or for carrying out tests with them must provide the necessary space and aeration and render possible the maintenance of suitable ecological and nutritional conditions. They must prevent the individuals from escaping, and they should — at least in

special cases—allow continuous observation without serious disturbance
of the insects. The material of the containers may be glass, polyethylene,
ceramics, concrete, cement-asbestos, metal (sheet metal or gauze),
or wood. Polyethylene may be destroyed after some time (Fig. 3). Experience indicates that small colonies should not be placed in containers
which are too large (Weesner, 1956; Osmun and Weesner in discussion;
Becker, 1965b) to enable them to keep fungal growth in their environment at a minimum and make use of the wood before it is too decayed.
Soil-dwelling species need space for moving and gallery building as part
of their natural behavior (Fig. 4). Large colonies of Rhinotermitidae and

Fig. 3

Fig. 3.   A: Polyethylene container with aeration holes in the lid enlarged by *Kalotermes
flavicollis*. B: Polyethylene container with soil gallery of *Reticulitermes lucifugus santonensis* projecting out of the lid.

Fig. 4.   A: Large, asbestos-concrete containers for termite cultures, with water barriers.
B: Diagram of asbestos-concrete containers for cultures of termites, with water barriers.
C: Galleries of *Reticulitermes* on the covering plate of an asbestos-concrete culture con-
tainer.

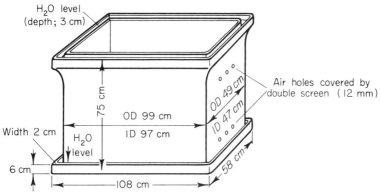

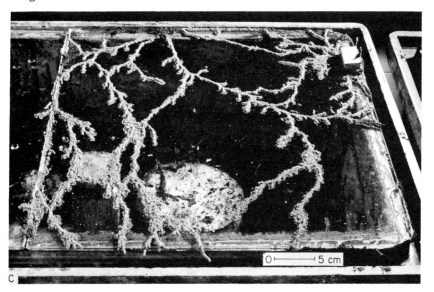

Fig. 4

Termitidae should be placed in containers of at least 0.3 m^3 capacity, and posts, tree branches, or other timber for nest and gallery building should be added.

Prevention of escape is made possible by closing the containers so that aeration is unimpaired, or by water barriers (Fig. 4). The lids of the tubes and flasks may be perforated, which can easily be accomplished in the case of polystyrene by means of a hot needle, or they may be provided with a well-fixed piece of metal gauze. Corrosion of the gauze must be watched for, and a bronze gauze is recommended. Glass aquariums with covers of glass ordinarily do not close so perfectly that aeration is impossible; but the termites may leave the aquariums in their galleries. Such containers require water barriers in order to prevent escape. The water barriers need not be broader and deeper than 3 – 5 cm. To provide a maximum of safety, large containers should have water barriers at both the bottom and the top (Fig. 4). This top barrier is, at the same time, an easily accessible drinking-water supply for the termites. Colonies that are very active in gallery building must be watched regularly since they may bridge the water barriers by galleries during a single night. If the swarming of alates must be prevented, special gauze covers should be applied before the flight takes place.

In many cases observation of the termites is necessary. This is possible to some extent through the walls of glass and plastic containers. For a better look at the bottom of the containers, where Rhinotermitidae normally build many galleries, mirrors may be installed (Herfs, 1950). For permanent observation of incipient colonies without frequent disturbance of the insects, culturing between glass plates has advantages (Adamson, 1941; Lüscher, 1949). A special aeration system (Fig. 5a) can be provided (Lüscher, 1949) or, under changed conditions, omitted (Becker, 1966f). Dimensions and distance between the glass plates depend on the size of the termites. The distance is maintained by glass strips and the whole system is held together by clips or by adhesive tape at two edges only.

F. COLLECTION AND HANDLING

During flight periods imagoes can easily be collected in the field for establishing laboratory colonies. When placed in containers with soil or filter paper, they do some flying and then shed their wings. If dealation does not take place, the wings may be carefully removed with tweezers. Aspirator tubes are suitable for collecting imagoes. If imagoes with wings are to be transported, it is best to put them into containers with slightly wet, crumpled filter paper.

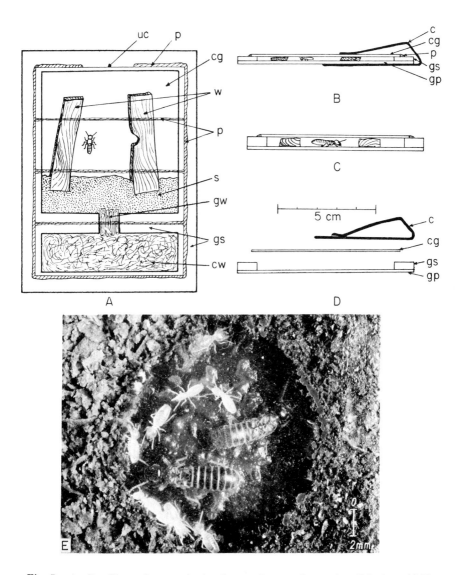

Fig. 5. A – D: Glass plate-termitaries for continuous observation (Lüscher, 1949). A: Plan of nest. B: Section through nest for *Kalotermes flavicollis* (height = 4 mm). C: Section through nest for *Zootermopsis angusticollis* (height = 4 mm). D: Details of a nest in section. E: Incipient colony of *Nasutitermes ephratae* in a simpler device (Becker, 1965). (c) Clamp made with hairpin; (cg) coverglass; (cw) cotton wool; (gp) glass plate; (gs) glass strip; (gw) glass wool; (p) paraffin wax for waterproofing; (s) sand; (uc) unsealed crack for aeration; (w) pieces of wood.

Favorable prerequisites for obtaining a termite species exist when the species builds nests which can be easily transported whole. This applies to the genera *Nasutitermes, Microcerotermes*, and *Termes* whose nests, constructed of brown carton material, are easily recognizable on trees, poles, or on the ground and which are easy to collect if their position is not too high on a tree; it even applies to *Coptotermes* species, whose nests are, however, more difficult to locate. Although the nests always contain only part of the workers of a colony, they may well be used for laboratory cultures because of the presence of reproductives. When only parts of the bigger nests are collected, the central part with the reproductives must be chosen; this part is characterized by the presence of eggs and larvae. Attention should be paid to the original position of the nest. Other species which do not have discrete nest structures can be collected and transported in the wood in which they live, or they can be removed from it. In the case of genera which develop neotenic reproductives, it is sufficient to take any groups which contain stages suitable for development into neotenics.

The containers in which termites may be transported or shipped for several days must be sufficiently aerated. The number of animals should not be too high. Moist wood or filter paper serves to supply them with water and food; cotton wool is less suitable. The interior of the container must, however, be dry. The animals must not be exposed to low temperatures, particularly when they come from tropical regions. When they are air-shipped, they must be kept in that part of the plane which is heated and pressure-conditioned.

Splitting the wood to get the termites out presupposes practical experience and skill to avoid injuring too many animals. Some of them may be removed from feeding tunnels by tapping them off. When the animals must be clean, that is, free from wood particles, soil, etc., e.g., for weighing purposes, they can be collected individually in smaller groups with a pair of soft steel tweezers. A simpler and more rapid method is to place sheets of paper on the nest material, soil, etc. (Gay *et al.,* 1955). The termites gather on the paper and can be easily shaken off by tapping.

For cultures with many animals, piles of small slices (5 – 10 cm thick) of attractive food should be used. The animals feeding in them are mostly of a similar caste composition and can be removed from the wood specimens by shaking and tapping. *Nasutitermes* animals gather after some hours on wood slices freshly exposed in the culture basin; at first soldiers are abundant, after some time they disappear almost completely and groups of workers of about 1000 animals can be collected in less than 5 minutes (Becker, 1966f). When large groups of animals are required, their average weight may serve as an indicator. Another, less exact method lies in apportioning animal groups in narrow glass tubes.

II. REARING AND BREEDING

A. REARING OF IMAGOES AND INCIPIENT COLONIES

Imagoes should not be collected from their nests before they are mature and the swarming period starts. The Kalotermitidae have reached maturity for swarming when the abdomen shrinks noticeably. This does not, however, apply to the Termitidae.

Imagoes must be kept at saturated humidity; water condensation on the container walls must, however, be prevented to keep the animals from sticking to the walls with their wings. Wing damage impairs wing shedding. Normally the animals must have flown before they shed their wings. Containers in which they can fly should not be too small. Inclined wood specimens or suspended strips of filter paper offer the animals an easy takeoff possibility. Readiness to fly is most pronounced in the late afternoon or in the evening. It may be induced by raising the relative humidity. An effect equal to flying is obtained when imagoes are held by one wing with a tweezer and are allowed to whir. The wings by which they are held should be alternated. Afterward, dealation often sets in quickly. When the animals still do not shed their wings, they may be broken off by taking one or two wings with a spring-steel tweezer and pulling them suddenly forward. The imagoes of several species of different termite families survived such an artificial dealation unharmed and developed into normal reproductives. Those animals which had not been artificially dealated usually died in the alate stage despite sufficient flight possibilities and flight action.

The dealated imagoes are placed in large, flat dishes on moist filter paper. Pairs forming tandems (Chapter 8) may be removed and placed together in culture, or the abdominal sternites may be examined under the microscope to determine the sex of the individuals (Chapter 2).

Those pairs which tend to gnaw into suitable material or to burrow into soil may be offered the choice of a suitable place in containers with wood, soil, or both; otherwise conditions may be created to facilitate nesting. In the case of *Cryptotermes* species or other Kalotermitidae, it is best to use suitable wood samples, i.e., wood which, preferably, is moderately attacked by brown-rot fungi, and to bore one hole each into them. The diameter of this hole should somewhat exceed the body diameter of the animals and be twice or three times as long as their body lengths (Wilkinson, 1962). The successful attack of a wood block by *Cryptotermes* species may be recognized by a brown sealing lamella.

A termitary consisting of wooden tongue blades has been described and used by McMahan (1961, 1962) for rearing *Cryptotermes* (Fig. 6); Hepburn (1954) described a combination of wood blocks and glass plates (Fig. 7); and Skaife (1957) utilized nests of plaster of paris with sawdust.

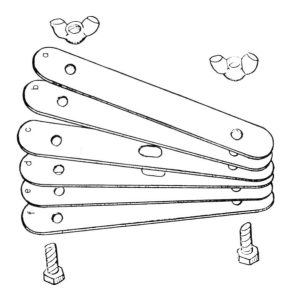

Fig. 6. Dismantled termitary of tongue blades (McMahan, 1962).

Otherwise, glass or plastic tubes that contain one termite pair each and that are sufficiently aerated are filled with a wood sample or moist soil with wood in or on it. When soil is used exclusively as in the case of *Macrotermes* and *Odontotermes* species, wood chips or wood dust may be added. A diameter of 2 cm and a height of 6 cm may be enough in the case of kalotermitids for the first 6 to 8 months. Larger imagoes, of course, need other dimensions. Another method that permits continuous observation with a minimum of disturbance entails placing of the culture

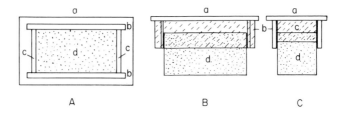

Fig. 7. Termitary for the observation of dry-wood termites (Hepburn, 1954). A: From above; B: from the side; C: from one end. (a) Cover plate; (b) side plates; (c) end plates; (d) wood block.

between glass plates, as was described earlier. Tubes or plates are kept in large, aerated containers with water or a saturated solution of potassium sulfate on the bottom; this keeps the relative humidity constant at 97–98%.

Cultures that are not continuously observed, especially species establishing abundant colonies with a long-lived, physogastric female, may be kept in small wooden boxes with soil and suitable food to be later transferred to larger containers (Becker, 1966f).

B. GROUPS AND COLONIES OF KALOTERMITIDAE (DRY-WOOD TERMITES)

Dry-wood termites of the family Kalotermitidae may be permanently kept in wood without soil. They are less susceptible to lower relative humidities than most of the other termites; for their successful development, however, these genera, which are usually resistant to dryness, also require humidities which are only slightly below the vapor saturation point.

The lower limit for the development of incipient colonies seems to be at 95% relative humidity for the genus *Cryptotermes*. Larger groups survive for some time at lower humidities. Other genera develop best at a wood moisture which is somewhat above the fiber saturation point of wood, i.e., at 100% relative humidity. For culturing *Cryptotermes* species, a relative humidity of 97–98%—which may be obtained by using a saturated potassium sulfate solution with precipitates (unsolved salts) for want of an appropriate, conditioned chamber—and a temperature of 26°–30°C proved to be suitable.

Kalotermes flavicollis develops better at almost 100% relative humidity or in wood whose water content is slightly above fiber saturation. The increased wood moisture can be obtained by using sterilized soil or gypsum. The gypsum must be absolutely free from iron compounds (Gösswald, 1943); this source of moisture cannot be recommended since the termites dig themselves into it and are difficult to get out. A very favorable temperature for incipient colonies of *Kalotermes flavicollis* is 26°C. Older colonies may be kept at a temperature between 20° and 30°C.

Incisitermes species may live for some period in moist wood; their moisture optimum obviously seems also to be slightly below 100% relative humidity, which corresponds to the fiber saturation point. Although *Neotermes, Rugitermes,* and *Bifiditermes* species may survive for some time in relatively dry wood, a water content somewhat above fiber saturation is recommended.

Suitable food consists of softwoods and hardwoods which contain no toxic substances, i.e., species of *Pinus, Picea, Abies, Betula, Fagus, Populus, Pirus, Malus*, etc. The wood samples are most nutritive when they have already suffered a 3−6% weight loss due to attack by either a brown-rot basidiomycete, or a nontoxic, soft-rot ascomycete or a fungus imperfectus.

C. GROUPS AND COLONIES OF TERMOPSIDAE (DAMP-WOOD TERMITES)

Among the Termopsidae the genus *Zootermopsis* has achieved importance for laboratory tests. Of the three species occurring in North America, *Z. angusticollis* and *Z. nevadensis* (Hagen) may be of a certain economic importance as building pests; usually, however, they live in tree stumps or in dead logs in the forest. The animals can be cultured in small groups of only a few individuals. They readily develop neotenic reproductives. Softwood which is slightly decayed by brown-rot fungi is recommended as a nutrient source. The animals are rather susceptible to mold fungi, and hardwood species which are easily infested by mold fungi endanger the cultures. The water content of the wood should be slightly above the fiber saturation point. The wood must be regularly dampened, larger pieces should be used which do not dry as rapidly as small ones, or the wood should be placed in or on moist soil. Because of the sensitivity of *Zootermopsis* to high temperatures, the cultures, except for short periods, should always be maintained at 18°−22°C.

D. GROUPS AND COLONIES OF RHINOTERMITIDAE (SOIL- AND WOOD-DWELLING TERMITES)

The collective term, soil-dwelling termites, is usually associated with the Rhinotermitidae. All species of this family tunnel the earth and build galleries consisting primarily of soil (Becker and Seifert, 1962). Reproductive individuals, eggs, and the young larvae remain in the wood in an unspecified place in the case of the genera *Heterotermes* and *Reticulitermes*, or they build nests which are the permanent center, as in *Coptotermes*. Species of the latter genus seldom or never produce neotenic reproductives (Gay *et al.*, 1955; Hrdý, 1966; Becker, 1966f), whereas these are easily developed in the two former genera.

Groups of *Heterotermes* and *Reticulitermes* may well be maintained over a long period due to the regular development of supplementary reproductives. *Coptotermes* species, which do not develop any neotenics, may be kept for a period of several months, sometimes up to 2 years in bigger groups, even without reproductive forms.

Rhinotermitid groups of 50 animals each may be cultured, although it is best to use at least 100, and if possible 200, 500, or a few thousand animals for test purposes (Osmun, 1957; and others). The greater the number of animals, the lower their mortality rate during the test (Becker, 1961; Schultze-Dewitz, 1962). Colonies of *Reticulitermes* and *Hetero-termes* which had been started with less than 10 larvae and workers have been successfully reared and developed up to the alate stage.

Soil-dwelling termites may also be maintained without soil. Sufficiently damp wood or filter paper enables them to survive for a lengthy period. However, as the building of galleries is one of their natural habits, they should be provided with soil, the composition of which need not necessarily be defined. Humus has an additional nutritive value because it contains plant substances and microorganisms. Pure sand collapses relatively easily when it is tunneled by the animals and may thus endanger them. When the moisture of the soil is adjusted, attention must be paid to the different water-holding capacities of the individual types of soil.

Softwoods and hardwoods may be used to feed the termites. The wood may be placed in or on the soil. Species which are highly susceptible to mold attack should not be used. If necessary, the samples may be sprayed with a spore suspension of mold species which has proved to be beneficial to termites. Moderate attack of wood by brown-rot Basidiomycetes or soft-rot fungi also favors and accelerates the development of Rhino-termitid species; the use of wood with $5-10\%$ weight loss is advisable.

The water content of the soil should be slightly below its water-holding capacity, and this content must be restored to its original amount from time to time. Moisture gradient tubes for prolonged maintenance of subterranean termites have been described by Pence (1957). The most favorable temperature for culturing *Reticulitermes* species is between $24°$ and $28°C$, for *Heterotermes* and *Coptotermes* species between $26°$ and $30°C$.

E. Groups and Colonies of Termitidae (Nest-Building Termites)

The Termitidae have permanent nests above and below the ground. These are the centers of social activities and have acquired a greater importance than in the other termite families with the exception, for example, of the genera *Coptotermes* and *Schedorhinotermes* (Harris, 1956a, 1961). Most of the Termitidae do not develop neotenic reproductives easily; the genus *Microcerotermes* is an exception to this. Large groups of Termitidae can be successfully maintained for some months, even in the absence of supplementary reproductives. Groups of *Nasu-*

titermes species which originally had young larvae, have survived for up to 2 years. Fungus-growing termites, like the genera *Odontotermes*, *Macrotermes*, and *Microtermes*, are far more difficult to culture than species without fungus gardens.

Maintenance of groups for laboratory tests has so far been successful with species of the genera *Nasutitermes, Microcerotermes,* and *Odonto-termes* (see later). Groups of at least 1000 workers with a proportionate number of soldiers are kept in smaller containers with soil and preferably with some nest material. Rearing and breeding in the laboratory was successful with *Microcerotermes* species in Paris and in Berlin-Dahlem and with *Nasutitermes* in Berlin-Dahlem, Basel, and Prague. When the species develop arboreal nests, the nests in the laboratory must also be established above the soil of the termitaries. The insects tend to build extensive galleries and must therefore be given sufficient room to move freely. Care must be taken to provide the termites with sufficient moisture and with access to a water reserve if possible. In well-developed colonies this is the water barrier which surrounds the container and to which the termites may build galleries.

Workers to be used for experiments may be removed from vigorous colonies of *Nasutitermes* and *Microcerotermes* without damaging the nest by tapping the specimens off the attacked wood. Approximately 1000 workers can thus be obtained within several minutes. When a *Nasutitermes* colony is populous, large quantities of workers may be tapped off only 1−2 hours after the insertion of new blocks. Soldiers can easily be collected by opening galleries or carton covers over attacked wood and by putting paper over these openings. The soldiers then flock to the paper and may be collected. The animals are not individually counted, but weighed in groups or measured in tubes when their weight (or quantity) is known.

III. TESTING

A. GENERAL VIEWS

Laboratory investigations should contribute in the most accurate way possible to a preliminary evaluation of the termite resistance of materials, including durable wood species and of the effectiveness of preservatives. Such investigations are not only carried out in industrialized countries of the northern hemisphere where termites do not occur, but also in countries where termites are widely distributed.

Laboratory investigations presuppose similar and uniform test conditions in order to obtain comparable and repeatable test results. Moreover, relatively short test periods are required; also, the materials to be tested are subjected to severe conditions to avoid a discrepancy between experimental and practical results. To fulfill the latter demand, it is necessary to use termite species which are economically important pests, to create test conditions which are likely to produce termite attack, and to subject the test material to previous conditioning and aging to simulate practical conditions. It may be useful to carry out the investigations step by step, starting with rough screening and finishing with semipractical tests.

As individual termite species must be expected to react differently to different materials and toxic substances, a large number of comparable results is required before general conclusions can be drawn from the results obtained with one termite species.

B. MATERIAL

Specimens of the material to be tested should be large enough to permit conclusions as to the presumable behavior of materials under practical conditions. On the other hand, it is useful to keep them as small as possible when damage is to be assessed by weighing. Size and dimensions of the test specimens must be in line with the test method.

The aggressiveness of termite groups or newly used termite species may be assessed by simultaneously testing some other material or timber species the resistance of which is known, or using treated wood whose repellency to certain termite species is known. In tests to determine the efficacy of wood preservatives, size and dimensions of specimens in existing test standards covering other organisms should be accepted. Experience gained in the field of impregnation and distribution of the preservative in the specimens as well as effects of leaching and evaporation may be considered. Existing standards should also be used for aging tests (Association Française de Normalisation, 1955; Deutscher Normenausschuss, 1941, 1961, 1963). For comparative purposes parallel tests should be carried out with untreated wood which has been given a preservative treatment (e.g., a defined creosote and a water-borne salt at constant concentrations).

C. TERMITE SPECIES

The number of termite species which has so far been regularly used for laboratory testing is small.

Mastotermes darwiniensis Froggatt, the only species of the family Mastotermitinae, proved very aggressive when used in Australia (Gay *et al.,* 1955).

Of the family Kalotermitidae, *Kalotermes flavicollis* is used in Germany (Gösswald, 1942, 1943, 1950; Becker, 1942a,b, 1960, 1961), in Switzerland (Lüscher, 1951; Ernst, 1957), in Czechoslovakia (Hrdý and Hrdá, 1960; Hrdý, 1963, 1964), in Italy (Rescia, 1959; Gallo, 1965), and in Spain (Benito Martinez, 1958). *Neotermes bosei* (Snyder) became a test organism in India (Sen-Sarma and Chatterjee, 1965). *Incisitermes minor* (Hagen) has long been used in the United States as a test species (Randall *et al.*, 1934; Ebeling and Pence, 1958).

Laboratory tests have been carried out with *Cryptotermes brevis* (Walker) in Puerto Rico (Wolcott, 1957) and in Spain (Benito Martinez, 1958) and with *C. havilandi* (Sjöstedt) in Nigeria (Butterworth *et al.*, 1966). *Cryptotermes dudleyi* Banks is bred for testing purposes in Berlin-Dahlem.

Among the Termopsidae, *Zootermopsis angusticollis* and *Z. nevadensis* served as laboratory species in the United States (Kofoid and Bowe, 1934), in Switzerland (Lüscher, 1951), and in Germany (Becker, 1961).

Of the Rhinotermitidae, species of the genera *Heterotermes*, *Reticulitermes*, and *Coptotermes* have been used for experiments. *Heterotermes indicola* (Wasmann), which is widely distributed and economically important in South-East Asia, is used regularly for test purposes in Berlin-Dahlem (Becker, 1962b, 1965d, 1966d,e) and Dehra Dun (Sen-Sarma, 1963).

Of the *Reticulitermes* species of North America, the following species have been employed: *R. flavipes* (Kollar) and *R. virginicus* (Banks) (Lund, 1957, 1958; Esenther, unpublished; Johnson, unpublished), and *R. hesperus* Banks (Kofoid, 1934; Ebeling and Pence, 1958). *Reticulitermes flavipes*, *R. hesperus*, and *R. tibialis* Banks are also used for laboratory testing in Berlin-Dahlem.

In Europe *R. flavipes*, which is established in Hamburg (Chapter 15), has frequently been used (Schmidt, 1960; Becker and Puchelt, 1961; Schultze-Dewitz, 1960a, 1961). *Reticulitermes lucifugus* (Rossi), occurring in South and West Europe, has been employed in several European countries (Becker, 1961; Ernst, 1957; Coudreau *et al.*, 1960; Hrdý, 1961b; Lüscher, 1951; Schmidt, 1953; Schultze-Dewitz, 1960b, 1961). *Reticulitermes lucifugus* var. *santonensis* Feytaud of the French Atlantic coast proved to be particularly aggressive (Coudreau *et al.*, 1960; Becker, 1961, 1965d, 1966e). *Reticulitermes clypeatus* Lash from southeastern Europe has been used for comparative purposes (Hrdý, 1961b). In Japan, *R. speratus* (Kolbe) is employed for laboratory testing (Shimizu, 1963).

Coptotermes acinaciformis (Froggatt) and *C. lacteus* (Froggatt) are regularly used in Australia (Gay *et al.*, 1955). In China (Budig, 1957) and in Czechoslovakia (Hrdý, 1966) tests are carried out with *C. formosanus* Shiraki. In Berlin-Dahlem *C. amanii* (Sjöstedt) from East Africa and *C. niger* Snyder from Central America serve for test purposes (Becker, 1966f).

Few Termitidae species have been used in the laboratory. *Microcerotermes edentatus* Wasmann was kept for a long time in Paris and would have been suitable for laboratory tests. *Microcerotermes beesoni* Snyder has been suggested for test purposes in India (Sen-Sarma and Chatterjee, 1965). Tests are planned in Berlin-Dahlem with *M. crassus* Snyder from Thailand and *M. fuscotibialis* (Sjöstedt) from West-Africa.

Odontotermes obesus (Rambur) has been employed in Kanpur (India). *Odontotermes transvaalensis* (Sjöstedt) has occasionally been used in Berlin-Dahlem (Becker, 1962a). *Nasutitermes exitiosus* (Hill) has long been employed in Australian laboratories (Holdaway, 1935; Gay *et al.*, 1955). *Nasutitermes ephratae* (Holmgren) from Central America has been cultured successfully and used as a test termite in Berlin-Dahlem (Becker, 1962a, 1963, 1966c). Recently some other *Nasutitermes* species have been bred in this laboratory.

Laboratory experience has so far been gained with less than 30 species. The number of species employed, however, has been constantly rising over the past years.

D. GROUP COMPOSITION

During the test, the groups of termites which serve as controls and are free from adverse test influences should remain sound and aggressive. The smaller the natural colonies are, the lower may be the number of individuals in the test groups. The ability to remain viable and aggressive in smaller groups is most pronounced in the Kalotermitidae and the Termopsidae, less so in the Termitidae. When the species are able to develop supplementary reproductives easily or relatively quickly, such as those of Kalotermitidae, *Zootermopsis, Heterotermes*, and *Reticulitermes* species, perfect colonies develop with regard to caste differentiation. Several authors assumed that only such still-functional communities are suitable for test purposes. The attack of wood, the test material, or a poisoning of the insects may, however, set in before the neotenics have been developed. Tests with *Coptotermes* and *Nasutitermes* species have revealed, on the other hand, that groups without sexually functional individuals may be kept alive for some months, as already mentioned, and can unhesitatingly be used as experimental groups.

In general, with increasing numbers of individuals in the test groups, there is a lower mortality rate and less of a weight loss due to water losses.

In certain tests a greater number of animals renders testing and evaluation more rigorous (Schultze-Dewitz, 1962; and others). Since repeated
attacks must be anticipated, large test groups are better suited to simulate
practical conditions. When Kalotermitidae are employed, however,
which usually live in small communities, tests with 100 or with even
10 animals in many cases do not yield divergent results.

Suitable and customary numbers for test groups are, e.g., 10, 25, or
100 individuals of the Kalotermitidae and *Zootermopsis*, 200—500
workers of species of the genera *Reticulitermes* and *Coptotermes* (with
Coptotermes as many as 6000—8000 individuals are used in Australia),
1000—3000 individuals of the *Heterotermes* species, and 1000—5000
animals of the *Nasutitermes* species. Generally speaking, we can distinguish between tests with small groups of 10—100 individuals, medium
groups of 100-1000 termites, and large groups of 1000—10,000 insects
(Gay *et al.*, 1955; Becker, 1962a; Hrdý, 1967).

The foregoing figures refer to pseudergates, larvae, and nymphs of the
Kalotermitidae and *Zootermopsis*, to workers and older larvae of the
Rhinotermitidae, and to workers of the Nasutitermitidae. The proportionate number of soldiers of the species concerned should then be
added. When some nymphs are added to *Heterotermes* or *Reticulitermes*
cultures, the development of supplementary reproductives is accelerated.

E. TESTING TECHNIQUES AND CONDITIONS

Tests can be carried out in two different ways. The termites are either
offered the choice of the material to be tested together with sufficient
food, or else the test material forms the only substance to feed on in a
compulsory feeding test. Selective feeding tests come nearer to natural
conditions, and results obtained may, in general, well be applied to practical conditions when the test arrangement is adapted to the living conditions of the respective termite species. A material that has been attacked
in a selective feeding test can safely be regarded as susceptible under
natural conditions. Compulsory feeding tests are, more or less, hunger
tests for the termites. These tests are only reasonable with those species
that are able to survive for some time without food. These tests, in which
the behavior of the insects can be observed in order to induce attack,
reveal whether or not a material can be damaged at all or how a poison
which the animals cannot evade acts.

Form and size of the containers in which tests are carried out depend
on the termite species used and the number of individuals employed.
Kalotermitidae, which can generally be kept without soil, may be cul-

tured in open or closed Petri dishes of glass or polystyrene with diameters of 5 – 10 cm. Tubes and other containers of the same materials may also be used for test purposes. Unlike imagoes, larvae, soldiers, and nymphs cannot climb up the walls of glass or polystyrene containers. The test method of culturing termites between two suitably spaced glass plates offers a distinct advantage: they may be observed without disturbance; however, the method will probably be suited only for special problems. Unless the containers can be placed in a conditioned room with constant, high humidities, hygrostat dishes (Fig. 8) are recommended; as it may be injurious to the termites to be kept on a metal fabric, termiteproof synthetic fabrics should be used.

Compulsory feeding tests with *Kalotermes flavicollis* (Gösswald, 1942, 1955, 1956) and with *Cryptotermes brevis* (Wolcott, 1943, 1947, 1953, 1957) have been carried out, permitting the insects to move freely in the dishes. In order to be able to recognize even superficial attack when it is restricted to small spots it is convenient to place glass rings, which are open on both sides, 1 cm in diameter and 1 cm high on the material to be tested (Becker, 1942a, 1950, 1952) (Fig. 9). Glass rings of this size can accommodate 10 kalotermitid individuals. Wider rings allow the use of larger groups. When tests are carried out to explore whether or not a material can be attacked at all, the escape reaction may be useful (Theden and Becker, 1961; Becker, 1962a). The glass rings are placed on the materials, leaving an opening on one side, which permits gnawing but prevents the termites from escaping (Fig. 9). In another arrangement (Gösswald and Kloft, 1959) the groups are not placed on the material but on plastic foils which are perforated; the diameters of the holes correspond to the head capsula of *Kalotermes* specimens and permit them to attack the material, especially textiles (Fig. 10).

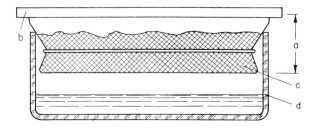

Fig. 8.   Hygrostat container or "Munich-dish" for keeping insects at a constant relative humidity above salt solution. (a) Height of test volume; (b) grooved cover; (c) glass jacket, the bottom of which is covered with wire gauze; (d) surface of water or salt solution.

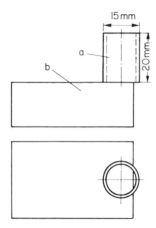

Fig. 9. Experimental arrangement for testing the resistance of material to termites by means of a compulsory method with Kalotermitidae (Becker, 1942a, 1950, 1962a). (a) glass cylinder; (b) test specimen.

In long-term tests Rhinotermitidae should be provided with soil to satisfy their building instinct. Termitidae should receive mound material or soil or both. Rhinotermitidae and Termitidae can also be cultured in larger petri dishes, *e.g., Reticulitermes* (Schmidt, 1960; Hrdý, 1961a). In France a test arrangement (Fig. 11) has been developed (Coudreau *et al.*, 1960) by which wood specimens can be tested for their natural durability and by which the effectiveness of a preservative can be determined using *Reticulitermes*. The termites can reach the wood specimens only by building soil gallery-runways.

Frequently cylindrical containers of plastic material or glass with a diameter of 9 cm and a height of 9 cm with a volume of approximately

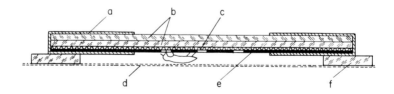

Fig. 10. Testing arrangement with metal/glass diapositive frame and perforated plastic foil (Gösswald and Kloft, 1959). (a) Metal frame; (b) small glass plates; (c) textile specimen; (d) gauze of the hygrostat dish; (e) perforated termite-resistant foil of plastics.

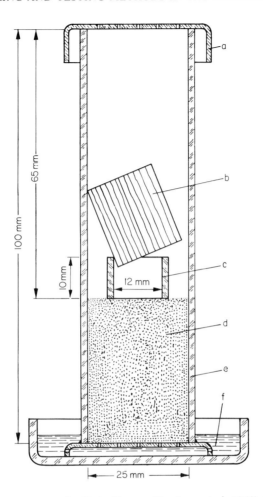

Fig. 11.   Testing arrangement for *Reticulitermes* (Condreau *et al.*, 1960). (a) Cover with fine holes; (b) wood specimen; (c) glass cylinder open at both ends; (d) humid sand; (e) glass tube with finely perforated bottom; (f) water.

600 cm³ have been used for Rhinotermitidae (Gay *et al.*, 1955; Lund, 1957, 1958; Becker, 1961, 1962b, 1966c) and for *Nasutitermes* (Gay *et al.*, 1955; Becker, 1963). The containers are partly filled with soil (Fig. 12). The test blocks may be buried in the soil or placed on it. The test may be a compulsory feeding one, or palatable wood may be added. The animals are thus not compelled to attack the test blocks because they are hungry.

Negative phototaxis, escape, and burial reactions were used also for *Reticulitermes*. Two proposed ways (Herfs, 1950) are to place textiles to be tested on soil into which the termites want to disappear or to wrap the fabric around plastic blocks. A modification of the glass ring method developed for *Kalotermes* has been used for tests with *Reticulitermes* (Hrdý, 1961a). For testing the natural resistance of timbers, sawdust has also been used (Schmidt, 1960; Sen-Sarma, 1963). During the test the relative humidity must be saturated for Rhinotermitidae and Termitidae, at least in that part of the container which is filled with soil. The animals must be in a position to cover their water requirements. Optimal values for the soil moisture have previously been mentioned. For dry-wood termites 97−98% relative humidity is most suitable. In case the test requires it, the termites may be kept at lower humidities for shorter periods.

The most favorable temperatures for tests are 25°−27°C for *Kalotermes flavicollis* and *Incisitermes minor*; 26°−30°C for *Cryptotermes*, *Heterotermes*, and *Coptotermes* species; 26°−28°C for *Reticulitermes* species; and 28°−30°C for *Microcerotermes* and *Nasutitermes* species. Investigators employed different temperatures for the same species or genus. In Australia, for example, 26° ± 0.5°C is used for *Coptotermes*, *Nasutitermes*, and *Mastotermes* species. Recommended temperatures for *Reticulitermes* species are 29°−30°C (Herfs, 1950); 30° ± 1°C (Lund, 1957, 1958); 28°C (Schmidt, 1953); 26°C (Becker, 1952, 1961; Schultze-Dewitz, 1960a,b; Hrdý, 1961b); and 23° ± 2°C (Association Française de Normalisation, 1955).

As the figures above show, 26°C would be a suitable temperature for all species with the exception of the genus *Zootermopsis* and should be considered when a standard temperature is chosen. A room conditioned to 26°C is, moreover, advantageous as work can be more easily carried out at this temperature than at higher temperatures.

F. OBSERVATION, RECORDING, AND EVALUATION

Observations can be made daily or after defined periods. Daily observations are necessary when the mortality rate of the insects under toxic influences is to be determined. They are necessary if it is desirable to know when the gnawing activity begins. During the testing, however, the

Fig. 12. A: Scheme for testing arrangement for Rhinotermitidae and Termitidae (Gay *et al.*, 1955; Becker, 1961, 1962c). B−D: Containers with *Heterotermes indicola*. B: From the side; C: Perforated lid with galleries or tubes; D: Bottom with runways in the soil. (a) Glass or plastic jar with perforated cover; (b) specimen of wood; (c) sand, soil or nest material. See pages 377 and 378.

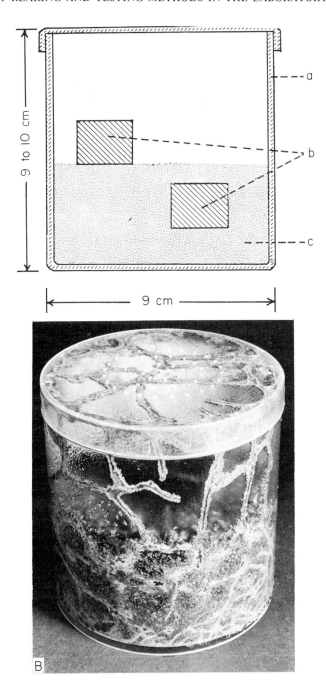

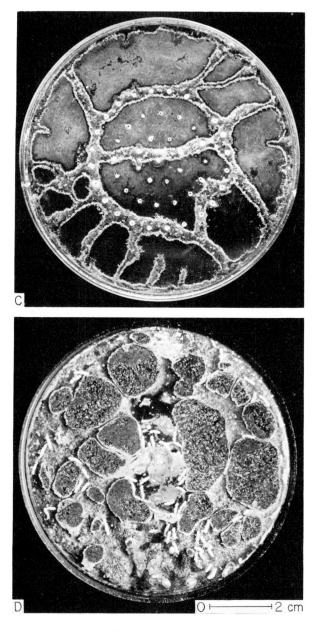

Fig. 12 (Continued)

termites should be disturbed as little as possible. The most suitable test period, 2, 4, 8, or 12 weeks, depends on the kind of test, on the material to be tested, and on the species employed.

After defined periods, essential statements can be made about the attack or rate of deterioration of the specimens by observation and description, by taking photos, and by measuring, planimetering, or weighing. When the weight of the samples of the material cannot be determined, due to the properties of the material, after kilndrying before and after the test, the specimens must be brought to constant equilibrium weight in a conditioning room.

In addition to unprotected material specimens, specimens with certain retentions of one or several preservatives with known toxicity effects should be used to determine the aggressiveness of the experimental termites. When the natural durability of wood species is to be explored, timbers of medium durability should be used in addition to others which are highly susceptible. The use of other materials for comparative purposes is also recommended.

The influence of climatic conditions on property changes of the test material, the aging effects, must be borne in mind when such tests are carried out and evaluated. Suitable simulation of the aging effects is necessary before final laboratory testing.

The evaluation and classification of a material depends on its use. When subterranean cables or those which are in contact with the ground show gnawing marks in the laboratory, it is an alarming sign, since the number of animals attacking under natural conditions may be extremely high. Superficial attack, which may be observed when preservatives which have no repellent effects are used, may be differently judged under practical conditions (Harris, 1956b). The killing of many animals under toxic influences may not necessarily have the same effects in big colonies, and deterioration may proceed slowly. Where termite attack is not very likely, the resistance of a material must be rated differently than in places where the occurrence of termites can be regarded as certain.

REFERENCES

Adamson, A. M. (1941). Laboratory technique for the study of living termites. *Ecology* 22, 411-414.

Association Française de Normalisation. (1955). Essai de résistance des matériaux aux termites. Essai des produits de protection contre ces insectes. Pr X 41-505.

Becker, G. (1942a). Der Einfluss verschiedener Versuchsbedingungen bei der "Termitenprüfung" von Holzschutzmitteln unter Verwendung von *Calotermes flavicollis* als Versuchstier. *Wiss. Abhandl. Deut. Materialpruefungsanstalt.* [2] 3, 55-66.

Becker, G. (1942b). Prüfung von Textilien auf "Termitenfestigkeit". *Melliand Textilber.* **23**, 523-527 and 573-577.

Becker, G. (1948). Über Kastenbildung und Umwelteinfluss bei Termiten. *Biol. Zentr.* **67**, 407-444.

Becker, G. (1950). Prüfung der "Tropeneignung" von Holzschutzmitteln gegen Termiten. *Wiss. Abhandl. Deut. Materialpruefungsanstalt.* [2] **7**, 62-76.

Becker, G. (1952). Untersuchungen über die Schutzwirkung von Pentachlorphenol gegen holzzerstörende Insekten. *Holz Roh- Werkstoff* **10**, 341-352.

Becker, G. (1953). Einige Beobachtungen über holzzerstörende Insekten (Termiten und Kafer) in Guatemala. *Z. Angew. Entomol.* **35**, 339-373.

Becker, G. (1960). Biologische Untersuchungen an Textilien. *In* "Handbuch der Werkstoffprüfung". 2nd ed., Vol. V, pp. 971-1007, Springer, Berlin.

Becker, G. (1961). Beiträge zur Prüfung und Beurteilung der natürlichen Dauerhaftigkeit von Holz gegen Termiten. *Holz Roh- Werkstoff* **19**, 278-290.

Becker, G. (1962a). Allgemeines über die Laboratoriumsprüfung der Beständigkeit von Werkstoffen und der Wirksamkeit von Schutzmitteln gegen Termiten. *Materialpruefung* **4**, 215-221.

Becker, G. (1962b). Laboratoriumsprüfung von Holz und Holzschutzmitteln mit der südasiatischen Termite *Heterotermes indicola* Wasmann. *Holz Roh- Werkstoff* **20**, 476-486.

Becker, G. (1962c). Beobachtungen über einige Termiten-Arten in Indien. *Z. Angew. Entomol.* **50**, 359-379.

Becker, G. (1963). Widerstandsfähigkeit von Kunststoffen gegen Termiten. *Materialpruefung* **5**, 218-232.

Becker, G. (1965a). Feuchtigkeitseinfluss auf Nahrungswahl und -verbrauch einiger Termiten-Arten. *Insectes Sociaux* **12**, 151-184.

Becker, G. (1965b). Die Haltung von Termiten im Laboratorium. *Z. Angew. Zool.* **52**, 385-398.

Becker, G. (1965c). Versuche über den Einfluss von Braunfäulepilzen auf Wahl und Ausnutzung der Holznahrung durch Termiten. *Mater. Organismen* **1**, 95-156.

Becker, G. (1965d). Prüfung der Wirksamkeit synthetischer Kontaktinsektizide auf vier Termiten-Arten. *Holz Roh- Werkstoff* **23**, 469-478.

Becker, G. (1966a). Einflüsse physikalischer Faktoren auf Termiten. *Mater. Organismen* **1**, 415-425.

Becker, G. (1966b). Über Beziehungen zwischen Tieren und Mikroorganismen im Holz. *Mater. Organismen* **1**, 481-496.

Becker, G. (1966c). Termiten-abschreckende Wirkung von Kiefernholz. *Holz Roh-Werkstoff* **24**, 429-432.

Becker, G. (1966d). Laboratory testing methods with termites in Berlin-Dahlem. *Proc. 2nd Workshop Termite Res., Biloxi, Miss., 1965*, pp. 67-70.

Becker, G. (1966e). Prüfung der Wirksamkeit wasserlöslicher Holzschutzmittel auf drei Termiten-Arten. *Materialpruefung* **8**, 445-454.

Becker, G. (1966f). Einige Beobachtungen und Versuchsergebnisse an Zuchten von *Coptotermes*-Arten (Isopt.) im Laboratorium. *Z. Angew. Zool.* **53**, 463-479.

Becker, G. (1967). Die Temperatur-Abhängigkeit der Frasstätigkeit einiger Termitenarten. *Z. Angew. Entomol.* **60**, 97-123.

Becker, G., and Kerner-Gang, W. (1964). Schädigung und Förderung von Termiten durch Schimmelpilze. *Z. Angew. Entomol.* **53**, 429-448.

Becker, G., and Puchelt, D. (1961). Grundlagenversuche für Laboratoriumsprüfungen mit zwei *Reticulitermes*-Arten. *Holzforsch. Holzverwert.* **13**, 110-117.

Becker, G., and Seifert, K. (1962). Über die chemische Zusammensetzung des Nest- und Galeriematerials von Termiten. *Insectes Sociaux* 9, 273-289.

Benito Martínez, J. (1958). Los termes en España. Biologia, daños y métodos para combatir la especia subterránea *Reticulitermes lucifugus*. *Serv. Plagas For.* B 29.

Buchli, H. (1952). *Antennopsis gallica*, a new parasite on termites. *Trans. 9th Intern. Congr. Entomol., Amsterdam, 1951* Vol. 1. pp. 519-524.

Buchli, H. (1956). Die Neotenie bei *Reticulitermes*. *Insectes Sociaux* 3, 131-143.

Buchli, H. (1958). L'origine des castes et les potentialités ontogéniques des termites européens du genre *Reticulitermes* Holmgren. *Ann. Sci. Nat. Zool. Biol. Animale* [11] 20, 261-429.

Buchli, H. (1960). L'effet du champignon parasite *Antennopsis gallica* sur les jeunes colonies de termites. *Compt. Rend.* 250, 1320-1321.

Budig, P. K. (1957). Ermittlungen und Untersuchungen zur Frage der Termitenfestigkeit. *Deut. Elektrotech.* 1, 265-268.

Butterworth, D., Kay, D., and MacNulty, D. (1966). Testing materials for termite resistance. Part 4. The resistance of some Nigerian timbers to *Cryptotermes havilandi* (Sjöst.). *Mater. Organismen* 1, 257-269.

Castle, G. B. (1934). The damp-wood termites of western United States, genus *Zootermopsis* (formerly *Termopsis*). *In* "Termites and Termite Control" (C. A. Kofoid, ed.), 2nd ed., pp. 273-310. Univ. of California Press, Berkeley, California.

Coudreau, J., Fougerousse, M., Bressy, O., and Lucas, S. (1960). Recherches en vue de déterminer une nouvelle méthode destinée à apprécier la résistance d'un bois aux destructions causées par les termites (*Reticulitermes lucifugus* Rossi). *Holzforschung* 14, 40-51.

Deutscher Normenausschuss. (1941). Prüfung von Holzschutzmitteln. Bestimmung der Auslaugbarkeit. DIN 52 176.

Deutscher Normenausschuss. (1961). Werkstoff-, Bauelemente- und Geräteprüfung. Klimabeanspruchung. Allgemeines, Begriffe. DIN 50 010.

Deutscher Normenausschuss. (1963). Prüfung von Textilien. Bestimmung der Widerstandsfähigkeit von Textilien gegen Schädigungen durch Mikroorganismen. Allgemeines und Probenvorbehandlung. DIN 53 930.

Ebeling, W., and Pence, R. J. (1958). Laboratory evaluation of insecticide-treated soils against the western subterranean termite. *J. Econ. Entomol.* 51, 207-211.

Ernst, E. (1957). Der Einfluss der Luftfeuchtigkeit auf Lebensdauer und Verhalten verschiedener Termitenarten. *Acta Trop.* 14, 97-156.

Esenther, G. R., Allen, T. C., Casida, J. E., and Shenefelt, R. D. (1961). Termite attractant from fungus-infected wood. *Science* 134, 50.

Gallo, F. (1965). *Tyrolichus casei* (Ouds.) nuovo parassita delle termiti. *Boll. 1st. Patol. Libro "Alfonso Gallo" (Rome)* 14, 134-142.

Gay, F. J., Greaves, T., Holdaway, F. G., and Wetherly, A. H. (1955). Standard laboratory colonies of termites for evaluating the resistance of timber, timber preservatives, and other materials to termite attack. *Australia, Commonwealth Sci. Ind. Res. Organ., Bull.* 277, 60.

Gösswald, K. (1942). Methoden der Untersuchungen von Termitenbekämpfungsmitteln. A. Prüfung von Materialien auf Termitenfestigkeit. *Kolonialforstl. Mitt.* 5, 343-377.

Gösswald, K. (1943). Richtlinien zur Zucht von Termiten. *Z. Angew. Entomol.* 30, 297-316.

Gösswald, K. (1950). Methoden der Prüfung von Textilien auf Termitenfestigkeit im fabrikneuen und im Gebrauchszustand. *Z. Angew. Entomol.* 31, 99-134.

Gösswald, K. (1955). Die Gelbhalstermite (*Calotermes flavicollis* Fabr.) als Versuchstier. *In* "Die Termiten" (H. Schmidt, ed.), pp. 165-192. Akad. Verlagsges., Leipzig.

Gösswald, K. (1956). Laboratory testing of termite resistance with the yellow necked termite *Calotermes flavicollis* Fabr. *Composite Wood (India)* 3, 65-70.

Gösswald, K., and Kloft, W. (1959). Zur Laboratoriumsprüfung auf Termitenfestigkeit mit *Kalotermes flavicollis* Fabr. *Entomol. Exptl. Appl.* 2, 268-278.

Grassé, P.-P. (1949). Ordre des Isoptères ou Termites. *In* "Traité de Zoologie" (P.-P. Grassé, ed.), Vol. IX, pp. 408-544. Masson, Paris.

Grassé, P.-P. and Noirot, C. (1958). La société de *Calotermes flavicollis* (insecte Isoptère), de sa fondation au premier essaimage. *Compt. Rend.* 246, 1789-1795.

Grassé, P.-P., and Noirot, C. (1960). L'isolement chez le Termite à cou jaune (*Calotermes flavicollis* Fab.) et ses conséquences. *Insectes Sociaux* 7, 323-331.

Harris, W. V. (1956a). Termites destructive to timber. *Rec. Brit. Wood Pres. Assoc., Rec. Ann. Conv. 1956*, pp. 145-157.

Harris, W. V. (1956b). Field tests for termite resistance. *Colonial Build. Notes, Dept. Sci. Ind. Res.* No. 39, 1-3.

Harris, W. V. (1958). Colony formation in the Isoptera. *Proc. 10th Intern. Congr. Entomol., Montreal, 1956* Vol. 1, pp. 435-439.

Harris, W. V. (1961). "Termites. Their Recognition and Control." Longmans, Green, London.

Hepburn, G. A. (1954). A new laboratory method for observing *Cryptotermes brevis* Walker. *J. Entomol. Soc. S. Africa* 17, 219-221.

Herfs, A. (1950). "Die Termitenstation der Farbenfabriken Bayer in Leverkusen." Leverkusen, 47.

Hickin, N. E. (1961). Maintenance of termite colonies in England for research purposes. *Pest Technol.* 3, 84-86.

Holdaway, F. G. (1935). Standard laboratory colonies of *Eutermes exitiosus* Hill for timber testing under controlled conditions. *J. Australian Inst. Agr. Sci.* 1, 34-35.

Hrdý, I. (1961a). A quick laboratory method of determining the termite resistance of materials (Isoptera). *Beitr. Entomol.* 11, 546-556.

Hrdý, I. (1961b). Zur Frage der natürlichen Dauerhaftigkeit einiger Hölzer aus China gegen Termiten (Isoptera). *Beitr. Entomol.* 11, 557-565.

Hrdý, I. (1963). Odolnost impregnovaných drevovláknitých desek proti termitum v laboratornich a terénních pokusech. (The resistance of wood-fibre boards impregnated against termites in laboratory and field tests.) *Zool. Listy* 12, 75-85.

Hrdý, I. (1964). Laboratory methods for testing the resistance of materials against termites. Review of the results of testing wood, impregnating agents and plastics. *Rozpravy Cesk. Akad. Ved.* 74, No. 11, 1-147.

Hrdý, I. (1966). Beitrag zur Bionomie von *Coptotermes formosanus*, Laboratoriumszucht und Verwendbarkeit dieser Art für die Prüfung der Termitenfestigkeit von Material. *Mater. Organismen* 1, 427-436.

Hrdý, I. (1967). Testing termite resistance of woods. *Rec. Brit. Wood Pres. Assoc.* pp. 113-118.

Hdrý, I., and Hdrá, J. (1960). (Die Wirkung von DDT und γ-HCH im Vergleich auf die Termiten *Kalotermes flavicollis* (Fabricius) und *Reticulitermes lucifugus* (Rossi). 2. Mitt. Beitrag zur Untersuchung der Widerstandsfähigkeit des Materials gegen Schadinsekten.) *Zool. Listy* 9, 209-215.

Kofoid, C. A., ed. (1934). "Termites and Termite Control," 2nd ed. Univ. of California Press, Berkeley, California.

Kofoid, C. A., and Bowe, E. E. (1934). Biological tests of treated and untreated woods. *In* "Termites and Termite Control" (C. A. Kofoid, ed.), 2nd Ed. pp. 517-544. Univ. of California Press, Berkeley, California.

Kovoor, J. (1964). Modifications chimiques provoquées par un termitidé (*Microcerotermes edentatus*, Was.) dans du bois de peuplier sain ou partiellement dégradé par des champignons. *Bull. Biol. France Belg.* **98**, 491-510.

Light, S. F. (1942-1943). The determination of the castes of social insects. *Quart. Rev. Biol.* **17**, 312-326; **18**, 46-63.

Light, S. F., and Illg, P. L. (1945). Rate and extent of development of neotenic reproductives in groups of nymphs of the termite genus *Zootermopsis*. *Univ. Calif. (Berkeley) Publ. Zool.* **53**, 1-40.

Light, S. F., and Weesner, F. M. (1947). Methods for culturing termites. *Science* **106**, 131.

Light, S. F., and Weesner, F. M. (1951). Further studies on the production of supplementary reproductives in *Zootermopsis* (Isoptera). *J. Exptl. Zool.* **117**, 397-414.

Lund, A. E. (1957). An accelerated wood-preservative termite study. *Forest Prod. J.* **7**, 363-367.

Lund, A. E. (1958). The relationship of subterranean termite attack to varying retentions of water-borne preservatives. *Proc. Am. Wood-Preservers Assoc.* **54**, 44-52.

Lund, A. E. (1959). Subterranean termites and fungi. Mutualism or environmental association. *Forest Prod. J.* **9**, 320-321.

Lund, A. E. (1962). Subterraneans and their environment. New concepts of termite ecology. *Pest Control* **30**, 30-34, 36, 60, and 61.

Lund, A. E. (1966). Subterranean termites and fungal-bacterial relationships. *Mater. Organismen* **1**, 497-502.

Lund, A. E., and Engelhardt, N. T. (1962). Subterranean termites and *Absidia coerulea* Bainier (Mucorales). *J. Insect Pathol.* **4**, 131-132.

Lüscher, M. (1949). Continuous observation of termites in laboratory cultures. *Acta Trop.* **6**, 161-165.

Lüscher, M. (1951). Termiten und Holzschutz gegen Termiten. *Holzforschung* **5**, 10-12.

Lüscher, M. (1956). Die Entstehung von Ersatzgeschlechtstieren bei der Termite *Kalotermes flavicollis* Fabr. *Insectes Sociaux* **3**, 119-128.

Lüscher, M. (1961). Air-conditioned termite nests. *Sci. Am.* **205**, 138-145.

McMahan, E. A. (1961). Laboratory studies of *Cryptotermes brevis* (Walker) Isoptera: Kalotermitidae) with special reference to colony development and behavior. *Dissertation Abstr.* **21**, 2414 (abstr.).

McMahan, E. A. (1962). Laboratory studies of colony establishment and development of *Cryptotermes brevis* (Walker) (Isoptera: Kalotermitidae). *Proc. Hawaiian Entomol. Soc.* **18**, 145-153.

Noirot, C. (1956). Les sexués de remplacement chez les termites supérieurs (Termitidae). *Insectes Sociaux* **3**, 145-158.

Osmun, J. V. (1957). Three entomological laboratory techniques. I. Rearing method for subterranean termites. *Proc. Indiana Acad. Sci.* **66**, 141-143.

Pence, R. J. (1957). The prolonged maintenance of the western subterranean termite in the laboratory with moisture gradient tubes. *J. Econ. Entomol.* **50**, 238-240.

Randall, M., Herms, W. B., and Doody, T. C. (1934). The toxicity of chemicals to termites. *In* "Termites and Termite Control" (C. A. Kofoid, ed.), 2nd ed., pp. 368-384. Univ. of California Press, Berkeley, California.

Rescia, G. (1959). II. Osservazioni sulla tossicitá dei tre isomeri alfa, beta, gamma dell'esaclorocicloesano verso il *Calotermes flavicollis* Fabricius. *Boll. 1st. Patol. Libro "Alfonso Gallo" (Rome)* **18**, 126-142.

Ruppli, E., and Lüscher, M. (1964). Die Elimination überzähliger Ersatzgeschlechtstiere bei der Termite *Kalotermes flavicollis* (Fabr.). *Rev. Suisse Zool.* **71**, 626-632.

Schmidt, H. (1953). Studien an Holzwerkstoffen in der "Termitenprüfung." Erste Mitteilung: Eigenschaften und Bewertung der Versuchstermiten (*Reticulitermes*). *Holz Roh-Werkstoff* 11, 385-388.

Schmidt, H. (1960). Ein Termiten-Test an Sägespänen verschiedener Holzarten. *Holz Roh-Werkstoff* 18, 59-63.

Schultze-Dewitz, G. (1960a). Form und Intensität des Termitenangriffs an Hölzern verschiedener Struktur und Rohdichte. 1. Mitt. Prüfungen an getrenntem Früh- und Spätholz. 2. Mitt. Prüfungen von Hölzern mit verschiedener Jahrringbreite und verschiedenem Spätholzanteil. 3. Mitt. Einfluss der Rohdichte des Holzes auf den Termitenangriff. *Holz Roh- Werkstoff* 18, 365-367, 413-415, and 445-446.

Schultze-Dewitz, G. (1960b). Vergleichende Untersuchungen der natürlichen Frassresistenz einiger fremdländischer Kernholzarten unter Verwendung von *Reticulitermes lucifugus* Rossi als Versuchstier. *Holzforsch. Holzverwert.* 12, 64-68.

Schultze-Dewitz, G. (1961). Untersuchungen über Unterschiede in der Frassleistung bei *Reticulitermes lucifugus* Rossi und *Reticulitermes flavipes* Kollar. *Holzforsch. Holzverwert.* 13, 29-31.

Schultze-Dewitz, G. (1962). Abhängigkeit des Versuchsergebnisses bei der Termitenprüfung von der Grösse der Prüfgemeinschaft. *Symp. Genet. Biol. Ital.* 11, 24-31.

Sen-Sarma, P. K. (1963). Studies on the natural resistance of timbers to termites. I. Observations on the longevity of the test termite, *Heterotermes indicola* (Wasm.), in the sawdust from forty common Indian timbers. II. Preliminary results of accelerated laboratory tests of 37 common Indian timbers against *Heterotermes indicola* (Wasm.). *Indian Forest Entomol. Bull.* [N.S.] 220.

Sen-Sarma, P. K., and Chatterjee, P. N. (1965). Studies on the natural resistance of timbers to termite attack. IV. Qualitative and quantitative estimations of resistance of sixteen species of Indian timbers against *Neotermes bosei* Snyder (Isoptera: Kalotermitidae) based on laboratory tests. *Indian Forester* 91, 805-813.

Shimizu, K. (1963). Studies on the caste differentiation in termites. III. Emergence of soldiers and supplementary reproductives of the Japanese termite, *Leucotermes (Reticulitermes) speratus* (Kolbe). *Japan. J. Appl. Entomol. Zool.* 7, 207-213.

Skaife, S. H. (1957). The Durban dry-wood termite *Kalotermes durbanensis* Haviland. *J. Entomol. Soc. S. Africa* 20, 373-390.

Smythe, R. V., and Coppel, H. C. (1965). The susceptibility of *Reticulitermes flavipes* (Kollar) and other termite species to an experimental preparation of *Bacillus thuringiensis* Berliner. *J. Invertebrate Pathol.* 7, 423-426.

Smythe, R. V., and Coppel, H. C. (1966). Pathogenicity of externally occurring fungi to *Reticulitermes flavipes*. *J. Invertebrate Pathol.* 8, 266-267.

Theden, G., and Becker, G. (1961). Kunststoffe, Prüfung auf Verhalten gegen Organismen. In "Kunststoffe, Struktur, physikalisches Verhalten und Prüfung," (R. Nitsche and K. A. Wolf, eds.), Vol. 2, pp. 376-409. Springer, Berlin.

Weesner, F. M. (1956). The biology of colony foundation in *Reticulitermes hesperus* Banks. *Univ. Calif. (Berkeley) Publ. Zool.* 61, 253-313.

Weidner, H. (1954). Die Bodentermite *Reticulitermes*, eine ernste Gefahr für die Gebäude in Hamburg. *Verhandl. Deut. Ges. Angew. Entomol.* 12, 55-61.

Weiser, J., and Hrdy, I. (1962). *Pyemotes*—mites as parasites of termites. *Z. Angew. Entomol.* 1, 94-97.

Wilkinson, W. (1962). Dispersal of alates and establishment of new colonies in *Cryptotermes havilandi* (Sjöstedt) (Isoptera, Kalotermitidae). *Bull. Entomol. Res.* 53, 265-286.

Williams, O. L., and Kofoid, C. A. (1934). Tests on wallboards and insulating materials. *In* "Termites and Termite Control" (C. A. Kofoid, ed.), 2nd ed., pp. 574-576. Univ. of California Press, Berkeley, California.

Wolcott, G. N. (1943). How to make wood unpalatable to the West Indian dry-wood termite, *Cryptotermes brevis* Walker. *Caribbean Forester* **4**, 145-147.

Wolcott, G. N. (1947). The permanence of termite repellents. *J. Econ. Entomol.* **40**, 124-129.

Wolcott, G. N. (1953). Termite repellent wood extractives. *J. Agr. Univ. Puerto Rico* **37**, 224-227.

Wolcott, G. N. (1957). Inherent natural resistance of woods to the attack of the West Indian dry-wood termite, *Cryptotermes brevis* Walker. *J. Agr. Univ. Puerto Rico* **41**, 259-311.

12

Feeding Relationships and Radioisotope Techniques

ELIZABETH A. MCMAHAN

I. INTRODUCTION

The normally functioning termite colony is a prime example of a homeostatically regulated, self-stabilizing system (Emerson, 1956, 1959, 1962). Its maintenance of optimal conditions of existence and reproduction rests on efficient social integration and division of labor. Among the chief homeostatic and integrative mechanisms of social insect colonies generally is the mutual exchange of nutrients between colony members. Réaumur noted the passing of food from adults to young in the social wasps as early as 1742, and later investigators described the passing of liquids in the opposite direction as well. Brian and Brian (1952) discuss the history of the concept of mutualistic feeding, from the theory of "oecotrophobiosis" championed by Roubaud (1908, 1910, 1916), who emphasized the role of larval secretions in promoting tending by adults, to Wheeler's (1928) enlargement of his own concept of "trophallaxis" to include tactile and chemical stimulation in addition to the transfer of food.

A. FUNCTIONS OF TROPHALLAXIS AMONG SOCIAL INSECTS

Trophallaxis permits efficient use of nutrients, recognition of colony mates (Emerson, 1929), interindividual communication (Ribbands, 1952,

1953, 1964), distribution of pheromones involved in caste differentiation (Pickens, 1932; Light, 1942–1943, 1944; Miller, 1942; Lüscher, 1955, 1958, 1960, 1961, 1962, 1964; Karlson and Butenandt, 1959; Butler, 1963; Wilson, 1965) and in caste elimination (Lüscher, 1958), and transfer of cellulose-digesting protozoans in termite families harboring them (Grassé and Noirot, 1945). It undoubtedly plays an important role in the phenomenon called the "group effect" (Grassé and Chauvin, 1944; Grassé, 1946; Buchli, 1958), which leads to greater working efficiency, greater longevity, and greater vigor of social insects in groups as opposed to individuals in isolation. Harris and Sands (1965) have summarized the role of trophallaxis in colony organization. The aspect of trophallaxis with which this chapter is chiefly concerned is food exchange.

B. Methods of Food Exchange among Termites

There are two methods by which termites exchange food: *stomodeal* and *proctodeal*. The stomodeal method is reported to occur in all families of termites and the proctodeal in all except the Termitidae. Grassé (1949) and Grassé and Noirot (1945) have described these processes. In stomodeal feeding the soliciting termite caresses with its antennae the head of the prospective donor or taps with its mandibles against the buccal region of the donor. This activity provokes a degorgement reflex resulting in the appearance of a droplet of fluid, which is passed from the donor's mouth to the recipient's (Fig. 1). Grassé describes stomodeal food as being of two types. Sometimes it is a clear fluid, which may be a little opalescent and viscous. This appears to be pure saliva secreted by the salivary glands and stored temporarily in the salivary reservoirs.

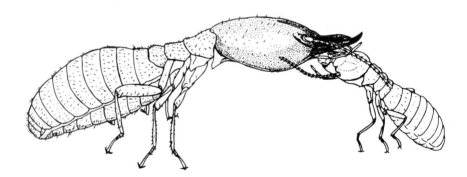

Fig. 1.   Little worker of *Bellicositermes natalensis* (Haviland) giving stomodeal food to a large soldier (Grassé, 1949).

struction of insect pests (for recent summaries and references, see Lindquist, 1958; Grosch, 1962; Jenkins, 1963; "Radioisotopes and Ionizing Radiations in Entomology," 1963; O'Brien and Wolfe, 1964).

Radioisotope studies of food transfer within colonies of social insects are still relatively new, but, while much of their contribution so far has been to confirm earlier findings, they have also expanded knowledge of food exchange behavior and give promise of continued usefulness. Part of their attractiveness to investigators of termite behavior lies in their potentiality for permitting the collection of quantifiable data under conditions that are nearly normal for these insects, whose cryptic mode of life makes direct observation difficult.

Most of the applications of radioisotopes to social insect behavior have involved the Hymenoptera: bees (Nixon and Ribbands, 1952; Oertel *et al.*, 1953; Courtois and Lecompte, 1958; Gösswald and Kloft, 1958a, 1961); ants (Wilson and Eisner, 1957; Gösswald and Kloft, 1958b, 1960, 1963; Berwig, 1959; Kannowski, 1959; Beck, 1961; Stumper, 1961; Chauvin and his colleagues, 1961; Chauvin and Lecompte, 1964, 1965, 1966; Mortreuil and Brader, 1962; Courtois and Lecompte, 1962; Naarmann, 1963); and wasps (Montagner, 1963a,b; Montagner and Courtois, 1963; Morimoto, 1960). This chapter, of course, will be concerned primarily with the application of radioisotopes to studies of termite feeding behavior (Gösswald, 1962; Gösswald and Kloft, 1958a, 1961, 1963; Alibert, 1959, 1960, 1963; McMahan, 1960, 1963, 1966). Like many other studies of termite behavior, these concern chiefly members of the so-called lower families, especially those of the Kalotermitidae. Greater ease in laboratory rearing and maintenance of the dry-wood species is, of course, the primary explanation. Except for Alibert's investigation (1963) of food exchange in the nest of *Cubitermes fungifaber* (Sjöstedt) (Termitidae), tests carried out up to 1967 have involved only *Kalotermes flavicollis* (Fabricius) and *Cryptotermes brevis*. The tests have been designed to answer questions such as the following: What are the feeding capabilities of different castes and instars? To what extent do all colony members participate in food exchange? Are consistent, detectable food-transfer patterns based on caste or instar? What is the rate of food distribution throughout the colony? Do members of different colonies or even of different species exchange food? The radioisotope tracer technique lends itself well to such feeding studies.

In all these studies an appropriate food source was impregnated with a nuclide and exposed to colony members for ingestion. It was subsequently traced by means of appropriate radiation detection instruments through its history of transferal.

A. Problems Involved

In addition to the requirement of relatively specialized and expensive equipment for radiation detection and the safety problems inherent in handling radioisotopes, there are certain other considerations that should be kept in mind by the investigator who wants to use nuclides to study feeding behavior.

1. Selection of Nuclides

The selection of a nuclide for use in a biological study usually depends upon a favorable combination of half-life, energy characteristics, and the need for an inert or for a metabolically active element. Other factors to be considered are safety, availability, ease of application and detection, and damage to the experimental animal (see O'Brien and Wolfe, 1964). Experimental studies designed specifically to determine which radioisotopes are best to use are mostly lacking.

Both beta and gamma emitters have been tried in social insect feeding studies. The beta nuclides have included P^{32} (Nixon and Ribbands, 1952; Gösswald and Kloft, 1958a,b, 1959, 1961; Alibert, 1959, 1960, 1963; Kannowski, 1959; Berwig, 1959; Morimoto, 1960; Beck, 1961; Stumper, 1961; Mortreuil and Brader, 1962; Naarman, 1963), C^{14} (Oertel et al., 1953), and Au^{198} (Courtois and Lecompte, 1958, 1962; Montagner, 1963a,b; Montagner and Courtois, 1963; Alibert, 1965; Chauvin and Lecompte, 1966). Gamma nuclides have included I^{131} (Wilson and Eisner, 1957; Gösswald and Kloft, 1963; Sen-Sarma and Kloft, 1965), Co^{57} (McMahan, 1963, 1966), and Sr^{85} (McMahan, 1963). Table I gives the characteristics of these nuclides. A chief advantage of gamma emitters lies in the fact that intact insects can be measured for radioactivity without the necessity of data correction for absorption of radiation by the insect's body (see Kloft, 1962).

Nuclides vary in their rates and means of elimination from the experimental animal. The effective half-life of a nuclide in a biological system depends both on its radioactive half-life and on its biological half-life, which reflects its metabolic activity. It may vary with the developmental stage of the organism, as Crossley (1963) has found with the beetle *Chrysomela knabi*. McMahan (1963) found in a study of isotope loss that *Cryptotermes brevis* nymphs which had fed on Sr^{85}-labeled wood lost an average of 45% of their originally acquired radioactivity in 2 days, while nymphs which had fed on Co^{57}-labeled wood lost less than 15% of theirs in the same interval. Most of the Sr^{85} loss was via fecal pellets, but a much smaller portion of the Co^{57} was lost in this way. Dissections of radioactive termites and measurement of radioactivity of isolated

TABLE I

CHARACTERISTICS OF RADIOISOTOPES[a] USED IN STUDIES OF
FEEDING BEHAVIOR OF SOCIAL INSECTS

Nuclide	Radiation (Mev)	Half-life
Au^{198}	β 0.97; γ 0.411	2.69 days
C^{14}	β 0.155	5568 years
Co^{57}	β 0.26; γ 0.014 − 0.131	270 days
I^{131}	β 0.33, 0.60, 0.15, 0.81; γ 0.080 − 0.720	8.08 days
P^{32}	β 1.712	14.30 days
Sr^{85}	γ 0.013 − 0.513	65 days

[a] From Comar (1955).

structures and regions showed that Sr^{85} tended to be concentrated chiefly in the Malpighian tubules and that Co^{57} was located chiefly in the hindgut. Both nuclides, but especially Co^{57}, appeared to be concentrated by the protozoans. Percentage of loss to other termites through proctodeal feeding was about the same for both nuclides: 7% and 5%, respectively, for large donors.

Nuclides may be excreted through the cuticle in addition to their loss via the digestive tract (see below). In drawing conclusions from feeding studies using different radioisotopes, then, one must take into account the nuclides used and their metabolic·behavior.

2. Acquisition of Radioactivity by Other than Stomodeal or Proctodeal Feeding

The acquisition of radioactivity by a termite exposed to another termite possessing radioactive gut contents cannot be interpreted as involving exclusively stomodeal or proctodeal food transfer unless experimental design permits it. P^{32}, for example, may be excreted through the cuticle of an insect which has ingested radioactive food (Berwig, 1959) and may, therefore, become available to colony mates via grooming or other contact. Similarly, if colony members ingest fecal material deposited within the nest, radioactivity may be acquired without the necessity of direct food exchange or even contact between individuals.

External contamination of body surfaces from radioisotope-impregnated food may also occur, to be passed along to colony mates through grooming. Alibert (1959) and Gösswald and Kloft (1958a, 1959) bypassed this danger by covering the radioactive filter paper, used as food, with plastic screens and allowing their termites to feed only through small holes (see Fig. 3).

Fig. 3. Method of exposing *Kalotermes flavicollis* to radioactive food (P³²) while avoiding outer contamination. (a) Glass base; (b) filter paper saturated with a radioactive phosphate solution; (c) termite-proof foil with holes; (d) glass ring for confining the test insect on the test piece (Gösswald and Kloft, 1958a).

3. Interpreting Variability in Acquisition of Radioactivity

Termites differ in the volume of their digestive tracts (Holmgren, 1909; Katzin and Kirby, 1939; Grassé, 1949; Gösswald, 1962; see also Chapter 3). Large *Cryptotermes brevis* nymphs, for example, have larger gut volumes than small nymphs, as expected, and acquire proportionately more radioactivity during feeding (McMahan, 1963). But soldiers and reproductives that may be similar in weight and size to nymphs obtain considerably less radioactivity as recipients during proctodeal feeding. This may reflect relative numbers of hindgut protozoans as well as gut volume if the protozoans are concentrating the nuclide. (See Section I, A, 1)

Figure 4 shows the differences in daily average uptake or loss of radioactivity by three large *Cryptotermes brevis* nymphs (av. wt. 6.16 mg), two small nymphs (av. wt. 3.20 mg), a pair of supplementary reproductives (av. wt. 4.15 mg), and a soldier (4.50 mg). These termites were originally confined together in a termitarium of Sr⁸⁵-labeled wood and were measured daily for acquisition of radioactivity. After 20 days of exposure to this radioactive food, they were placed together in a nonradioactive termitarium, and their individual radioactivity was again measured daily. Differences in feeding ability (rate and capacity) are reflected in the graph. If the question to be answered by the nuclide-feeding experiment requires only a yes or no answer (for example: Has radioactivity been acquired?) then these individual variations are not troublesome, but, if strength of feeding relationship is to be measured in terms of degree of acquisition of radioactivity, then account must be taken of all the age, caste, and molting differences that may influence the results.

Feeding studies, moreover, have shown wide variations in the degree of feeding and, hence, in the amounts of radioactivity acquired by nymphs that appeared to be very similar in size and stage of development (McMahan, 1966). Gösswald (1962) has pointed out the difficulty of making up perfectly comparable test groups in his studies of termite attack on wood. Some of the feeding variation is due, doubtless, to differences in molting cycle; premolting individuals cease feeding. In any case, lack of homogeneity in acquisition of radioactivity by apparently similar termites seems to be a characteristic finding in these studies.

4. Radiation Effects on Behavior

Finally, there is the possibility that the termites' investigated behavior is being affected by the radiation to which they are exposed during confinement on a radioactive cellulose source or following ingestion of radio-

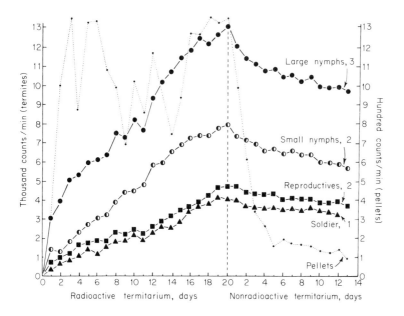

Fig. 4. Average daily gain and loss of radioactivity (Sr⁸⁵) by different types of *Cryptotermes brevis* individuals confined together, first in a radioactive (wooden cup) termitarium and then in a nonradioactive one. Solid circles represent three large nymphs; half-black circles, two small nymphs; squares, a male and a female supplementary reproductive; triangles, a soldier; dotted line, pellets. The figures on the ordinate represent thousand counts per minute for all except the pellet data. In this case the ordinate figures represent hundred counts per minute (McMahan, 1963).

active food. Insects are unusually resistant to lethal effects of radiation (see O'Brien and Wolfe, 1964, for summaries), requiring rather massive doses before succumbing. The degree of resistance, however, depends not only on species, but also on age, developmental stage, nutritional status, oxygen tension, temperature, and genome number. Grosch and Sullivan (1952) reported that adult *Habrobracon* wasps which had ingested up to 1500 μc of P^{32} in honey lived as long as or longer than controls. Following irradiation at doses of about 100,000 r, however, Grosch (1956) found that the wasps exhibited a lack of interest in food, and that lethargy appeared to be characteristic of wasps which had received doses above this level.

Nuclide concentrations and doses used in termite feeding studies have usually been considerably less than these amounts. However, Arnason *et al.* (1949) found that the calculated concentration of P^{32} expected to reduce emergence of adult *Drosophila* to 50% when larvae were fed on radioactive medium was about 3.3 μc/ml, a dosage comparable to those used in some of the termite studies. The *Drosophila* effects probably were due chiefly to internal beta radiation, but results of other investigations (King, 1954) suggest that the conversion of phosphorus to sulfur during P^{32} decay may also play a damaging role. Biological half-life, as well as energy, of the nuclide involved would also help to determine the degree of injury sustained.

In the termite studies no obviously abnormal behavior was noted, and feeding relationships shown by the radioisotope studies have tended to confirm earlier observations in which no isotopes were used. It seems likely that the levels of radiation involved were so low that no important behavioral deviations resulted. It must be kept in mind, however, that even low doses may affect behavior, as Hug (1959) showed with ants. When both weakly irradiated and nonirradiated areas were available to them, ants tended to congregate in the latter. Future studies may even show that social insects are unusually sensitive to radiation effects. In a preliminary study, in which part of a *Nasutitermes costalis* (Holmgren) colony was exposed to a Co^{60} source, McMahan (1968) found that only 6000 r was sufficient to kill all irradiated termites within 6 days if the entire dose was given in 1.5 hours. This is considerably below the dosage usually found to be lethal to insects. The need for further studies of termite radiosensitivity are indicated.

B. APPLICATION OF RADIOISOTOPES TO TERMITE FEEDING STUDIES

1. Feeding Capabilities of Different Castes and Instars

The inability or disinclination of termite soldiers, of youngest instars, and of functional reproductives to feed directly on environmental cellulose, and their consequent dependence upon colony mates, was of course known before radioisotopes became available as food tracers. Grassé (1949, p. 498) summarizes these data for the Kalotermitidae, the Termopsidae (Hodotermitidae), the Rhinotermitidae, and for several subfamilies of the Termitidae (see also Chapter 3). Insofar as they have gone at present, the more recent studies using the nuclide tracer technique have confirmed these findings.

Alibert (1959) studied feeding capabilities of *Kalotermes flavicollis*, using P^{32}. She exposed groups of termites (segregated according to developmental stage) to filter paper which had been soaked in a solution of the nuclide (specific activity: 1 mc/ml). External contamination was prevented by forcing the termites to feed through a small hole of head diameter cut in plastic foil, which was stretched over the radioactive paper (see Fig. 3). Gösswald and Kloft (1959) suggest that the perforations through which the termites fed served as innate releasing mechanisms for "food tunnel gnawing." They have used this same method for testing resistance of textiles and other materials to *Kalotermes*.

Subsequent measurement of the termites for radioactivity showed that first instar young, soldiers, preimagoes (termites in a short stage preceding the adult stage), and alates never fed directly from the paper. Second instars acquired only small amounts of radioactivity. The most active feeders, according to the intensity of radioactivity recorded, were 3rd, 4th, and 5th instars and pseudergates, but "nymphs" (older individuals on the way to becoming alates) also fed actively after a preadaptation time of 2 days. Even functional reproductives of more than 3 years of age were shown to have the ability to feed directly on a cellulose source, but they too required a prior isolation time of 65−70 hours before apparently reverting in their feeding role from receiver to active supplier of food. Although alates did not feed on the radioactive filter paper before they had had an opportunity to swarm, they apparently did so afterward, indicating that reproductive founders of incipient *Kalotermes flavicollis* colonies feed directly on cellulose for a time. They are known to provide their first young with proctodeal food, the means by which these young obtain symbiotic flagellates (Goetsch, 1936; Grassé and Noirot, 1945). Alibert (1960), in her P^{32} studies of feeding relations between reproductives and young in incipient (6−18 months) colonies, confirmed this observation.

McMahan (1963) isolated groups of *Cryptotermes brevis* soldiers in small balsa-wood cups which had been soaked in a solution of Sr^{85} and dried. No radioactivity was acquired during the isolation period of 7 days, indicating failure to feed on wood, but as soon as nymphs were introduced into the cups the radioactivity of the soldiers rose in concert with that of the nymphs.

Studies by Alibert (1963) on nests of the termitid humivore, *Cubitermes fungifaber,* showed that only workers fed directly on the P^{32}-labeled humus provided. Reproductives, alates, adult soldiers, "white soldiers," and young received stomodeal food from the workers.

Nuclide studies have also confirmed the observation that molting termites do not feed for several days before and after the event (Gösswald and Kloft, 1959; McMahan 1960, 1963). It has already been mentioned that cessation of feeding during molting has proved to be one of the problems facing investigators using radioisotopes to study food transfer. Not only does feeding of all types cease for the molting individual, but gut contents are voided and donation of food to colony mates also ceases. During the period of emptying the intestine just prior to the molt, however, the molting nymph appears to stimulate an actual increase in trophallactic activity on the part of other termites. They eagerly solicit the hindgut material, rich in flagellates, through proctodeal feeding, thereby conserving it for use by the colony. This finding was reported by Alibert (1965) who used Au^{198} as a tracer.

2. Patterns of Food Exchange

All members of a termite colony participate in food exchanges, either as donors, as recipients, or as both (except when molting). Certain definite patterns of food exchange exist, of course: the functional workers feed directly on the cellulose source and pass along stomodeal and/or proctodeal food to other workers and to other colony members. Some individuals receive predominantly stomodeal and some predominantly proctodeal food. Furthermore, the inhibition theory of caste differentiation, among the lower termites at least (Lüscher, 1962; see also Chapter 9), seems to require that all castes serve as donors of pheromone-bearing nutrients. May there not be patterns of feeding within these general patterns, however, based on seasonal or developmental variations in food solicitation or donation? Among the lower termites, are soldiers and reproductives (having smaller gut volumes and exclusively "second-hand" proctodeal food to offer) less frequently solicited for food than workers? Are large workers or nymphs more frequently solicited than smaller ones? Is there, in other words, a sort of peck order in feeding relationships within the colony? Perhaps answers to these and similar questions will lead to clues to such problems as why one individual and not another becomes the first soldier of an incipient colony (Weesner, 1956), what brings about soldier "flares," and additional information about the basis of caste ratios.

A beginning has been made in the search for such patterns in feeding behavior using radioisotopes. Alibert's study (1960) of feeding relationships between founding reproductives and their first offspring in *Kalotermes flavicollis* has already been mentioned (Section II, B, 1). Not only did the reproductives provide proctodeal food (P^{32}-labeled) to these young, but the young transmitted proctodeal food to the reproductives as well.

Feeding relationships within the mature *Cubitermes fungifaber* colony were also studied by Alibert (1963). She found that colony members were fed either saliva or regurgitated stomodeal food by the workers which had eaten radioactive (P^{32}) humus, the type of food received depending on the caste and stage of development of the recipient. The queen was first to show radioactivity derived from salivary feeding by workers, and this feeding appeared to be continuous. Alates, close to swarming, and white soldiers also gave evidence of extensive salivary feedings. The youngest instars and the king received smaller amounts of saliva, while adult soldiers and some workers received regurgitated food. Alibert's distinction between the two types of stomodeal food was based upon the time required for radioactivity to be exhibited by the various colony members. Regurgitated radioactive food could be detected early in the experiment, whereas radioactive salivary fluid did not appear until $25-30$ hours after exposure of the nest to the radioactive food source. These "latency times" were borne out by dissection of workers at varying times after exposure to the radioactive humus and measurement of their gut contents, hemolymph, and saliva.

McMahan (1963) attempted to test the hypothesis that proctodeal feeding patterns exist in *C. brevis* based on nymphal size (or instar). She set up experimental situations in which a large and a small donor, each with gut contents labeled with a different isotope (Sr^{85} or Co^{57}), were confined in nonradioactive wooden cups with one large and one small nonradioactive nymph. Respective sizes are indicated in Fig. 2. The amount of radioactivity (counts per minute) transferred from donor to recipient in a given feeding combination was considered to be an indication of the relative strength of that particular relationship. Although large recipients acquired more total radioactivity than small ones and large donors "delivered" more radioactivity than small ones, when the data were evaluated in terms of counts per minute per milligram of body weight, the data for the two sizes were comparable. McMahan concluded that in these tests termite size did not appear to influence significantly either the direction or the extent of food transfer. Further comparative tests should be conducted in which instar is precisely identified and different castes are also included.

3. Rate of Food Transfer within the Colony

According to the theory of inhibition, caste ratios are regulated by the amount of pheromone produced by members of a given caste and circulated via trophallaxis to all colony members. Theoretically, as the colony grows, the average amount of pheromone reaching members eventually drops below the inhibitory threshold, and other members of the caste in question develop. Both colony size and rate of food exchange, then, might logically be expected to be correlated with caste ratio, which for soldier to nonsoldier, at least, appears to be a relatively characteristic figure for each species. The ratios range from about 1 soldier per 1000 nonsoldiers in the case of *Cephalotermes rectangularis* (Sjöstedt) (Grassé, 1949) to about 1 per 2 or 3 in the case of *Tenuirostritermes tenuirostris* (Desneux) (Weesner, 1953; Light and Weesner, 1955). In line with the inhibition theory, one might expect species having low soldier to nonsoldier ratios to have high rates of food exchange and vice versa. Radioisotopes provide a relatively easy means of studying such rates. Wilson and Eisner (1957) have shown by this means that ant species differ widely in rate of food transfer.

Alibert (1959) investigated food transfer rates within the *Kalotermes flavicollis* colony. After making certain individuals radioactive by having them feed for 1 or 2 days on radioactive (P^{32}) filter paper, she returned them to their original (nonradioactive) colony in the ratio of one donor to 10 colony mates. After 12 hours, 40% of the colony was radioactive, after 20 hours, 70%, and after 35 hours, 100%.

Similar studies were made by McMahan (1966) using artificial colonies numbering from 25–200 *Cryptotermes brevis* nymphs. The ratio of labeled (Co^{57}) to nonlabeled individuals was much less than Alibert's since only one radioactive donor was placed in each "colony." Variation in rate of spread of radioactivity was found within each treatment, but 25-member colonies were capable of reaching 100% saturation in 96 hours and 200-member colonies of reaching 50% saturation in the same interval. The average amount of radioactivity per termite decreased significantly with increase in colony density, indicating chain transmissions along longer sequences of nonradioactive individuals in the larger groups. Wilson and Eisner (1957) found the same thing with ants. If spread of radioactivity in these tests is analogous with spread of pheromones, these studies give quantitative evidence that as colony size increases the average amount of transmitted substance received per individual does indeed decrease.

It is hard to compare Alibert's and McMahan's rates of food transfer for *Kalotermes flavicollis* and *Cryptotermes brevis*, respectively, since experimental conditions were dissimilar. According to the inhibition hypothesis, since *C. brevis* has a smaller soldier to nonsoldier ratio than *K. flavicollis* (approximately 1:45 and 1:20, respectively) one might expect the food transfer rate to be higher in the former species. *Cryptotermes brevis* also has a smaller average colony size, which makes colony saturation with a given transmitted substance more quickly attained. This also might help to explain the differing caste ratios. More comparative tests are needed.

In any case, the food transfer rate in the termites studied so far appears to be slower than that reported for the bee colony. Nixon and Ribbands (1952), using a ratio of one radioactive donor to about 4100 originally unlabeled bees, found that 52% of the colony was labeled after about a day. Ants, too, show a generally faster rate of food transfer than termites (Wilson and Eisner, 1957), but the rate varies widely according to species. Gösswald and Kloft (1963) report that in their studies of ants, rate of food exchange was conditioned by temperature, time, and number of individuals within the group.

Gösswald and Kloft (1963) studied the rate of loss of radioactivity from termites in groups as compared to that in isolated individuals. They caged radioactive (I^{131}) nymphs of *Kalotermes flavicollis*, some in single isolation and some in groups containing nonlabeled individuals as well. They found the biological half-life of the isotope in the isolated individuals to be much less than that in the groups. McMahan (1960) and Sen-Sarma and Kloft (1965) carried out similar experiments with similar results. These investigators interpret the lengthened half-life among grouped termites as resulting from repeated circulation of the radioactive food among the members of the group, and Gösswald and Kloft conclude that the greater economy in the use of food and other substances is doubtless a factor contributing to the "group effect" in social insects, mentioned earlier. Wilson and Eisner (1957) point out that this chain transmission of food results in an increased uniformity of gut contents within the colony, a process which may have important sociological implications.

4. Transfer of Food between Different Colonies or Species

So far, no termite work has been published showing transfer of radioactive food from members of one colony to those of another or across species lines. A number of studies not involving isotopes have indicated that there is usually intercolony and interspecies antagonism (Emerson 1929; Pickens 1954), although there have been reports of possible fusion of colonies whose galleries are closely adjacent, and there are techniques for inducing colony acceptance of foreigners (Emerson, 1939, p. 191). The ability or degree of tendency to transfer food, as shown by a transfer of radioactivity, might conceivably be a means of indicating termite phylogenetic relationships.

Internest transfer of radioactive food has been demonstrated in ants. Kannowski (1959) found that when P^{32}-labeled honey was introduced into mounds of *Lasius minutus*, ants in adjacent mounds also became labeled. This indicates that single colonies may consist of several mounds which interconnect below the ground surface. Mortreuil and Brader (1962), Gösswald and Kloft (1963), and Chauvin and Lecompte (1965) carried out similar studies with confirmatory results. Chauvin *et al.* (1961) found evidence also that radioactivity was transmitted across species lines, between *Formica polyctena* and *F. rufa*.

III. CONCLUSION

So far radioisotope techniques have been applied in the study of only a few termite species, chiefly those most easily reared in the laboratory. These tracer techniques are especially suited to the clarification of termite feeding relations involving interindividual transfer of nutrients. In spite of the problems inherent in nuclide work, radioisotopes will doubtless continue increasingly to help bring about understanding of the interplay of social factors that are responsible for the homeostatically balanced entity that is the termite colony.

REFERENCES

Alibert, J. (1959). Les échanges trophallactiques chez le Termite à cou jaune (*Calotermes flavicollis* Fabr.) étudiés à l'aide du phosphore radio-actif. *Compt. Rend.* 248, 1040-1042.

Alibert, J. (1960). Les échanges trophallactiques entre Termites sexués et larves de jeunes fondations de colonies et de sociétés plus agées (*Calotermes flavicollis* Fabr.). *Compt. Rend.* 250, 4205-4207.

Alibert, J. (1963). Echanges trophallactiques chez un termite superieur. Contamination par le phosphore radio-actif de la population d'un nid de *Cubitermes fungifaber*. *Insectes Sociaux* 10, 1-12.

Alibert, J. (1965). Mue et trophallaxie proctodéale chez *Calotermes flavicollis*. *Compt. Rend.* 261, 3207-3210.

Andrew, B. J. (1930). Method and rate of protozoan refaunation in the termite *Termopsis angusticollis* Hagen. *Univ. Calif. (Berkeley) Publ. Zool.* 33, 449-470.

Arnason, T. J., Irwin, R. L., and Spinks, J. W. T. (1949). Some effects of P^{32} on the development of *Drosophila*. *Can. J. Res.* D27, 186-194.

Beck, H. (1961). Vergleichende untersuchungen ueber einige verhaltensweisen von *Polyergus rufescens* Latr. und *Raptiformica sanguinea* Latr. *Insectes Sociaux* 8, 1-11.

Berwig, W. (1959). Untersuchungen über cuticulare Stoffabgabe bei Ameisenweibchen durchgeführt mit Radioisotopen. *Naturwissenschaften* 46, 610-611.

Brian, M. V., and Brian, A. D. (1952). The wasp, *Vespula sylvestris* Scopoli: Feeding, foraging, and colony development. *Trans. Roy. Entomol. Soc. London* 103, 1-26.

Buchli, H. R. (1958). L'origine des castes et les potentialities ontogéniques des termites européens du genre *Reticulitermes* Holmgren. *Ann. Sci. Nat. Zool. Biol. Animale* [11] 20, 263-429.

Butler, C. G. (1963). Pheromones in sexual processes in insects. *Symp. Roy. Entomol. Soc. London* 2, 6-73.

Chauvin, R., and Lecompte, J. (1964). Sur les échanges du deuxième degré entre colonies-filles de *Formica polyctena*, étudiés au moyen des radio-isotopes. *Insectes Sociaux* 11, 97-104.

Chauvin, R., and Lecompte, J. (1965). Evolution des échanges entre différentes colonies-filles de *Formica polyctena*, mesurée à l'aide des radio-isotopes. *Insectes Sociaux* 12, 197-199.

Chauvin, R., and Lecompte, J. (1966). Echanges protidiques entre fourmilières de *Formica polyctena*, mesurés a l'aide de radio-isotopes. *Insectes Sociaux* 13, 1-4.

Chauvin, R., Courtois, G., and Lecompte, J. (1961). Sur la transmission d'isotopes radio-actifs entre deux fourmilières d'espèces différentes (*Formica rufa* et *Formica polyctena*). *Insectes Sociaux* 8, 99-107.

Comar, C. L. (1955). "Radioisotopes in Biology and Agriculture." McGraw-Hill, New York.

Courtois, G., and Lecompte, J. (1958). Sur un procédé de marquage des abeilles butineuses au moyen d'un radioisotope. *Compt. Rend.* 247, 147-149.

Courtois, G., and Lecompte, J. (1962). Etude des échanges de nourriture entre butineuses de *Formica polyctena* travaillant dans des secteurs différents mais appartenant a la même fourmilière. *Insectes Sociaux* 9, 323-327.

Crossley, D. A., Jr. (1963). Use of radioactive tracers in the study of insect-plant relation-ships. *Proc. Symp. Radiation and Radioisotopes Applied to Insects of Agricultural Importance, Athens, 1963* pp. 43-53. IAEA, Vienna.

Emerson, A. E. (1929). Communication among termites. *Trans. 4th Intern. Congr. Entomol. 1928 Ithaca* 2, 722-727.

Emerson, A. E. (1939). Social coordination and the superorganism. *Am. Midland Naturalist* 21, 182-209.

Emerson, A. E. (1956). Regenerative behavior and social homeostasis of termites. *Ecology* 37, 248-258.

Emerson, A. E. (1959). The evolution of adaptation in population systems. *In* "Evolution after Darwin" (S. Tax, ed.) pp. 307-348. Univ. of Chicago Press, Chicago, Illinois.

Emerson, A. E. (1962). Human cultural evolution and its relation to organic evolution of termites. *Proc. New Delhi Symp., 1960* pp. 247-254. UNESCO, Paris.

Goetsch, W. (1936). Beiträge zur biologie des Termitenstaates. *Z. Morphol. Oekol. Tiere* 31, 490-560.

Gösswald, K. (1962). On the methods of testing materials for termite resistance with particular consideration of the physiological and biological data of the test technique. *Proc. New Delhi Symp., 1960* pp. 169-178. UNESCO, Paris.

Gösswald, K., and Kloft, W. (1958a). Radioaktive Isotope zur Erforschung des Staaten-lebens der Insekten. *Umschau Forschr. Wiss. Tech.* 58, 743-745.

Gösswald, K., and Kloft, W. (1958b). Neue Untersuchungen über die sozialen Wechsel-beziehungen im Ameisenvolk, durchgefuhrt mit Radio-Isotopen. *Proc. 10th Intern. Congr. Entomol., Montreal, 1956* Vol. 2, p. 543. Mortimer, Ltd, Ottawa.

Gösswald, K., and Kloft, W. (1959). Zur laboratoriumsprüfung von textilien auf Termitenfestigkeit mit *Kalotermes flavicollis* Fabr. *Entomol. Exptl. Appl.* 2, 268-278.

Gösswald, K., and Kloft, W. (1960). Untersuchungen mit radioaktiven Isotopen an Waldameisen. *Entomophaga* 5, 33-41.

Gösswald, K., and Kloft, W. (1961). Einblicke in das Staatenleben von Insekten auf Grund radiobiologischer Studien. *Imkerfreund* 1, 7-12.

Gösswald, K., and Kloft, W. (1963). Tracer experiments on food exchange in ants and termites. *Proc. Symp. Radiation and Radioisotopes Applied to Insects of Agricultural Importance, Athens, 1963* pp. 25-42. IAEA, Vienna.

Grassé, P.-P. (1946). Sociétés animales et effet de groupe. *Experientia* 2, 77-82.

Grassé, P.-P. (1949). Ordre des Isoptères ou Termites. *In* "Traité de Zoologie" (P.-P. Grassé, ed.), Vol. IX, pp. 408-544. Masson, Paris.

Grassé, P.-P., and Chauvin, R. (1944). L'effect de group et la survie des neutres dans les sociétés d'Insectes. *Rev. Sci.* 82, 461-464.

Grassé, P.-P., and Noirot, C. (1945). La transmission des flagellés symbiotiques et les aliments des termites. *Bull. Biol. France Belg.* 79, 273-292.

Grosch, D. S. (1956). Induced lethargy and the radiation control of insects. *J. Econ. Entomol.* 49, 629-631.

Grosch, D. S. (1962). Entomological aspects of radiation as related to genetics and physiology. *Ann. Rev. Entomol.* 7, 81-106.

Grosch, D. S., and Sullivan, R. L. (1952). The effect of ingested radiophosphorus on egg production and embryo survival in the wasp *Habrobracon. Biol. Bull.* 102, 128-140.

Harris, W. V., and Sands, W. A. (1965). The social organization of termite colonies. *Symp. Zool. Soc. London* 14, 113-131.

Haskins, C. P., and Whelden, R. M. (1954). Note on the exchange of ingluvial food in the genus *Myrmecia. Insectes Sociaux* 1, 33-37.

Holmgren, N. (1909). Termiten studien. I. Anatomische Untersuchungen. *Kgl. Svenska Vetenskapsakad. Handl.* 44 [3], 1-215.

Hug, O. (1959). Biological effects of small radiation doses. *Intern. At. Energy Agency, Bull.* 1, No. 1, 7-10.

Jenkins, D. W. (1963). Use of radionuclides in ecological studies of insects. *In* "Radioecology" (V. Schultz and A. W. Klement, eds.), pp. 431-440. Reinhold, New York.

Kannowski, P. B. (1959). The use of radioactive phosphorus in the study of colony distribution of the ant *Lasius minutus. Ecology* 40, 162-165.

Karlson, P., and Butenandt, A. (1959). Pheromones (ectohoromones) in insects. *Ann. Rev. Entomol.* 4, 39-58.

Katzin, L. I., and Kirby, H. (1939). The relative weights of termites and their protozoa. *J. Parasitol.* 25, 444-445.

King, R. C. (1954). Studies with radiophosphorus in *Drosophila*. III. The lethal effect of P^{32} treatment upon developing flies. *J. Exptl. Zool.* 126, 323-335.

Kloft, W. (1962). Technical problems of radioisotopes measurement in insect metabolism. *Proc. Symp. Radioisotopes and Radiation in Entomology, Bombay, 1960* pp. 163-172. IAEA, Vienna.

Light, S. F. (1942-1943). The determination of castes of social insects. *Quart. Rev. Biol.* 17, 312-326; 18, 46-63.

Light, S. F. (1944). Experimental studies on ectohormonal control of the development of supplementary reproductives in the termite genus *Zootermopsis* [formerly *Termopsis*]. *Univ. Calif. (Berkeley) Publ. Zool.* 43, 413-454.

Light, S. F., and Weesner, F. M. (1955). The incipient colony of *Tenuirostritermes tenuirostris* (Desneux). *Insectes Sociaux* 2, 135-146.

Lindquist, A. W. (1958). Entomological uses of radioisotopes. *In* "Radiation Biology and Medicine" (W. D. Claus, ed.), pp. 688-707. Addison-Wesley, Reading, Massachusetts.

Lüscher, M. (1955). Die entstehung von Ersatzgeschlechtstieren bei der Termite *Kalotermes flavicollis* Fabr. *Insectes Sociaux* 3, 119-128.

Lüscher, M. (1958). Uber die Enstehung der Soldaten bei Termiten. *Rev. Suisse Zool.* 65, 372-377.

Lüscher, M. (1960). Hormonal control of caste differentiation in termites. *Ann. N. Y. Acad. Sci.* 89, 549-563.

Lüscher, M. (1961). Social control of polymorphism in termites. *Symp. Roy. Entomol. Soc. London* 1, 57-67.

Lüscher, M. (1962). Hormonal regulation of development in termites. *Symp. Genet. Biol. Ital.* 10, 1-11.

Lüscher, M. (1964). Die spezifische wirkung männlicher und weiblicher Ersatzgeschlechtstiere auf die Entstehung von Ersatzgeschlechtstieren bei der Termite *Kalotermes flavicollis* (Fabr.). *Insectes Sociaux* 11, 79-90.

McMahan, E. A. (1960). Unpublished portion of Ph.D. Dissertation, University of Hawaii. Deposited with University Microfilms, Inc., Ann Arbor, Michigan.

McMahan, E. A. (1963). A study of termite feeding relationships, using radioisotopes. *Ann. Entomol. Soc. Am.* 56, 74-82.

McMahan, E. A. (1966). Food transmission within the *Cryptotermes brevis* colony (Isoptera: Kalotermitidae). *Ann. Entomol. Soc. Am.* 59, 1131-1137.

McMahan, E. A. (1968). Radiation and the termites at El Verde. *In* "A Tropical Rain Forest" (H. T. Odum, ed.). A.E.C. Office of Technical Information, Washington, D.C. (in press).

Miller, E. M. (1942). The problem of castes and caste differentiation in *Prorhinotermes simplex* (Hagen). *Bull. Univ. Miami* 15, 1-27.

Montagner, H. (1963a). Contribution à l'étude du déterminisme des castes chez les Vespides. *Compt. Rend. Soc. Biol.* 157, 147-150.

Montagner, H. (1963b). Etude préliminaire des relations entre les adultes et le couvain chez les guêpes sociales du genre *Vespa*, au moyen d'un radio-isotope. *Insectes Sociaux* 10, 153-166.

Montagner, H., and Courtois, G. (1963). Données nouvelles sur le comportement alimentaire et les échanges trophallactiques chez les guêpes sociales. *Compt. Rend.* 256, 4092-4094.

Morimoto, R. (1960). Experimental study on the trophallactic behavior in *Polistes* (Hymenoptera, Vespidae). *Acta Hym. Fukuoka* 1, 99-103.

Mortreuil, M., and Brader, I. M. (1962). Marquage radioactif des fourmis dans les plantations d'Ananas. *Proc. Symp. Radioisotopes and Radiation in Entomology, Bombay, 1960* pp. 39−45. IAEA, Vienna.

Naarmann, H. (1963). Untersuchungen über Bildung und Weitergabe von Drüsensekreten bei *Formica* (Hymenopt. Formicidae) mit Hilfe der Radioisotopenmethode. *Experientia* 19, 412-413.

Nixon, H. L., and Ribbands, C. R. (1952). Food transmission within the honeybee community. *Proc. Roy. Soc.* B140, 43-50.

Noirot, C. (1952). Les soins et l'alimentation des jeunes chez les Termites. *Ann. Sci. Nat. Zool. Biol. Animale* [11] 14, 405-414.

O'Brien, R. D., and Wolfe, L. S. (1964). "Radiation, Radioactivity, and Insects." Academic Press, New York.

Oertel, E., Emerson, R. B., and Wheeler, H. E. (1953). Transfer of radioactivity from worker to drone honeybees after ingestion of radioactive sucrose. *Ann. Entomol. Soc. Am.* 46, 596-598.

Pickens, A. L. (1932). Observations on the genus *Reticulitermes* Holmgren. *Pan-Pacific Entomologist* 8, 178-180.

Pickens, A. L. (1954). Intraspecific problems in the taxonomy of insect caste. *Insectes Sociaux* 1, 71-74.

"Radioisotopes and Ionizing Radiation in Entomology." (1963). Bibliog. Ser. No. 9, IAEA, Vienna.

Réaumur, R. A. F. de (1742). "Memoires pour servir à l'histoire des insectes." Paris.

Ribbands, C. R. (1952). Division of labour in the honeybee community. *Proc. Roy. Soc.* B140, 32-43.

Ribbands, C. R. (1953). "The Behavior and Social Life of Honeybees." Bee Res. Assoc., London.

Ribbands, C. R. (1964). Role of recognition of comrades in the defense of social insect communities. *Symp. Zool. Soc. London* 14, 159-168.

Roubaud, E. (1908). Gradation et perfectionnement de l'instinct chez les Guêpes Solitaires d'Afrique du genre *Synagris*. *Compt. Rend.* 147, 695-697.

Roubaud, E. (1910). Évolution de l'instinct chez les Guêpes sociales d'Afrique du genre Belonogaster Sauss. *Compt. Rend.* 151, 553-556.

Roubaud, E. (1916). Recherches biologiques sur les Guêpes solitaires et sociales d'Afrique. *Ann. Sci. Nat. Zool.* 1 [10], 1-160.

Sen-Sarma, P. K., and Kloft, W. (1965). Trophallaxis in pseudoworkers of *Kalotermes flavicollis* (Fabricius) (Isoptera: Kalotermitidae) using radioactive I^{131}. *Proc. Zool. Soc., Calcutta* 18, 41-46.

Stumper, R. (1961). Radiobiologische Untersuchungen über den sozialen Nahrungshaushalt der Honigameise, *Proformica nasuta* (Nyl.), *Naturwissenschaten* 48, 735-736.

Weesner, F. M. (1953). The biology of *Tenuirostritermes tenuirostris* (Desneux) with emphasis on caste development. *Univ. Calif. (Berkeley) Publ. Zool.* 57, 251-302.

Weesner, F. (1956). The biology of colony foundation in *Reticulitermes hesperus* Banks. *Univ. Calif. (Berkeley) Publ. Zool.* 61, 253-314.

Wheeler, W. M. (1928). "Insect Societies, Their Origin and Evolution." Kegan Paul, London.

Wilson, E. O. (1965). Chemical communication in the social insects. *Science* 149, 1064-1071.

Wilson, E. O., and Eisner, T. (1957). Quantitative studies of liquid food transmission in ants. *Insectes Sociaux* 4, 157-166.

13

Biochemical Studies in Termites

B. P. MOORE

I. INTRODUCTION

Biochemical studies in termites have lagged behind those in most other major orders of insects, presumably because the Isoptera are predominantly tropical in distribution and few species are available, regularly and in quantity, at most well-equipped research laboratories. However, this difficulty is now being overcome, to some extent, by modern means of fast transport and also by the establishment of study groups in areas where termites naturally abound. Thus, the next decade may confidently be expected to witness an increasing tempo of research in this interesting area of insect biochemistry.

At present the information available is still largely of an analytical nature; it is very fragmentary and relates to comparatively few termite species, which frequently have been examined only incidentally, in studies mainly concerned with other orders. Therefore, it is not possible to present an integrated picture of the whole of termite biochemistry, even in general terms, and this chapter cannot do more than aim to cover the main avenues of current research with an indication, wherever possible, of promising areas for future work.

II. FOOD AND DIGESTION

Termites have become relatively specialized in their feeding habits (Chapter 3) in comparison with their close relatives, the cockroaches, which are largely omnivorous. They subsist almost entirely upon wood, either living or dead, or the woody tissues of plants, intact or partly degraded and in the form of humus or dried animal dung. Such materials are rich in lignin and in carbohydrate, especially cellulose, but poor in vitamins, protein, and other forms of organic nitrogen, and the termites have therefore needed to evolve some special metabolic adaptations in order to meet these nutritional imbalances.

Of the major wood constituents, lignin alone is not digested by termites. It passes the gut with little change to form, in the case of wood-eating species, the bulk of the feces, which, in turn, provide the raw material for nest building and other constructional activities (Cohen, 1933).

A. DIGESTION OF CELLULOSE

Termites derive their main source of both metabolic water and available energy from cellulose, yet none have been shown to secrete the specific enzymes (cellulases) necessary to hydrolyze the β-glucosidic linkages of the polysaccharide. They rely upon other organisms to do this for them.

Wood-eating termites of the more primitive families sustain large protozoan faunas in their specially enlarged and modified hindguts (Chapter 3 and Volume II). Some, at least, of these protozoans live in a state of true symbiosis with their termite hosts; they depend upon their hosts for shelter and for supplies of raw food but are entirely responsible for cellulase production. In an elegant series of papers, over forty years ago, Cleveland (1923 – 1924, 1925) showed that these symbionts ingest the wood particles provided by their hosts and degrade the cellulose to glucose, which is partly converted to glycogen. Bound wood-sugars, such as xylose, are also released during the digestion process. All of these metabolites are produced far in excess of the requirements of the protozoan symbionts and are thus available to their termite hosts for metabolic purposes.

Workers of the most advanced termite family, the Termitidae, do not possess intestinal protozoans, yet many of the species feed upon wood and are able to break down cellulose. Cellulase activity has been demonstrated in extracts of at least one such species (Tracey and Youatt, 1958), but it is not yet clear whether the enzyme is produced by the termites themselves or by their intestinal flora. However, it is interesting to note, in this context, that cellulose utilization in this species [*Nasutitermes exitiosus* (Hill)] is much more efficient than in *Coptotermes lacteus* (Froggatt), which relies upon protozoans for digestion. Inner-mound matrix from *N. exitiosus* colonies contains about 6% of residual cellulose (Holdaway, 1933), whereas that of *C. lacteus* retains at least 18%. Laboratory colonies of *N. exitiosus*, when provided with no other food than their own nest material, are far outlived by corresponding colonies of *C. lacteus*, but when the species are provided with each other's nest materials the times of survival are reversed (Gay *et al.*, 1955). The mode of cellulase production in the protozoan-free termites is clearly worthy of further investigation.

Termites that feed upon humus rely, in effect, upon soil bacteria and fungi to achieve cellulose breakdown, although the process could not be classed as one of symbiosis. Certain species of Macrotermitinae have taken the association a stage further and deliberately cultivate elaborate subterranean fungus gardens for their food (Chapter 16).

B. NITROGEN ECONOMY

Termites are certainly able to subsist and even multiply on foods with low nitrogen content, but early claims that they were able to live indefinitely on a diet of pure cellulose, with the implication that they or their symbionts were able to fix atmospheric nitrogen, have been discounted. The "pure cellulose" used in the rearing tests was mostly cotton or laboratory filter paper, which Hungate (1941) has subsequently shown regularly to contain appreciable amounts of nitrogen in combination. According to this author, laboratory colonies of the American dampwood termite *Zootermopsis* were unable to make extensive growth on a diet of sound wood containing only 0.03 – 0.06% of nitrogen, although they persisted for some months. However, the natural presence of fungi in the wood or the artificial addition of yeast, both of which led to an increase in available nitrogen, enabled growth of the termites to proceed normally.

Controlled cannibalism is undoubtedly an important factor in the nitrogen economy of most termites. In many species, the injured and the dead and supernumerary members of any caste are habitually eaten, and, in times of nutritional hardship, quite extensive cannibalism may take place. Cook and Scott (1933) and Hendee (1934) have shown that termites deprived of nitrogenous food show an increase in cannibalism. Nitrogenous metabolites are thus recycled. Chitinase activity has been demonstrated in extracts from mature workers of two species (Tracey and Youatt, 1958; Waterhouse *et al.*, 1961). Since mature workers no longer molt, the chitinase is unlikely to be associated with molting fluid and is therefore presumably a component of the digestive juices, where it must play an important part in the nitrogen-recycling process. It is probably equally important in fungus-feeding termites for digestion of chitin present in the primary food.

On the other hand, there is no evidence to support the suggestion made by Leach and Granovsky (1938) that termites might be able to reutilize uric acid and its derivatives, either directly or by the aid of symbionts. These compounds, the normal end products of nitrogen metabolism in terrestrial insects, are certainly present in appreciable amounts in termites. Jucci (1921) reported the presence of urate deposits in the fat-bodies of many termites, and Hungate (1941) has detected uric acid in the feces of *Zootermopsis*. Several grams of uric acid were isolated from *N. exitiosus* during the course of large-scale processing for scent-trail pheromone (Moore, 1966), and the compound may safely be assumed to form a waste product.

Uric acid

III. HEMOLYMPH COMPONENTS

A. AMINO ACIDS

Termite hemolymph, in common with that of insects, generally, contains relatively high concentrations of amino acids. Fujii (1964) detected the following among total amino acids from worker hemolymph in *Copto-termes formosanus* Shiraki: threonine (22.5%), lysine (15%), serine (14.1%), valine (12.9%), alanine (12.1%), cystine (11.9%), leucine (8.5%), and tyrosine (2.7%). Corresponding material from the soldiers was more simple and contained only serine (58.1%), threonine (22.9%), and leucine (19%). This relative simplicity is no doubt a reflection of the restricted metabolism of the soldier caste.

B. PIGMENTS

In general, termites are less pigmented than insects of most other pterygote orders, and extracts from the completely dark-adapted species are frequently colorless. However, alcoholic extracts from *Nasutitermes* species are often bright orange-yellow in color and contain both water-soluble and fat-soluble pigments.

Riboflavin, biopterin, and a number of apparently new pteridines have been detected (Piraux and Hahirwa, 1964) in several African species of Termitinae and Macrotermitinae. The biochemical significance of these compounds is not at all clear, as indeed is the case with insect pteridines in general. However, it is noteworthy that the termite flavin and pteridines are much more abundant in nymphs and imagoes than in the blind castes. Their presence may therefore be associated with light sensitivity and vision.

The highly fluorescent nasutins were first isolated (Moore, 1962) from alcoholic extracts of *N. exitiosus*. Subsequently, they were identified as hemolymph components and were detected in all castes except alates and in all stages of development. Nasutin A, the major component, was first assigned the tentative constitution $C_{16}H_8O_7$, but this was later amended (Moore, 1964a) to $C_{14}H_6O_6$, and the substance was shown to be the dilactone (Fig. 1A) of 2,2'-dicarboxy-4,6,4',6'-tetrahydroxydiphenyl. Nasutins B and C were identified as 3,4,3'-tri-*O*-methylellagic and 3,3'-di-*O*-methylellagic acids, respectively (Fig. 1B,C).

Nasutin A proved to be identical, on direct comparison, with a pigment isolated earlier by Lederer (1942) from castoreum, a secretion of the Canadian beaver; it is a bright yellow substance, insoluble in water but readily soluble in mildly aklaline solutions, with production of a deep orange coloration that is also responsible for some of the color of the termite extracts.

The nasutins, when present in insect extracts, are readily detected by their formation of spots with characteristic R_f values in paper chroma-tography. These spots are brilliantly blue-fluorescent under ultraviolet light, and their size affords a rough measure of the amounts of nasutins present. Table I lists the species in which nasutins have been detected

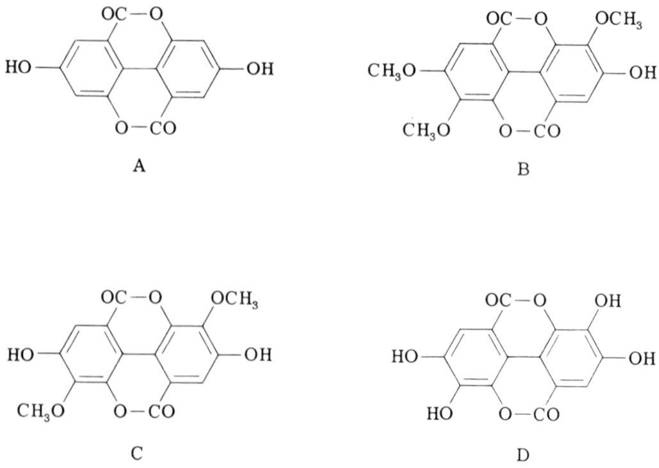

Fig. 1. A: nasutin A; B: nasutin B; C: nasutin C; D: ellagic acid.

TABLE I

OCCURRENCE OF NASUTINS IN THE NASUTITERMITINAE

Genus and species	Nesting habit	Primary food	Colonies tested	Colonies positive	Nasutins rating[a]
Nasutitermes					
exitiosus	Terrestrial	Dead wood	20	20	++++
fumigatus	Terrestrial	Dead wood	2	2	++
graveolus	Arboreal	Dead wood	2	2	+++
walkeri	Arboreal	Dead wood	2	2	++++
dixoni	Terrestrial	Detritus	2	0	−
longipennis	Terrestrial	Dry grass	2	0	−
magnus	Terrestrial	Dry grass	3	1	(+)
triodiae	Terrestrial	Dry grass	2	2	+
Tumulitermes					
pastinator	Terrestrial	Dry grass	2	0	−
westraliensis	Terrestrial	Dry grass	1	0	−
Occasitermes					
occasus	Terrestrial	Dry grass	1	0	−

[a]Based upon strength of relevant spots in thin-layer chromatography: ++++ = all tests very strong; + = all tests weak; (+) = tests weak or negative; − = all tests negative.

by this technique; the compounds appear to be restricted to the genus *Nasutitermes*, and they occur abundantly only in the wood-feeding species. However, nasutins have been detected in traces in *N. magnus* (Froggatt) and *N. triodiae* (Froggatt), both of which are thought to be exclusively grass feeders.

The biochemical derivation of the nasutins is still obscure, but it seems likely that they are metabolites of some phenolic constituent of the food timber. Chemically, these compounds are closely related to ellagic acid (Fig. 1D)—a substance that abounds in eucalypt timbers—and they may well share with it a common mode of biogenesis. Feeding experiments with appropriately chosen, isotopically labeled precursors could be expected to provide an answer, but, although such trials are relatively easily carried out with laboratory termites, they have not yet been undertaken. However, it is already clear that the nasutins are not obtained directly from the food material, for, although appropriate tests have been made, no nasutins have been detected in chaff or in various eucalypt timbers upon which the termites feed. Moreover, no nasutins are detectable in *Coptotermes lacteus*, which frequently occurs close by *Nasutitermes exitiosus* in nature and feeds upon essentially the same food timbers.

The question of the possible biochemical role (if any) of the nasutins is also an open one at present, but, in view of their phenolic nature, it seems likely that these substances may function as antibiotics, although no such activity has yet been detected in *in vitro* tests with a limited number of pathogens. On the other hand, the fact that nasutins occur regularly as components of the hemolymph, in a small but well-defined group of termites, rather militates against the alternative possibility that these substances may be no more than functionless byproducts of wood digestion.

C. VITAMINS

The vitamin requirements of termites have not been determined, but these insects are known to contain most members of the vitamin B group. This accounts for their importance as an item of diet for many tropical animals, including aboriginal man. Spector (1956) gives the following values (mg/100 gm dry animal tissue) for an unspecified termite: biotin, 0.066; inositol, 215; niacin (nicotinic acid plus nicotinamide), 17.5; pantothenic acid, 8.8; riboflavin, 2.65; and thiamine, 1.28. These levels are, in general, comparable with those of other insects but are a good deal higher than those of normal human tissues. Some of these vitamins may be synthesized by the termites' symbionts.

No requirement for the fat-soluble vitamins (A, D, E, and K) has yet been demonstrated in any insect (Gilmour, 1960), although β-carotene is apparently essential for growth and pigmentation in the locust *Schistocerca* (Dadd, 1957). This carotenoid, which is a precursor for vitamin A in higher animals, is abundant in some termites of the Nasutitermitinae (Moore, 1966; unpublished), but its role there has not been diagnosed.

A water-soluble, heat-stable factor, "Vitamin T," capable of accelerating growth in insects and vertebrates, has been isolated by Goetsch (1947) from a number of different fungi and the insects, including termites, that feed upon them. "Vitamin T" has not been chemically identified, but it appears to be a mixture of growth-promoting substances. Claims that it acts directly in termite caste control have not been substantiated (Lüscher, 1961), although, since it is a nutritional factor, it could be expected to have some effect on colony vigor and thereby influence, for example, the level of alate production.

IV. LIPIDS

The synthesis and subsequent breakdown of lipid materials form an important aspect of termite metabolism. Accumulated depot fats provide, for many species, energy reserves to cover the inactive season and to sustain newly independent imagoes in their colonizing activities. Other groups of lipids are involved in waterproofing the cuticle, in chemical defense, and in various pheromonal roles. Phospholipids are presumably important in cell architecture, but these have not yet been investigated in termites. Since the lipid content of most termite primary foods is low, the required compounds must be derived biosynthetically, presumably mainly from carbohydrate.

A. FAT COMPONENTS

In general, the fat content of termites is not high by insect standards, and it varies a good deal between species and with the season and the level of nutrition. Recoveries from solvent extractions of *N. exitiosus* varied between 1 and 3% by weight, the lower values occurring at the end of winter when the depot fats were largely exhausted (Moore, unpublished). *Coptotermes lacteus* was much less variable in this respect and yielded only 0.4–0.6%, by weight, of fat. The latter species appears to rely much less upon depot fat for overwintering metabolism—a property that may well be linked with the higher cellulose reserves present in its nest material (Section II, A). The fats from the two species did not differ greatly in composition, but, in comparison with those of other insects, the degree of unsaturation present was rather high (Table II).

B. CUTICULAR LIPIDS

Termites owe their ability to thrive in arid areas to the protection derived from their nest structures, the materials of which include special waterproofing polysaccharides in the outer walls. When removed from their environment, these insects are generally very susceptible to desiccation, for their cuticle is exceptionally soft and its water-retaining properties are poor. However, a few freely foraging forms, such as the black, diurnal species of *Hospitalitermes* and *Grallatotermes*, are better provided in this respect: their cuticles are quite strongly sclerotized and they habitually spend long periods in the open without suffering undue dehydration.

Hydrocarbons predominate in the cuticular lipids of *N. exitiosus* and the majority of these are unsaturated (Moore, unpublished). Gas chromatographic analysis of the saturated fraction (see Fig. 2) has shown all normal paraffins, from C_{24} to C_{47}, to be present. The odd carbon-number compounds predominate, and there is an overall peak occurrence at C_{39}, with a secondary maximum at C_{29}. The unsaturated hydrocarbons, when hydrogenated, showed a similar molecular distribution pattern. These unsaturated hydrocarbons formed too complicated a mixture for satisfactory analysis by direct mass spectroscopy, but were suitably fractionated by preparative thin-layer chromatography on silica gel. Mass spectroscopic analysis then showed degrees of unsaturation ranging from four to eight double bonds at each of the higher carbon numbers, and the major component was identified as a quadrupally unsaturated, unbranched hydrocarbon, $C_{39}H_{72}$. This major component was ultimately purified to better than 70% by repeated chromatography, the main contaminant being the C_{41} homolog. The almost complete transparency of the mixture above 200 mμ indicated complete lack of conjugated unsaturation, and ozonolysis gave adipic (C_6, dibasic), pelargonic (C_9, monobasic), and lauric (C_{12}, monobasic) acids as the main degradation products. The major hydrocarbon component of *N. exitiosus* cuticular grease is therefore $\Delta^{10,16,22,28}$-nonatriacontatetraene.

$$CH_3 \cdot (CH_2)_8 \cdot CH{=}CH \cdot (CH_2)_4 \cdot CH{=}CH \cdot (CH_2)_4 \cdot CH{=}CH \cdot (CH_2)_4 \cdot CH{=}CH \cdot (CH_2)_{10} \cdot CH_3$$

$\Delta^{10,16,22,28}$-Nonatriacontatetraene

TABLE II

Composition of Fatty Acids from Hydrolysis of Insect Fats[a]

Fatty acids	Isoptera[b]		Orthoptera		Lepidoptera		Coleoptera	
	Coptotermes lacteus	Nasutitermes exitiosus	Sphenarium purpurascens	Melanoplus atlantis	Acentrocneme hesperiaris	Carpocapsa pomonella	Mylabris pustulata	Pachymeris dactris
Saturated								
C_{12}		1						24
C_{14}	1	13	2.9					21
C_{16}	15	2	14.8		30		13	8
C_{18}	2		11.4	7.3	4	12	32	
C_{20}				12.2				
C_{22}				2.8				
Unsaturated[c]								
C_{16}			9.6 (−2.0 H)	4.1 (−2.0 H)				
C_{18}	78 (−3.3 H)	80 (−3.4 H)	35.5 (−2.9 H)	29.9 (−2.8 H)	66 (−2.6 H)	88 (−2.6 H)	54 (−2.0 H)	47 (−2.2 H)
C_{20}			25.8 (−4.7 H)	38.4 (−3.8 H)			1 (−8.0 H)	
C_{22}				5.3 (−3.7 H)				

[a] Data for Isoptera from Moore (unpublished), others from Gilmour (1960).

[b] Fats from the Isoptera contained traces of unidentified acids belonging to other series.

[c] Figures in parentheses indicate degrees of unsaturation.

The function of such long-chain hydrocarbons has not yet been established, but it seems likely that these compounds would play some part in limiting water losses through the cuticle; they may also serve

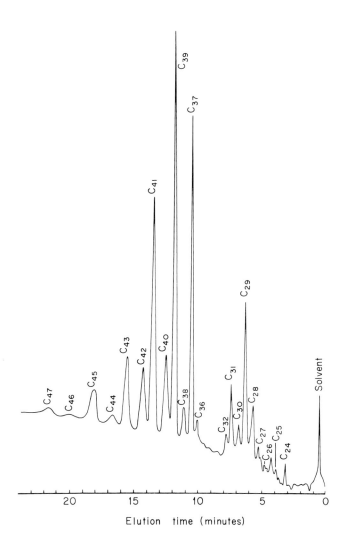

Fig. 2. Gas chromatogram of the saturated hydrocarbon fraction from the cuticular lipids of *Nasutitermes exitiosus*. Column: 2 meters of 10% silicone (SE 30) on "Gas-chrom P" (80–120 mesh); nitrogen flow 50 ml/minute; temperature programmed from 250°– 340° at 10° per minute.

as vehicles for certain pheromones, particularly those associated with the laying of scent trails (Section VI, B).

C. STEROIDS

The specific steroid requirements of termites have not been studied systematically, but they are presumably met, in nature, by metabolism of phytosterols present in the food materials. Likewise, the question of the relative roles of the termites and their symbionts in converting these phytosterols into the essential animal sterol cholesterol remains un-answered. However, although termites undoubtedly synthesize lower terpenoids in quantity for communication and defense (Sections V, VI), there is no reason to suppose that they depart from all other insects in possessing an ability to effect the basic sterol biosynthesis from open-chain precursors.

Mass spectrometric analysis of total sterols from wood-fed *Kalotermes flavicollis* (Fabricius) (Duperon *et al.*, 1964) indicated a cholesterol con-tent of at least 70%, with stigmasterol, β-sitosterol, and an unidentified sterol containing an extra methylene group in the ring system, as minor components. Similar analysis of material from the cricket *Gryllus do-mesticus*, fed upon salad, indicated at least 90% of cholesterol, with the phytosterols present only in trace amounts.

V. DEFENSIVE SECRETIONS

Defense in termites is associated with the soldier caste, which has been evolved specially for the purpose. However, a few species are known (*Speculitermes,* and some other genera of *Amitermitinae*) where soldiers are so infrequent (considerably below 0.1% of total individuals in some cases) that they would appear to be virtually functionless. Here, the soldier caste is presumably in the process of elimination; its duties may have been assumed by the workers, or perhaps the high protective efficiency of the nest structure has rendered it redundant.

The primitive mode of defense in termites is undoubtedly based upon purely mechanical action of the soldier mandibles, and this mode is still retained by the majority of species. Large soldiers immobilize their enemies by inflicting savage bites, whereas the smaller kinds rely more upon permanent attachment, via their pincerlike mandibles, to achieve the same effect. Soldiers of some highly specialized Termitinae (*Capri termes*, etc.) possess curious, highly asymmetrical mandibles that pro-duce a snapping action when forcibly crossed. This action is apparently used to flip attacking arthropods away from entrances to the termites' nest.

The mechanical mode of defense is supplemented by chemical means in at least two distinct groups of termites (Mastotermitidae and some Rhino-termitidae) and is completely superseded by them in a third, the Nasuti-termitinae. Soldiers of these three groups have independently evolved a sticky secretion that more or less encompasses and immobilizes the foe, but the chemical basis of the secretion is entirely different in each group. Here we have a very nice example of parallel evolution within the order.

A. DEFENSE IN *MASTOTERMES*

Mastotermes soldiers produce almost pure *p*-benzoquinone from glands opening into the buccal cavity (Moore, 1968). This material, in contact with amino acids and proteins of the saliva, soon produces a dark, rubberlike material that is applied to the adversary when the soldier termite strikes. Any excess, unreacted quinone undoubtedly acts as an irritant.

The existence of quinones in *Mastotermes* is of interest in adding yet another group of arthropods to the tally of those utilizing these highly active substances as a basis for defense. Among the insects, quinone-bearing species have been detected in the following other orders: Blat-taria, Dermaptera, Hemiptera, and Coleoptera. Although many of these instances are undoubtedly cases of parallel evolution, the existence of quinones in *Mastotermes*, the most primitive termite, and in at least one group of cockroaches, may be of some phylogenetic significance, for it is generally held, on paleontological and morphological evidence, that termites and cockroaches share a close common ancestry.

B. DEFENSE IN *COPTOTERMES*

Soldiers of *Coptotermes lacteus* and related species produce a milk-like latex when disturbed. This latex is exuded from a pore, the fontanelle, on the front of the head capsule and is applied to an adversary in a fashion similar to that of *Mastotermes*. Chemical analysis of the *Copto-termes* secretion (Moore, 1968) has shown it to consist of a suspension of lipid material in an aqueous solution of mucopolysaccharide. The lipid fraction has virtually the same composition as the cuticular lipids of the species, and its purpose appears to be to lend a more resilient texture to the dried latex, which forms a tenacious coating on any adversary coming into contact with it. The mucopolysaccharide incorporates mainly glucosamine units, into which it is broken down by acidic hydrolysis. No chemical toxicity appears to be associated with the *Coptotermes* secretion.

C. Defense in the Nasutitermitinae

Soldiers of the highly specialized Nasutitermitinae have become entirely dependent upon chemical means for defense. Their mandibles are degenerate and nonfunctional, and the greater part of their head capsule is occupied by the very large cephalic gland. The opening of this gland, homologous with the fontanelle of other groups, is produced into a long tubular, beaklike process, the nasus (Fig. 3), through which is shot the defensive secretion. The latter soon forms an exceedingly sticky thread that attacking arthropods find almost impossible to remove. After firing, the soldier termite removes the near end of the thread by wiping the nasus upon the substrate and then retires into the nest, for it is apparently unable to produce a rapid series of shots. However, the highly effective nature of their defensive secretion, coupled with the high proportion of soldiers reared by these insects, has enabled them to reach the forefront of development in their order, and they may be counted among the most advanced termites that exist today.

The nasute soldier secretion is based upon terpenoids, and, in the cases of Australian species that have been examined, the bicyclic hydrocarbon α-pinene (Fig. 4A) has been identified as the major volatile component. β-Pinene (Fig. 4B) also occurs in lesser amounts, together with limonene (Fig. 4C) and other monocyclic isomers (Table III). The volatile fraction of the secretion has been found to vary quite widely within a given species, but this is probably not at all critical for purposes of defense. However, such variation in composition of the soldier volatiles may well form the basis of colony specific odors that are known to exist.

The sticky, resinous properties of the soldier secretions that are enhanced upon evaporation of the volatile components are due to the presence of a number of closely related polyacetoxy diterpenoids that have not yet been fully characterized (Moore, 1968). These substances are undoubtedly an integral part of the secretion for they are extractable, with chloroform, from crushed heads of freshly frozen soldiers. An alternative mechanism of polymerization *in situ* (Moore, 1964b), after the firing process, may therefore be discounted. A claim in the literature (Schildknecht, 1962) that the steroid 24-methylenecholesterol also occurs in the nasute soldier secretion does not appear to have been substantiated. No toxic activity appears to be associated with the secretion for the termites fed, without ill effect, upon filter paper saturated with the

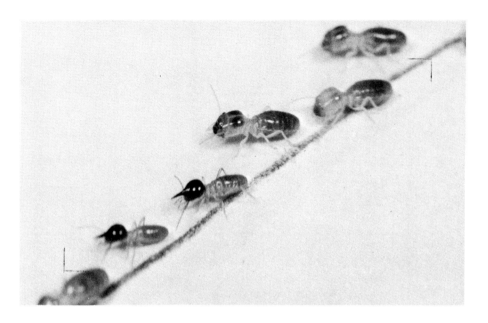

Fig. 3. Soldiers and workers of *Nasutitermes exitiosus* compared. Soldiers possess a hollow, beaklike projection on the front of the head, from which they shoot threads of a sticky defensive secretion.

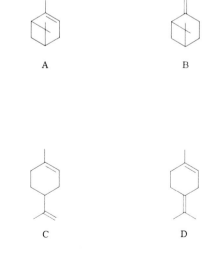

Fig. 4. Some terpenes from termitid soldiers: A: α-pinene; B: β-pinene; C: limonene; D: terpinolene.

TABLE III
VOLATILE TERPENES FROM TERMITID SOLDIERS[a]

Genus and species	Number of colonies examined	Volatile components (%)					
		α-Pinene	β-Pinene	Limonene	Terpinolene	α-Phellandrene	Myrcene
Nasutitermes							
exitiosus	4	65–73	9–12	11–15	–	–	–
graveolus	2	42–97	2–48	2–9	–	Trace	–
longipennis	2	67–84	16–17	0–15	Trace	1	–
magnus	1	52	20	–	4	Trace	–
triodiae	2	35–99	1–64	Trace	–	–	–
walkeri	2	30–80	9–34	16–30	Trace	–	–
Tumulitermes							
pastinator	2	95–96	1–2	2–3	–	–	–
Amitermes							
herbertensis	2[b]	–	–	–	98–99	1–2	–
laurensis	1	10	Trace	59	Trace	29	–
vitiosus	2[b]	13–25	Trace	13–17	6–10	43–45	8–12
Drepanotermes							
rubriceps	2	–	–	83–99	1–8	0–8	–
Termes							
cheeli	1	None detected					
Microcerotermes							
turneri	1	None detected					

[a] Data from Moore (1968).
[b] Composite samples comprising soldiers from several colonies.

nonvolatile components (Ernst, 1959). However, behavioral experiments with the living soldiers do suggest that the odor of the secretion serves as an alarm signal, for test glass rods, coated with fresh secretion and presented to the nasutes, receive more "shots" than do untreated controls. Similar results have been obtained with artificial pinene preparations.

It seems clear that the terpenoid components of the defensive secretions are synthesized in the soldiers' cephalic glands, for, although such compounds are widespread in plant tissues, they are unlikely to persist in dead and weathered wood or chaff, upon which the various nasute species of termites feed. Moreover, soldiers of these species have degenerate mouthparts and are quite unable to ingest the primary food: they are fed by workers on predigested materials. Since the workers do not themselves contain the terpenoids in detectable amounts, they presumably provide precursors from which the soldiers are able to elaborate their defensive materials. Feeding experiments with C^{14}-labeled acetate, mevalonate, and other plausible precursors would be of interest here for very little is known concerning the mode of terpene biosynthesis in insects, although it is generally assumed to follow a pathway similar to that occurring in plants (Gilmour, 1965).

VI. PHEROMONES AND ATTRACTANTS

The widespread occurrence of chemical signal substances, or "pheromones" (Karlson and Lüscher, 1959), in insects is now firmly established, and chemical means of communication have come to be recognized as a very important factor in the biology of most groups. Pheromones are fundamental to social insect life, where they provide a means for integrating effort and regulating development throughout the nest, and their elaboration, to comparable levels of specialization, in two such distinct orders as the Isoptera and the Hymenoptera provides one of the most striking examples of parallel evolution on record.

The termite society may ultimately prove to be even more dependent upon pheromones than are those of the Hymenoptera, where visual signals are still important. Already, a wealth of data has accumulated from studies on manipulated laboratory colonies to show that almost every aspect of termite development and behavior is mediated by chemical signals. Unfortunately, biochemical studies have lagged far behind. Comparatively few termite pheromones have been isolated so far, and even fewer have been chemically identified, to provide something of a perspective of the types of structure involved.

A. PRIMER PHEROMONES

Primer pheromones may be defined as chemical signals that do not give rise to an immediate behavioral response in the recipient, but serve instead to trigger or govern a chain of physiological responses that ultimately lead to changes in development and associated behavioral repertoire. These pheromones are the mediators of caste control in social insects, and there is evidence to support their importance as such in both lower and higher termites (Chapters 9 and 10). However, it is evident that the modes of caste control in termites are very plastic and they are further complicated, in comparison with those of Hymenoptera, by interactions between two sexes (see Lüscher, 1961) so that their study has proved exacting and difficult. Moreover, the long time required for the rearing of thrifty colonies from founding royal pairs has hindered attempts to isolate the pheromones involved.

Light (1944) fed extracts from parts of secondary female reproductives of *Zootermopsis* to standard groups of the corresponding larval termites and noted the numbers of secondary reproductives reared after 3 weeks. He obtained nearly complete inhibition with extracts from head plus thorax, but not with those from other parts. Lüscher (1955), working with *Kalotermes*, fixed primary reproductives of both sexes in wire screens that separated groups of the larval termites, so that the heads were in contact with one group and the abdomens with the other. He obtained complete inhibition, in rearing of secondary reproductives, only when both male and female abdomens were in contact with a given group. The combined results of these two investigators do much to confirm that reproductives of these primitive termites produce inhibitory pheromones in their heads or thoraxes that, when passed via the anus to larval termites, are responsible for caste control.

Regulation of soldier production is also likely to be mediated by pheromones, for, although the proportions of soldiers reared vary widely from one group of termites to another (e.g., less than 0.1% in *Amitermes laurensis* Mjöberg to about 20% in some species of *Nasutitermes*), they are remarkably constant within species, in colonies of comparable age and size. However, the evidence for the existence of an inhibitory "soldier substance," corresponding to those produced by reproductives, is much less adequate.

Castle (1934) first observed that incipient colonies of *Zootermopsis angusticollis* (Hagen) produce one soldier from the earliest brood but no further members of this caste during the rest of the year. However, if the first soldier is removed, usually another is soon reared, and the process may be repeated several times. Similar results were obtained by Light and Weesner (1955) with *Reticulitermes hesperus* Banks, although the habitually much lower soldier numbers in this species rendered the outcome less clear-cut. Gay and Moore (unpublished) examined the situation in *Nasutitermes exitiosus*, where the natural proportion of soldiers is about 15%. Standard laboratory colonies were set up with 4 gm of healthy workers and various proportions of juveniles and soldiers, all insects being freshly separated from a single natural mound. After a period of 8 weeks under optimal conditions, the colonies were dismantled and assessed. The results (Table IV) showed that colonies deprived of soldiers reared significant, though rather variable, numbers of this caste and that survival of soldiers was high when no juveniles were present but that this survival was significantly lower when juveniles were initially present. The last effect may be ascribed to competition, presumably for food, since both juveniles and soldiers needed to be sustained by trophallaxis with the workers, whose numbers were rather limited. The results of this and similar experiments do suggest the existence of an inhibitory soldier pheromone, but they also serve to underline the difficulties of bioassay of such pheromones and the importance of nutritional factors in caste regulation. Feeding experiments with extracts of soldiers have so far led to rather variable and inconclusive results.

B. RELEASER PHEROMONES

Releaser pheromones cause a more or less immediate, though transient, behavioral response in the recipient animal. Their action is reversible and they give rise to no long-term morphological changes. In termites they probably mediate most short-term interactions between individuals, including sex attraction, alarm, trail laying, recognition of the royal pair, trophallaxis, and disposal of the injured and the dead.

Long-range sex attraction, comparable with that occurring in the Lepidoptera, is unknown in termites, where the alates are weak fliers with a limited range on the wing. However, short-range sex attractants do appear to be involved in the establishment of tandem pairs between newly dealated imagoes after the colonizing flight. Such pairs are to be seen making their way for cover, with the male so closely following the female as to appear coupled to her. Temporary loss of contact with his partner causes the male to make sweeping searching movements, while the female raises the tip of her abdomen in an apparent "calling" attitude until contact is reestablished. The male is not, apparently, following a scent trail but responding directly to a short-range attractant, but nothing is known concerning the origin or nature of the pheromone involved.

When sufficiently stimulated, termites exhibit curious oscillatory move-

TABLE IV

SOLDIER REARING AND SURVIVAL IN LABORATORY COLONIES OF *Nasutitermes exitiosus*

Initial composition	Colony[a]	Final composition after 8 weeks			
		Workers	Soldiers	Nymphs	Totals
4-gm (approx.	a_1	673	3	0	676
840) workers	a_2	676	6	1	683
	a_3	707	5	3	715
	a_4	688	0	0	688
	a_5	673	3	1	677
		3417	17	5	3439
4-gm workers	b_1	752	12	5	769
plus 150	b_2	736	9	0	745
juveniles	b_3	756	11	0	767
	b_4	672	8	1	681
	b_5	772	12	0	784
		3688	52	6	3746
4-gm workers	c_1	752	97	2	851
plus 150	c_2	701	101	1	803
juveniles	c_3	709	95	1	805
plus 100	c_4	756	93	2	851
soldiers	c_5	760	92	2	854
		3678	478	8	4164
4-gm workers	d_1	656	96	1	753
plus 100	d_2	696	105	0	801
soldiers	d_3	711	107	0	818
	d_4	708	99	0	807
	d_5	694	90	0	784
		3465	497	1	3963

[a] The production of soldiers and nymphs in small numbers by the a colonies is attributed to the presence of a few advanced juveniles in the worker material. The effect should be allowed for in all other colonies.

ments that soon bring about a greatly increased level of activity throughout the colony. Two types of movement have been detected (Howse, 1965) in *Zootermopsis angusticollis*: a short-lived longitudinal oscillation in response to a low-intensity stimulus to the antennal sensilla and a longer, complex movement after a large disturbance. The latter is associated with the laying of a scent trail (a means of recruitment in the species) and only takes place in contact with another individual, which is then normally induced to follow the trail. The mechanism is obviously associated with alarm.

In some species these oscillatory movements are accompanied by emission of a volatile alarm pheromone, and the Australian Harvester termite [*Drepanotermes rubriceps* (Froggatt)] affords the best documented example. Soldiers of this species (Fig. 5) are very active and aggressive when disturbed, approaching the level of formicine ants in mobility and pugnacity. They show oscillatory movements and emit, from the fontanelle, traces of a volatile scent reminiscent of oranges. The scent consists almost entirely of the monoterpenoid hydrocarbon, limonene (Fig. 4C; Moore, 1968) (Table III), and presentation of this substance to the soldiers causes them to enter a short-lived snapping and biting frenzy. α- and β-Pinenes are much less effective as stimulants, and therefore there seems little reason to doubt that limonene is the true alarm pheromone of the species. Similarly, the alarm scent of *Amitermes herbertensis* Mjöberg has been identified as almost pure terpinolene (Fig. 4D), an isomer of limonene that has hitherto been detected only as a minor component in natural products.

Alarm reaction is not readily demonstrated in species of the Nasutitermitinae for nasute soldiers are much less excitable than are their amitermitine counterparts. However, Ernst (1959) has shown these soldiers are stimulated to fire further shots, when presented with a glass rod loaded with their own defensive secretion, and similar presentation of α-pinene, the main volatile component of the secretion (see Section V) causes a like response.

Fig. 5. Soldiers of the Australian Harvester termite, *Drepanotermes rubriceps,* in characteristic alert posture.

The association of alarm pheromone activity with components of a defensive secretion seems eminently reasonable, for the two functions, alarm and defense, are closely linked in nature. Nevertheless, these two functions have assumed different emphasis in different species, and an examination of soldier habits in the Termitidae reveals a complete spectrum of evolution. The nasute forms, with their massive cephalic glands, place the emphasis upon defense, with alarm as a subsidiary role. Some Amitermitinae (e.g., *Amitermes vitiosus* Hill) also produce copious amounts of an odorous, sticky secretion that appears to serve both purposes, but others, notably *Drepanotermes*, have dispensed with (or have never acquired) the resinous components and produce only comparatively small amounts of alarm pheromone. In *Amitermes laurensis*, soldier numbers are habitually so low that the caste would appear functionless. Volatile terpenes are still detectable in these soldiers (Table III), but they are probably of little significance in the biology of the species.

Worker and soldier termites of all families possess a sternal gland that is associated with the laying of scent trails. According to Noirot and Noirot-Timothée (1965), one of these glands is situated on each of the third, fourth, and fifth sternites in *Mastotermes*. *Stolotermes, Porotermes*, and *Hodotermes* have a single gland on the fourth sternite, and all other termites have one at the base of the fifth. Extracts of the excised glands have been shown to possess trail-laying activity in the following genera: *Mastotermes* (Moore, unpublished), *Zootermopsis* (Lüscher and Müller, 1960; Stuart 1963a), *Reticulitermes* (Smythe and Coppel, 1966), *Coptotermes* (Moore, unpublished), *Drepanotermes* (Moore, unpublished), and *Nasutitermes* (Stuart, 1963a; Moore, 1966). Such activity may well prove to be general throughout the Isoptera.

The existence of trail-laying mechanisms in primitive termites that nest in the food material (usually rotten wood) and do not forage seemed at first surprising, but Stuart (1963b) has shown that in these species trail laying is facultative and is a means of recruitment of both soldiers and workers to breaches in the nest structure. This may be presumed to be the ancestral habit, and more specialized termites have subsequently adapted it to the purpose of foraging. In the advanced *Nasutitermes* the sternal gland has become very diffuse and it lacks a discrete orifice; its secretion spreads over most of the hindbody and perhaps to all parts, along with the cuticular waxes (Section IV, B), and is automatically applied to a substrate at every contact. These termites would therefore appear to be obligate trail layers.

The scent-trail pheromones are highly active substances that function at extreme dilution. Using large batches (12 kg) of the Australian *Nasu-*

titermes exitiosus, Moore (1966) succeeded in isolating, in milligram quantities, a substance that was active in the trail-laying test (Fig. 6) over the range 10^{-8} to 10^{-5} gm/ml in inert solvent. Above or below these limits there was no response from the parent termites. The same substance was detected in other species of *Nasutitermes*, toward which it also showed activity, and also in *Coptotermes lacteus*, which registered no response. The substance was shown to have a monocyclic diterpenoid hydrocarbon ($C_{20}H_{32}$) constitution and to possess four isolated double bonds; it is believed to be a true scent-trail pheromone, but proof of this must await the determination of the complete structure and its unambiguous synthesis. However, the occurrence of terpenoid hydrocarbons in at least three important roles in higher termites is certainly noteworthy.

Termites are known to be attracted by quite an array of food odors, particularly those associated with fungus-infected wood. In some cases, extracts from these materials show trail-laying activity indistinguishable from that elicited by extracts of the insects themselves. Leaf alcohol, hex-3-enol, shows such activity: it is attractive to both *Kalotermes flavicollis* and *Microcerotermes edentatus* Wasmann and its presence in the former and in gallery material of the latter has been established by Verron and Barbier (1962). Since the synthetic *cis*-isomer of the alcohol also showed great attractiveness, the natural product is assumed to possess this configuration.

Fig. 6. Biological test for scent-trail activity with *Nasutitermes exitiosus*. The termites are shown emerging from the stock chamber to follow an artificial trail laid from a concentrate of their own scent-trail pheromone in inert solvent.

Becker (1964) has tested eight hydroxy aromatic compounds that are known to occur in fungus-infested wood, with positive results in many cases; five species of termites were used, and vanillic, *p*-hydroxybenzoic, *p*-coumaric, and protocatechuic acids showed the highest general attractiveness. The corresponding aldehydes were either repellent or only feebly attractive.

$$\begin{array}{l} H \\ \diagdown \\ C-CH_2-CH_2-OH \\ \parallel \\ C-CH_2-CH_3 \\ \diagup \\ H \end{array}$$

cis -Hex-3-enol

Extracts of pine blocks, artificially infected with the brown-rot fungus *Lenzites trabea*, are known to be attractive to a wide variety of termites (Esenther *et al.*, 1961), but the substance responsible for this activity has not been identified. However, Smythe and Coppel report (1966) that, according to gas chromatographic studies, the active materials present in the infected timber and in the sternal glands of *Reticulitermes* are probably identical. It seems likely, therefore, that some, if not all, termite scent-trail pheromones will prove to be metabolites derived from food materials.*

A recent chance discovery that workers of *Reticulitermes flavipes* (Kollar) would follow traces drawn from certain ball-point pens subsequently led to the identification (Becker, 1966) of diethyleneglycol monoethyl and monobutyl ethers as the active constituents of the ink solvent. These substances showed trail-laying activity with a wide variety of Termopsidae, Kalotermitidae, Rhinotermitidae, and Termitidae, but the one species of Mastotermitidae gave no response.

Although this surprising discovery still awaits a satisfactory explanation, it should be noted that the levels of activity shown by the synthetic ethers are by no means comparable with that of the natural scent-trail pheromone of *N. exitiosus*. Perhaps these ethers mimic, in some way, a naturally occurring termite food attractant, such as the above-mentioned *cis*-hex-3-enol. In any event, it appears unlikely that they would play any part in the natural biology of the termites which react to them.

---

*The termite attractant present in *Lenzites*-infected timber has recently been identified as *n-cis*-3,*cis*-6,*trans*-8-dodecatriene-1-ol by Matsumura, Coppel and Tai (*Nature*, 1968, **219**, 963-964).

REFERENCES

Becker, G. (1964). Termiten-anlockende Wirkung einiger bei Basidiomyceten-Angriff in Holz entstehender Verbindungen. *Holzforschung* 18, 168-172.

Becker, G. (1966). Spurfolge-Reaktion von Termiten auf Glykol-Verbindungen. *Z. Angew. Zool.* 53, 495-498.

Castle, G. B. (1934). The damp-wood termites of western United States, genus *Zootermopsis* (formerly, *Termopsis*). *In* "Termites and Termite Control" (C. A. Kofoid, ed.), 2nd ed., pp. 273-310. Univ. of California Press, Berkeley, California.

Cleveland, L. R. (1923). Symbiosis between termites and their intestinal protozoa. *Proc. Natl. Acad. Sci. U.S.* 9, 424-428.

Cleveland, L. R. (1924). The physiological and symbiotic relationship between the intestinal protozoa of termites and their host with special reference to *Reticulitermes flavipes* Kollar. *Biol. Bull.* 46, 178-201 and 203-227.

Cleveland, L. R. (1925). The method by which *Trichonympha campanula*, a protozoan in the intestine of termites, ingests solid particles of wood for food. *Biol. Bull.* 48, 282-293.

Cohen, W. E. (1933). An analysis of termite (*Eutermes exitosus*) mound material. *J. Council Sci. Ind. Res., Australia* 6, 166-169.

Cook, S. F., and Scott, K. G. (1933). The nutritional requirements of *Zootermopsis angusticollis*. *J. Cellular Comp. Physiol.* 4, 95-110.

Dadd, R. H. (1957). Ascorbic acid and carotene in the nutrition of the desert locust, *Schistocerca gregaria* Forsk. *Nature* 179, 427-428.

Duperon, P., Hugel, M. F., Sipal, Z., and Barbier, M. (1964). Analyse des sterols d'insectes phytophages par Spectrometoie de masse. *Comp. Biochem. Physiol.* 11, 257-262.

Ernst, E. (1959). Beobachtungen beim Spritzakt der Nasutitermes-Soldaten. *Rev. Suisse Zool.* 66, 289-295.

Esenther, G. B., Allen, T. C., Casida, J. E., and Shenefelt, R. D. (1961). Termite attractant from fungus-infected wood. *Science* 134, 50.

Fujii, N. (1964). Free amino acids in formosan termite. II. Determination of free amino acids in egg, worker, and soldier of Formosan termite by one-dimensional ascending paper chromatography. *Miyazaki Daigaku Nogakubu, Kenkyu Jiho* 9, 213-216.

Gay, F. J., Greaves, T., Holdaway, F. G., and Wetherly, A. H. (1955). Laboratory testing

Gilmour, D. (1960). "The Biochemistry of Insects." Academic Press, New York.

Gilmour, D. (1965). "The Metabolism of Insects." Oliver & Boyd, Edinburgh and London.

Goetsch, W. (1947). Ein neuentdecker Wirkstoff (Vitamin-T-Komplex). *Experientia* 3, 326-327.

Hendee, L. (1934). Caste determination and differentiation with special reference to the genus Reticulitermes (Isoptera). *J. Morphol.* 56, 267-293.

Holdaway, F. G. (1933). The composition of different regions of mounds of *Eutermes exitiosus* Hill. *J. Council Sci. Ind. Res., Australia* 6, 160-165.

Howse, P. E. (1965). On the significance of certain oscillatory movements of termites. *Insectes Sociaux* 12, 335-346.

Hungate, R. E. (1941). Experiments on the nitrogen economy of termites. *Ann. Entomol. Soc. Am.* 34, 467-489.

Jucci, C. (1921). Sulla presenza di depositi uratici nei tessuto adipose dei termitidi. *Atti Accad. Nazl. Lincei, Rend., Classe Sci. Fis., Mat. Nat.* [5] 30, 213-215.

Karlson, P., and Lüscher, M. (1959). "Pheromones": A new term for a class of biologically active substances. *Nature* 183, 55-56.

Leach, J. G., and Granovsky, A. A. (1938). Nitrogen in the nutrition of termites. *Science* 87, 66-67.

Lederer, E. (1942). Sur les constituants du castorèum. II. Les pigments; isolement et constitution chimiques. *Bull. Soc. Chim. Biol. (Trav.)* **24**, 1155-1162.

Light, S. F. (1944). Experimental studies on ectohormonal control of the development of supplementary reproductives in the termite *Zootermopsis* (formerly *Termopsis*). *Univ. Calif. (Berkeley) Publ. Zool.* **43**, 413-454.

Light, S. F., and Weesner, F. M. (1955). The production and replacement of soldiers in incipient colonies of *Reticulitermes hesperus* Banks. *Insectes Sociaux* **2**, 347-354.

Lüscher, M. (1955). Zur Frage der Übertragung sozialer Wirkstoffe bei Termiten. *Naturwissenshaften* **42**, 186.

Lüscher, M. (1961). Social control of polymorphism in termites. *In* "Insect Polymorphism" (J. S. Kennedy, ed.), pp. 57-67. Roy. Entomol. Soc., London.

Lüscher, M., and Müller, B. (1960). Ein spurbildendes Sekret bei Termiten. *Naturwissenshaften* **47**, 503.

Moore, B. P. (1962). Coumarin-like substances from Australian termites. *Nature* **195**, 1101-1102.

Moore, B. P. (1964a). The chemistry of the nasutins. *Australian J. Chem.* **17**, 901-907.

Moore, B. P. (1964b). Volatile terpenes from *Nasutitermes* soldiers (Isoptera, Termitidae). *J. Insect Physiol.* **10**, 371-375.

Moore, B. P. (1966). Isolation of the scent-trail pheromone of an Australian termite. *Nature* **211**, 746-747.

Moore, B. P. (1968). Studies on the chemical composition and function of the cephalic gland secretion in Australian termites. *J. Insect Physiol.* **14**, 33-39.

Noirot, C., and Noirot-Timothée, C. (1965). Le gland sternal dans l'évolution des Termites. *Insectes Sociaux* **12**, 265-272.

Piraux, M., and Hahirwa, A. (1964). Ptérines chez les Termites. *In* "Etudes sur les Termites africains" (A. Bouillon, ed.). pp. 125-138. Masson, Paris.

Schildknecht, H. (1960). Untersuchungsmethoden zur Aufklarung Chemischer Abwehrstoffe von Insekten. IX. Mitterlung über Insektenabwehrstoffe. *Proc. 11th Intern. Congr. Entomol., Vienna, 1960* Vol. 3, pp. 269-275 Inst. di Entomol. Agraria, Pavia.

Smythe, R. V., and Coppel, H. C. (1966). Some termites may secrete trail-blazing attractants to lead others to food sources. *Pest Control* **34** [10], 73-78.

Spector, W. S., ed. (1956). "Handbook of Biological Data." Saunders, Philadelphia, Pennsylvania.

Stuart, A. M. (1963a). Origin of the trail in the termites of *Nasutitermes corniger* (Motschulsky) and *Zootermopsis nevadensis* Hagen, Isoptera. *Physiol. Zool.* **36**, 69-84.

Stuart, A. M. (1963b). Studies on the communication of alarm in the termite *Zootermopsis nevadensis* (Hagen), Isoptera. *Physiol. Zool.* **36**, 85-96.

Tracey, M. V., and Youatt, G. (1958). Cellulase and chitinase in two species of Australian termites. *Enzymologia* **19**, 70-72.

Verron, H., and Barbier, M. (1962). L'hexene-3 ol-1, substance des Termites *Calotermes flavicollis* et *Microcerotermes edentatus*. *Compt. Rend.* **254**, 4089-4091.

Waterhouse, D. F., Hackman, R. H., and McKellar, J. W. (1961). An investigation of chitinase activity in cockroach and termite extracts. *J. Insect Physiol.* **6**, 96-112.

14

Water Relations in Termites

MARGARET S. COLLINS

I. INTRODUCTION

The distribution patterns of termite genera show that temperature and moisture are the major physical factors limiting dispersal (Emerson, 1955; Calaby and Gay, 1959). The importance of moisture can be recognized on a smaller scale when nesting behavior (Noirot, 1958-1959), timing of colonizing flights and postflight behavior (Bodot, 1966; Nutting, 1966a), as well as seasonal cycles in production of young (Bodot, 1966) are considered or laboratory culture is undertaken. Accordingly, a number of investigators have studied various aspects of water relations in termites, beginning with Williams (1934), who compared desiccation tolerance in two species of *Reticulitermes*. A brief review of the work of Gösswald (1941), Ernst (1956, 1957), and Klee (1960) is contained in a study of survival, under differing humidities, of the European dry-wood termite *Kalotermes flavicollis* (Fabricius) by Sen-Sarma (1964).

Termite species differ considerably in moisture requirements, some being able to live in wood above ground in the driest, hottest portions of the Sonoran desert of North America and Mexico (Nutting, 1966b), while others are restricted to mesic or wetter regions and frequently to subterranean nests.

II. SURVIVAL COMPARISONS

When experimentally challenged by low humidity and constant high temperature, sharp differences in survival time can be demonstrated between species. Tables I and II include data on *Kalotermes flavicollis* and representatives of four families of the North American fauna. The genera of Kalotermitidae (Table I) differ in tolerance of drying, with *Kalotermes* and *Neotermes* species being comparatively short-lived, while species of *Incisitermes, Marginitermes, Pterotermes,* and *Cryptotermes* are much longer-lived under experimental or cultural dryness. Of the Rhinotermitidae (Table II), *Heterotermes aureus* (Snyder) survives longer than other species, with *Reticulitermes tibialis* Banks next. The work of Becker (1965) suggests that *Heterotermes indicola* (Wasmann) has a higher moisture requirement and probably less desiccation tolerance than *Heterotermes aureus* although direct comparisons are not available.

TABLE I

SURVIVAL TIME DURING EXPERIMENTAL DRYING AT $34°-35°C$ AND $0-4\%$ RELATIVE HUMIDITY OF VARIOUS SPECIES OF KALOTERMITIDAE AND *Zootermopsis laticeps*[a]

Species	Caste	Sample size	Average survival time (days)
Zootermopsis laticeps	Nymphs	10	1.15
Kalotermes approximatus	Nymphs	10	1.90
Kalotermes flavicollis	Nymphs	1	About 2
	Nymphs	10	About 3
Neotermes castaneus	Nymphs	10	3.1–4.4
Neotermes jouteli	Nymphs	10	4.4–15.6
Incisitermes minor	Nymphs and imagoes	10	10
Incisitermes schwarzi	Nymphs	10	11.6
Cryptotermes cavifrons	Nymphs and imagoes	10	9.6
	Nymphs	10	21.5
Incisitermes snyderi	Nymphs	10	Half group dead at 22
Cryptotermes brevis	Nymphs	10	1 Dead after 30

[a] Data for *Kalotermes flavicollis* from Sen-Sarma (1964); data for other species from Collins (1958, 1966, and unpublished) and Collins and Richards (1966).

TABLE II

SURVIVAL TIME DURING EXPERIMENTAL DRYING AT 34°–35°C AND 0–4% RELATIVE HUMIDITY OF VARIOUS SPECIES, CASTES, AND GROUP SIZES OF *Reticulitermes* SPP., *Heterotermes aureus* (RHINOTERMITIDAE), AND *Gnathamitermes perplexus* (TERMITIDAE)

Species	Caste	Stage	Sample size	Average survival time (minutes)
R. hageni	Workers, soldiers		25	240–279
R. virginicus	Workers, soldiers		30	360–376
	Nymphs		25	374
	Nymphs		20	342–390
	Nymphs		4	645
	Imagoes	1–2 Days	20	288
	Imagoes	Postflight (old)	20	258
	Imagoes	At flight	4	270
	Workers		4	330
R. flavipes	Workers		20	336
	Workers, soldiers		25	182–374
	Nymphs		4	375
	Imagoes	Teneral	4	275
	Imagoes	1–3 Days	20	354
	Imagoes	1–3 Days	4	350
	Workers		4	435
R. tibialis	Nymphs		4	855
	Workers		5	518
	Workers		4	690
R. arenincola	Nymphs		4	540
	Workers		4	405
H. aureus	Workers		5	756
G. perplexus	Workers		5	392

The Hodotermitid *Zootermopsis laticeps* (Banks) survives drying little longer than species of Rhinotermitidae. In Hodotermitidae, Rhinotermitidae, and Termitidae, survival without food or water at 0–4% relative humidity at 34°C extends for minutes or hours; in the more desiccation-tolerant species of Kalotermitidae, survival extends for days or weeks, and for some, starvation would precede desiccation (Strickland, 1950; Collins, 1958, and unpublished observations; Collins and Richards, 1963, 1966).

Survival time during experimental drying is conditioned by rate of water loss, the amount of water that can be lost before immobility, body size, ability to restrict loss of water in defecation, group size, and behavior during drying (Dunmore and Collins, 1951; Collins, 1959; Collins and Richards, 1963, 1966). These will be considered in the sections to follow.

III. FACTORS INFLUENCING SURVIVAL TIME DURING EXPERIMENTAL
DRYING

A. RATE OF WATER LOSS

1. Procedures and Observations

Data on termites indicate that rate of water loss is of primary importance in determining survival time under dry conditions. In this respect, termites tolerant of dryness resemble desert-invading arthropods as described in Edney (1967). Loss rates were determined at $0-4\%$ relative humidity at 34°C in still air by measuring the weight loss (Collins and Richards, 1963, 1966). Termites of a wide range of sizes have been considered, and meaningful comparisons require that loss rates be expressed as amount per unit surface per unit time. Tables III – VI give ranges of initial weights, estimated surface areas, "k" values (the constant employed in the formula $S = k \cdot W^{2/3}$, where $S =$ surface area and $W =$ body weight), lowest rate of loss observed in untreated individuals, and ranges in rate of loss following treatment with peanut oil or alumina. Loss rate is expressed as $mg/cm^2/hr$. Surface area estimates were based on measurements of projected outlines of emptied, flattened cuticles. Averages of k are presented. This constant varies with caste and species; further, k changes with age within an instar, especially in imagoes (Table V) that go from a heavy, fat-filled condition immediately following metamorphosis to the condition at which they may fly, at about 7 days in some species. Termites maintained for long periods of time under unfavorable conditions tend to differ in k values from their caste counterparts from flourishing colonies or the field. While errors are unavoidable using either direct measurement or the constant and the formula, they apparently are not great enough to obscure relations between castes and species. The various species occupy comparable ranks using either measure. Data on averaged loss rates on all species are summarized in Table VII.

Rate of loss was determined on individuals killed by a 30-minute exposure to HCN fumes. Killing the animal before weight loss determination prevented variability in rates resulting from activity and perhaps differing spiracular responses to dry air in different species. It also protected against the deposition of fecal droplets in response to noises, an alarm reaction easily evoked in some species, especially *Neotermes castaneus* (Burmeister). Rate of loss decreases with time in groups desiccated while living (Collins, 1958). This decrease could be due to respiratory regulation; decreasing activity or huddling with drying; reduction in rate with decrease in amount available to be lost; the purely physical response of reduction in transpiration rate as the integument becomes

TABLE III

Ranges of Initial Weights and Estimated Surface Areas of Workers of Various Species of North American Termites, k Values, Lowest Rate of Loss in Untreated Animals, and Rate of Loss after Treatment with Peanut Oil or Alumina[a]

Family and Species[b]	Initial weight (mg)	Surface area (cm²)	k value[c]	Rate of weight loss (mg/cm²/hr)		
				Untreated	Treated Peanut Oil	Alumina
Rhinotermitidae						
R. hageni	1.00–1.20	0.06	5.38[d]	1.45	–	–
H. aureus						
Single	1.80–2.05	0.06–0.13	5.66	0.00	–	13.92
Groups of 5	1.76–1.96	0.10–0.11	–	0.11	–	–
R. arenincola	2.00–2.70	0.11–0.13	7.25	1.02	2.40–3.75	7.20–16.40
R. tibialis	2.15–2.68	0.10–0.13	6.40	1.14	2.16–10.60	5.84–14.70
R. virginicus	2.52–3.30	0.12–0.14	6.54	0.98	1.96–3.80	9.82–14.60
R. flavipes	2.96–3.35	0.11–0.13	5.65	1.80	2.56–3.50	15.80–24.90
R. hesperus	2.30–3.60	0.10–0.15	5.67	0.98	1.23–3.91	21.43–36.00
Termitidae						
A. minimus	0.95–1.20	0.06–0.07	6.29	0.00	2.14–4.48	8.45–13.85
A. wheeleri	1.70–2.00	0.06–0.10	6.56[d]	0.00	0.00–1.63	15.00–29.03
G. perplexus						
Single	2.20–3.15	0.09–0.13	6.23	0.00	1.14–4.17	5.40–20.10
Groups of 5	2.02–2.55	0.09–0.15	–	1.41	–	9.43

[a] After Collins and Richards (1963) and Collins (1966 and unpublished).
[b] A, Amitermes; G, Gnathamitermes; H, Heterotermes; R, Reticulitermes.
[c] See text for explanation of k value.
[d] Determination on only one individual.

TABLE IV

Ranges of Initial Weights and Estimated Surface Areas of Nymphs and Larvae of Various Species of North American Termites, k Values, Lowest Rate of Loss in Untreated Animals, and Rate of Loss after Treatment with Peanut Oil or Alumina[a]

Family and species[b]	Initial weight (mg)	Surface area (cm²)	k value[c]	Rate of weight loss (mg/cm²/hr)		
				Untreated	Treated	
					Peanut oil	Alumina
Kalotermitidae						
I. milleri	2.03– 2.97	0.08–0.13	6.03	0.00	1.40– 1.90	5.40–10.10
C. cavifrons						
Old	2.94– 6.12	0.16–0.31	9.30	0.00	0.19– 3.16	7.23– 8.27
Young	3.43– 5.92	0.17–0.24	7.37	0.00	1.92– 4.17	15.39–31.51
C. brevis	4.87– 9.85	0.21–0.29	6.72	0.00	2.41– 5.89	17.27–20.04
I. snyderi young	7.35–11.05	0.30–0.39	7.97	0.00	1.26– 3.14	8.46–20.13
K. approximatus	6.82–13.95	0.25–0.44	7.55	0.00	1.37[d]	19.26–27.68
I. schwarzi						
Old	7.96–14.76	0.33–0.56	8.31	0.16	0.69– 0.83	9.29–11.10
Young	11.72–14.10	0.40–0.44	7.55	0.04	2.28–12.13	14.88[d]
Par. simplicicornis	10.00–15.90	0.27–0.41	6.20	0.00	1.51– 2.80	24.17–28.43
N. jouteli	11.32–13.95	0.41–0.52	8.20	0.00	5.13–14.62	22.15[d]
N. castaneus young	16.17–22.85	0.48–0.61	7.56	0.65	2.79– 4.65	18.25–22.53
Pt. occidentis	35.65–50.45	0.68–0.91	6.53	0.00	10.09–11.42	18.65–22.26
Hodotermitidae						
Z. angusticollis	63.30–78.10	1.03–1.19	6.52	1.01	4.66– 5.04	21.40[d]
Z. laticeps	55.15–80.20	1.11–1.44	6.67	1.87	3.64– 4.14	12.30–23.50
Rhinotermitidae						
R. arenincola	2.35– 2.91	0.13	7.06	0.88	6.55[d]	12.80–15.30
R. hageni	2.46– 3.01	0.13–0.15	—	0.75	6.70– 9.40	11.90–16.50

Pro. simplex	2.83– 3.47	0.12–0.18	7.31	0.81	2.14– 4.03	8.20–13.93
R. hesperus	3.30– 4.20	0.16–0.22	7.36	0.69	3.29– 4.81	16.67–20.62
R. flavipes						
Old	4.36– 6.46	0.17–0.23	–	2.06	2.14– 2.80	9.24–12.20
Young	–	–	–	1.69	4.22– 5.40	–

[a] After Collins and Richards (1963, 1966); Collins (1966 and unpublished).
[b] *C*, *Cryptotermes*; *I*, *Incisitermes*; *K*, *Kalotermes*; *N*, *Neotermes*; *Par*, *Paraneotermes*; *Pro*, *Prorhinotermes*; *Pt*, *Pterotermes*; *R*, *Reticulitermes*; *Z*, *Zootermopsis*.
[c] See text for explanation of *k* value.
[d] Determination on only one individual.

TABLE V

RANGES OF INITIAL WEIGHTS AND ESTIMATED SURFACE AREAS OF IMAGOES OF DIFFERENT AGES AND VARIOUS SPECIES OF NORTH AMERICAN TERMITES, k VALUES, LOWEST RATE OF LOSS IN UNTREATED ANIMALS, AND RATE OF LOSS AFTER TREATMENT WITH PEANUT OIL OR ALUMINA[a]

Family and species[b]	Ages of imagoes	Initial weight (mg)	Surface area (cm²)	k value[c]	Untreated	Treated Peanut oil	Treated Alumina
Kalotermitidae							
I. milleri	11 Days or older	2.66– 2.83	0.18–0.19	9.40	0.16	1.75[d]	8.33[d]
C. cavifrons	Teneral	3.06– 4.40	0.14–0.18	6.77	0.00	14.91–26.22	28.80–36.46
	2–5 Days	3.76– 3.91	0.14–0.15	5.94	0.20	19.90[d]	18.99
	6–10 Days	2.42– 3.32	0.13–0.16	7.16	0.10	8.30– 9.30	–
I. snyderi	Teneral	7.72–10.52	0.27–0.33	6.84	0.00	10.33–27.46	16.81–39.83
	2–5 Days	5.90– 8.78	0.26–0.35	7.30	0.11	6.31–12.22	15.19–30.50
	6–10 Days	7.28– 8.66	0.31–0.35	8.40	0.56	7.59– 7.90	17.00[d]
C. brevis	11 Days or older	3.90– 6.46	0.25–0.33	9.05	0.14	1.56– 3.94	6.10–18.98
	Teneral	7.00– 8.80	0.19–0.29	5.81	0.00	35.29–40.69	19.79–39.88
	6–10 Days	6.55[d]	0.31[d]	–	0.00	2.92[d]	–
Par. simplicicornis	11 Days or older	4.32– 5.90	0.29–0.31	10.10	0.00	1.46– 2.97	8.14–17.71
K. approximatus	6–10 Days	5.40– 5.70	0.30–0.31	9.71	0.50	2.45[d]	13.95[d]
	Teneral	7.26[d]	0.26[d]	–	1.99[d]	26.78[d]	–
I. minor	2–5 Days	6.92– 7.21	0.30–0.31	–	0.53	4.72– 5.89	–
I. schwarzi	6–10 Days	7.35– 7.95	0.29–0.35	8.34	0.00	2.61– 3.65	18.75–20.55
	Teneral	7.88–14.88	0.27–0.41	7.01	0.34	17.85–24.50	32.78–46.13
	2–5 Days	9.52–10.62	0.31–0.34	6.98	0.37	9.48–10.79	20.19–24.60
	6–10 Days	10.42–11.37	0.41–0.45	8.19– 9.40[e]	0.54	9.40–10.50	–
M. hubbardi	11 Days or older	9.30–13.72	0.42–0.54	8.19– 9.40[e]	0.22	1.36–15.60	13.07[d]
	Teneral	13.35–16.15	0.34–0.39	6.03	0.00	20.41–33.06	30.63–43.83

N. jouteli	2–5 Days	10.40–13.40	0.32–0.39	7.06	0.00	4.13–8.82	18.25–25.97
	11 Days or older	9.35–10.55	0.32–0.43	8.42	0.00	3.87–7.03	17.79–20.66
N. castaneus	Teneral	13.25–20.10	0.31–0.42	5.64	0.54	11.13–18.95	49.78[a]
	2–5 Days	12.11–18.93	0.44–0.56	8.63	0.24	3.74[a]	18.14–19.90
	Teneral	13.72–23.80	0.46–0.66	8.00	0.51	11.80–24.10	21.14–37.40
	2–5 Days	13.56–20.71	0.49–0.63	8.30–8.60[e]	0.48	9.40–10.80	18.40–19.30
	6–10 Days	13.80–15.78	0.50–0.54	8.60	0.52	4.90–7.70	–
Alates	11 Days or older	10.60–12.24	0.52–0.57	10.81	0.60	3.57–3.99	14.88–20.28
Dealates	11 Days or older	14.95–19.30	0.50–0.62	8.60	0.82	2.74–2.78	–
Pt. occidentis	Teneral	30.50–38.75	0.65–0.80	6.96	0.23	24.72–42.99	24.01–42.07
	2–5 Days	26.80–40.10	0.76–0.96	7.44–9.36[e]	0.16	5.70–22.33	8.08–22.14
	6–10 Days	32.60[d]	0.81[d]	7.91[d]	0.00[d]	18.14[d]	–
Hodotermitidae							
Z. angusticollis	Teneral	75.30–82.40	1.16–1.45	6.88	1.16	14.87–23.27	42.80[d]
	6–10 Days	42.50–55.30	0.94–1.12	7.71	0.80	10.04[d]	24.41[a]
Rhinotermitidae							
R. hageni	Teneral	2.36–2.85	0.14–0.16	–	3.49	12.70–13.60	15.40–18.90
	2–5 Days	1.75–2.12	0.13	–	1.72	3.30–7.50	–
	6–10 Days	1.30–1.92	0.12–0.14	9.72	0.91	3.40–5.00	–
	11 Days or older	1.27–1.74	0.12–0.14	–	1.15	2.72–4.36	9.16–12.70
R. flavipes	Teneral	4.96–6.35	0.23–0.27	–	4.36	8.88–11.50	–
	2–5 Days	4.38–5.42	0.24–0.28	–	2.27	8.09[d]	–
	6–10 Days	3.37–5.42	0.21–0.27	–	1.36	–	–
R. arenincola	2–5 Days	2.20–2.40	0.15	–	1.29	4.37[d]	13.50[d]
	6–10 Days	2.55–3.22	0.14–0.18	–	1.98	4.20–5.36	–
R. virginicus	2–5 Days	3.40–4.36	0.19–0.23	–	1.56	–	–
	6–10 Days	3.37–3.91	0.20–0.21	–	1.23	4.17[d]	–
	11 Days or older	2.39–4.09	0.16–0.22	–	0.97	4.33–7.04	5.40–10.70

[a] After Collins and Richards (1963, 1966); Collins (1966 and unpublished).

[b] C, Cryptotermes; I, Incisitermes; K, Kalotermes; M, Marginitermes; N, Neotermes; Par, Paraneotermes; Pt, Pterotermes; R, Reticulitermes; Z, Zootermopsis.

[c] See text for explanation of k value.

[d] Determination on only one individual.

[e] Higher value for older individual.

TABLE VI

RANGES OF INITIAL WEIGHTS AND ESTIMATED SURFACE AREAS OF SUPPLEMENTARY REPRODUCTIVES OF VARIOUS SPECIES OF NORTH AMERICAN TERMITES, k VALUES, LOWEST RATE OF LOSS IN UNTREATED ANIMALS, AND RATE OF LOSS AFTER TREATMENT WITH PEANUT OIL OR ALUMINA[a]

Family, species[b], and age	Initial weight (mg)	Surface area (cm²)	k value[c]	Rate of weight loss (mg/cm²/hr)		
				Untreated	Treated	
					Peanut oil	Alumina
Kalotermitidae						
I. milleri	2.12[d]	0.08[d]	—	0.91[d]	4.39[d]	—
C. cavifrons Old	2.45[d]	0.17[d]	9.30[d]	0.27[d]	1.69[d]	—
C. brevis						
Old	4.30—4.85	0.27—0.39	9.50[d]	0.00	3.02[d]	7.16[d]
Young	5.60[d]	0.21[d]	—	0.71[d]	—	29.14[d]
N. jouteli						
2 Months old	14.36[d]	0.35[d]	—	0.17[d]	7.41[d]	—
9 Months old	15.06—16.20	0.43—0.46	—	0.26	3.78[d]	16.00[d]
Rhinotermitidae						
R. hageni	1.35—1.72	0.10—0.11	—	0.95	3.06—3.23	8.40—15.46
R. arenincola	2.89—3.85	0.14—0.15	—	0.69	7.65[d]	16.43[d]
R. virginicus	5.51—5.78	0.22	—	2.81	14.93[d]	17.20[d]
R. tibialis	3.18—6.18	0.18—0.23	—	0.94	7.07—13.90	11.00—16.60

[a]After Collins and Richards (1963, 1966); Collins (unpublished).

[b]C, Cryptotermes; I, Incisitermes; N, Neotermes; R, Reticulitermes.

[c]See text for explanation of k value.

[d]Determination on only one individual.

TABLE VII

AVERAGE WEIGHT LOSS OF UNTREATED WORKERS OR NYMPHS FOR VARIOUS SPECIES OF TERMITES[a,b]

Less than 0.50	0.51–1.00	1.01–1.50	1.51–2.00	2.01–2.50
Kalotermitidae	Kalotermitidae	Rhinotermitidae	Hodotermitidae	Hodotermitidae
C. brevis	K. approximatus	R. hesperus	Z. angusticollis	Z. laticeps
C. cavifrons	N. castaneus	R. hageni	Termitidae	Rhinotermitidae
I. minor	Rhinotermitidae	Pr. simplex	G. perplexus	R. flavipes
I. snyderi	R. arenincola	R. virginicus	A. minimus	
I. milleri	R. tibialis	Termitidae		
I. schwarzi		A. wheeleri		
N. jouteli				
Par. simplicicornis				
Pt. occidentis				
M. hubbardi				
Rhinotermitidae				
H. aureus				

[a] A, Amitermes; C, Cryptotermes; G, Gnathamitermes; H, Heterotermes; I, Incisitermes; K, Kalotermes; M, Marginitermes; N, Neotermes; Par., Paraneotermes; Pr., Prorhinotermes; Pt., Pterotermes; R, Reticulitermes; Z, Zootermopsis.

[b] In mg/cm²/hr.

drier, a phenomenon described by Richards (1958); or to some combination of these and perhaps unknown factors. Sen-Sarma suggests that spiracular regulation is the major factor in tolerance of low humidities seen in *Kalotermes flavicollis;* however, with living termites considered in groups, identification of individual causative elements can be difficult.

It would be desirable to have determinations of rate of loss at different temperatures as 34°C may lie above the transition temperature of the epicuticular waterproofing of some species. However, rate losses at this temperature parallel moisture needs in laboratory culture and in nature; thus, rate of loss so determined can be considered a significant item in habitat specification.

Great variability between individuals was observed, especially in younger representatives within an instar. Variability decreased with age. Rate of loss could be increased by application of a number of agents, but peanut oil and alumina were selected to avoid experimental errors arising from the continued solvent evaporation that follows use of volatile solvents like CCl_4 or $CHCl_3$. (The manner in which waterproofing mechanisms are affected by peanut oil and alumina is discussed in Section II, A, 2.) As termites aged within an instar, vulnerability to the chosen rate-increasing agent decreased (Tables IV and V). These findings suggested that the waterproofing mechanism was delicate, but became less so with age. The problem of obtaining an undamaged animal is very great, however, and extreme care in handling is required. Only if an animal loses no weight during an experimental interval is one sure that the waterproofing is intact. Practically, however, the lowest value of a series of observations on termites handled carefully is the best approximation that can be obtained of the loss rate using this particular technique.

In general, species in family Kalotermitidae showed lower loss rates when untreated and greater loss rates following application of peanut oil or alumina than species of Rhinotermitidae, Hodotermitidae, or Termitidae. Species within each of these families differed, especially in the Kalotermitidae. In this family, *Kalotermes approximatus* (Snyder) showed a comparatively high rate of loss when untreated, and a response to peanut oil and alumina intermediate in magnitude between that shown by the more desiccation-resistant species within the family and species of Rhinotermitidae, Hodotermitidae, and Termitidae. Available data on *K. flavicollis* suggest that it will behave like *K. approximatus* in this regard. Reproductive nymphs (Table IV) usually lost water less rapidly than imagoes (Table V), although some individuals, even the delicate teneral imagoes, showed no weight loss during an experimental interval. This indicates the existence of an efficient waterproofing, undamaged at the time of the experiment. These findings illustrated the desirability of scrutiny of the cuticle of the several age groups and castes.

2. Cuticular Structure

The termite imago possesses a sclerotized integument consisting of a procuticle, the outer layers of which develop some shade of brown or black, and an outer epicuticle, a layer that appears as a refractile line in the light microscope. The thickness of the cuticle varies in different regions of the body, but, when a single area is chosen for measurement and comparison of cuticular thickness between different ages, castes, and species, cuticular thickness is seen to be related to body size. The cuticle of nymphs develops little pigment; though unsclerotized, it is as thick as that of an imago of comparable size and seems to have the same layers. Pore canals large enough to be seen with the light microscope may be observed in many North American species, especially the larger ones. In some species a cement layer develops externally. This can be revealed using Wigglesworth's technique of extracting the cuticle with boiling chloroform, then treating the animal with an ammoniacal silver solution. The distribution and development of the cement layer among termite species are shown in Table VIII. Sections through cuticles with and without cement layers are shown in Fig. 1.

Recent advances in knowledge of the ultrastructure of the epicuticle (Locke, 1965) provide possible mechanisms for phenomena observed when termites are treated with peanut oil or exposed to fine alumina particles and then dried. Electron microscopy of a spread of insect species reveals that the epicuticle consists of a clearly defined, dense layer, the cuticulin, resolvable as a double layer overlying a homogeneous region that ranges up to 1 μ in thickness. These layers were found to be penetrated by filaments of wax $60-130$ Å in diameter. The wax filaments give rise to the surface wax layer. Locke visualizes these filaments as liquid crystals of lipid and water in the middle phase, physically continuous with the lipids on the surface of the insect. The molecular arrangement is such that free diffusion of lipid can occur in any direction towards regions where the lipid ceases to be in the liquid-crystalline phase. Phase changes to either a reversed middle phase or a complex hexagonal phase, as a response to environmental humidity, temperature, or cuticular condition, could permit the flow of water through the crystal. A tightly packed, lipid monolayer is believed to be the main barrier to water loss (Beament, 1961). This monolayer lies over the openings of the lipid-water liquid-crystals. Crystalline waxes and a complex of wax and cement would serve as protective layers external to the water barrier.

Locke describes the consequences of immersing an insect in oil as solution and loss of the surface wax and a rapid flow of cuticular lipids outside. These lipids vacate spaces which water subsequently passes through, giving rise to bubbles when the insect is left in the oil, or, in the case of peanut oil treatment, to increased transpiration rates during dry-

TABLE VIII

DISTRIBUTION AND DEVELOPMENT OF THE CEMENT LAYER IN SOME NORTH
AMERICAN TERMITES

No cement layer observed in any preparation	Cement layer delicate, frequently not observable in preparations	Cement layer heavy to very heavy, usually observable in preparations
Rhinotermitidae	Rhinotermitidae	Hodotermitidae
Reticulitermes hesperus	*Prorhinotermes simplex*	*Zootermopsis angusticollis*
	Reticulitermes arenincola	*laticeps*
Termitidae	*flavipes*	Kalotermitidae
Amitermes minimus	*hageni*	*Cryptotermes brevis*
	virginicus	*cavifrons*
	Termitidae	*Incisitermes minor*
	Gnathamitermes perplexus	*milleri*
		schwarzi
		snyderi
		Marginitermes hubbardi
		Neotermes castaneus
		jouteli
		Paraneotermes simplicicornis
		Pterotermes occidentis
		Rhinotermitidae
		Heterotermes aureus
		Reticulitermes tibialis

ing as a result of damage to the waterproofing. Tables IV and V show that the effectiveness of peanut oil in increasing transpiration rate declines with age within an instar. In terms of Locke's model, it could be suggested that the crystalline waxes and the wax-cement complex become progressively less soluble in peanut oil, and these layers, when well-developed, prevent uncovering of many of the wax canals. Species differences in composition of the cement could account for the different responses to peanut oil shown by different termite species of the same

Fig. 1. Photomicrographs of sections of the cuticle of various species of termites prepared to reveal the cement layer. Arrows point to the cement layer. The bar on each figure represents 100 μ. 1: *Reticulitermes virginicus* worker showing cement as delicate granules around the posterior end of the abdomen. 2: *R. flavipes* nymphs showing granular appearance of the delicate cement layer at the posterior end of the abdomen. 3: *R. flavipes* nymph showing the ventral region of the thorax through the leg bases. Note the absence of any cement layer in this region. 4: *R. tibialis* secondary reproductive showing heavy scaly material of the cement layer slightly lifted up from the cuticle. 5: The same (as in part 4) at higher magnification. 6: *Neotermes jouteli* nymph, section in the abdominal region. 7: *N. castaneus* imago, section mounted in air to increase contrast. 8: *Cryptotermes brevis*, old nymph, section in the abdominal region. See pages 447 and 448.

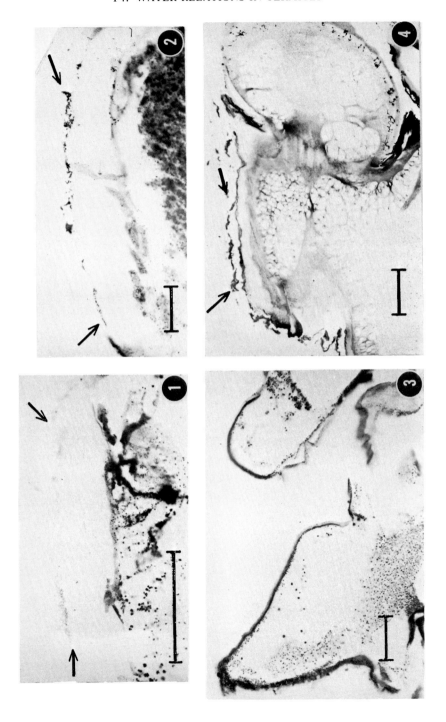

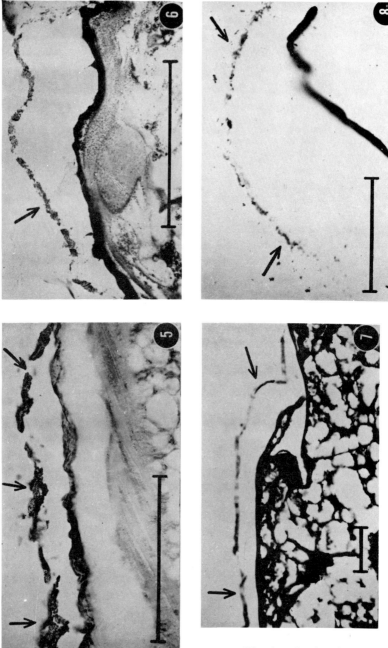

Fig. 1. (Continued)

caste and age. Experimental data indicate that it takes several days for the cement to be organized enough to protect the water barrier against peanut oil.

Locke's model suggests that sorptive dusts desiccate insects by dragging the middle-phase wax filaments through their canals, leaving them filled with water which could then evaporate readily. Ebeling (1961) had previously related the rapid desiccation of insects following exposure to sorptive dusts to removal of wax over the pore canal system. The wax canals or filaments would constitute a set of organized channels external to the procuticular pore canals, and this arrangement could account for the huge increases in rate of loss following exposure of insects with highly impermeable cuticles to peanut oil or alumina.

The lower loss rates shown by nymphs when compared to imagoes of the same species may reflect the possession of less-damaged cuticular waterproofing in the nymphs, probably as a result of their being usually older within their instar than the imagoes used in the experiments.

B. WATER CONTENT AND TOLERANCE OF LOSS

In insects the hemolymph constitutes a fluid reserve that can be drawn upon extensively without impairment of respiration, locomotion, or other activities (Mellanby, 1939). This seems to be true for termites, as individuals can walk after sustaining a fluid loss sufficient to produce marked flattening of the abdomen. Pence (1956) found that giving such a dehydrated individual water would permit restoration of body form, and the termite lived after rehydration.

Water content of some castes and species is shown in Table IX. While the fat-free body weight before and after drying would constitute a better method of expressing water content (Bursell, 1964), the only data available involve simple whole-body weight differences before and after drying. Fat content varies between castes and between age groups within a caste.

Data on *Reticulitermes flavipes* (Kollar) in Table X show that reproductive nymphs tolerate a smaller percentage weight loss than either imagoes or workers before reaching the end point (Dunmore and Collins, 1951). The value found here is close to that found by Ebeling and Wagner (1959) working with *Incisitermes minor* (Hagen) nymphs, who died after a 30% weight loss. Thus, this feature could not be a determinant in the usually greater resistance to desiccation shown by nymphs in comparison to imagoes. When species are compared, no relationship between water content and survival time is evident.

TABLE IX

PERCENTAGE OF THE BODY WEIGHT LOST WHEN TERMITE SPECIES ARE DRIED TO CONSTANT WEIGHT, ARRANGED IN ORDER OF INCREASING DESICCATION RESISTANCE[a]

Family and species	Caste	Number	% Body weight lost
Rhinotermitidae			
Reticulitermes tibialis	Workers	10	80.0
	Workers	15	78.8
Heterotermes aureus	Workers	30	68.0
Hodotermitidae			
Zootermopsis laticeps	Nymphs	4	78.8
Kalotermitidae			
Kalotermes approximatus	Nymphs	15	67.2
Neotermes castaneus	Larvae	6	84.2
Neotermes jouteli	Larvae	6	88.7
Incisitermes schwarzi	Imagoes	10	66.4
	Nymphs	6	67.9
Incisitermes minor	Nymphs	9	70.9
	Nymphs	9	70.9
	Imagoes	9	72.5
Cryptotermes cavifrons	Nymphs	10	72.0
Pterotermes occidentis	Imagoes	5	77.6
Cryptotermes brevis	Larvae and nymphs	10	65.8

[a]See Table X for *Reticulitermes flavipes*, which has the lowest desiccation resistance.

TABLE X

AVERAGE SURVIVAL TIME AND PERCENTAGE WEIGHT LOSS FOR GROUPS OF 50 INDIVIDUALS OF *Reticulitermes flavipes*[a]

Caste	Number of groups of 50	Initial weight (mg)	Survival time (minutes)	% Weight lost at	
				Last death	Constant weight
Workers	1	106.5	160 ± 6.7	55.8	75.7
	1	125.4	217 ± 6.6	55.1	77.6
	1	133.7	224 ± 8.9	59.8	77.3
	1	137.6	226 ± 6.9	—	—
	1	155.5	280 ± 9.7	—	—
	1	156.5	406 ± 24.8	68.7	76.2
	1	166.1	394 ± 12.5	57.1	78.2
	1	175.4	428 ± 15.1	66.3	78.5
	8	144.6	292 ± 6.5	59.2	77.7
Nymphs	7	325.1	430 ± 4.0	34.6	70.2
Imagoes					
Young	3	279.3	593 ± 12.0	57.9	75.4 (N, 50)[b]
Old	4	143.8	354 ± 5.3	50.7	71.7

[a]Dunmore and Collins (1951).

[b]Only one group of 50 was dried to constant weight

C. BODY SIZE

Given comparable rates of loss, the larger the animal the longer it will survive under conditions of extreme dryness (Dunmore and Collins, 1951). This feature, first observed in samples of workers of *Reticulitermes flavipes*, may be of importance in specifying differential desiccation resistance in *Reticulitermes* species. Table X shows survival time and percentage weight loss for groups of 50 workers of different initial weights and averaged data for groups of 50 of different castes in *R. flavipes*. Reference to Tables II – VI will show that the species of *Reticulitermes* all lose water at about the same rate except for *R. flavipes*, which has a consistently higher rate. Survival times of samples of these species parallel body sizes. *Reticulitermes tibialis* showed the least variability between samples, and seems to be the most desiccation tolerant as a result of possessing better protection for the waterproofing and moderate size.

In spite of the fact that transpiration is a surface phenomenon, body sizes, and thus surface-volume ratios, were not relatable to rate of loss.

D. ABILITY TO RESTRICT EXCRETORY WATER LOSS

Species of Rhinotermitidae normally void liquid feces, but after experimental drying these termites may show a plug of hard dry material protruding from the anus. Species of Kalotermitidae normally void dry hard pellets, but living ones must be handled quietly and with extreme caution when desiccation tolerance comparisons are being made, due to the habit of voiding liquid excrement as an alarm reaction to such stimuli as opening the incubator or desiccator. Stuart (1967) reports similar behavior in two species of *Zootermopsis*, and shows how this response can initiate building behavior as a means of defense. Species differences in the ease with which this response can be invoked may play an important role in determining differential survival during experimental drying.

Termites possess rectal glands of varying degrees of morphological complexity. At their most elaborate these glands consist of six conical pads of cells projecting into the lumen of the gut separated from each other by elaborately convoluted channels. The structure of the rectal glands is described in Chapter 4. Further details are provided in Noirot and Noirot-Timothée (1960, 1966a,b), Noirot et al. (1967), and Noirot-Timothée and Noirot (1967). Evidence that the cells of these glands function in ion transport is presented in Noirot and Noirot-Timothée (1966b). The function of the rectal glands in resorption of water in insects, established by Wigglesworth, Ramsay, and others, is well reviewed in Stobbart and Shaw (1964). In termites elaborate rectal glands with tall papillae and elaborate intimas have been observed in *Mastotermes darwiniensis* Froggatt (slides provided by Dr. C. Noirot), *Zootermopsis angusticollis* (Hagen), and *Z. laticeps,* and all twelve of the species of Kalotermitidae of North America thus far observed, as well as in *Kalotermes flavicollis* from Europe. In the Rhinotermitidae, *Prorhinotermes simplex* (Hagen) has tall elaborate rectal pads, but the intima and its channels are much less elaborate than they are in species of Kalotermitidae or the other lower families. Species of *Reticulitermes* have simple low cellular pads with relatively simple intimas. Desert-dwelling species of Termitidae and Rhinotermitidae in North America are provided with low, relatively simple, rectal pads but well-developed, complex intimas. In these species, as in the Kalotermitidae, the posterior portion of the rectum is surrounded by heavy bands of circular muscle and provided with radially arranged bundles of muscle inserted on the body wall and attached to the rectum at points just external to the convoluted channels between the rectal papillae. The rectal glands are heavily tracheated and closely invested with the posterior terminations of the Malpighian tubules, although the tubules do not actually penetrate the rectal wall as they do in the Lepidoptera and Coleoptera (Wigglesworth, 1956). African and Australian species of the Termitidae exhibit great variability in the relative height of the rectal pads and the complexity of the channels in the intima, but in no case yet observed are the arrangements of papillae and intima as elaborate as those seen in the lower families.

Species of Kalotermitidae that are tolerant of high environmental humidity void excrement as pellets when the humidity is low but as formless masses when the humidity is high (Hetrick, 1961, for *K. approximatus*; Collins, unpublished observations for other North American species). This habit may constitute an important route for the escape of excess water, permitting some species to survive in high humidities (*Incisitermes, Kalotermes, Paraneotermes, Neotermes, Cryptotermes cavifrons* Banks). *Pterotermes occidentis* (Walker) (Nutting, 1966a,b, and personal communication), *Marginitermes hubbardi* (Banks) (Collins, unpublished observation), and *Cryptotermes brevis* (Walker) (Collins, 1958, and unpublished observations) cannot be cultured successfully under conditions of high environmental moisture. *Cryptotermes brevis* maintained at 86% relative humidity in a desiccator becomes progressively more bloated and finally succumbs to paralysis and death from what Buxton (1932) has termed "water poisoning." According to Bursell (1964), this effect occurs when metabolic water is produced in quantities that cannot be eliminated by evaporation so that the water content rises above normal levels. It will be of interest to determine whether this intolerance of high environmental humidities can be related to lack of flexibility in retention of metabolic water.

E. GROUP SIZE

Survival under dry conditions is longer for termites tested in groups than for individuals tested singly (Grassé and Chauvin, 1944; Sen Sarma, 1964; Collins, unpublished observations). Grassé and Chauvin have suggested that sensory stimuli are of importance, while other investigators have emphasized trophallactic exchange. Where clustering behavior, or "huddling" (Pence, 1956) occurs in groups exposed to dry air, a reduction of exposed evaporating surface may act to extend survival time. Data on respiratory rates of grouped and isolated termites would be desirable in this connection.

F. BEHAVIOR DURING DRYING

Insect behavior is sometimes strongly influenced by environmental humidity. When low humidity triggers increased activity, an insect is provided with a means of leaving areas that provide less than optimal conditions; however, this response would decrease survival time during experimental drying. Those species that respond to low humidities by reducing activity and static "huddling" would withstand experimental drying longer than those species that respond with increased locomotory activity. In general, experimental samples of Rhinotermitidae and Termitidae species were more active than samples of species in family Kalotermitidae. Imagoes and workers were more active than reproductive nymphs (Collins, 1958).

Responses to different humidities in several species of termites have been determined by Ernst (1956). He reported that *Nasutitermes arborum* (Smeathman) (Termitidae), *Zootermopsis nevadensis* (Hagen) (Hodotermitidae), *Reticulitermes lucifugus* (Rossi) (Rhinotermitidae), and *Kalotermes flavicollis* (Kalotermitidae) differ in the time elapsing before selection of the wet region of a humidity gradient, with *Nasutitermes* responding first, within an hour, and the others following in the order listed. *Kalotermes flavicollis* took 3 days. Reversal of eccritic humidity from dry to wet occurred in some species when the hydration level fell. As Bursell (1964) suggests, the time relations here seem to be related to rate of loss of water if the insects Ernst used lose water at rates similar to those shown by members of their respective families for which data are available. A similar situation has been observed in *Cryptotermes brevis* (Collins, unpublished observation). Here, nymphs will cluster on lumps of agar if previously maintained in very dry atmospheres; they do not show this response if maintained in the original wood at moderate humidities (above 50%).

When groups of living termites are dried, trophallactic exchange could make fluid from one available to the remainder of the group, and, by draining one at the time, the life of the group could be prolonged. Casual observation of groups of Kalotermitidae during desiccation suggests that the smaller members of the group become compressed and die first—so any altruism inherent in this behavior is not only nonconscious, but probably also unwilling. Prolonged survival of the group would allow the decrease in loss rate with time to come into play, and, in the field, increase the chances of persistence until favorable conditions returned, perhaps through a rain. Kofoid's observation (1934) that colonies of *Zootermopsis* found after prolonged droughts contained only large reproductive nymphs may be an example of the result of these forces in action.

IV. CULTURAL REQUIREMENTS IN THE LABORATORY

Becker (1965) has shown that termite species vary with respect to optimal soil water content, and that this content is influenced by soil type (Chapter 11). The significant feature is the amount of water present in relation to the amount of water the soil could hold. Termites find optimal conditions in sand with a lower water content than is selected when they are cultured in soil that contains humus. This important finding may suggest a line of attack on factors involved in the apparent paradox that termites usually have a fairly high moisture requirement, but that Arizona, which is largely desert, has more species than any other state in this country. Further, the Arizona fauna includes representatives of the higher termite families that tolerate drying rather poorly. Measurement of soil humidities under cow chips in different stages of drying and utilization and at different depths would be very desirable in this connection, along with comparative data on CO_2 tolerance and on high-temperature tolerances and a rescrutiny of the ability to absorb moisture from saturated or near-saturated atmospheres. Cook and Scott (1932) showed that *Zootermopsis* lacked this ability. Beament (1964) suggested that being able to absorb moisture from the atmosphere may be a capacity common to most arthropods, and it may be that termites with a more transpiration-retarding cuticle than *Zootermopsis* will prove to have it.

Pence (1957) reports that the optimal humidity for *Reticulitermes hesperus* Banks is 97.5%. Skaife (1955) found that *Amitermes hastatus* (Haviland) (as *A. atlanticus* Fuller) colonies select the humid portions of artificial nests in which a humidity gradient is set up.

In general, species of Termitidae, Rhinotermitidae, and Hodotermitidae considered so far have a high and constant environmental moisture requirement. *Reticulitermes* species are so dependent upon atmospheric moisture that they cannot be cultured in dry environments, even in the presence of abundant food and water. Bursell (1964) suggests that insects showing this feature do so as a result of the large energy expenditures associated with regulatory processes called into play by low humidities.

Genera of Kalotermitidae differ sharply in moisture needs: the North American species of *Neotermes, Paraneotermes, Kalotermes,* and *Incisitermes* and *Cryptotermes cavifrons* survive best when there is abundant environmental moisture, with optimal humidities of $90-97\%$; but some species within these genera can live for long periods of time at humidities well below the optimum; and there are at least three species that cannot survive in very humid atmospheres, succumbing to "water poisoning" or attacks of fungi. These three, *Pterotermes occidentis* (Nutting, personal communication), *Marginitermes hubbardi,* and *Cryptotermes brevis,* require dry surroundings with occasional access to water, which they will gather around and drink, or lumps of agar too small to raise the humidity of the culture dish to a high level. These lumps are utilized in sealing the group off if there are enough termites, and the state of hydration will permit.

V. PHYLETIC CONSIDERATIONS

The ability to survive at a high temperature and low humidity for impressively long intervals and to live in surroundings where free water is rare or absent appear in several species of the termite fauna of North America. These species have in common a highly transpiration-retarding cuticle; elaborate rectal glands; usually reduced activity in dry atmospheres; and moderate to large size. It seems safe to assume that these individuals produce large amounts of metabolic water, although direct evidence on this point has not been obtained. Termite species less well adapted to survive in dry environments may possess well-developed rectal glands (species of *Neotermes, Kalotermes, Zootermopsis,* and *Heterotermes aureus; Gnathamitermes perplexus* (Banks); and *Prorhinotermes simplex*), but without the effectively transpiration-retarding cuticular water-proofing, survival in habitats exposed to appreciable intervals of dryness is unlikely.

Many of the species of the Arizona fauna survive by adoption of subterranean habits; by utilizing the moisture contained in cow chips; by living in dead branches of live trees (Nutting, 1965); or by adjusting activity cycles to favorable seasons of the year. The nest is an effective means of creating a favorable microclimate (Fyfe and Gay, 1938; Emerson, 1958; see also Volume II).

The most primitive living termite, *Mastotermes darwiniensis,* is subterranean in habits. Termites of the families Hodotermitidae, Rhinotermitidae, and Termitidae seem to share a common origin from the primitive isopteran stock, and the species so far studied show a variable but relatively high moisture demand.

The ability to survive in dry surroundings seems to be an evolutionary specialization. In the family Kalotermitidae two distinct clusters of genera are indicated on morphological grounds in Krishna's 1961 revision. With the exception of *Pterotermes,* the genera for which data are available fall into the same two distinct groups on the basis of moisture requirements: the very moisture-dependent *Neotermes, Kalotermes, Paraneotermes, Calcaritermes* group and the more desiccation-tolerant *Incisitermes, Marginitermes, Cryptotermes* group. Data on Kalotermitid genera not represented in the North American fauna and information on *Cryptocercus punctulatus* Scudder will be necessary to complete the picture.

In the three species of the North American fauna best adapted for survival in dry surroundings, there seems to have been a loss of the ability to tolerate high environmental humidities.

REFERENCES

Beament, J. W. L. (1961). The water relations of insect cuticle. *Biol. Rev.* **36**, 281-320.

Beament, J. W. L. (1964). The active transport and passive movement of water in insects. *Advan. Insect Physiol.* **2**, 67-129.

Becker, G. (1965). Feuchtigkeitseinfluss auf Nahrungswahl und -verbrauch einiger Termiten-arten. *Insectes Sociaux* **12**, 151-184.

Bodot, P. (1966). Etudes écologique et biologique des Termites des savanes de Basse Cote-d'Ivoire. Ph.D. Dissertation, Université D'Aix-Marseille.

Bursell, E. (1964). Environmental aspects: Humidity. *In* "The Physiology of Insecta" (M. Rockstein, ed.), Vol. 1, pp. 324-357. Academic Press, New York.

Buxton, P. (1932). Terrestrial insects and the humidity of the environment. *Biol. Rev.* **7**, 275-320.

Calaby, J. H., and Gay, F. J. (1959). Aspects of the distribution and ecology of Australian termites. *In* "Biogeography and Ecology in Australia" (A. Keast, R. L. Crocker, and C. S. Christian, eds.), pp. 211-223. Junk Publ., The Hague.

Collins, M. S. (1958). Differences in toleration of drying and rate of water loss between species of termites (*Reticulitermes, Kalotermes, Neotermes, Cryptotermes*). *Anat. Record* **132**, 423-424 (abstr.).

Collins, M. S. (1959). Studies on water relations in Florida termites. I. Survival time and rate of water loss during drying. *Quart. J., Florida Acad. Sci.* **21**, 341-352.

Collins, M. S. (1966). Water loss and cuticular structure in North American termites—a preliminary report. *Proc. 2nd Workshop Termite Res., Biloxi, Mississippi, 1965* pp. 25-33. Natl. Acad. Sci.—Natl. Res. Council, Washington, D. C.

Collins, M. S., and Richards, A. G. (1963). Studies on water relations in North American termites. I. Eastern species of the genus *Reticulitermes* (Isoptera, Rhinotermitidae). *Ecology* 44, 600-604.

Collins, M. S., and Richards, A. G. (1966). Studies on water relations in North American termites. II. Water loss and cuticular structure in eastern species of the Kalotermitidae (Isoptera). *Ecology* 47, 328-331.

Cook, S., and Scott, K. (1932). The relation between absorption and elimination of water by *Termopsis angusticollis*. *Biol. Bull.* 63, 505-512.

Dunmore, L. A., and Collins, M. S. (1951). Caste differences in toleration of drying in *Reticulitermes flavipes* (Kollar). *Anat. Record* 111,

Ebeling, W. (1961). Physicochemical mechanisms for the removal of insect wax by means of finely-divided powders. *Hilgardia* 30, 531-564.

Ebeling, W., and Wagner, R. E. (1959). Rapid desiccation of drywood termites with inert sorptive dusts and other substances. *J. Econ. Entomol.* 52, 190-207.

Edney, E. B. (1967). Water balance in desert arthropods. *Science* 156, 1059-1066.

Emerson, A. E. (1955). Geographical origins and dispersions of termite genera. *Fieldiana, Zool.* 37, 465-519.

Emerson, A. E. (1958). The evolution of behavior among social insects. *In* "Behavior and Evolution" (A. Roe and G. Simpson, eds.), pp. 311-335. Yale Univ. Press, New Haven, Connecticut.

Ernst, E. (1956). Die Reaktionen von Vier Termitenarten in der Feuchtigkeitsorgel. *Insectes Sociaux* 3, 229-231.

Ernst, E. (1957). Der Einfluss der Luftfeuchtigkeit auf Lebensdauer unter verhalten verschiedener Termitenarten. *Acta Trop.* 14, 97-156.

Fyfe, R. V., and Gay, F. J. (1938). "The Humidity of the Atmosphere and the Moisture Conditions within Mounds of Eutermes exitiosus Hill," Pamphlet 82. Council Sci. Ind. Res., Australia.

Gösswald, K. (1941). Einfluss verschiedener Temperatur und Luftfeuchtigkeit auf Termiten. *Mitt. Biol. Zentralanstalt Land- Forstwirtsch., Berlin-Dahlem* 65, 33.

Grassé, P.-P., and Chauvin, R. (1944). L'effet de groupe et la survie des neutres dans les sociétés d'insects. *Rev. Sci.* 82, 461-464.

Hetrick, L. A. (1961). *Kalotermes approximatus* infests Roseaceous trees *Florida Entomologist* 44, 53-54.

Klee, O. (1960). Uber den Einfluss der Temperature und der Luftfeuchtigkeit auf die toxische Wirkung organischsynthetischer Insektizide. *Z. Angew. Zool.* 47, 183-229.

Kofoid, C. A., ed. (1934). "Termites and Termite Control." Univ. of California Press, Berkeley, California.

Krishna, K. (1961). A generic revision and phylogenetic study of the family Kalotermitidae (Isoptera). *Bull. Am. Museum Nat. Hist.* 122, 303-408.

Locke, M. (1965). Permeability of the insect cuticle to water and lipids. *Science* 147, 295-298.

Mellanby, K. (1939). The functions of insect blood. *Biol. Rev.* 14, 243-260.

Noirot, C. (1958-1959). Remarques sur l'écologie des Termites. *Ann. Soc. Roy. Belg.* 539, 151-169.

Noirot, C., and Noirot-Timothée, C. (1960). Mise en évidence d'ultrastructures absorbantes dans l'intestin postérieur des insects. *Compt. Rend.* 251, 2779-2781.

Noirot, C., and Noirot-Timothée, C. (1966a). Présence de mucopolysaccharides acides dans la cuticle intestinale des insectes. Étude histochimique et ultrastructurale. *Compt. Rend.* D263, 768-770.

Noirot, C., and Noirot-Timothée, C. (1966b). Revêtement de la membrane cytoplasmique et absorption des ions dans les papilles rectales d'un Termite (Insecta, Isoptera). *Compt. Rend.* **D263**, 1099-1102.

Noirot-Timothée, C., and Noirot, C. (1967). Liaison de mitochondries avec des zones d'adhésion intercellulaires. *J. Microscopie* **6**, 87-90.

Noirot, C., Noirot-Timothée, C., and Kovoor, J. (1967). Revêtement particulaire de la membrane plasmatique en rapport avec l'excretion dans une region specialisée de l'intestine moyen des Termites supérieurs. *Compt. Rend.* **D264**, 722-725.

Nutting, W. L. (1965). Observations on the nesting site and biology of the Arizona damp-wood termite *Zootermopsis laticeps* (Banks) (Hodotermitidae). *Psyche* **72**, 113-125.

Nutting, W. L. (1966a). Colonizing flights and associated activities of termites. I. The desert damp-wood termite *Paraneotermes simplicicornis* (Kalotermitidae). *Psyche* **73**, 131-149.

Nutting, W. L. (1966b). Distribution and biology of the primitive dry wood termite *Pterotermes occidentis* (Walker) (Kalotermitidae). *Psyche* **73**, 165-179.

Pence, R. J. (1956). The tolerance of the drywood termite, *Kalotermes minor* Hagen, to desiccation. *J. Econ. Entomol.* **49**, 553-554.

Pence, R. J. (1957). The prolonged maintenance of the western subterranean termite in the laboratory with moisture gradient tubes. *J. Econ. Entomol.* **50**, 238-240.

Richards, A. G. (1958). The cuticle of arthropods. *Ergeb. Biol.* **20**, 1-26.

Sen-Sarma, P. K. (1964). The effects of temperature and relative humidity on the longevity of pseudoworkers of *Kalotermes flavicollis* (Fabr.) (Isoptera) under starvation conditions. *Proc. Natl. Inst. Sci. India* **B30**, 300-314.

Skaife, S. H. (1955). "Dwellers in Darkness." Longmans, Green, London.

Snyder, T. E. (1961). Supplement to the annotated subject-heading bibliography of termites, 1955-1960. *Smithsonian Misc. Collections* **143**, 1-114.

Stobbart, R. H., and Shaw, J. (1964). Salt and water balance: Excretion. *In* "Physiology of Insecta" (M. Rockstein, ed.), Vol. 3, pp. 190-255. Academic Press, New York.

Strickland, M. J. (1950). Differences in toleration of drying between species of termites (Reticulitermes). *Ecology* **31**, 373-385.

Stuart, A. M. (1967). Alarm, defense and construction behavior relationships in termites (Isoptera), *Science* **156**, 1123-1125.

Wigglesworth, V. B. (1956). "Insect Physiology," 5th ed., Wiley, New York.

Williams, O. L. (1934). Some factors limiting the distribution of termites. *In* "Termites and Termite Control" (C. A. Kofoid, ed.), 2nd ed., pp. 42-49. Univ. of California Press, Berkeley, California.

15

Species Introduced by Man

I. INTRODUCTION

The history of termite introductions to new countries extends over more than 100 years for there are two well-authenticated records of established exotic species which date from the first half of the nineteenth century — *Reticulitermes flavipes* (Kollar), a North American species found near Vienna, Austria in 1837, and *Heterotermes perfidus* (Silvestri), a species of uncertain origin but definitely introduced, which appears to have been present in St. Helena from about 1840. Within recent years there has been an increase both in the records of introductions and the numbers of species involved so that at present there are published references to some 42 positively identified and possibly 8 unidentified species, which have been introduced to new areas or countries.

In many instances these references are to species intercepted at ports of entry, to species which have failed to become established in exotic environments, or to species whose original home is uncertain. However, there are at least 17 species for which there is unequivocal evidence of their establishment in new habitats. These occur mainly in the Kalotermitidae and Rhinotermitidae, and particularly in the genera *Cryptotermes* and *Coptotermes*.

The ease and success with which dry-wood termites, such as *Cryptotermes*, are moved from place to place are associated with their ability to tolerate relatively low-moisture conditions for lengthy periods, with their habits of infesting timber and furniture isolated from the ground, and with the fact that the small size of their colonies frequently results in entire colonies being transported in a single, small wooden article.

The spread of subterranean termites, which normally require access to a constant source of moisture, has been achieved by such means as the invasion of tubs or pots containing plants growing in soil, the invasion of timber which has been in contact with the ground for some time prior to shipment, or the infestation of timber of a high moisture content in ships.

In general, termites appear to have fairly prescribed environmental requirements so that introduced species are more likely to succeed in establishing themselves in environments which are climatically similar to their native habitat. At times this similarity may be the result of artificial factors such as heating systems; this certainly appears to have been an important factor in the establishment of *Reticulitermes flavipes* in Hamburg, Germany.

Introduced species frequently become of considerable economic importance, although they are rarely able to invade native habitats and are almost always restricted to the man-modified environments of houses, buildings, and cultivated crops. This restriction seems to be more definite in continental areas than in islands or islandlike areas and may be due to biotic barriers (resulting from the presence of closely related native species), which are strong in continental areas, but relatively weak in the simpler island communities (Emerson, 1949).

The species of termites that have been introduced to new habitats are listed in Table I. This table shows for each species the country or countries known or believed to be the original home as well as the countries to which it has been introduced, with some indication of the date of such introduction where this is known. It also indicates whether or not the species has merely been intercepted or is considered to be established in the new country. Where the origin of a species is obscure or there is some doubt as to whether it is an introduction and, if so, whether it is established, this is indicated in the table by a question mark.

II. INDIVIDUAL HISTORIES OF INTRODUCTION OR INTERCEPTION

The history and manner of introduction or interception of all species known to have been involved in artificial dispersal have been given in detail elsewhere with complete bibliography (Gay, 1967). Many of these case histories, which refer solely to interceptions, are based on one or two records only and do not warrant detailed consideration here. Instead, attention will be focused on those species which have been very firmly established and/or widely distributed in new areas through man's activities.

A. MASTOTERMITIDAE

1. Mastotermes darwiniensis Froggatt

Mastotermes darwiniensis, which is restricted to Australia, is widely distributed throughout the tropical zone of the continent, both inland and close to busy ports such as Townsville, Queensland and Darwin, Northern Territory. This termite, which normally lives in logs and the stems and branches of trees and shrubs, is capable of causing severe damage to constructional timber and is the most important economic species in tropical Australia.

In 1961 a series of all castes which had been collected from a store in Lae, New Guinea was identified as *M. darwiniensis.* The presence of alates in this collection indicated that the infestation had been established for some time. Subsequently, the discovery of a single alate specimen in the insect collection of the Department of Agriculture, Stock, and Fisheries which had been collected at Lae early in 1959 indicated an even earlier date of introduction than at first believed.

A survey of the infestation showed that two areas, of approximately 30 and 20 acres, respectively, were involved; the former, a commercial area occupied by stores, a timber mill, and various minor industries; the latter, a relatively undeveloped area with only a few houses and small sheds. In both areas there was evidence of attack on structural timber in buildings, posts in the ground, and living trees and shrubs, including hibiscus, pawpaw, kapok, guava, and rain trees. Numerous small colonies were detected in both areas as well as one very large colony in a log dump near the center of the commercial area. This colony appeared to be the focal point from which the general infestation had spread.

The log dump, which covered an area of about one acre, consisted of Australian eucalypts imported into Lae toward the end of World War II. There is strong evidence that these logs formed part of a shipment sent to Darwin earlier in the war, subsequently found to be surplus to requirements and then reconsigned to Lae. There is little doubt that during the period in Darwin some of the logs became infested with *M. darwiniensis,* either as incipient colonies headed by primary reproductives or more probably as "budded" colonies headed by neotenic reproductives. The colony or colonies survived the passage to Lae and there produced at

TABLE I

List of Termite Species Which Have Been Introduced to Other Countries[a]

Species	Country or countries of origin	Country or area of introduction	Status Established	Status Intercepted	Authority
Mastotermes darwiniensis Froggatt	Australia	New Guinea: Lae (prior to 1959)	+		Division of Entomology, CSIRO (1961)
Kalotermes flavicollis (F.)	Mediterranean area and Asia Minor	England: Liverpool (1961)		+	Harris (1962)
Kalotermes sp.	Tahiti	Hawaii: Honolulu (1927)		+	Ehrhorn (1934)
Kalotermes sp.	Mexico	Hawaii: Honolulu (1930)		+	Ehrhorn (1934)
Kalotermitidae	East Africa	England: Kew Gardens (1874)		+	McLachlan (1874)
Kalotermitidae	?	England: Bethnal Green (1955)		+	Harris (1962)
		New York: Niagara Falls (1952)		+	Snyder (1952b)
Incisitermes immigrans (Snyder)	Hawaii, Marquesas, Galapagos, Central and South America	Jarvis Island	?		Light (1935)
		?Fanning Island	+		Light (1935)
Incisitermes minor (Hagen)	U.S.A. (western states)	Ohio: Cleveland (1952)		+	Snyder (1952b)
		Oklahoma (1957)		+	Anonymous (1957)
		Arkansas: Fort Smith (1962)		+	Anonymous (1962)
		Maryland: Bethesda (1962)		+	Anonymous (1962)
		Iowa: Storm Lake (1962)		+	Anonymous (1962)
		Texas: San Antonio (1963)		+	Anonymous (1963)
Incisitermes nigritus (Snyder)	Guatemala	California: San Francisco (1945)		+	Snyder (1946)
Neotermes insularis (Walker)	Australia	New Zealand (prior to 1853)	+		Clark (1938), Hill (1942)
Neotermes jouteli (Banks)	Bahamas, Cuba, Mexico, southern Florida	England		+	Harris (1955a,b and in litt.)

Cryptotermes brevis (Walker)	West Indies and Caribbean, South and Central America			Reference
Hawaii (ca. 1900)	+			Fullaway (1926)
Hawaii: Honolulu (1926)		+		Ehrhorn (1934)
Hawaii: Honolulu (1927)		+		Ehrhorn (1934)
Florida: Key West (1919)	+			Banks and Snyder (1920)
California: Berkeley (1936)		+		Light (1936)
Louisiana	+			Emerson (1936)
Tennessee: Memphis (1952)		+		Snyder (1952a)
Missouri: St. Louis (1952)		+		Snyder (1952a)
Wisconsin: Madison (1952)	?			Snyder (1952a)
California		+		Snyder (1952a)
Connecticut		+		Snyder (1952a)
North Carolina		+		Snyder (1952a)
New York		+		Snyder (1952a)
Ohio		+		Snyder (1952a)
West Virginia		+		Snyder (1952a)
Canada: Belleville, Ont. (1952)	?			Snyder (1952a)
Washington, D.C. (1954)		+		Snyder (1954a)
Maryland: Kensington (1962)		+		Anonymous (1962)
China	+			Light (1931)
Marquesas Islands	+			Light (1932)
Midway Islands (1951)	+			Keck (1952)
Fiji (1932, 1937)	?			Lever (1939b)
?British Guiana: Georgetown (1920)	+			Emerson (1936)
?Brazil: São Paulo, Minas Gerais	+			Araujo (1958)
?Venezuela: Caracas, Cua, etc.	+			Martorell (1939)
St. Helena: Jamestown		+		Harris (1953, 1958)
England: Lancing, Sussex (1957)		+		Harris (*in litt.*)
England: Watford, Mx. (1960)		+		Hickin (1963)
South Africa: Durban (before 1920)	+			Coaton (1948)

TABLE 1 (*Continued*)

Species	Country or countries of origin	Country or area of introduction	Status Established	Status Intercepted	Authority
Cryptotermes brevis (Walker) (*continued*)	West Indies and Caribbean, South and Central America (*continued*)	Various localities in Natal, Zululand, Cape Province (1943–1961)	? ? ?		Hepburn, G. A. (*in litt.*) Hepburn, G. A. (*in litt.*) Hepburn, G. A. (*in litt.*)
		Congo: Boma	?		Coaton (1948)
		Sierra Leone: Njala	?		Coaton (1948)
		Canary Islands	+		Benito Martínex (1957)
		Peru: Lima	?		Coaton (*in litt.*)
		El Salvador: Chilata (1942)	?		Coaton (*in litt.*)
		Australia: Maryborough, Qld. (before 1964)	?		Division of Entomology. CSIRO (1965)
		Australia: Hornsby, N.S.W. (1933)	?		Division of Entomology. CSIRO (1965)
		New Caledonia: Nouméa (before 1933)	+		Division of Entomology. CSIRO (1965)
		Easter Island (before 1965)	+		I. E. Efford (*in litt.*)
Cryptotermes cynocephalus Light	Philippines	Ceylon	?		Ahmad (1953)
		New Britain: Rabaul	?		Hill (1942)
		Hawaii: Honolulu (1930)		+	Ehrhorn (1934)
		Holland: Amsterdam (1959)		+	Harris (*in litt.*)
Cryptotermes domesticus (Haviland)	?Indo–Malayan	?Fanning Island	+		Kirby (1925)
		?Marquesas Islands	+		Light (1932)
		Panama: Taboga Island (before 1926)	+		Araujo (*in litt.*)
		Samoa	+		Hill (1942)

Species	Locality			Reference
	Solomon Islands: Tulagi	+		Hill (1942)
	New Britain: Rabaul	+		Hill (1942)
	Fiji: Suva	+		Hill (1942)
	Australia: Thursday Island	+		Hill (1942)
	Oeno Island	?		Light and Zimmerman (1936)
	Austral Islands	?		Light and Zimmerman (1936)
	Society Islands	+		Light and Zimmerman (1936)
	Flint Island	?		Light and Zimmerman (1936)
	Tahiti	+		Light and Zimmerman (1936)
	Guam	+		Swezey (1940)
	Australia: Darwin (1959)		+	Division of Entomology, CSIRO (1959)
Cryptotermes dudleyi Banks	(?)Oriental region: Ceylon to Philippines			
	Panama (before 1890)	+		Emerson (1936)
	Costa Rica: San José (1925)	+		Snyder (1926)
	Trinidad: St. Augustine	?		Emerson (*in litt.*)
	Australia: Darwin (before 1913)	?		Hill (1942)
	Australia: Thursday Island (before 1933)	?		Hill (1942)
	East Pakistan: Khulna (1955)	+		Sen-Sarma and Mathur (1957)
	India: Orissa and Lower Bengal (1956, 1957)	+		Sen-Sarma and Mathur (1957)
	Kenya, Tanzania, and Somalia (numerous records)	+		Wilkinson, W. (*in litt.*)
	Uganda (1963)		+	Wilkinson, W. (*in litt.*)
	Marshall Islands: Arno Atoll	?		Emerson (*in litt.*)
	Mauritius	?		Emerson (*in litt.*)
	Madagascar	?		Emerson (*in litt.*)
	Cocos (Keeling) Islands	?		Harris (*in litt.*)
Cryptotermes havilandi (Sjöstedt)	Eastern countries of Africa and Belgian Congo			
	Madagascar	+		Moszkowski (1955)
	Fernando Póo (1873)	+		Moszkowski (1955)

TABLE I (*Continued*)

Species	Country or countries of origin	Country or area of introduction	Status		Authority
			Established	Intercepted	
Cryptotermes havilandi (Sjöstedt) (*continued*)	Eastern countries of Africa and Belgian Congo (*continued*)	Nigeria: Port Harcourt	+		Moszkowski (1955)
		Senegal: Thiès	?		Moszkowski (1955)
		Comoro Islands	+		Moszkowski (1955)
		Europa Islands	+		Moszkowski (1955)
		Trinidad: several localities	+		Moszkowski (1955)
		British Guiana: Kartabo	?		Moszkowski (1955)
		Surinam: Paramaribo	?		Moszkowski (1955)
		?India: Sundarbans, Bengal	+		Moszkowski (1955)
		Ivory Coast	?		Araujo (1958: *in litt.*)
		Brazil: Santos and Guaratuba	?		Araujo (1958: *in litt.*)
		Tobago: Speyside	?		Adamson (1940)
		?India and East Pakistan	?		Chhotani (1963)
Cryptotermes sp.	?Mexico	Germany: Hamburg		+	Wichmann (1957)
	South America	England: Melton Mowbray Leics. (1957)		+	Harris (*in litt.*)
Glyptotermes tuberculatus Froggatt	Australia	New Zealand	?		Kelsey (1944)
Bifiditermes condonensis (Hill)	Australia	New Zealand	?		Kelsey (1944)
Ceratokalotermes spoliator (Hill)	Australia	New Zealand: Otahuhu (1960)		+	F. J. Gay and K. M. Harrow (*in litt.*)
Zootermopsis angusticollis (Hagen)	Western North America: British Columbia to lower California	Japan: Hiroshima (1937)		+	Esaki (1937)
		Pennsylvania: Philadelphia		+	Snyder (1952a)
		Ohio: Oxford		+	Snyder (1952a)
		Texas: Dallas		+	Snyder (1954b)

Species	Distribution	Locality			Reference
		Indiana: Indianapolis		+	Snyder (1954b)
		Michigan: Howell		+	Snyder (1954b)
		Missouri: Kansas City		+	Snyder (1954b)
		Kansas: Wichita		+	Snyder (1954b)
		England: Bethnal Green London (1955)		+	Harris (1955b)
Zootermopsis (?) *angusticollis* (Hagen)	(As above)	Germany: Hamburg (1956)		+	Wichmann (1957)
		Australia: Sydney (1963)		+	CSIRO records (1963)
		Australia: Tamworth, N.S.W. (1966)		+	CSIRO records (1966)
Porotermes adamsoni (Froggatt)	Australia (east coastal areas)	Australia: Adelaide (1935)		+	CSIRO records (1936)
		Australia: Chester Hill, Sydney (1956)		+	CSIRO records (1956)
		New Zealand	?		Kelsey (1944) and D.S.I.R. records (1958)
Heterotermes perfidus (Silvestri)	?	Australia: Adelaide (1944)	+		CSIRO records (1944)
		St. Helena (ca. 1840)			McLachlan (1874)
					Emerson (1936)
					Harris (1953)
		Madagascar	+		Cachan (1949)
		Mauritius	+		Moutia (1936)
		U.S.A.: Massachusetts	+		Emerson (*in litt.*)
Heterotermes philippinensis (Light)	Philippines				
Reticulitermes arenincola Goellner	U.S.A.: Michigan and Indiana				
Reticulitermes hesperus Banks	U.S.A. (western states)	Hawaii: Honolulu (1926)	+		Ehrhorn (1934)
Reticulitermes flavipes (Kollar)	U.S.A. (eastern states), northern Mexico, and Guatemala	Austria: Vienna (1837)		+	Emerson (1936)
		Germany: Hamburg (1937)			Weidner (1937)
		Germany: Mannheim	?		Wichmann (1957)
		Austria: Hallein (?1950)	?		von Kurir (1958)
		Canada: Ontario (1935–1938)	+		Urquhart (1953, 1954)
		Canada: Ottawa, Ont. (1961)		+	MacNay (1961)

TABLE 1 (*Continued*)

Species	Country or countries of origin	Country or area of introduction	Status — Established	Status — Intercepted	Authority
Reticulitermes lucifugus (Rossi)	Germany: Hamburg	U.S.A.: California (prior to 1908)		+	Banks and Snyder (1920)
Reticulitermes speratus (Kolbe)	Japan, Korea	Hawaii: Honolulu (1922)		+	Whitney (1929)
Reticulitermes sp.	U.S.A.: Maryland	Hawaii: Honolulu (1925)		+	Ehrhorn (1934)
Coptotermes acinaciformis (Froggatt)	Australia	New Zealand: Auckland	+		Kelsey (1944)
Coptotermes (?) *acinaciformis* (Froggatt)	Australia	Fiji, Suva	?		Lever (1939a)
Coptotermes amanii (Sjöstedt)	Tanganyika, Zanzibar	South Africa, Durban (1960)		+	Coaton (*in litt.*)
Coptotermes crassus Snyder	Honduras, western Mexico	Texas: Houston (1956)		+	Dorward (1956)
Coptotermes formosanus Shiraki	Japan, Formosa, south China	Hawaii: Honolulu (ca. 1900)	+		Oshima (1920)
					Fullaway (1926)
		Hawaii: Honolulu (1927)		+	Ehrhorn (1934)
		Guam	+		Clagg (1958)
		Midway Islands	+		Clagg (1958)
		Marshall Islands	+		Clagg (1958)
		South Africa: Simonstown (1925)	+		Coaton (1950)
		South Africa: Komatipoort (1958)	+		Coaton (*in litt.*)
		?Ceylon	?		Ahmad (1953)
		U.S.A.: Texas (1965)	?		Anonymous (1965)
		U.S.A.: Louisiana (1966)	+		Anonymous (1966)
Coptotermes frenchi Hill	Australia	New Zealand: Auckland	+		Kelsey (1944)

Species	Origin	Locality	Established	Reference
Coptotermes havilandi Holmgren	SE. Asia and Indonesia	Marquesas Islands (prior to 1932)	+	Light (1932)
		Mauritius (prior to 1936)	+	Moutia (1936)
		Réunion	?	Paulian (1957)
		Barbados	+	Tucker (1939)
		Jamaica	+	Adamson (1948)
		Brazil: São Paulo, Santos	+	Araujo (1958)
		Brazil: Rio de Janeiro	?	Gonçalves and Silva (1962)
Coptotermes heimi (Wasmann)	India and West Pakistan	?Java		Kemner (1934)
Coptotermes lacteus (Froggatt)	Australia	Singapore	+	Lever (1952)
		New Zealand: Auckland		Clark (1938)
Coptotermes testaceus (Linnaeus)	Trinidad, Tobago, and South America (British Guiana)	Barbados	+	Saint (1940)
Coptotermes vastator Light	Philippines	Hawaii: Honolulu (1918)		Ehrhorn (1934)
		Hawaii: Honolulu (prior to 1963)	+	Bess (1965)
Coptotermes sp.	?	Australia: Sydney	+	Division of Entomology, CSIRO (1965)
Termes hispaniolae (Banks)	Central and South America, islands in West Indies	Barbados (1939–1940)	+	Saint (1940)
Nasutitermes columbicus (Holmgren)	Colombia, Panama, Costa Rica	Germany: Hamburg (1902)	+	Wichmann (1957)
Nasutitermes corniger (Motschulsky)	Mexico, Central America, Bolivia	Honolulu	+	Swezey (1945)
		Washington, D.C.	+	Swezey (1945)
		New Jersey	+	Swezey (1945)
Nasutitermes costalis (Holmgren)	West Indies, Central and South America	England: Spalding, Lincs. (1942)	+	Riley (1943)
Nasutitermes fulviceps (Silvestri)	Argentina, Brazil, Uruguay, Paraguay	Germany: Hamburg (1899)	+	Wichmann (1957)

TABLE I (*Continued*)

Species	Country or countries of origin	Country or area of introduction	Status		Authority
			Estab-lished	Inter-cepted	
Nasutitermes nigriceps (Haldeman)	Central and South America, islands in West Indies	Florida: Miami (1958)		+	Anonymous (1958)
Nasutitermes octopilis Banks	British Guiana	Barbados (1939 – 1940)		+	Saint (1940)
Nasutitermes walkeri (Hill)	Australia	New Zealand: Hawkes Bay	?		Kelsey (1944)
Nasutitermes sp.	Borneo	California		+	Swezey (1945)
Trinervitermes sp.	?	England: Croydon, Surrey (1948)		+	Sweeney (1948)

[a]Comprised of those which have become established together with those intercepted in transit (modified from Gay, 1967).

least one flight of winged adults which gave rise to the numerous small colonies evident in both areas of infestation when the original survey was made in 1962. A vigorous and thorough control campaign has eliminated most of this infestation in Lae, so that at the present time (1968) only small pockets remain.

B. KALOTERMITIDAE

1. Incisitermes immigrans (Snyder)

Incisitermes immigrans is recorded from areas on the Pacific coast of Central and South America, from islands in the Pacific from Hawaii through Fanning and Jarvis Islands to the Marquesas, and from the Galapagos Islands.

Some aspects of the present distribution of this species are obscure, as is also its center of origin, although the logical place would appear to be the Pacific coastal regions of Central and South America. The Jarvis Island record refers to infested wood from a wrecked schooner and undoubtedly represents an introduction. Transport by ocean currents may explain the presence of this species on the Hawaiian and Marquesas Islands, but not on Fanning Island, which lies in the counterequatorial current. It is possible, therefore, that the species was introduced to Fanning Island also through human agencies (Light, 1935).

2. Incisitermes minor (Hagen)

Incisitermes minor is found in the western United States and lower California. It is the most common dry-wood termite in California and is responsible for extensive damage to poles and, to a lesser extent, to timber in buildings.

Over the past 15 years this termite has been introduced on numerous occasions to cities in central and eastern United States. Infestations which have been reported from Cleveland, Ohio; Niagara Falls, New York; Fort Smith, Arkansas; Bethesda, Maryland; Storm Lake, Iowa; San Antonio, Texas; and Oklahoma have been traced to sources such as wooden chests, furniture, and grape boxes brought in from the West Coast. All these infestations appear to have been dealt with effectively soon after discovery, and there is no published evidence of the permanent establishment of *I. minor* in the eastern United States.

3. Neotermes insularis (Walker)

Neotermes insularis has a wide distribution in coastal and near-coastal districts of eastern and northern Australia, from Victoria to the Northern

Territory. It occurs commonly in dead stumps, firewood, and rotting logs, but is often an important pest of living trees, particularly eucalypts, because of the extensive gallery systems it produces, especially in the upper portions of the bole.

This species was described by Walker in 1853 from winged forms collected in New Zealand, and there have been many records of its occurrence there since then. Almost all of these refer to small colonies found in hardwood poles imported from Australia. Some of these eucalpt poles had been in service for more than 15 years and contained nymphs in all stages of development as well as winged adults. It appears, therefore, that *N. insularis* is established in New Zealand and may well have been so for over a century. There are no records of the species attacking indigenous trees in New Zealand, and, conversely, in Australia there are no records of it attacking utility poles or pole crossarms.

4. Cryptotermes brevis (Walker)

Cryptotermes brevis occurs throughout the West Indies and Caribbean regions, and in South and Central America. This dry-wood termite, which is a serious pest of timber in service and furniture wherever it occurs, appears to have been more widely and more frequently introduced to new countries than any other species of termite (Fig. 1). As a consequence, it is difficult in some instances to determine whether it is a native or introduced species.

Cryptotermes brevis was first recorded from the continental United States in 1919 when winged adults were collected from a house in Key West, Florida. This and other records from Florida and Louisiana were all from buildings and suggest that it was introduced from the West Indies. Since this original discovery, *C. brevis* has been detected or intercepted at widely separated places in the United States. In the period from 1936 to 1962 it was found at Berkeley, California; Memphis, Tennessee; St. Louis, Missouri; Madison, Wisconsin; Washington, D. C.; and in cities in Connecticut, North Carolina, New York, Ohio, and West Virginia. These infestations were in articles of household and office furniture as well as in constructional timber in buildings, and their origins could be traced to places such as the Caribbean region, Peru, Hawaii, and Asia.

In Hawaii itself the species has been present from about 1904 and is believed to have been introduced, at about that time or possibly a little earlier, in the course of Oriental commerce. Some weight is given to this belief by the fact that *C. brevis* has been intercepted in Hawaii, at least twice since the original introduction, in goods brought in from the Orient. These facts would suggest that it is a fairly widely and successfully established species in the Orient. However, the only published record of

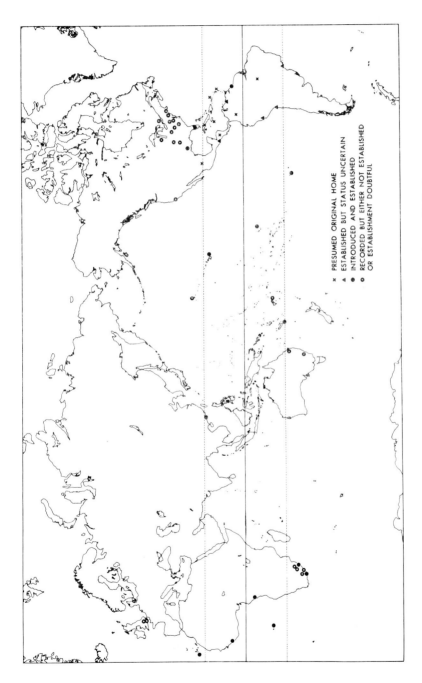

Fig. 1. Distribution map of *Cryptotermes brevis* (Walker).

its occurrence in that region is that of Light (1931) who considered it was of Chinese origin and "may be expected to be a 'house termite' in China as in Honolulu." Its early history and precise status in the Orient remain obscure, although the paucity of records suggest that it is not a native species.

There are several records of the occurrence of *C. brevis* in the Pacific area. It was collected in the Marquesas Islands in 1929 when alates were found swarming around a light and was probably introduced there as in Hawaii. In 1932 it was detected in Fiji in house timbers and again in 1937 in furniture, but there is no evidence that it has become established. In 1951 it was found infesting woodwork on Midway Island. There are two records of its presence in Australia, the first in 1946 near Sydney, New South Wales in a chair imported from New Caledonia 13 years previously; the second in 1964 in the timbers of a house at Maryborough, Queensland. The origin of the latter infestation is unknown. There is no evidence of establishment at the first of these two localities. In the latter town, however, a survey following the initial discovery revealed a small number of infested houses, but the prospects of eradication are good. In 1965 a very extensive infestation of *C. brevis* was detected in the Administrative Buildings of the South Pacific Commission in Noumea, New Caledonia. In view of the fact that furniture infested with this termite was imported into Australia from New Caledonia as early as 1933 (see above), there is little doubt that *C. brevis* is firmly established there. In 1965 *C. brevis* was also recorded as commonly occurring in the buildings of a village on Easter Island. This appears to be an established infestation which almost certainly developed from infested timber brought from Chile by a naval vessel that visits the island annually.

The Central and South American records for this species suggest that in some areas it is an introduced rather than a native species. In Guyana (British Guiana), where it was found at Georgetown in 1920, it does not appear to be established in wild areas of the country (Emerson, 1936). In Brazil, where Araujo has recorded its presence in the State of São Paulo, it has only been found in man-made structures. Similarly, in Venezuela it is reported to be very abundant in furniture and wooden buildings in many regions, but there are no references to it occurring in native habitats (Martorell, 1939). *Cryptotermes brevis* is also recorded from Lima, Peru and Chilata, El Salvador and, on the evidence of the Easter Island infestation, is presumed to be present in Chile. There is, however, no indication of its status in any of these countries.

In 1939 *C. brevis* was collected from constructional timber at two different sites on the island of St. Helena. It has been suggested that these infestations stem from infested timber taken from a captured vessel brought to the island during the Napoleonic war (Harris, 1958). If this is so, it is surprising that the species remained undetected for so long. It seems more probable that the introduction took place in more recent times.

There are two records of the introduction of *C. brevis* into England: one in 1957 in balsa wood from South America and one in 1960 in a wooden gramophone case from Trinidad.

The history of the introduction and spread of this dry-wood termite in South Africa is well documented (Coaton, 1948). The first specimens were found in Durban in 1918 so that the original infestation probably occurred during World War I. There was very little additional evidence of its presence for more than 10 years after this, but from 1930 onward sporadic new infestations were reported from the business areas of Durban adjacent to the original center of establishment, and by 1938 several of the largest commercial buildings in the city were showing signs of severe infestation. By 1947 the infestation had spread to the outer residential suburbs, and extensive damage was being caused to both hardwoods and softwoods in structural timber, wooden fittings, and furniture. In the same year, infestations were reported also from Ifafa Beach, 60 miles from Durban, and from Port Elizabeth, some 550 miles from Durban, although the latter infestation was subsequently estimated to be from 15 to 20 years old. It appears likely that both these infestations arose from the transport of infested timber from Durban. Since then, the Plant Protection Research Institute of South Africa has recorded the following occurrences of *C. brevis:* East London, Cape Province about 1950 and 1952; King Williamstown, Cape Province 1951; Hluhluwe Game Reserve, Zululand 1952; Pietermaritzburg, Natal about 1957; and Kwambonambi, Zululand about 1961. With a single exception these infestations all related to furniture brought from Durban.

Elsewhere in the African continent, *C. brevis* has been recorded from Boma, Congo and Njala, Sierra Leone. These undoubtedly represent introductions, as does a record from the Canary Islands.

5. *Cryptotermes cynocephalus* Light

Cryptotermes cynocephalus is a dry-wood termite native to the Philippines, where it has been collected from numerous localities attacking isolated boards in houses. This termite has been introduced into Ceylon, and has been found in the woodwork of a building in Rabaul, New Britain, but there are no details of its present status in either country. In addition there are two records of its interception, once in Honolulu, Hawaii in

1930 in wood attached to orchids from the Philippines and once at Amsterdam, Holland in 1959 in timber of unstated origin.

6. *Cryptotermes domesticus (Haviland)*

Cryptotermes domesticus occurs widely throughout the Indo-Malayan region and in numerous islands and island groups over a wide area of the Pacific, but the center of origin of the species is somewhat uncertain. It is a variable species which has been described under ten different specific names, and this circumstance has tended to mask recognition of the possibility that in some parts of its present range of distribution it is an introduction.

It was originally described from Singapore and Sarawak in 1898 and was said to be common in every house, but there was no reference to its occurrence in native habitats. Similarly, in the Hainan province of mainland China it was thought to be restricted to man-made structures. The only reference to its occurrence in exclusively native habitats, such as old stumps, dead trunks, timbers, and decayed portions of trees, is from Botel-Tobago Island, off the coast of Formosa (Hozawa, 1915). It is possible, therefore, that the center of origin of the species is the coastal region and/or the associated islands of southeast Asia.

Elsewhere, *C. domesticus* has been found chiefly in furniture and buildings or in cultivated trees and shrubs, as is indicated from the following records which cover the period 1925 – 1959: Fanning Island, from *Tournefortia* logs and coconut stumps; Marquesas Islands, from *Sapindus* log and mango; Guam, from buildings; Samoa, from furniture; Oeno Island, from *Tournefortia* log; Austral Islands, from dead coffee tree; Society Islands, from ornamental trees and shrubs and structural timber; Flint Island, from *Tournefortia* log and coconut; Tahiti, from structural timber; Darwin, Australia, from a sewing machine cabinet imported from Singapore; and Tulagi, Solomon Islands; Rabaul, New Britain; Suva, Fiji, all from furniture and buildings.

There is little doubt that most, if not all, of these records represent introductions and that the wide dispersal of this termite through the Pacific area has been aided by the movement of goods of commerce or household furniture.

7. *Cryptotermes dudleyi Banks*

Cryptotermes dudleyi is also a rather variable species which has been referred to under eight different specific names. Snyder (1949) records it from the Neotropical, Indo-Malayan, Papuan, and Australian regions, but its original habitat has not been definitely established. The most probable center appears to be the Indo-Malayan region between Ceylon and the Philippines, from which center it has been widely dispersed through commerce.

It was introduced into Panama prior to 1890, and, although it is now common in houses in the Canal Zone, it has not been found there in wild situations. In 1925 alates were captured in a house in San José, Costa Rica, and the presence of the species there could logically be linked with its successful establishment in Panama. In the adjacent Caribbean region it has been recorded from St. Augustine, Trinidad, and its absence from other islands in the West Indies suggests that it is an introduction.

There are three records of *C. dudleyi* from the Indo-Pakistan subcontinent: in 1955 it was found infesting posts and sawed timber at Khulna, East Pakistan (this is believed to be an introduction brought in after World War II) and in 1957 it was recorded at two localities in India — Barkuda Island, Chilka Lake, Orissa Province and Mangrove Forests, Sundarbans, Lower Bengal. The last-named record refers to infestations commonly found in bamboo and wooden buildings close to creeks and rivers in Sundarbans, and this association with man-made structures is characteristic of an introduced species.

The Australian records of *C. dudleyi* all appear to refer to introductions. In 1913 it was found at Darwin, Northern Territory in the trunk of a living coconut palm and in the stem of an indigenous shrub. Despite detailed searches on at least two subsequent occasions, it has not been seen again in this area. Very small colonies have been detected on two occasions elsewhere: one in the timbers of a building on Thursday Island and one in a native curio imported into Sydney, New South Wales from New Guinea. In the Pacific area there is a record of its presence on Arno atoll, Marshall Islands.

The species appears to have been introduced into the Cocos-Keeling Islands, as the British Museum (Natural History) collection contains an alate male from that locality.

In East Africa the first record of *C. dudleyi* was in stored timber at Tanga, Tanganyika (Harris, 1950). It was later found to be well established in many coastal towns in Somalia, Kenya, and Tanganyika (now part of Tanzania), and is considered to be an introduced species which has been present for a long time, and probably brought in by the dhow traffic. In 1963 this termite was found inland in Uganda in the woodwork of a motor omnibus which had been imported some 7 or 8 years previously. It is believed that the body work of this bus was built in one of the coastal towns where *C. dudleyi* is well established.

Cryptotermes dudleyi is present in both Mauritius and Madagascar, and these records appear to represent introductions, probably from ports on the East African coast.

8. *Cryptotermes havilandi (Sjöstedt)*

Cryptotermes havilandi appears to be native to the eastern countries of Africa and to the rain forests of the Congo Republic. Throughout this area it is widespread in wild habitats, occurring in living branches, dead parts of living trees, dry wood in stumps, fallen logs, but only rarely in human habitations.

The indications are that this species was introduced by man into Madagascar, the western coast of Africa, South America, and islands off the coast of South America. *Cryptotermes havilandi* was probably brought to Madagascar by early travelers who journeyed in wooden rafts or boats, and this could account for its presence on Europa Island and the Comoro Islands, which lie between Madagascar and the African mainland (Moszkowski, 1955). Its occurrence in native habitats in Madagascar may be explained by the fact that in two other areas, namely, Kartabo, Guyana (British Guiana) and Port of Spain, Trinidad, *C. havilandi* has become established in a semiwild situation and also by the fact that exotic species are able to successfully invade native habitats in island communities with an impoverished fauna.

At Kartabo, Guyana this termite was collected at two sites from very old timber in man-made structures which had fallen into neglect and been invaded by native genera and species. It was also found in a recent building at the biological station, but was never found in adjacent native forest in 3 years' intensive collecting.

At Port of Spain, Trinidad this termite was found in dead stumps in a part of the botanical garden. Elsewhere on the island it has been responsible for extensive damage to houses. It is considered to be an introduction to this island as well as to the island of Tobago, where it has been recorded as attacking timber in a bungalow.

On the mainland of South America the records of *C. havilandi* all appear to represent introductions: Paramaribo, Surinam in a church organ; Santos, São Paulo, Brazil in wood prepared for furniture; and Guaratuba, D. F. Brazil in a timber support or stay.

The first record of the invasion of man-modified habitats by *C. havilandi* was from Africa in 1872. Alates emerging from wood which had been completely riddled by this termite were attracted to the light in a room at Victoria, Cameroon. The species has been collected from Nigeria, Senegal, Ivory Coast, and Gold Coast, and appears to be the common domestic dry-wood termite of West Africa and to have been introduced to all the above-mentioned countries. Records of *C. havilandi* from buildings in Dar es Salaam and Mombasa in East Africa are questionable and appear to relate to *C. dudleyi.*

Although Moszkowski (1955) recorded *C. havilandi* from India and concluded from "knowledge of the geographical location of the native habitat . . . (that this) would indicate that this species was introduced," this interpretation cannot be accepted. The material on which her conclusions were based was collected in what is obviously a wild habitat; the termite was described by Snyder as a new species, *Cryptotermes bengalensis,* which Moszkowski placed in synonymy with *C. havilandi.* More recent workers have rejected this synonymy and consider *C. bengalensis* as a valid species. Moreover, additional collections have been made from native trees and from localities some hundreds of kilometers inland which leave no doubt that this is a native species and not *C. havilandi.*

9. Other Kalotermitidae

Species of Kalotermitidae, other than those already referred to in detail, have been intercepted or detected on several occasions. In some instances they have not been identified beyond family level, but most have been assigned to a genus and often to a species. They include the following: *Kalotermes flavicollis* (Fabricius), a native of the Mediterranean region, intercepted at Liverpool, England in 1961 in wooden boxes containing currants from Greece; *Kalotermes* sp., intercepted at Honolulu, Hawaii in 1929 in a wooden box from Tahiti and in 1930 in wood attached to orchids from Mexico; *Neotermes jouteli* (Banks), a Central American and Caribbean species, detected in wood of *Lignum vitae* imported into England from San Domingo; *Incisitermes nigritus* (Snyder), native to Guatemala, intercepted at San Francisco, California in 1945 in logs of *Guaiacum officinale* from Guatemala; *Cryptotermes* sp., found at Hamburg, Germany in 1949 in postbags previously held for some time in Mexico; *Cryptotermes* sp., found at Melton Mowbray, Leics, England in 1957 in Parana pine from South America; *Glyptotermes tuberculatus* Froggatt, a native of the coastal areas of New South Wales, Australia, recorded from New Zealand in 1940. All castes were found in an Australian hardwood pole which collapsed during a gale. There is no evidence, to date, that this species is established in New Zealand. *Bifiditermes condonensis* (Hill), an endemic species in coastal areas of Australia, recorded from New Zealand in 1944. Nymphs and soldiers were collected from recently imported utility poles of Australian hardwood on two occasions, but the establishment of the species is doubtful. *Ceratokalotermes spoliator* (Hill), native to the coastal and tableland districts of eastern Australia, recorded from New Zealand in 1960 as a small colony of nymphs and soldiers in a power pole. There is no evidence of establishment in New Zealand. And Kalotermitidae – In 1874 alates and nymphs of a dry-wood termite were found in a trunk of *Trachylobium* sp. brought to England from East Africa, and in 1955 a tropical dry-wood termite was found in a timber yard in a suburb of London.

C. TERMOPSIDAE

1. *Zootermopsis angusticollis (Hagen)*

Zootermopsis angusticollis is a damp-wood termite with a wide distribution along the Pacific coast of North America, from Vancouver to the Mexican border. Generally the colonies are found in logs and stumps of pine or fir, but where constructional timber remains damp for long periods this species is also capable of causing extensive damage to buildings. Although *Z. angusticollis* has very high requirements for moisture, it can withstand a wide range of temperature conditions.

The species has been introduced to new areas on many occasions, but there is no evidence so far that it has become established in any of these. In view of its tolerance of varying climatic conditions, this failure to become established may be due to the early detection of introductions.

In 1937 it was found at Hiroshima, Japan infesting timber recently imported from Oregon, United States.

Between 1951 and 1954 at least ten introductions were made to the central and eastern United States in heavy timber planking shipped from Oregon. Infested timber was found at Philadelphia, Pennsylvania (twice); Oxford, Ohio; Dallas, Texas; Indianapolis, Indiana (three times); Howell, Michigan; Kansas City, Missouri; and Wichita, Kansas.

In 1955 *Z. angusticollis* was found in imported softwood (possibly Douglas fir) from western Canada in a timber yard in Bethnal Green, London, and in 1956 it was found in the sapwood of *Chamaecyparis lawsoniana* at Hamburg, Germany.

There are two positive records of introduction to Australia, one in 1963 to Sydney, New South Wales and one in 1966 to Tamworth, New South Wales; both were in Douglas fir timber. In addition there are two records which are probably referable to *Z. angusticollis*, one from Adelaide, South Australia in 1935 and one from Chester Hill, New South Wales in 1956. Both the latter records also relate to infestations in Douglas fir logs or timber.

2. *Porotermes adamsoni (Froggatt)*

Porotermes adamsoni occurs in coastal and near-coastal districts of southeastern Australia. Normally it is found in decaying logs and in dead and living *Eucalyptus* trees. However, under favourable moisture conditions it can cause serious damage to utility poles and to bridge and other constructional timber.

It has been introduced to New Zealand on at least four occasions: in railway sleepers sent to the South Island in 1937; in tramway sleepers and power poles shipped to Auckland (two records) sometime prior to 1944; and in chalkboard crates consigned from Australia to Wellington in 1958. There is no indication, however, of whether the species has succeeded in establishing itself in New Zealand.

D. RHINOTERMITIDAE

1. *Heterotermes perfidus (Silvestri)*

Heterotermes perfidus, which was described by Silvestri in 1936 from material from St. Helena, is certainly an introduced species although its origin is still not clear.

There has been some taxonomic confusion over this termite, which at various times has been referred to as *H. tenuis* (Hagen), a South American species, and as *H. platycephalus* Froggatt, an Australian species. There is no doubt now, however, that *H. perfidus* is a valid species not referable to any other described species of *Heterotermes*.

This termite is believed to have been introduced into St. Helena about 1840 when a captured slaver was brought into the port of Jamestown, where it was condemned and dismantled, and the timbers landed in the town. These timbers proved to be infested with a termite which escaped, became well established, and so destructive that by 1875 it was estimated to have caused damage amounting to £60,000 sterling. It is now widely distributed on the island, damaging both houses and furniture, but its original home still remains a mystery.

2. *Heterotermes philippinensis (Light)*

Heterotermes philippinensis is native to the Philippines, where it frequently causes damage to constructional timber in buildings.

It was introduced into Madagascar some time prior to 1949, but there does not appear to be any information on precisely when and how this happened. The species is now well established and responsible for appreciable damage to buildings and their contents.

Heterotermes philippinensis was also introduced into Mauritius, where it was first collected in 1933, although it was probably established much earlier. It is widely distributed through the island now, particularly in lowland districts. In the main, it damages wooden buildings, but instances of attack on living plants of manioc (*Manihot utilissima*) have been reported.

3. Reticulitermes arenincola Goellner

Reticulitermes arenincola typically occurs in sandy situations along the southern shore of Lake Michigan (United States). Colonies of this termite found near Forest Hills, Massachusetts in 1918 are believed to have been transported in soil around plants sent to the Arnold Arboretum.

4. Reticulitermes flavipes (Kollar)

Reticulitermes flavipes is widely distributed in eastern North America from the Canada-United States border to Mexico and Guatemala. It is not only commonly found in logs and stumps, but also causes appreciable damage to utility poles and constructional timber.

This species was originally described in 1837 from winged forms collected in hothouses of the Royal Palace at Schoenbrunn, near Vienna. These termites were found in wooden tubs in which plants had been sent, presumably from North America. The infestation was eradicated but not before considerable damage to buildings had occurred. In 1955 there was a renewed occurrence of *Reticulitermes* damage in Austria, this time at Hallein, where infested timber was found in factory buildings. By 1957 the infestation had spread to several adjacent buildings and several hundred nests had been discovered. The manner in which this infestation originated is unknown, but, on the assumption that the species concerned was *R. flavipes*, it was thought to have been introduced about 1950−1951 in wooden boxes from Hamburg, where the species is well established (von Kurir, 1958). More recently, however, it has been claimed by Thurich (1960) that the species at Hallein is *R. lucifugus* (Rossi). This is a Mediterranean species which has not previously been recorded from Austria so that, irrespective of the identity of the species of *Reticulitermes,* the infestation at Hallein represents a successful establishment after introduction from another country.

The infestation of *R. flavipes* in Hamburg, referred to above, was discovered in 1937 in wooden boards of a conduit in the municipal heating system. Three explanations of the possible origin of this infestation have been advanced:

1. It developed from supporting beams in the heating system which were infested when imported from North America.

2. Termites were present in timbers imported for use as ships' masts, and some of these timbers were incorporated in buildings.

3. It came from the yards of timber merchants or wood carvers handling foreign timber.

By 1953 two well-defined centers of infestation about 2.5 km apart were known in Hamburg, and serious damage was occurring in both centers (Weidner, 1953). The species is now well established in the city, and a survey and eradication service has been created specifically to deal with the problem. Elsewhere in Germany, *R. flavipes* has been reported from Mannheim, where it was found under the bark of logs of *Pinus echinata* imported from Virginia, United States.

The Canadian records of *R. flavipes,* which date from 1938 or a little earlier, are all from waterfront localities in Ontario and are all considered to be introductions.

5. Reticulitermes hesperus Banks

Reticulitermes hesperus, which is common in the Pacific coast region of the United states, was intercepted at Honolulu, Hawaii in 1926 in wooden plant stakes from California.

6. Reticulitermes lucifugus (Rossi)

Reticulitermes lucifugus is widely distributed throughout the Mediterranean regions of Europe, Asia Minor, and Africa.

A report that this species was introduced into California prior to 1908 in wooden crates of chemicals from Hamburg, Germany appears to be based on a misidentification. *Reticulitermes lucifugus* does not occur in Germany, whereas *R. flavipes* is well established in Hamburg and was probably the species involved. There is no evidence that this introduction became established.

7. Reticulitermes speratus (Kolbe)

Reticulitermes speratus, which is widely distributed in Japan and also recorded from Korea, was intercepted at Honolulu, Hawaii in 1929 in a flowering *Prunus* sp. from Japan.

8. Reticulitermes sp.

Reticulitermes sp. was intercepted at Honolulu, Hawaii in 1925 in packaging around plants sent from Maryland, United States.

9. Coptotermes acinaciformis (Froggatt)

Coptotermes acinaciformis is widely distributed throughout Australia and is the most economically important species of termite in the continent. It is responsible for widespread damage to timber in service as well as to living trees.

It was introduced into New Zealand sometime prior to the mid-1930's when it was found at numerous places in the Auckland and New Plymouth districts attacking houses, trees, utility poles, and tramway sleepers. There is no doubt that this termite was introduced from Australia in rail or tramway sleepers and in poles (Miller, 1941), either as small incipient colonies or as groups of workers, soldiers, and reproductive nymphs. Under New Zealand conditions, functional neotenic reproductives appear to be produced very readily both in *C. acinaciformis* and in the other introduced Australian species of *Coptotermes* (*C. frenchi* and *C. lacteus*) so that the introduction of groups of the latter type referred to above could produce foci of infestation. By 1939 it had become so firmly established and was causing so much damage that the Government organized a survey and eradication campaign to deal with the problem. The campaign, which has continued for more than 25 years, has not succeeded in eradicating *C. acinaciformis* from New Zealand, but has brought about a marked reduction in the numbers of foci of infestation and in the amount of damage caused.

An active nest of what is believed to have been *C. acinaciformis* was found in part of the staging of the main wharf at Suva, Fiji in 1939. There are also other records of its detection in Suva in eucalypt logs shipped from Australia.

10. Coptotermes amanii (Sjostedt)

Coptotermes amanii is native to Tanzania. Early in 1960 it was intercepted at Durban in a crate which had been reconsigned to South Africa from an East African port.

11. Coptotermes crassus Snyder

Coptotermes crassus is recorded from Honduras and Western Mexico in stumps, posts, and within the trunks of living trees.

This termite was found in a dry dock at Houston, Texas in 1956 and can reasonably be assumed to have been taken there in a ship from a foreign port. Within 2 years the infestation had spread to timbers in an adjacent pier and shipyard. However, the entire infestation appears to have been eradicated by fumigation (Padget, 1960).

12. Coptotermes formosanus Shiraki

Coptotermes formosanus has a wide distribution throughout Japan, Formosa, and the southern mainland of China. It is an extremely destructive species which attacks not only buildings and furniture but living trees as well.

This termite was recorded from Honolulu, Hawaii in 1913 and may well have reached the island as early as 1900 in Oriental commerce. By 1926 it had spread throughout Honolulu, in 1928 it was recorded from the island of Kauai, and 2 years later from Lanai. The two latter records indicate the facility with which this species is transported by ships; this is supported by records of active infestations in (1) a coal barge in the harbour at Honolulu in 1927 and (2) in ships plying between Hawaii and California. All the Hawaiian records refer to damage to furniture or timber in service, and there is no published information indicating a spread to wild habitats.

Elsewhere in the Pacific area, *C. formosanus* has been recorded from Guam, Midway Island, and the Kwajalein Naval Station in the Marshall Islands. These records date from the early 1950's, and it is believed that the introductions resulted from the large scale movements of goods and supplies during World War II.

Coptotermes formosanus has probably been introduced into Ceylon as there are no records of the species from the Indo-Pakistan subcontinent prior to its discovery in Ceylon (Ahmad, 1953). There is no evidence, however, of the manner of introduction nor when it might have occurred.

In South Africa this species was found at Simonstown, Cape Province in 1925. The infestation was traced to timber which had been landed in 1924 from a vessel that had previously operated for several years between Hong Kong and Ceylon. Some of the timber was sold as firewood and the rest dumped in the dockyard area. Subsequently, infestations developed in close proximity to both these parcels of timber and affected living trees as well as timber in buildings. In 1927 extensive damage to timber in the dockyard area necessitated vigorous control measures, which were so successful that no recurrence of activity was reported for more than 20 years. Since 1949, however, there have been instances of renewed activity in the Naval Dockyard area, and control operations are continuing.

A second introduction of *C. formosanus* into South Africa occurred at Komatipoort, in the Eastern Transvaal, sometime prior to 1958, presumably in infested wood brought in through the port of Lourenzo Marques in Mozambique. In 1958 infestation was found in a living tree and in trap stakes in a built-up area of the town. The subsequent capture, in 1960, of an alate in a light trap leaves little doubt that the species is established in Komatipoort.

In 1960 *C. formosanus* was found infesting the bulkhead of a Fisheries Research Vessel at Mombasa, Kenya. This vessel was formerly in service in the Far East, where presumably the infestation had taken place.

The first record of the establishment of this species in mainland United States was in 1965, when all castes were recorded from large wooden beams in a shipyard warehouse in Houston, Texas. This infestation was destroyed by fumigation. A year later, however, *C. formosanus* was reported from four localities in New Orleans and the West Lake area of Louisiana. In 1967 winged forms were collected from two sites in Charleston, South Carolina. There is no information on the origin of these infestations, which are clearly widespread and well established. The adaptability and reproductive potential of this species are considered to constitute a threat to buildings along the entire Gulf and Pacific coasts and as far north as Boston on the Atlantic coast (Beal, 1967).

13. Coptotermes frenchi Hill

Coptotermes frenchi occurs widely in eastern and southern Australia, and is responsible for appreciable damage to living eucalypts and to constructional timber.

This termite was recorded from tramway sleepers in Auckland, New Zealand in 1933, and it is reasonably certain that it was introduced in infested logs and sleepers imported from Australia in the same way as *C. acinaciformis*. By the early 1940's all castes had been collected from houses, trees, tramway sleepers, and power poles, indicating that the species was well established in Auckland.

14. Coptotermes havilandi Holmgren

Coptotermes havilandi is native to southeast Asia and Indonesia, and is recorded from within the trunks of trees and from old wood. This species was found in Mauritius in 1936, but its wide distribution there suggests that it had been present for many years (Moutia, 1936). In addition to attacking timber, living trees, and sugar cane, it has been found on several occasions in remote areas of native forest or woodland; this raises some doubt as to whether it is an introduced species.

Coptotermes havilandi was recorded from the island of Réunion in 1957, and this probably represents an introduction. The species is established in the West Indian islands of Barbados and Jamaica, where it appears to have been introduced about 1939—1940.

In South America, *C. havilandi* is present in Brazil, where it was first reported in 1958. It is recorded as attacking timber, books, stored cotton seed, and avocado trees, but there is no information on the manner in which or when it reached Brazil.

15. Coptotermes heimi (Wasmann)

Coptotermes heimi is widely distributed through India and parts of West Pakistan. The species, as now defined (Roonwal and Chhotani, 1962), includes the collections previously referred to as *C. parvulus* Holmgren. This termite is very destructive to timber in houses or manufactured articles and to many trees and shrubs.

Coptotermes heimi has been collected near Semerang, Java, and this may be within its normal range of distribution. However, the discovery of an active colony of this species in a ship at the Singapore Naval Base in 1949 indicates that it could have reached Java in the same way.

16. Coptotermes lacteus (Froggatt)

Coptotermes lacteus is restricted to the coastal and adjacent tableland areas of southeastern Australia. Its attacks are virtually restricted to dead wood in logs and stumps, and it is not considered to be of any economic significance in Australia.

The species was discovered in Auckland, New Zealand in 1939 in building timbers, and additional collections, which included all castes, were made in 1939 and 1944. There is little doubt that the species is established in New Zealand, but the mode of entry is unknown.

17. Coptotermes testaceus (Linnaeus)

Coptotermes testaceus is widely distributed in South America and is frequently responsible for considerable damage to buildings. It is also present in the West Indian islands of Trinidad, Tobago, and Grenada and is thought to be native to the islands or to have been introduced a long time ago (Adamson, 1938). This termite was intercepted in shipments of firewood entering Barbados from British Guyana in 1939–1940.

18. Coptotermes vastator Light

Coptotermes vastator is widely distributed in the Philippines, where it is considered to be the most important economic species of termite. It has been intercepted on numerous occasions from 1918 onward by Plant Quarantine officials at Honolulu, Hawaii. In 1963, hundreds of alates were collected from an infested building in Honolulu and the inference is that this species is now established there.

19. Coptotermes sp.

In 1965 workers and immature reproductive nymphs of an unidentified species of *Coptotermes* were detected at Sydney, Australia in household effects shipped from Hong Kong.

E. Termitidae

1. Termes hispaniolae (Banks)

Termes hispaniolae occurs in Central and South America and on some islands in the West Indies. In 1939—1940 it was intercepted in shipments of firewood entering Barbados from British Guyana.

2. Nasutitermes columbicus (Holmgren)

Nasutitermes columbicus occurs in Colombia, Panama, and Costa Rica. In 1902 it was intercepted at Hamburg, Germany in orchid plants from Colombia.

3. Nasutitermes corniger (Motschulsky)

Nasutitermes corniger occurs in Mexico and Central America as far south as Bolivia. It has been intercepted on numerous occasions in mainland United States and in Honolulu on plants, mainly orchids, imported from Central America.

4. Nasutitermes costalis (Holmgren)

Nasutitermes costalis is found throughout the West Indies and adjacent countries of Central and South America. In 1942 a small group of workers and soldiers was discovered in Lincolnshire, England in packaging material which had recently arrived from Martinique.

5. Nasutitermes fulviceps (Silvestri)

Nasutitermes fulviceps is native to Argentina, Brazil, Paraguay, and Uruguay. In 1899 it was intercepted at Hamburg, Germany in orchid plants imported from Brazil.

6. Nasutitermes nigriceps (Haldeman)

Nasutitermes nigriceps is widely distributed throughout the Neotropical region. It was collected from a dead orchid pseudobulb in Miami,

Florida in 1958 and has been intercepted in Florida several times in wood coming from Puerto Rico. However, there is no evidence that the species is established in Florida.

7. Nasutitermes octopilis Banks

Nasutitermes octopilis is known only from Guyana. In 1939–1940 it was intercepted in a shipment of firewood sent from that country to the island of Barbados.

8. Nasutitermes walkeri (Hill)

Nasutitermes walkeri is restricted to eastern Australia and is not considered to be of any economic significance. There is a single record of this species from New Zealand, where soldiers and workers were collected from a power pole at Hawkes Bay some time prior to 1941. There has been no further record of the presence of this species in New Zealand, so that the inference by Hill (1942) that the species is established there should be treated with reservation.

9. Nasutitermes sp.

An undetermined species of *Nasutitermes* was intercepted in California in 1945 in orchid plants shipped from Borneo.

10. Trinervitermes sp.

Trinervitermes is predominantly an Ethiopian genus, with a few species also occurring in the Indo-Malayan region. Specimens of an undetermined species of this genus were discovered in Surrey, England in 1948.

III. GENERAL CONCLUSIONS FROM THE STUDY OF INTRODUCTIONS

Three points emerge from the above case histories. First, it is clear that the termites most likely to be introduced are species of *Cryptotermes* and *Coptotermes*. These termites are so readily transported from place to place and have been so successful in establishing themselves in new habitats that in some instances it is difficult to determine their original home (e.g., *Cryptotermes domesticus* and *C. dudleyi*) and in others the countries of introduction have functioned as stepping stones to wider distribution. For example, *Cryptotermes brevis*, which is essentially a Neotropical species, is thought to have reached Hawaii by way of China or Hong Kong, and *Coptotermes formosanus*, an Oriental species, has been intercepted on the Pacific Coast of North America in ships trading between there and Hawaii, where it is well established.

In at least three species there have been significant changes in behavior or biology after introduction which have increased the economic significance of the termites concerned. The Australian species, *Coptotermes acinaciformis* and *C. frenchi*, appear to rely mainly on supplementary reproductives for colony foundation in New Zealand, whereas in Australia such forms are very uncommon and colony foundation is almost invariably by winged reproductives. A third species, *Coptotermes lacteus*, which under Australian conditions seldom, if ever, attacks structural timber, has been reported on several occasions attacking timber in buildings and utility poles in New Zealand.

In view of the ease with which species of *Cryptotermes* and *Coptotermes* may be transported over long distances and the plasticity of behavior or biology which some of them exhibit, it is apparent that any country in which they occur, either as indigenous or introduced species, must be regarded as a potential source of harmful termites for dispersal to other countries.

The second point concerns the manner in which introductions have taken place. It is obvious that the commonest method of transport from place to place is in timber, either in the log, sawed or fabricated into articles of various kinds; the wide recognition of this fact by quarantine authorities has been responsible for the repeated interception of potential pest termites.

The other important modes of entry are in plants and ships. The almost universal prohibition on the importation of plants growing in soil has restricted, to some extent, the opportunities for transporting subterranean termites. Nevertheless, live plants still play a significant role as carriers of termites; this is especially true for orchids, which are a particularly favorable means for transporting species of *Nasutitermes*.

The significant role which ships have played in the dispersal of termites is not merely restricted to the carriage of termite-infested cargoes, but has also been influenced by the occurrence of infestations in the woodwork of the ships themselves. Not only dry-wood termites have spread in this way, but at least four species of *Coptotermes* — *C. crassus, C. formosanus, C. havilandi,* and *C. heimi* — have shown their ability to take advantage of the favorable moisture conditions which ships provide. Subsequent establishment from ship-dwelling colonies has been either as a result of incorporating infested ships' timbers in buildings on shore, or by flights of winged adults from ships in port.

The final point is that, with remarkably few exceptions, all successful introductions and establishments have taken place in islands or on the coastal fringes of continental areas. In part this reflects the significant role which ships have played as the physical means of transport from country to country. In addition, however, it supports the suggestion, made earlier, that biotic barriers to successful establishment are much weaker in the impoverished or simpler communities of islands and islandlike areas than they are in the main continental land masses.

REFERENCES

Adamson, A. M. (1938). Notes on termites destructive to buildings in the Lesser Antilles. *Trop. Agr. (Trinidad)* **15**, 220-224.

Adamson, A. M. (1940). A second report on the termites of Trinidad, British West Indies. *Trop. Agr. (Trinidad)* **17**, 12-15.

Adamson, A. M. (1948). Notes on the termite fauna of the Lesser Antilles. *Trop. Agr. (Trinidad)* **25**, 53-55.

Ahmad, M. (1953). Two new cases of introduction of termites. *Spolia Zeylan.* **27**, 35-36.

Anonymous. (1957). *U.S. Dept. Agr. Coop. Econ. Insect Rept.* **7**, 651.

Anonymous. (1958). Infestation report. Termites, Florida. *Pest Control* **26**, No. 10, 86.

Anonymous. (1962). *U.S. Dept. Agr. Coop. Econ. Insect Rept.* **12**, 261, 1172, 1217, and 1252.

Anonymous. (1963). *U.S. Dept. Agr. Coop. Econ. Insect Rept.* **13**, 119.

Anonymous. (1965). *U.S. Dept. Agr. Coop. Econ. Insect Rept.* **15**, 907-908.

Anonymous. (1966). *U.S. Dept. Agr. Coop. Econ. Insect Rept.* **16**, 562-563.

Araujo, R. L. (1958). Contribuicãio à biogeographia dos térmitas da São Paulo, Brasil. Insecta-Isoptera. *Arch. Inst. Biol. (Defesa Agr. Animal), SÃo Paulo* **25**, 185-217.

Banks, N., and Snyder, T. E. (1920). A revision of the Nearctic termites. *U.S. Natl. Museum Bull.*, **108**, 1-228.

Beal, R. H. (1967). Formosan invader. *Pest Control* **35**, No. 2, 13-17.

Benito Martínez, J. (1957). El termes de madera seca *(Cryptotermes brevis)* en las islas Canaries. *Montes* **13**, 147-161.

Bess, H. A. (1965). Second species of subterranean termite established in Hawaii. *P.C.O. News* **25**, No. 10, Oct. Suppl.

Cachan, P. (1949). Les termites de Madagascar. *Mem. Inst. Sci. Madagascar* **A3**, 177-275.

Chhotani, O. B. (1963). Miscellaneous Note 19. The termite *Cryptotermes havilandi* (Sjöstedt) from the interior of India. *J. Bombay Nat. Hist. Soc.* **60**, 287-288.

Clagg, C. F. (1958). Termites from western Pacific islands. *Proc. Hawaiian Entomol. Soc.* **16**, 338-339.

Clark, A. F. (1938). Termites in New Zealand. *New Zealand J. Forestry* **4**, 177-179.

Coaton, W. G. H. (1948). *Cryptotermes brevis*, a new wood-borer problem in South Africa. *Bull. Dept. Agr. Forestry S. Africa* **290**, 1-18.

Coaton, W. G. H. (1950). Infestation of buildings in South Africa by subterranean wood-destroying termites. *Bull. Dept. Agr. Forestry S. Africa* **299**, 1-89.

Dorward, K. (1956). Spread and new finds of some insects in the United States in 1956. *Agr. Chem.* **11**, 57.

Ehrhorn, E. M. (1934). The termites of Hawaii, their economic significance and control, and the distribution of termites by commerce. *In* "Termites and Termite Control" (C. A. Kofoid, ed.), 2nd ed., pp. 321-324. Univ. of California Press, Berkeley, California.

Emerson, A. E. (1936). Distribution of termites. *Science* **83**, 410-411.

Emerson, A. E. (1949). Evolution of interspecies integration and the ecosystem. *In* "Principles of Animal Ecology" pp. 695-792. Saunders, Philadelphia, Pennsylvania.

Esaki, T. (1937). The large termite *Zootermopsis angusticollis* (Hagen) introduced from Oregon, U.S.A. to Japan. *Kontyu* **11**, 344-346.

Fullaway, D. T. (1926). Termites or white ants in Hawaii. *Hawaiian Forester Agr.* **23**, 68-88.

Gay, F. J. (1967). A world review of introduced species of termites. *Bull. Commonwealth Sci. Ind. Res. Organ.* **286**, 1-88.

Gonçalves, C. R., and Silva, A. G. A. (1962). Observacoes sobre Isopteros do Brasil. *Arch. Museu Nacl., Rio de Janeiro* **52**, 193-208.

Harris, W. V. (1950). Dry-wood termites. *E. African Agr. J.* **16**, 50-52.

Harris, W. V. (1953). A note on termites from St. Helena. *Proc. Roy. Entomol. Soc. London* A28, 13-14.

Harris, W. V. (1955a). An American termite in imported timber. *Wood* **20**, 366-367.

Harris, W. V. (1955b). Exhibit of living *Kalotermes* near *jouteli* and preserved *Zootermopsis angusticollis* from imported timber. *Proc. Roy. Entomol. Soc. London* C20, 36-37.

Harris, W. V. (1958). More about dry-wood termites. *E. African Agr. J.* **23**, 161-166.

Harris, W. V. (1962). Termites in Europe. *New Scientist* **13**, 614-617.

Hickin, N. E. (1963). "The Insect Factor in Wood Decay," pp. 270-272. Hutchinson, London.

Hill, G. F. (1942). "Termites (Isoptera) from the Australian Region." Council Sci. Ind. Res., Melbourne, Australia.

Hozawa, S. (1915). Revision of the Japanese termites. *J. Coll. Sci., Imp. Univ. Tokyo* **35**, 1-61.

Keck, C. B. (1952). Midway Island insects. *Proc. Hawaiian Entomol. Soc.* **14**, 351.

Kelsey, J. M. (1944). The identification of termites in New Zealand. *New Zealand J. Sci. Technol.* B25, 231-260.

Kemner, N. A. (1934). Systematische und biologische studien über die Termiten Javas und Celebes. *Kgl. Svenska Vetenskapsakad. Handl.* [3] **13**, 1-241.

Kirby, H. (1925). *Cryptotermes hermsi* sp. nov. A termite from Fanning Island. *Univ. Calif. (Berkeley) Publ. Zool.* **26**, 437-441.

Lever, R. J. A. W. (1939a). Termites or white ants. *Colony Fiji, Agr. J.* **10**, 18-19.

Lever, R. J. A. W. (1939b). Entomological notes. A Central American white ant in Fiji. *Colony Fiji, Agr. J.* **10**, 36-37.

Lever, R. J. A. W. (1952). New or recently introduced insect pests in Singapore, absent from the Federation of Malaya. *Malayan Agr. J.* **25**, 214-217.

Light, S. F. (1931). Present status of our knowledge of the termites of China. *Lingnan Sci. J.* **7**, 581-600.

Light, S. F. (1932). Termites of the Marquesas Islands. *Bull. Bishop Museum, Honolulu* **98**, 73-86.

Light, S. F. (1935). The Templeton Crocker expedition of the Californian Academy of Sciences, 1932, No. 20. The termites. *Proc. Calif. Acad. Sci.* [4] **21**, 235-256.

Light, S. F. (1936). A tropical termite in California. *Pan-Pacific Entomologist* **12**, 125-126.

Light, S. F., and Zimmerman, E. C. (1936). Termites of southeastern Polynesia. *Occasional Papers Bishop Museum* **12**, 1-12.

McLachlan, R. (1874). A brood of white ants (termites) at Kew. *Entomologist's Monthly Mag.* **11**, 15-16.

MacNay, C. G. (1961). Import interceptions. *Can. Insect Pest Rev.* **39**, 135-136.

Martorell, L. F. (1939). Insects observed in the state of Aragua, Venezuela, South America. *J. Agr. Univ. Puerto Rico* **23**, 184-185.

Miller, D. (1941). The species of termites in New Zealand. *New Zealand J. Forestry* **4**, 333-334.

Moszkowski, L. I. (1955). *Cryptotermes kirbyi*, new species from Madagascar and *C. havilandi* Sjöstedt from Africa and introduced into Madagascar, India and South America (Isoptera, Kalotermitidae). *Mem. Inst. Sci. Madagascar* **E6**, 15-41.

Moutia, A. (1936). Termites in Mauritius. *Bull. Dept. Agr., Mauritius (Sci. Sect.)* **21**, 1-30.

Oshima, M. (1920). A new species of immigrant termite from the Hawaiian Islands. *Proc. Hawaiian Entomol. Soc.* **4**, 261-264.

Padget, L. J. (1960). Program for eradication of *Coptotermes crassus* Snyder. *Down to Earth* **16**, 11-14.

Paulian, R. (1957). La faune entomologique de l'Ile de la Réunion. *Mem. Inst. Sci. Madagascar* **E8**, 29.

Riley, N. D. (1943). On the occurrence of *Nasutitermes costalis* Holmgren in England. *Proc. Roy. Entomol. Soc. London* **A18**, 95.

Roonwal, M. R., and Chhotani, O. B. (1962). Indian species of the termite genus Coptotermes. *Indian Council Agr. Res., Entomol. Monographs* **2**, 1-115.

Saint, S. J. (1940). Entomological section. *Rept. Dept. Sci. Agr., Barbados* pp. 9-10.

Sen-Sarma, P. K., and Mathur, R. N. (1957). Further record of occurrence of *Cryptotermes dudleyi* (Banks) in India (Insecta: Isoptera: Kalotermitidae). *Current Sci. (India)* **26**, 399.

Snyder, T. E. (1926). New termites from Guatemala, Costa Rica, and Colombia. *J. Wash. Acad. Sci.* **16**, 18-28.

Snyder, T. E. (1946). A small dark-coloured new *Kalotermes* from Guatemala. *Proc. Entomol. Soc. Wash.* **48**, 158-160.

Snyder, T. E. (1949). Catalog of the termites (Isoptera) of the world. *Smithsonian Misc. Collections* **112**, 1-490.

Snyder, T. E. (1952a). *Zootermopsis angusticollis* (Hagen) infesting Douglas fir lumber at Philadelphia, Pa. *Proc. Entomol. Soc. Wash.* **54**, 56.

Snyder, T. E. (1952b). Non-subterranean termites at home and abroad. *Pest Control* **20**, No. 9, 23 and 26.

Snyder, T. E. (1954a). Termite notes. *Pest Control* **22**, No. 11, 28.

Snyder, T. E. (1954b). Note. *Zootermopsis* introduced into eastern U.S. *Proc. Entomol. Soc. Wash.* **56**, 47.

Sweeney, R. C. H. (1948). Soldiers of *Nasutitermes* (*Trinervitermes*) (Isoptera) in England, with a note on artificial termitaria. *Entomologist's Monthly Mag.* **84**, 164-166.

Swezey, O. H. (1940). A survey of the insect pests of cultivated plants in Guam. *Hawaiian Planters' Record* **44**, 151-182.

Swezey, O. H. (1945). Insects associated with orchids. *Proc. Hawaiian Entomol. Soc.* **12**, 343-403.

Thurich, L. (1960). Vergleichende morphologische Betrachtung der Soldaten der europäischen und vorderasiatischen *Reticulitermes*-Arten. *Entomol. Mitt. Zool. StInst. Zool. Museum Hamb.* **30**, 1-16.

Tucker, R. W. E. (1939). Report of the Entomological Section, Department of Science and Agriculture, Barbados, for the year ending 31st March, 1939. *Agr. J. Barbados* **8**, 56-60.

Urquhart, F. A. (1953). The introduction of the termite into Ontario. *Can. Entomologist* **85**, 292-293.

Urquhart, F. A. (1954). A new locality record for the termite in Ontario. *Can. Entomologist* **86**, 576.

von Kurir, A. (1958). Termitengefahr für Österreich und somit für Sentraleuropa durch die gelbfüssige Termite (*Reticulitermes flavipes* Kollar). *Holzforsch. Holzverwert.* **10**, 8-15.

Walker, F. (1853). List of the specimens of Neuropterous insects in the collection of the British Museum, Part 3, 501-529, Termitides, British Museum, London.

Weidner, H. (1937). Termiten in Hamburg. *Z. Pflanzenkrankh. Pflanzenschutz* **47**, 593-596.

Weidner, H. (1953). Die Bodentermite *Reticulitermes* eine ernste Gefahr für die Gebaude in Hamburg, *Entomol. Z.* **62**, 191-192.

Whitney, L. A. (1929). Note. *Reticulitermes speratus* Kolbe intercepted from Japan. *Proc. Hawaiian Entomol. Soc.* **7**, 222.

Wichmann, H. E. (1957). Unbekannte Wege der Termiten—einschleppung. *Anz. Schaedlingskunde* **30**, 183-185.

16

The Association of Termites and Fungi

WILLIAM A. SANDS

I. INTRODUCTION

The environment of termites normally includes a wide variety of fungi, some of which compete with them for the plant remains that provide their food. Such competition may lead to habitat partition and subsequently to the evolution of symbiosis, parasitism, or pathogenic relationships. It is common to find intermediate stages in the development of some of these states, and, consequently, there is difficulty in deciding what constitutes a genuine association as opposed to coincidence and in classifying the associations under appropriate headings. In practice it is preferable to cast the net as widely as possible, indicating dubious associations where they occur. Representatives of all the classes of fungi are found associated with termites. The field of study has only recently begun to pass from the stage of collected observational data to experimentation and offers plenty of scope for further work. Some of this has been stimulated by the idea that the use of attractant fungal extracts combined with suitable poisons might provide highly specific control measures; the possibility of biological control of termites with fungal parasites and pathogens has also been considered by several workers.

495

The truly symbiotic nature of the relationship between the subfamily Macrotermitinae and the fungal genus *Termitomyces* is at last becoming clear. However, there remains some controversy as to the mechanics of fungus-comb construction and, consequently, of its phylogenetic significance.

In an age when raw materials for processing into foodstuffs are gathered from all parts of the world, it is important that they should not be contaminated in any way at their sources. Some exceedingly potent fungal toxins have been found, and termites have been suspected of facilitating the spread of such fungi by accidental transport of spores during their attacks on crop plants. However, the fungi associated with termites are not all detrimental to humanity, some having been found to possess medicinal and culinary properties.

It has been necessary to be selective in preparing a list of references since the literature on the subject is surprisingly extensive. The bibliographies of Snyder (1956, 1961) provide good coverage up to 1960, and only the more important publications prior to this date are given.

II. FUNGI IN RELATION TO NUTRITION OF TERMITES

Whether the ancestors of all termites were associated with symbiotic protozoans, as is popularly supposed, or not, it seems certain that they must always have had to adapt their feeding habits and digestive processes to partially decomposed food. This food consists almost entirely of plant remains, commonly wood, and it has usually been attacked by fungi and other microorganisms to some extent by the time the termites find it. Cellulose and lignin are among the less easily digestible materials; the breakdown of their stable complex molecules to a point where they can be metabolized requires more energy than the breakdown of starches, sugars, and proteins utilized by other plant-feeding insects. Thus, the presence of fungi has often proved beneficial to termites, and differing levels of dependency have evolved, culminating in the symbiosis described under the second subheading. On the other hand, some fungi produce breakdown products which are repellent or poisonous to termites.

A. BEHAVIORAL RESPONSE TO AND DEPENDENCE ON FUNGI

Some groups of termites are more obviously associated with fungi than others. The Termopsidae and Rhinotermitidae in particular are usually found in wood which clearly shows the effects of decay by various rot-producing fungi. On the other hand, some Kalotermitidae live in wood which is apparently sound and fungus-free. However, Hendee (1933) showed that although fewer fungi could be isolated from colonies of *Incisitermes minor* (Hagen) than from those of *Reticulitermes hesperus* Banks or *Zootermopsis angusticollis* (Hagen) they were present in significant numbers (17 fungal genera, as compared with 25 genera and 22 genera, respectively, from the same number of colonies of the two latter termite species). There was no evidence of any specific relationship between these termites and the genera of fungi recorded, of which *Penicillium* and *Trichoderma* were the commonest. Hendee (1934, 1935) also investigated experimentally the role of some of these fungi in the diet of *Z. angusticollis* and concluded that their presence was essential. Better growth and viability were both obtained when the termites fed on rotten Monterey pine or Douglas fir than when they fed on either sound wood or filter paper. The mold *Trichoderma lignorum* (Tode) Harz on otherwise sound wood also provided some benefit.

Apart from their dietary effects, Hendee suggested that the fungi might also break down harmful extractives in the wood. The latter effect was found by Williams (1965) to be critical in the case of *Coptotermes niger* Snyder feeding upon *Pinus caribaea* Morelet in British Honduras. The heartwood of this tree is both toxic and repellent to these termites by reason of its turpentine and resin content. However, when broken down by the cubical brown-rot fungus *Lentinus pallidus* Berk. and Curt., the heartwood becomes the preferred feeding and nest site of the termite. Much of the carbohydrate content is broken down by cubical brown rot, causing the percentage by weight of nitrogen in the wood with the fungus to rise compared with the original wood. Hungate (1940) noted that the percentage by volume of nitrogen does not change in rotted wood and that the weight loss of over 30% must be due to decomposition of carbon compounds. Williams (1965) commented that enough cellulose would remain undigested to supply the needs of the termites. In the case of white-rot fungi, it is the lignin which is broken down, providing extra assimilable carbohydrate to the termites. Williams also demonstrated the nutritional importance of the rot fungus in *Pinus caribaea* to *C. niger* in a series of replicated "survival" experiments of the assay type. In these the value of a food material was assessed on the basis of the mean time taken for the test samples of termites (in this case, ten replications of fifty individuals each for each food) to reach 50% mortality. The use of the 50% level, or "median mortality time," is standard practice in bioassay of drugs and pesticides because it is less subject to extraneous variations resulting from aging samples, disease, and other uncontrolled factors than is the 100% mortality level. The rotten heartwood promoted significantly longer survival than sound or rotten sapwood or heartwood from which the repellent extractives had been removed with solvents. The value of the bark as a food material increased with age owing to progressive deterioration of the outer layers, presumably again by fungi.

Experimental assays of fungi in the environment of other termites have been reported recently, though with fewer replications and less attention to statistical significance than those described above. Since in this type of assay there are often wide variations and sudden inexplicable losses of replicates, the techniques used are important in assessing the reliability of the results. However, less rigorous experiments may provide useful preliminary screening of larger numbers of species to be followed up by more detailed tests or other methods. Lund (1960b) used paired replicates of ten individuals of a species of *Reticulitermes* to test five species of fungi in agar culture. From the times taken to reach 100% mortality he concluded that *Poria incrassata* is helpful to the termites and *Lentinus lepideus* Fr. antagonistic. *Lenzites trabea* Pers. ex Fr., *Polyporus versicolor* (L) Fries, and *Poria monticola* Murr. also appeared to be better than the controls. The apparent deleterious effect of *Lentinus lepideus* was investigated further (Lund, 1962) by the use of its metabolite, methyl cinnamate, to control *R. flavipes* (Kollar) and *R. virginicus* (Banks). He also notes that the longevity of both species is reduced by the presence of *Aspergillus* sp. and *Penicillium* sp.

In an extensive series of screening experiments, Becker and Kerner-Gang (1964) tested the influence on termite longevity of about 30 species of Ascomytes and some *Fungi Imperfecti,* partly represented by several strains, amounting altogether to more than 60 fungus cultures. They used 4 species of termites, *Kalotermes flavicollis* (Fabricius), *Heterotermes indicola* (Wasmann), *Reticulitermes lucifugus* var. *santonensis* Feytaud, and *Nasutitermes ephratae* (Holmgren). The groups of termites used to test each fungus were of uniform size within species, numbering 10, 100, 50, and 100, respectively, the difference being due to availability of material. Only 1 group of each species of termites was used to test each fungus in each experiment, but control groups on starvation diets and on pure cellulose were kept, and some of the experiments were repeated. Thus although no tests of statistical validity could be applied, some of the results confirmed others. The authors stated that the influence of some fungi varied with the species of termite; some were favorable and some toxic. *Trichoderma* species were mostly toxic; *Aspergillus flavus* Link had highly toxic, neutral, and "markedly favorable" strains. Other species of *Aspergillus* and several of *Penicillium* had varied effects. A "markedly favorable" influence occurred with the tested strains of *Aspergillus ustus* (Bainier) Thom and Ch., *Alternaria humicola*

Oudem., *Chaetomium* sp., *Dactylium fusarioides* Frag. et Cif., *Memnoniella echinata* (Riv.) Gall., and *Trichurus* sp. Most of these fungi are cellulose decomposing species, commonly known as "soft rot."

A slightly different approach was tried by Kovoor (1964), in studying the comparative effects of *Microcerotermes edentatus* (Wasmann) and 2 fungi, *Ganoderma applanatum* (Pers.) Pat. and *Trametes trabea* (Pers.) Bres. on wood of poplar (*P. virginiana* Foug.). Weighed groups of about 800 termites consisting of mixed worker and soldier castes were kept for periods up to 3 months in dishes with moistened sterilized sand and provided with sawdust of sound or fungus infested wood. Samples of sterilized poplar wood incubated with each of the fungi provided the latter material. Up to 11 replications of the termites were used, but it is not clear whether this number was standard in all tests. Analyses of the wood before and after fungal action and of residues from the termite cultures were made to determine the proportions of their main constituents. It was found that the termites preferred to feed on decayed rather than healthy wood. They were attracted by wood whose breakdown products resulting from fungal attack were principally cellulose and pentosans; that is, the breakdown is in the same direction as their own digestion of wood. The attractive substance from *T. trabea* infested wood was extractable in an alcohol-benzene mixture. Wood decayed by *G. applanatum* was toxic to termites and unattractive to them; the toxic substance was also soluble in alcohol-benzene, and after extraction of this fraction *G. applanatum*-decayed wood was used by the termites in the normal way. In wood attacked by *T. trabea,* lignin was strongly attacked, and the termites only slightly modified what was left. It appeared that *Microcerotermes*, which has an intestinal flora of bacteria, could, with their help, break down other constituents of the wood in addition to cellulose.

Several of the authors cited above have noted that termites are attracted to certain rot fungi. This aspect of termite behavior has stimulated the attention of a number of workers in recent years with a view to its possible exploitation as a means of control, and attempts have been made to identify the attractive substances. Esenther *et al.* (1961) noted that runways of *Reticulitermes* spp. on trees tend to go straight to decaying wood, and suggested that a gradient of attractive material may help the termites to find their food supply. Eight species of fungi isolated from rotting wood or termites were used to infest autoclaved blocks of Western pine (*P. monticola*) sapwood. After *Lentinus lepideus, Lenzites trabea, Polyporus versicolor, P. gilvus, Poria monticola, Penicillium* sp., *Aspergillus* sp., and *Spicaria* sp. had grown for 2–3 weeks, the wood blocks were washed and placed with 250 termites in a "multiple-choice situ-

ation." After 2 minutes the termites were mainly concentrated around
the blocks attacked by *L. trabea*. The same reaction was obtained to
aqueous or benzene-ether extracts of *L. trabea* blocks, even in extreme
dilutions; 1 gm of dry wood in 6 liters of water produced a solution of
which 0.03 ml was still attractive. The extracts provoked similar reactions
in *Reticulitermes flavipes, R. virginicus,* and *Nasutitermes columbicus*
(Holmgren).

Gas chromatographic fractionation of *L. trabea* extract was undertaken by Watanabe and Casida (1963). At least 6 steam-volatile fractions
were found. Attractants were also found in the fungus on artificial media,
in wood alone, and in termites. Some compounds containing propenyl or
styryl radicles, such as cinnamyl alcohol and isosafrole, were active, as
also were 6-ionones and certain camphor analogs. The authors considered
that the attractiveness of camphor might be due to a minor impurity.
Further tests of extracts from *L. trabea* infested wood were carried out
by Esenther and Coppel (1964), using *Reticulitermes* spp., *Incisitermes
minor* and *Zootermopsis angusticollis*. Like Becker and Kerner-Gang,
they found that the responses of the termites were variable. *R. flavipes*
could detect 50 μg of wood equivalent or as little as 0.001 μg of gas
chromatography extract. The termites also responded to 0.08 μg of the
following synthetic attractants: *d*-camphor, cinnamyl alcohol, acetate
and cinnamate, 3-methyl ionone, *trans*-isosafrole, 2-methyl-2-hepten-
6-one, *N*-crotyl-*p*-toluidine. Again, there was variation in the response
in spite of the controlled conditions. Biting behavior was only initiated
on suitable materials, from which the authors conclude that decayed
wood contains both an "orienting" and a feeding stimulus. The same research team has extended the study in several directions. The response
of 21 termite species to aqueous *L. trabea* extracts was investigated by
Allen *et al.* (1964), who obtained a response index for each species, based
on the number of termites visiting a cellulose assay pad dampened with
extract. This was expressed as a percentage of the remaining number of
termites in the test dish, including those visiting a control pad dampened
with plain water. Their response index has the disadvantage that in com-
bining the control figures with the remainder it confounds any response
to wet cellulose with that to the fungus. Furthermore, it takes no account
of the fact that random movements of the termites would give rise to
visits to the assay pads in the proportion of their area to that of the dish.
The result is that positive values of their response index up to 7.1 indicate
a nil response. A better index is obtained by taking the difference between
the attractant pad and the control as a percentage of the total number of
termites placed in the dish. This response index gives a zero value for
nil response and in other cases both positive and negative values the

latter probably showing a genuine repellency. Although statistical tests of significance cannot be applied on the figures available, the new index has been calculated and indicated apparent positive responses in *Neotermes connexus* Snyder, *Incisitermes immigrans* (Snyder), *Reticulitermes flavipes*, *R. tibialis* Banks, *R. speratus* (Kolbe), *Coptotermes formosanus* (Shiraki), and *C. vastator* Light. A negative index of value similar to these was obtained for *Glyptotermes satsumensis* (Matsumura). Most of the strongly reacting species are Rhinotermitidae, with one or two Kalotermitidae also. Perhaps the most important new finding was that the effect of the attractant varied not only within genera, but markedly within species of termites. Further work by Smythe *et al.* (1965) showed that the response also varied with external factors such as temperature (increased effect) and light intensity (decreased effect). The castes of *R. flavipes* reacted differently, the secondary reproductives most strongly, followed by workers and soldiers. The stimulus provided by their fellows promoted quicker response in larger samples of termites.

Smythe *et al.* (1967) have tested 22 species of fungi, some represented by different strains, with 4 species of termites, *R. flavipes, R. virginicus, R. hesperus,* and *Z. angusticollis.* The 2 latter species did not react particularly strongly to any fungal extract, although the response indices (theirs) to some, such as *Lentinus lepideus* and *Lenzites trabea,* would seem large enough to be significant. The latter fungus elicited the common response from *R. flavipes,* which also reacted to *Daedalea quericina* (L.) Fr. *R. virginicus* responded to both *Poria monticola* and *P. cocos* (Schw.) and to a mixture of them.

To summarize the foregoing: although there is no evidence of any symbiosis between the termite species mentioned and the primarily basidiomycete, saprophytic, wood-rotting fungi, there is no doubt that several termite species are nutritionally dependent on them. Other termites, although not necessarily dependent on fungi, do benefit from their presence, and there is clear evidence that adaptive behavioral responses to substances produced by the fungi have developed in diverse termite species. However, the variation in these responses makes their value in control measures questionable at the moment. The direct contradiction between the effects on *Reticulitermes* ascribed to *Lentinus lepideus* and its cinnamate extractives by Lund (1960a, 1962) and Allen *et al.* (1964) or Smythe *et al.* (1967) may arise from this variation or from differences in experimental technique. One point which does not appear to have been made by any of these authors is that familiarity may play a large part in the response of a sample of termites from any one area or colony. If a colony had recently been feeding on wood decayed by a particular fungus, its members would be likely to have become habituated to it in the same way as they do to their own colony odor, and this habituation could persist for some time until another main source of food had been discovered. This would account for the discrepancies noted between species or within them. It might even lead to "colony specialization" in a particular kind of rotting wood, which could be a first stage in the evolution of symbiosis and would permit the coexistence of several colonies of the same or related species in one habitat.

Before leaving the subject of the nonsymbiotic use of fungi by termites, mention must be made of the record by Ribaldi (1956) of *Actinomucor corymbosus* (Harz) Naumov from a nest of *R. lucifugus* in Italy. The fungus "appeared to be a source of vitamins and proteins especially for the young." A somewhat similar account of a fungus in cultures of *R. flavipes* was given by von Kurir (1963). The fungus was identified as *Termitomyces* sp., but this identification appears very doubtful in view of the known symbiotic relationship of that genus with Macrotermitinae.

There remains one further curious case of nonsymbiotic relationship between termites and fungi, and this occurs in the nasute genus *Hospitalitermes,* dark-colored termites that forage in the open air in daylight. Petch (1913b) and Kalshoven (1958) studied several species occurring in the Indo-Malayan region. They appear to prefer feeding on algae but, since these are in short supply in their habitats, their staple diet is made up of lichens, which are symbiotic algal-fungal combined structures. Sooty molds on the surface of wood and bark are also consumed.

Although most of this account has been concerned with three families of termites, it will be well known to any entomologist who has collected them in the tropics that this by no means exhausts the subject. There are many other genera that appear to be confined to rotting wood or leaves and which have probably evolved some degree of dependence on the fungi concerned.

B. Symbiosis

From earliest times, symbiotic relationships have exercised a fascination for naturalists, and that between the Macrotermitinae and the fungal genus *Termitomyces* Heim is no exception. The history of its discovery and gradual elucidation has been reviewed from time to time as research has proceeded. Doflein (1906) and Petch (1906, 1913a) were among the earliest authors to make these appraisals, followed by Bugnion (1913), Hegh (1922), Bose (1923), Bathellier (1927), Heim (1940a), Grassé (1937, 1944, 1949), Coaton (1961), Roonwal (1962), and Batra and Batra (1966).

The first discovery of the spongelike "fungus-gardens" of Macro-termitinae, built from vegetable residues and supporting a mycelium with white nodules of conidia and conidiophores, was made by König (1779) in the East Indies. He believed that the fungus was the food of the young termites. Soon afterward, Smeathman (1791) described similar structures in the mounds of *"Termes bellicosus"* in West Africa. He believed that the fungus gardens, or "combs," were nurseries and also observed the food "magazines" of stored plant fragments in the upper parts of the nest. The first attempts to describe and classify some of the fungi found associated with the fungus combs were made by Berkeley (1847), and by Berkeley and Broome (1871a,b, 1875). Subsequent descriptions of similar fungi by several authors created a number of snynonyms, thirteen of them being combined by Petch (1906, 1913a) under the name of *Collybia albuminosa* (Berk.) Petch, which was recorded as growing from the nests of various *Odontotermes* species in Ceylon. Petch also noted the association between the small "mushroom," *Entolomola microcarpum* Berk. and Broome, and the presence of termites, while regarding its status as a termite fungus as unproved. This was not fully established until the observations of Bottomley and Fuller (1921), who found the fructifications of this fungus developing on the fragments of comb brought up out of the nests by *Odontotermes* species during the rainy season in South Africa.

In the next two decades, the fungus combs of a number of species of Macrotermitinae were described from Africa, Asia, and the Far East by various authors. Some of these named fungi found on the combs, but the majority did not do so. On the other hand, several of the fungi were described, while the associated termites were unknown or misidentified. The position was reviewed and clarified in a series of papers by Heim (1940a,b,c, 1941–1942, 1942, 1948, 1951b, 1952a,b, 1958, 1963), who created the genus *Termitomyces* for all the Basidiomycetes symbiotic on the combs of Macrotermitinae and described a number of new species, associating them with their termite hosts where possible. He also divided *Termitomyces* into two subgenera: *Praetermitomyces* for the single species mentioned above (*E. microcarpum*, Fig. 1C) and *Eutermitomyces* for the remaining species which, like *T. albuminosa*, fructify at the tips of long stipes or "pseudorhiza" that grow out from the fungus combs, through the mounds or the soil above the nest (Fig. 1A, B). The central part of the cap of some of these larger species is hardened, thickened, and to some extent pointed as an adaptation to penetrating the soil. This structure, termed the "perforatorium" by Heim, varies in form and degree of development among species and so is taxonomically important in the

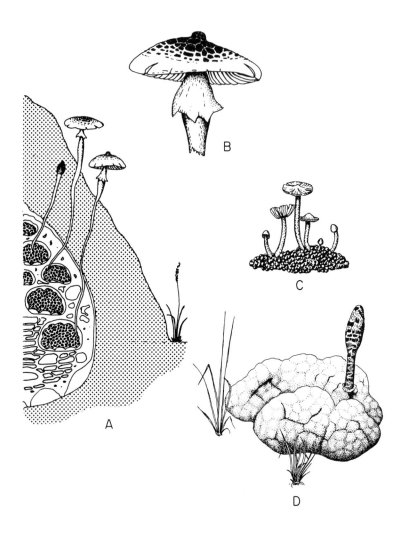

Fig. 1. Some of the fungi associated with termites. A: *Termitomyces (Eutermitomyces) letestui* growing out of a mound of *Macrotermes natalensis*, from the fungus combs *in situ*. B: *T. (E) letestui*, cap enlarged to show detail including "perforatorium." C: *T. (Praetermitomyces) microcarpus* on fragments of fungus comb brought to the soil surface by *Odontotermes* sp. (same scale as B). D: *Podaxon pistillaris* growing from an abandoned mound of *Trinervitermes geminatus*. E: *Termitaria* sp., fructification on the head of a

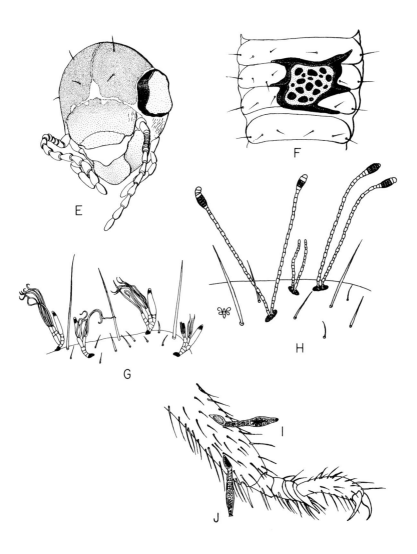

worker caste of *Nasutitermes* sp. F: *Mattirolella silvestrii* on the abdomen of a soldier of *Rhinotermes marginalis*. G: *Laboulbenia* sp. on the abdomen (part of one tergite shown) of *Odontotermes* sp. H: *Antennopsis gallica* on an abdominal tergite of *Reticulitermes lucifugus santonensis*. I: *Coreomycetopsis oedipus*. J: *Laboulbeniopsis termitarius*. I and J are on the leg of the soldier of *Nasutitermes costalis*.

group. Cheo (1942) established that the conidial stage described as *Aegerita duthei* Berk. [or *Termitosphaera duthei* (Berk.), as it was called by Ciferri, 1935] is in fact the same species as *Termitomyces albuminosa* (Berk.) Heim.

Termitomyces medius was described by Grassé and Heim (1950) as a species somewhat intermediate between the two subgenera, though belonging to *Eutermitomyces*. It has a short stipe, developing from fungus comb chambers in the outer layers near the surface of the nest of *Ancistrotermes latinotus* (Holmgren).

The list is given in Table I of the described species of *Termitomyces* together with their termite hosts when these have been established. It is a surprisingly short list, considering the amount which has been written on the subject, and the relationships with the termite host species are very imperfectly known. There appears to be a tendency for species of fungi to be associated with genera of termites, as was noted by Grassé (1959). Exceptions to this, such as *T. albuminosa* associated with *Microtermes*, are probably the result of misidentifications of the fungus. Heim (1952a) considered that the size and form of the fungi are to some extent influenced by the size and position of the combs from which they grow, and that variations between species arise partly from differing stages of adaptation to the "cavernicolous" condition. *Odontotermes* appears to have adapted to some change, biochemical or morphological, in *T. microcarpus* in the rainy season when it is about to fructify, by developing the habit of shaving away the outer layers of its fungus combs and spreading them on the surface of the soil above the nest. Harris (1961) suggested that intensified foraging in the area where basidiospores had recently been discharged would result in reinoculation of the new combs. However, the same species, *Odontotermes badius* (Haviland), was recorded by Coaton (1961) as symbiotic with both *T. microcarpus* and *T. albuminosa*. The only experimental evidence was provided by Sands (1960), who found that although *Ancistrotermes guineensis* (Silvestri) in laboratory-reared cultures would feed and survive on fungus comb of *A. crucifer* (Sjöstedt) the fungus did not grow on the sterile comb constructed by the termites. When supplied with fragments of comb from another nest of their own species, the termites, by feeding on it, immediately inoculated their own comb, on which the fungus grew profusely thereafter. This argues specific symbiosis on the part of the fungus, whereas the termites are not so particular.

The sterility of the combs in these laboratory-reared cultures also suggests that their alate founders carry no inoculum of viable spores. Lüscher (1951a) had a similar experience with *Pseudacanthotermes spiniger* (Sjöstedt). Batra and Batra (1966) have disputed this suggestion on the grounds that they, in common with a number of earlier authors, have found conidia in the gut of swarming alates and in crevices in their integument. Heim (1942) recorded that identical cultures of the fungi on artificial media could be obtained from conidia or basidiospores. The conidia are, however, fragile, thin-walled spores, and, although they may be viable when taken from swarming alates, it seems doubtful that they could remain so in a dormant state for the two or three months that elapse between swarming and the building of the first fungus comb in the incipient colony. The apparent absence of *Termitomyces* from Madagascar was noted by Heim (1938) in his comments on the work of Jumelle and Perrier de la Bathie (1907a,b, 1910). The occurrence of *Microtermes* in Madagascar was explained by Harris and Sands (1965) by the habit of the male alate, which clings to the abdomen of the female during flight, thus ensuring the distribution of pairs rather than single-tons. If the fungus is truly absent from Madagascar, this could only be explained by the lack of a viable inoculum in colonizing pairs.

All species of *Termitomyces* fructify early in the rainy season, as do many other fungi. Since no mycelium of this genus has ever been identified "in the wild," the discharge of basidiospores at this time would have no value unless it enabled the distribution of the fungi to new colonies when spores are collected along with food material by foraging termites. Thus it would be hard to explain the adaptation of the fungi to soil penetration, with long "pseudorhiza" and the "perforatorium," unless it were necessary to disperse basidiospores. If the transfer to new colonies were normally by conidia, the adaptation to symbiosis would be more likely to have occurred through the loss of a "perfect" phase. The occurrence of fertile comb in laboratory-reared colonies of *Macrotermes* described by Grassé and Noirot (1955) can be attributed to the widespread distribution of basidiospores of this common species. Failure to obtain spores might be a factor further restricting the spread of young colonies of less abundant species.

It was shown by Bathellier (1927) and Heim (1942) that the white nodules, which are normally made up of conidiophores and conidia on the fungus comb, are also the primordia of the agaric phase. Bathellier thought that this did not grow from normal nests, but Grassé (1945) stated that he was wrong; in those fungi that develop directly from the comb, many nodules begin to grow out, but most are eaten off by the termites, and only one or two get away from any comb. Earlier authors believed that the termites weed the comb to keep down alien fungi. Grassé (1937) found that the mycelium, which permeates the entire comb, is mixed with finer hyphae of *Xylaria* species, generally considered to be saprophytic rather than symbiotic. There are many other fungal

TABLE I

LIST OF DESCRIBED SPECIES OF *Termitomyces* TOGETHER WITH THEIR TERMITE HOSTS, IF KNOWN, AND WHERE THESE SPECIES HAVE BEEN RECORDED IN THE LITERATURE

Fungal species	Termite host species	Where recorded
Subgenus: *Praetermitomyces*		
Termitomyces microcarpus (Berkeley and Broome) Heim	*Odontotermes badius* (Haviland) *O. transvaalensis* (Sjöstedt) *O. vulgaris* (Haviland)	All three species first recorded in Bottomley and Fuller (1921)
Subgenus: *Eutermitomyces*		
T. citriophyllus Heim	Unknown	
T. clypeatus Heim	Unknown	
T. entolomoides Heim	"*Macrotermes* sp." (this identification is probably wrong)	Heim (1963), but fungus comb photo.[a] in Heim (1952a) is *Protermes* sp.
T. globulus Heim & Goossens	Unknown	
T. letestui (Patouillard) Heim	*Macrotermes natalensis* (Haviland)	Heim (1948)
T. mammiformis Heim	*Pseudacanthotermes* sp., probably *militaris* (Hagen)	Heim (1940c)
T. mammiformis form *albus* Heim	Unknown	
T. medius Grassé & Heim	*Ancistrotermes latinotus* (Holmgren)	Grassé and Heim (1950)
T. robustus (Beeli) Heim	*Acanthotermes acanthothorax* (Sjöstedt)	Heim (1958), but comb photos.[a] not this genus
T. robustus var. *fuliginosus* Heim		
T. schimperi (Patouillard) Heim	*Macrotermes natalensis* (Haviland)	Heim (1958)
T. striatus (Beeli) Heim	*Pseudacanthotermes militaris* (Hagen)	Heim (1948)
T. striatus form *annulatus* Heim		
T. striatus form *griseus* Heim		
T. striatus form *ochraceus* Heim		
T. striatus var. *aurantiacus* Heim		
T. albuminosa (Berkeley) Heim (*eurhizus* and *cartilagineus*, both synonyms, Petch, 1913)	*Odontotermes redemanni* (Wasmann) *O. obscuriceps* (Wasmann) *O. horni* (Wasmann) *O. sundaicus* Kemner *Microtermes insperatus* Kemner *Odontotermes obesus* (Rambur) *O. badius* (Haviland)	Both in Petch (1906) Bathellier (1927) Both in Kemner (1934) Bose (1923) Coaton (1961)
T. eurhizus (Berkeley) Heim	*O. gurdaspurensis* Holmgren	Batra and Batra (1966)

[a]Comb photograph(s)

spores to be found in the comb, on the termites, and in the surrounding nest material, as was shown by Das *et al.* (1962) and recently by Batra and Batra (1966). The latter authors found that in *Odontotermes* nests the defensive oral secretion of the soldier caste and soil recently manipulated by workers with the addition of saliva both exert a fungistatic effect on genera of fungi other than *Termitomyces*. It is interesting that Randall and Doody (1934) noted an odor of acetic or a related acid when gut contents of termites were acidified. They suggested that acetates or butyrates are produced in the digestion of cellulose. The secretion of soldiers of *Odontotermes* also has this smell, and we may speculate that a by-product of cellulose digestion has come to be involved in both defense and the adaptation of *Termitomyces* to a habitat otherwise apparently inimical to fungi. The carbon dioxide content of the mound was also found to inhibit spore germination in many foreign fungi.

The foregoing remarks have been concerned mainly with the taxonomy and biology of *Termitomyces;* now it is appropriate to consider the role of the fungus in the life of the termite colony. There has been a tendency, when contemplating the nest structures of social insects, to regard them as something fixed or static like human dwellings. This they seldom are, and the misconception has sometimes led to wrong interpretations being placed on their functions. The fungus combs of Macrotermitinae are just such a case, where the assumption that the comb is a static structure has held up appreciation of its true function for half a century.

The earliest investigators thought that the combs were nurseries and that the function of the mycelium and nodules was to feed the young, but it soon became obvious that the small volume of the fungus produced could not provide the main food supply for even the young stages of a large colony. Authors were at pains to point this out from Petch (1906) onward, and other explanations were sought. Grassé (1937) suggested that the fungus provided nutritional adjuvants or (1945) vitamins. Heim (1942) considered that the comb was merely part of the architecture, and that the fungus was a tolerated commensal, expelled when overgrown. Ghidini (1938) thought that the comb served as humidity control, while Lüscher (1951b) believed that this function was combined with heat production, maintaining a constant high temperature in the nest.

Meanwhile, Kalshoven (1936) pointed out that the fungus combs of *Macrotermes, Odontotermes,* and *Microtermes* were eaten away from below by the termites, when they reached a certain stage of maturity, either being simultaneously built up at the upper surface or replaced by new comb in the space beneath. These important observations appear to have escaped the attention they deserved from some workers, and it was not until 20 years later that Grassé and Noirot (1957) rediscovered the dynamic nature of fungus comb in all the genera that they studied. They also found that new deposits on the upper comb are dark brown or gray in *Protermes, Macrotermes, Odontotermes,* and *Acanthotermes,* aging under the influence of the fungus to pale beige, whereas in *Ancistrotermes* and *Microtermes* new material is pale, aging to dark gray. Sands (1956) and Ausat *et al.* (1960) have shown experimentally that fungus comb with mycelium and nodules is an important part of the diet of *Odontotermes* since without it, even when supplied with alternative food, they survived no longer than when starved. Further work by Grassé and Noirot (1958) confirmed that the apparent stability of the comb results from continuous replacement of material removed from below by new additions above. They showed by staining techniques that the action of the fungus is to break down lignin, freeing more cellulose. The fungus nodules were found to be confined to the "middle-aged" zone. They also pointed out that cellulose is certainly digested by the termites, probably by bacteria in the hindgut, since the rectal contents show almost no debris giving the reaction of cellulose, but are strongly positive for lignin. Grassé (1959) remarked that new material on the upper parts of the comb is lignin-staining and contains very little or no cellulose. It appeared that *Termitomyces* was not essential to *Macrotermes* since a culture had been kept alive in Paris for 18 months on rotten wood alone.

The continuous cycle of comb construction was further studied by Alibert (1964) who used fluorescein staining to show the fate of food material in the colony. When only the upper surfaces of combs of *Macrotermes mülleri* (Sjöstedt) or *M. lilljeborgi* (Sjöstedt) were stained, no staining appeared in the gut of the termites. Fluorescein from the lower surface of the comb was found in the gut of the termites within 48 hours, as it also was when the "leaf confetti" was stained. The latter material is heaped up in certain chambers in the nest, presumably being temporarily stored after foraging. Although the stain from the "leaf confetti" first appeared in the gut after 48 hours, it did not appear on the comb until 60 hours or more after staining. The stimulus to feeding by the termites was shown to arise from the state of the comb rather than its position since inverted combs replaced in a nest continued to be used in the normal way.

One aspect of the symbiosis remains, namely the true nature of the comb material, that has not been discussed. The earliest authors believed the comb to be fecal in origin, in common with the internal lining and shelving in the nests of the majority of other termites. The contrary idea that the fungus combs were built from undigested plant material after prolonged mastication was first put forward by Bathellier (1927). He stated that all termites other than *Cryptotermes* produce semiliquid brown feces which dry to a hard dark brown substance known as "carton," containing less vegetable material in more finely divided form than occurs in fungus comb. This statement is incorrect. Many workers from Petch (1906, 1913a,b) on have noted the similarity between the rectal pouch contents of Macrotermitinae and their fungus combs, including Grassé (1937). However, Grassé then proceeded to restate Bathellier's theory on the grounds that the "normal" feces of *Macrotermes* were dark brown and semiliquid. This opinion has been reiterated in most of the subsequent works on the subject by this authority on termite biology. The arguments in favor of the older theory of fecal origin were set out in detail by Sands

(1960), who appears to be the only investigator ever to have watched and photographed the process of fungus comb construction. In *Ancistrotermes guineensis* the workers were observed repeatedly while they deposited their fecal pellets to build the comb. No chewed wood was ever added to the comb during many hours of observation. The matter was therefore regarded as settled until Grassé and Noirot (1961) published the statement that the observations described above were wrong. Their reason for this was the oft-repeated and incorrect one that in the Macrotermitinae the rectal contents are always limited in quantity, rich in mineral particles, and form reddish spots when deposited, and that they never contain large vegetable fragments. The impression that this is so must have arisen from examination of inadequate samples of scarcely mature worker termites from the fungus combs alone. These authors also considered that the green-colored combs found in the nests of *Macrotermes* that foraged upon fresh grass proved that no passage through the gut had occurred, "removing all doubt, if any had remained."

The true origin of the comb is an important fact when considering the evolution of termite behavior. Except in emergencies such as a broken nest, there is no termite known that habitually uses its undigested food as a building material. Even in the Kalotermitidae and Termopsidae that live entirely inside wood, it is the feces that are used for plugging holes, building partitions, etc. The evolution of a symbiotic relationship with another organism must be a gradual process, involving mutual adaptations. Saprophytic fungi must have invaded part of the normal nest structure of an ancestral termite before they could become symbionts. It would thus be necessary to believe that a termite group, now extinct, arose in which the food was not eaten, as before, but built into special structures which provided a medium for fungal growth, and that the symbiosis then arose to the mutual benefit of termites and fungi. The lack of theoretical parsimony is obvious when this theory is compared with the alternative: that the fecal carton common to most termites' nests was invaded at some stage by fungi which then became symbiotic.

Other published evidence points the same way. The staining reactions of new comb and feces described by Grassé (1959) were both strongly lignin-positive with little cellulose. Undigested woody material, on the other hand, normally contains $40-60\%$ cellulose and only $20-30\%$ lignin. According to Becker and Seifert (1962), these percentages are roughly reversed in the feces of many other termites, and the same probably applies to the newly deposited comb material of Macrotermitinae. The delay between gut staining and the appearance of fluorescein on the new fungus comb observed by Alibert (1964), where termites fed on stained "leaf confetti," would be most likely to occur if the comb is fecal. The persistence of green pigment in the feces of grass- and leaf-eating insects is common. In *Trinervitermes* described by Sands (1965), the "black" fecal lining of the nests is in fact the concentrated, very dark green residue of grass.

To sum up, there can be no doubt of the symbiotic relationship between the termites and *Termitomyces* which grows on the fecal fungus combs of Macrotermitinae. These combs are an integral part of the normal food cycle of the colony. The first stage of digestion by the breakdown of cellulose takes place in the initial passage through the gut. The function of the fungus appears to be mainly the breakdown of lignin, but it probably also supplies nitrogenous materials and possibly other factors such as vitamins. The reuse of feces in this way appears to have replaced the proctodeal feeding common in other termites. Such evidence as there is seems to indicate that the growth of *Termitomyces* on combs in new colonies probably arises from the introduction of basidiospores rather than inoculation with conidia by the parent alates. The diversity of appearance and texture of the combs can also best be explained on the basis of their fecal origin and the differing degrees of symbiosis with the fungi.

III. FUNGI SAPROPHYTIC IN TERMITE NEST STRUCTURES

The bodies of termites inevitably become contaminated with many fungal spores in the course of foraging and burrowing activities. These spores are often deposited in the nest structure and have been recovered and identified by mycologists as occurring in termite mounds. However, the fungi that are known to be genuine obligate or facultative saprophytes of termite nests only form a small part of such extensive lists. Moreover, many of them have been recognized as such for a long time, and relatively few new additions have been made in recent years. Some of the species or genera have been recorded many times from all parts of the world, and therefore only the more important references to them are given. The history of the saprophytic fungi closely parallels that of *Termitomyces* since they were usually studied at the same time. Berkeley (1843) and Berkeley and Broome (1871a,b, 1875, 1886) described a number of species of *Xylaria, Podaxon,* and others as being associated with termite nests. Petch (1913a) summarized the work up to that time and synonymized a number of species. He recognized two species of *Xylaria* as valid, namely *X. nigripes* Klotsch and *X. furcata* Fr. These Ascomycete Pyrenomycetes grow out of abandoned fungus combs of *Odontotermes* species. They produce long black stalks arising from a gray mycelium and bearing cylindrical stromata at the tips when they reach the surface of the soil. The stromata, 4—15 cm high, may bear gray conidia or develop asci later, turning black when the ascospores extrude from the perithecia. In *X. furcata* the stromata are dichotomously branched. Petch also recognized a single species of *Peziza, P. epispartia* Berk. and Br., that develops with *Xylaria* but from a yellow mycelium. It produces a disc-shaped yellow ascophore up to 1.5 cm in diameter on the soil surface. Two species of *Podaxon* were accepted, *P. carcinomalis* Fr., recorded by Berkeley and Broome from termite mounds in Queensland, and *P. termitophilum* Jum. and P.d.l.B., from mounds in open grassland in Madagascar. These Gasteromycetes develop an elongated oval, somewhat shaggy, grayish-brown fruiting body on a stalk, the whole protruding up to 30 cm from the mound surface. The last fungal species, somewhat doubtfully regarded by Petch as associated with termites, was *Neoskofitzia termitum* v. Höhnel. It is a small reddish-brown Ascomycete, developing perithecia up to 400 μ diameter.

Bottomley and Fuller (1921) recorded the growth of *Podaxon pistillaris* (L. ex Pers.) Fries. and *P. carcinomalis* from mounds of *Trinervitermes rhodesiensis* (Sjöstedt). *Podaxon termitophilum* was regarded by Heim (1938) as an obligate saprophyte on Madagascar termite heaps, whereas *P. carcinomalis* and *P. indicus* (Spreng) were facultatively so. He recorded several other Basidiomycete saprophytes from Madagascar, namely *Psalliota termitum* Dufour, *Gyrophragmium delilei* Mont., *Leucocoprinus* sp., and *Xerocomus* sp., but these have not been found elsewhere.

Several authors recorded *Xylaria nigripes* from mounds of various Macrotermitinae from China to South Africa, and Heim (1952a) added another species, *X. obovata* Berk. as a rare obligate saprophyte in the Congo. A curious, small Basiodiomycete, *Marasmius pahouinensis* De Seynes, was described from an arboreal nest of *Microcerotermes* in the Ivory Coast. Three species of *Xylaria* from tropical America were reported by Dennis (1956) to be associated with old termite nests. *Xylaria rhizomorpha* (Mont.) Mont., *X. braziliensis* (Teiss.) Lloyd, and *X. rhizocola* (Mont.) Fr. were described as terrestrial species with small or very small ascospores and strongly mammiform perithecia; the termite builders of the nests were not recorded. Dennis then (1958) turned his attention to the African members, and noted that *Xylaria* should be included in the genus *Xylosphaera* Dum. together with several other synonyms. *Xylosphaera nigripes* was already known, *X. braziliensis* was given as a new record on *Macrotermes* mounds, and *X. thyrsus* was thought to be a termite saprophyte. The development and liberation of the conidia of *X. furcata* from the mounds of *Macrotermes natalensis* was studied in Ghana by Dixon (1965). Conidia were discharged violently by the sudden rounding off of the cell walls between spore and sporophore.

In a recent paper Batra and Batra (1966) recorded again the presence of *Neoskofitzia termitum* among many other fungi found in the mounds of *Odontotermes gurdaspurensis* Holmgren. Last, Alasoadura (1966) noted 16 records of *Podaxon pistillaris* from small mounds in Nigerian savanna, which he attributed to *Pseudacanthotermes*. This is most improbable since this genus of termites does not normally build mounds in Nigeria. On the other hand, *Podaxon* is a common sight growing from the small mounds of *Trinervitermes geminatus* (Wasmann) and *T. trinervius* (Rambur) (Fig. 1D). This fungus seems to occur in places where the grass-feeding and harvesting genera of Nasutitermitinae are found, and many of the records are from their mounds. The host genus in Madagascar is probably *Coarctotermes;* in Africa, India, Ceylon, and Malaysia *Trinervitermes;* and in Australia perhaps *Tumulitermes*.

IV. FUNGI PARASITIC ON OR PATHOGENIC TO TERMITES

The borderline between parasitism and pathogenicity is not sharp and seems to be determined largely by two characteristics: the rapidity with which the organism causes the death of the host and the means of doing so. Fungi that permeate and poison the host quickly are thought of as pathogens, whereas those using its substance without marked toxic effects until their development is complete tend to be classed as parasites.

The fungi known to be parasitic on termites are few, but there is no doubt that many more await discovery. The earliest known was the Ascomycete Pyrenomycete, *Laboulbenia hageni* (Laboulbeniales) found by Thaxter (1895) on *Macrotermes bellicosus* (Smeathman) from Mozambique. It was not illustrated but was described as brownish, with multiple-branched appendages arising from basal cells up to 65 μ in length. In a subsequent paper Thaxter (1920) described the genus *Termitaria*, which has since become well known (Fig. 1E). The fungus forms grayish or brownish plates with a flat surface and a dark brown or black rim, closely applied to the cuticle of any part of the termite's body. The platelike mature form consists of columnar cells that arise from a flat, primary, thalluslike, brown structure. This forms a thin substratum that firmly adheres to the cuticle. The outer layers of columnar cells have thicker walls and produce within themselves spores that escape through openings at their outer ends. Thaxter remarked that there was no indication that the parasite penetrated the integument of the host, which was not seriously inconvenienced. However, he noted that the cells of host tissue beneath the integument adjacent to the fungus were hypertrophied. The form of the fungus becomes elongated on appendages. Its relationships were difficult to assess, being a *Fungus Imperfectus*, probably belonging among the Leptostromaceae. Two species were described; the first, *T. snyderi*, had blunt or flat terminations to the vertical sporogenous filaments and occurred on *Reticulitermes flavipes* and *R. virginicus* from America and *R. lucifugus* from Sardinia. The second was *T. coronata*, in which the sporogenous hyphae terminated in a crown of several minute brown-tipped points, and it was found on *Nasutitermes costalis* (Holmgren) from Grenada. In the same paper Thaxter described two further small parasitic fungi both found at the tips of the legs of *N. costalis* from the same locality. They very closely resemble each other, being single columns of cells ending in club-shaped sporogonia and arising from one end of an ovoid foot, flattened on the side, applied to the cuticle of the host. One, *Coreomycetopsis oedipus* (Fig. 1I), consists of 10−15 hyaline or yellowish cells including the foot, the apical 6 or 7 forming the sporogonium; the total length of the fungus is up to 135 μ. The other species, *Laboulbeniopsis termitarius* (Fig. 1J), is about the same size and shape but consists of only four pale, brownish, elongated cells; the terminal pore of the sporogonium also has a small, flared rim.

A new species of *Termitaria* was named *T. thaxteri* by Reichensperger (1923) from *Nasutitermes rippertii* (Rambun), *N. arenarius* (Hagen), and *Cornitermes cumulans* (Kollar) in Brazil, and he also noted the existence of unnamed species on *Nasutitermes* and *Hodotermes* in Africa. It was shown by Feytaud and Dieuzeide (1927) that *Termitaria* penetrates the cuticle of the host by a kind of rooting pedicle. The adipose tissue is invaded and altered by mycelium. The hypodermis and cuticle are altered to make way for the pedicle, and around the break cells disappear, the color becomes abnormal, and large amebocytes are found. *Termitaria thaxteri* Reich. was found on *Neotermes samoanus* (Holmgren) by Tate (1928). Colla (1929) added *Porotermes quadricollis* (Rambur) and *Neotermes hirtellus* (Silvestri), both from South America, to the named hosts of *T. snyderi* Thax., and *Nasutitermes corniger* (Motschulsky), *N. guayanae* (Holmgren), *N. surinamensis* (Holmgren), and *N. luzonicus* (Oshima) to those of *T. coronata* Thax. He also described a new parasite, *Mattirolella silvestrii* from *Rhinotermes marginalis* (Linne) in British Guiana. This is related to *Termitaria*, but the platelike structure is irregularly stellate in outline, and the fertile columnar hyphae are completely enclosed in cavities formed by sterile hyphae that are intensely black in color. The fungus is confined to the thorax, abdomen, and appendages of the termites (Fig. 1F). Another *Termitaria*,

T. pacedensis, was mentioned by Pickens (1952), but no details of this "species" have been found. Heim (1952b) stated that *Termitaria* is an internal parasite, entering through the alimentary canal, invading the fatty tissues, and finally breaking down the exoskeleton to emerge as sporogenic hyphae bearing chlamydospores.

A curious fungal parasite belonging to a new order, Gloeohaustoriales, was described by Heim and Buchli (1951) and Heim *et al.* (1951), and further details of its relationships, morphology, and effects on the termites were given by Heim (1951a, 1952b) and Buchli (1952, 1960a). This is *Antennopsis gallica* Heim and Buch., which occurs on all parts of the body of all castes of *Reticulitermes lucifugus santonensis* and will also grow on *Kalotermes flavicollis*. It consists of erect, dark brown conidiophores developing as pairs of parallel columns of cylindrical cells, terminating in clavate, spore-bearing heads, transversely septate into 10–20 pigmented cells. The columns are always paired, arising from the 2 central cells of an ellipsoidal, suckerlike foot of 4 cells of constant size and shape. This structure was named the "haustorium." The early life history of the fungus is unknown, but there is no sign of the fungus inside or outside the insects other than the haustoria, with conidiophores in various stages of development (Fig. 1H). The fungus secretes a thick mucus which impedes the termites by gumming down appendages, and young colonies die out as a result of heavy infestations. Another species, *Antennopsis grassei*, was named by Buchli (1960a) from Madagascar, where it was found on *Postelectrotermes amplus* (Sjöstedt), *Neotermes desneuxi* (Sjöstedt), and *Postelectrotermes longiceps* (Paulian). It differed from *A. gallica* in having a haustorium of only 3 cells, each of which commonly gives rise to a conidiophore. The conidia are unpigmented, with thinner walls, and the fungus does not seem to produce mucus.

In a more recent paper (Buchli, 1966) the same author has reviewed the known fungal parasites of termites and provided more information on the biology of *Antennopsis*. He considers that the part of the fungal life history at present unknown may take place in moist wood, because unidentified but characteristic spores occur consistently in the tunnels of infected termite colonies. New colonies can be experimentally infected by transference to such contaminated wood. In the same paper two new fungal parasites are described. The first is *Antennopsis gayi*, which resembles *A. gallica* in having a haustorium of 4 cells, but only 1 of the 2 central cells produces a pale brown conidiophore. The clavate conidial head consists of 7–15 colorless or pale brown cells and may be constricted in the middle. This fungus is found upon *Coptotermes elisae* (Desneux) and *C. obiratus* Hill in New Guinea. The second new parasite belongs to the genus *Laboulbenia* and differs from *L. hageni* in having longer multiple-branched appendages. These are male sexual organs carrying antheridia, the female organ being the flask-shaped perithecium containing an oogonium, which, after fertilization, produces sticky ascospores which escape and adhere to the cuticle of the host to form new parasites. This fungus was found upon *Odontotermes badius* from Ethiopia, and is that illustrated in Fig. 1G. Because it frequently arises in pairs from a double-celled haustorium, Buchli has named it *Laboulbenia geminata*. However, it should be noted that under the International Code of Botanical Nomenclature the names of plants are not valid unless accompanied by a Latin description, which was omitted in the case of *L. geminata, A. grassei,* and *A. gayi.*

A fungus which has intermediate status between parasite and pathogen is the Ascomycete Pyrenomycete, *Cordycepioideus bisporus,* described by Stifler (1941) as having killed a reproductive pair of *Macrotermes natalensis* in Tanzania. It resembles *Cordyceps* in developing clusters of erect clavate branched or simple stromata, cream in color with dark perithecia producing black ascospores.

Of the truly pathogenic fungi, the Phycomycetes *Entomophthora aphidis* and *Sporotrichum globuliferum* killed *Reticulitermes flavipes,* according to Forbes (1895). *Entomophthora coronata* (Cost) similarly killed Cuban *Nasutitermes* studied by Kevorkian (1937), who considered that it could also be saprophytic. This is a fungus very commonly found in laboratory cultures of termites and quite possibly also affects colonies in nature. Another *Entomophthora* was found by Alston (1947) to kill 100% of samples of *Coptotermes curvignathus* (Holmgren) in Malaya in 48 hours, and Yendol and Paschke (1965) obtained 97% mortality in 84 hours in *R. flavipes* infected with *E. coronata,* whereas *E. virulenta* Hall and Dunn was not pathogenic. However, these fungi are mostly nonspecific insect pathogens. In the remaining references the distinction between pathogenicity and mere toxicity becomes somewhat vague. An indication of this was given in the first section of this chapter where certain fungi were found experimentally to be "unfavorable" to termite survival. Lund and Engelhardt (1962) found that *R. virginicus* and *R. flavipes* both reached 100% mortality in $5\frac{1}{2}$ days when in contact with *Absidia coerulea* Bainier (Mucorales). Beal and Kais (1962) found that the same 2 species of termites infected with spores of *Aspergillus flavus* died more rapidly than controls. Various species of *Aspergillus* are known to be facultative pathogens of animals. Samples of *R. flavipes* exposed for 5 minutes to cultures of fungi by Smythe and Coppel (1966) showed increased mortality. The fungi concerned were given as *Gleomastix* sp., *Cunninghamella echinulata, Cephalosporium, Poecilomyces varioti, Penicilliun* sp., *P. oxalicum,* and *P. frequentans.*

Two Hyphomycetes, *Beauvaria bassiana* and *Metarrhizium anisopliae*, were tested against *Reticulitermes lucifugus santonensis* by Toumanoff (1965) and Toumanoff and Rombaut (1965). Samples of 20 termites were used to assay various strains and formulations of the fungi. When spores and hyphae were placed with damp pine sawdust supplied to the termites, mortalities between 10 and 20% occurred in 2 or 3 days and all were dead in 16 days. More rapid mortality was reported when spores and sawdust were intimately mixed. The authors stated that the effect arose from the toxicity of the spores before or immediately after germination on the cuticle since no mycelium penetrated the bodies of the termites until after death. In further experiments 5 species of *Poecilomyces*, 3 of *Beauvaria*, 2 of *Spicaria*, and 1 each of *Metarrhizium*, *Cephalosporium*, *Myrothecium*, and *Fusarium* were tested, and kills of 100% in 1−16 days were recorded, according to species. The onset of symptoms was accelerated by mixing bacteria such as *Salmonella*, *Shigella*, *Staphylococcus*, or *Vibrio* with the fungi. The validity of these results cannot be assessed because the authors did not indicate whether any of the assay samples were replicated or whether controls were included in the experiments. No statistical tests of the results were mentioned.

V. TERMITES AS CARRIERS OF FUNGI

The extreme virulence to warm-blooded animals, including man, of the toxin produced by *Aspergillus flavus* only became generally known a few years ago when the effect of contaminated groundnut meal on Christmas turkeys threatened to curtail the festivities. Subsequent investigations showed that termite damage to the plant before harvest in the drier growing areas caused the nuts to pass through a stage of drying when the growth of the fungus was maximized. Furthermore, it was suspected that the termites themselves might carry the fungus. Sellschop (1965) reported that the mouthparts of *Odontotermes latericius* (Haviland), which attacked the plants and scarified the pods, were loaded with spores. However, the fungus is in any case very common in soil, and it seems likely that it would reach the vulnerable plants without the help of the termites as carriers, although they may make some contribution in this respect.

In an investigation of attack on Honduras pine by *Coptotermes niger* carried out by Williams (1965), it was found that the termite was secondary to the brown-rot fungus *Lentinus pallidus*. The brown-rot fungus most commonly made its entry into damaged trees around the edges of fire scars. In this it was probably aided to some extent by the carriage of spores and hyphal fragments to all parts of the outside by the tree by the foraging activities of the termites. Lund (1960a) showed experimentally that sound pinewood exposed to *Reticulitermes* species for some days became infected with rot fungi.

Other termites have been suspected of transmitting fungus diseases of agricultural and tree crops, but none of these coincidences of termite attack and fungal disease has been investigated experimentally. Examples, such as various species of *Neotermes* and *Kalotermes* on Cocoa and Tea, *Microcerotermes* on tea, and subterranean termites associated with red rot on sugar cane, may be mentioned, but the relationship cannot be substantiated.

VI. USE OF TERMITE FUNGI BY MAN

It is not only the Macrotermitinae that have discovered the alimentary value of *Termitomyces*. However, it is the fructifications produced in the rainy season that are esteemed as delicacies by men in all those parts of the world, from South Africa to China, where they are found. Many authors from Berkeley and Broome onwards have mentioned this. In some parts of Africa the agarics are collected and sold in the native markets, either fresh or dried. Heim compared their gustatory properties in several of his taxonomic papers and noted their use in the Congo. More recently, Alasoadura (1966) observed that they are a common sight in Nigerian markets at the appropriate season. They are also popular in Uganda, though curiously not in Kenya and Tanzania. Cheo (1948) records that *T. albuminosa* is a well-known delicacy in China and is preserved dry by salting. He also notes that a decoction of *Xylosphaera nigripes* is used for relieving spasms in children, a fact not recorded from any other part of the world, but suggesting that this fungus may have properties worthy of further investigation.

REFERENCES

Alasoadura, S. C. (1966). Studies in the Higher Fungi of Nigeria II. Macrofungi associated with termite nests. *Nova Hedwigia* 11, 387-393.

Alibert, J. (1964). L'évolution dans le temps des meules à champignons construites par les termites. *Compt. Rend.* 258, 5260-5263.

Allen, T. C., Smythe, B. V., and Coppel, H. C. (1964). Response of twenty-one termite species to aqueous extracts of wood invaded by the fungus *Lenzites trabea* Pers. ex Fr. *J. Econ. Entomol.* 57, 1009-1011.

Alston, R. A. (1947). A fungus parasite on *Coptotermes curvignathus* Holmg. *Nature* 160, 120.

Ausat, A., Cheema, P. S., Koskhi, T., Petri, S. L., and Ranganathan, S. K. (1960). Laboratory culturing of termites. *Proc. New Delhi Symp., 1960* pp. 121-125. UNESCO, Paris.

Bakshi, B. K. (1951). Fungi in the nest of *Odontotermes obesus*. *Indian Phytophathol.* **4**, 1-4.

Bathellier, J. (1927). Contribution à l'étude systématique et biologique des termites de l'Indo-Chine. *Faune Colonies Franc.* **1**, 125-365.

Batra, L. E., and Batra, S. W. T. (1966). Fungus-growing termites of tropical India and associated fungi. *J. Kansas Entomol. Soc.* **39**, 725-738.

Beal, R. H., and Kais, A. G. (1962). Apparent infection of subterranean termites with *Aspergillus flavus* Link. *J. Insect Pathol.* **4**, 488-489.

Becker, G., and Kerner-Gang, W. (1964). Schädigung und Förderung von Termiten durch Schimmelpilze. *Z. Angew. Entomol.* **53**, 429-448.

Becker, G., and Seifert, K. (1962). Uber die chemische Zusammensetzung des Nest- und Galeriematerials von Termiten. *Insectes Sociaux* **9**, 273-289.

Berkeley, M. J. (1843). On two Hymenomycetons fungi belonging to the Lycoperdaceous group. *Hooker's J. Botany, London* **2**, 200-205.

Berkeley, M.J. (1847). Decades of fungi. Ceylon fungi. *Hooker's J. Botany, London* **6**, 479-514.

Berkeley, M. J., and Broome, C. E. (1871a). Note. *Trans. Linnean Soc. London (Botany)* **27**, 149-152.

Berkeley, M. J., and Broome, C. E. (1871b). The fungi of Ceylon. *J. Linnean Soc. London (Botany)* **11**, 494-567.

Berkeley, M. J., and Broome, C. E. (1875). Enumeration of the fungi of Ceylon. *J. Linnean Soc. London (Botany)* **14**, 29-140.

Berkeley, M. J., and Broome, C. E. (1886). List of fungi from Queensland and other parts of Australia; with descriptions of New Species. Part III. *Trans. Linnean Soc. London (Botany)* [N.S.] **2**, 217-224.

Bose, S. R. (1923). The fungi cultivated by the termites of Barkuda. *Records Indian Museum* **25**, 253-258.

Bottomley, A. M., and Fuller, C. (1921). The fungus food of certain termites. *S. African J. Nat. Hist.* **3**, No. 1, 139-144 and 223.

Buchli, H. (1952). *Antennopsis gallica,* a new parasite on termites. *Trans. 9th Intern. Congr. Entomol., Amsterdam, 1900* Vol. 1, pp. 519-524.

Buchli, H. (1960a). L'effet du champignon parasite *Antennopsis gallica* sur les jeunes colonies de termites. *Compt. Rend.* **250**, 1320-1321.

Buchli, H. (1960b). Une nouvelle espèce de champignon parasite du genre *Antennopsis* Heim sur les termites de Madagascar. *Compt. Rend.* **250**, 3365-3367.

Buchli, H. (1966). Notes sur les parasites fongiques des Isoptères. *Rev. Ecol. Biol. Sol.* **3**, 589-610.

Bugnion, E. (1913). Les moeurs des termites champignonnistes (de Ceylan). *Bibl. Univ. Rev. Suisse* pp. 1-32.

Cheo, C. C. (1942). A study of *Collybia albuminosa* (Berk.) Petch, the termite growing fungus, in its connection with *Aegerita duthiei* (*Termitosphaeria duthiei* (Berk.) Ciferri). *Sci. Red. Acad. Sin.* **1**, 243-248.

Cheo, C. C. (1948). Notes on fungus growing termites in Yunnan, China. *Lloydia* **11**, 139-147.

Ciferri, R. (1935). Sulla posizione sistematica dell '*Aegeritha duthiei*,' fungo dell 'ambrosia' dei termitai. *Atti Ist. Botan. Univ. Pavia* **6**, 229-246.

Coaton, W. G. H. (1961). Association of termites and fungi. *African Wild Life* **15**, No. 1, 39-54.

Colla, S. (1929). Su alcuni funghi parassiti delle Termiti. *Boll. Lab. Zool. Portici* 22, 39-48.

Das, S. R., Maheshwari, K.,L., Nigam, S. S., Shukla, R. K., and Tandon, R. N. (1962). Micro-organisms from the fungus gardens of the termite *Odontotermes obesus* (Rambur). *Proc. New Delhi Symp., 1960* pp. 163-166. UNESCO, Paris.

Dennis, R. W. G. (1956). Some *Xylarias* of tropical America. *Kew Bull.* 11, 401-444.

Dennis, R. W. G. (1958). Some *Xylosphaeras* of tropical Africa. *Rev. Biol. (Lisbon)* 1, 175-208.

Dixon, P. A. (1965). The development and liberation of conidia of *Xylosphaera furcata* (Fr.) Dennis. *Brit. Mycol. Soc. Trans.* 48, 211-217.

Doflein, F. (1906). Die Pilzzüchtenden Termiten. *Ostasienfaht Erlebn. Beob. Naturf. China, Japan, Ceylon* pp. 454-473.

Esenther, G. B., and Coppel, H. C. (1964). Current research on termite attractants. *Pest Control* 32, No. 2, 34, 36, 38, 42, 44, and 46.

Esenther, G. B., Allen, T. C., Casida, J. E., and Shenefelt, R. D. (1961). Termite attractant from fungus-infected wood. *Science* 134, 50.

Feytaud, J., and Dieuzeide, R. (1927). Sur un champigon parasite du *Reticulitermes lucifugus* Rossi. *Rev. Zool. Agr.* 26, No. 11, 161-163.

Forbes, S. A. (1895). The white ant in Illinois (*Termes flavipes* Kollar). *Rept. Illinois State Entomologist,* pp. 190-204.

Ghidini, G. M. (1938). La presumbile funzione delle spugne legnose nei nidi dei Metatermitidi. *Riv. Biol. Coloniale (Rome)* 1, 261-267.

Grassé, P. -P. (1937). Recherches sur la systématique et la biologie des termites de l'Afrique occidentale française. Première partie: Termitinae. *Ann. Soc. Entomol. France* 106, 1-100.

Grassé, P. -P. (1944). Recherches sur la biologie des termites champignonnistes (Macrotermitinae). *Ann. Soc. Nat. Zool. Biol. Animale* [11] 6, 97-171.

Grassé, P. -P. (1945). Recherches sur la biologie des termites champignonnistes (Macrotermitinae). *Ann. Soc. Nat. Zool. Biol. Animale* [11] 7, 115-146.

Grassé, P. -P. (1949). Ordre des Isoptères ou Termites. *In* "Traité de Zoologie" (P. -P. Grassé, ed.), Vol. IX, pp. 408-544. Masson, Paris.

Grassé, P. -P. (1959). Une nouveau type de symbiose: La meule alimentaire des termites champignonnistes. *Nature* 3293, 385-389.

Grassé, P. -P., and Heim, R. (1950). Un *Termitomyces* sur meules d'un *Ancistrotermes* Africain. *Rev. Sci.* 88, No. 1, 3-13.

Grassé, P.-P., and Noirot, C. (1955). La fondation de nouvelles sociétés par *Bellicositermes natalensis* Hav. *Insectes Sociaux* 2, 213-219.

Grassé, P.-P., and Noirot, C. (1957). La signification meules à champignons des Macrotermitinae (ins., Isoptères). *Compt. Rend.* 224 [14], 1845-1850.

Grassé, P.-P., and Noirot, C. (1958). Le meule des termites champignonnistes et sa signification symbiotique. *Ann. Sci. Nat. Zool. Biol. Animale* [11] 20, 113-128.

Grassé, P.-P., and Noirot, C. (1961). Nouvelles recherches sur la systématique et l'éthologie des termites champignonnistes du genre *Bellicositermes* Emerson. *Insectes Sociaux* 8, 311-359.

Harris, W. V. (1961). "Termites: Their Recognition and Control." Longmans, Green, New York.

Harris, W. V., and Sands, W. A. (1965). The social organization of termite colonies. *Symp. Zool. Soc. London* 14, 113-131.

Hegh, E. (1922). "Les Termites." Imprimerie Industrielle et Financière, Bruxelles, Belgium.

Heim, R. (1938). Observations sur la flore mycolgique malgache. VI. Les champignons des termitières. Première note. Basidiomycetes. *Bol. Soc. Broteriana* [2] 13, 45-68.

Heim, R. (1940a). Culture artificielle des mycotètes d'un agaric termtophile Africain. *Compt. Rend.* 210, 410-412.

Heim, R. (1940b). Les champignonnières des termites et les grands champignons d'Afrique tropicale. *Rev. Botan. Appl.* **20**, 121-127.

Heim, R. (1940c). Etudes descriptives et expérimentales sur les Agarics Termitophiles d'Afrique tropicale. *Mem. Acad. Sci.,* Paris **64**, 1-74.

Heim, R. (1941-1942). Nouvelles études descriptives sur les Agarics termitophiles d'Afrique tropicale. *Nouv. Arch. Museum Hist. Nat. Paris* **18**, 107-166.

Heim, R. (1942). Les champignons des termitières. Nouveaux aspects d'un problème de biologie et de systématique générale. *Rev. Sci.* **80**, 69-86.

Heim, R. (1948). Nouvelles réussites culturales sur les *Termitomyces. Compt. Rend.* **226**, 1488-1491.

Heim, R. (1951a). Le nouvel ordre des Gloeohaustoriales. *Compt. Rend.* **233**, 1245-1248.

Heim, R. (1951b). Les *Termitomyces* de Congo Belge recoltes par Mme. Goossens-Fontana. *Bull. Jardin Botan. Bruxelles* **21**, 205-220.

Heim, R. (1952a). Les *Termitomyces* du Cameroun et du Congo Francais. *Denkschr. Schweiz. Naturforsch. Ges.* **80**, 1-29.

Heim, R. (1952b). Classement raisonné des parasites, symbiotes, commensaux et saprophytes d'origine fongique associés aux termites. *6th Congr. Intern. Palot. Comp., Madrid, 1952* pp. 15-21. Imp. J. Pueyo, Madrid.

Heim, R. (1958). Fasc. 7: *Termitomyces. In* "Flore Iconographique des Champignons du Congo," p. 139-151. Jardin. Botan. Etat, Bruxelles.

Heim, R. (1963). Les *Termitomyces* de la République Centrafricain I. *Cah. Maboke* **1**, 20-26.

Heim, R., Buchli, H., Duche, J., and Laboureur, P. (1951). Memoire sur l'*Antennopsis* ectoparasite du termite de Saintonge. *Bull. Soc. Mycol. France* **67**, 336-364.

Hendee, E. C. (1933). The association of the termites *Kalotermes minor, Reticulitermes hesperus* and *Zootermopsis angusticollis* with fungi.

Hendee, E. C. (1934). The association of termites and fungi. *In* "Termites and Termite Control" (C. A. Kofoid, ed.), 2nd ed., pp. 105-116. Univ. of California Press, Berkeley, California.

Hendee, E. C. (1935). The role of fungi in the diet of the common damp-wood termite, *Zootermopsis angusticollis. Hilgardia* **9**, 499-525.

Hungate, R. E. (1940). Nitrogen content of sound and decayed coniferous woods and its relation to loss in weight during decay. *Botan. Gaz.* **102**, 382-392.

Jumelle, H., and Perrier de la Bathie, H. (1907a). Les termites champignonnistes à Madagascar. *Compt. Rend.* **144**, 1449-1451.

Jumelle, H., and Perrier de la Bathie, H. (1907b). Les champignons des termitières de Madagascar. *Compt. Rend.* **145**, 274-276.

Jumelle, H., and Perrier de la Bathie, H. (1910). Termites champignonnistes et champignons des termitières à Madagascar. *Rev. Gen. Botan.* **22**, 30-64.

Kalshoven, L. G. E. (1936). Onze Kennis van de Javaansche Termieten. *Handel. Ned.—Ind. Natuurw. Cong.* **7**, 427-435.

Kalshoven, L. G. E. (1958). Observations on the black termites, *Hospitalitermes* spp., of Java and Sumatra. *Insectes Sociaux* **5**, 9-30.

Kemner, A. (1934). Systematische und biologische Stüdien über die Termiten Javas und Celebes. *Kgl. Svenska Vetenskaps akad. Handl.* [3] **13**, 1-124.

Kevorkian, A. G. (1937). Studies in the Entomophthoraceae. I. Observations on the genus *Conidiobuolus. J. Agr. Univ. Puerto Rico* **21**, 191-199.

König, J. G. (1779). Naturgeschicte der sogenannten weissen Ameisen. *Beschäft. Berlin. Ges. Naturf. Freunde* **4**, 1-28.

Kovoor, J. (1964). Modifications chimiques provoquees par un termitide *Microcerotermes edentatus*) dans du bois de peuplier sain ou partiellement degradé par des champignons. *Bull. Biol. France Belg.* 98, 491-509.

Lund, A. E. (1960a). Termites and wood destroying fungi. *Pest Control* 28, No. 2, 26-28.

Lund, A. E. (1960b). Termites and their attack on sound wood. *Pest Control* 28, No. 6, 40, 42, and 44.

Lund, A. E. (1962). Subterranean termites and their environment. New concepts of termite ecology. *Pest Control* 30, No. 2, 30-34, 36, and 60-61.

Lund, A. E., and Engelhardt, N. T. (1962). Subterranean termites and *Absidia coerulea* Bain. (Mucorales). *J. Insect Pathol.* 4, 131-132.

Lüscher, M. (1951a). Beobachtungen über die Kolonie-gründung bei verschiedened aftricanischen Termitenarten. *Acta Trop.* 8, 36-43.

Lüscher, M. (1951b). Significance of "fungus gardens" in termite nests. *Nature* 167, 34-35.

Petch, T. (1906). The fungi of certain termite nests (*Termes redemanni* Wasm. and *T. obscuriceps* Wasm.). *Ann. Roy. Botan. Gard. Peradeniya, Ceylon* 3, No. 2, 185-270.

Petch, T. (1913a). Termite fungi, a resumé. *Ann. Roy. Botan. Gard. Peradeniya, Ceylon* 5, No. 6, 303-341.

Petch, T. (1913b). White ants and fungi. The black termite (*Eutermes monoceros* Koen.) of Ceylon. *Ann. Roy. Botan. Gard. Peradeniya, Ceylon* 5, 389-420.

Pickens, A. L. (1952). Biochemical control of caste in the social life of an insect community. *J. Elisha Mitchell Sci. Soc.* 68, No. 2, 133-135.

Randall, M., and Doody, T. C. (1934). Hydrogen-ion concentration in the termite intestine. *In* "Termites and Termite Control" (C. A. Kofoid, ed.), 2nd ed., pp. 99-104. Univ. of California Press, Berkeley, California.

Reichensperger, A. (1923). Neue eigenartig Parasiten von Termiten. *Mém. Soc. Fribourg. Sci. Nat. (Botan.)* 26, 103-114.

Ribaldi, M. (1956). Sulla presenza di particolari fruttificazioni di *Actinomucor corymbosus* (Harz) Naumov in un termitaio a Spello (Perugia). I. Alcune ozzervazione sull'aspetto naturale e colturale del fungo. *Note. Sper. Entomol. Agr.* 9, 32.

Roonwal, M. L. (1962). Biology and ecology of Oriental termites. No. 5. Mound structure, nest and moisture-content of fungus combs in *Odontotermes obesus,* with a discussion on the association of fungi with termites. *Records Indian Museum* 58, 131-150.

Sands, W. A. (1956). Some factors affecting the survival of *Odontotermes badius. Insectes Sociaux* 3, 531-536.

Sands, W. A. (1960). The initiation of fungus comb construction in laboratory colonies of *Ancistrotermes guineenis* (Silvestri). *Insectes Sociaux* 7, 251-259.

Sands, W. A. (1965). Alate development and colony foundation in five species of *Trinervitermes* (Isoptera, Nasutitermitinae) in Nigeria, West Africa. *Insectes Sociaux* 12, 117-130.

Sellschop, J. P. F. (1965). Field observations on conditions conducive to the contamination of groundnuts with the mould *Aspergillu: flavus. S. African Med. J. (Suppl. S. African J. Nutr.).* 774-776.

Smeathman, H. (1791). Some account of the termites which are found in Africa and other hot climates. *Phil. Trans. Roy. Soc. London* 71, 139-192.

Smythe, R. V., and Coppel, H. C. (1966). Pathogenicity of externally occurring fungi to *R. flavipes. J. Invertebrate Pathol.* 8, 266-267.

Smythe, R. V., Allen, T. C., and Coppel, H. C. (1965). Response of the eastern subterranean termite to an attractive extract from *Lenzites trabea*-invaded wood. *J. Econ. Entomol.* 58. 420-423.

Smythe, R. V., Coppel, H. C., and Allen, T. C. (1967). The response of *Reticuliterems* spp. and *Zootermopsis angusticollis* (Isoptera) to extracts from woods decayed by various fungi. *Ann. Entomol. Soc. Am.* **60,** 8-9.

Snyder, T. E. (1956). Annotated, subject-heading bibliography of termites, 1350 B.C. to A.D. 1954. *Smithsonian Misc. Collections* **130,** 1-305.

Snyder, T. E. (1961). Supplement to the annotated, subject-heading bibliography of termites, 1955 to 1960. *Smithsonian Misc. Collections* **143,** No. 3, 1-137.

Stifler, C. B. (1941). A new genus of Hypocreales. *Mycologia* **33,** 82-86.

Tate, P. C. (1927). On *Ectomyces calotermi*, n. g., n. sp., an Ascomycete parasitic on *Calotermes samoanus* Holmgren, Isoptera, Protermitidae. *Parasitology* **19,** 54-60.

Tate, P. C. (1928). Notes on the genera *Ectomyces* and *Termitaria*, fungi parasitic on termites. *Parasitology* **20,** 77-78.

Thaxter, R. (1895). Notes on the Laboulbeniaceae, with descriptions of new species. *Proc. Am. Acad. Arts Sci.* **30,** 470-471.

Thaxter, R. (1920). Second note on certain peculiar fungus parasites of living insects. *Botan. Gaz.* **69,** No. 1, 3-9.

Toumanoff, C. (1965). Action de divers champignons entomophages sur *Reticulitermes santonensis* Feytaud. *Ann. Parasitol. Humaine Comparée* **40,** 611-624.

Toumanoff, C., and Rombaut, J. (1965). Action de certains champignons entomophages, cultivés sur les milieux appropriés attractifs, sur le termite de Saintonge, *Reticulitermes santonensis* Feytaud. *Ann. Parasitol. Humaine Comparée* **40,** 611-624.

Von Kurir, A. (1963). Der Pilz *Termitomyces* als Nabrung für die larven der Gelbfüssigen Termite (*R. flavipes* Kol.). *Holzforsch. Holzverwert.* **15** No. 5, 101-107.

Watanabe, T., and Casida, J. E. (1963). Response of *Reticulitermes flavipes* to factors in fungus-infected wood and synthetic chemicals. *J. Econ. Entomol.* **56,** 300-307.

Williams, R. M. C. (1965). "Termite Infestation of Pines in British Honduras," Overseas Res. Publ. No. 11. H. M. Stationery Office, London.

Yendol, W. G., and Paschke, J. D. (1965). Pathology of an *Entomophthora* infection in the Eastern Subterranean Termite, *Reticulitermes flavipes* (Kollar). *J. Invertebrate Pathol.* **7,** 414-422.

17

The Biology of Termitophiles

DAVID H. KISTNER

I. TERMITOPHILES IN GENERAL

A. DEFINITION OF THE TERM TERMITOPHILE

The word termitophile could be defined as any animal other than a termite that is normally found in a termite nest. This definition has the advantage of operational precision; if it were accepted then all organisms taken from a termite nest would be drawn to the attention of appropriate workers, and many facts about the ecological relationships of the termites, which have been thrown away in the past through field decisions that such and such are not "significant," would now be known. For example, Professor J. K. A. Van Boven of the Université de Louvain (personal communication, 1967) has taken as many as a hundred species of ants from a single *Macrotermes* sp. nest in the Congo. Obviously, many of these species probably nest in all sorts of places besides termite nests, but the possibility exists that some of them are quite specific.

However, the word termitophile is usually used to indicate some obligatory relationship of an animal to the termite society. Thus, an animal has to be found in a termite nest during at least one complete stage of its life cycle before it is considered to be a termitophile. This is the classic way in which the term has been used. The advantage of this definition is that it eliminates animals that are only using the termite nest as shelter (called termitariophiles, a term used by Araujo in Volume II) and certain soil-inhabiting insects that appear to be just as frequent in other soil as in the earthen mounds of some of the fungus growing termites, i.e., *Microtermes* sp. in *Macrotermes* sp. mounds. With this definition, the scope of any study is more restricted. However, even now, a large number of species of so-called obligatory termitophiles are only presumed to be obligatory by virtue of their morphology or by their presumed relationships to other species which are "typical" termitophiles. It thus appears that the precise status of many species will be determined only after careful field work.

In general, for the purposes of this chapter, only those species that are known to conform to the second definition will be discussed in detail, but, for their general interest, all the variety of arthropods that have been called termitophiles will be discussed. It must be remembered that their relationships to their termite hosts are virtually unknown so that many will be shown eventually to conform only to the first and more general definition.

B. VARIETIES OF TERMITOPHILES

Over the years, a wide variety of arthropods have been reported from termite nests. The first catalog of such organisms was compiled by Kraatz (1857) and contained principally the species of Aleocharinae (Staphylinidae) known or suspected to be from termite nests up to that date. This was followed in 1894 by a large and comprehensive catalog by Wasmann. Additions were made to this list by Warren (1919) and Hegh (1922). Since then, no general catalogs have appeared, probably because the volume of the material has increased to the point where only specialized groups can be handled by any single individual. I will not attempt to catalog the species, but a listing of the groups is given in Table I.

Such a list, in addition to showing the variety of forms, also shows that termitophilous species have evolved independently at least 29 times. If

TABLE I

MAJOR GROUPS OF ARTHROPODS RECORDED FROM TERMITE NESTS

Class	Order	Families
Crustacea	Isopoda	
Diplopoda		
Arachnida	Acarina	
	Araneida	
	Chelonethida	
	Solpugida	
Insecta	Coleoptera	Brenthidae, Cantharidae, Carabidae, Cetonidae, Chrysomelidae, Cossiphodidae, Curculionidae, Erotylidae, Histeridae, Lathridiidae, Limexylidae, Melandryidae, Pselaphidae, Ptilliidae, Rhysopaussidae, Scaphidiidae, Scarabaeidae, Scydmaenidae, Silphidae, Staphylinidae, Tenebrionidae
	Collembola	
	Diptera	Phoridae, Syrphidae
	Heteroptera	
	Homoptera	Cossidae, Jassidae
	Hymenoptera	Formicidae
	Lepidoptera	Tiniidae
	Thysanura	

one takes into consideration the fact that the Staphylinidae exhibit at least 12 convergent evolutions to this type of life (Seevers, 1957) and that the Phoridae exhibit at least 2, the minimum number of times termitophily has evolved is 40 times. The actual number of independent invasions of the termite colony is probably much higher. The comparison of some of these different forms yields interesting information on convergent evolution which will be discussed later.

II. COLLECTING TERMITOPHILES

In spite of the fact that many specimens of termitophiles have been collected, there is surprisingly little in the literature about how such collecting is done.

The most lucid description was given by Bugnion (1913), who collected *Termitoxenia perideniyae* (Wasmann), a phorid fly, from *Odontotermes taprobanes* (Walker) (as *T. redemanni* Wasmann*) nests in Ceylon. He described opening the nest and removing the fungus gardens, which

---

*A. E. Emerson has informed me that *Odontotermes redemanni* (Wasmann) is a synonym of *Odontotermes taprobanes* Walker.

were placed in boxes and carried back to the laboratory. He remarked that it was possible to keep the fungus for 48 hours without regulating the humidity. The fungus was sorted and the small *Termitoxenia* were captured with a pair of forceps. Bugnion stressed the importance of assaying the nest in the field and maintained that if no specimens were found in half an hour of searching through the fungus gardens it was better to seek out another nest.

Emerson (1935) found certain *Thyreoxenus* in a migratory column of *Nasutitermes* sp. as well as other termitophilous forms in a trail over sandy ground at about 7:00 A.M. (Emerson, 1967, personal communication). The migratory columns are rarely seen, but are probably not rare occurrences at night. Other investigators, particularly Cameron (1932), reported capturing some termitophiles in the foraging columns.

Our experience is confined to the Old World tropics. I have never found foraging columns very profitable and have never personally seen a migration of any species of termite. We therefore concentrate on the total dissection of the nest. First, the nest is assayed in the field, but the decision as to whether to continue with a particular nest is dictated by local conditions and the time available. In dry areas, such as South Africa, the yield per nest is typically very low, so if a nest is rejected because a half-hour sort through the fungus gardens has yielded nothing, nearly all nests would be rejected and no specimens would be collected. In wetter areas, such as Ceylon, where we also collected, yields are much higher and one can pick and choose particularly productive nests. Even in wet areas, though, there is a risk of throwing away some rare material if you reject an unpromising nest. The preferred method then is to sort through patiently even if initial assays are unfavorable.

By dissecting the nest completely and keeping careful records of the position of each specimen, a more accurate account of the ecology of the termitophiles can be compiled. For instance, in *Macrotermes* colonies not all of the termitophiles are found in the fungus gardens. Some can be found in the royal cells, in the passageways, and in the auxiliary brood chambers adjacent to the fungus gardens. The precise location of each species has an interesting way of varying from one species to another, not only with reference to the termitophile species but also to the species of termite.

After the nest is carefully dissected, part of the material is taken into the laboratory or lodging and sorted further. Yellow plastic trays have proved most useful in this regard as the color contrasts well with most termites and termitophiles. We have found plastic better than metal for this purpose because it is lighter, more easily transported, and cheaper.

It is useful to have sides on the tray, rather than using a cloth, as the steep sides discourage escape by the faster termitophiles. Specimens are captured from the trays by the use of straight-tubed aspirators. Extremely small specimens can be picked up with a moistened camel's hair brush.

Smaller nests (e.g., *Cubitermes* and *Nasutitermes*) where the structural subdivisions are not as obvious are carried back to the laboratory intact. There they are sorted out, each piece is broken, and its contents are shaken out into the trays. This is a slow process, and we have used Berlese funnels advantageously from time to time. The nest is broken over the top of the funnel and allowed to dry. In the Congo this was difficult because the humidity was so high that it took from a week to 10 days to dry out a *Cubitermes* nest. Recently, in South Africa we sampled *Trinervitermes* nests by using a Berlese funnel in combination with tear gas (chloropicrin). We found it worked best if the nest was broken only sufficiently to get it or part of it over the screen with the open cells of the nest directed into the funnel. Then about an ounce of chloropicrin was poured onto the top of the nest. Nests were totally evacuated and all the termites and termitophiles were gathered in a quart of alcohol within 12 hours.

We consider Berlese sampling only an auxiliary method for two reasons: one cannot see the specimens alive, and it takes more time to sort the dead samples. When a nest is sorted alive, the movement of the termitophiles is of considerable help in spotting them. The specimens may be captured, and the majority of the termites, except for a small sample to identify the hosts, can be thrown away. With the Berlese technique, the end product consists of a quart- or pint-sized jar of dead termites, debris, and hopefully some termitophiles. This all must be sorted under a microscope by experienced sorters. The Berlese technique does permit later sorting in the home laboratory, thus conserving valuable field time.

Termitophiles captured alive with the termites were studied alive as long as possible or necessary. Many species will not survive long in the laboratory, but with better facilities longer observations may prove feasible. Specimens should be fixed in Bouin's fluid where possible. Even if the specimens are to be eventually stored dry, the delicate specimens retain their shapes better if they are fixed in Bouin's fluid first. After the specimens have been fixed in Bouin's for a few days, they can be left in it or transferred into alcohol. Pasteels (1966) recommends the use of alcoholic Bouin's to dissolve the epicuticle and permit faster penetration. Material which has been fixed in Bouin's has the further advantage that sections may be made for study of the internal morphology.

III. THE EVOLUTION OF SELECTED TERMITOPHILES

Of all of the groups of Arthropods that are associated with termites, perhaps the best known are the Staphylinidae. These are known chiefly from the adults, so that even here there are sizable gaps in our knowledge. Nevertheless, the adults have been sufficiently studied so that phylogenies could be worked out and matched to the phylogeny of the termites, thus yielding some interesting generalizations. The bulk of this work was done by the late Professor Charles H. Seevers and everything that will be said in this section, unless otherwise cited, can be found in papers by Seevers (1937, 1938, 1939, 1941, 1945, 1946, 1957, 1960, 1965). That Seevers was able to produce such fine papers over the years was due in no small way to the field activities and personal interest of Professor Alfred E. Emerson who has collected about 25% of the known species.

A. THE INVASION OF TERMITE NESTS BY STAPHYLINIDAE

Seevers showed that there were at least 11 independent entries of staphylinid beetles into termite nests. The array of these entries, which are now represented by subfamilies, tribes, and subtribes of the Staphylinidae, is shown in Fig. 1. It is interesting to note that all of the families and subfamilies of termites have been invaded except the Kalotermitidae and the Serritermitidae (not shown). The Hodotermitidae are not shown invaded, but the recent recapture of *Termitotelus* sp. with *Microhodotermes viator* (Latreille) in Southwest Africa by Coaton and Sheasby has verified this association. It is omitted from the diagram because its tribal status is uncertain but it nevertheless represents another independent invasion.

While it is still not possible to pinpoint the relationships of each of the tribes and subtribes because of confusion in the classification of the free-living Aleocharinae. the tribe Myrmedoniini will undoubtedly occupy a central position in the future. Koblick and Kistner (1965) have already shown the relationship of the Pygostenini to the Myrmedoniini, and studies are under way in this laboratory which, upon completion, will show the relationship of the Termitodiscini with the Myrmedoniini. The Termitopaediini, Pseudoperinthini, Termitonannini, and Termitohospitini will probably also be shown to be derived from myrmedoniine stock in the future but probably from different branches of the tribe than the Termitodiscini or the Pygostenini. However, even though all have ancestry in the Myrmedoniini, they still represent separate invasions, with the exception of the Termitondina, which may share a common ancestry with the Termitodiscini. The ancestry of the Corotocini will be especially

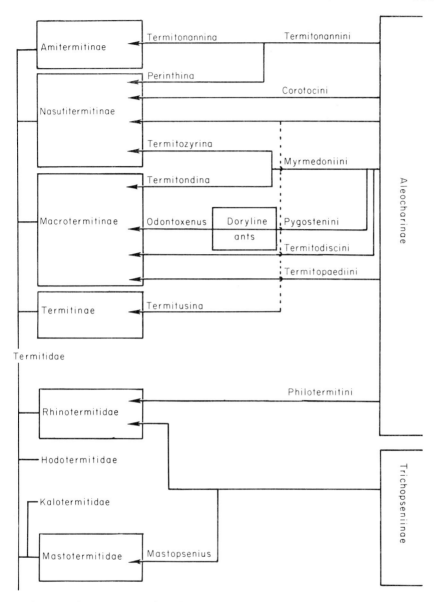

Fig. 1. Primary host relationships of most of the major categories of termitophilous Staphylinidae. On the left is a phylogenetic arrangement of some of the families and subfamilies of the termites. The phylogeny of the termites is distorted by the placement of the Amitermitinae above the Nasutitermitinae, but this simplifies the diagram of the Staphylinid invasions. On the right are two subfamilies of the Staphylinidae. Each arrow represents an invasion of the societies of a particular taxon of termites by a tribe or a subtribe of Staphylinidae [modified from Seevers (1957)].

difficult to work out, but it will probably prove to be a tribe other than the Myrmedoniini.

Both the morphology and the ecology of free-living members of the tribe Myrmedoniini make this tribe especially attractive as ancestors of termitophiles (as well as myrmecophiles). The tribe has numerous genera and species that are predacious and have evolved various degrees of prey specificity varying by genus and species from no specificity whatsoever to predation on a single subgenus of ants and a single genus of termites. Thus, we have observed the genus *Termozyras* Cameron feeding only on fungus-growing termites and refusing other prey even though it does not live in termite nests. There are many other examples of this type for which data have been collected, but the basic taxonomy must be completed before they are published. A certain degree of prey specificity provides an ecological setting from which the further evolution of termitophily becomes not only plausible but probable.

It will also be noted in Fig. 1 that the Pygostenini invaded the Macrotermitinae (*Odontotermes* only) from the doryline ant niche. This was first documented by Wasmann (1904a,b) and further elaborated by Kemner (1929a,b). The host transfer was discussed by Kistner (1958), who stated that this transfer must have taken place after *Odontotermes* reached India during the Miocene extension of grasslands across the Arabian subpeninsula. Kistner (1958) also showed that another Pygostenine genus, *Typhloponemys* Rey, was also transferred. Cameron (1927) described a species of *Derema* (*Demerinda*) belonging to the tribe Deremini. which showed that still another tribe, the majority of whose members are found with doryline ants. had been transferred to termites. Thus, it is probable that a whole faunal interchange between doryline ants and *Odontotermes* took place. Whether this interchange took place several times or only once cannot be determined at the present time.

After the initial entry into the termite nest, the further evolution of each termitophilous taxon most probably occurred within the context of the evolution of the termites. This phenomenon has been demonstrated best for the tribes Corotocini and Termitonannini (Seevers, 1957).

B. The Phylogeny of the Tribe Corotocini

The tribe Corotocini as defined by Seevers (1957) contains many of the most spectacular species of physogastric termitophilous Staphylinidae. Most members of the tribe are found in association with the Nasutitermitinae. Seevers divided the tribe into 6 subtribes as shown in Fig. 2. This figure shows also the manner in which modifications of the tarsal

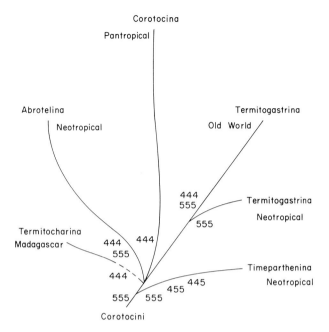

Fig. 2. Phylogeny of the subtribes of the Corotocini. Numbers indicate the tarsal formulas present in members of each subtribe [slightly modified from Seevers (1957)].

formula took place as well as the geographic distribution of each of the subtribes in terms of the faunal regions. Figure 3 shows the host relationships of four of the subtribes superimposed on a dendrogram of the Nasutitermitinae. It should be noted that the only exception to the parallel evolution principle is found in the subtribe Timeparthenina, where 2 genera, represented by 1 species each and known only from the type series, have been recorded from the nests of *Anoplotermes*.

The relationships between the genera of the subtribe Timeparthenina can be seen in Fig. 4. The host genera can be observed readily as can the overall form of the termitophiles.

More generalized corotocine genera, such as *Termitophya* (Fig. 5), are found with the other line of Nasutitermitinae evolution. This more generalized stock most probably gave rise to the rest of the tribes.

The relationships between the genera of the subtribe Termitogastrina are shown in Fig. 5. This subtribe evolved only with *Nasutitermes* in the New World, but is additionally found with *Trinervitermes, Bulbitermes, Grallatotermes,* and *Hospitalitermes* in the Old World. The New World branch retains many primitive features, whereas many of the Old

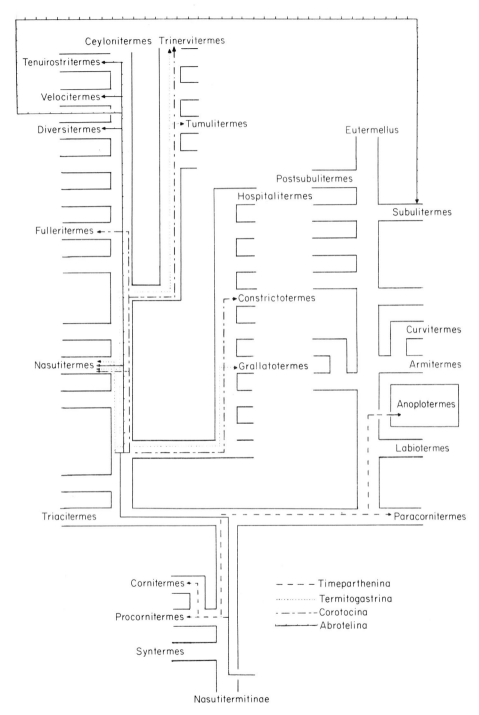

Fig. 3. Host relationships of the subtribes of the tribe Corotocini [from Seevers (1957)].

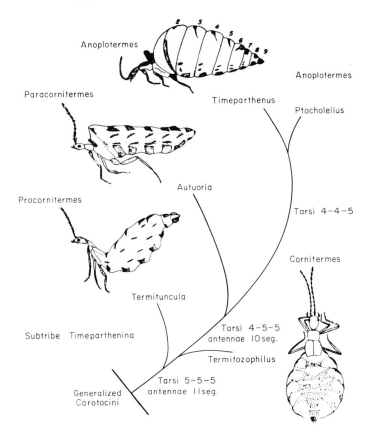

Fig. 4.   Phylogeny of the genera of the subtribe Timeparthenina [modified from Seevers (1957)].

World genera have been considerably modified with the development of extensive physogastry in *Paracoratoca*. However, the most primitive of the Old World stock, such as the genus *Idiogaster*, look much like their New World counterparts.

The relationships between the genera of the subtribe Corotocina are summarized in Fig. 6. This subtribe contains the most specialized staphylinid termitophiles. Again the most primitive member of the group is found in South America, although the African genus *Termitopullus* is also relatively primitive. Various specializations of general biological interest have been observed in this group. *Corotoca* has been shown to be larviparous; in fact, one can see the larvae developing within the

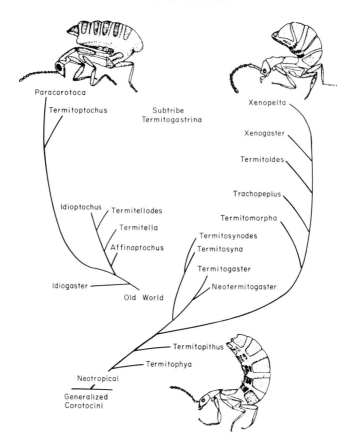

Fig. 5. Phylogeny of the genera of the subtribe Termitogastrina [slightly modified from Seevers (1957)].

translucent abdomen of some of the females. The genera *Thyreoxenus*, *Termitomimus*, *Spirachtha*, and *Spirachthodes* are believed to exhibit postimaginal growth. This belief is strengthened by the presence of several intermediate stages present in preserved series that permit the construction of a graded series between stenogastric and physogastric states. An examination of these individuals shows that besides the changes in the physogastric abdomen, there are also changes in some of the chitinized parts. These include changes in the proportions of the legs and changes in the metasternum. Current theories of growth of insects would require another molt to secure such changes. It would therefore be useful, if possible, to observe these changes in living individuals to see if these changes are due to postimaginal growth or to some kind of balanced genetic polymorphism. Similar postimaginal growth has been documented for the Termitoxeniinae (Diptera, Phoridae) by Mergelsberg (1935) for the genera *Termitophilomyia*, *Termitostroma*, and *Termitosagma*, but he shows, and I have confirmed, that the growth here occurs only in the membranous parts of the abdomen and does not involve the legs or other chitinized parts. *Thyreoxenus* and *Oideprosoma*, alone of the termitophiles so far, exhibit the development of enlarged membranous, presumably glandular areas of the thorax as well as the abdomen.

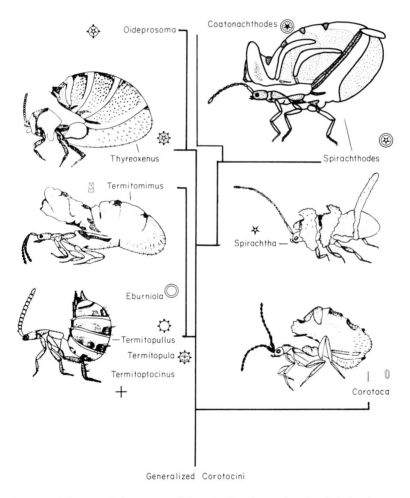

Fig. 6. Phylogeny of the genera of the subtribe Corotocina. Symbols by the generic names are those used in the distribution map (Fig. 8) [modified from Seevers (1957)].

The distribution of the Corotocini except for the subtribe Corotocina is shown in Fig. 7, while the distribution of the subtribe Corotocina is shown in Fig. 8. The presence of closely related species of termitophiles in such diverse areas of the world indicates that the ancestral stock of these beetles arose and invaded Nasutitermitinae nests very early in the distributional history of the termites. From the geographic distribution data, we know that they would have had to disperse over the Bering land bridge when tropical conditions prevailed; which is believed to have occurred during the Cretaceous. Also, in order to reach Australia and the Solomon Islands, the beetles would have had to be with Nasuti-termitinae stock prior to the end of the Cretaceous. That sea gaps apparently prevent the invasion of mature nests of species that might disperse its reproductives through flight over relatively short sea barriers is shown by the fact that although *Thyreoxenus parviceps* Mann is found commonly with *Nasutitermes costalis* (Holmgren) in Trinidad, the same species of termite lacks any species of *Thyreoxenus* in nearby Grenada. Thus it would appear that the termite-termitophile association has to move across land connections (Emerson, 1967, personal communication).

The subtribe Abrotelina is entirely neotropical in distribution and has evolved in association with New World termites of the *Nasutitermes* branch of the Nasutitermitinae. While these species show the phylogenetic interdigitation with New World *Nasutitermes*-related genera that the Termitogastrina show, they add a few new dimensions in that they are also found with *Diversitermes*, *Velocitermes*, and *Tenuirostritermes*. The subtribe Termitocharina contains only one genus and species and its relationship may well be with the Abrotelina, but this will not be known until some good field work is done. If this is so, then the origin of this subtribe would be early in the history of the *Nasutitermes* branch of the Nasutitermitinae. As the Abrotelina now stand, there is no way to date their origin.

C. The Phylogeny of the Tribe Termitonannini

Whereas the tribe Corotocini all exhibit some degree of physogastry, most members of the tribe Termitonannini do not exhibit any and are limuloid in form. This tribe is further subdivided into two subtribes, the Termitonannina and the Perinthina, whose relationships are shown in the dendrogram in Fig. 9. The host relationships are summarized for the tribe in Fig. 10. One can see from the dendrogram and the host relationships that the Termitonannina and the Perinthina had a common origin in the New World topics. The Termitonannina speciated wholly

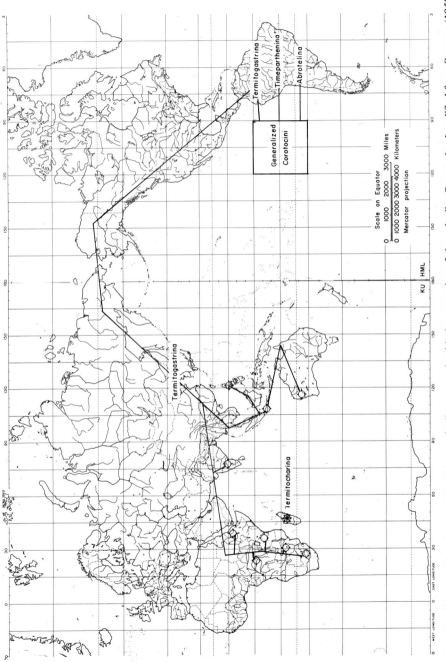

Fig. 7. Distribution of the Corotocini, phylogenetically arranged, with the exception of the subtribe Corotocina [modified from Seevers (1957)].

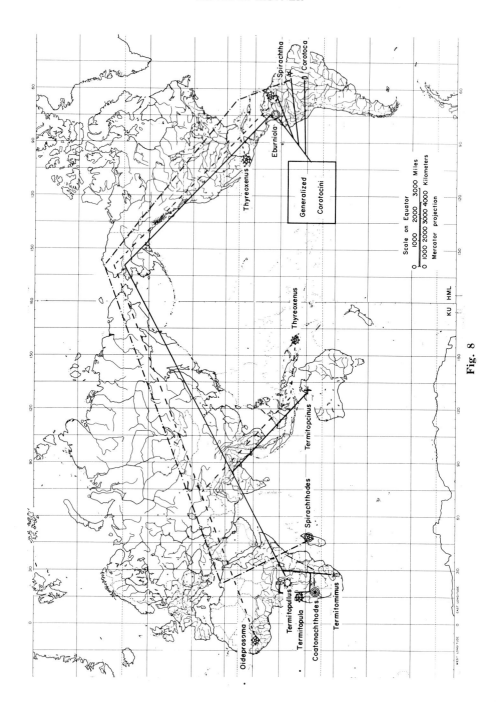

Fig. 8

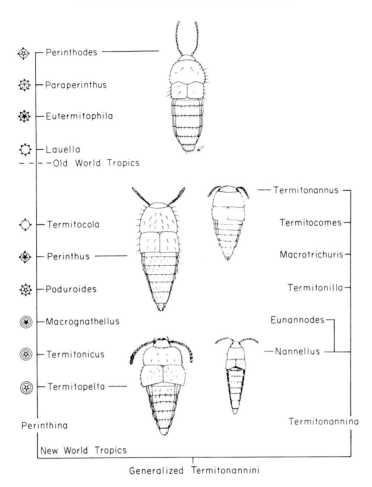

Fig. 9. Phylogeny of the subtribes and genera of the tribe Termitomannini. Symbols by the generic names of the Perinthina are those used in the distribution map (Fig. 11) [Modified from Seevers (1957)].

within the New World tropics, mostly with members of the *Subulitermes* branch of the Nasutitermitinae. The Perinthina, on the other hand, speciated both in the New World and the Old World (see distribution in Fig. 11), which points to an early origin of the group. The host specificity of the Termitonannina is not clear, due to the fact that a large number of the more primitive members of the Subtribe are found with *Anoplotermes*.

Fig. 8. Distribution of the genera of the subtribe Corotocina, phylogenetically arranged [modified from Seevers (1957)].

However, the host specificity of the Perinthina is clear (Fig. 10).

D. THE PROBLEM OF *Anoplotermes*

You will note that members of both tribes Corotocini and Termitonan-nini are associated with *Anoplotermes*. Ahmad (1950) places *Anoplotermes* in the subfamily Amitermitinae on the *Speculitermes-Synhamitermes* branch of the phylogenetic tree. Most modern termite systematists agree with this view, which is based on the structure of the worker mandible. Weidner (1966, Fig. 14 and 336) disagrees with this view and places *Anoplotermes* near *Armitermes*, citing Goetsch's study (1939) and the termitophile evidence.

To a termitophile specialist, Weidner's interpretation (1966) has great appeal. It would explain the presence of primitive Termitonannina in *Anoplotermes* nests, whereas the most specialized forms (*Termitonannus*) are in *Anoplotermes* and *Subulitermes* nests. The placement of *Anoplotermes* in the Amitermitinae makes necessary the hypothesis that host transfer took place at least twice, once in the Corotocini from *Paracornitermes* to *Anoplotermes* and once again in the Termitonannina from *Anoplotermes* to *Labiotermes* and *Subulitermes* as the most primitive forms are with *Anoplotermes*.

Aside from the morphology of the termites, which is the province of the termite specialists, there are several factors that favor the host transfer hypothesis. First is the fact that *Anoplotermes* often nests within the mounds of other termites. Thus it would be in a position to pick up termitophiles from other species and in turn infect other species with its own termitophiles. Second is the fact that the Corotocini and Termitonannini have not been captured from the same *Anoplotermes* colonies, which would favor the view of transfer by chance and not coevolution of the entire fauna over long periods of time. Third, the presence of *Mormellus bicolor* Silvestri with *Subulitermes microsoma* (Silvestri) in Brazil would tend to substantiate the fact that host transfer can take place as its closest relatives are found with *Diversitermes* and *Velocitermes* on the *Nasutitermes* branch of the phylogenetic tree. Finally, the presence of Termitonannini in *Speculitermes* nests as well as *Anoplotermes* nests would tend to substantiate the presence of primitive members of this group in that branch of the phylogenetic tree and to substantiate the relationship of *Anoplotermes* to *Speculitermes*. Since no one has doubted the systematic position of *Speculitermes*, this would tend to reinforce the host transfer hypothesis also.

In any event, I do not think that the termitophile evidence should be used to attest to the veracity of Goetsch's experiments.

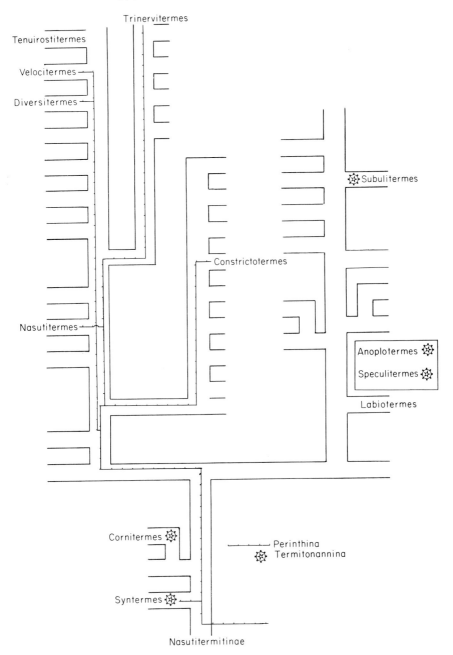

Fig. 10. Host relationships of the Termitonannini [slightly modified from Seevers (1957)].

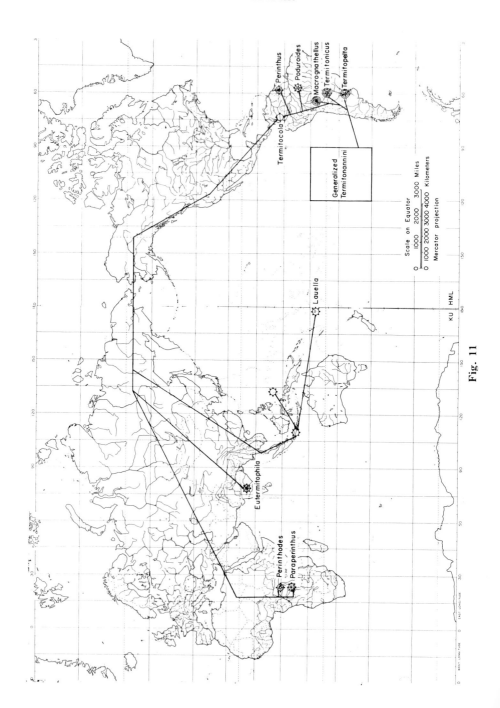

Fig. 11

E. CONCLUSIONS

Two principal conclusions can be deduced from the above types of studies. The first is that the termitophiles are of ancient origin and have speciated within the framework of the phylogenetic pattern of their hosts over long periods of time. Thus, as the termites were somehow isolated and underwent specific and generic differentiation, the associated termitophiles also underwent specific and generic differentiation. This happened regardless of the body types exhibited by the various termitophiles. The second is (Figs. 8 and 11) that ecological assemblages of organisms without genetic continuity can evolve in association with one another. Thus, the three lines moving across the Bering Land bridge in Fig. 8 are connected only by the ecological setting presented by the termites, and the zoogeography of the termitophiles precisely parallels that of the termite hosts as developed by Emerson (1955).

These conclusions are inherent in the other tribes and subtribes, but for a variety of reasons, these are not sufficiently well known and the situation is therefore not as crystal clear as in the examples presented above. For a summary of the exisiting published data, the interested reader is referred to Seevers (1957).

IV. TERMITE-TERMITOPHILE INTEGRATING MECHANISMS

One of the most interesting aspects of the association of organisms of differing genetic continuity is the basis of the association. In other words, why should termites tolerate the inclusion of foreign organisms in their societies?

Two principal adaptations emerge. One is the physogastry previously mentioned. Another is the limuloid body shape. Both of these adaptations have arisen convergently (Fig. 12) many times in both the Coleoptera and the Diptera, as has been pointed out many times (Wasmann,

Fig. 11. Distribution of the genera of the subtribe Perinthina, phylogenetically arranged [modified from Seevers (1957)].

Fig. 12. Photographs showing the overall appearance of the two principal body type modifications occurring in termitophiles (see page 546):
  A. *Thaumatoxena* sp., showing the limuloid form
  B. *Termitomimus entendveniensis* Trägårdh, showing physogastry
  C. *Termitodiscus braunsi* Wasmann, showing the limuloid form
  D. *Termitostroma schmitzi* Reichensperger, showing physogastry

This series shows the convergent development of these phenomena as the species on the bottom are beetles, whereas the species on the top are flies (original photos).

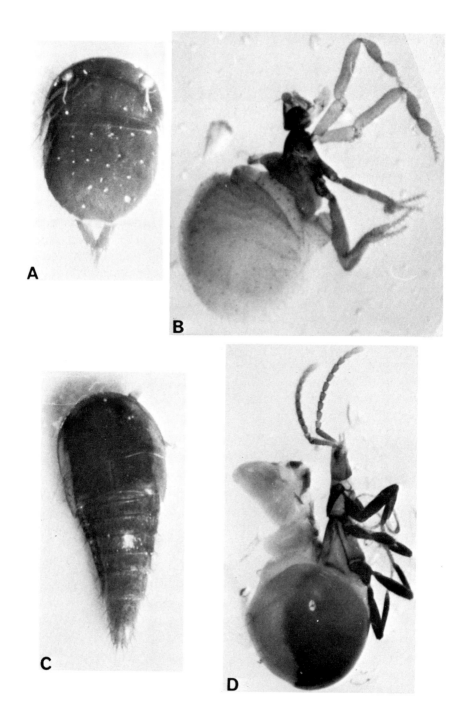

Fig. 12. (See page 545 for legend.)

1900, and elsewhere; Trägårdh, 1907) but most recently by Leleup (1965, p. 171–172). Unfortunately, one of Leleup's termitophiles [i.e., *Trilobitideus mirabilis* (Wasmann)] is actually a myrmecophile, but the basic truth in the comparison holds nevertheless. Both of these adaptations have been the subject of a great deal of speculation.

A. PHYSOGASTRY

The condition of certain Diptera and Coleoptera associated with termites, wherein the abdomen is greatly enlarged, particularly the membranous parts but not only these, has traditionally been called physogastry. Physogastry is believed to be caused by the hypertrophy of the fat body in some species, the enlargement of the reproductive system in others (Mergelsberg, 1935), and a combination of the two in still others (Trägårdh, 1907).

Whatever the cause of the enlargement, Wasmann (1895, and elsewhere) called the physogastric species symphiles and assumed that the termites licked the expanded abdomens and received some substance from them. Thus, the symphiles and the termites exhibited a mutualistic relationship whereby the symphiles received lodging and food in exchange for the secretion of some substance which the termites licked. Unfortunately, the evidence for this hypothesis has been scanty. Termitophiles are extremely delicate and cannot usually be observed without cracking open the termite nest. Observations, then, usually have to be made in petri dishes with both the host and the termitophiles under artificial conditions.

The following observations have been made. Wheeler (1928) reported Emerson's observations of *Constrictotermes cavifrons* (Holmgren) transporting *Spirachtha mirabilis* Mann to shelter within the nest in the same manner that the termites picked up the smaller nymphs and carried them to shelter (observations are here amplified by personal communication). He also observed the beetles being licked by the termites under the microscope. The termites licked the membranous parts of the body, the abdominal appendages, and the antennae and legs.

Emerson (1935) reported his observations of *Nasutitermes guayanae* (Holmgren) licking *Thyreoxenus major* Mann. He also observed *Thyreoxenus parviceps* being licked by *Nasutitermes costalis* (Holmgren) as well as being fed by regurgitations from the termites. Apparently, a lot of licking went on in this colony, for he saw the beetles lick each other as well as termite nymphs without harming them. He further observed this species of beetle bend its abdomen to one side and deposit a small drop of fluid to which the termites gave no visible reaction.

Thyreoxenus parviceps was also observed in migration with its host. *Thyreoxenus pulchellus* Mann was observed (also by Emerson) to walk slowly among its host termites [*Nasutitermes ephratae* (Holmgren)] and to raise its abdomen and move it forward so that periodically it was well in front of its head. Once, when it did this, the beetle deposited a drop of grayish-white liquid upon the head of a worker, whereupon two other workers licked it off.

Emerson (1929) reported that *Termitogaster emersoni* Mann was not only licked by its host, *Nasutitermes ephratae,* but that there was also communication between the two species. Thus, when the staphylinid would rapidly bend and jerk its legs, a behavior very characteristic of termites, the termites would respond by intensively licking the body, legs, and antennae of the beetle.

In the Philippines my wife and I observed workers of *Macrotermes gilvus* (Hagen) licking specimens of *Neodioxeuta oudemansi* Franssen. We also observed workers of *Trinervitermes bettonianus* (Sjöstedt) licking a new species of *Idiogaster* Wasmann in Kenya. However, we did not observe *Trinervitermes trinervoides* (Sjöstedt) licking the membranous parts of *Paracorotoca akermani* (Warren) in South Africa; this confirms observations of Warren (1920). The *Paracorotoca* did not avoid the termites as Warren suggested, but actually seemed to seek out their company and were groomed and palpated by both workers and soldiers as shown in Fig. 13. Worker termites were seen frequently licking a leg of the presumed *Paracorotoca* larvae (Fig. 13), but neither the adults or the larvae were observed receiving food from the termites.

For the Termitoxeniinae (a subfamily of Phoridae, Diptera), the food habits were established early when Bugnion (1913) reported finding fungus conidia in the intestine of *Termitoxenia peradeniyae* associated with *Odontotermes taprobanes* Walker in Ceylon. He extracted oblong objects from the gut of freshly dissected specimens and compared this extract with an extract made from the small, white fungus heads from the fungus gardens of the termites. No one has reported seeing the termites lick these remarkable physogastric phorid flies in the field, but Emerson (1967, personal communication) observed *Odontotermes patruus* (Sjöstedt) licking *Termitosagma ephippium* Schmitz in the Congo. My wife and I have observed *Odontotermes culturarum* (Sjöstedt) licking *Termitosagma henningsi* Reichensperger and *Termitostroma schmitzi* Reichensperger at Amani, Tanzania.

Thus, while some physogastric genera are licked, others may not be, so the precise function of physogastry may vary from one taxon to another.

Some interesting work is being done by Pasteels (1966) at the Université Libre de Bruxelles. This work has not yet been published, but I

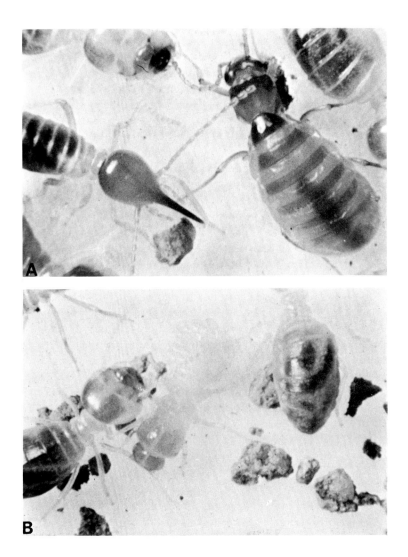

Fig. 13. *Paracorotoca akermani* (Warren):

A. Adult having its antenna groomed by a worker termite while being palpated by a soldier termite with both its antenna (over the pronotum) and its maxillary palpi (over the mesothoracic leg)

B. Presumed larva being licked on its leg by a worker termite. All photographed alive by the author in the laboratory of Dr. W. G. H. Coaton, Plant Protection Research Institute, Pretoria, Republic of South Africa. So far as I know, these are the first photographs of living termite-termitophile interactions that have ever been published.

had the privilege of visiting his laboratory, viewing his slide preparations, and reading his thesis. He has studied the histology of the abdomens of several termitophilous species and has been able to identify glands in various positions along the abdomen as well as pores by which some of the glands can discharge. Pores of the same type had been demonstrated previously by Trägårdh (1907) in *Termitomimus entendveniensis,* but Trägårdh did not find glands. His explanation of the pores was that they were used to provide passage of fat or another derivative of the fat body as a fluid to the exterior of the body where the termites could lick it.

Warren (1920, p. 323) demonstrated the following glands in *Paracorotoca akermanni:* (1) mandibular, (2) cephalic, (3) tergal scent glands of abdominal segment VI, and (4) sternal glands of abdominal segment X, developed in the female but absent in the male. He was also able to demonstrate pores by which these glands could discharge. Strangely enough, he did not choose to interpret these glands as an adaptation to termitophily, possibly because he did not know or investigate these glands in free-living Staphylinidae.

McIndoo (1923) did another histological study of the abdominal appendages of *Spirachtha mirabilis.* He suggested that materials could pass from the blood into hypodermal cells and through the cuticle. He did not demonstrate definitive glands or pores.

Pasteels' work, when published, will permit better interpretation because he compares termitophilous, myrmecophilous, and free-living forms and is then able to distinguish glands unique to termitophily from those characteristic of many free-living Aleocharinae.

Several histological studies have been made of the physogastric abdomen of the Termitoxeniiae (Assmuth, 1913; Bugnion, 1913; Mergelsberg. 1935). These studies were oriented toward the problem of whether the Termitoxeniinae were (Assmuth, Mergelsberg) or were not (Bugnion) hermaphroditic. This subject was reviewed in depth by Borgmeier (1964). Mergelsberg studied egg development as well and thought that the development of physogastry was correlated with egg development. Both Assmuth and Bugnion showed large cells placed superficially under the hypodermis. Many of these larger cells were shown to be situated in relation to large setae. However, neither came to any conclusion as to whether these cells were glands or not or whether or not the cells were discharged through the associated setae. This work should be repeated with material collected in Bouin's fluid to facilitate better preservation and extended to other species of Termitoxeniinae.

It can therefore be said that evidence is slowly accumulating to support the ideas of Wasmann and Wheeler about the role of physogastry as an integrating mechanism of the termite-termitophile association. We have field observations showing that some of the genera at least are licked and that these lick in turn; thus, there is a mutual exchange of exudates. We know that the termitophiles are lodged and that some of the genera are fed by the termites. Thus, we know that both parties receive something and that neither party is apparently harmed. Since the mouthparts of most of the physogastric species are regressed to the point where they would be useless for killing prey, we know that the termites are essential to the termitophiles. Furthermore, the carefully controlled humidity and temperature of the termite nest is also necessary for many of the physogastric species as they do not live long when removed from it. Certainly, the exudates produced by the termitophiles are not vital to the termites as many colonies, even of species that often harbor termitophiles, lack them. So, whether we consider this relationship mutualistic or not seems to hinge on whether the exudate produced by the termitophile is beneficial to the termites or not. So far all we can say is that the exudate is not apparently harmful.

B. LIMULOID BODY SHAPE

Limuloid means shaped like a king crab *(Limulus)*. In general, any staphylinid or other insect with a teardrop shaped body has been placed in this category. It probably is too loose a term and category, but, until adequate studies have been done, it is a useful term. Termitophilous limuloid forms are usually broad in front and narrow behind as well as dorsoventrally flattened. Most myrmecophilous limuloid forms are not dorsoventrally flattened but other features are similar. Associated with the overall change in body form are the following: (1) shortening and compaction of the antennae, sometimes with a reduction in the number of antennomeres, sometimes not; (2) shortening of the leg axes usually accompanied by the development of the projections of the femur and tibia so that the whole leg can be folded inside protective flanges; (3) broadening and flattening of the hind coxae; (4) broadening of the relative size of the pronotum so that it sometimes covers the entire head or otherwise modifying the head so that its outline is indistinct from the pronotum; and (5) reduction of the mesothoracic peritremes. To see the facies of two convergent examples of these changes in both Staphylinidae and Phoridae, see Fig. 12.

Because of the convergent evolution of this body form many times in many groups of both termitophiles and myrmecophiles, Wasmann (1895, and elsewhere) called it *"trutztypus"* or defensive form. The assumption here was that forms exhibiting this body form were not as well adapted to life in the termite colony and used their body form to evade destruction.

Forms exhibiting such body modifications were also called synocketes by Wheeler (1910).

Actual field observations of species with limuloid body shapes are even scarcer than observations of physogastric species. Some interesting observations were made by Grassé and Poisson (1940) on *Termitogerrus lepidulus* with *Macrotermes natalensis* (Haviland) in the Ivory Coast. They reported that this species eats the small, round fungus heads in the fungus gardens and they were able to see them feeding upon conidia, blastopores, and fungus filaments. They also saw them grooming their hosts by moving their mandibles over the legs and bodies of both workers and nymphs. They suggested that the beetles may have been feeding upon fungus spores adhering to the bodies of their hosts. They deliberately state that they saw no evidence of the termites licking the beetles. Such grooming behavior would tend to negate the idea that these beetles were living a harried existence which their shape would tend to alleviate. Furthermore, because the fungus gardens are the scene of intense termite activity, one would tend to think of the beetles as integrated termite guests.

We have studied *Termitodiscus heimi* Wasmann associated with *Odontotermes obesus* (Rambur) in India and *Termitodiscus escherichi* Wasmann associated with *Odontotermes taprobanes* in Ceylon. We were able to see them eating fungus in the field and able to confirm this with gut smears. However, we noticed a definite avoidance reaction when they came in close contact with the termites. They were extremely fast on their feet, and, when they would detect a termite worker or soldier in their vicinity, they scurried for cover in the folds of the fungus combs very quickly. We noticed the same avoidance reaction with *Termitodiscus braunsi* (Wasmann) association with *Odontotermes transvaalensis* (Sjöstedt) in South Africa. In no instance did we observe the termites catch a *Termitodiscus*, and we were therefore unable to see if the body shape would afford protection.

To say that *Termitodiscus* is not integrated within the colony on the basis of the avoidance reaction would be premature. Ordinarily, *Odontotermes* builds fungus gardens in a semispherical pattern out from and above the royal cell. Most of the young are raised in fungus gardens nearest to the royal cell. It is in these fungus gardens that the majority of *Termitodiscus* are found. If the avoidance reaction were stronger, one would expect them to be found in the most peripheral fungus gardens where termites are scarce and even Scaphidiidae closely resembling free-living species are frequent. The fact that *Termitodiscus* choose fungus gardens with more termite activity would indicate a more integrated existence than one would suppose from the avoidance reaction alone. We have never found them within the royal cell, however. This subject was recently reviewed in more detail in a revision of this genus by Kistner (1967).

It is clear from the foregoing that many more observations are needed before any conclusions can be reached as to the function of the body shape for protecting the termitophile and as to the role that these termitophiles play in the termite society.

C. PHORESY

Phoresy, as used by entomologists, means simply that one species rides upon another and does not imply that this is a necessary feature of their life history as suggested by Henry (1966), although it does not exclude that possibility.

Phoresy was first reported for *Odontoxenus triarticulatus* Kemner associated with *Odontotermes javanicus* Holmgren in Java by Kemner (1929a, b). This finding has since been confirmed by us on *Odontoxenus termitophilus* Wasmann associated with *Odontotermes obesus* at Khandala, India. The species not only rides on the heads of worker termites as reported by Kemner but also walks around on the body, where we have seen them on the thorax and abdomen as well as the head. Phoresy in this instance is associated with a limuloid body form but I have not treated it in the discussion of limloid body form because I have shown (Kistner, 1966) that phoresy can develop in different evolutionary lines of myrmecophiles independent of the limuloid body shape. This has been confirmed by Akre and Rettenmeyer (1966) for certain myrmecophiles associated with New World Army ants.

The above particular phoretic association is aided by the presence of specially modified tarsal setae in *Odontoxenus*. These setae are greatly expanded both in length and in width. We have observed through the microscope that these setae leave damp footprints on the termite head when the beetle moves upon a termite and therefore concluded that they function to secrete something which gives the beetle a firmer footing upon the termite.

Emerson (1949, p. 720) reported that *Termitonicus mahout* Mann was seen riding on the heads of worker termites of *Velocitermes beebei* (Emerson) and also seen imbibing nutritive liquids passed by mouth between the termites. Here again, phoresy is not dependent upon body form, as *Termitonicus* is even less limuloid than the majority of the other Termitonannini.

Seevers (1941) reported observations made by Emerson to the effect that *Termitopsenius acanthoscelis* Seevers was seen to ride upon the back of *Rhinotermes marginalis* (Linné) at Kartabo, British Guiana.

He also observed that the same species could jump more than an inch when disturbed for several minutes. *Rhinotermopsenius saltatorius* Seevers, a physogastric species from the same locality and host, was observed to jump even farther. No explanation was offered for this behavior.

Thus phoresy, while rare, may be an important adaptation for those species which exhibit it. With further careful observation, it may be shown to be more common than is presently known.

D. MIMICRY

While mimicry of various sorts has been shown to be an important integrating mechanism of the ant society with reference to the ant-myrmecophile association (Kistner, 1966), this has been a relatively neglected idea for termitophiles.

The idea was first suggested for termitophiles by Trägårdh (1907) with reference to *Termitomimus entendveniensis* Trägårdh associated with *Trinervitermes trinervoides* Sjöstedt from the Republic of South Africa. If one looks at a specimen of *T. entendveniensis* from the lateral surface (see Fig. 12), the recurved abdomen can be seen to be divided into three distinct regions, which Trägårdh named the pseudocaput, pseudothorax, and pseudoabdomen. He then went on to state that this form is very much like a young termite larva and that this probably was an adaptation used to deceive the tactile sense of the termites.

There is nothing to disprove this idea in the literature. Trägårdh (1907) also did histological studies of the abdomen of the same species and of various glands and suggested that the fat body secreted substances desired by the termites. He further suggested that the glands were not in any way connected with the termitophilous life of *Termitomimus*. Thus, he was aware of other possible integrating mechanisms.

We recently studied the presumed larvae of *Paracorotoca akermani* associated with the same species of termite in South Africa. Here there is a striking resemblance between the larvae and the nymphs of the termite. The head of the larvae together with the thorax mimic the head of the termite (see Fig. 13). Furthermore, the worker termites react to the larvae exactly as they would react to young nymphs. We were unable to prove that this is an integrating mechanism, and the problem is complicated by the presence of abdominal appendages of unknown function. However, we believe the resemblance is striking, and the whole subject of mimicry is worthy of further exploration in the future.

V. CONCLUDING REMARKS

Our knowledge of termitophiles is still in the descriptive stage, and our fund of information on the behavior of these interesting creatures is fragmentary at best.

Further studies of termitophiles should shed light on the evolution of the termites as well as the termitophiles. Studies of the behavior of the termitophiles and their role within the termite colony should be useful in our understanding of the integrating mechanisms of termite societies as well as our understanding of insect exocrine glands.

Perhaps if we can understand the integrating mechanisms of ant and termite societies, we might be able to use such information to solve, or at least understand, some of the pressing integration problems of our own.

REFERENCES

Ahmad, M. (1950). The phylogeny of termite genera based on imago-worker mandibles. *Bull. Am. Museum Nat. Hist.* **95**, 37-86.

Akre, R. D., and Rettenmeyer, C. W. (1966). Behavior of Staphylinidae associated with army ants (Formicidae: Ecitonini). *J. Kansas Entomol. Soc.* **39**, 745-782.

Assmuth, J. (1913). *Termitoxenia assmuthi* Wasm. Anatomisch-histologische Untersuchungen. *Abhandl. Kaiserl. Lepold.—Carolinis. Deut. Akad. Naturforsch. Halle* **98**, 187-316.

Borgmeier, T. (1964). A generic revision of the Termitoxeniinae, with the description of a new species from Burma (Dipt. Phoridae). *Studia Entomol.* **7**, 72-95.

Bugnion, E. (1913). *Termitoxenia*. Etude anatomo-histologique. *Ann. Soc. Entomol. Belg.* **57**, 23-44.

Cameron, M. (1927). Descriptions of two new genera of termitophilous Staphylinidae from India. *Entomologists' Monthly Mag.* **63**, 222-224.

Cameron, M. (1932). "The Fauna of British India, Including Ceylon and Burma. Staphylinidae, 3." Sidgwick & Jackson, London

Emerson, A. E. (1929). Communication among termites. *Trans. 4th Intern. Congr. Entomol., Ithaca, N. Y., 1928* Vol. 2, pp. 722-727.

Emerson, A. E. (1935). Termitophile distribution and quantitative characters as indicators of physiological speciation in British Guiana termites. *Ann. Entomol. Soc. Am.* **28**, 369-395.

Emerson, A. E. (1949). Evolution of interspecies integration and the ecosystem. *In* "Principles of Animal Ecology," pp. 695-729. Saunders, Philadelphia, Pennsylvania.

Emerson, A. E. (1955). Geographic origins and dispersions of termite genera. *Fieldiana, Zool.* **37**, 465-521.

Götsch, W. (1939). Neuartige Termitensoldaten aus Kunstnestern. *Zool. Anz.* **128**, 209-216.

Grassé, P.-P., and Poisson, R. (1940). Recherches sur les insectes termitophiles. I. Une nouvelle espèce de *Termitodiscus* et son ethologie. *Bull. Soc. Entomol. France* **45**, 82-90.

Hegh, E. (1922). "Les Termites." Imprimerie Industrielle et Financiere, Bruxelles, Belgium.

Henry, S. M., ed. (1966). "Symbiosis." Vol. I. Academic Press, New York.

Kemner, N. (1929a). Die Lebensweise des *Doryloxenus* auf Java and Wasmann's Hypothese über seinen Wirtswechsel. *Entomol. Tidskr.* **50**, 214-223.

Kemner, N. (1929b). On *Doryloxenus* from Java and Wasmann's hypothesis of host change of this genus of beetles. *Proc. 4th Intern. Congr. Entomol., Ithaca, N. Y., 1928* Vol. 2, pp. 832-835.

Kistner, D. H. (1958). The evolution of the Pygostenini (Coleoptera: Staphylinidae). *Ann. Musée Roy. Congo Belge: Sér. in 8°, Sci. Zool.* **68**, 1-198.

Kistner, D. H. (1966). A revision of the African species of the aleocharine tribe Dorylomimini (Coleoptera: Staphylinidae). II. The genera *Dorylomimus, Dorylonannus, Dorylogaster, Dorylobactrus* and *Mimanomma*, with notes on their behavior. *Ann. Entomol. Soc. Am.* **59**, 320-340.

Kistner, D. H. (1967). A revision of the termitophilous tribe Termitodiscini (Coleoptera: Staphylinidae). Part I. The genus *Termitodiscus* Wasmann; its systematics, phylogeny, and behavior. *J. N. Y. Entomol. Soc.* **35**, 204-235.

Koblick, T. A., and Kistner, D. H. (1965). A revision of the species of the genus *Myrmechusa* from tropical Africa with notes on their behavior and their relationship to the Pygostenini (Coleoptera: Staphylinidae). *Ann Entomol. Soc. Am.* **58**, 28-44.

Kraatz, G. (1857). Beiträge zur Kenntnis der Termitophilen, *Linn: Entomologist* **11**, 44-56.

Leleup, N. (1965). La faune entomologique cryptique de l'Afrique intertropicale. *Ann. Musée Roy. Afrique Centr.: Sér. in 8°, Sci. Zool.* **141**, 1-186.

McIndoo, N. E. (1923). Glandular structure of abdominal appendages of a termite guest. *Zoologica* **3**, 367-381.

Mergelsberg, O. (1935). Über die postimaginale Entwicklung (Physogastrie) und den Hermaphroditismus bei afrikanischen Termitoxenien (Dipt.). (Zugleich ein Beitrag zur Entwicklung der Eizelle.) *Zool. Jahrb.* **60**, 345-398.

Pasteels, J. (1966). Le système glandulaire exocrine des Aleocharinae (Coleoptera: Staphylinidae) et son evolution chez quelques espèces termitophiles. Suivi d'une étude systématique des Aleocharinae termitophiles recoltées au Gabon. Sc.D. dissertation, Université Libre de Bruxelles, Faculté des Science.

Seevers, C. H. (1937). New species of termitophilous Staphylinidae from tropical America and the Solomon Islands. *Ann. Entomol. Soc. Am.* **30**, 1-23.

Seevers, C. H. (1938). The termitophilous Coleoptera occurring in the United States. *Ann. Entomol. Soc. Am.* **34**, 318-349.

Seevers, C. H. (1939). New genera and species of Neotropical physogastric termitophiles. *Am. Museum Novitates* **1018**, 1-9.

Seevers, C. H. (1941). Taxonomic investigations of some termitophilous Staphylinidae of the subfamilies Aleocharinae and Trichopseniinae (new subfamily). *Ann. Entomol. Soc. Am.* **34**, 318-349.

Seevers, C. H. (1945). New genera and species of Trichopseniinae from American and Australian termite nests. *Pan-Pacific Entomologist* **21**, 63-72.

Seevers, C. H. (1946). New aleocharine beetles from Central and South American termite nests. (Staphylinidae). *Rev. Entomol. (Brazil)* **17**, 247-265.

Seevers, C. H. (1957). A monograph on the termitophilous Staphylinidae (Coleoptera). *Fieldiana, Zool.* **40**, 1-334.

Seevers, C. H. (1960). New termitophilous Staphylinidae of zoogeographic significance (Coleoptera). *Ann. Entomol. Soc. Am.* **53**, 825-834.

Seevers, C. H. (1965). New termitophilous Aleocharinae from Angola (Coleoptera: Staphphylinidae). *Publ. Cult. Companhia Diamantes Angola* **69**, 129-138.

Trägårdh, I. (1907). Description of *Termitomimus*, a new genus of termitophilous, physogastric Aleocharini, with notes on its anatomy. *Zool. Stud. Tillag. Prof. T. Tullberg, Upsala*, pp. 172-190.

Warren, E. (1919). Termites and termitophiles. *S. African J. Sci.* **16**, 93-112.

Warren, E. (1920). Observations on the comparative anatomy of the termitophilous Aleocharine *Paracorotoca akermani* (Warren). *Ann. Natal Museum* **4**, 297-366.

Wasmann, E. (1894). "Kritisches Verzeichniss der Myrmekophilen und Termitophilen Arthropoden." Felix L. Dames, Berlin.

Wasmann, E. (1895). Die Myrmekophilen und Termitophilen. *Compt. Rend. 3rd Congr. Intern. Zool., Leyden, 1896*, 410-440.

Wasmann, E. (1900). *Termitoxenia*, ein neues flügelloses, physogastres Dipterengenus aus Termitennestern. I. Theil. Äussere Morphologie und Biologie. *Z. Wiss. Zool.* **67**, 599-617.

Wasmann, E. (1904a). Zur Kenntnis der Gäste der Treiberameisen und ihrer Wirthe am obern Congo nach den Sammlungen und Beobachtungen von P. Herm. Kohl, C. SS. C. bearbeitet. *Zool. Jahrb. Suppl.* **7**, 611-682.

Wasmann, E. (1904b). Die phylogenetische Umbildung ostindischer Ameisengäste in Termitengäste. *Compt. Rend. 6th Congr. Intern. Zool., Berne, 1904*, pp. 436-448.

Weidner, H. (1966). Betrachtungen zur Evolution der Termiten. *Deut. Entomol. Z.* [n.s.] **13**, 323-350.

Wheeler, W. M. (1910). "Ants, Their Structure, Development, and Behavior." Columbia Univ. Press, New York.

Wheeler, W. M. (1928). "The Social Insects." Kegan Paul, Trench, Trubner & Co., London.

AUTHOR INDEX

Numbers in italics refer to pages on which the references are listed.

Subject Index

A

Abdomen, *see also* various structures
  external anatomy, 20, 42–44
  nerves of, 174–178
Abortive sperm, 149
Abrotelina, 533, 534, 538, 539
Absidia coerulea, 517
Absorption of nutrients, 79–80
Acanthotermes, see also Acanthotermes
    acanthothorax
  digestive system, 65
  food habits, 51
  fungi and, 509
  sternal glands, 101
Acanthotermes acanthothorax
  dimorphism, sexual, 312
  fungi and, 508
  soldiers, 321, 322, 334, 342
  white-soldiers, 321
Acarina in termite nests, 427
Accessory glands
  female, 128, 136, 141, 143, 144, 259
  male, 138, 144–149, 152–155
  neuters, 156
Accessory lobes of brain, 168
Acetic acid in paunch, 78
Achrestogonimes, 151, 241
Acorhinotermes, soldier, 31
Actinomucor corymbosus, 502
Adultoids, 156, 285, 324, 328, 329, 333
Aegerita duthei, 506
Affinoptochus, 536
Africa, *see* various countries; Vol. II
Afrosubulitermes
  digestive system, 71
  food habits, 51
Agar, in cultures, 353
Ahamitermes
  digestive system, 66
  food habits, 51
  nesting site, 262

preflight behavior, 241
Alarm behavior, 204, 206, 219–225, 228,
  451
Alates, *see also* Imagoes, Flight
  appearance in colonies, 235–237,
    335–337
  development and number, 237–238, 253
  feeding of, 238, 314
  fungi, transport of, 507
  protozoa and, 238
Aleocharinae, 530, 531, 550
Algae, as food for termites, 502
Allodontermes infundibuli, flight funnels,
  239
Allognathotermes, 4, *see also Allognatho-*
    termes hypogeus
  digestive system, 69
  nymphs, production of, 336
Allognathotermes hypogeus
  digestive system, 69
  dimorphism, sexual, 313
  flight, 249, 254
  pairing, 255, 257
Alpha lobe of brain, 166, 167
Alternaria humicola, 498
Altitude, effect on flights, 242–243
Amidon, degradation of, 78
Amino acids in hymolymph, 410–411
Amitermes, see also various species
  alate production, 336
  castes or polymorphism, 326–328
  digestive system, 66, 74
  food habits, 50, 51, 314
  soldiers and emergence, 240
Amitermes emersoni
  flight and related activities, 241–244,
    248–250, 252, 254, 258
  soldiers and emergence, 240
Amitermes evuncifer
  digestive system, 66
  dimorphism, sexual, 312
  neuters, development of, 326

*As there is disagreement regarding the generic designation of this species it has been listed according to the authors' preference.

*See Vol. II for a complete list of included genera.

*As there is disagreement regarding the generic designation of this species it has been listed according to the author's preference.

†See Vol. II for a complete list of included genera.

N

---

*See Vol. II for a complete list of included genera.

O

Occasitermes, digestive system, 70

Occasitermes occasus, tests for nasutins, 412

Ocelli, ocellus, 21, 22, 23, 30, 31, 33, 170, 181

Ocellus, median, 24

Odontotermes, 11, *see also* various species
cultures, 364, 368
fungi and, 503, 504, 506, 508, 509, 512
termitophiles and, 532

Odontotermes angustatus, flight, 254

Odontotermes assmuthi
dealation, 258
egg laying rate, 269, 270
flight, 244
pairing, 260
preflight behavior, 239

Odontotermes badius
dealation, 257
flight cones, 239
fungi and, 506, 508, 517
pairing, 255, 257, 260
preflight behavior, 239

Odontotermes culturarum and termitophiles, 548

Odontotermes gurdaspurensis and fungi, 508, 514

Odontotermes horni
frontal gland, 96
fungi and, 508

Odontotermes javanicus and termitophiles, 553

Odontotermes latericius and fungi, 518

Odontotermes magdalenae
division of labor, 318
soldiers, 94, 323

Odontotermes obesus, 7
alates, number of, 237
anatomy, 30, 33, 42, 72
cellobiase in, 76
colony size, 275
digestive system, 65
egg laying rate, 272
flight, 244
fungi and, 508
soldiers, number of, 275
termitophiles and, 552, 553
use in testing, 371

Odontotermes patruus, 548

Odontotermes redemanni
fungi and, 508
glands, 93, 105, 111, 114
head segmentation, 30
reproductive system, 129, 130, 131, 135, 145, 149
soldiers, 93

Odontotermes sundaicus and fungi, 508

Odontotermes taprobanes and termitophiles, 527, 548, 552

Odontotermes transvaalensis
fungi and, 508
termitophiles and, 552
use in testing, 371

Odontotermes vulgaris, and fungi, 508

Odontoxenus spp., 531, 553

Odor, colony, 194

Odor trail, *see* Trail laying

Oeno Island, termites introduced, 465

Oenocytes, 105

Oideprosoma, 537, 540

Olfactory lobes, 171

Ommatids, ommatidia, 178, 179

Oocytes, 129–131, 133

Oothecal-like egg mass, 2, 143

Ophiotermes
castes, 329
digestive system, 67, 72

Optic lobes, 170

Optic nerve, 161

Oral segment, 30

Orcytes, 75

Organ of Johnston, 181, 184–186

Orient, termites exported, 472, 474, *see also* various countries

Orthognathotermes
mandibles, imago and soldier, 27
soldier, 218

Orthotermes, see also O. depressifrons
digestive system, 67
soldiers
feeding of, 52
sex of, 329
workers, 329

Orthotermes depressifrons, soldiers, 329

Oscillatory movements, 213–214, 425–427

Ovarioles, 126–136

Ovary, 126–136, 305–306

Oviducts, 126, 136, 138, 140, 142

P

P[32] in feeding studies, 392–394, 396–399, 402
Pairing, 198–201, 255–257
Palatum, 30, 33
Palpifer, 22
Panama, 242
  termites
    exported, 469, 488
    introduced, 477, 464
Panoisitic ovary, regions of, 129
Pantolenic acid, 413
Papillae, rectal, *see* Rectal papillae
Paracapritermes
  digestive system, 67
  glands, 550
Paracornitermes, and termitophiles, 534, 535
Paracornitermes-branch of Nasutitermitinae, 28
Paracornitermes-Subulitermes branch of Nasutitermitinae, 28
Paracorotoca, 535, 536, 548–550, 554
Paraglossa, 22, 26, 30
Paraguay, termites exported, 469, 488
Paraneotermes simplicicornis
  alates, 237, 241
  colony size, 273
  cuticle, 446
  dealation, 258
  flight, 243, 245, 246, 248–250, 252
  nesting site, 201, 261, 262
  soldier ratio, 273
  tandems, 260
  water dynamics, 438, 440, 443, 452
Paraperinthus, 541, 544
Paraproct, 43, 144
Parasites, 110–111, 119, 345, 347, 357, 514–518
Parietal, 21
Parthenogenesis, 139, 201, 267, 295, 297
Paunch, 53, 59, 61, 64–66, 68, 69, 71, 78, 80
  pH in, 75, 76
Pedicels
  of antennae, 23
  of ovarioles, 129, 133
Pedunculate bodies, 163–167
Peg organs, 182–183

Pellets, fecal, 80, 389, *see also* Feces
Penicillium spp., 497–499, 517
Penis, 155
Pentosanes, utilization of, 78
Pericapritermes, see also various species
  digestive system, 67
  soldiers, 31–32, 52, 217, 218, 323, 329
  workers, 329
Pericapritermes magnificus, digestive system, 72
Pericapritermes urgens
  digestive system, 68
  oocyte development, histochemistry of, 133
  rectal papillae, 82
  soldier, 32, 335, 336
Periesophageal ring, 171
Perinthina, 531, 538, 541, 543
Perinthodes, 541, 544
Perinthus, 541, 544
Perinuclear vitellarium zone of oocyte, 132
Periplaneta americana, transplant experiments, 296
Peritrophic membrane, 58
Peru, termites
  exported, 472
  introduced, 464
Peziza epispartia, 513
pH of gut, 75–76
Pheromones, 89, 106, 197, 199, 343, 400, 418, 423–430
  alarm, 201, 425–428
  aphrodisiac, 202
  caste and, 106, 225–227, 235, 294, 296, 303, 304, 306, 343, 344, 389, 400
  primer, 424–425
  releaser, 425–430
  sex, 104, 106, 197, 199
  trail laying, 8, 204–209, 410, 428–429
Philippines, termites
  exported, 464, 465, 469, 475, 477, 481, 486, 487
  introduced, 465, 467
Philotermitini, 531
Phoresy of termitophiles, 553–554
Phoridae in termite nests, 527
Photosensitive organs, 178–181
Phototropic behavior, 245
Phragmosis, phragmotic, 31, 323

S

*See Vol. II for a complete list of included genera.

*See Vol. II for a complete list of included genera.